SAP PRESS e-books

Print or e-book, Kindle or iPad, workplace or airplane: Choose where and how to read your SAP PRESS books! You can now get all our titles as e-books, too:

- By download and online access
- For all popular devices
- And, of course, DRM-free

Convinced? Then go to www.sap-press.com and get your e-book today.

Material Requirements Planning with SAP S/4HANA®

SAP PRESS is a joint initiative of SAP and Rheinwerk Publishing. The know-how offered by SAP specialists combined with the expertise of Rheinwerk Publishing offers the reader expert books in the field. SAP PRESS features first-hand information and expert advice, and provides useful skills for professional decision-making.

SAP PRESS offers a variety of books on technical and business-related topics for the SAP user. For further information, please visit our website: www.sap-press.com.

Jawad Akhtar, Martin Murray
Materials Management with SAP S/4HANA:
Business Processes and Configuration (2nd Edition)
2020, 939 pages, hardcover and e-book
www.sap-press.com/5132

Justin Ashlock
Sourcing and Procurement with SAP S/4HANA (2nd Edition)
2020, 716 pages, hardcover and e-book
www.sap-press.com/5003

Bernd Roedel, Johannes Esser
Inventory Management with SAP S/4HANA
2019, 494 pages, hardcover and e-book
www.sap-press.com/4892

Mahesh Babu MG
PP-DS with SAP S/4HANA
2020, 476 pages, hardcover and e-book
www.sap-press.com/4951

Caetano Almeida

Material Requirements Planning with SAP S/4HANA®

Editor Emily Nicholls
Copyeditor Melinda Rankin
Cover Design Graham Geary
Photo Credit Shutterstock.com/1105171211/© nadianb
Layout Design Vera Brauner
Production Kelly O'Callaghan
Typesetting SatzPro, Krefeld (Germany)
Printed and bound in the United States of America, on paper from sustainable sources

ISBN 978-1-4932-1886-8

© 2020 by Rheinwerk Publishing, Inc., Boston (MA)
1st edition 2020

Library of Congress Cataloging-in-Publication Data
Names: Almeida, Caetano, author.
Title: Material requirements planning with SAP S/4HANA / Caetano Almeida.
Description: 1st edition. | Bonn ; Boston : Rheinwerk Publishing, 2020. |
Includes index.
Identifiers: LCCN 2020021393 (print) | LCCN 2020021394 (ebook) | ISBN
9781493218868 (hardcover) | ISBN 9781493218875 (ebook)
Subjects: LCSH: SAP HANA (Electronic resource) | Material requirements
planning--Data processing.
Classification: LCC TS161 .A39 2020 (print) | LCC TS161 (ebook) | DDC
650.0285--dc23
LC record available at https://lccn.loc.gov/2020021393
LC ebook record available at https://lccn.loc.gov/2020021394

All rights reserved. Neither this publication nor any part of it may be copied or reproduced in any form or by any means or translated into another language, without the prior consent of Rheinwerk Publishing, 2 Heritage Drive, Suite 305, Quincy, MA 02171.

Rheinwerk Publishing makes no warranties or representations with respect to the content hereof and specifically disclaims any implied warranties of merchantability or fitness for any particular purpose. Rheinwerk Publishing assumes no responsibility for any errors that may appear in this publication.

"Rheinwerk Publishing" and the Rheinwerk Publishing logo are registered trademarks of Rheinwerk Verlag GmbH, Bonn, Germany. SAP PRESS is an imprint of Rheinwerk Verlag GmbH and Rheinwerk Publishing, Inc.

All of the screenshots and graphics reproduced in this book are subject to copyright © SAP SE, Dietmar-Hopp-Allee 16, 69190 Walldorf, Germany.

SAP, the SAP logo, ABAP, Ariba, ASAP, Concur, Concur ExpenseIt, Concur TripIt, Duet, SAP Adaptive Server Enterprise, SAP Advantage Database Server, SAP Afaria, SAP ArchiveLink, SAP Ariba, SAP Business ByDesign, SAP Business Explorer, SAP BusinessObjects, SAP BusinessObjects Explorer, SAP BusinessObjects Lumira, SAP BusinessObjects Roambi, SAP BusinessObjects Web Intelligence, SAP Business One, SAP Business Workflow, SAP Crystal Reports, SAP EarlyWatch, SAP Exchange Media (SAP XM), SAP Fieldglass, SAP Fiori, SAP Global Trade Services (SAP GTS), SAP GoingLive, SAP HANA, SAP HANA Vora, SAP Hybris, SAP Jam, SAP MaxAttention, SAP MaxDB, SAP NetWeaver, SAP PartnerEdge, SAPPHIRE NOW, SAP PowerBuilder, SAP PowerDesigner, SAP R/2, SAP R/3, SAP Replication Server, SAP S/4HANA, SAP SQL Anywhere, SAP Strategic Enterprise Management (SAP SEM), SAP SuccessFactors, The Best-Run Businesses Run SAP, TwoGo are registered or unregistered trademarks of SAP SE, Walldorf, Germany.

All other products mentioned in this book are registered or unregistered trademarks of their respective companies.

Contents at a Glance

1. Introduction to MRP with SAP S/4HANA 19
2. MRP Basics 29
3. Master Data and Basic Settings 55
4. Configuring MRP 131
5. Running MRP 189
6. Evaluating the MRP Results 225
7. Managing Planned Orders 303
8. Advanced MRP Features 323
9. Demand Management 347
10. Demand-Driven MRP 379
11. Long-Term Planning 413
12. Predictive Material and Resource Planning 441
13. Administering MRP 459
14. Enhancing MRP 493
15. Migrating to SAP S/4HANA 505

Dear Reader,

Grocery shopping is a serious business lately.

A global health crisis has renewed my focus on limiting trips to our local supermarket. The result? A burgeoning fascination with grocery lists.

Gone are casual drop-ins to grab items for a single meal; suspended is on-the-spot dinner planning inspired by the produce section. These days I've become hyper-vigilant about preparing a detailed shopping list that has both the breadth and depth to last my household several weeks. I've been consulting new recipes, calculating routine consumption, estimating freezer space, and researching substitutes for high-demand dry goods. Aligning the types, quantities, and availability of needed ingredients has become a new outlet for planning and creativity.

If you, like me, have started thinking about grocery lists as food replenishment proposals, you're reading the right book. So tell me—what did you think about *Material Requirements Planning with SAP S/4HANA*? Your comments and suggestions are the most useful tools to help us make our books the best they can be. Please feel free to contact me and share any praise or criticism you may have.

Thank you for purchasing a book from SAP PRESS!

Emily Nicholls
Editor, SAP PRESS

emilyn@rheinwerk-publishing.com
www.sap-press.com
Rheinwerk Publishing · Boston, MA

Contents

Preface 15

1 Introduction to MRP with SAP S/4HANA   19

1.1 MRP Basics 19
1.2 MRP within the Supply Chain in SAP Systems 20
1.3 MRP with SAP S/4HANA 24
    1.3.1 Classic MRP 24
    1.3.2 MRP Live 24
    1.3.3 MRP Cockpit 25
    1.3.4 Demand-Driven MRP 27
    1.3.5 Predictive Material and Resource Planning 28
1.4 Summary 28

2 MRP Basics   29

2.1 MRP Procedures 29
    2.1.1 Material Requirements Planning 30
    2.1.2 Master Production Scheduling 31
    2.1.3 Consumption-Based Planning 33
    2.1.4 Demand-Driven MRP 34
2.2 The MRP Planning Process 35
    2.2.1 Reading the Planning File 36
    2.2.2 Calculating the Net Requirements 37
    2.2.3 Calculating the Procurement Quantity 39
    2.2.4 Determining the Replenishment Proposal Type 41
    2.2.5 Scheduling Replenishment Proposals 43

Contents

		2.2.6	Exploding the BOM	50
		2.2.7	Creating Exception Messages	52
2.3	**Summary**			53

3   Master Data and Basic Settings   55

3.1	**Material Master**			56
	3.1.1	MRP Type		62
	3.1.2	Lot-Sizing Procedures		76
	3.1.3	Procurement Types and Special Procurement Types		85
	3.1.4	Scheduling Parameters		87
	3.1.5	Net Requirements Calculation		90
	3.1.6	MRP Area		93
3.2	**Procurement Master Data**			95
	3.2.1	Internal Procurement		97
	3.2.2	External Procurement		112
	3.2.3	Quota Arrangement		121
3.3	**Planning File**			126
3.4	**Summary**			128

4   Configuring MRP   131

4.1	**Overall Plant Parameters**		132
	4.1.1	Maintain Environment	134
	4.1.2	Maintain Master Data	136
	4.1.3	Maintain Planned Orders	141
	4.1.4	Maintain Planning Run	142
4.2	**MRP Group**		158
	4.2.1	Consumption Mode/Adjustment Horizon	160
	4.2.2	Horizons	160
	4.2.3	Determine Production Storage Location	162
	4.2.4	Convert Planned Order	163

	4.2.5	Program Plan: Independent Requirements Split	163
	4.2.6	Evaluation	164
	4.2.7	Planning Run	164
	4.2.8	External Procurement	169
	4.2.9	Availability Check	170
4.3	**MRP Type**		170
4.4	**Lot-Sizing Procedure**		174
4.5	**Availability Check**		178
4.6	**MRP Areas**		180
4.7	**Parallel Processing**		185
4.8	**Summary**		187

5 Running MRP — 189

5.1	**MRP Live versus Classic MRP**		189
5.2	**Classic MRP**		193
	5.2.1	Control Parameters	194
	5.2.2	Single-Item/Single-Level Planning	197
	5.2.3	Single-Item/Multilevel Planning	199
	5.2.4	Single-Item Interactive Planning	202
	5.2.5	Multilevel Sales Order/Project Planning	204
	5.2.6	Total Planning Run	206
	5.2.7	Master Production Scheduling	209
5.3	**MRP Live**		211
	5.3.1	MRP Dispatcher	211
	5.3.2	MRP Live Control Parameters	212
	5.3.3	Running MRP Live in SAP GUI	214
	5.3.4	SAP Fiori	216
5.4	**Planning PP/DS Materials in MRP Live (One MRP Run)**		221
5.5	**Summary**		223

6 Evaluating the MRP Results ... 225

6.1	Exception Messages	225
6.2	Rescheduling Checks	230
6.3	The Stock/Requirements List	235
	6.3.1 Individual Access	236
	6.3.2 Collective Access	254
6.4	MRP List	260
6.5	Information and Settings for Materials in MRP on SAP HANA	263
6.6	Order Report	264
6.7	Pegged Requirements	268
6.8	Evaluation of the Planning Situation	270
6.9	MRP Cockpit	272
	6.9.1 Shortage	273
	6.9.2 Accessing SAP Fiori Applications for MRP	275
	6.9.3 Monitor and Manage Material Coverage	277
	6.9.4 Monitor and Manage Internal Requirements	282
	6.9.5 Monitor and Manage External Requirements	284
	6.9.6 Monitor and Manage Production or Process Orders	285
	6.9.7 Display MRP Master Data Issues	289
	6.9.8 Manage Change Requests	290
	6.9.9 Detect MRP Situations	293
6.10	Summary	301

7 Managing Planned Orders ... 303

7.1	Planned Orders	303
7.2	Planned Order Availability Check	308
7.3	Planned Order Conversion	311
7.4	Additional Options for Mass Processing	317
7.5	Summary	321

8 Advanced MRP Features — 323

8.1	Subcontracting Planning	323
8.2	Planning Calendar	329
8.3	BOM Explosion Number	333
8.4	Parts Interchangeability	336
	8.4.1 Creating an MPN-MRP Set	336
	8.4.2 Planning an MPN-MRP Set	339
8.5	Range of Coverage Profile (Dynamic Safety Stock)	341
8.6	Summary	346

9 Demand Management — 347

9.1	What Is Demand Management?	348
9.2	Planning Strategies	352
	9.2.1 Planning with Final Assembly (Strategy 40)	355
	9.2.2 Net Requirements Planning (Strategy 10)	356
	9.2.3 Gross Requirements Planning (Strategy 11)	358
	9.2.4 Make-to-Order Production (Strategy 20)	359
	9.2.5 Planning without Final Assembly (Strategies 50 and 52)	361
	9.2.6 Planning with a Planning Material (Strategies 60 and 63)	363
	9.2.7 Planning at Assembly Level (Strategies 70, 74, and 59)	365
	9.2.8 Assembly-to-Order (Strategies 81 through 86)	367
9.3	Creating a Demand Plan	368
	9.3.1 Splitting Independent Requirements	373
	9.3.2 PIR Reorganization	373
9.4	Configuring Demand Management	374
9.5	Summary	377

10 Demand-Driven MRP   379

10.1 What Is DDMRP? 379
    10.1.1 Buffer Calculation 381
    10.1.2 The DDMRP Process 384

10.2 Setting Up DDMRP 386
    10.2.1 Product Classification 386
    10.2.2 Mass Maintenance of Products 394
    10.2.3 Buffer Proposal Calculation 396

10.3 Running DDMRP 400

10.4 Integrating DDMRP with SAP IBP 409

10.5 Summary 410

11 Long-Term Planning   413

11.1 Creating a Long-Term Planning Scenario 414

11.2 Running Long-Term Planning 419

11.3 Processing Simulative Planned Orders 422

11.4 Evaluating the LTP Results 426
    11.4.1 Evaluating Work Center Capacity 429
    11.4.2 Transferring the LTP Results to the Logistics Information System 430

11.5 Cleaning Up the Long-Term Planning Scenario 435

11.6 Summary 438

12 Predictive Material and Resource Planning   441

12.1 Prerequisites to Run pMRP 442

12.2 Creating a pMRP Simulation 443

12.3 Processing pMRP Simulations 448

| 12.4 | Releasing the pMRP Simulation | 456 |
| 12.5 | Summary | 457 |

13 Administering MRP — 459

13.1 Housekeeping MRP — 459
- 13.1.1 Keeping the Planning File Consistent — 460
- 13.1.2 Managing Background Jobs — 461
- 13.1.3 Deleting Old MRP Lists — 464

13.2 Troubleshooting MRP — 464
- 13.2.1 Material Not Planned — 465
- 13.2.2 Inconsistencies — 467
- 13.2.3 MRP Live Support Functions — 473

13.3 Improving MRP Performance — 478
- 13.3.1 Classic MRP — 478
- 13.3.2 MRP Live — 482
- 13.3.3 Frequent Causes and Solutions — 490

13.4 Summary — 492

14 Enhancing MRP — 493

14.1 Enhancing Classic MRP — 494
14.2 Enhancing MRP Live — 498
14.3 Enhancing the SAP Fiori Applications of the MRP Cockpit — 501
14.4 Summary — 504

15 Migrating to SAP S/4HANA — 505

15.1 Performing Readiness Check — 505

15.2		**Assessing Simplifications in MRP**	507
	15.2.1	Planning File	507
	15.2.2	Storage Location Planning	509
	15.2.3	Subcontracting	511
	15.2.4	Production Versions	511
	15.2.5	External Procurement	512
	15.2.6	Total Requirements Cleanup	513
15.3		**Reviewing Custom Code**	515
15.4		**Evaluating New MRP Features**	516
	15.4.1	MRP Live	516
	15.4.2	Demand-Driven MRP	517
	15.4.3	Predictive Material and Resource Planning	517
	15.4.4	SAP Fiori and the MRP Cockpit	518
15.5		**Summary**	519

Appendices

A	**Roadmap for MRP in SAP S/4HANA**	521
B	**The Author**	525

Index	527

Preface

Imagine that you are the person responsible for a car manufacturer's production line.

Your sales team informs you how many cars they plan to sell in the next months, and now you need to ensure that you will produce enough cars to fulfill the demand. For every car that you need to produce, there is a huge variety of components: the wheels, the brakes, the engine, the windshield—not to mention thousands of minor parts, like screws, bolts, nuts, and so on.

It would be virtually impossible to manually determine how much of each component you need to buy or produce and when. From a business perspective, there are additional challenges: If you buy too many components, you will spend too much money, which will affect the company's profits. If you buy them too early, you will overwhelm the warehouse, causing logistical problems. On the other hand, if you do not buy enough components or if you buy them too late in the schedule, your production line will stop, and you will not be able to deliver the cars on time for your customers.

To address those challenges, the material requirements planning (MRP) concept was created in the sixties by Joseph Orlick. MRP allows companies to effectively plan the quantities of products to be manufactured and purchased, aiming to achieve the highest service level at the lowest possible cost. In the context of a car manufacturer, MRP can tell you how many tires you have to buy and when each one of those tires is needed so that you can fulfill all your forecasted demand and avoid overstocking.

After it was formulated, MRP was adopted as a central planning tool by many companies; since then, it has also evolved to become material resources planning, which includes additional functions like capacity planning, master production scheduling, and sales and operations planning.

In the SAP world, MRP has been part of SAP ERP since its earlier releases. Over time, there were many incremental changes and improvements to MRP, but the core functionality had remained the same since SAP R/3. When SAP introduced the new SAP HANA database, there was a huge opportunity to redesign MRP to take advantage of the SAP HANA in-memory capabilities, so a new version of MRP called MRP Live was created. In comparison to what became known as "classic" MRP, the changes implemented in MRP Live were mostly technical and focused on performance improvements—but the core MRP logic remained the same.

Preface

In 2015, SAP released a successor to SAP ERP called SAP S/4HANA, built specifically to run on SAP HANA. In SAP S/4HANA, using MRP Live became the best practice for materials planning, even though the old MRP functionality from previous releases was still available. Besides MRP Live, several simplifications were implemented in SAP S/4HANA that had a direct impact on MRP. In addition, there were several improvements to the MRP user interface, and a new set of browser-based applications collectively called the MRP Cockpit was introduced.

Every subsequent annual release of SAP S/4HANA introduces new features and applications for MRP. In 2017, a new concept for materials planning called demand-driven MRP (DDMRP) was introduced in SAP S/4HANA, offering a whole new philosophy for materials planning. Additional DDMRP features were released in 2018, and the new Predictive Material and Resource Planning (pMRP) was finally released in 2019.

My previous e-book, *Introducing Material Requirements Planning (MRP) with SAP S/4HANA*, published by SAP PRESS, focused exclusively on the new features introduced in SAP S/4HANA (up to release 1709). But I decided it was time to write a complete MRP implementation guide rather than an introduction to the changes, and that is what I have undertaken with this book.

If you are not yet familiar with MRP in SAP ERP, this book will provide a complete implementation guide, explaining the most basic MRP concepts, the master data required to run MRP in an SAP S/4HANA system, and the whole configuration behind MRP. If, on the other hand, if you are an experienced MRP consultant, you will also find useful information in this book. You will understand the impacts of the SAP S/4HANA simplifications on MRP, and we will go through each of the new MRP features introduced in SAP S/4HANA, like MRP Live, DDMRP, and the new pMRP.

If you are a materials planner, this book is also for you: you will learn how to run MRP in SAP S/4HANA and how to effectively evaluate the MRP results. After reading this book, you should have an overall understanding of the MRP concepts, and you should be able to configure and run MRP in an SAP S/4HANA system.

This book also offers a lot of technical information about MRP that I have acquired during my career, which will be interesting for both novice and experienced MRP consultants. I'll talk about the most common problems that may affect MRP, how to troubleshoot and solve those issues, and how to work on improving MRP performance.

Let's review the roadmap for the book. We will start in Chapter 1 by focusing on the MRP concepts, with a brief introduction about MRP and how it interacts with other areas and tools in the SAP ERP system. In Chapter 2, we'll discuss how basic MRP planning happens, which will serve as a foundation for later explanations of key variants in SAP S/4HANA.

In Chapter 3, we will move into more practical and implementation-focused content, beginning with the MRP-related master data. In Chapter 4, we will talk about the required Customizing settings to set up MRP in an SAP S/4HANA system.

After that, Chapter 5 will explain in detail how to run MRP in an SAP S/4HANA system, and Chapter 6 will explain how to evaluate the MRP results. We will focus on both classic MRP and MRP Live, and we will talk about the evaluation using the old SAP GUI transactions and the new SAP Fiori applications of the MRP Cockpit. Chapter 7 will cover the planned order, which is the main planning object generated by MRP for in-house produced materials.

Having covered basic MRP concepts and its implementation, execution, and evaluation, the book will then focus on advanced MRP scenarios in Chapter 8, such as subcontracting, range of coverage, and parts interchangeability. We will then talk about some SAP S/4HANA features that are complementary to MRP, such as demand management in Chapter 9 and long-term planning in Chapter 10. In Chapter 11 and Chapter 12, we will cover how to leverage the new SAP S/4HANA features: DDMRP and pMRP, respectively.

Chapters 13 and 14 will be more technical. Here we will talk about the administration of MRP (housekeeping, troubleshooting, and performance) and enhancements that can be implemented in the standard MRP. In those chapters, I tried to share my experience working with MRP in SAP Product Support to help you to avoid the common issues that may arise in daily MRP administration and to resolve some of the most frequent problems that we face when implementing and managing MRP in SAP S/4HANA. There is a special focus on performance, for both MRP Live and classic MRP, because this is very often a concern when running MRP. We will also talk about classic MRP's BAdIs, MRP Live's AMDP BAdIs, and common scenarios in which those BAdIs can be used to enhance MRP.

We will close the book in Chapter 15 by talking about the migration to SAP S/4HANA and summarizing the simplifications that will have an impact on an upgrade to SAP S/4HANA. We will also discuss how to address all those changes and new features in an implementation or upgrade project. This chapter can be used as a quick migration guide: we will talk about which actions should be taken, such as the reports that must be executed during the migration; master data that should be created; and the concerns about the custom code implemented in MRP.

In summary, this book should be useful for someone who is a beginner in MRP, as we will go through the basic MRP concepts, but also for someone who is already familiar with MRP and just wants to get in touch with the new MRP features in SAP S/4HANA, like MRP Live, DDMRP, or pMRP.

Acknowledgments

Before we start learning about MRP in SAP S/4HANA, I would like to thank all my SAP colleagues, especially those who work to develop new MRP features and to support the customers who are already using MRP. They have answered hundreds of e-mails in which I asked questions, suggested new features, or simply shared customer feedback about MRP.

I would also like to thank my editor, Emily Nicholls, and the whole SAP PRESS publishing team, as they helped me to write this book by providing suggestions, insights, and editing.

Finally, a very special thank-you goes to my wife, Elizabeth, who spent her nights lonely while I was involved in this project. Without her support, I would not have been able to accomplish it.

Caetano Almeida
July 2020

Chapter 1
Introduction to MRP with SAP S/4HANA

Material requirements planning (MRP) is the central planning tool used widely across companies of many different industries. The main objective of MRP is to ensure that we will have enough of the materials that we need, with the best possible service level, and at minimal cost.

We will begin this book in this chapter by explaining core MRP concepts (Section 1.1), situating them in the context of the broader supply chain as run in SAP systems (Section 1.2), and then turning our attention to MRP as it exists in SAP S/4HANA (Section 1.3).

1.1 MRP Basics

MRP will start by planning the top-level materials (i.e., the finished products), taking all the requirements—a forecast in a make-to-stock (MTS) production environment or a sales order in a make-to-order (MTO) environment—as inputs and checking if we have enough stock to cover them. If there is not enough stock, the system will check if there is any planned receipt—such as a production order or purchase order—that can cover the requirement. When there is not enough stock and no planned receipt, MRP will generate a replenishment proposal to let us know that we need to buy or produce this material.

For a finished product that is manufactured internally, the replenishment proposal created by MRP is a planned order. For each planned order, MRP will calculate the dates based on a predefined lead time in order to ensure that we will start the production on time to meet the requirement. For each planned order, MRP will determine the components based on a predefined list called a *bill of materials* (BOM). It will create dependent requirements for each component, indicating the date and quantity needed.

The dependent requirements generated by MRP will then act as inputs for MRP to plan the components. MRP will plan the semifinished products, level by level, until reaching the raw material level. At this point, the system will generate purchase requisitions, informing us that we need to buy those materials from a supplier.

This is the basic process of a deterministic MRP type, where the main input will be requirements for a finished product and the output will be planned orders or purchase requisitions for this finished product for all component levels.

During the MRP run, exception messages will be triggered whenever an issue arises that cannot be solved automatically. For example, if MRP determines that the start date of a planned order should be in the past (which would be impossible), it triggers an exception message to inform the planner (known as an MRP controller) about it. After the MRP run, a planner should evaluate the MRP results and check if any action should be performed to resolve the issue.

This process is repeated cyclically, and whenever a new requirement is created for a material or there is a relevant change in the stock or a planning element, it is marked to be included in the next planning run. In most companies, MRP is usually executed on a daily basis to plan all the changed materials, plus once a week to replan all the materials, irrespective of the changes.

1.2 MRP within the Supply Chain in SAP Systems

MRP is one of the planning tools that SAP provides for companies to manage their whole supply chain, from forecasting and production planning through purchasing, manufacturing, and finished goods delivery to the customer.

Let's walk through this supply chain flow as performed in SAP S/4HANA and outlined in Figure 1.1. From a production planning perspective, everything will start with a forecast of the quantities that should be produced in each period (e.g., months, weeks, or days). This forecast was traditionally created in sales and operations planning (S&OP) functionality offered as part of SAP ERP or SAP Advanced Planning and Optimization (SAP APO).

S&OP is still available in SAP S/4HANA, and integration of SAP S/4HANA with SAP APO is still supported, but SAP recommends that S&OP be run in the successor of SAP APO: a cloud solution called SAP Integrated Business Planning (SAP IBP). SAP IBP generates the forecast that can be used as an input for the planning process in SAP S/4HANA.

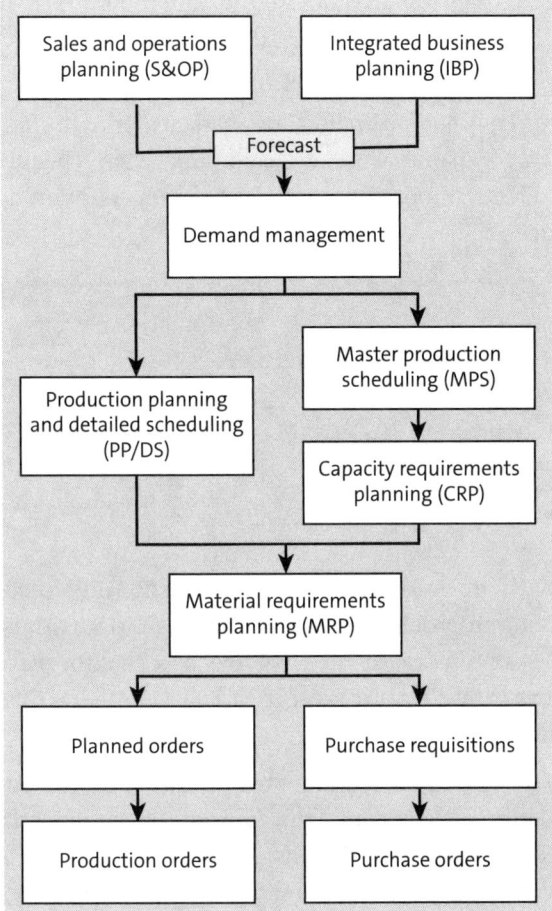

Figure 1.1 Production Planning in SAP S/4HANA

The forecast generated by S&OP (either in SAP APO or in SAP S/4HANA) or by SAP IBP is then transferred to a functionality within SAP S/4HANA called demand management, where this forecast will become what we call *planned independent requirements* (PIRs). Each material will have a planning strategy, and this planning strategy will determine which type of PIR is created and how this material will be planned; for example, we can plan to produce our material to stock (MTS production) or to start the production only after we receive a sales order (MTO production).

In an MTS scenario, we usually rely on the forecast to start the production ahead of time, but in an MTO scenario, this is not always true. In a pure MTO scenario, we will

1   Introduction to MRP with SAP S/4HANA

only start the production when we receive a sales order, so the only input for MRP will be the sales order. Alternatively, we might use a forecast in an MTO scenario to start the procurement of some components ahead of time.

After we generate the independent requirements in demand management, we start the actual materials planning. Often, companies will use master production scheduling (MPS) for planning finished products, important semifinished products, or products that will use bottleneck production lines.

> **Note**
>
> Technically speaking, MPS and MRP in SAP S/4HANA are pretty much the same thing, and they even can be executed in the same transaction.
>
> However, because neither MPS nor MRP take into account capacity restrictions, it is advisable to split the planning run between MPS and MRP and to run capacity leveling for the products planned with MPS *before* running MRP.

MPS will plan the products mentioned previously, just like deterministic MRP would plan them, generating replenishment proposals whenever it finds a shortage. After we finish the MPS planning run, we can run capacity leveling to ensure that the plan proposed by MPS will not exceed the critical resources capacity. Figure 1.1 shows this capacity leveling as a step between MPS and MRP.

With capacity leveling, we might have to shift some planned order dates in the event of a capacity overload, so we will automatically adjust the dates of the component requirements. Therefore, when MRP is executed, it will consider those adjusted dates and generate a realistic plan that will already consider capacity restrictions. This way, we will be generating purchase requirements for our suppliers with the actual required dates, according to our plant capacity.

> **Tip**
>
> Capacity leveling can also be executed as a background job, so it is possible to have MPS, capacity leveling, and MRP executed as a sequence of background jobs that run overnight.

As also shown in Figure 1.1, an alternative to MPS is to use the Production Planning and Detailed Scheduling (PP/DS) tool, formerly part of SAP APO, which SAP embedded into the SAP S/4HANA digital core. PP/DS supports advanced planning features that are not available in MPS or MRP, such as planning with finite capacity (i.e., considering capacity restrictions on the work centers), planning considering the batch shelf life, or planning with complex heuristics.

Whereas PP/DS in SAP APO was a separate application running in a different system than MRP, MRP Live in SAP S/4HANA can plan both advanced planning PP/DS materials and MRP materials. PP/DS provides not only tools for materials planning, but also tools for optimizing the production schedule, which means that it also can be used for capacity planning.

After PP/DS optimization or capacity leveling, the production plan should be adjusted to consider capacity restrictions, and the load in our production work centers should be leveled. All the requirement dates for the components should also be adjusted accordingly. We can run MRP to plan those components, generating planned orders for the components produced internally and purchase requisitions for materials procured externally.

After evaluating the MRP results and any exception messages generated during the planning run, the MRP controller will resolve any conflicts, and the planned orders will be converted to production orders so that the manufacturing process can start. The production order is the object that we will use to manage the whole manufacturing process; it will also serve as a costing object, collecting all the costs related to the process.

Simultaneously, the purchase requisitions generated by MRP for the raw materials will be converted to purchase orders so that the external procurement of those materials can start. This ensures that we have the required quantity to manufacture our products.

Finally, once the procurement and manufacturing activities have been completed, the products will be delivered into stock. In an MTO scenario, they can be immediately delivered to the customer because we have had a sales order since we started the manufacturing process. In an MTS scenario, the finished product will go to a warehouse, where it will wait for a sales order to be created so that it can be delivered to a customer. Once the product is finally issued to be delivered, the PIRs (forecast) will be reduced.

Now that we have discussed how MRP is positioned within the supply chain and how it interacts with other systems and planning tools within SAP S/4HANA, we will deep-dive into the MRP concepts in the new suite.

1 Introduction to MRP with SAP S/4HANA

1.3 MRP with SAP S/4HANA

In the earlier releases of SAP ERP, MRP referred to one specific planning tool. In contrast, SAP has already delivered many new features and tools related to MRP since the first logistics-inclusive release of SAP S/4HANA was launched in 2015.

In this section, we offer a basic introduction to these new concepts. They are among the most important innovations delivered in SAP S/4HANA, and we will refer to them many times later in this book.

1.3.1 Classic MRP

SAP S/4HANA and the latest releases of SAP ERP introduced a new MRP functionality called MRP Live, which was basically the same concept and the same logic, but improved for better performance on an SAP HANA database. Since then, the previously existing MRP and its transactions have become known as classic MRP to help differentiate between the versions.

Classic MRP has a set of transactions that we can use to plan our materials, allowing us to plan an entire plant, a single material, or a material and its components. It was entirely developed in ABAP, the SAP programming language used originally to develop SAP ERP, and it was designed to be executed in SAP GUI, the software installed on an end user's computer to access SAP S/4HANA.

All the classic MRP transactions are still available and supported in SAP S/4HANA, but it is no longer the target architecture for the future. Instead, it has been defined as part of the SAP S/4HANA Compatibility Pack to help current SAP customers transition to the new suite and its newer technologies. Although classic MRP can still be used in SAP S/4HANA, it is not recommended as a long-term solution; all the innovation in MRP will center on MRP Live.

Companies looking for a quick migration to SAP S/4HANA with minimal impact in the conversion project may consider classic MRP as a temporary solution, but a migration to the new MRP Live should be considered part of the future roadmap.

1.3.2 MRP Live

MRP is traditionally executed as a background job over night, planning all the changed materials within one or more plants. To calculate the shortages for each material, it needs to read all the relevant planning elements, such as sales orders and production orders. Basically, every document that may consume or receive a certain quantity of material into stock is relevant for MRP and should be read from the database. This means that MRP should select large chunks of data from the database, and because of that and the complex algorithms executed during the planning run, MRP may take a long time to complete.

When SAP created the SAP HANA database, there was a huge opportunity to improve MRP performance using the power of SAP HANA's in-memory parallelization. Therefore, SAP decided to redesign MRP, pushing the MRP logic into the database layer and creating MRP Live.

MRP Live was first available in SAP ERP when running on SAP HANA, but it had to be activated with a business function. In SAP S/4HANA, MRP Live is active by default and is the recommended solution for materials planning. The MRP logic that will be outlined in this book is the same for classic MRP and MRP Live, but MRP Live's main advantage is its performance improvement.

Besides performance, MRP Live offers other benefits, such as the fact that there is a new transaction with more flexible selection criteria that replaces all the classic MRP transactions. Recall that SAP S/4HANA also brought the PP/DS functionality from SAP APO into its code; the new MRP Live is also capable of planning materials with PP/DS heuristics, which means that we can have a single planning run to plan all the materials.

Finally, another key advantage lies in what is to come. The new MRP Live has been defined by SAP as the *future architecture*, which means that all the innovation in this area will be focused on MRP Live, rather than classic MRP. Therefore, it is highly recommended that new SAP S/4HANA implementations use MRP Live as their default planning tool.

1.3.3 MRP Cockpit

Innovations in SAP S/4HANA were focused not only on MRP performance, but also on usability and user interface improvements.

In SAP ERP, the traditional user interface was SAP GUI, a program installed on the end user computer and used to access SAP ERP. In SAP GUI, we could run MRP and evaluate the results using different transactions—but a common complaint from end users was that those transactions were cumbersome and not intuitive or user-friendly.

1 Introduction to MRP with SAP S/4HANA

SAP S/4HANA was designed with a strong emphasis on leveraging cloud computing technologies to support SAP customers' future IT landscapes. Therefore, there is a new web-based user interface called SAP Fiori. In SAP Fiori, the transactions were replaced by applications, and there is a strong focus on usability and improving the overall user experience (even though we can still call the old transactions in SAP Fiori). We can still use the old SAP GUI in SAP S/4HANA, but we can also access it through the web browser using different devices, like a tablet or a smartphone, by logging into the SAP Fiori launchpad.

A new set of MRP applications collectively called the MRP Cockpit was delivered in the latest versions of SAP ERP. With SAP S/4HANA, these applications were enhanced and new applications were created as an alternate way to evaluate MRP results. For the SAP Fiori applications of the MRP Cockpit, SAP has placed a strong focus on identifying and resolving shortages that may lead to supply chain disruptions. Figure 1.2 shows the Monitor Material Coverage app.

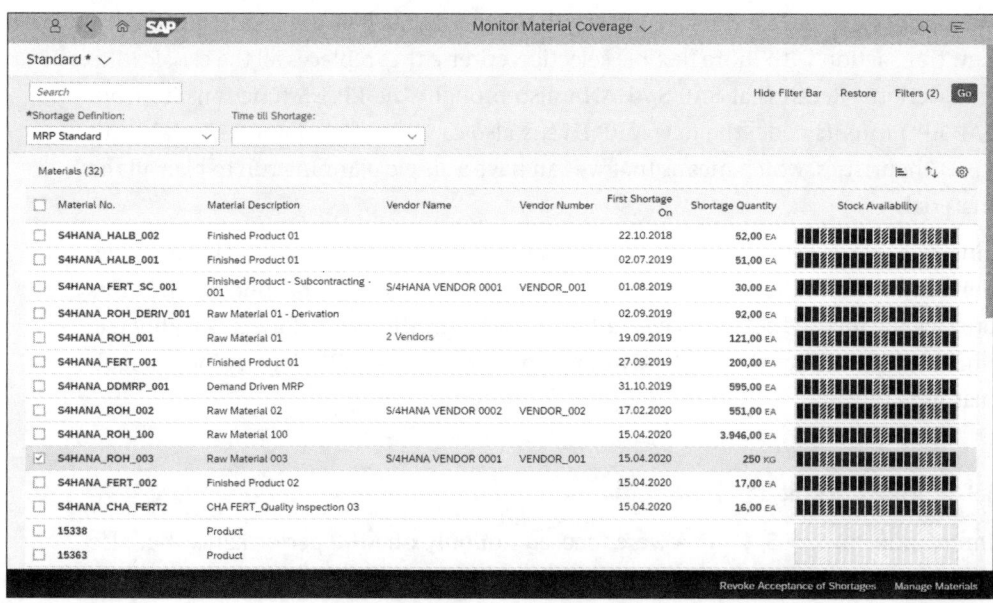

Figure 1.2 Example of an SAP Fiori App in the MRP Cockpit

The SAP Fiori applications of the MRP Cockpit were created with a *role-based* approach: different applications were designed considering the different roles of users that execute a business process step or transaction within the organization.

SAP delivers standard business roles. For example, we have a generic role for the production planner, which will allow access to all the MRP Cockpit applications, but we also have a role specifically created for the planner responsible only for external procurement, which will only include the applications relevant for materials procured externally.

These SAP Fiori applications were also developed while focusing on improving the user experience and productivity and thus offer additional features, such as charts and visual highlights of issues.

It is highly recommended to take advantage of these UI improvements and to use the SAP Fiori launchpad in any SAP S/4HANA implementation. We will talk about these applications in more detail in Chapter 6.

1.3.4 Demand-Driven MRP

Since MRP was introduced in SAP ERP, there were incremental improvements, but no major change in the MRP logic. In the last decade, however, a new concept called *demand-driven MRP* (DDMRP) became popular in companies of different industries, and it was finally introduced in SAP S/4HANA 1709.

Traditional MRP is usually based on a forecast (or on an actual sales demand in MTO scenarios), and the lower-level products are planned according those forecasted quantities. Any changes in the forecasted quantities for the finished products may lead to huge changes and exceptions for the lower-level products. If the forecasted quantities are incorrect, we may end up with excess stock or low service levels.

The new DDMRP tries to create stock buffers for strategic materials, allowing the demand to be fulfilled by the buffer. These stock buffers will protect the lower-level products from any changes to the finished products' demand and help reduce the total replenishment lead time. Because the demand generally can be fulfilled by the buffer, DDMRP helps us to increase service levels, keeping optimal stock levels for our products.

SAP S/4HANA offers a new set of SAP Fiori applications that will help classify and define which specific products should be buffered, automatically calculate the buffer quantities, and plan and execute the replenishment in order to maintain the buffer levels. Technically speaking, the new DDMRP is a new MRP type in which a maximum stock level, a reorder point, and a safety stock are automatically calculated by the system according to the average daily usage of each product.

We take a deep dive into those concepts in Chapter 10, in which we will discuss how to implement and use DDMRP in SAP S/4HANA.

1.3.5 Predictive Material and Resource Planning

Although MRP is basically an operational tool, we often need to carry out simulations to understand how a change at the demand plan will affect the MRP results. For example, we might need to understand if our suppliers will be able to provide enough raw material or if we will have enough capacity in our plant to manufacture the forecasted quantities.

In SAP ERP, a tool called Long-Term Planning (LTP) was used for simulation purposes. It was basically a simulated MRP, with very similar transactions and results. Although LTP is still available in SAP S/4HANA, a new functionality called *Predictive Material and Resource Planning* (pMRP), released in SAP S/4HANA 1909, can also be used for simulation purposes.

The new pMRP provides an improved graphical interface and a strong focus on capacity simulations, and it can be used to validate a demand plan. It also can be used in conjunction with the new DDMRP, allowing a forecast to influence the DDMRP buffer calculation.

As of the time of writing (summer 2020), the first version of pMRP had been released, but the roadmap published by SAP mentions that there are further improvements planned for the next releases, including improvements in the SAP Fiori applications and supplier collaboration scenarios. We will discuss pMRP further in Chapter 13.

1.4 Summary

This chapter provided an overview of the basic MRP concept and how it is positioned in the supply chain within SAP S/4HANA. We have discussed MRP's main inputs and outputs and how it works with other tools in the current SAP S/4HANA architecture.

We also went through the new tools available in SAP S/4HANA and clarified some important concepts that will be mentioned throughout this book. In the following chapters, we will learn how to implement and use MRP in SAP S/4HANA, including the new tools mentioned in this chapter.

Chapter 2
MRP Basics

This chapter introduces the different MRP procedures available in SAP S/4HANA. It also explains the MRP logic and the process executed internally by MRP when planning a material.

We started the previous chapter with a basic introduction to MRP, including an overview of how it works in SAP S/4HANA. However, there are different MRP procedures that can be chosen when we plan a material in SAP S/4HANA, and each procedure has a different logic. In Section 2.1, we will explain the differences between each of these procedures.

In addition, when we run MRP for a material, the sequence of steps and the internal logic executed internally by the algorithms implemented by SAP is the same for all the MRP procedures. It is important that we understand this internal MRP logic so that we can understand and evaluate the MRP results after the execution. Therefore, Section 2.2 will be dedicated to explaining the planning process executed by MRP. We will go through each step executed by MRP during the planning run, from reading the planning file to identifying which materials should be planned to generating exception messages for materials with issues.

2.1 MRP Procedures

When we are creating a new material in SAP S/4HANA and we want it to be planned by MRP, we need to extend the MRP views for this material. It is critical that we define something called the *MRP type* in the first MRP view. Standard MRP types are delivered by SAP in Customizing, but we can also create custom MRP types by defining our own specific settings.

Each MRP type must be assigned to an MRP procedure, which determines how a material will be planned by MRP: when a shortage is identified or when a replenishment proposal should be created.

2 MRP Basics

We are going to talk about the MRP type later in Chapter 3, when we discuss the MRP master data, but we need to first discuss the logic behind each MRP procedure. In this section, we will go through the standard MRP procedures, which is the basis for understanding how each MRP type works.

> **Note**
>
> SAP delivers standard MRP procedures that should be selected when creating an MRP type. Although we can have several MRP types referencing a single MRP procedure and can create our own MRP type that references a standard procedure, it is not possible to create a *new* MRP procedure.

2.1.1 Material Requirements Planning

The main MRP procedure is generally called *deterministic MRP* or simply MRP. This procedure, which we discussed in Chapter 1, is used by the most common MRP type in SAP ERP, MRP type PD. Figure 2.1 shows the MRP type Customizing (Transaction OMDQ), with reference to MRP procedure **D—Material Requirements Planning**.

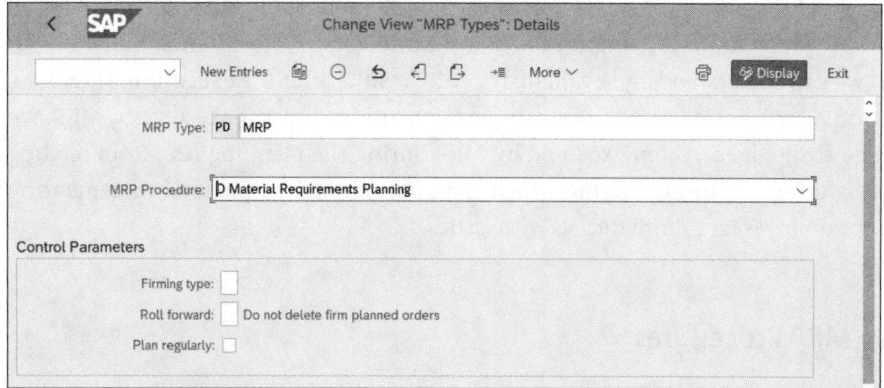

Figure 2.1 MRP Procedure in MRP Type Customizing

There are several different MRP types for this procedure, each one with a different combination of settings, and we will go through these MRP types in Chapter 3. For now, note that all the MRP types using procedure D will have a simple and straightforward logic:

1. The first thing that SAP S/4HANA will do when planning a material with this kind of MRP procedure is perform a *net requirements calculation* to identify on which

exact dates we will have a shortage of materials. (We will discuss the net requirements calculation later in this chapter.)

2. Whenever there is a shortage (if the existing stock plus the firm receipts cannot cover the requirements), MRP will trigger the creation of a new replenishment proposal. A material setting called the *lot-sizing procedure* will be used to determine the replenishment proposal quantity.

3. With the quantity determined, the system needs to determine the start and finish dates of the new replenishment proposal in a step called *scheduling*. These dates are determined based on lead times set for the material.

4. After the replenishment proposal scheduling, if this material is manufactured internally, MRP will determine the necessary components based on the BOM. This process is called *BOM explosion*; for each component, MRP will generate dependent requirements.

5. These components will also be planned by MRP, taking the dependent requirements as an input for the net requirements calculation, until we reach the raw material level. This is where MRP will generate purchase requisitions as replenishment proposals and where we will no longer have a BOM explosion.

In order to work, the deterministic MRP needs an input—generally either a forecast or a sales requirement for the finished product. Dependent requirements created during the BOM explosion will act as the input for the semifinished products and raw materials. Therefore, the planning results for the finished products will be directly tied to the planning results of the components, and any change in the finished product demand plan will lead to changes in the components.

2.1.2 Master Production Scheduling

Master production scheduling (MPS) in SAP S/4HANA is a special MRP procedure, with a logic very similar to deterministic MRP. The steps described previously for the deterministic MRP are also carried out when we are planning MPS materials. The main difference is that MPS materials can be planned separately by a different set of transactions in classic MRP, or in a separate planning run if we are using MRP Live.

The idea is to use MPS to plan finished products, products that will use bottleneck production lines, or critical semifinished products—and to plan them *before* planning the MRP materials. Because the MPS/MRP run considers infinite capacity (i.e., it will not check the capacity in the work centers during the planning run), we can run capacity leveling before planning the MRP materials, as shown in Figure 2.2.

2 MRP Basics

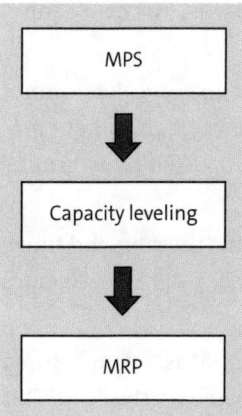

Figure 2.2 Capacity Leveling between MPS and MRP

When running capacity leveling after the MPS execution, we will ensure that the planned orders will be scheduled for a date on which they can actually be executed. By adjusting the dates of the planned orders, we will also adjust the dependent requirement dates so that the components will be planned considering realistic requirement dates.

For example, if we have too many sales orders for a material in a given week, SAP S/4HANA will generate enough planned orders to cover those sales orders, even if we do not have the capacity in the plant to manufacture everything in the same week. When the components are planned, we will also have a large quantity of dependent requirements in the same week, leading to a large shipment to be delivered by the supplier in that week.

By leveling the capacity, we will dispatch the planned orders created by MRP to weeks in which they can actually be produced, smoothing the production plan. This means that when we plan the components, we might split the shipment into smaller deliveries, avoiding problems in the warehouse.

> **Note**
> Capacity leveling is part of the PP-CRP component and another planning tool that is still part of SAP S/4HANA, even though it is no longer target architecture for the future. We can schedule capacity leveling to be executed as a background job, after planning the MPS materials and before planning MRP materials.

2.1.3 Consumption-Based Planning

The deterministic MRP will calculate the replenishment quantities based on the requirements—a sales order requirement or a forecast for a finished product, or a dependent requirement or reservation for a component.

Before the creation of the deterministic MRP, however, companies used to use the material *consumption* to determine the replenishment quantities for all the materials. The most popular method was the reorder point, in which we determine a certain target quantity (the reorder point) for each material. Whenever the stock falls below this quantity, replenishment is triggered.

Consumption-based planning methods are still available today and are frequently used, generally (but not only) for products that are cheaper and used very frequently, such as nails or screws. In SAP S/4HANA, we have a group of MRP procedures that are considered consumption-based planning, and the reorder point is one of these MRP procedures.

There are several standard MRP types with the MRP procedure **B—Reorder Point Planning** that follow this logic. There are MRP types for which we will manually set the reorder point, and other MRP types where the system can automatically calculate the reorder point based on past consumption data. In addition, we can determine if the MRP type will only compare the stock with the reorder point during the net requirements calculation or if it will also consider external requirements. This MRP type will often be used together with a lot-sizing procedure that will replenish to the maximum stock level so that the stock will not fall below the reorder point very often, avoiding an excessive number of small replenishment proposals.

Another consumption-based procedure is **S—Forecast-Based Procedure**. When using an MRP type with this procedure, we need to run a forecast before the MRP execution, in which the system will determine the forecast requirements based on the past material consumption. MRP will react to those forecast requirements and generate replenishment proposals. There are many different forecast models available to determine the forecast, from a simple moving average to a complex seasonal trend model. We can manually determine which model should be used or allow the system to select the best model based on our material consumption history. The forecast is used not only for materials using a forecast-based MRP type, but also to support the automatic calculation of the reorder point in some of the consumption-based MRP types mentioned earlier.

The last of the consumption-based MRP procedures is **R—Time-Phased MRP**, which is not often used. With this procedure, we plan a material in regular cycles. It is generally useful if a material is always produced or delivered at regular intervals—for example, on a specific day of the week. An MRP type with a time-phased MRP procedure can be considered a consumption-based MRP type when it plans based the on forecast requirements generated by the material forecast. However, it can also work as a (deterministic) MRP procedure because it can also plan by considering the actual requirements as an input.

We will provide examples of the most important consumption-based MRP types later in Chapter 3, when we talk about the MRP-related master data.

2.1.4 Demand-Driven MRP

Demand-driven MRP (DDMRP) is a relatively new concept and was not available in SAP ERP. It was first introduced in SAP S/4HANA 1709, and subsequent releases added improvements for this planning procedure and the SAP Fiori applications that support it.

When using a DDMRP procedure, we select strategic materials that will receive a stock buffer. In the context of DDMRP in SAP S/4HANA, when we say that we will *buffer* a material, it means that we will be adding an MRP type with the DDMRP procedure for this material.

This buffer is divided into three different zones: green represents a maximum stock level, yellow represents the reorder point, and red represents a safety stock.

The whole DDMRP process starts with the classification of our materials according to the following criteria: lead time, usage in BOMs, variability, and value. This classification will help us to determine if a specific material should be buffered or not. Based on this classification, the system will determine factors that will be used for the buffer calculation.

Before the actual MRP execution, we will have to schedule a buffer calculation, in which the system automatically calculates the size for each zone. This buffer calculation will consider the average daily usage of each material, plus the variability factor and the lead-time factor, derived from the material classification. When the buffer is calculated, we will know the maximum stock level, the reorder point, and the safety stock, which will be used by MRP in the net requirements calculation.

Although the DDMRP procedure is *similar* to a consumption-based procedure, because MRP will react to a reorder point, it is not *exactly* a consumption-based procedure. MRP will also react to an actual demand in the past and to qualified demands within a spike horizon.

The idea behind DDMRP is that we will no longer rely on a forecast to plan our products because the demand will be covered by the buffer. This buffer will also help to protect the lower-level materials from changes to the higher-level materials' demand by absorbing the changes.

Chapter 10 will be entirely dedicated to explaining the benefits of DDMRP and the details of its implementation in SAP S/4HANA.

2.2 The MRP Planning Process

So far, we have discussed the different MRP procedures available in SAP S/4HANA, from the traditional or deterministic MRP procedure to the newest DDMRP procedure. No matter which MRP type is selected or which procedure is used, MRP will always follow a predefined sequence of steps during the planning run.

The following steps are executed when we trigger MRP execution, no matter whether we are running classic MRP or MRP Live:

1. Read the planning file.
2. Calculate the net requirements.
3. Calculate the procurement quantity.
4. Determine the replenishment proposal.
5. Schedule the replenishment proposals.
6. Explode the BOM.
7. Generate the exception messages.

In this section, we will go through each of these steps to have a better understanding of the internal logic executed by MRP. This way we will be able to better interpret the MRP results, and we will be prepared to go through the MRP master data in the next chapter. There, we will discuss the calculation behind each MRP type and lot-sizing procedure in detail.

2.2.1 Reading the Planning File

MRP is traditionally executed as a background job, which can take a long time to complete (the more materials are selected to be planned, the longer the execution of the planning run). We do not, however, need to plan all the materials every time MRP is executed; one possibility is to plan only those materials for which an MRP-relevant change happened since the last planning run.

The *planning file* is a special table that will be created whenever a valid MRP type is set for a material, and it will be marked whenever an MRP-relevant change is posted for this material. For example, when a goods movement is posted, adding or removing a certain quantity from stock, then the planning file will be marked. Whenever a document that should add or remove stock in the future is created, such as a sales order, a production order, or a purchase order, then the planning file will be marked. This way, MRP knows exactly which materials have been changed and should be included in the next planning run.

Materials are classified in the planning file according to the concept of the *low-level code*: a finished product will have low-level code 000, its direct components will have low-level code 001, and so on. Raw materials that have no components will have the highest low-level code.

When MRP is executed in SAP S/4HANA, we can choose between a regenerative planning run (in which all the materials will be planned) or a net change planning run (in which only those materials for which the planning file is marked will be planned). Therefore, the first step within the MRP execution will be to read the planning file in order to identify which materials should be included in the planning run. The planning file will be read following the low-level code sequence, starting from materials with the lowest low-level code, in order to ensure that a component will never be planned before its parent products.

Figure 2.3 shows the planning file entry for a material in SAP S/4HANA, including the low-level code, the **Net Change** flag, and additional flags available in the planning file that are used by MRP when planning a material.

> **Note**
>
> In SAP ERP, we could also choose to plan only those materials which had an MRP-relevant change within a planning horizon, but this option is no longer available in SAP S/4HANA due to a simplification.

2.2 The MRP Planning Process

Plan. file entries								
Material	S4HANA_ROH_001							
Plnt	0001							
No. of entries	5							
NETCH plnng file ent	5							
NETPL plnng file ent	5							
Current data from 27.04.2020 At 05:12 Tim								

R Cde	Material	MRP Area	MPS ind.	NChge plng	NChgePHor.	ResetProps	ExplodeBOM	Planning date
B 004	S4HANA_ROH_001	0001	☐	X	X	X		
B 004	S4HANA_ROH_001	0001-0003	☐	X	X			
B 004	S4HANA_ROH_001	0001/0001	☐	X	X			
B 004	S4HANA_ROH_001	VENDOR_001	☐	X	X	X		
B 004	S4HANA_ROH_001	VENDOR_002	☐	X	X	X		

Figure 2.3 Planning File Entry for Material in SAP S/4HANA

When an MRP-relevant change is made to the master data, special flags are set in the planning file. If it is a change in the BOM, for example, a flag will be set to inform the system that the BOM should be re-exploded in the existing planned orders. Some changes in the MRP settings in the material master, however, will require the existing replenishment proposals to be deleted and recreated to ensure that the new settings are considered during the planning run. Both flags are read during this step of the planning run.

When the planning file is being read, there are also some checks related to some specific MRP procedures. In the planning file, we will identify if a material is using an MPS procedure; those materials will be planned only if the planning scope considers MPS materials. There are also checks for materials using a time-phased procedure, for which MRP will check the date and ensure that it is the correct date to plan each material.

The planning file **Net Change** flag will also be unchecked after MRP plans a material in order to ensure that it is no longer planned in a net change planning run—until there is an MRP-relevant change for the material that checks the planning file again.

We will go over the main transactions and reports that are generally used to create and manage the planning file entries in Chapter 3 when discussing the MRP-related master data.

2.2.2 Calculating the Net Requirements

Net requirements calculation can be considered the core of the MRP algorithm. It is during the net requirements calculation step that MRP will identify on which exact dates there will be a shortage of stock, and the creation of a new replenishment proposal will be necessary to ensure that service levels will not be affected.

During this step, MRP will check if the plant stock plus the existing firm replenishment elements can cover the requirements. If the required quantity cannot be covered by the plant stock plus the firm receipts on a specific date, then we have a shortage. The system will have to reschedule an existing firm proposal in the future or generate a new planned order or purchase requisition to cover this shortage.

When we talk about a requirement, we are talking about a planning element that should remove a certain quantity from the stock in the future. For the finished products, common requirements are sales orders, deliveries, or planned independent requirements (PIRs). For a semifinished product or raw material, a requirement will be usually a reservation or a dependent requirement. A stock transfer may also represent a requirement in the supplying plant.

Replenishment elements are all those elements that should bring a certain quantity into the stock in the future. We may have firm receipts (e.g., a production order or a purchase order) or planned receipts (e.g., a planned order or a purchase requisition). For example, when we finish the execution of a production order, we usually post a goods receipt that will increase the stock available in the plant. When this happens, the production order will no longer be relevant to MRP and will not be considered in the net requirements calculation.

> **Note**
> There are different types of stock that can be considered available by MRP. Besides the unrestricted stock, which is always considered available, we can define in Customizing if MRP will consider blocked stock, stock in transfer, or restricted stock available.

The net requirements calculation logic can be a little bit different depending on the MRP procedure selected. For an MRP procedure, the basic calculation to identify a shortage will be stock plus the existing receipts minus the requirements and the safety stock. If the result of this calculation is negative, it means that we will have a shortage and replenishment should be triggered.

In a reorder point procedure, however, the system will simply add the stock to the existing receipts and compare the results with the reorder point. If this sum is lower than the reorder point, it means that replenishment should be triggered. It is also possible to change a reorder point's MRP type settings to include requirements in the calculation, as we will discuss in Chapter 4. In this case, we will add the stock and the receipts, subtract the requirements, and then compare with the reorder point.

If we compare the net requirements calculation in an MRP procedure with the net requirements calculation in a reorder point procedure, there is a major difference: when using an MRP procedure, the system will trigger a new replenishment proposal for each period in which we have a shortage, but if we are using a reorder point procedure, then replenishment should only be triggered once, when the available quantity falls below the reorder point.

The logic used for the net requirements calculation of a forecast-based procedure is similar to the logic used by an MRP procedure, with the main difference that only the forecast will be considered as a requirement. This means that replenishment will be triggered whenever a forecast requirement is greater than the stock plus the receipts.

There are also some variations on the results of the net requirements calculation depending on the planning strategy selected for the material:

- For example, when we are using an MTO strategy, we will not consider the plant stock in the net requirements calculation because the sales order requirement will be assigned to a special individual stock segment.
- When using gross requirements planning, which is an MTS strategy, the plant stock will not be included at all in the net requirements calculation because the idea behind the planning strategy is to produce based on the forecast, no matter how much we already have in stock.

There is another planning strategy in which sales orders are intentionally left out of the net requirements calculation, and we will see examples of additional special cases later in Chapter 9, when we discuss demand management and planning strategies.

2.2.3 Calculating the Procurement Quantity

After the net requirements calculation, MRP has identified when we will have a shortage and the shortage quantity. MRP will generate new replenishment proposals to cover the shortage, but the quantity will not necessarily match the shortage quantity.

To calculate the quantity of the newly created replenishment proposal, MRP will use the **Lot-Sizing Procedure** material master setting, which allows us to define which logic will be used for this calculation. (Note that SAP delivers standard lot-sizing procedures that are ready to be assigned to the material master and used, but we can also create our own lot-sizing procedures in Customizing.)

Lot-sizing procedures are divided into the following categories:

- Static lot-sizing procedures
- Period lot-sizing procedures
- Optimum lot-sizing procedures

The *static lot-sizing procedures* have the most straightforward calculation: the quantity is derived from the shortage quantity or from a quantity predefined in the material master settings. The most frequently used static lot-sizing procedure is the *lot-for-lot* procedure, in which the system will generate a new replenishment proposal with the exact shortage quantity.

With a DDMRP or reorder point MRP type, we will often use the *replenish to maximum stock level* procedure, in which a maximum stock level is defined for a material (or calculated by DDMRP) and the system tries to generate a new replenishment proposal to reach this stock level.

Another common static lot-sizing procedure is the *fixed* procedure, in which we define a fixed quantity in the material master and MRP will always generate replenishment proposals with this quantity. If a shortage quantity is not met with a single replenishment proposal, several proposals can be created with the fixed quantity. This option is often used when a machine in the production line always produces in batches of a predetermined quantity or a vendor always delivers in batches of the same quantity.

The *period lot-sizing procedures* are used when we want to have a single replenishment proposal to cover the shortages within a whole period. For example, if we want to have a single replenishment proposal per week, we can use a *weekly* lot-sizing procedure; if we want to have a single proposal for the whole month, we can use a *monthly* lot-sizing procedure.

We also have a special period lot-sizing procedure that will allow us to create our own period using a planning calendar. With this option, we can define that MRP will always generate replenishment proposals on one or more fixed days of the week. This option is very useful if we have an agreement with a supplier to have a component always delivered on specific days of the week.

Finally, the *optimum lot-sizing procedures* will try to determine the best replenishment proposal quantity based on the storage and setup costs. These procedures are not often used because the calculation is far from simple, and it might be difficult to determine the exact storage and setup costs. There are different optimum procedures to choose from, and the difference between them is mainly the cost criterion.

We will see examples of the MRP calculation using the different standard lot-sizing procedures available in SAP S/4HANA in Chapter 3, when we talk about the MRP master data.

Besides the lot-sizing procedure itself, additional settings in the material master can be used to influence the replenishment proposal quantity. For example, we can use a *minimum* or *maximum lot size quantity* to ensure that the replenishment proposals will never be lower than the minimum or exceed the maximum quantity, no matter what the selected procedure is.

SAP S/4HANA also offers the option to use a *rounding value* in the material master so that replenishment proposals are always rounded to a quantity that is a multiple of this value. We can also use a *rounding profile* for additional rounding-related features, such as a defining a threshold for rounding or using a dynamic rounding profile.

For materials produced internally, we often have some kind of quantity loss during the manufacturing process. MRP can plan ahead for this additional quantity to ensure that we will have enough of the product at the end of the manufacturing process. This can be done by adding a scrap percentage in the material master, which will be added into the quantity of a planned order generated by MRP.

The quantity calculation will be executed for each replenishment proposal created by MRP, and each one may have a different quantity, depending on the shortage quantity and other variables involved in the calculation.

With the replenishment proposal quantity calculated, MRP will continue to the next step: determining which specific replenishment proposal should be generated.

2.2.4 Determining the Replenishment Proposal Type

At this point, we already know that there is a shortage for a material and that a replenishment proposal with a certain quantity should be generated. The next problem that MRP needs to resolve is determining which specific replenishment proposal should be generated.

MRP considers two main settings to determine the replenishment proposal to be generated:

- The *procurement type* is very straightforward: it determines if a material will be procured internally, be procured externally, or if both types of procurement can be accepted.
- The *special procurement type* allows us to handle specific scenarios—for example, a stock transfer scenario, in which a material is procured externally, but the supplier is another plant within the organization.

The procurement type is a mandatory field and must be selected for a material that should be planned by MRP. If we are using a material with internal procurement, MRP will simply generate planned orders, which are generally converted to a production or process order but can also be used for repetitive manufacturing.

For external procurement, however, there are different options for replenishment proposals that can be generated by MRP, depending on the source of supply selected. In the simplest case, MRP will generate purchase requisitions directly for a material that is to be procured externally. If we are using classic MRP, when we execute MRP we can also choose if we will first generate planned orders and then convert those planned orders to purchase requisitions.

When a material allows both procurement types, MRP will generate planned orders and we will choose later whether they will be converted to planned orders or purchase requisitions.

> **Note**
> MRP Live does not support the creation of planned orders for materials procured externally and will generate purchase requisitions for schedule lines directly.

For external procurement, MRP also supports the creation of a different replenishment proposal called a *schedule line* if we have a scheduling agreement with the supplier; this will not require a purchase order to be created.

With the replenishment proposal determined by MRP, we may also have the determination of a source of supply. For internally procured materials, MRP will try to determine a production version, which will tell us what BOM and routing is to be used. For externally procured materials, we have more options to determine the source of supply: we can use an info record, a contract, a source list, or a scheduling agreement to determine the supplier.

There are cases in which a material can have a variety of sources of supply procured either externally or internally, depending on the required quantity or the plant capacity to produce the material. For external procurement, we can use a source list to prioritize a source of supply over a period of time. Alternatively, we can use something called *quota arrangement* to distribute the quantities among the different sources of supply for both external and internal procurement. We will discuss source lists and quota arrangements later in Chapter 3.

The special procurement type is optional, and it is used together with a procurement type. If a material uses a special procurement type, then we usually have a special scenario to be taken care of by MRP when planning this material. For internal procurement, it is possible to produce or to withdrawal a material from anther plant; to treat it as a phantom assembly, which is not actually handled in stock; or to directly produce it to build another product.

For external procurement, we can have a stock transfer generated to bring this material from another plant; to create a subcontracting purchase requisition; to use direct procurement, in which we will procure a component directly to produce another material; or to use a consignment scenario.

In Chapter 3, we will provide more details about the procurement types and special procurement types, and we will also talk in detail about the master data involved in the source determination process in SAP S/4HANA.

Now that MRP knows which kind of replenishment proposal should be generated, it can continue to the next step, scheduling, in which the replenishment proposal dates will be calculated.

2.2.5 Scheduling Replenishment Proposals

So far we have seen that MRP will read the planning file to determine which materials will be planned, run the net requirements calculation to identify the shortages, calculate the procurement quantity, and then determine the procurement type, defining which replenishment proposal should be created. These replenishment proposals will also need a start and a finish date, and it is during a process called *scheduling* that those dates will be calculated.

The scheduling of the replenishment proposal may have some variations, depending on the MRP procedure or the procurement type selected for a material. In this section, we will go through these variations to understand how these dates are calculated by MRP.

In a traditional deterministic MRP procedure, MRP will find the shortages and generate a replenishment proposal to cover each shortage. In this case, the shortage date will be the starting point for the scheduling process, and MRP will consider the shortage date the replenishment proposal finish date. It will then read the lead times set on the material master and run backward scheduling to calculate the replenishment proposal basic start date. *Backward scheduling* basically means that it will subtract the lead times from the finish (shortage) date in order to calculate the start date, as shown in Figure 2.4.

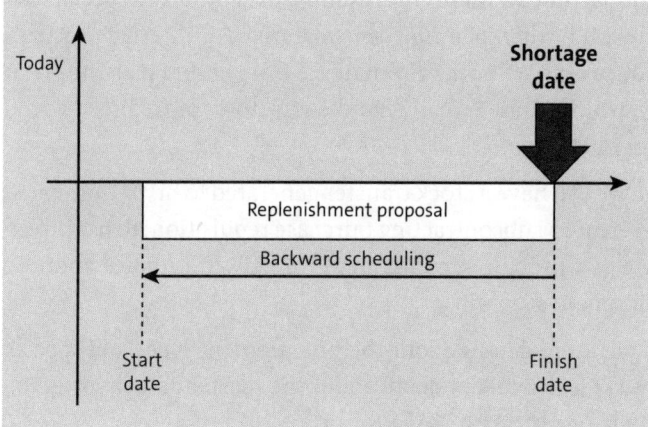

Figure 2.4 Backward Scheduling

There are situations, however, in which backward scheduling will determine a start date for the replenishment proposal in the past. Of course, this is usually not desirable: we cannot start producing a material yesterday! When this kind of situation happens, MRP will automatically consider the current date as the replenishment proposal and switch to *forward scheduling* in order to calculate the replenishment proposal finish date. We also frequently refer to this as *today scheduling* because we are using today as the starting point for scheduling.

> **Tip**
> We can choose in Customizing if we want to allow MRP to generate a replenishment proposal with a start date in the past, even though this is not actually realistic. Some companies use this option to minimize the number of exception messages triggered by MRP, and the planner usually manually reschedules these replenishment proposals later.

In this scenario, MRP will consider today as the basic start date and add the lead time to calculate the finish date. We can see a simplified forward scheduling model in Figure 2.5. In this case, the shortage date will not match the finish date, and MRP will throw an exception message to inform the user about it.

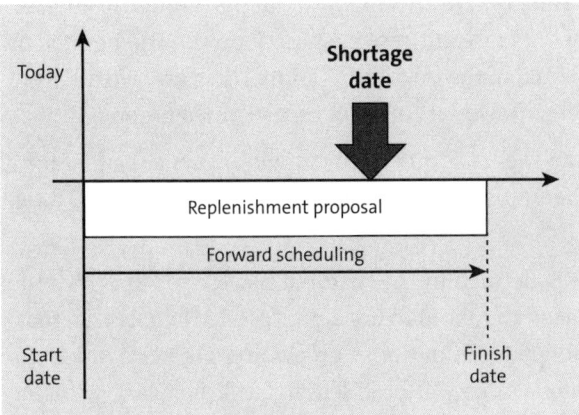

Figure 2.5 Forward Scheduling

A similar logic with forward scheduling starting from today will be used by any MRP type with a reorder point procedure. As we discussed in the previous section, the net requirements calculation for a reorder point MRP is different: it will only compare the stocks plus replenishment proposals with the reorder point. If MRP identifies that the stock is below the reorder point (i.e., there is a shortage), then procurement must start immediately; therefore, today scheduling will be used.

If we are using a period lot-sizing procedure, the replenishment proposal finish date may not match the shortage. We can define in Customizing for the period-based lot-sizing procedures if the replenishment proposal finish date should match the requirement, if it should fall in the beginning of the period (e.g., the first day of the month in monthly lot sizing), or if it should fall on the last day of the period. There is also a special setting in which we can define that the start of the replenishment proposal should be the first day of the period and the finish date should be the last day of the period. We will see those lot-sizing-specific settings in Chapter 4.

So far, we have referred to the times maintained in the material master and used for scheduling using the term *lead times*, but in fact this is very generic. There are different times that can be considered for scheduling, each with a specific purpose. In addition, the different times are considered for an externally procured replenishment

2 MRP Basics

proposal when compared with an internally procured proposal. Let's discuss in detail the scheduling and the times considered for each replenishment proposal.

Scheduling for In-House Production

When we talk about *in-house production*, we are talking about parts that will be manufactured within the company. In this case, the replenishment proposal generated by MRP will be a planned order, as noted in the previous section. There are two different ways to schedule a planned order and two sets of dates on a planned order.

This first scheduling will calculate the basic dates only and is always executed for a planned order. In basic dates scheduling, we will consider the following times to calculate the order dates:

- The *in-house production time* is defined in the material master and specifies the number of days that will be taken to manufacture a product. In the material master, we can enter a lot-size-independent in-house processing time, for which the number of days in the planned order will be fixed and will not vary with the replenishment proposal quantity. It is also possible to provide a lot-size-dependent in-house processing time, for which the number of days in the planned order will be proportional to the quantity.

- The *goods receipt processing time* is a buffer of a number of days that will represent the time between finishing the production of a material and the time it becomes available in stock. It can represent, for example, the time spent in quality inspection or the time spent to properly store a material in in the warehouse.

- The *opening period* comes from a setting defined in the material master called the *scheduling margin key*. It is used to determine the opening date—in other words, the date on which a planned order should be converted to production order.

Figure 2.6 shows the backward scheduling for in-house production, illustrating how the mentioned times are used to calculate the basic dates. Starting from the shortage date, we will subtract the goods receipt processing time and get the actual planned order finish date. From the finish date, we will then calculate the planned order start date by subtracting the in-house production time. Finally, using the opening period, we will calculate the planned order opening date.

> **Note**
>
> The opening period is not relevant when today scheduling is executed because the planned order must be immediately converted to a production or process order.

2.2 The MRP Planning Process

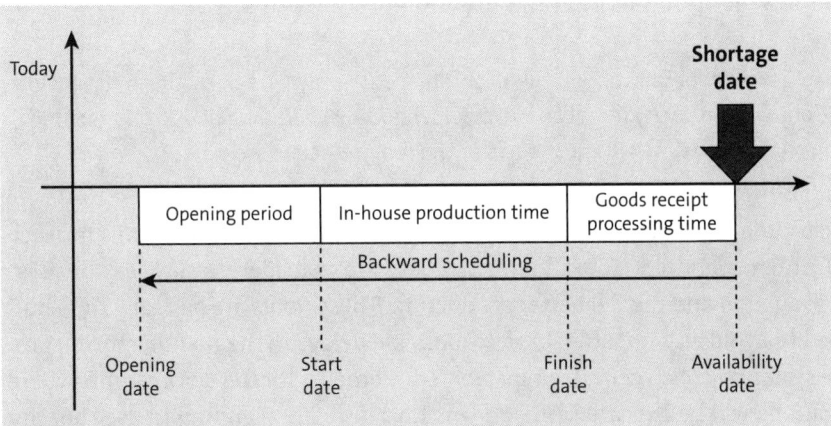

Figure 2.6 Backward Scheduling for In-House Production

After the calculation of the basic dates, MRP can run an additional step called *lead-time scheduling*, in which it will calculate a second set of dates called *production dates*. Lead-time scheduling is an optional step; we can choose whether it will be executed or not when we trigger the MRP run.

During lead-time scheduling, the system will read a master data element called the *routing*, in which we will define the different operations that should be executed to produce a material and the time spent on each operation. Although the basic dates calculation is made in days, the production dates calculation is carried out with the precision of seconds—meaning that we will have the production start *date* and also the production start *time* down to the second.

Ideally, the in-house production time should be as close as possible to the lead time calculated from the routing to avoid any divergence between the basic dates and the production dates. In fact, it is even possible to automatically update the in-house production time in the material master with the lead time from the routing.

By default, when running lead-time scheduling, the system will run backward scheduling—considering the basic start date as the production finish date and then calculating the basic start date. If there is any difference between the basic start date and the production start date, we can define in Customizing that system should automatically adjust the basic dates to match the production dates. It is also possible to change the scheduling Customizing settings to run forward scheduling, starting from the basic start date and letting the system calculate the production finish date.

> **Note**
> The system will generally adjust the basic start date only. The basic finish date will only be adjusted in a very rare scenario in which today scheduling had to be executed and the basic finish date was pushed after the requirement date.

When lead-time scheduling is executed during MRP, we will see the details for each planned order operation, and additional floats are considered, such as the float before production and the float after production. These *floats* are basically time buffers added to avoid any impact caused by possible delays in the manufacturing process. The system can also generate capacity requirements for the work centers where the operations will be executed. This means that if we are planning to use capacity leveling, then running lead-time scheduling is a prerequisite.

During the planned order scheduling, the system will also determine the dates for the component requirements. If we are using basic dates scheduling only, then the dependent requirement dates will refer to the planned order basic start date in order to ensure that all the components will be available when the order execution starts.

When using lead-time scheduling, however, we can assign each component to a specific routing operation; therefore, the dependent requirement dates may refer to the operation dates or to the start date, depending on the settings chosen in Customizing. It is also possible to define an offset of days for a component in the BOM so that it can be available earlier or after the order or operation start.

We have covered scheduling for in-house production, so now let's turn our attention to scheduling for external procurement.

Scheduling for External Procurement

For external procurement, we will only have basic dates scheduling, so we will only calculate the basic dates for purchase requisitions or schedule lines. For a regular MRP procedure, backward scheduling will be executed, starting from the shortage date, and today scheduling can be executed if the start date falls in the past.

The following times will be considered when scheduling an externally procured purchase requisition:

- The *goods receipt processing time* is the same goods receipt processing time considered during the scheduling of an internally procured replenishment proposal.

- The *planned delivery time* is the time that the vendor will take to deliver the product, measured in calendar days. It is basically the time between sending the purchase request to the vendor and receiving the product in the warehouse. We can specify it at a material level or specify a different planned delivery time per vendor or per contract/agreement.
- The *purchasing processing time* represents the internal time spent by the purchasing department to receive the purchase order, negotiate, and send it to the supplier. It is a fixed time maintained per plant in Customizing.
- The *opening period* is the period of time in which a planned order should be converted to purchase requisition in order to initiate the procurement. This value comes from the scheduling margin key assigned to the material master.

Note

If we are using MRP Live, then the system will automatically generate purchase requisitions when we are working with external procurement, so the opening period is no longer relevant. The opening period will also not be relevant when running forward scheduling.

Figure 2.7 illustrates backward scheduling for external procurement, showing that the system starts on the shortage date and subtracts the goods receipt processing time.

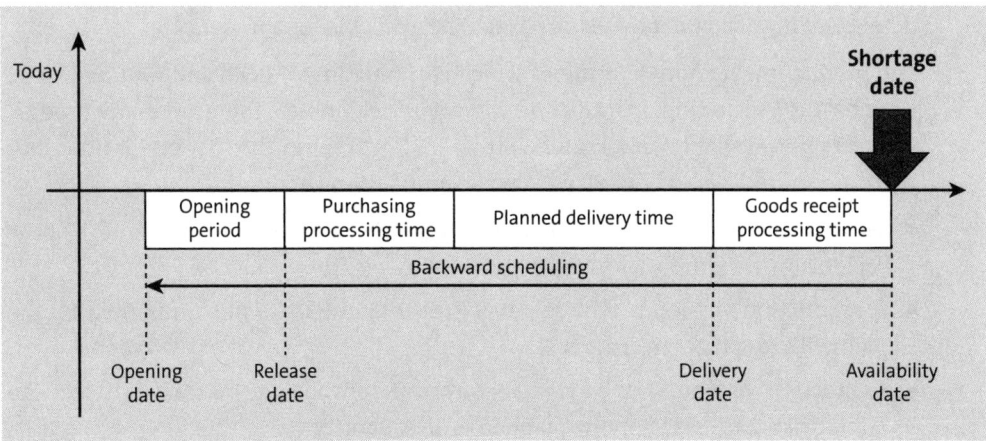

Figure 2.7 Backward Scheduling for External Procurement

After that, the planned delivery time and the purchasing processing time are subtracted to calculate the release date—in other words, the date on which we should have a released purchase order to start procurement. The opening period shown in the figure will be relevant when using planned orders in classic MRP.

2.2.6 Exploding the BOM

For materials procured internally, MRP will generate planned orders to cover the shortage. Those planned orders will generally have *components*, which are the materials that are consumed to manufacture the finished or semifinished products. MRP will generate dependent requirements for those components so that they can also be planned by MRP.

To determine the list of the planned order components, MRP will read the BOM and generate the dependent requirements. We call this process *BOM explosion*.

> **Note**
>
> Subcontracting purchase requisitions will also go through BOM explosion because MRP needs to determine which components must be sent to the vendor.

In SAP ERP, we had many different ways to determine which BOM should be exploded for a given material, but this logic was simplified in SAP S/4HANA. To have a BOM determined by MRP in SAP S/4HANA, it is mandatory that an additional master data element called the *production version* be available for a material.

The production version determines which combination of BOM and routing can be used by MRP, including quantity and validity restrictions. If there are many production versions available for a material, then MRP will select the first one it finds, but there are some ways to prioritize a specific production version:

- We can define a quota arrangement for a material, distributing a percentage of the replenishment proposals for each production version.
- A production version can be manually set in a PIR and will be inherited by the planned order that covers this PIR.
- Production versions can be created with different lot sizes. MRP will select the appropriate one based on the planned order quantity.

2.2 The MRP Planning Process

> **Warning**
> If MRP cannot find a valid production version for a material, then the BOM cannot be exploded and there will be no components in the planned order. If this happens, an exception message will be created for the planned order, informing the planner that the BOM could not be exploded.

When the BOM is exploded, MRP will determine which BOM components are relevant for production and will generate dependent requirements for those components. A BOM might list alternative items (only one of which is relevant for the planned order) or include a discontinued part that needs to be replaced; the BOM explosion will generate the necessary list of requirements.

In addition, there is another SAP S/4HANA feature called *variant configuration*, which allows us to create object dependencies for components. These object dependencies will allow the planned order components to vary according to the characteristics defined in the sales order.

There is also a special type of component called *phantom assembly*, which is generally used to simplify BOM maintenance. If a component is a phantom assembly, MRP will not generate a dependent requirement for this component. Instead, it will read the phantom assembly's BOM and bring the components directly into the planned order. This means that the phantom assembly will never be received into stock. It is used to better organize the BOM structure, allowing us to avoid huge BOMs and providing a better way to maintain complex BOMs. This is a special procurement type that will be discussed later in Chapter 3.

As mentioned when we discussed planned order scheduling, the planned order components will also have a date determined by MRP, which is the date on which we expect to use this component. This date can be either the order start date, or the operation date if we run lead-time scheduling. We have a special setting in the BOM called *lead-time offset*, which allows us to bring the dependent requirement date forward or to displace it. This feature can be useful if we want to ensure that we will have the component in stock before we start the planned order/operation or if we know that we will only consume it at a later stage. The lead-time offset value is defined in days.

We can also use something called the *distribution key*, which will allow MRP to split the dependent requirement into smaller quantities between the order start and finish dates. This is useful if the component is not consumed entirely when the order starts, but continuously throughout the process.

When the dependent requirements are created, MRP can also determine from which storage location each component will be consumed. There are different ways to determine the component storage location, as we will discuss in Chapter 7.

Those dependent requirements generated during the BOM explosion are the main input for MRP to determine which materials should be planned next; they will usually be the main requirements for the components. When we convert a planned order to production order, dependent requirements will become an order reservation, which is later used to consume those components for the order.

Once we have all the shortages identified, the replenishment proposals created to cover them, and the dependent requirements created with the BOM explosion, we can say that a material has been planned by MRP. However, when MRP finds any problem or a situation that needs to be reviewed by the planner, it will trigger the creation of exception messages. Let's discuss that now.

2.2.7 Creating Exception Messages

Although MRP is a smart application that can handle most of the problems that may happen when planning a material, there are situations in which it needs to bring the planner's attention to a specific situation or even terminate the planning run because of an error. In this case, it will trigger an *exception message*, which will be displayed for the planner in the MRP evaluation transactions.

Exception messages are divided into groups, where each group represents a specific type of issue. An exception message is always triggered with reference to a specific planning element. The logic to trigger those exceptions is hard-coded into the MRP algorithm, which means that we cannot trigger a custom exception or influence the creation of exception messages.

> **Note**
> The creation of exception messages will not necessarily happen as the last step in the MRP run. In fact, exceptions may be triggered throughout the planning run, during the different MRP steps detailed in Section 2.2.1 through Section 2.2.6. For example, if there is a problem with the BOM, an exception can be triggered during the BOM explosion. If there is a problem with the date calculation, the exception can be created during the replenishment proposal scheduling.

Some situations described earlier in this chapter may lead MRP to trigger an exception message for a material. For example, if a production version does not exist for a material, then MRP cannot explode the BOM, which will trigger an exception message to alert the planner that a production version does not exist for that planned order.

The most commonly triggered exception messages are related to the rescheduling of replenishment proposals. If MRP finds a shortage but there is a firm replenishment proposal in the future that can cover it, a rescheduling exception will be triggered. This message will include a rescheduling date so that the planner can manually adjust the replenishment proposal dates to cover the shortage (remember that MRP cannot change firm replenishment proposals without manual intervention).

If the start date of a replenishment proposal created by MRP would fall in the past, it automatically switches to today scheduling, so the replenishment proposal finish date may not match the requirement date. This is another situation in which MRP will trigger a rescheduling exception message, to inform the planner that this replenishment proposal is related to a shortage on a specific date.

There are also situations in which MRP cannot continue planning a specific material due to an error. Therefore, the system triggers a termination exception message to tell the planner that this material could not be planned. A classic example of a termination is when we have too many replenishment proposals being created by MRP on the same date (usually due to lot-sizing issues), and the number of replenishment proposals exceeds the maximum value allowed in Customizing.

With all the replenishment proposals, dependent requirements, and exception messages created for a material, MRP can restart the process outlined earlier for the next material. It will start by reading the planning file, then calculate the net requirements, and so on.

2.3 Summary

This chapter provided a basic overview of the MRP logic, starting with the main MRP procedures available in SAP S/4HANA. We also went through the whole process carried out during the MRP run when planning a material.

The idea behind this chapter is to provide some fundamental knowledge for new users or consultants who do not know exactly how MRP works, so it was more focused on the theoretical knowledge; we did not talk about transaction codes or specific Customizing settings. Starting in Chapter 3, we will go deeper into the concepts introduced here and focus on practical knowledge, going through the details of each transaction and the Customizing related to MRP in SAP S/4HANA.

In the next chapter, we start the hands-on MRP experience by discussing all the master data related to MRP, including the MRP tabs in the material master, BOMs, routings, production versions, quota arrangements, and all the master data mentioned in this chapter.

Chapter 3
Master Data and Basic Settings

Master data may represent different entities in the SAP S/4HANA system, and it is the system foundation. In this chapter, we will walk through the most important MRP master data, which needs to be created before we can execute the planning run. We also will discuss the impact of the master data settings on the MRP results.

SAP S/4HANA relies on different types of data, such as customizing data, master data, and transactional data. Customizing is usually the first type to be created, during the implementation phase. It lets us tailor business processes to company needs and usually remains untouched when there are no process changes.

Transactional data represents the business transactions posted on a daily basis, such as sales orders, production orders, or purchase orders. It is frequently created and changed and is usually created with reference to master data.

Master data is generally used to describe entities, such as a product, an employee, or a customer, and it holds both information about the entity (such as a description) and settings that tell the system how to process this specific entity. It is usually referenced in business transactions and it remains unchanged for longer periods.

This chapter will show the most important master data from an MRP perspective, and it will explain the most important settings that may affect the MRP run. Section 3.1 covers the material master, which is the actual object of the planning run, and walks through the most important MRP settings, including the MRP areas, which became fundamental in SAP S/4HANA. We will continue in Section 3.2 by explaining the procurement master data in SAP S/4HANA for both internal and external procurement. Finally, in Section 3.3 we will look at the planning file and discuss its importance for the MRP run.

3.1 Material Master

The most important master data in SAP S/4HANA, at least from the logistic point of view, is the material master. It represents a product that can be purchased, produced, stocked, sold, or costed, and many other business transactions can be posted with reference to a material.

As the name suggests, MRP is centered on the material master. Requirements such as a forecast or a sales order are created with reference to a material, and the MRP run will generate replenishment proposals for this material in order to cover the shortages.

The following are the most important material types in SAP from an MRP perspective:

- **Finished products**
  These are usually products manufactured by the company and sold to customers. The standard material type for a finished product is FERT.

- **Semifinished products**
  These products are also manufactured internally, but they are generally not sold; they are used as components for finished or other semifinished products. The standard material type HALB identifies semifinished products.

- **Raw materials**
  These are materials that a company purchases from a supplier and uses to produce semifinished or finished products. The standard material type for raw materials is ROH.

Other standard material types can also be considered by MRP. It is even possible to create a custom material type for a specific process. But these three types are the most commonly used in manufacturing processes.

The material master is created in Transaction MM01, and there are four tabs in the material master to store the MRP-relevant settings. Figure 3.1 shows the details of the **MRP 1** tab in the material master. In addition to general data, this is where we will find information about the MRP procedure, lot sizes, and MRP areas in the corresponding sections of the screen. We will explore those areas in more detail later in this chapter.

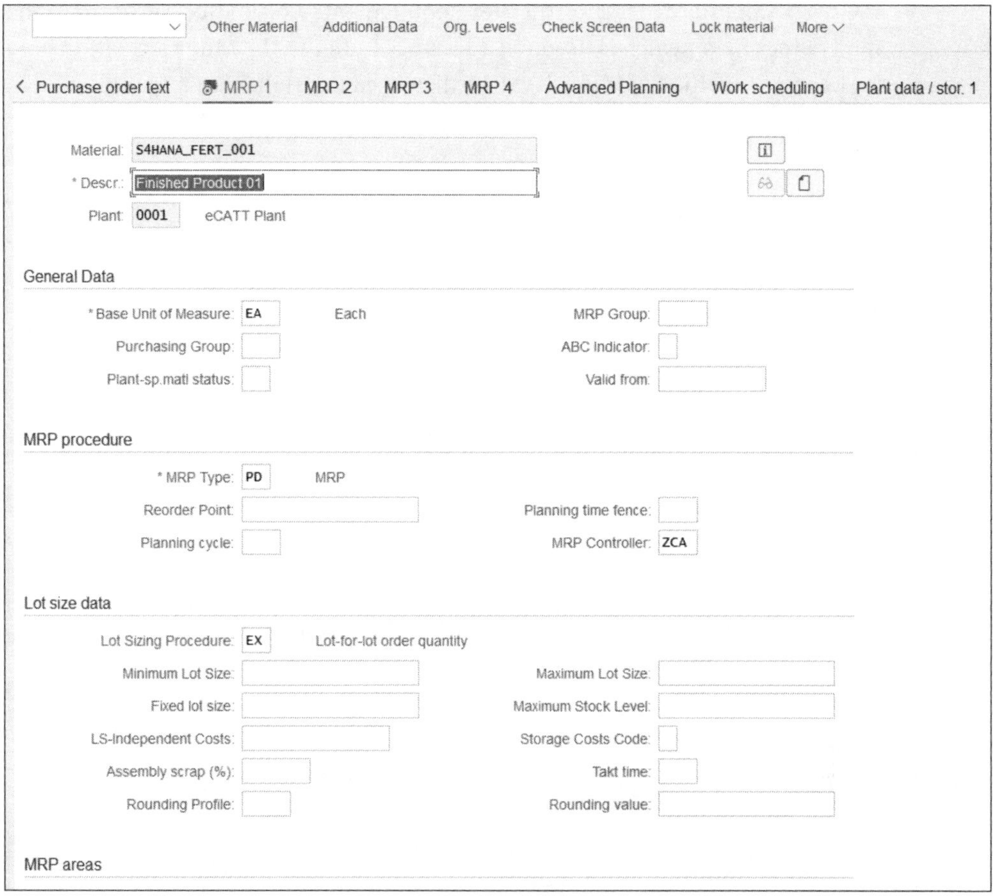

Figure 3.1 The MRP 1 Tab in the Material Master

The **MRP 2** tab shown in Figure 3.2 displays details about procurement, scheduling, and net requirements calculation in the corresponding sections:

- In the **Procurement** section, we can indicate if a material will be produced internally or purchased, for example, or which storage location should be used by MRP for this product.
- In the **Scheduling** section, we can record the default values for internal and external procurement, including how much time a material takes to be produced internally or procured externally and how much time it takes to receive it in the warehouse. These parameters will be discussed in detail in Section 3.1.4.

- The most important fields of the **Net Requirements Calculation** section are the **Safety Stock** field (which is used to add a stock buffer in the MRP calculation) and the **Coverage Profile** field (which will be discussed in detail in Chapter 8).

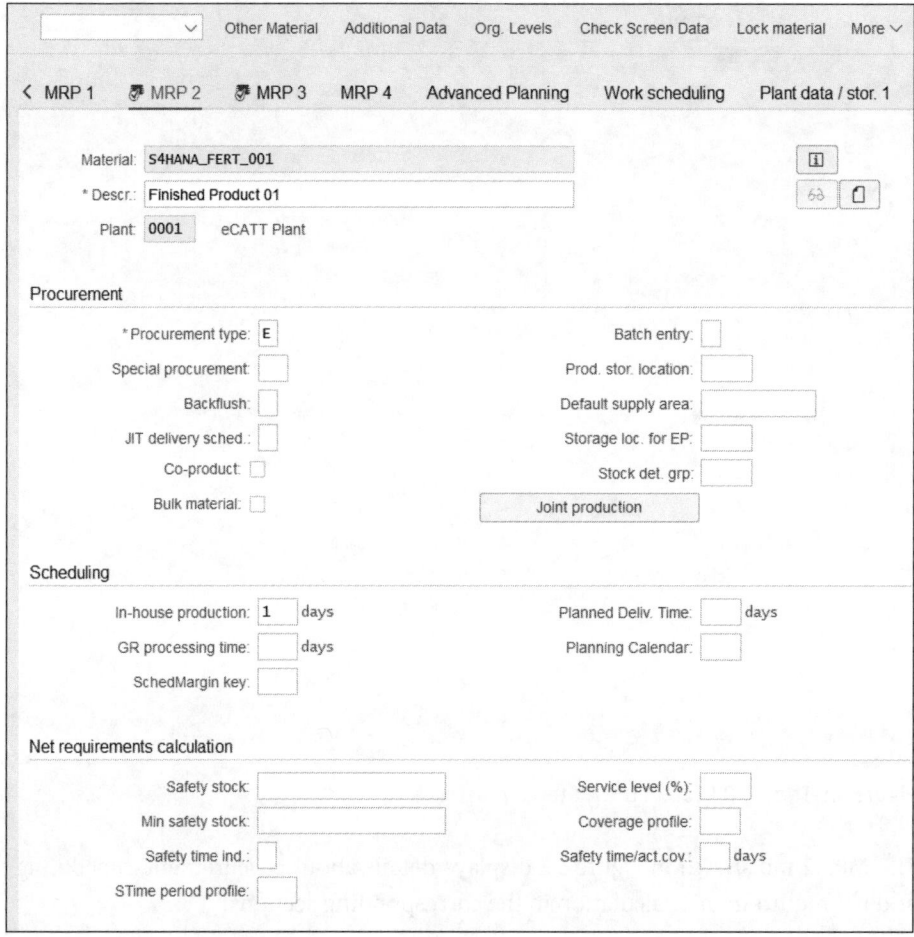

Figure 3.2 The MRP 2 Tab in the Material Master

The **Planning** section is the most important section of the **MRP 3** tab in the material master, as shown in Figure 3.3. This section contains settings related to demand management, which we will explore in Chapter 9. Another important section of this tab is

3.1 Material Master

Availability Check, which stores settings related to the ATP check that are used not only by MRP but also in many different areas across the system.

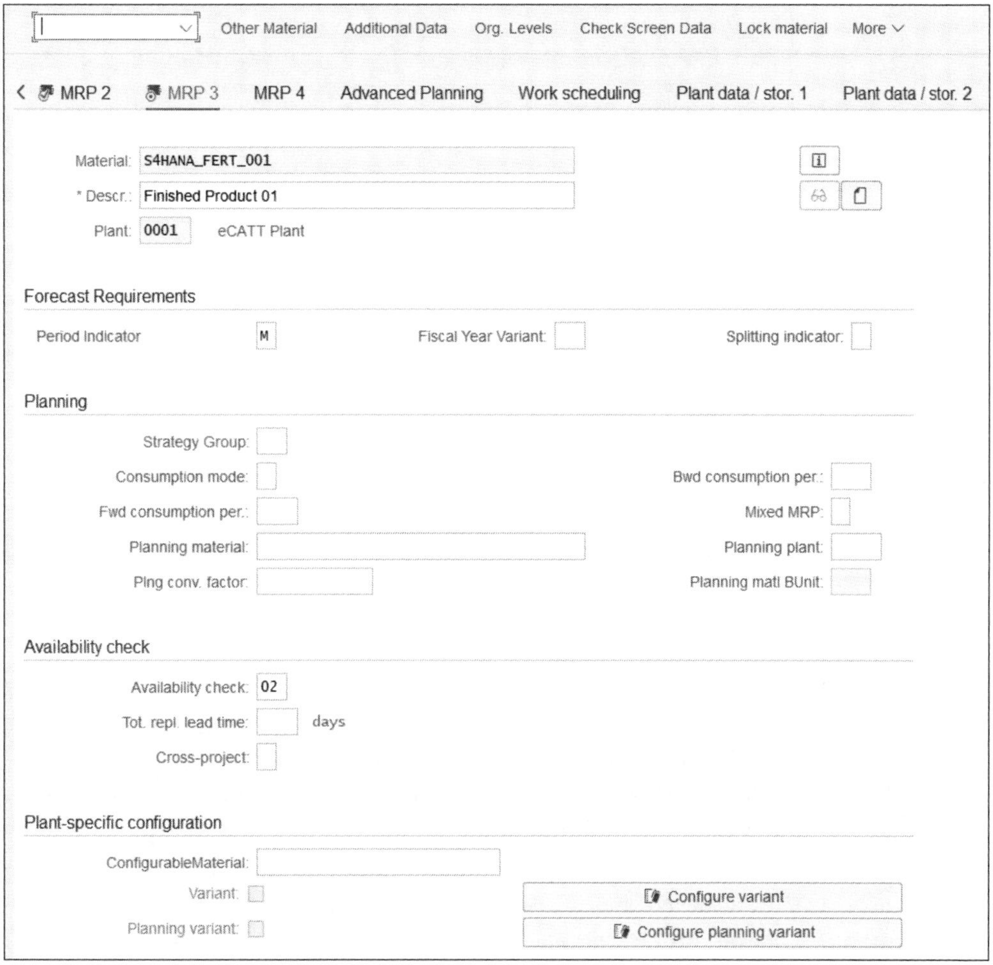

Figure 3.3 The MRP 3 Tab in the Material Master

Finally, the **MRP 4** tab shown in Figure 3.4 displays information related to BOM explosion/dependent requirements, discontinued parts, and repetitive manufacturing.

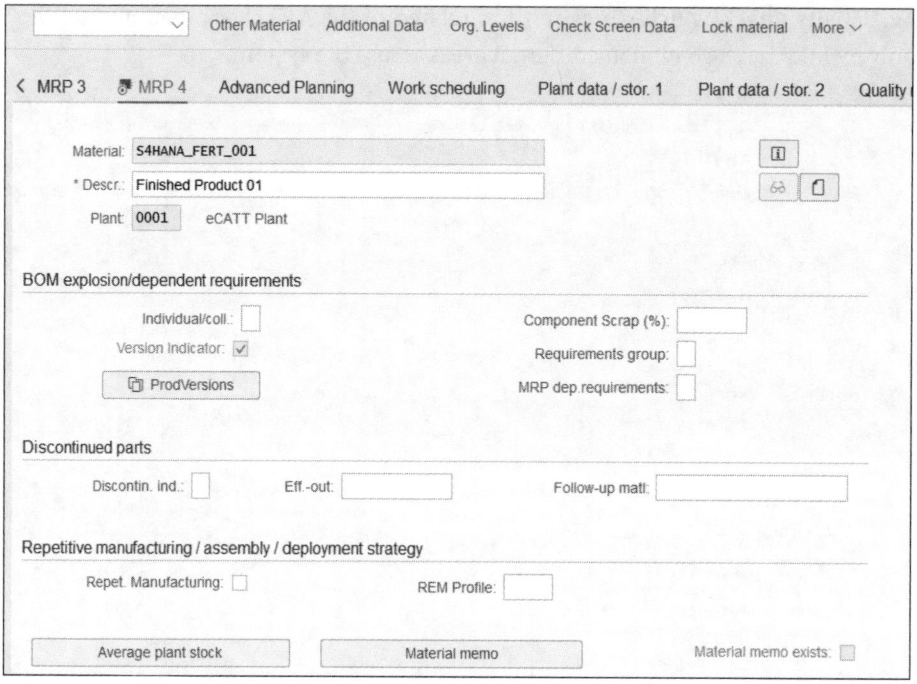

3   Master Data and Basic Settings

Figure 3.4 The MRP 4 Tab of the Material Master

> **Note**
>
> If we compare the material master MRP tabs of an SAP S/4HANA system with the MRP tabs of an SAP ERP system, we will see that several fields are missing from SAP S/4HANA, especially in the **MRP 4** tab.
>
> This is basically because SAP tried to reduce the effort of material master maintenance in SAP S/4HANA, removing fields that were no longer relevant due to simplifications. SAP Note 2267246 provides more information about these simplifications implemented in the material master.

In addition to the four MRP tabs, the **Forecasting** tab in the material master is also relevant for MRP. This tab generally should be extended to the material master when using a forecast-based MRP type; we will explore the different MRP types in the following section.

Figure 3.5 shows the **Forecasting** tab and all the fields relevant to the forecast. Here we define, for example, the forecast model to be used to when the forecast is executed, the number of historical periods to be analyzed, the number of forecast periods, and additional information related to the forecast. In this tab, we can also manually include or change the forecast values and the consumption values or manually execute the forecast by clicking the respective buttons.

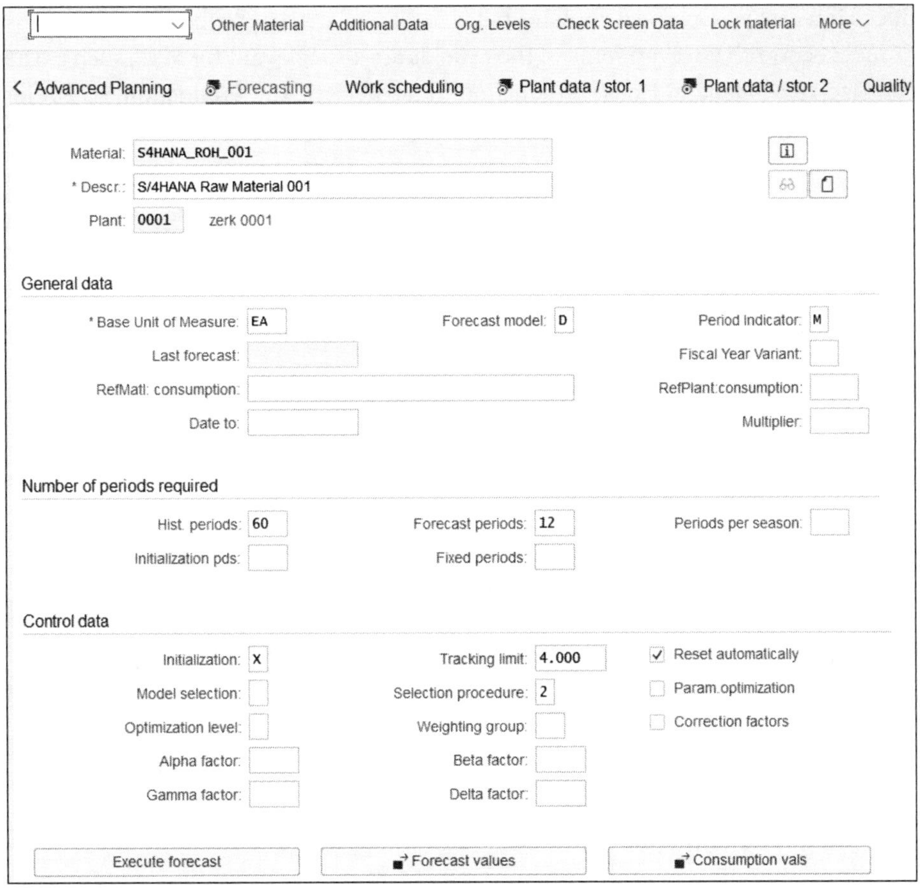

Figure 3.5 The Forecasting Tab in the Material Master

> **Warning**
>
> According to SAP Note 2268100, SAP plans to replace the current material forecast solution in the future. The future solution should perform the forecasting algorithm

3   Master Data and Basic Settings

> in SAP HANA by utilizing SAP HANA's forecasting library, improving the material forecast performance. In the meantime, the material forecast transactions, such as Transaction MP30, can still be used because there is no functional equivalent yet in SAP S/4HANA.

Finally, the **Work Scheduling** tab in the material master is relevant for materials produced internally only, and it contains fields mostly related to production and process order execution. However, some of those fields are also relevant for MRP, such as the **Lot Size Dependent In-House Production Time** field or the **Production Scheduler Supervisor** field.

In the following sections, we will describe the main MRP settings in the material master, such as the MRP type or the lot-sizing procedure, and we will discuss the impact of changing those settings in the MRP results.

3.1.1   MRP Type

As we discussed in Chapter 2, there are several different MRP procedures, such as the traditional MRP, master production scheduling, or consumption-based planning.

The MRP procedure to be used for planning during the MRP run is defined by the selection of an MRP type. For each MRP procedure, there are different MRP types available in the standard Customizing delivered by SAP, each one with small variations in the Customizing settings. If we cannot find a specific MRP type to fulfill particular business requirements, we can create a new one in Customizing. Table 3.1 shows the complete list of MRP types delivered by SAP in SAP S/4HANA and how they match with MRP procedures.

MRP Type	MRP Type Description	MRP Procedure
D1	Demand-driven replenishment, fixing type 1	C—Demand-driven replenishment
M0	MPS, fixing type 0	M—Master production scheduling
M1	MPS, fixing type 1	M—Master production scheduling
M2	MPS, fixing type 2	M—Master production scheduling
M3	MPS, fixing type 3	M—Master production scheduling

Table 3.1 Standard MRP Types Delivered by SAP in Customizing

3.1 Material Master

MRP Type	MRP Type Description	MRP Procedure
M4	MPS, fixing type 4	M—Master production scheduling
ND	No planning	N—No MRP
P1	MRP, fixing type 1	D—Material requirements planning
P2	MRP, fixing type 2	D—Material requirements planning
P3	MRP, fixing type 3	D—Material requirements planning
P4	MRP, fixing type 4	D—Material requirements planning
PD	MRP	D—Material requirements planning
R1	Time-phased planning	R—Time-phased materials planning
R2	Time phased with auto reorder point	R—Time-phased materials planning
RE	Replenishment planned externally	W—Replenishment (IS Retail)
RF	Replenishment with dynamic target stock	W—Replenishment (IS Retail)
RP	Replenishment	W—Replenishment (IS Retail)
RR	Time-phased replenishment with dynamic target stock	W—Replenishment (IS Retail)
RS	Time-phased replenishment planning	W—Replenishment (IS Retail)
V1	Manual reorder point with external requirements	B—Reorder point planning
V2	Automatic reorder point with external requirements	B—Reorder point planning
VB	Manual reorder point planning	B—Reorder point planning
VI	Vendor-managed inventory	W—Replenishment (IS Retail)
VM	Automatic reorder point planning	B—Reorder point planning
VS	Seasonal MRP	R—Time-phased materials planning

Table 3.1 Standard MRP Types Delivered by SAP in Customizing (Cont.)

3   Master Data and Basic Settings

MRP Type	MRP Type Description	MRP Procedure
VV	Forecast-based planning	S—Forecast-based planning
X0	Without MRP, with BOM explosion	X—Without MRP, with BOM explosion

Table 3.1 Standard MRP Types Delivered by SAP in Customizing (Cont.)

> **Note**
>
> MRP types with procedure W (replenishment) are specific to SAP's industry solution for retail customers. The Retail industry solution is active by default in SAP S/4HANA, but this topic is out of scope of this book.
>
> MRP type X0 is generally used when a material is planned by PP/DS; MRP will only explode the BOM for planned orders generated by PP/DS.

MRP Types with Procedure MRP

The standard MRP types with the MRP procedure will start with the character *P*. The most basic and most commonly used MRP type is PD, also known simply as MRP or deterministic MRP. This very simple MRP type produces very straightforward MRP results, so we will start exploring the MRP types using PD in the material master.

When using this MRP type, whenever there is a requirement, the system will compare it with the available quantity; that means the on-hand stock plus the receipts. If the requirement is larger than the available quantity, then we will have a shortage. For each shortage, MRP will create a new replenishment proposal to cover the shortage. The quantity of the replenishment proposal created by MRP will be defined by the lot-sizing procedure set for the material in the **MRP 1** tab.

> **Note**
>
> For simplification purposes, we will use lot-sizing procedure EX on the examples shown in this section so that the replenishment proposal quantity is always equal to the shortage quantity. We will explore different lot-sizing procedures in the following section.

Figure 3.6 shows the stock and requirements situation for material S/4HANA_FERT_001 *before the MRP run*. The first line shows use that we have 50 EA of stock available for our material. The following lines show that we have a forecast (independent requirement) of 100 EA on 03.06, 01.07, and 01.08.

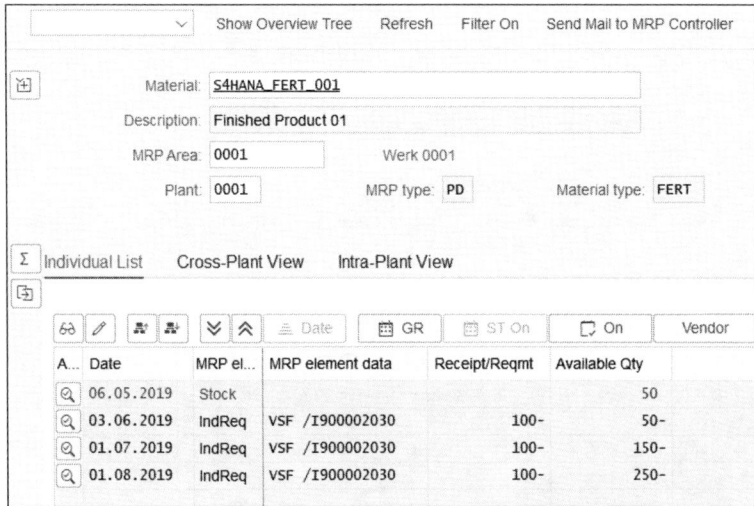

Figure 3.6 Stock/Requirements for Material S/4HANA_FERT_001 before the MRP Run

Pay special attention to the value of the **Available Quantity** column, which shows the projected quantity for a given date considering the on-hand stock, the requirements, and the receipt elements. On 03.06, for example, we have a negative projected available quantity of -50, because we only have 50 EA of stock available, a forecast of 100, and no replenishment element. This means that we have a projected shortage of -50 for this date.

Now, let's analyze the stock and requirements situation for the same material *after the MRP run*. As shown in Figure 3.7, for every date on which we would have a negative available quantity, MRP created a new replenishment proposal (in this case, a planned order) to cover all the shortages. Because we are using lot-sizing procedure EX for our material, the replenishment proposal quantity was exactly the shortage quantity, meaning that the target available quantity was always zero.

Besides MRP type PD, there are additional MRP types with the same procedure, such as P1, P2, P3, and P4. This means that the same logic will be used to identify the shortages and to create replenishment proposals. The main difference is that when we use those MRP types, we will also consider a time fence for our material. The *time fence* is a firm period in which MRP will not create new replenishment proposals. The planning time fence is a period of workdays, and it is maintained in the **MRP 1** tab of the material master (see Figure 3.1).

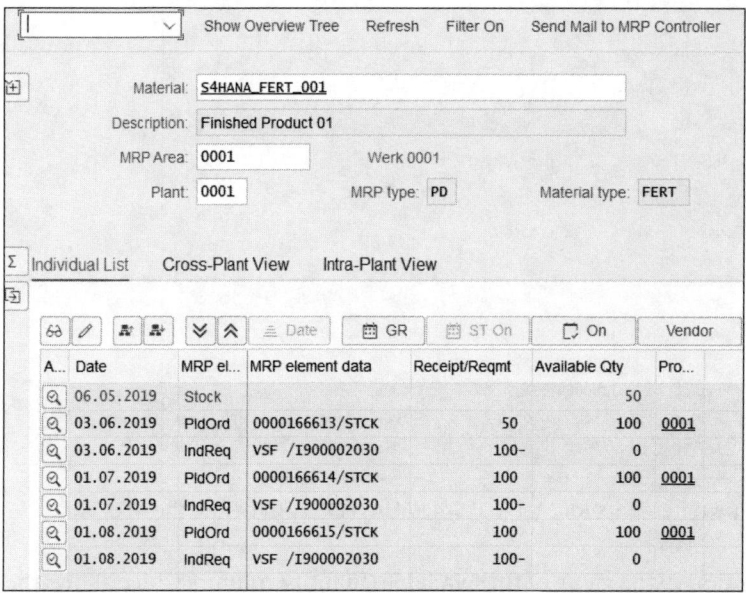

Figure 3.7 Stock/Requirements for Material S/4HANA_FERT_001 after the MRP Run with MRP Type PD

Each one of these standard MRP types has a different *firming type* defined in Customizing, codifying the way that MRP type will treat replenishment proposals within the time fence:

- MRP type P1 will use firming type **1—Automatic Firming and Order Proposals Rescheduled Out**. This means that any existing planned order that falls into the time fence will be automatically considered firm and will not be changed by MRP. If there is a shortage within the time fence, a new planned order will be created, but it will be rescheduled out (i.e., it will be created outside the time fence).

- MRP type P2 uses firming type **2—Automatic Firming without Order Proposal**, which means that any existing planned order that moves into the time fence will be automatically firmed, but MRP will not cover new shortages within the time fence.

- MRP type P3 uses firming type **3—Manual Firming and Order Proposals Rescheduled Out**. This is similar to MRP type P1, but only planned orders that are manually firmed will be kept within the time fence. Newly created planned orders or unfirmed planned orders within the time fence will be rescheduled out.
- MRP type P4 uses firming type **4—Manual Firming without Order Proposal**. It will delete any unfirmed planned order within the time fence, and it will not cover shortages within the time fence.

Figure 3.8 shows the MRP results when using MRP type P1 and a planning time fence of 30 days. The blue line that corresponds to **End of Planning Time Fence** identifies when this 30-day period ends. The independent requirement of 100 EA in 03.06 lies within the time fence and is causing a shortage of 50 EA, but MRP only created a new planned order on the same date to cover it on 24.06, outside the time fence. On the following day, the time fence will move to 25.06 and this planned order will be automatically firmed because it will now lie within the time fence.

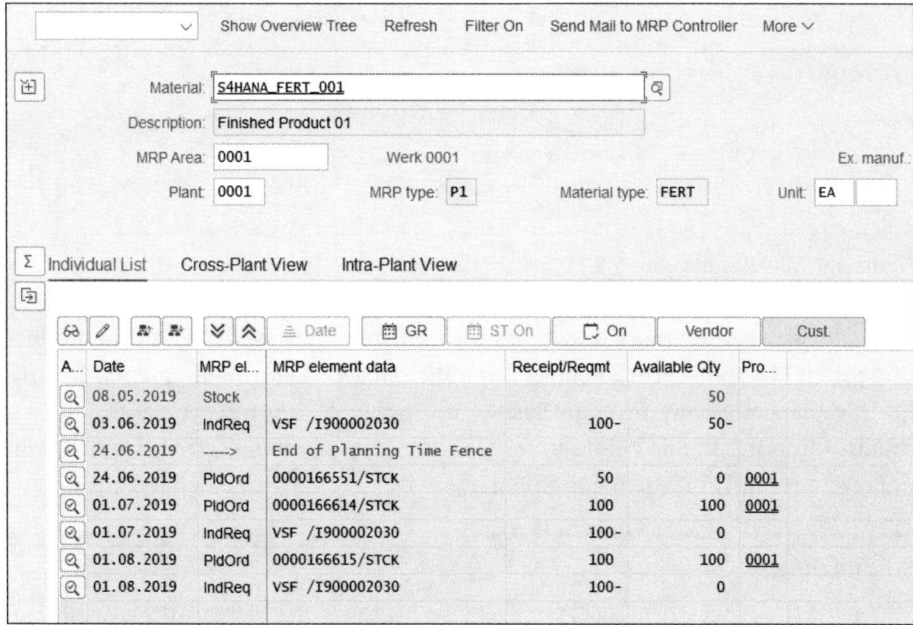

Figure 3.8 MRP Results with MRP Type P1

Now let's analyze the same scenario with MRP type P2, which uses a different firming type. As shown in Figure 3.9, when we are using MRP type P2 and the same time fence of 30 days, we will have the same shortage of 50 EA within the time fence, caused by the independent requirement on 03.6. The difference here is that MRP did not create a new planned order outside the time fence to cover this requirement. With the firming type used by MRP type P2, shortages within the time fence will not be covered at all by MRP and the planner will have to manually manage those situations.

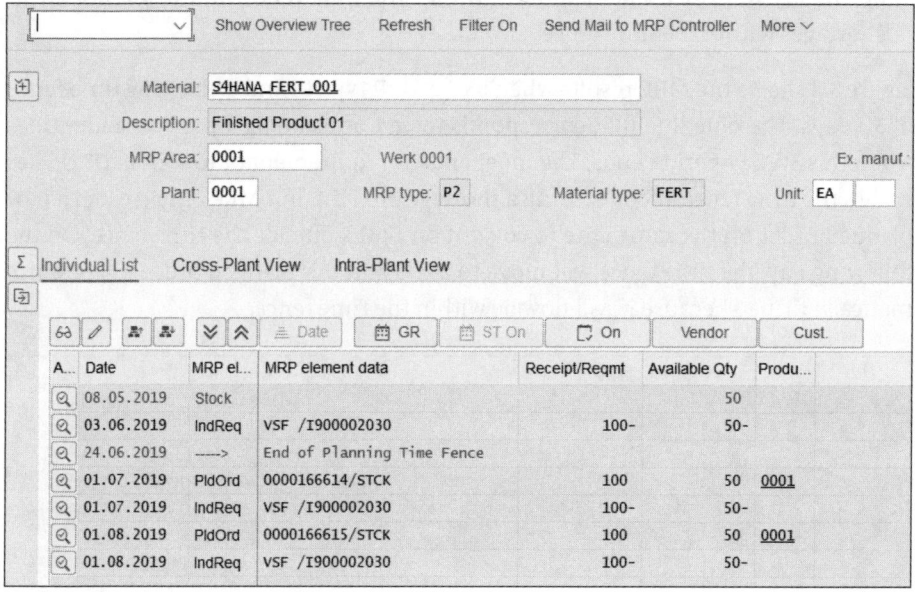

Figure 3.9 MRP Results with MRP Type P2

The main idea behind those MRP types with a firming type is to have a firm production plan in the short term and not allow MRP to react on late requirements, disturbing the plan originally firmed. Usually, the usage of a firming type and a firm production plant should be discussed with the sales department because MRP will not react promptly on late requirements.

> **Example**
>
> Imagine that a weekly production plan is defined in a plant every Monday, which means that the MRP controller firms and schedules all the planned orders. On Tuesday, a new sales order arrives for the current week, leading to a shortage situation. If we are using the regular MRP type PD, then MRP will simply generate a new planned order to cover this requirement, affecting the existing production plan.

> On the other hand, if we are using an MRP type with firming and a planning time fence of seven days, then MRP will create a new planned order outside the time fence—or it may not create a new planned order, depending on the firming type being used. This means that the production plan for the week will not be affected, and the MRP controller will have to deal with this exception when planning for the next week.

Master Production Scheduling

SAP S/4HANA offers a set of MRP types with the master production scheduling (MPS) procedure. The logic behind the MPS MRP types is similar to the logic used by deterministic MRP types, except that materials with those MRP types will be planned in a separated planning run. In classic MRP, there are different transactions to process MPS materials; in MRP Live, a selection criterion is available for selecting only MPS materials in the planning run.

As already explained in Chapter 2, the idea behind this separation is that MPS can be executed first for a set of products that should be prioritized, such as the most important or valuable finished products or products that use bottleneck resources. After the MPS run, capacity leveling can be executed for those bottleneck resources, and the planner can review and adjust the plan for those products. With the capacity issues resolved, MRP then will be executed, considering the adjusted requirement dates for the components.

The main MRP type for the MPS MRP procedure is M0, which would be equivalent to the deterministic MRP type PD. MRP types M1, M2, M3, and M4 would be the equivalents to P1, P2, P3, and P4, respectively, with similar firming types.

Consumption-Based MRP Types

Three different consumption-based MRP types are available in the standard SAP S/4HANA:

- Reorder point planning procedure (the most common and simplest)
- Time-phased planning procedure
- Forecast-based planning procedure

Let's first talk about the *reorder point* planning procedure. With this kind of MRP procedure, we need to have a reorder level defined, either manually in the material master or automatically by the system. For every goods issue posted to a material with this MRP type, SAP S/4HANA will compare the current stock level with the reorder point, and it will trigger replenishment once the stock falls below the reorder point.

Figure 3.10 illustrates the stock level of a material with an MRP reorder point. In this chart, stock is gradually consumed until reaching the reorder level. Once the reorder level is reached, replenishment is triggered by MRP. After the replenishment lead time, the stock comes back to the original level.

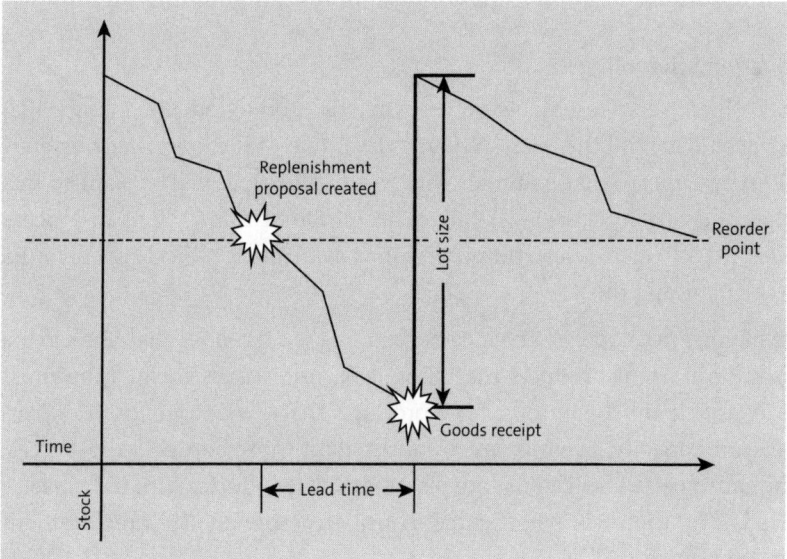

Figure 3.10 Reorder Point Planning

SAP S/4HANA delivers different MRP types for the reorder point procedure; among them, the simplest is MRP type VB. When using this basic reorder point MRP type, we need to manually input a reorder point in the material master. Figure 3.11 shows the **MRP 1** tab of the material master, where we define the MRP type and the reorder point together. In this example, a reorder point of 40 EA has been defined for the material, which means that a new replenishment proposal will be created by MRP once the stock level falls below 40 EA.

> **Tip**
> The reorder point can be calculated as the product of the average daily consumption of a material and its lead time. To avoid shortages caused by any delay in replenishment, we can add a small quantity to the reorder point to represent a safety stock.

3.1 Material Master

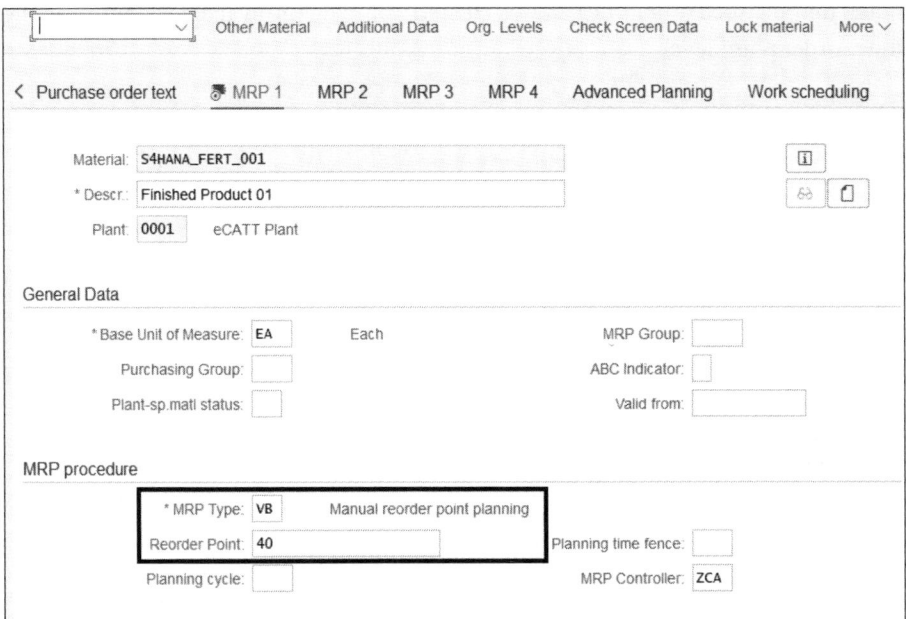

Figure 3.11 Reorder Point in the Material Master

Now let's analyze an example with material S4HANA_FERT_001, MRP type VB, and the manual reorder point of 40 EA defined in the material master. Figure 3.12 shows the stock and requirements situation after the MRP run for the material. The current stock level is 50 EA and there are two different sales orders of 30 EA. Note that MRP did not create any new replenishment proposal for the material because the current stock level is above the reorder point level.

We emphasized the **Available Quantity** column in Figure 3.6. When analyzing the deterministic MRP, note that the forecast requirements are leading to a negative available quantity. In Figure 3.12, note now that there are two sales orders that would lead to a shortage on 19.06, but MRP did not react to this shortage. That is because those sales orders are not relevant for the MRP calculation when using MRP type VB. MRP will compare the stock with the reorder point and only the stock with the reorder point, not taking any requirement into consideration during the net requirements calculation.

Now imagine that the stock/requirements situation for the material has been changed and that a goods issue of 20 EA has been posted. The stock now falls to 30 EA, which is below the reorder point defined in the material master. Figure 3.13 shows

71

that a new planned order of 10 EA was created, bringing the available quantity above the reorder point level.

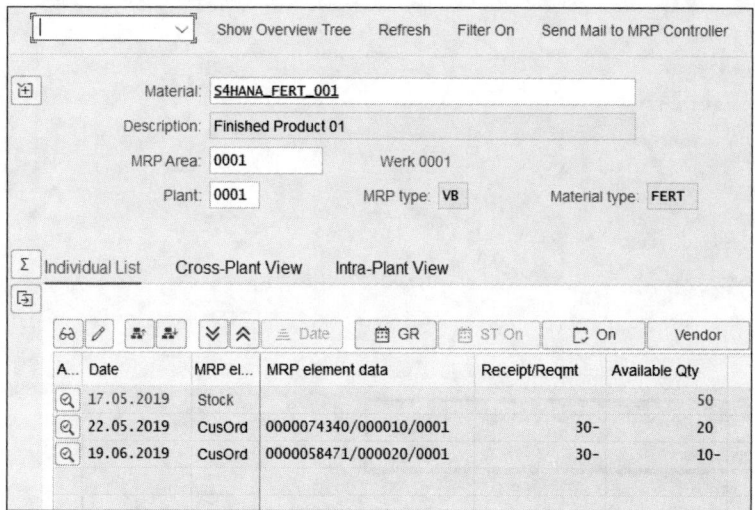

Figure 3.12 Stock/Requirements Situation for Material S/4HANA_FERT_001 and MRP Type VB

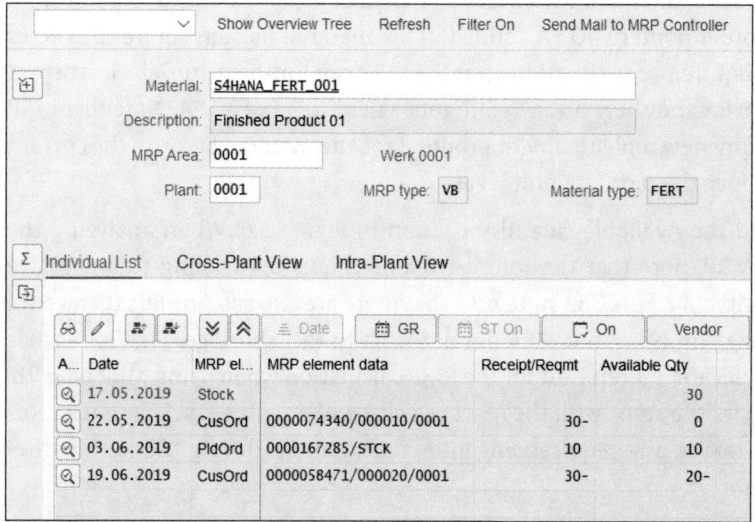

Figure 3.13 MRP Results for Material S4HANA_FERT_001 with Stock below the Reorder Point Level

> **Note**
>
> For simplification purposes, we are using lot-sizing procedure EX in this example so that MRP generates a new replenishment proposal with the exact missing quantity. In real-life situations, however, this combination of a reorder point with lot-sizing procedure EX generally is not desired because it will trigger replenishment very frequently.
>
> The reorder point MRP is frequently used with a lot-sizing procedure that replenishes up to the maximum stock level or with a minimum or fixed lot size in order to avoid frequent replenishments.

While MRP type VB will not consider replenishment elements during the calculation, there are standard MRP types for the reorder point procedure that will consider external requirements during the calculation. The standard MRP type V1, for example, will consider external requirements within the replenishment lead time during the net requirements calculation. In this case, MRP will not only compare the current stock with the reorder point level but also consider any sales order within the replenishment time.

Let's get back to the previous example, in which we had 50 EA on stock and two sales orders of 30 EA for material S4HANA_FERT_001. Considering that we have an in-house production time of 10 business days for the material, the first of those sales orders would be within the replenishment lead time and it would be considered by MRP during net requirements calculation.

> **Tip**
>
> We can show the **End of Replenishment Lead Time** line in the MRP evaluation transactions, such as the Stock/Requirements List, as shown in Figure 3.14. It will help identify, for example, which requirements were considered during the MRP run when using MRP type V1. We can activate this feature in the **Settings** menu or by clicking the respective button on the screen.

As shown in Figure 3.14, even though the stock is not yet below the reorder point, MRP created a new planned order because there is a sales order within the replenishment lead time. This means that soon we will have a goods issue leading the stock to fall below the reorder point. This sales order was included in the net requirements calculation because of the MRP type settings, and that is why a new planned order was created.

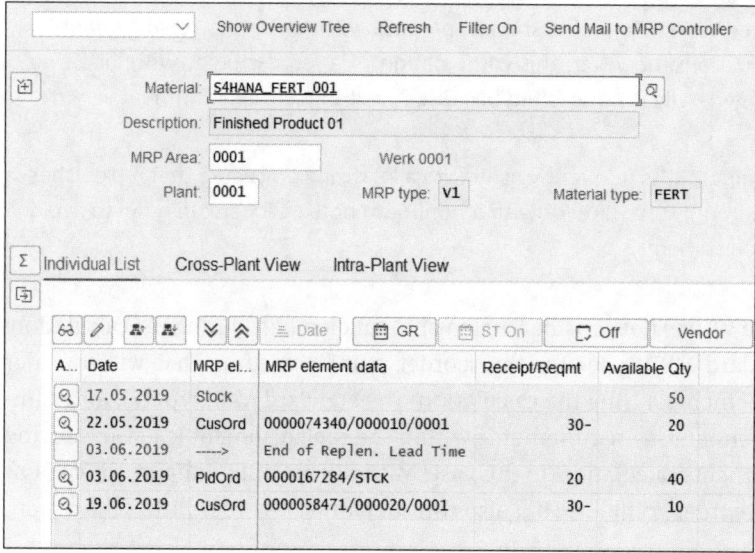

Figure 3.14 MRP Results with MRP Type V1

While VB and V1 are MRP types in which the reorder point should be manually set in the material master, SAP also offers standard MRP types in which the reorder point can be calculated automatically by the system, such as MRP type V2, for example. This MRP type will require a forecast to be executed before the MRP run, however. Past data will be analyzed according to the forecast model defined in the material master, and the system will automatically calculate the reorder point.

> **Note**
> SAP S/4HANA offers the new demand-driven MRP (DDMRP), in which a reorder point can also be automatically calculated by the system based on the past consumption data. We will discuss DDMRP in more detail in Chapter 10.

There are different options available for reorder point MRP types in Customizing, and we can define, for example, which external requirements will be considered or if they will be considered within the replenishment lead time or in the total horizon. We will discuss these options in Chapter 4, in which we will learn how to configure MRP in SAP S/4HANA.

In some situations, such as if a material is produced in the plant only once a month or if a vendor delivers the product on a fixed day of the week, we may need to plan a material in fixed cycles. In these cases, we may use the MRP types with the *time-phased* MRP procedure, in which a *planning date* is defined in the planning file. This planning date is defined when the material is created, and this material will only be planned by MRP when this planning date is reached. For those MRP types, we will have to define a planning cycle in the **MRP 1** tab of the material master. The planning cycle is basically a *planning calendar*; we will walk through the creation of a planning calendar in Chapter 7.

Standard MRP types R1 and R2 are examples of MRP types with time-phased procedures. In those MRP types, it is also mandatory to create a forecast, and only the forecast requirements will be considered in the calculation. It is also possible, however, to have all the requirements relevant to MRP when using an MRP type with a time-phased procedure by setting the **Time-Phased with Requirements** flag in the MRP type Customizing.

SAP S/4HANA also offers *forecast-based* MRP procedures, which are very common in retail and fashion industries. With this MRP procedure, MRP will react on forecast requirements, generated by a forecast carried out for the material. This forecast will use a forecast model defined in the **Forecasting** tab of the material master (see Figure 3.5), and the system will analyze past consumption data and predict the future consumption. The forecast will generate *forecast requirements* for the material, and MRP will plan the replenishment according to those forecast requirements.

The forecast requires that past consumption records (goods issues) are available for the material master, and each forecast model requires a minimum number of historical consumption periods for initialization. If there is no past consumption, then the consumption values can be entered manually in the material master.

When using a forecast-based MRP type, we need to execute the forecast before the MRP execution. The forecast can be executed manually for a material in the **Forecasting** tab of the material master or in Transaction MP30. The most common option is to run mass forecasting using Transaction MP38 or to schedule a periodic execution in the background with program RMPROG01. Figure 3.15 shows the MRP results with the forecast-based MRP type VV; here we can see the forecast requirements and the replenishment elements created by MRP to cover those requirements.

3   Master Data and Basic Settings

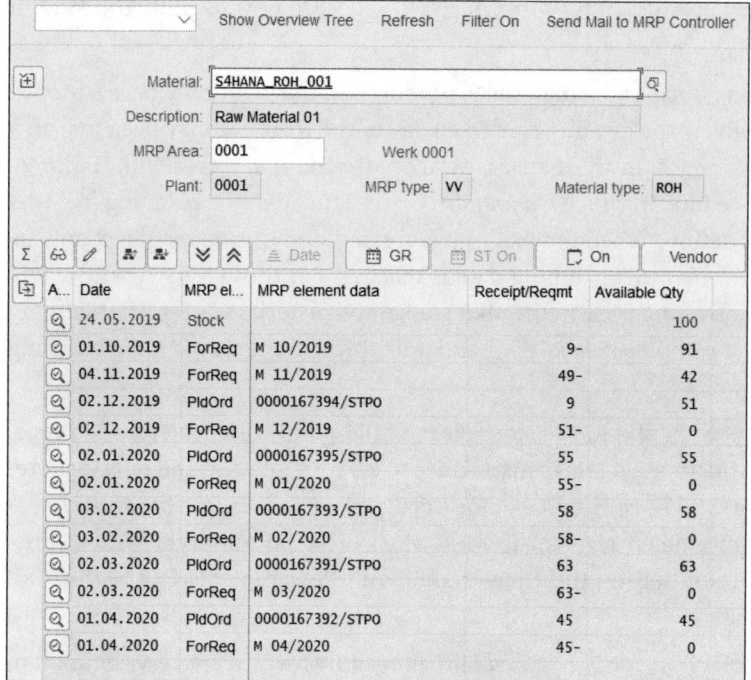

Figure 3.15 MRP Results with Forecast-Based MRP Type VV

3.1.2 Lot-Sizing Procedures

In Section 3.1.1, we noted that the MRP type determines when MRP should trigger a new replenishment proposal.

Another very important MRP setting is the *lot-sizing procedure*, which determines the quantity of the replenishment proposal generated by MRP. In all of the MRP type examples shown in Section 3.1.1, the replenishment proposal was created by MRP with exactly the missing quantity, but this is not the only option available. We might want to procure an additional quantity for costing purposes or add a safety stock, or we might want to cover all the requirements within a week with a single replenishment proposal, for example.

The lot-sizing procedure will allow us to define rules for the quantity of the replenishment proposal created by MRP. The lot-sizing procedures available in SAP S/4HANA can be grouped into the following categories:

- Static lot-sizing procedures
- Period lot-sizing procedures
- Optimum lot-sizing procedures

In the following sections, we will discuss these different categories and walk through examples of the most commonly used lot-sizing procedures. We will discuss the lot-sizing procedure Customizing settings in detail in Chapter 4.

Static Lot-Sizing Procedures

In the static lot-sizing procedures, the quantity will be calculated according to the quantity specifications defined in the material master.

The most common of these lot-sizing procedures provided by SAP is the *lot-for-lot order quantity* (EX), in which the system will procure the exact missing quantity. (The abbreviation EX comes from the German word *exakte*, meaning *exact* in English.) This is the lot-sizing procedure used in the example shown in Figure 3.7. In the figure, there was a missing quantity of 50 EA on 03.06, and MRP created a new planned order with this exact quantity. The main characteristic of this lot-sizing procedure is that the system will procure *exactly* the missing quantity.

One important remark is that the MRP net requirements calculation happens on a daily basis. This means that MRP will calculate the shortage quantity by adding together all the requirements on the same day. Therefore, when there are several requirements in the same day, MRP will generate a single replenishment proposal covering all those requirements, even if we are using a lot-for-lot procedure, such as the standard EX.

Another very common lot-sizing procedure is the fixed lot size FX, or *fixed order quantity*. This generally is used when a machine can only produce a fixed quantity of the product or when the vendor can only deliver in a specific quantity due to logistical limitations. When a fixed lot size is used, we need to also indicate the **Fixed Lot Size** setting in the material master, as shown in Figure 3.16.

With a fixed lot size, if the requirement is smaller than the lot size, we will have one replenishment proposal with the fixed quantity defined in the material master. If the requirement quantity is higher than the fixed quantity, we will have two or more replenishment proposals created by MRP, until the shortage is cleared. Figure 3.17 shows the MRP results when using the material master settings defined in Figure 3.16: a fixed lot size of 50 EA. There is a dependent requirement of 120 EA, for which MRP created three different planned orders of 50 EA.

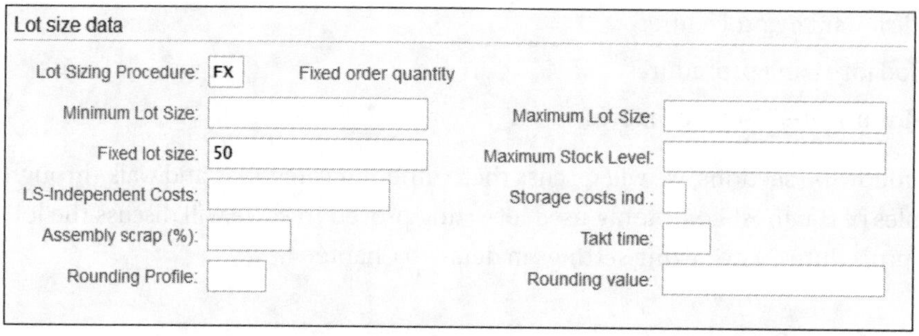

3 Master Data and Basic Settings

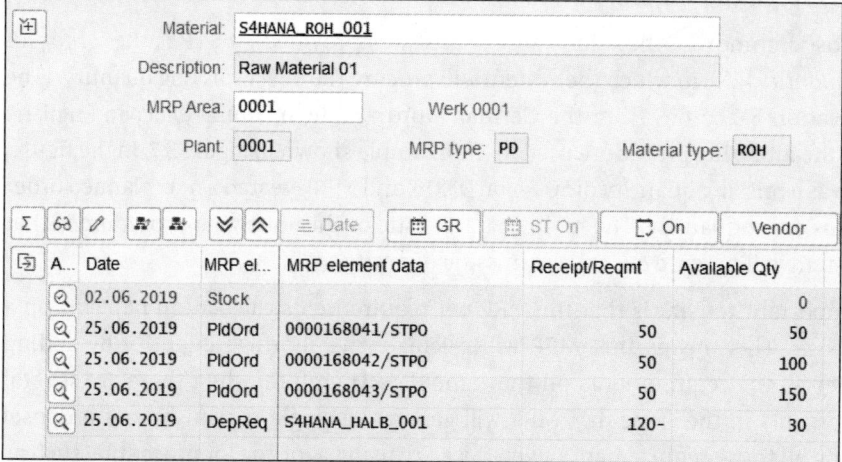

Figure 3.16 Fixed Lot Size in the Material Master

A...	Date	MRP el...	MRP element data	Receipt/Reqmt	Available Qty
🔍	02.06.2019	Stock			0
🔍	25.06.2019	PldOrd	0000168041/STPO	50	50
🔍	25.06.2019	PldOrd	0000168042/STPO	50	100
🔍	25.06.2019	PldOrd	0000168043/STPO	50	150
🔍	25.06.2019	DepReq	S4HANA_HALB_001	120-	30

Figure 3.17 MRP Results with a Fixed Lot Size of 50 EA

Note

In the example in Figure 3.17, there is a remaining available quantity of 50 EA because the requirement is not a multiple of the fixed lot size.

To avoid this remaining quantity for the product after covering all the requirements, check the **Last Lot Exact** flag in the lot-sizing procedure. MRP will use the fixed lot sizing, but the last replenishment proposal will be created with exactly the missing quantity. This setting is relevant not only for a fixed lot-sizing procedure but also when defining a maximum or a minimum lot size, for example.

A variation of the fixed lot-sizing procedure would be the lot-sizing procedure FS, for *fixing and splitting*. With this lot-sizing procedure, we can not only define that system will split the replenishment proposals, but also define that they will be produced in regular intervals. This is useful, for example, when we have limit on the quantity that can be produced in a given day. When using this lot-sizing procedure, we will need to set values in the **Fixed Quantity**, **Rounding Value**, and **Takt Time** fields in the material master, where the rounding value will represent the quantity to be split, the takt time will be the interval between the splits, and the fixed lot size will be used to calculate the total replenishment proposal quantity. (The German word *takt* represents the rate at which a certain product should be produced.)

Figure 3.18 shows the MRP results when using lot-sizing procedure FS, a fixed lot sizing of 100, a takt time of 1, and a rounding value of 50. Here, there is a requirement of 140, and due to the fixed quantity of 100, the replenishment quantity calculated by MRP is 200. Due to the rounding value of 50, this quantity is split between four different replenishment proposals of 50 EA. Due to the takt time of one day, these proposals are created with one day of difference between each other, as shown in the **Date** column.

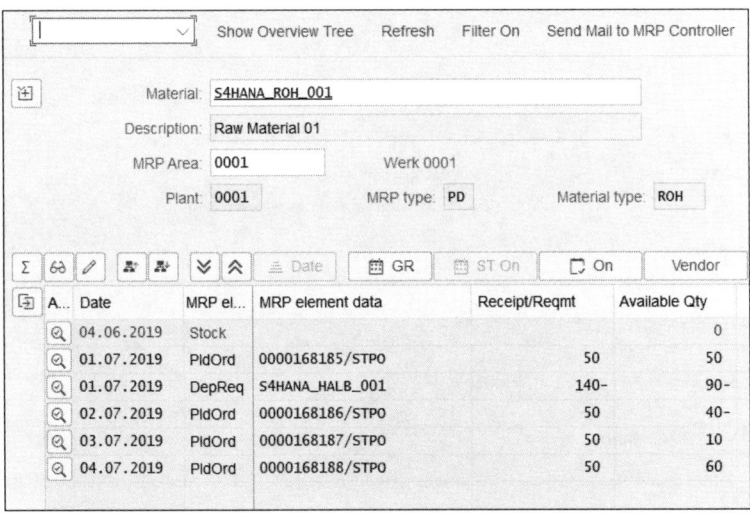

Figure 3.18 MRP Results with Lot-Sizing Procedure FS and Takt Time

Lot-sizing procedure HB, or replenishment to maximum stock level, is commonly used in conjunction with a reorder point MRP type. This lot-sizing procedure requires a maximum stock level to be defined in the material master. In the case of a shortage,

MRP will generate a replenishment proposal for which the quantity will be enough to reach the maximum stock level. In the lot-sizing procedure Customizing, we can define if the maximum stock level will be calculated before or after covering the requirements.

Figure 3.19 shows an example with material S/4HANA_ROH_001, a raw material planned with a reorder point MRP type. For this material, we have defined a reorder point of 100 EA and lot-sizing procedure HB, with a maximum stock level of 300. Considering that we have only 50 EA on stock and that this quantity is already below the material reorder point, MRP needs to create a new replenishment proposal that will replenish up to the maximum stock level of 300. Because we already have 50 EA on stock, the quantity calculated by MRP for the newly created purchase requisition will be 250 EA.

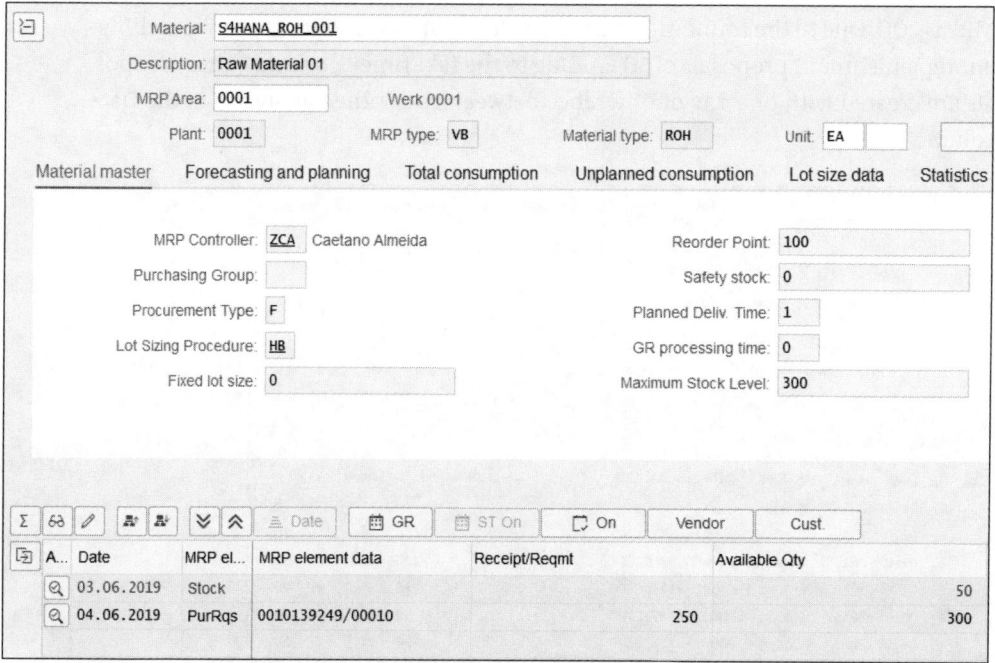

Figure 3.19 MRP Results Create Purchase Requisition to Replenish to the Maximum Stock Level

Period Lot-Sizing Procedures

When we use the static lot-sizing procedures described in the previous section for a raw material (i.e., a component of many different products and for which we will have a large number of reservations and dependent requirements), we may end up with too many replenishment proposals. This can result in additional effort for the purchasing department to handle all these requisitions, and the MRP controller might struggle to understand the MRP results and handle all the MRP exceptions.

In those cases, we suggest considering a period lot-sizing procedure to combine several requirements within a given period and generate a single replenishment proposal to cover them all. SAP S/4HANA offers the following standard period lot-sizing procedures:

- **Daily lot size (TB)**
  MRP will combine all the requirements on the same day and generate a single replenishment proposal.
- **Weekly lot size (WB)**
  MRP will combine all the requirements in the same week and generate a single replenishment proposal.
- **Monthly lot size (MB)**
  MRP will generate a single replenishment proposal to cover all the requirements within the same month.
- **Period lot size according to the planning calendar (PK)**
  A planning calendar allows us to define a flexible period to be used in the lot-sizing procedure. MRP will combine all the requirements within this period and generate a single replenishment proposal. This is useful, for example, when a supplier always delivers a product on a specific day of the week. We will discuss the creation of a planning calendar in Section 3.1.4.

Now let's analyze an example of a period lot-sizing procedure for material S4HANA_ROH_001, considering a deterministic MRP type PD. For this material, we have defined a monthly lot sizing MB; Figure 3.20 shows that there are three different dependent requirements in the month of July. To cover those dependent requirements, MRP created a single planned order on the first day of the month, considering the total shortage quantity for the month.

The default setting of the standard period lot-sizing procedure is to create the replenishment proposal at the beginning of the period, which is why this planned order was created on July 1. However, this system behavior can be changed in Customizing.

Figure 3.21 shows the details of the lot-sizing procedure Customizing (Transaction OMI4). The **Period Start = Availability Date** setting has been defined for the **Scheduling** field, and that is what controls that the replenishment proposal will be created at the beginning of the month. By changing the settings defined in this field, we can choose, for example, that the replenishment proposal will be created on the first requirement date or at the end of the period.

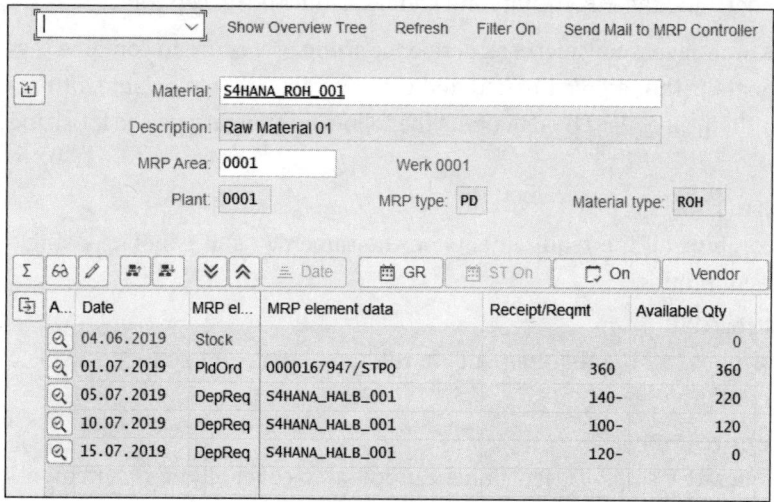

Figure 3.20 MRP Results with Monthly Lot-Sizing Procedure

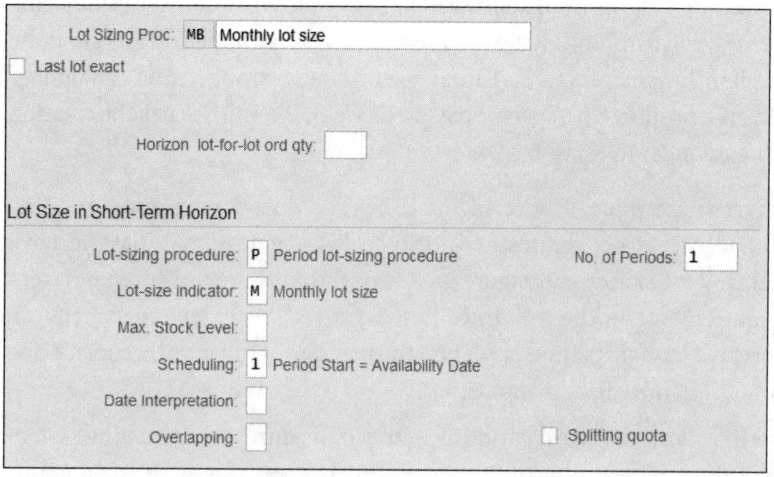

Figure 3.21 Lot-Sizing Procedure Customizing

Another important setting shown in Figure 3.21 for a period lot-sizing procedure is the number of periods. For example, the standard monthly lot-sizing procedure combines all the requirements within a single month into a single replenishment proposal. However, if we want to combine the requirements of two months, we can create a new lot-sizing procedure by copying lot sizing procedure MB, and then setting the **No. of Periods** field to 2. The same setting is also valid for a weekly or daily lot-sizing procedure if we want to create a new lot-sizing procedure with two or more weeks or days.

Optimum Lot-Sizing Procedures

Optimum lot-sizing procedures are generally used when we need to optimize the replenishment proposals to minimize costs. When using these lot-sizing procedures, MRP can consider the impact of the *lot-size independent costs* and *storage costs*, creating a replenishment proposal with the smallest possible total cost according to the different costing criteria.

When using one of these lot-sizing procedures, we need to set the **Lot-Size Independent Costs** and the **Storage Cost Code** values in the **MRP 1** tab of the material master:

- The *lot-size independent cost* represents a cost associated with each individual replenishment proposal, irrespective of the quantity: the cost associated with the creation of a single purchase order, for example.
- The *storage cost code* represents the cost to keep a material stored in the warehouse. It is a percentage based on the quantity stored and the unit price.

While the lot size independent value is directly defined in the material master, the storage cost code is a Customizing entry defined in the lot-sizing procedure Customizing (Transaction OMI4). The following standard optimal lot-sizing procedures are available in SAP S/4HANA:

- **Dynamic lot size creation (DY)**
  With this lot-sizing procedure, MRP will group requirements until the additional storage costs become greater than lot-size independent costs.
- **Groff reorder procedure (GR)**
  When using the Groff reorder procedure, MRP will group requirements into a single lot until the increase in the average costs per period is larger than the decrease in the lot-size independent costs per period.

- **Part period balancing (SP)**
  MRP will group requirements until the sum of the storage costs will be equal to the lot-size independent costs.

- **Least unit cost procedure (WI)**
  With this lot-sizing procedure, MRP will calculate the total costs, adding the lot-size independent cost to the total storage costs. MRP will group requirements and try to reach the minimum total cost per unit.

> **Tip**
>
> In the lot-sizing procedure Customizing, we can define a lot-sizing procedure for the short term and a different procedure for the long term. For example, we can set a lot-for-lot procedure for the current month, but a weekly procedure after that to minimize the replenishment proposals created far in the future.

Additional Lot-Sizing Settings

Besides the lot-sizing procedure, additional settings are available in the material master, and these settings can be combined with different lot-sizing procedures. The following settings are available:

- **Minimum Lot Size**: Replenishment proposals will be always created with at least the quantity defined in the **Minimum Lot Size** field. For example, if we have defined a minimum quantity of 100 and lot-sizing procedure EX in the material master, then the replenishment proposal quantity will be at least 100, even if the shortage quantity is below 100.

- **Maximum Lot Size**: When using a maximum lot size, the replenishment proposal will not exceed this quantity. By setting the **Maximum Lot Size** field to 50, for example, MRP will create several replenishment proposals of 50 if the shortage quantity exceeds this quantity.

- **Rounding Value**: MRP will always round the replenishment proposal quantity to a multiple of the rounding value defined in the material master. For example, if the rounding value is 10 and the shortage quantity is 77, then MRP will round the replenishment proposal to 80 because 80 is the nearest multiple of 10 that can cover the shortage.

- **Rounding Profile**: We can create a rounding profile in Customizing (Transaction OWD1) to define different rounding values, depending on the shortage quantity.

The rounding profile can be static, meaning that the quantity thresholds and the rounding values are manually defined, or it can be dynamic, meaning that we define a rounding off method in Customizing—such as rounding to a multiple of the order/sales unit, for example.

- **Assembly Scrap**: Assembly scrap is generally used when there is a loss during manufacturing and we want to plan an additional quantity of product. The planned order quantity will be increased by the percentage defined in the **Assembly Scrap** field in the material master, and the **Scrap Quantity** field in the planned order will store this additional quantity.

3.1.3 Procurement Types and Special Procurement Types

In the previous sections, we mentioned *replenishment proposals* several times, but there are different types of replenishment proposals. MRP will choose the kind of replenishment proposal to be created based on the procurement type assigned to the material master.

The procurement type is defined in the **MRP 2** tab of the material master, and it is usually a mandatory field. MRP considers the following standard procurement types:

- **In-house production (E)**
  This special procurement type is used for materials produced internally. When this procurement type is used, MRP will generate planned orders with profile LA, which can be converted to production orders or process orders. If repetitive manufacturing is active for a material, then planned orders of type PE will be generated, which can be used in repetitive manufacturing backflush.

- **External procurement (F)**
  This procurement type basically means that a material is purchased, and it is selected by default for raw materials with type ROH. For materials with this procurement type, MRP will generate planned orders of type NB (which can be converted to purchase requisitions), purchase requisitions, or schedule lines (when a scheduling agreement is active for a material).

- **Both procurement types (X)**
  Procurement type X basically means that a material can be either purchased or produced internally. A material with this procurement type will consider the same logic used by procurement type E, and planned orders will be created.

Besides the procurement type, SAP S/4HANA also offers special procurement types for special planning processes. The special procurement type is also defined in the

MRP 2 tab of the material master, but it is not a mandatory field because it is used only for very specific scenarios. SAP offers the following special procurement types:

- **Consignment**
  When using this special procurement type, MRP will create consignment purchase requisitions—that is, purchase requisitions with item category K.

- **Subcontracting**
  With this special procurement, MRP will generate subcontracting purchase requisitions. The BOM is exploded in the requisition so that the components can be sent to the vendor. We will discuss the subcontracting scenario in Chapter 8.

- **Stock transfer**
  SAP provides a standard special procurement for stock transfers, in which MRP will generate stock transfer requisitions to be used when a material is supplied by another plant.

- **Phantom assembly**
  This special procurement type is used when one semifinished product has a BOM, but we do not want a planned order created for this product. The semifinished product components will be copied directly to the planned order of the parent product, and the phantom assembly will not be managed as a stock item, meaning we will not receive it or consume it from stock.

- **Direct procurement**
  With a direct procurement special procurement, the material will not be received in stock. MRP will plan those components on a special stock segment, which is linked to the parent order requirement. This material will never reach stock because it will be directly consumed to the production order.

- **Direct production/collective order**
  This special procurement is similar to direct procurement because the component will not be actually received in stock; MRP will plan it on a special stock segment. The difference is that the component will be produced internally and a semifinished production order will be linked to the parent material production order, creating a collective order.

- **Withdrawal from alternative plant**
  This special procurement type is used when a component should be planned and consumed in a different plant. Dependent requirements for this specific component will be created for the alternative plant, where it will be actually procured.

- **Production in alternative plant**
  When this special procurement type is selected, a material is planned in the plant

where the shortage happens, but the actual production happens in a different plant. Components are planned and goods issues are posted in the production plant, but the goods receipt is posted in the planning plant.

SAP delivers a set of standard special procurement types in Customizing that can be used directly in the material master. However, when using the special procurement types stock transfer, withdrawal from alternative plant, and production in alternative plant, we might have to create a custom special procurement type in Customizing (Transaction OMD9), wherein we will define the sourcing plant for the stock transfer or the alternative plant for production and withdrawal.

Figure 3.22 shows a custom special procurement type in Customizing, where we have defined that Plant 0003 is the sourcing plant for a stock transfer that originated in Plant 0002.

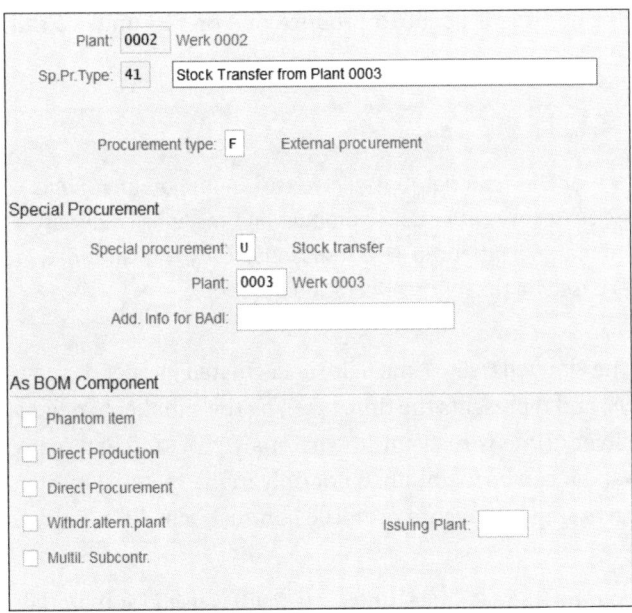

Figure 3.22 Special Procurement Type Customizing

3.1.4 Scheduling Parameters

We saw in Chapter 2 how MRP calculates the dates of a replenishment proposal, and we will find the fields related to replenishment proposal scheduling in the **MRP 2** tab of the material master. These fields are basically used to calculate the basic dates of a planned order or purchase requisition created by MRP, since lead time scheduling will use the operation times defined in the routing.

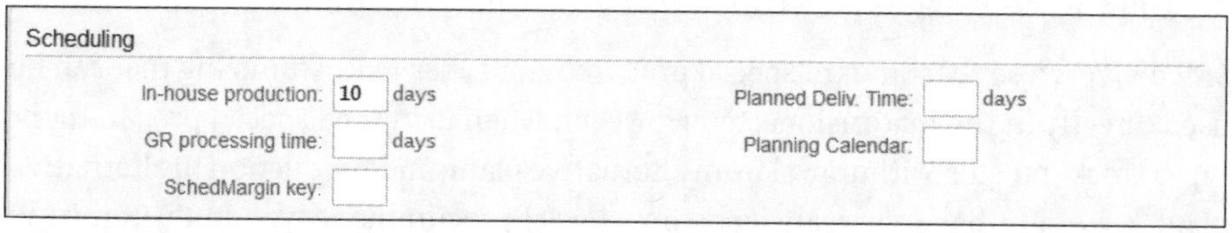

```
Scheduling
    In-house production:  10   days          Planned Deliv. Time:        days
    GR processing time:        days          Planning Calendar:
    SchedMargin key:
```

Figure 3.23 Scheduling Parameters in the Material Master

The **In-House Production Time** field shown in Figure 3.23 is used to calculate the dates of a material produced internally (materials with procurement type E). It represents the number of working days necessary to manufacture this specific product. The in-house production time defined in the **MRP 2** tab is lot size independent, which means MRP will assume that the same time is spent to produce one or 100 units of this material.

> **Note**
>
> In the **Work Scheduling** tab of the material master, we can find additional fields where we can define a lot-size-dependent in-house production time, which will vary according to the quantity of material produced. Use Transaction CA97N to automatically calculate those values based on the routing operation duration.

The *planned delivery time* (the **Planned Deliv. Time** field) is calculated in calendar days (rather than in working days) and represents the time taken by the supplier to deliver a product. The planned delivery time is relevant for materials procured externally (with procurement type F) and it can be maintained not only in the material master, but also in the supplier purchasing info record or in the contract/scheduling agreement.

The *goods receipt processing time* (the **GR Processing Time** field) is used for materials procured externally and for materials produced internally. It is maintained in working days and it represents the time for the material to become actually available for consumption after the goods receipt. It can represent, for example, the time spent in quality inspection or moving the product to the warehouse.

The *planning calendar* (the **Planning Calendar** field) is used in conjunction with a period lot-sizing procedure to define flexible periods for the lot size calculation. We will see the creation of a planning calendar later in Chapter 8.

The *scheduling margin key* (the **Sched/Margin Key** field) is created in Customizing and is used to determine floats for scheduling a replenishment proposal. A scheduling margin key can be created in customizing Transaction OMDC and contains the following fields:

- **Opening Period**: It is relevant for both in-house production or external procurement and is used to calculate the opening period—that is, how many days before the planned order start it should be converted to a production order or purchase requisition. MRP evaluation transactions, such as the Stock/Requirements List, will show a column with the opening date of a planned order.

- **Release Period**: The release period is only used when a material is managed with production/process orders. It is used to calculate the release period—that is, when a production or process order should be released. This information is also displayed in a column in the MRP evaluation transactions.

- **Float after Production**: The float after production is used when lead-time scheduling is executed for an in-house production planned order. It is a buffer of days calculated by the system between the end of the last order operation and the actual order finish date.

- **Float before Production**: Similar to the float after production, this is used during lead-time scheduling, but it represents a buffer between the order start and the start of the first order operation.

Figure 3.24 shows the MRP results in the Stock/Requirements List for material S4HANA_FERT_001.

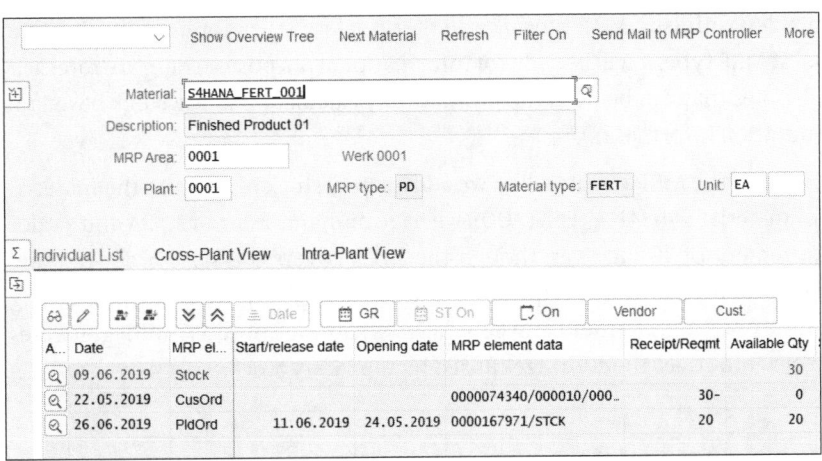

Figure 3.24 Start/Release and Opening Dates Calculated for a Planned Order

Additional columns are shown for a planned order in which the dates in the **Start/Release Date** and **Opening Date** fields were calculated according to the number of days defined in the **Sched/Margin Key** field.

> **Tip**
>
> The **Start/Release Date** and **Opening Date** columns are hidden by default. Show them by simply clicking and dragging the line between the **MRP Element** and **MRP Element Data** columns to the right.

3.1.5 Net Requirements Calculation

Some settings in the material master can also affect the net requirements calculation in the following ways:

- By including an additional requirement (such as a safety stock) into the net requirements calculation
- By making requirements not relevant to MRP
- By considering those requirements some days earlier

We can find those settings under the **MRP 2** tab of the material master, under the **Net Requirements Calculation** section.

The most frequently used of these settings is **Safety Stock**. When we add a safety stock into the material master, MRP will basically plant for this quantity, adding a stock buffer that covers an unexpected demand spike. The safety stock is generally used with a deterministic MRP type. If we enter a safety stock for a material with a reorder point MRP type, it will be only for informational purposes. There are forecast-based MRP types that can be used to automatically calculate a safety stock based on past consumption information.

Figure 3.25 shows the MRP results when we add a safety stock of 20 EA to the material master. For material S/4HANA_FERT_001, we have on-hand stock of 30 EA and a sales order requirement of 30 EA. Even though the stock covers the sales order requirement, we can see a safety stock requirement in the Stock/Requirements List adding up to the sales order requirement and generating a shortage of 20 EA. MRP generates a planned order to cover the shortage caused by the safety stock.

3.1 Material Master

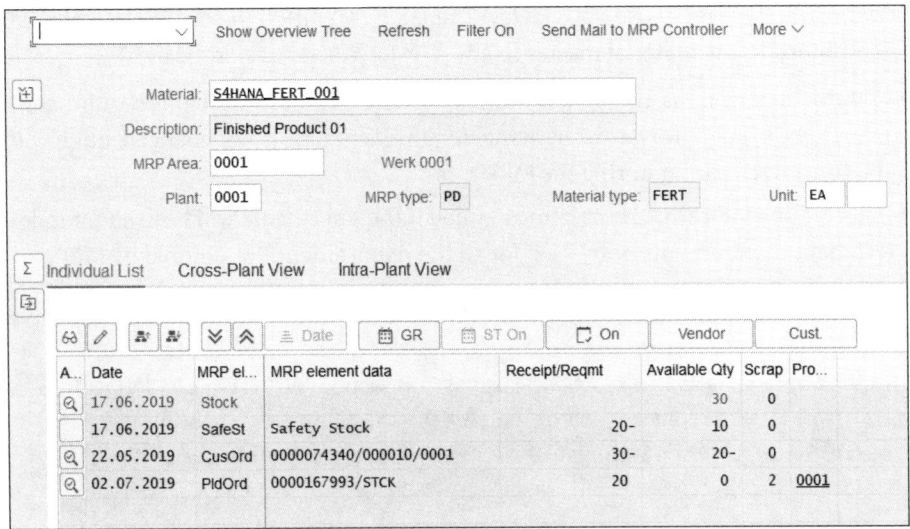

Figure 3.25 MRP Results with a Safety Stock of 20 EA

> **Tip**
>
> In customizing Transaction OMI1, we can define that a percentage of the safety stock will be available for planning in order to avoid the creation of a new replenishment proposal only to cover the safety stock. For example, if the safety stock is 20 and we have defined that 50% of the safety stock will be available for planning, then a new replenishment proposal will only be created if the shortage created by the safety stock exceeds 10.

Instead of a fixed safety stock, we can also use a dynamic safety stock for a material by adding a range of coverage profile. With this setting, MRP will calculate a safety stock that will cover the daily average requirements for a given period defined in the range of coverage profile. We will discuss the creation of a range of coverage profile and how this dynamic safety stock works later in Chapter 8.

Instead of considering those additional requirements, we can also add a *safety time* to the material so that the requirements can be brought forward on time during the net requirements calculation and MRP can consider them a little bit earlier in order to prevent any shortage caused by a delay. There are two different settings that should be combined in the material master to have a safety time considered by MRP:

- **Safety Time**: This is the actual number of working days that the requirement should be brought forward. The actual requirement date is not changed, but it will be considered earlier during the MRP run.
- **Safety Time Indicator**: This setting defined if the safety time will be used for independent requirements only, used for all the requirements, or ignored by MRP.

> **Tip**
>
> In the MRP evaluation transactions, such as Transaction MD04, we can define if we will see the requirements with or without the safety time by choosing the menu option **Settings • User Settings • Date**. There is also a button to switch the safety time on or off.

There are situations in which we may not want to have dependent requirements generated for a specific material or do not want to consider those dependent requirements during the MRP run.

When we do not want to have dependent requirements generated for a material, we usually set the **Bulk Material** flag in the **MRP 2** tab of the material master. This setting is generally used for very cheap and widely used components for which we cannot control the exact quantity consumed on each order (e.g., nails or packaging tape). Those materials can be planned with a reorder point MRP type and they will be consumed against a cost center instead of backflushed to an order. Whenever the stock reaches the reorder level, they will be replenished, and we will not need those dependent requirements.

There are also situations in which we simply do not want to have the dependent requirements relevant to MRP, but we will want to have the component planned when the planned order becomes a production order and still want to have it consumed against the order. In this case, we can use the **MRP Dependent Requirements** field in the **MRP 3** tab of the material master. With this setting defined for a component, MRP will generate dependent requirements for this material, but it will not consider them during the net requirements calculation. We will see those requirements in the MRP evaluation transactions, but they will not affect the available quantity.

3.1.6 MRP Area

SAP S/4HANA offers the possibility to segregate a storage location or a subcontractor, from an MRP perspective, and to plan those separately under a different organizational unit called an *MRP area*. We need to create MRP areas in advance in Customizing, and then assign the MRP areas in the **MRP 1** tab of the material master, as shown in Figure 3.26.

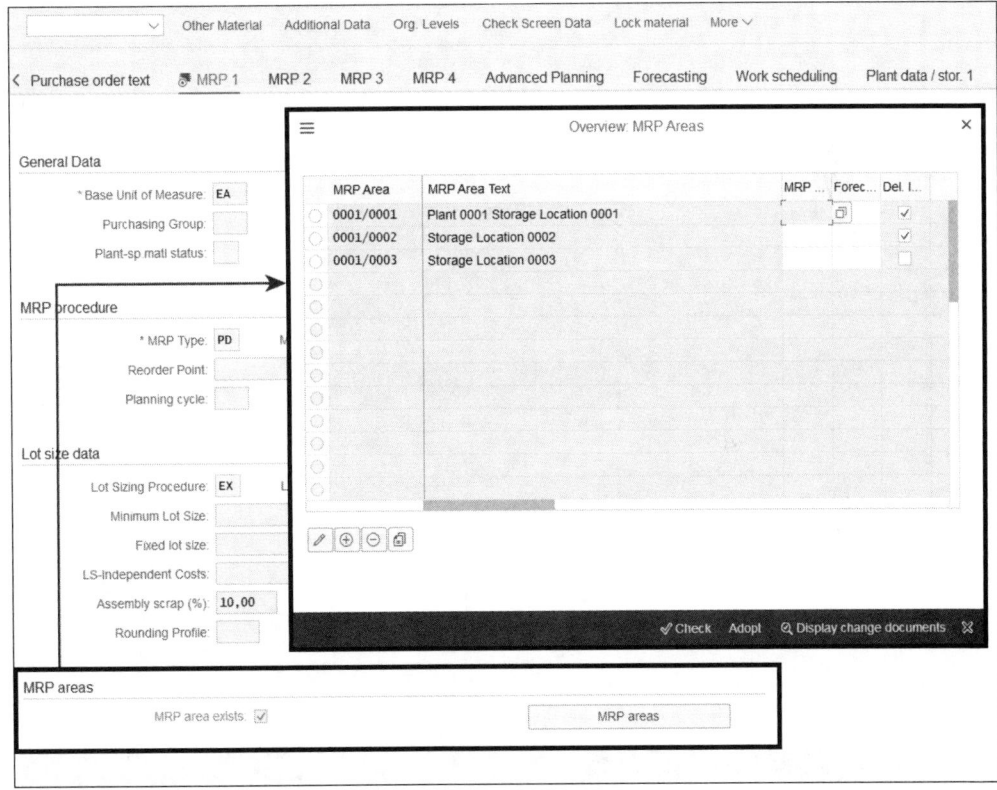

Figure 3.26 MRP Areas in the Material Master

We can assign different MRP planning parameters for each one of these MRP areas, such as a different lot-sizing procedure or a different MRP type. Figure 3.27 shows the MRP area maintenance screen (**Change MRP Area**) in the material master, where we can see different tabs with MRP settings. Notice in the MRP area that most of the settings available in the **MRP 1** tab of the material master are also available for the MRP area.

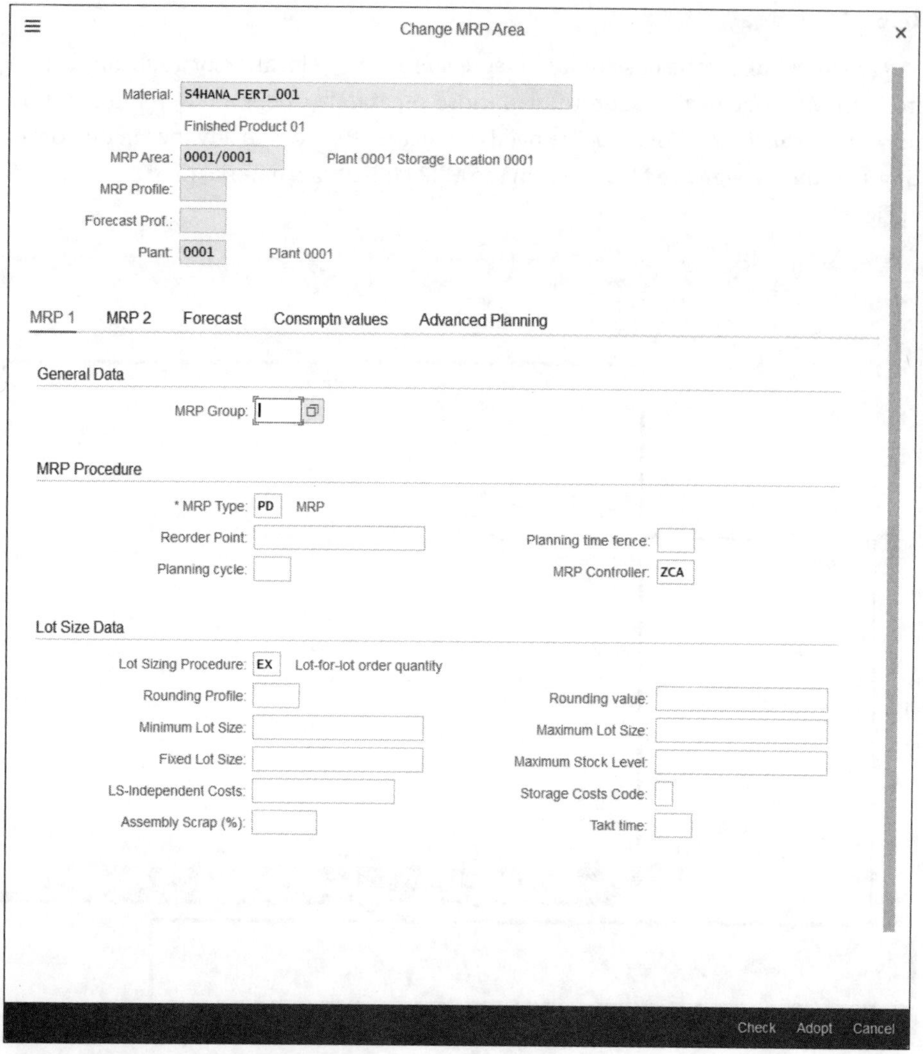

Figure 3.27 MRP Area Settings in the Material Master

SAP S/4HANA also offers report RMMDDIBE for the mass maintenance of the MRP area settings in the material master. With this report, we can copy the MRP area settings with a reference, create or change them with an MRP or forecast profile, create or change them with data, and set or reset the deletion indicator, as shown in Figure 3.28.

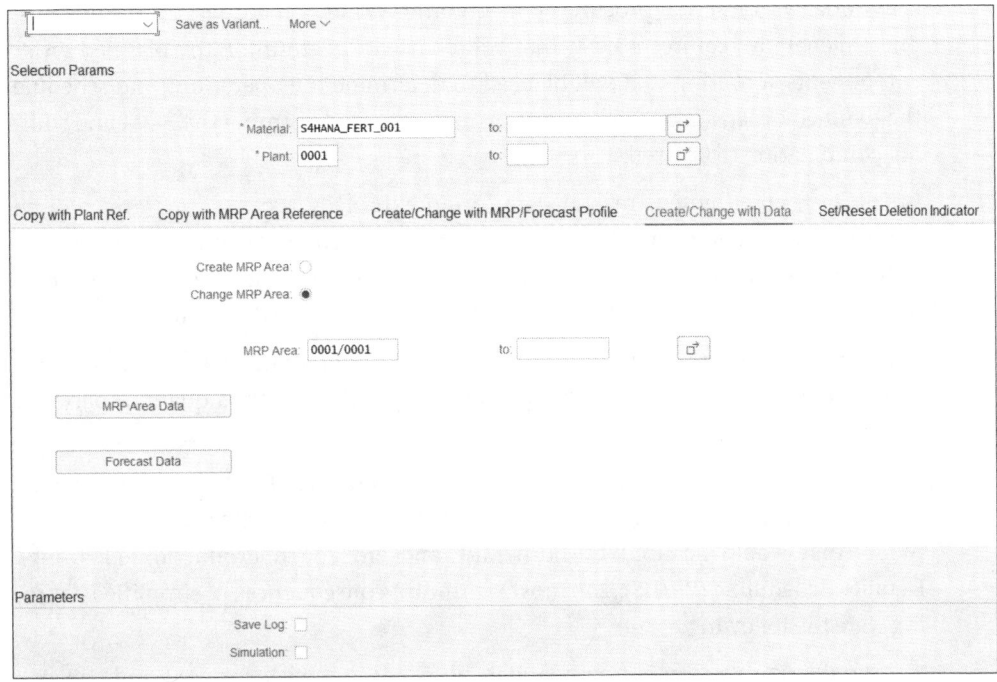

Figure 3.28 Mass Maintenance of MRP Areas with Report RMMDDIBE

We will discuss the creation of MRP areas in Customizing later in Chapter 4.

3.2 Procurement Master Data

With the material master created and the proper settings in the MRP views, it should already be possible to run MRP in order to generate replenishment proposals to cover shortages. However, each replenishment proposal created by MRP may require some additional master data so that all the procurement details can be considered in the production plan. In this section, we will go through the procurement-related master data and understand what is required to have a BOM exploded in the planned order or a vendor selected for a purchase requisition.

We noted in Section 3.1 that we can define the procurement type of a product in the material master and that, depending on the procurement type selected for a product, it will require a specific set of master data for the source of supply determination.

A material with internal procurement—in other words, a material that we will produce—generally requires a BOM that will be used to determine the planned order components, a routing that will be used to determine the operations and schedule the planned order, and a production version that will determine the BOM and routing combination to be used.

In contrast, procurement master data for an externally procured material will be basically used to determine the vendor and the replenishment element to be created. MRP can use an info record, a contract, a scheduling agreement, a source list, or a quota arrangement during the external procurement source determination.

When there are several possible sources of supply, either for internal or external procurement, we can use a quota arrangement to split the procured quantity between the different sources of supply.

One of the major simplifications implemented for MRP in SAP S/4HANA was the simplified sourcing. The idea behind this simplification was to create a unified sourcing model that would be used by both MRP and embedded Production Planning/Detailed Scheduling (PP/DS). The most significant consequences of simplified sourcing were the following:

- A production version is now mandatory for internal procurement and subcontracting. The BOM will be selected according to the production version only, and the **Alternative Selection** field that was available in SAP ERP was removed from the material master because it is no longer relevant.
- A source list is no longer mandatory for external procurement. In SAP ERP, it was mandatory to have a source list for external procurement so that MRP could select a vendor. In SAP S/4HANA, the source list is no longer mandatory: it is enough to have an info record, a purchasing contract, or a scheduling agreement to have a vendor selected by MRP. The source list can still be used to prioritize a source of supply for a given period of time.
- An existing quota arrangement will be automatically selected by MRP, and it is no longer necessary to mark in the material master if quota arrangements should be considered by MRP.

The source of supply determination with simplified sourcing follows this logic for external procurement:

1. MRP checks for the quota arrangement and tries to create replenishment proposals according to the quotas.

2. MRP checks for the source list and creates replenishment proposals according to the source list.
3. MRP tries to find a scheduling agreement and generates delivery schedules.
4. MRP tries to find a contract and generated purchase requisitions with a reference to the contract.
5. MRP tries to find valid info records and tries to create purchase requisitions.

In case of internal procurement (or subcontracting), the system will try to find a valid production version, but it will also consider a quota arrangement to prioritize a specific production version.

We will discuss simplified sourcing in more detail and the changes for internal and external procurement in the following sections.

3.2.1 Internal Procurement

When we talk about materials procured internally—that is, manufactured within the company—we need to know which components will be required to produce a material and what sequence of operations should be executed to build it. This information is stored in the BOM and the routing, respectively, which are read during the MRP run when creating new planned orders for a material procured internally. Because the same product can be manufactured with different component combinations and with different sequences of operations, *production versions* basically tell us which combinations of BOM and routing are allowed and can be selected by MRP.

In this section we will explain the BOM, routing, master recipe (similar to the routing, but used in process industry), and production version settings that are relevant to MRP.

Bill of Materials

The BOM is key master data for MRP. It provides a list of components that will be read when a planned order is created. MRP will generate a dependent requirement for each component, and those components will be also planned by MRP, leading to a multilevel MRP planning run. The process of reading a BOM and generating dependent requirements is called BOM explosion.

BOMs are used in different application areas, and there are different categories of BOMs available in SAP S/4HANA. For example, equipment BOMs and functional location BOMs are used in plant maintenance activities. From an MRP perspective, however, only the following categories of BOMs are relevant:

- A *material BOM* is created with reference to a material. It is basically a structured list of the components necessary to manufacture this product, including the quantities and other settings relevant to MRP.
- A *sales order BOM* is very similar to a material BOM, but it is created with a reference to the sales order number and sales order item. This kind of BOM will be used only in a make-to-order scenario, in which the planned order is created with reference to the sales order special stock.
- A *work breakdown structure* (WBS) *BOM* is similar to the sales order BOM, but it is created with a reference to the WBS element. It is generally used in an engineering-to-order scenario, where there is a link between the planned order and the project special stock.

Material BOMs are created in Transaction CS01, changed in Transaction CS02, and displayed in Transaction CS03. Sales order BOMs are created in Transaction CS61, and WBS BOMs are created in Transaction CS71. In the next chapter, we will walk through the Customizing settings to activate the usage of sales order and WBS BOMs during the MRP run.

> **Note**
>
> In SAP ERP, there was a **Selection Method** setting in the material master that we could use to determine how the BOM should be selected by MRP. This setting is no longer available in SAP S/4HANA; the BOM will be selected according to the production version only. If MRP cannot find a valid production version for a material, then the BOM will not be exploded by MRP when creating a planned order.
>
> When using a sales order or WBS BOM, however, a production version is not required.

BOMs can have two different technical types: a *multiple BOM* basically represents the alternative lists of components that can be used to manufacture the same product, whereas a *variant BOM* can be used to represent several different materials that are very similar and share a large number of components.

When creating a material BOM, we need to input the material number for which we want to create the BOM, the plant, and the BOM usage, as shown in Figure 3.29. The **BOM Usage** field defines in which application areas we can use a specific BOM; we generally use BOM usage 1 for material BOMs to be used for MRP planning because it allows the BOM to be used in production. SAP offers those predefined BOM usages, but we can also create custom BOM usages in Customizing. If we are working with multiple BOMs for the same material, we need to input a number into the **Alternative BOM** field.

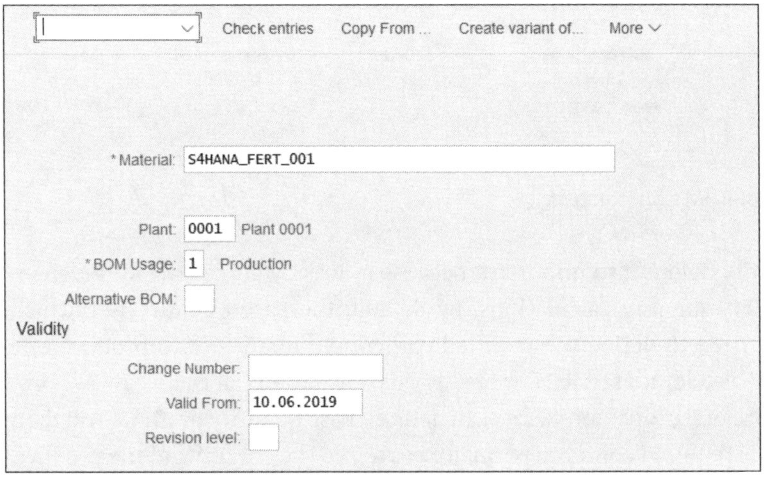

Figure 3.29 BOM Creation in Transaction CS01

> **Tip**
> We can control and log the history of changes made to a BOM using a change number. If we want to make the **Change Number** field mandatory in BOM transactions, we need to use the authorization object C_STUE_NOH. When the NOHIS field is empty for this authorization object, then an error message will be triggered for the user who is trying to create or change a BOM if the change number is not used.

Figure 3.30 shows the list of BOM items. We have the option to go the BOM header by choosing the respective option from the menu. The header holds important information, such as the BOM status, the base quantity, and the document assignment. By default, a BOM is created with status 1, which means it is released, but if we are still working on this BOM and do not want it to be used anywhere else, we can set a status that blocks its use.

3   Master Data and Basic Settings

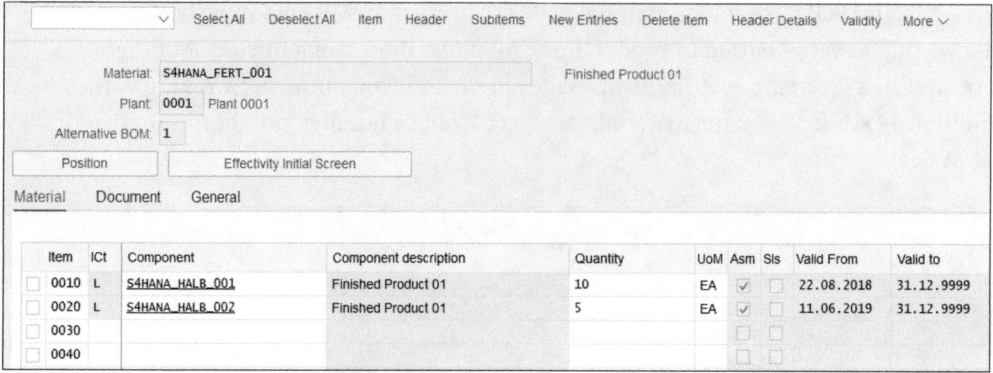

Figure 3.30 List of BOM Components

The **Base Quantity** field is also important because it directly affects the MRP-dependent requirement quantity calculations. By default, the base quantity is 1, which means that we need to define the required component quantities to produce one unit of the BOM header material. However, if we have a material that is always produced in a lot size of 10, for example, we can define a base quantity of 10; we will then have to enter the required component quantities to produce 10 units of the product.

> **Tip**
> We can create a new BOM status in customizing Transaction OS24, defining exactly in which areas we will be able to use the BOM. In addition, we can change the default base quantity of a BOM and the default status in customizing Transaction OS28.

BOM Items

There are different types of BOM items, such as material items, document items, class items, or text items. From an MRP perspective, we will generally focus on the *material items*, which are BOM items with reference to a material number and which can also be planned by MRP.

The input for a material item is very simple: we basically need to define the **Item Category**, **Quantity**, and **Unit of Measure** fields. The following item categories are available for a material item:

- **Stock items (L)**

  These are the most frequently used items in BOMs. For these components, MRP will generate dependent requirements, and those requirements can be used during component planning to ensure that they are available when necessary. The dependent requirements will become a reservation when the planned order is converted to a production order.

- **Nonstock items (N)**
  This kind of component is not kept in stock; therefore, MRP will generate a purchase requisition for external procurement directly in the production or planned order, instead of generating a dependent requirement. This item category is similar to the special procurement direct procurement that we can set in the material master.

- **Variable size items (R)**
  For this kind of item, MRP can calculate the quantity automatically based on the sizes and formulas entered.

- **Plant maintenance structure elements (I)**
  Items only used for structuring a plant maintenance assembly, which are not relevant for production.

- **Intramaterials (M)**
  This kind of item is used in process manufacturing for components that will only exist temporarily between two operations.

> **Note**
> When we add a material as a component in the BOM, SAP S/4HANA will automatically calculate the low-level code, which identifies the sequence used to plan materials during the MRP run. Finished products that are not components of any BOM will receive the low-level code 000 and will be planned first. The components of those finished products will receive low-level code 001 and will be planned in sequence.

We generally create a BOM item with the quantity as a *positive* number. When a planned order is created for the parent material, a dependent requirement will be generated for this component, indicating that this component will be consumed from the stock. However, we can also create a BOM item with a *negative* quantity. In this case, MRP plans a goods receipt for those products instead of a goods issue for the component when a planned order is created for the parent material. The negative quantity can be used in the following cases:

- **By-product**
  This is usually some kind of waste or leftover material generated during the manufacturing process, which will return to stock so that it can be sold, reused, or

3   Master Data and Basic Settings

disposed of. The by-product valuation will be based on the price defined in the material master.

- **Coproduct**
  This is used when the same manufacturing process can generate two different products. To use a coproduct in the BOM, check the **Co-product** flag in the **MRP 2** tab of the material master and create an apportionment structure by clicking the **Joint Production** button on the same tab of the material master, as shown in Figure 3.31. The coproduct will share a percentage of the production order costs, as defined in the apportionment structure. If we want to use this component as a coproduct in any specific BOM, despite the negative quantity, we will also have to check the **Co-product** flag in the BOM item details; otherwise, it will be used as a by-product.

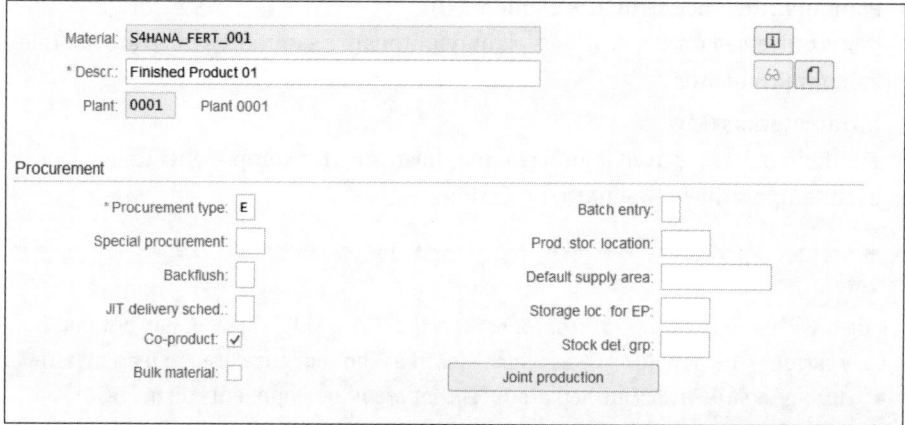

Figure 3.31 Coproduct Settings in the Material Master

By double-clicking the item number or selecting the item and choosing the **Item** menu option, we find additional settings for the BOM items on the next screen. The following settings, shown in Figure 3.32, are the most important from an MRP perspective:

- **Operation Scrap %** and **Component Scrap %**: Besides the **Assembly Scrap** field defined in the material master, there are additional fields where we can enter the scrap at the BOM item level.

- **Fixed Quantity**: This flag can be checked when the component quantity will be fixed, and it should not vary according to the order quantity.

- **Recursiveness Allowed**: In some situations, the parent material may also be a BOM component. This scenario happens especially in the chemical industry. In those situations, we need to check this flag to inform MRP that this is intentional and that the recursiveness check should not be carried out during the MRP run.
- **Lead-Time Offset** and **Operation Lead-Time Offset**: These fields can be used when a specific component should be available before or after the order or operation starts. It can be a positive value, when the component is required some days after the order or operation starts, or a negative value, when the component is required before the start.
- **Alternative Item Group**: Click this button to create an alternative item group. This is used when two different BOM items can be used as alternatives for each other.
- **Distribution Key**: When using a distribution key for a component, instead of having the whole requirement quantity on a single date, the quantity will be split into partial quantities between the order start and finish date. This split will be according to the distribution function defined in the distribution key Customizing.
- **Special Procurement**: Some special procurement types can also be defined in the BOM item details if the special procurement should only be valid for a material when it is a component of this specific BOM. The most commonly used are phantom assembly, direct production, or direct procurement.

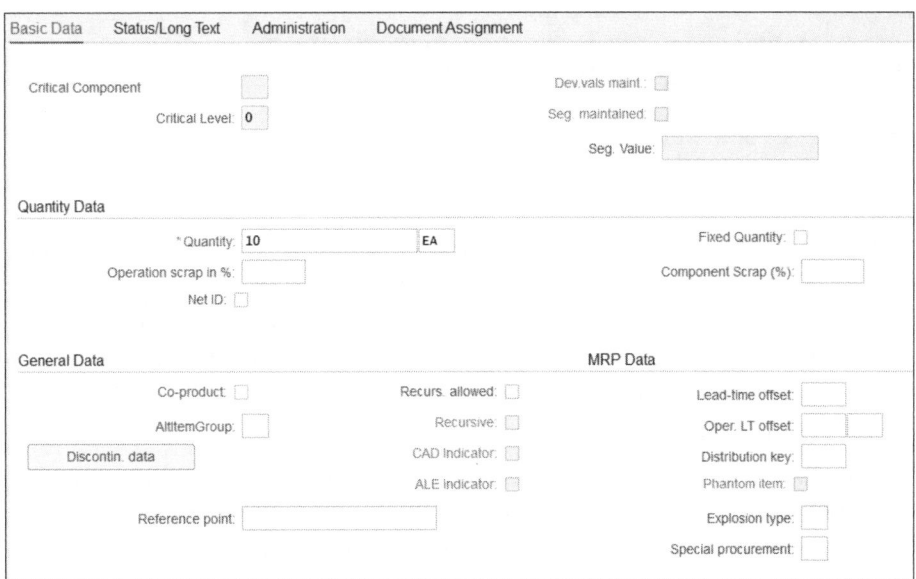

Figure 3.32 BOM Item Details

In the **Status/Long Text** tab, we can find additional MRP settings for the component, such as the **Bulk Material** flag (which can be used when we want to define a component as bulk for this BOM only) or the production storage location, which defines from which storage location a component will be issued.

Multilevel BOM Design

BOM components that are produced in-house can also have their own BOMs, leading to what we call a *multilevel BOM*. We have a lot of flexibility to design our material BOMs, which has a direct impact in MRP planning and manufacturing daily operations.

For example, if we choose to have a flat BOM, where the raw material is a direct component of the finished product BOM, as shown in Figure 3.33, then we will not have semifinished products in our product structure. Consequently, we will not be able to plan or to build any inventory buffer for our semifinished materials. On the other hand, designing a flat BOM creates a very lean product structure. Simplified master data maintenance will reduce the number of stock postings and orders created to manufacture a single product.

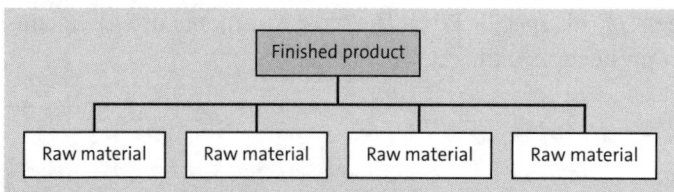

Figure 3.33 Flat BOM with No Semifinished Products

Alternatively, we can define our BOM with many levels of semifinished products, as shown in Figure 3.34, proving the flexibility of planning each semifinished product independently. We can use a different MRP type or lot-sizing policy, allowing us to build stock buffers for the semifinished products that can absorb demand spikes. This way, we will have an additional level of control because we will manage the stock of semifinished products and the stock reports will provide information about what has been already produced.

The increased number of semifinished products, however, will also mean that the MRP controller will have to plan for more materials, dealing with more planned orders and more exception messages after the MRP run. From the manufacturing execution perspective, we will have more production orders to release, confirm, and complete and more goods movements being posted to manufacture one single product.

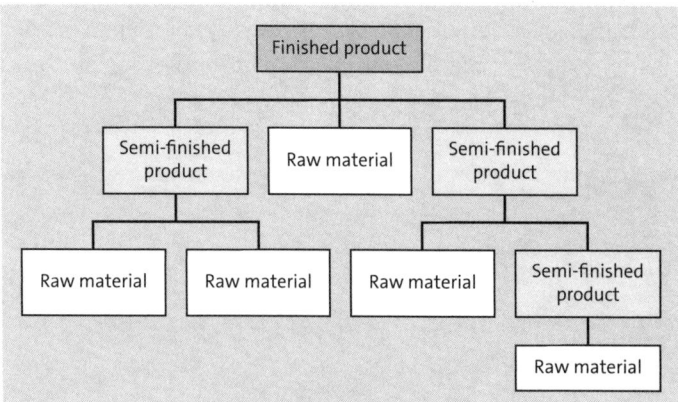

Figure 3.34 Multilevel BOM with Two Levels of Semifinished Products

There is no right or wrong when we talk about BOM design; each option has advantages and disadvantages. Most companies try to reach a balance: avoiding too many BOM levels, but strategically adding a semifinished product in the BOM structure whenever there is a planning or stock management advantage.

Routings, Rate Routings, and Master Recipes

Whereas the BOM describes the necessary components to build a product, the *routing* describes the list of steps (or operations) that should be performed to manufacture this product. From an MRP perspective, the routing is important because each operation will have a duration; the planned order dates can be calculated during lead-time scheduling according to the duration of the routing operations.

Routings are basically used by production orders in discrete manufacturing, whereas repetitive manufacturing uses a similar object called the rate routing, and the process industry uses master recipes.

Routing operations are executed sequentially, one after another, and a routing should have at least one main sequence of operations, but it can also have alternative or parallel sequences. Figure 3.35 shows the routing operation overview, illustrating the three operations that should be executed on the main sequence.

3 Master Data and Basic Settings

> **Note**
>
> In a master recipe, we will have different phases below the operations, and we will have to manually create relationships between the phases. This master recipe design allows for the flexibility required by food and chemical companies, for example, because we can plan for the different phases to start or finish together.

Ope...	SOp	Work Center	Plant	Con...	Standard...	Description	Lo...	PRT	Cl...	Ob...	Pe...	Cu...	Su...	Base Quantity	Un...	Setup	Unit	Activity...	Machine	Unit	Activity...	Labor	Unit
0010		WC01	0001	PP01		Operation 1								1	EA	10	MIN		30	MIN			
0020		WC02	0001	PP01		Operation 2								1	EA				40	MIN			
0030		WC03	0001	PP03		Operation 3								1	EA	20	MIN		20	MIN			
0040			0001											1	EA								
0050			0001											1	EA								
0060			0001											1	EA								
0070			0001											1	EA								
0080			0001											1	EA								

Figure 3.35 Routing Operation Overview

Each routing operation will be executed on a work center, and each work center has a standard value key, with the different activities (e.g., setup or machine processing) that can be executed during the manufacturing process. When creating a routing, we need to determine the time planned for each one of those activities, which is used to calculate the total operation duration. The duration is calculated according to the formulas defined in the work center; SAP provides standard formulas to calculate the setup and processing duration, but we can create custom formulas if necessary.

> **Note**
>
> Besides the calculation of the operation duration during lead-time scheduling, the standard values are also used to determine the capacity requirements for capacity leveling and for the production order costing purposes.

Figure 3.36 shows the routing operation details with the standard values.

Planned orders created by MRP will have two different sets of dates: *basic dates* and *production dates*. During the MRP run, SAP S/4HANA will first calculate the planned order basic dates using the in-house production time defined in the material master; then it can calculate the production dates when running MRP with lead-time scheduling.

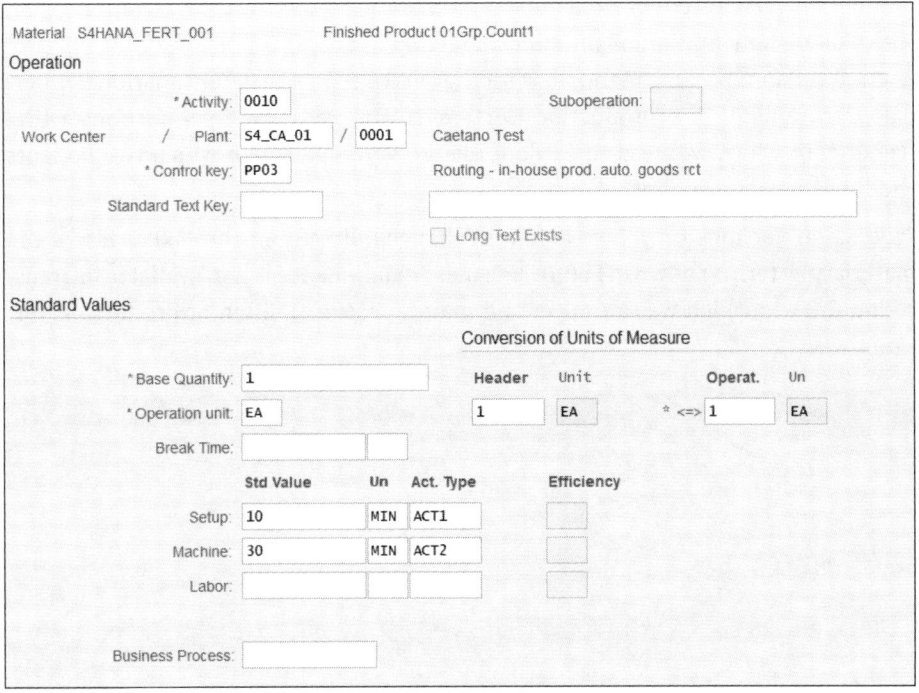

Figure 3.36 Standard Values in the Routing Operation Details

Depending on the planned order scheduling parameters defined in Customizing (Transaction OPU3), the planned order basic dates can be adjusted to match the planned order production dates so that they reflect the accurate planned order duration calculated according to the routing operation standard values. If there is a big difference between the in-house production time and the total duration calculated with routing, there might be problems with the planned order dates; therefore, we recommend keeping the in-house production time as close as possible to the routing. One best practice is to use Transaction CA97N to automatically update the in-house production time in the material master based on the routing scheduling.

Production Version

Many companies may have different alternative BOMs to manufacture a product, and each one may require a different routing with different operations or different standard values to build this product. To determine which combinations of BOM and routing can be used by MRP to generate planned orders, we need to create additional master data: the production version.

Production versions could already be used in SAP ERP to select the BOM. However, with the implementation of simplified sourcing in SAP S/4HANA, the usage of production versions became mandatory for the BOM alternative determination in internal procurement. The production version is also required in a subcontracting scenario, in which we need to explode the BOM to determine which components should be sent to a vendor.

Production versions can be created and changed directly in the **MRP 2** tab of the material master. As shown in Figure 3.37, mass maintenance is also available in Transaction C223, in which we can select and maintain several different production versions.

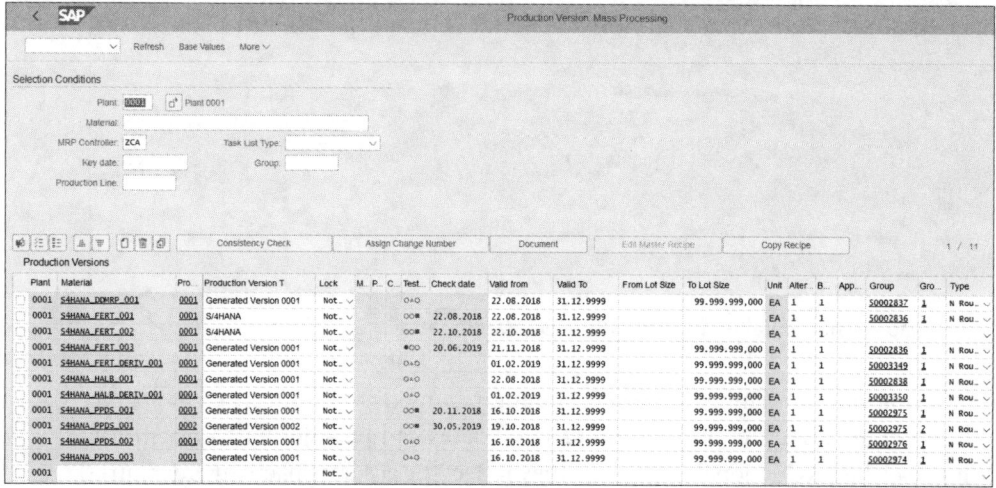

Figure 3.37 Mass Maintenance of Production Versions

When maintaining production versions in Transaction C223, we can select one or more production versions and directly maintain the values for each selected version in the grid or double-click the line to maintain each version individually in the detail screen, as shown in Figure 3.38.

> **Note**
>
> The only change introduced in production versions in SAP S/4HANA was the possibility of locking them for automatic sourcing only. In SAP ERP, it was only possible to lock a production version for any kind of usage, while SAP S/4HANA offers the additional possibility to lock it just for automatic sourcing. This way, the production

version cannot be selected by MRP, but can still be used when we manually create a production order, for example.

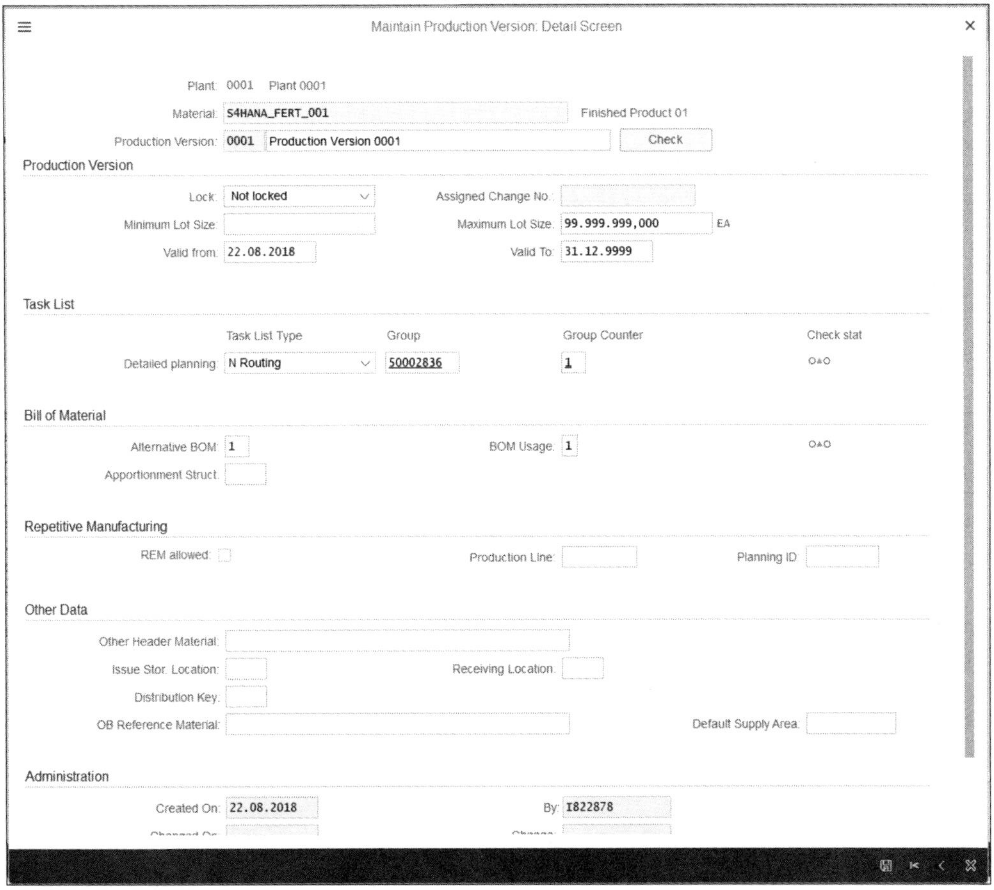

Figure 3.38 Detail Screen of the Production Version Maintenance

When creating a new production version, we need to define the validity dates, the lot size for which it should be selected, the alternative BOM, and the desired routing. It is very important to ensure that the BOM and the routing selected are valid for the whole production version validity and for the lot size defined for the production version; otherwise, the production version will be inconsistent. To ensure that the production version will be consistent, we can trigger a consistency check for a single production version by clicking the **Check** button in the detail screen (the top-right

3 Master Data and Basic Settings

corner of Figure 3.38) or by clicking the **Consistency Check** button in the Transaction C223 mass processing screen shown in Figure 3.37.

The results of the production version consistency check are shown in Figure 3.39. In this example, the BOM does not exist for the whole production version validity period, leading to an inconsistency. There is a **Test** column in Transaction C223 showing the test results; production versions with inconsistencies will show a red traffic light (see Figure 3.37).

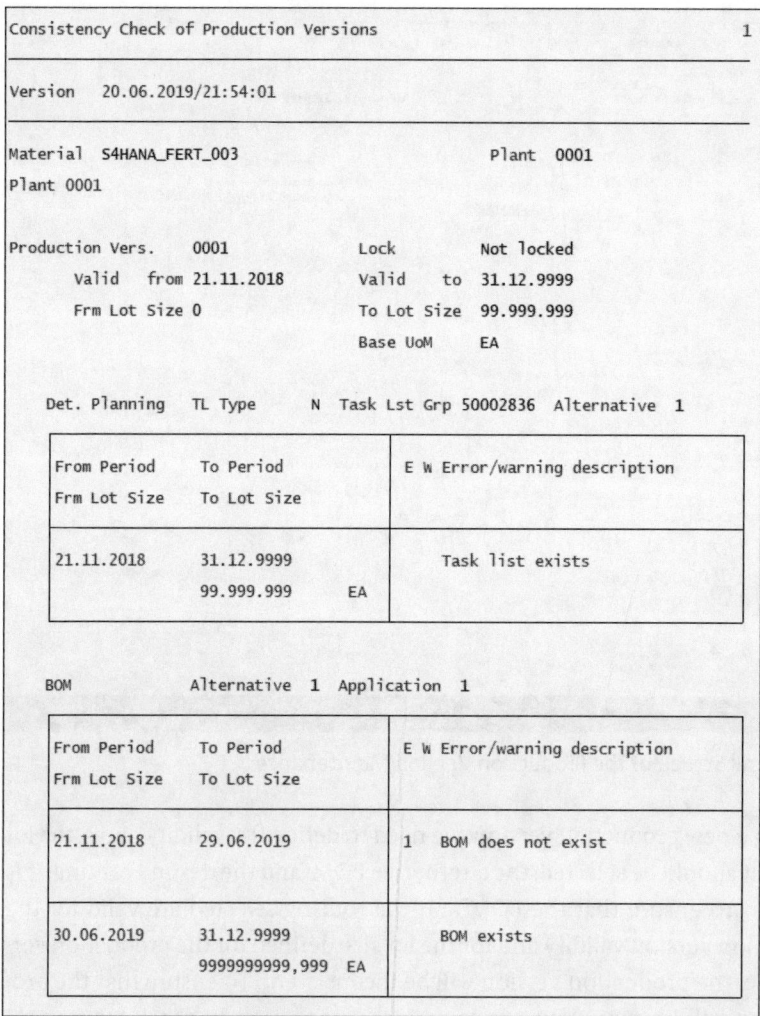

Figure 3.39 Production Version Consistency Check

Since the usage of production versions became mandatory for production planning in SAP S/4HANA, new reports were introduced to support the mass creation of production versions in order to accelerate migration from SAP ERP to SAP S/4HANA or facilitate new SAP S/4HANA implementations.

When SAP introduced the logistic processes in SAP S/4HANA 1511, report CS_BOM_PRODVER_MIGRATION was created to generate production versions based on existing BOMs. This report would create all the necessary production versions, but only with the BOM. Because most companies are using lead-time scheduling based on the routing (or master recipe), and the routing is selected according to the production version in SAP S/4HANA, this was a key limitation of this report. Because of this shortcoming, SAP soon created a new version of this report, which would create production versions based on the BOM and routing combination.

Report CS_BOM_PRODVER_MIGRATION02 was introduced with SAP Note 2463759 and is now available for all SAP S/4HANA releases (see Figure 3.40). This new version of the report provides much more flexible criteria to select the materials for which the production versions should be chosen, including limitations for material, BOM, and routing. This report also offers the option to select the following migration criteria:

- **Only Production Versions with Routing**: With this flag checked, a production version will only be created when a valid routing exists. This means that the report will not create production versions with the BOM only.
- **Only Production Versions where None Exists**: When this option is selected, the report will not create a production version if another already exists for the same BOM, even if the existing production version is only valid in the past.
- **Only BOMs Allocated to Routings**: When this option is selected, the report will only create production versions when there is an allocation of a BOM component to a routing operation.
- **Based on Production Orders**: When this option is selected, the report will only create a production version for BOM and routing combinations that were already used in production orders. This option would only be useful in the case of a migration to SAP S/4HANA because it checks for already existing production orders.
- **Also Repetitive Materials**: This option is used to create production versions for repetitive manufacturing materials.
- **Also Display Unchanged PVs**: When this option is selected, existing production versions that are not changed will be displayed in the results list.

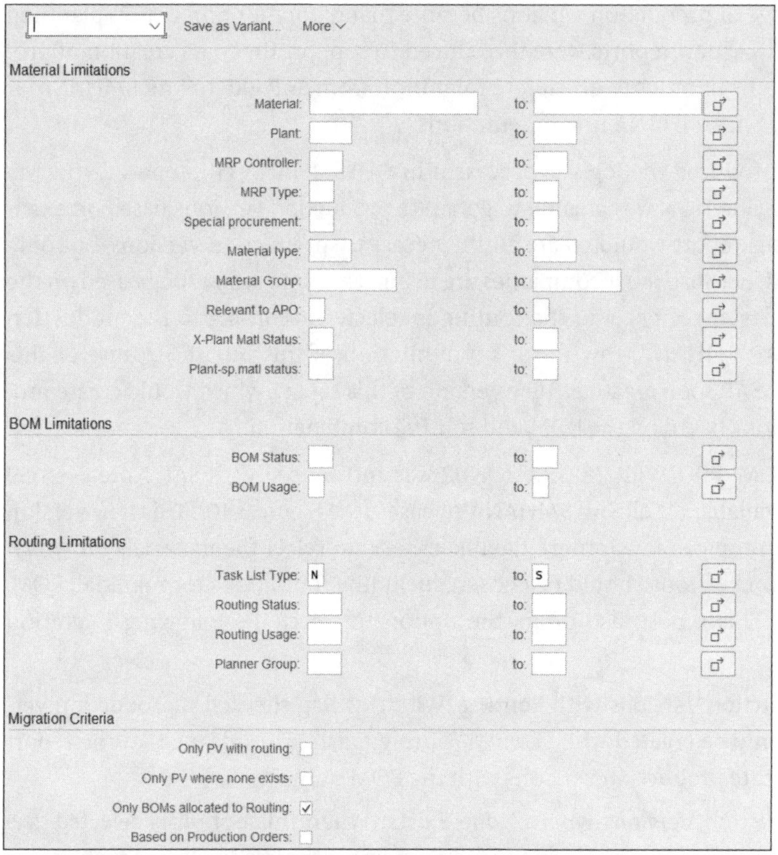

3   Master Data and Basic Settings

Figure 3.40 Report CS_BOM_PRODVER_MIGRATION02

This report can be executed in the background if we need to create a large number of production versions; we also have the option to execute it in simulation mode if we need to the results before running in update mode. There is also an option to select if we just want to create new production versions or if existing production versions will be also updated. This option may be used, for example, if production versions were previously created without a routing using report CS_BOM_PRODVER_MIGRATION.

3.2.2   External Procurement

When we talk about externally procured materials, we are talking about materials that are generally purchased and which will generate purchase requisitions, planned orders with external procurement, or delivery schedules. For this kind of procurement

3.2 Procurement Master Data

element, MRP can determine the vendor that will supply the material using the purchasing info record, the source list, the purchasing contract, or a scheduling agreement.

From an MRP perspective, it is not mandatory to have any kind of external procurement master data: MRP can create planned orders or requisitions without a supplier, and the purchasing department can determine it later when converting the requisition to purchase order. However, it is a best practice to have the source of supply determination set during the MRP run so that MRP can adjust the replenishment proposal dates according to the supplier lead time.

In this section, we will explore the external procurement master data and how it can influence the MRP results, determining the vendor or even the type of replenishment element that will be generated to cover a shortage.

Info Record

The *info record* is purchasing master data that will be used to store information about a specific vendor and material combination. An info record is required when converting a purchase requisition to a purchase order, and it can be used to determine if a specific supplier can be considered by MRP as a valid source of supply. Info records are usually created in Transaction ME11, and we should maintain the **Vendor**, **Material**, **Purchasing Organization**, **Plant**, and **Info Record Category** fields. We can also set the **Info Record Number** when using an external number range. Figure 3.41 shows the purchasing info record creation in Transaction ME11.

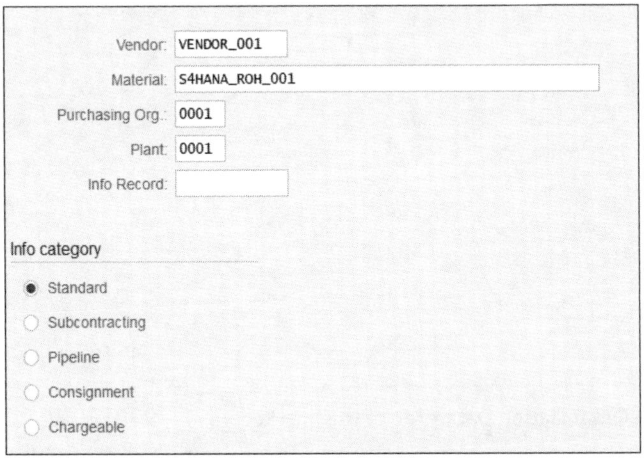

Figure 3.41 Info Record Creation in Transaction ME11

There are different tabs available in the info record, but the MRP-relevant information is stored under the **Purchasing Organization Data 1** tab shown in Figure 3.42. In this tab, we can define a planned delivery time for this specific material and vendor combination; this information can be considered by MRP to determine the dates of a replenishment proposal.

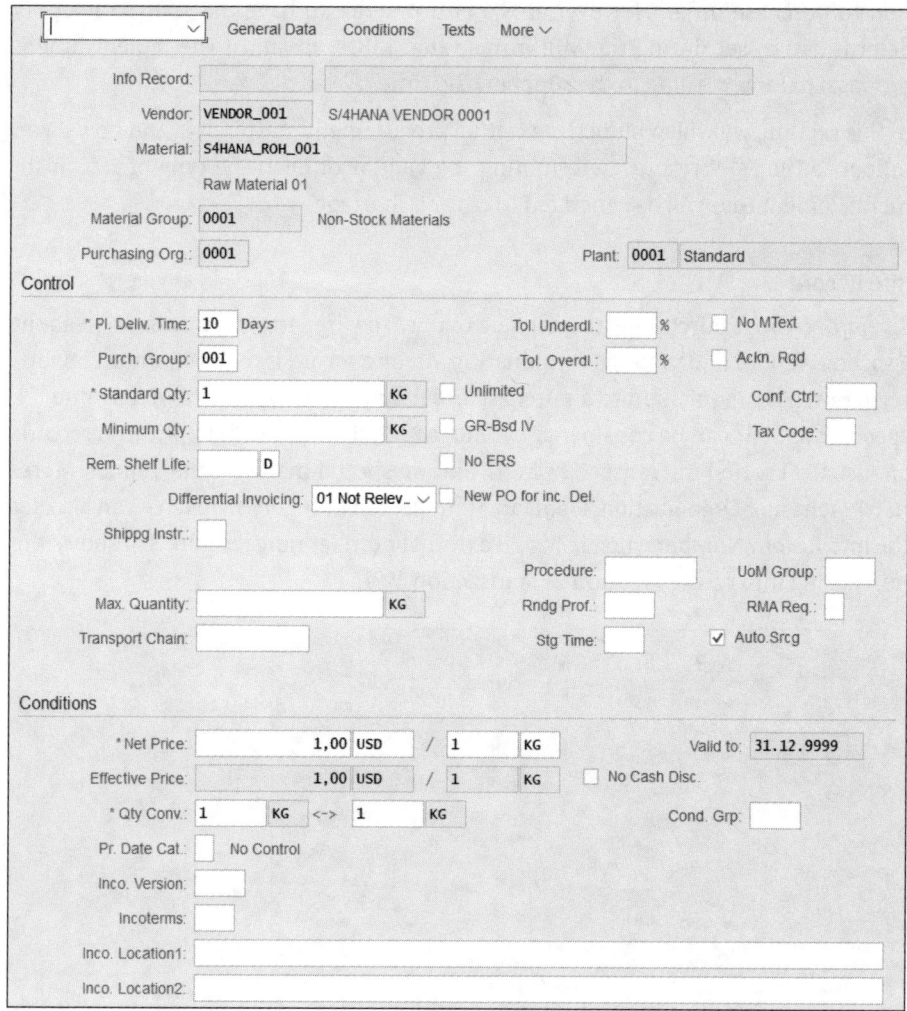

Figure 3.42 The Purchasing Organization Data 1 Tab of the Info Record

> **Note**
> In SAP ERP, we had the option to define in Customizing whether the planned delivery time set in the info record or in the contract/scheduling agreement would be considered (or not) by MRP. This option is no longer available in SAP S/4HANA due to a simplification; now, the planned delivery time from the info record/scheduling agreement will always be considered.

In SAP ERP, the creation of the info record was not enough to have the supplier selected by MRP as a valid source of supply. In SAP ERP, it was mandatory to have least a source list, indicating that this supplier should be considered during the MRP source of supply determination. This system behavior, however, was changed with SAP S/4HANA's simplified sourcing. In SAP S/4HANA, the new **Auto Sourcing** flag was introduced in the info record. When we check this flag, the vendor is automatically considered by MRP during the source determination, even when there is no source list for this vendor and material combination. However, if there are several vendors with the **Auto Sourcing** flag checked in the info record, we still need to create a source list or an info record to prioritize a specific source of supply.

> **Note**
> By default, MRP will not copy the info record number to the purchase requisition, even if this info record is considered during the source determination.
>
> This is standard system behavior that aims to improve the MRP performance, and it does not cause any problems because the info record number is not required in the purchase requisition. This system behavior is explained in SAP Note 82857 (MD01: Info Record no. Not in Purchase Requisition).

Source List

The *source list* is basically a list of the possible sources of supply allowed for a specific material. Source lists are created and changed in Transaction ME01, and the maintenance is very simple. The source list was mandatory in SAP ERP for the source determination during the MRP run, but the design changed a little bit in SAP S/4HANA with simplified sourcing.

With the introduction of simplified sourcing in the first SAP S/4HANA release, the source list was completely removed from the MRP source determination. The original idea in SAP S/4HANA was that the info record would be used to determine if a source of supply should be relevant to MRP, and the quota arrangement would be used to prioritize a specific source of supply when several are relevant to MRP.

However, with the info record, we do not have an accurate validity control as we have in the source list. In the info record, there is no control for the validity dates for the automatic selection of the source of supply. In addition, with simplified sourcing, MRP would consider the purchasing contract and the scheduling agreement by default as valid sources of supply, and there was no way to avoid them being considered.

Therefore, SAP changed the original simplified sourcing design with SAP Note 2607657, allowing the source list to be used to prioritize a source of supply during a given period of time and also allowing us to control when a purchasing contract or scheduling agreement should not be considered by MRP. In the current SAP S/4HANA releases, the source list is not mandatory for source determination, but it can still be used in those situations.

Source list maintenance is very simple: we only need to set the **Valid From** and **Valid To**, **Vendor**, and **Purchasing Organization** fields, as shown in Figure 3.43. Depending on the source of supply, additional fields can be entered, such as the planning plant in the case of a stock transfer or the scheduling agreement and item.

Material:	S4HANA_ROH_001			Raw Material 01									
Plant:	0001			Plant 0001									

Source List Records

	Valid from	Valid to	Vendor	POrg	PPl	OUn	Agmt	Item	Central Contr...	Cent. Contrac...	Fix	Blk	MRP	MRP Area
☐	01.08.2019	30.10.2019	VENDOR_001	0001							☐	☐	1	
☐	31.10.2019	31.12.2019	VENDOR_002	0001							☐	☐	1	
☐											☐	☐		

Figure 3.43 Sources of Supply in the Source List

From a planning perspective, the **MRP** field is the most important part of the source list because it determines whether the source of supply should be considered by MRP. This field can also control if a scheduling agreement should be considered or ignored by MRP. If there is an entry in the source list for a given vendor and the **MRP** field determines that this is a valid source of supply, it will be selected by MRP during source determination, even if the **Automatic Sourcing** flag is not set in the info record.

The validity is a very important point to be discussed, not only for the source list but for the whole external procurement source determination. During the MRP run, whenever a shortage is found, this date is used to determine the source of supply. After the source of supply determination, the planned delivery time will be used to calculate the start date of the replenishment proposal. If the start date of the replenishment proposal is in the past, MRP may recalculate the finish date, considering today as the start date. In extreme cases, we may have a requirement in the past causing a shortage and the purchase requisition starting today, which means that the source of supply determination date is completely outside the requisition dates.

Figure 3.44 shows the results of the MRP run for material S/4HANA_ROH_001, where there is a requirement on 17.06.2019 leading to a shortage. Considering the source list for this material (shown in Figure 3.43), the validity start of the first valid source of supply is 01.08.2019.

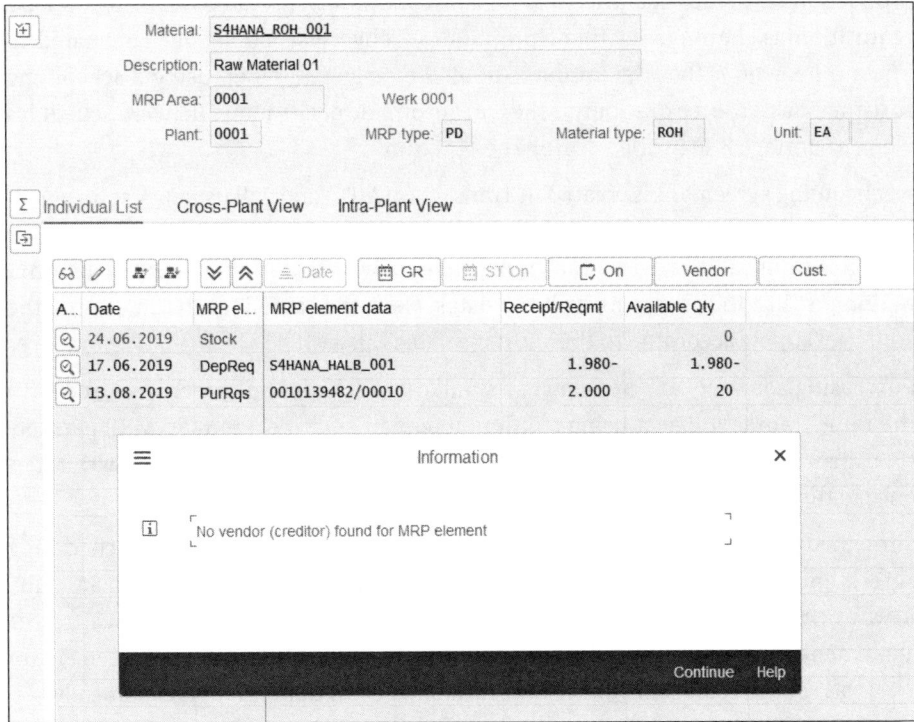

Figure 3.44 MRP Results with a Source List outside the Validity Date

To cover the shortage, MRP created a new purchase requisition on 13.08.2019, for which it could not find a valid source of supply. Although the purchase requisition finish date is within the source list validity, the source of supply was not considered by MRP because the actual source determination happened on 17.06.2019—the shortage date. The purchase requisition date was shifted to the future to avoid it starting in the past. SAP S/4HANA must determine the source of supply before scheduling the replenishment proposal because the planned delivery time may vary according to the source of supply.

This system behavior is valid not only for source lists but also for contracts, scheduling agreements, and quota arrangements.

Scheduling Agreements and Contracts

A *scheduling agreement* is a purchasing agreement with a specific vendor to supply a product under predefined price and logistic conditions. Instead of using a purchase requisition as the replenishment proposal, a delivery schedule will be created to inform the vendor that the product should be delivered. When using a scheduling agreement as a source of supply, MRP can automatically generate delivery schedules when a shortage is identified during the MRP run.

A scheduling agreement is created in Transaction ME31 and will usually use an agreement type such as the standard type LP or a similar one. We also need to determine the agreement validity date, which is considered by MRP during the source determination just like the source list validity dates. Here, the same logic to determine the source of supply according to the shortage date is also valid.

Purchasing contracts are created very similarly to scheduling agreements and with the same transaction, just using a different agreement type. From an MRP perspective, the main difference is that MRP will generate purchase requisitions with reference to the contract instead of generating schedule lines.

Simplified sourcing also affected the logic used by MRP to determine if a scheduling agreement or a contract should be considered as a valid source of supply. In SAP ERP, it was necessary to create a scheduling agreement and to add a reference to this agreement in the source list, making sure that the value of the **MRP** field (see Figure 3.43) was set to **Record Relevant to MRP. Schedule Lines Generated Automatically.**

3.2 Procurement Master Data

In SAP S/4HANA, this is no longer necessary; it is enough to have the scheduling agreement created for it to be considered by MRP as a valid source of supply and to have delivery schedules generated by MRP Live. The source list is still required in SAP S/4HANA—for example, if we have a scheduling agreement but do not want to have schedule lines created on a given period. If this is the case, we just need to create a source list entry with a reference to the agreement and leave the **MRP** field empty.

Within each scheduling agreement, we can have many different items with different materials. For each item, we will determine settings such as the **Item Category**, **Target Quantity**, **Net Price**, and **Storage Location** fields. MRP can consider different item categories, such as subcontracting or consignment, but the scheduling agreement will be only considered by MRP if the item category matches the special procurement type defined in the material master. Figure 3.45 shows the scheduling agreement item for material S4HANA_ROH_001.

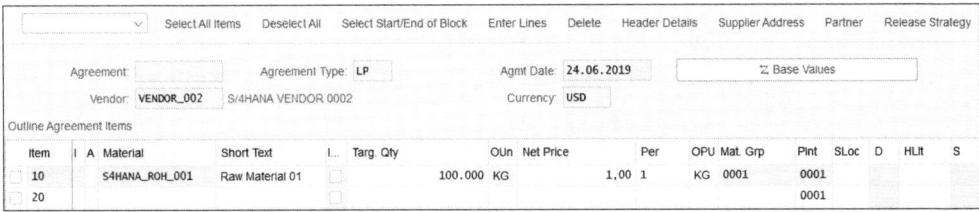

Figure 3.45 Scheduling Agreement Item

> **Warning**
> Although we can maintain a target quantity in the scheduling agreement item, this information is not considered by MRP during the source determination, and MRP can generate schedule lines that will exceed the agreement target quantity. If we want to limit the quantity of delivery schedules generated by MRP for a given agreement, we can use a quota arrangement.

In the scheduling agreement's **Additional Data** tab, we can find more fields that are relevant to MRP, as shown in Figure 3.46. Here, we can define a planned delivery time and a goods receipt processing time that can be considered by MRP, depending on the Customizing settings. Besides that, we can also set the **Firm Zone**, **Trade-Off Zone**, and **Binding on MRP** fields.

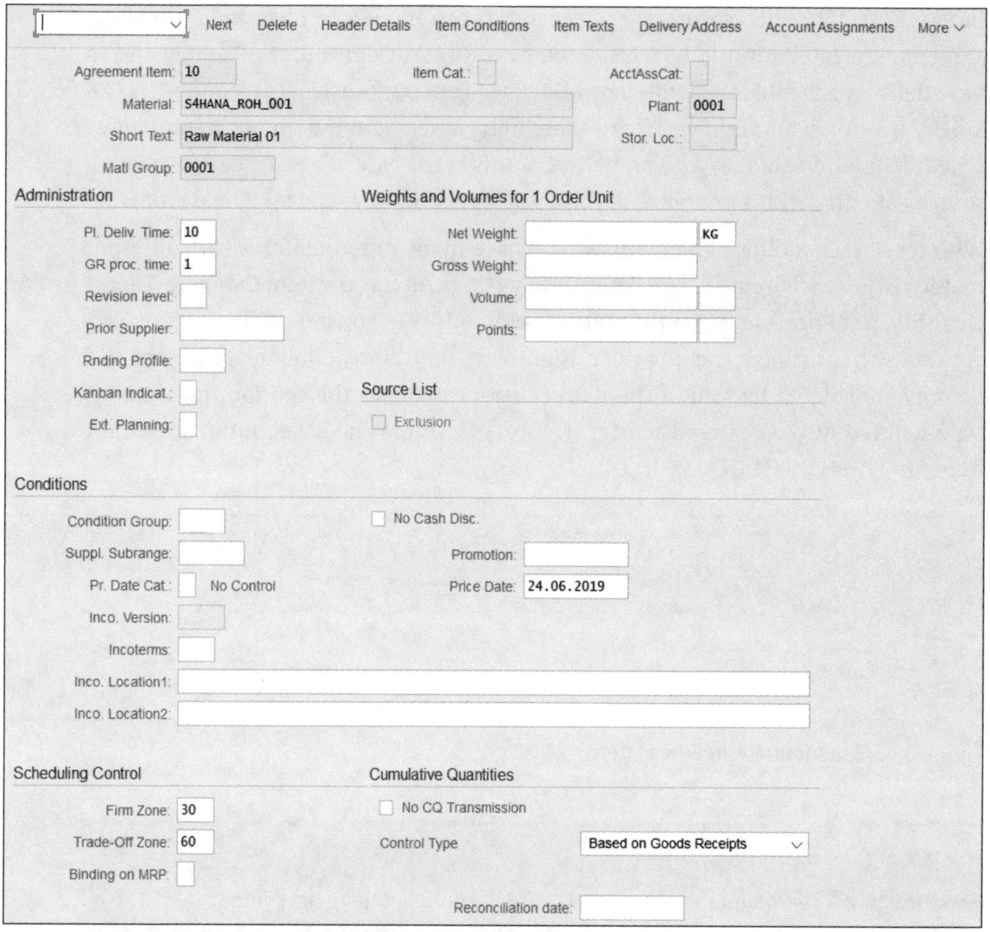

Figure 3.46 Scheduling Agreement Additional Data

The **Firm Zone** field represents a period in calendar days for which the schedule lines are firm and the vendor can start the product manufacturing. The **Trade-Off Zone** field represents a period in calendar days for which the vendor can start the procurement of the parts involved in the manufacturing. Depending on the value defined for the **Binding on MRP** field, delivery schedules within the firm zone of the trace-off zone can be changed by MRP or not. The following settings are possible for this field:

- Blank: Schedule lines after trade-off zone can be changed by MRP
- 1: Schedule lines within trade-off zone can be changed by MRP
- 2: Schedule lines can always be changed by MRP

> **Note**
>
> Another important setting in the scheduling agreement from the MRP perspective is the **SC Supplier** flag (also known in previous releases as **SC Vendor**), found under the **Delivery Address** tab. If this flag is checked, MRP considers that this scheduling agreement should be considered only in a third-party scenario, in which this component should be delivered directly to a subcontractor. MRP will not consider this agreement a valid source of supply in any other scenario, as this is specific for components delivered to the subcontractor.

3.2.3 Quota Arrangement

We now have discussed the master data for internal and external procurement, but the quota arrangement was intentionally left out. That is because the quota arrangement can be used to prioritize sources of supply for both internal and external procurement. The quota arrangement basically allows us to distribute the replenishment proposals created to cover a shortage between different sources of supply based on a predefined percentage.

In SAP ERP, a quota arrangement would be only selected by MRP during source determination if the **Quota Arrangement Usage** field indicated that quota arrangements should be considered by MRP. This logic was introduced in earlier releases of SAP ERP to allow the user to select when to use quota arrangements because using a quota arrangement could lead to performance issues in MRP.

One of the simplifications introduced by SAP S/4HANA simplified sourcing means that it is no longer required to define in the material master if the quota arrangement should be read by MRP; a quota arrangement will be automatically selected by MRP during the source determination, within the validity date range. This system behavior was changed in SAP S/4HANA because with the technology improvements and with the SAP HANA database, using a quota arrangement is no longer a performance bottleneck for MRP.

Quota arrangements are created and changed in Transaction MEQ1, and we can define several different validity periods. For each period, we can define a minimum quantity split so that the replenishment proposals will not be split between the different sources of supply when using a splitting quota if the quantity is below this minimum quantity. Figure 3.47 shows the quota arrangement validity periods in Transaction MEQ1.

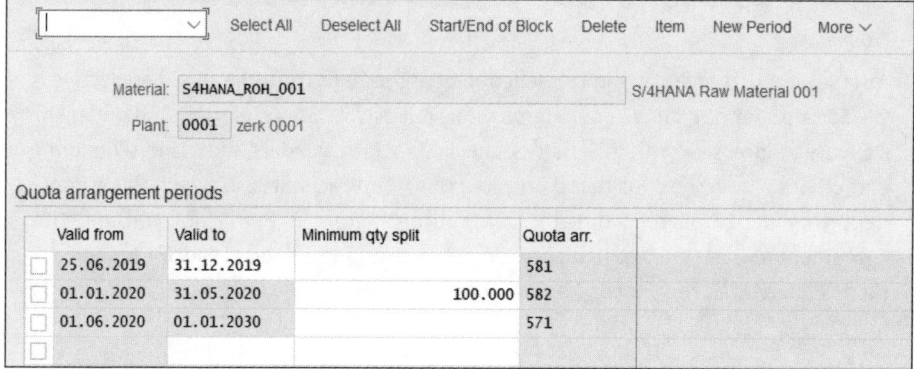

Figure 3.47 Quota Arrangement Periods in Transaction MEQ1

For each validity period, we can determine *items*; each item will represent a possible source of supply and the respective procurement type, special procurement type, and allocated quota, as shown in Figure 3.48.

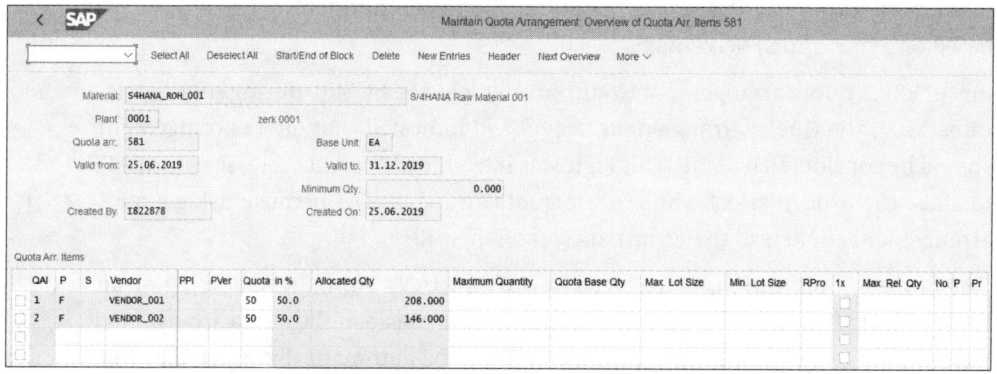

Figure 3.48 Quota Arrangement Items

> **Tip**
> We can mix sources of supply with different procurement types in the same quota arrangement. We can determine, for example, that a percentage of a material will be manufactured internally and the rest will be subcontracted.

There are two different procedures available for a quota arrangement: the allocation quota arrangement and the splitting quota arrangement.

3.2 Procurement Master Data

With the *allocation quota arrangement*, whenever MRP finds a shortage, it will choose one of the sources of supply defined in the quota arrangement. Whenever a source of supply is chosen and a new replenishment proposal is created, the allocated quantity is updated for this item, and MRP will always ensure that this quantity is allocated according to the quotas defined for each item.

Figure 3.49 shows the MRP results with the allocation quota arrangement. Note that for every shortage, MRP created a single replenishment proposal, choosing one of the sources of supply defined in the quota arrangement. For the replenishment proposal created to cover the subsequent shortage, MRP would choose the next source of supply, trying to keep the balance of the allocated quantity.

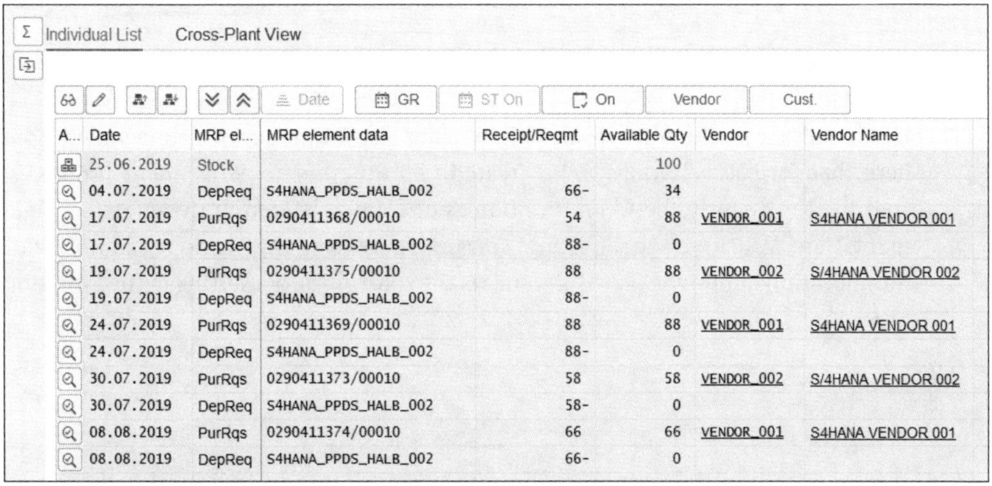

A...	Date	MRP el...	MRP element data	Receipt/Reqmt	Available Qty	Vendor	Vendor Name
	25.06.2019	Stock			100		
	04.07.2019	DepReq	S4HANA_PPDS_HALB_002	66-	34		
	17.07.2019	PurRqs	0290411368/00010	54	88	VENDOR_001	S4HANA VENDOR 001
	17.07.2019	DepReq	S4HANA_PPDS_HALB_002	88-	0		
	19.07.2019	PurRqs	0290411375/00010	88	88	VENDOR_002	S/4HANA VENDOR 002
	19.07.2019	DepReq	S4HANA_PPDS_HALB_002	88-	0		
	24.07.2019	PurRqs	0290411369/00010	88	88	VENDOR_001	S4HANA VENDOR 001
	24.07.2019	DepReq	S4HANA_PPDS_HALB_002	88-	0		
	30.07.2019	PurRqs	0290411373/00010	58	58	VENDOR_002	S/4HANA VENDOR 002
	30.07.2019	DepReq	S4HANA_PPDS_HALB_002	58-	0		
	08.08.2019	PurRqs	0290411374/00010	66	66	VENDOR_001	S4HANA VENDOR 001
	08.08.2019	DepReq	S4HANA_PPDS_HALB_002	66-	0		

Figure 3.49 MRP Results with Allocation Quota Arrangement

With a *splitting quota*, MRP will ignore the allocated quantity and, for each shortage, will split the replenishment proposals between the different sources of supply. We can activate a splitting quota by setting the respective flag in the lot-sizing procedure Customizing (Transaction OMI4). By default, the **Splitting Quota** setting is not checked in the standard lot-sizing procedures. We might have to create our own lot-sizing procedure as a copy of the standard one and set this flag to use a splitting quota, as shown in Figure 3.50.

3 Master Data and Basic Settings

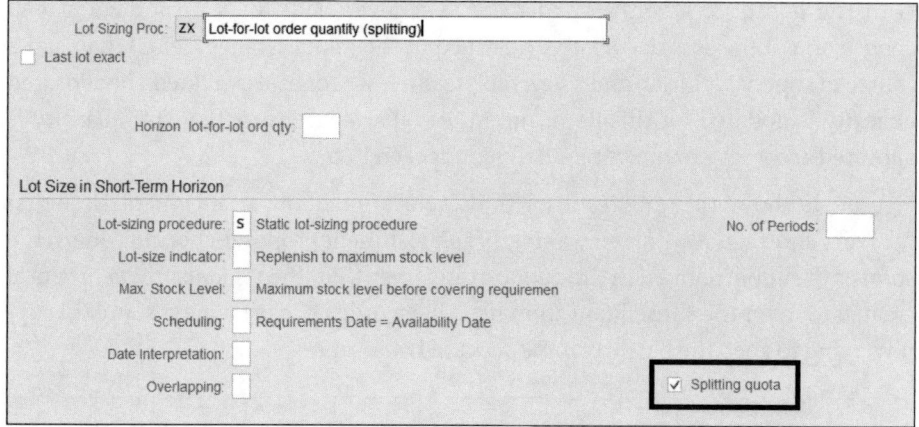

Figure 3.50 Splitting Quota in Lot-Sizing Procedure

Figure 3.51 shows the MRP results when using a splitting quota arrangement; note here that for each shortage, MRP created two different replenishment proposals, splitting the quantity between the sources of supply defined in the quota arrangement. Here, MRP used the same quota arrangement from the previous example with the allocation quota; the only difference is the splitting quota setting in the lot-sizing procedure.

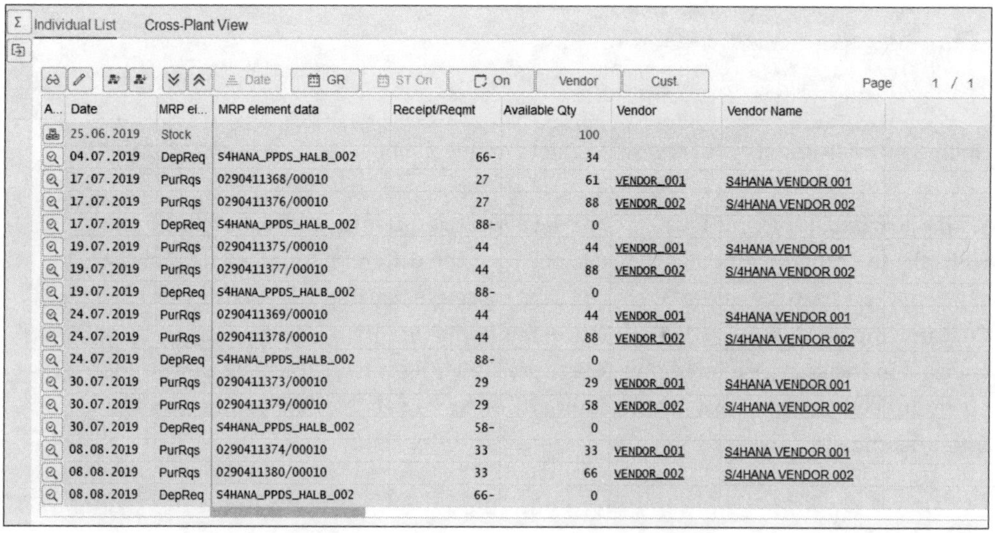

A...	Date	MRP el...	MRP element data	Receipt/Reqmt	Available Qty	Vendor	Vendor Name
	25.06.2019	Stock			100		
	04.07.2019	DepReq	S4HANA_PPDS_HALB_002	66-	34		
	17.07.2019	PurRqs	0290411368/00010	27	61	VENDOR_001	S4HANA VENDOR 001
	17.07.2019	PurRqs	0290411376/00010	27	88	VENDOR_002	S/4HANA VENDOR 002
	17.07.2019	DepReq	S4HANA_PPDS_HALB_002	88-	0		
	19.07.2019	PurRqs	0290411375/00010	44	44	VENDOR_001	S4HANA VENDOR 001
	19.07.2019	PurRqs	0290411377/00010	44	88	VENDOR_002	S/4HANA VENDOR 002
	19.07.2019	DepReq	S4HANA_PPDS_HALB_002	88-	0		
	24.07.2019	PurRqs	0290411369/00010	44	44	VENDOR_001	S4HANA VENDOR 001
	24.07.2019	PurRqs	0290411378/00010	44	88	VENDOR_002	S/4HANA VENDOR 002
	24.07.2019	DepReq	S4HANA_PPDS_HALB_002	88-	0		
	30.07.2019	PurRqs	0290411373/00010	29	29	VENDOR_001	S4HANA VENDOR 001
	30.07.2019	PurRqs	0290411379/00010	29	58	VENDOR_002	S/4HANA VENDOR 002
	30.07.2019	DepReq	S4HANA_PPDS_HALB_002	58-	0		
	08.08.2019	PurRqs	0290411374/00010	33	33	VENDOR_001	S4HANA VENDOR 001
	08.08.2019	PurRqs	0290411380/00010	33	66	VENDOR_002	S/4HANA VENDOR 002
	08.08.2019	DepReq	S4HANA_PPDS_HALB_002	66-	0		

Figure 3.51 MRP Results with Splitting Quota Arrangement

> **Warning**
> MRP does not consider quota arrangements at the MRP area level. If necessary, SAP Note 505667 provides a modification that allows the quota arrangement to be considered at the MRP area level during the MRP run.

The quota arrangement also provides the following settings that are considered during the MRP run:

- **Maximum Quantity**: This setting can be used when we want to limit the usage of a source of supply up to a certain quantity.
- **Maximum Lot Size**: We can limit the lot size of the replenishment proposals created for a specific vendor using the **Maximum Lot Size** setting. If the shortage quantity exceeds the maximum lot size, the remaining quantity will be redistributed between the remaining sources of supply, according to the quotas.
- **Minimum Lot Size**: This is similar to the minimum lot size defined in the material master. If the shortage quantity is below the minimum lot size, the replenishment proposal will be increased to match this minimum quantity.
- **Rounding Profile**: This setting is similar to the rounding profile defined in the material master, and it can be used to round the replenishment proposal quantity.
- **Indicator "Once-Only" (1X)**: This setting can be set if we want to avoid a source of supply being used several times to cover the same shortage.
- **Maximum Released Quantity**: This setting can be used to define a maximum released quantity for a source of supply in a given period. We should also define the period and the number of periods for the maximum released quantity.
- **Priority**: We can define a priority for each quota arrangement item so that MRP will create replenishment proposals following this priority.

> **Tip**
> Because MRP does not consider the scheduling agreement target quantity, we can use the quota arrangement to limit the maximum quantity and thus limit the quantity of schedule lines created for a certain agreement.

3.3 Planning File

Recall from Chapter 2 that MRP will select materials to be planned based on the planning file entries. The *planning file* is basically a table that is updated whenever an MRP-relevant change, such as a goods movement or a change on a planning element, is posted for a material. This entry will let MRP know that there was a change for this material since the last planning run and that this material should be planned again.

Whenever we set a valid MRP type for our material, a planning file entry is automatically created if MRP is activated for the plant. If we set MRP type ND (no MRP), the planning file entry will be automatically deleted because a material with this MRP type is not relevant to MRP.

The planning file entry can be displayed in Transaction MD21, as shown in Figure 3.52.

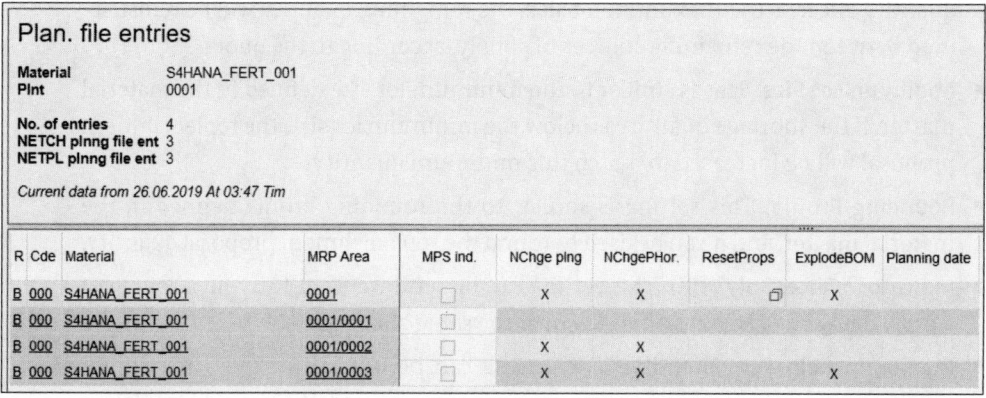

Figure 3.52 Planning File Entries in Transaction MD21

This was the same transaction used in SAP ERP, and here we will use the following fields:

- **Low-Level Code**: This is the lowest level of a material in any BOM and determines the sequence used in MRP to select materials for planning.
- **MPS Indicator**: This is set when a material uses an MRP type with an MPS procedure.
- **Net Change Planning**: This is the most important flag of the planning file and is set when an MRP-relevant change is posted for a material, indicating that it should be planned again by MRP.

- **Reset Proposals**: This indicates that all the existing unfirmed planned orders and requisitions should be deleted and recreated.
- **Explode BOM**: This is set automatically whenever a BOM is changed, indicating that the BOM should be re-exploded, independent of the planning type selected for the MRP run.
- **Planning Date**: This is used for time-phased materials to identify the date of the next planning run.

We can use Transaction MD20 to manually create a planning file entry or set the planning file flags, ensuring that it will be included in the next planning run.

> **Note**
>
> Planning file entries are generally automatically updated when we post a goods movement.
>
> For materials planned with a deterministic MRP, however, when the goods movement is posted to an order or a reservation, the planning file is only updated if the goods movement quantity is more or less than the planned quantity or if it is posted on a date different than the planned date. If we want to ensure that the planning file entry will be always updated when a goods movement is posted, we can check the **PFE Always** flag in customizing Transaction OMIY. Here, we can also define tolerances for overdelivery and underdelivery.

In SAP S/4HANA, the planning file was completely redesigned for better performance in an SAP HANA database. Planning file entries are now saved in the new table PPH_DBVM, which was simplified for update performance and consistency.

There are also new reports that can be used to set up the planning file or simply to run a consistency check. The new report PPH_SETUP_MRPRECORDS can be used to set up the planning file entries and also checks for planning file consistency. This report replaces all the reports previously used in SAP ERP to set up, convert, or check for the planning file consistency. Report PPH_SETUP_MRPRECORDS_SIMU is the equivalent version for long-term planning.

> **Warning**
>
> Any custom report built in SAP ERP based on old planning file tables DBVM/DBVL or MDVM/MDVL should be revised to read the new table PPH_DBVM.

If we are running a system conversion for SAP S/4HANA, we can use reports PPH_CONVERT_MRPRECORDS and PPH_CONVERT_MRPRECORDS_SIMU to convert the old SAP ERP planning file entries from table DBVM to table PPH_DBVM. The new reports will not only create the entries in table PPH_DBVM, but also copy the existing flags set in table DBVM.

> **Tip**
> SAP suggests that report RMMDVM10 should be executed in advance to run a consistency check in planning file table DBVM before the conversion.

In SAP ERP, Transactions MDAB and MDRE were used to schedule jobs to set up the planning file entries and to run a consistency check, respectively. Those transactions were replaced in SAP S/4HANA by Transaction PPH_MDAB, which can schedule a job with program PPH_SETUP_MRPRECORDS, which runs both actions together.

SAP Note 2268088 (S4TWL—Planning File) gives additional information about the planning file simplification in SAP S/4HANA.

3.4 Summary

This chapter explained how to create the basic MRP master data, from the material master (where we have the most important MRP settings) to internal and external procurement and finally to the planning file.

We have covered the differences between the most important MRP types, how MRP uses lot-sizing procedures to calculate the replenishment quantities, how the procurement and special procurement types influence which kind of replenishment proposal will be created, and additional settings in the material master.

From the procurement master data point of view, we have gone through the changes implemented in SAP S/4HANA by simplified sourcing and the impacts in source determination. We saw the details of a BOM and routing and how to create a production version. We have gone through all the master data used to determine the vendor and additional sources of supply for external procurement.

Finally, we saw the simplifications implemented in the planning file, the new transactions and reports that should be used to set up and check for the planning file consistency in SAP S/4HANA, and how to convert the SAP ERP planning file to SAP S/4HANA.

In the next chapter, we will explain how to configure MRP. We will show in more detail the relevant Customizing settings related to the MRP master data, such as the MRP types and lot-sizing procedures.

Chapter 4
Configuring MRP

This chapter gives step-by-step instructions for configuring MRP in SAP S/4HANA. We will start with overall plant parameters, which are the foundation of the MRP run. Then we explain the Customizing steps related to the master data and to the MRP planning process described in previous chapters.

As discussed in the previous chapter, customizing data is usually created during the SAP implementation project. It defines the business processes' design and tailors the system behavior according to company business requirements. The MRP configuration is nothing more than the creation of this customizing data in the SAP Customizing Implementation Guide (SAP IMG). Figure 4.1 shows the **Material Requirements Planning** path in the SAP IMG.

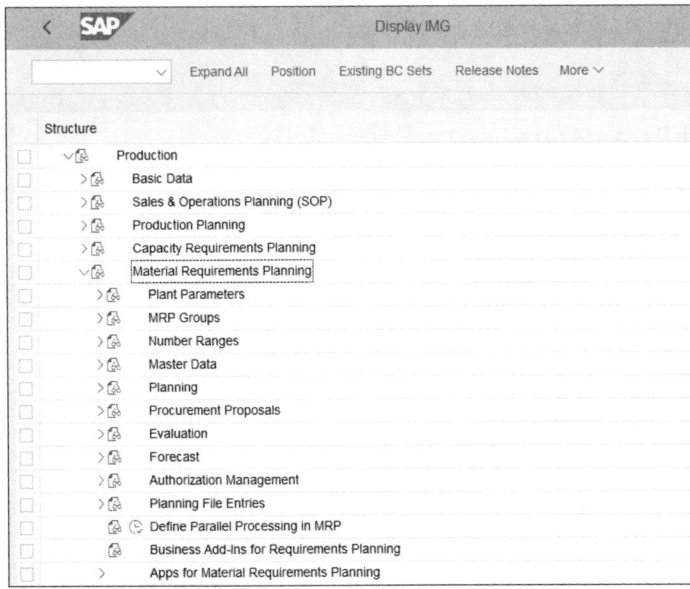

Figure 4.1 Material Requirements Planning in the SAP IMG

> **Tip**
> Use Transaction OPP1 to open the SAP IMG directly in the Customizing tree for MRP.

For MRP, the plant is the main organizational structure, so all MRP customizing is tied to the plant. We will start this chapter in Section 4.1 by describing how to maintain the MRP plant parameters in Customizing. We will also introduce the MRP group in Section 4.2 and explain how to use it to define Customizing settings for a specific group of materials.

We will then come back to the topics discussed in the previous chapters. In Section 4.3, we review the Customizing related to the MRP types and special procurement types, continuing with all the Customizing settings related to the MRP planning process, such as the already mentioned lot-sizing procedures (Section 4.4) and availability checks (Section 4.5).

A very important topic of discussion in this chapter will be the Customizing of MRP areas. The usage of MRP areas is required in SAP S/4HANA for storage location planning and for subcontracting, so we will discuss in detail the creation of MRP areas in Customizing in Section 4.6.

Finally, we will go through some general MRP-related configuration related to the planning file entries and the parallel processing used by classic MRP in Section 4.7. By the end of this chapter, we will have MRP configured and ready for execution.

4.1 Overall Plant Parameters

As mentioned in the beginning of this chapter, all the MRP customizing is plant-dependent, so we can define different MRP settings for each plant. The most important MRP settings for each plant are clustered in a single transaction, in which we can maintain all those parameters at once. This Customizing activity can be found under the MRP Customizing tree in the **Plant Parameters** folder, or we can access it directly using Transaction OPPQ.

> **Note**
> In SAP ERP, the Customizing step to configure MRP for a new plant was to activate MRP for this plant in the customizing Transaction OMDU. This Customizing step is no longer required in SAP S/4HANA, which considers that MRP is active for all plants by default.

4.1 Overall Plant Parameters

When accessing Transaction OPPQ, on the first screen we have the option to create, change, display, or copy the plant parameters for MRP. Because the plant is usually created through copying, an entry usually will already exist for the plant and we can maintain it directly. If an entry does not exist for the plant, we suggest you use another plant as a template through the copy option.

The plant maintenance screen shown in Figure 4.2 is divided into different screen areas (**Maintain Environment**, **Maintain Master Data**, **Maintain Planned Orders**, and **Maintain Planning Run**), in which each button will point to a Customizing activity. In the following sections, we will describe in detail each of those Customizing steps and the impact of those settings in MRP.

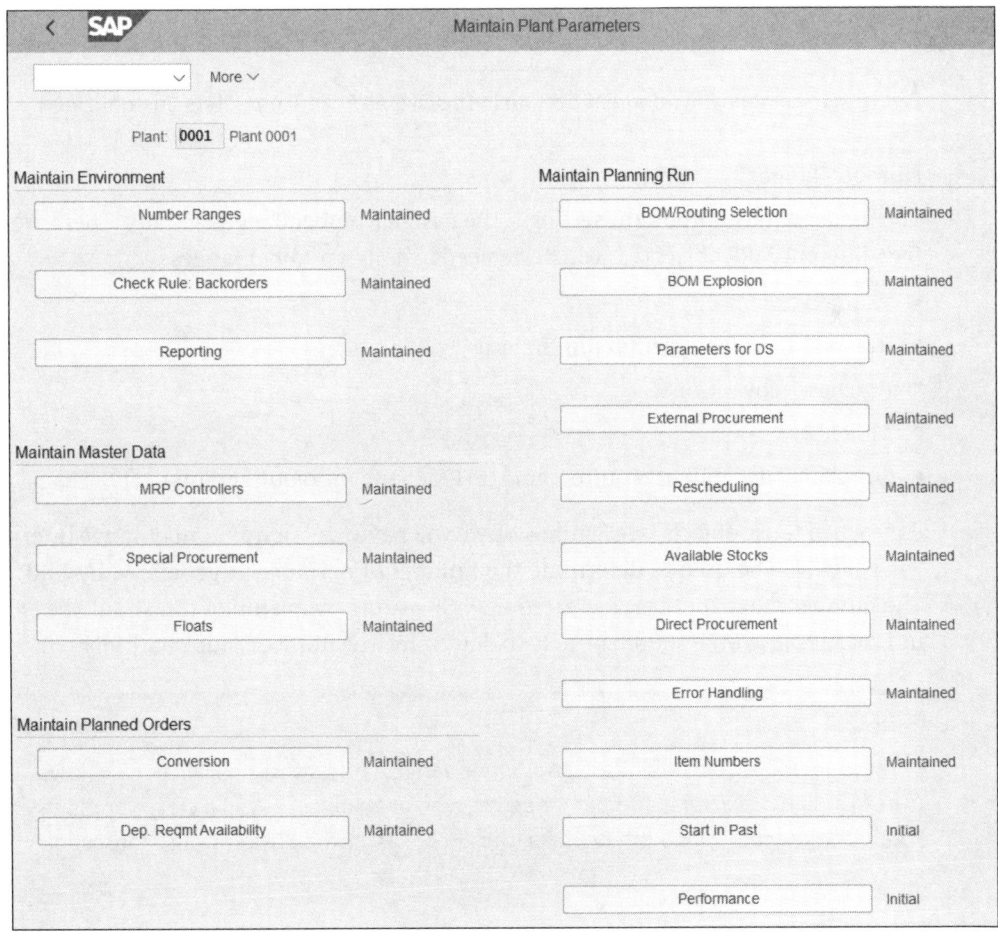

Figure 4.2 Maintain Plant Parameters during Customizing

4.1.1 Maintain Environment

The **Maintain Environment** section shown in Figure 4.3 lists the general MRP settings. In this section, we will discuss the details behind those Customizing activities.

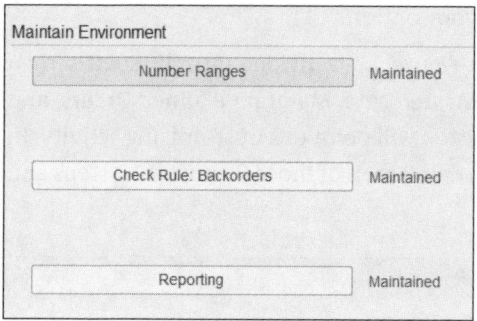

Figure 4.3 Maintain Environment Section in the Overall Plant Parameters Customizing

Number Ranges

The first and most important setting is the **Assign Number Ranges** activity. There are five different MRP objects for which we need to assign number ranges:

- Planned orders
- Reservations/dependent requirements
- Purchase requisitions
- MRP Lists
- Simulative dependent requirements (LTP-dependent requirements)

For each of those objects (see Figure 4.4), we will have to assign a number range interval, which will be used to determine the number of new objects generated by MRP. The number range for objects created by MRP during the planning run should be all internal because MRP should be able to determine the numbers automatically.

> **Tip**
> The Customizing activity to assign number ranges in Transaction OPPQ only allows us to assign an existing number range interval for an object. We can create or maintain the number range intervals for those objects in the customizing Transaction OMI2.

4.1 Overall Plant Parameters

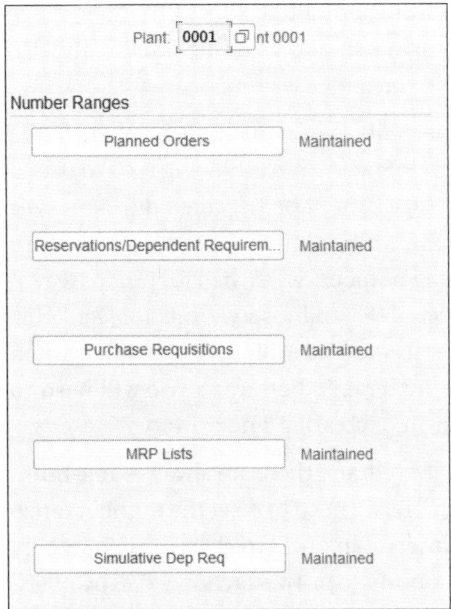

Figure 4.4 MRP Number Ranges

SAP delivers the following number ranges in Customizing, which are generally used without changes:

- Planned orders: Internal number range 1 with an interval from 1 to 19999999
- MRP Lists: Internal number range 1 with an interval from 1 to 9999999999
- Reservations and dependent requirements: Internal number range 1 with an interval from 1 to 9999999999
- Purchase requisitions: Internal number range 1 with an interval from 10000000 to 19999999

Under the Customizing activity to assign a number range interval for a planned order, we have the option to assign different intervals for planned orders created by MRP and long-term planning (LTP). The same interval can be used for both types of planned orders, and in this case, this interval will be shared by both order types. If we want to differentiate those planned order types by number, we should assign a different interval for each one.

Note that although the number range is considered a Customizing activity, it is not automatically transported. That is because the current number for each interval may not be the same in different systems, so a transport could lead to number range inconsistencies. If needed, number range intervals should be transported manually, and the current number should be adjusted in the target system.

For all the number range objects, there is a percentage of remaining numbers in the interval defined in Customizing for which SAP S/4HANA should trigger a warning message. For design reasons, a warning message cannot be triggered during classic MRP execution in the background, so the classic MRP execution is terminated with a short dump when this percentage of remaining numbers is reached for purchase requisitions (object BANF), planned orders (object PLAF), and reservations (object RESB). MRP Live, however, will not consider this warning and will only terminate when there are no more numbers available in the interval. In both cases, we will need to manually adjust the number range, extending it or creating a new interval.

In addition, the number ranges in MRP are buffered, and there are always some numbers stored in the number range buffer. Therefore, we need to reset the number range buffer after any change to a number range interval in order to clear those numbers stored before the change. The global reset can be done in Transaction SM56 by pressing the [F5] key; entering the client, object, and range; and selecting the **Global Reset** indicator.

Checking Rule: Backorders

The second Customizing activity in the **Maintain Environment** section in Figure 4.3 is **Checking Rule: Backorders**, during which we will define a specific available-to-promise checking rule to be used when updating backorders in Transaction CO06. This checking rule is not the one generally used for the planned order availability check and is used for backorders only.

Reporting

The third and last Customizing activity in this section is reporting. These Customizing settings are related to the MRP evaluation transactions, so we will explore them later in Chapter 6.

4.1.2 Maintain Master Data

Under the **Maintain Master Data** section of the plant maintenance screen, we will perform the plant-dependent Customizing settings that are related to the MRP master data, as shown in Figure 4.5.

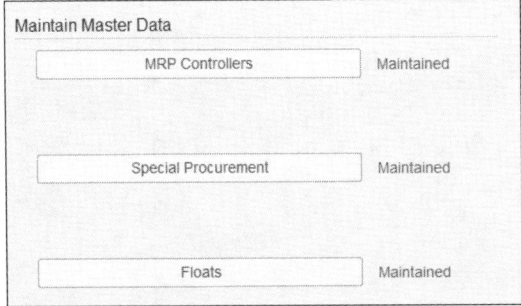

Figure 4.5 Maintain Master Data Section in the Overall Plant Parameters Customizing

MRP Controllers

The first setting is one of the simplest and at the same time most important MRP settings. In the **Maintain MRP Controllers** activity, we will create or change the MRP controller, a mandatory field on the **MRP 1** tab of the material master. The MRP controller, also known as the planner, is the person responsible for planning and analyzing the MRP results for a set of materials and for taking actions to resolve problems and exceptions that may occur during the MRP run.

The definition of the MRP controller is very important because it is used as a key selection criterion in many production planning transactions, such as the collective entry of the Stock/Requirements List, the planned order mass processing transaction, and even the MRP execution with MRP Live. Therefore, before creating the MRP controller in Customizing, we need to think about the products that will planned and who will be responsible for those materials.

Adding too many materials for a single MRP controller may lead to a situation in which the planner cannot handle all the problems and exceptions. It could also lead to performance issues when executing the MRP mass processing transactions. On the other hand, only adding a few materials to each MRP controller may increase the total number of MRP controllers, which is also not desirable.

In this Customizing activity, we will create and maintain the MRP controllers and assign an MRP controller for missing parts in this plant. Figure 4.6 shows the details for the MRP controller Customizing settings. These settings will not influence the system behavior and will instead maintain data about the MRP controller itself, such as the **Telephone** and the **Recipient Name** fields.

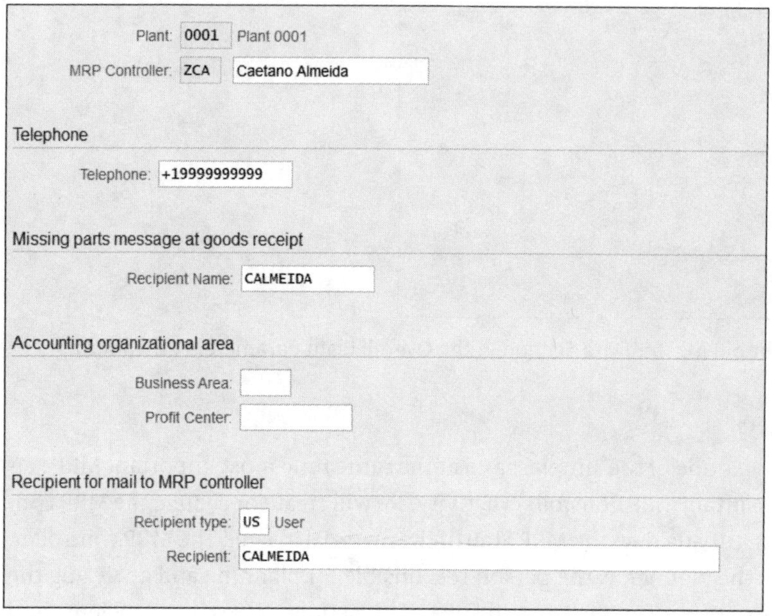

4 Configuring MRP

Plant:	**0001** Plant 0001
MRP Controller:	**ZCA** Caetano Almeida

Telephone

Telephone:	+19999999999

Missing parts message at goods receipt

Recipient Name:	CALMEIDA

Accounting organizational area

Business Area:	
Profit Center:	

Recipient for mail to MRP controller

Recipient type:	US User
Recipient:	CALMEIDA

Figure 4.6 Details of the MRP Controller Customizing

Some companies decide to use generic MRP controller titles, such as Finished Products MRP Controller or Raw Material MRP Controller, whereas other companies choose to create MRP controllers with a reference to the actual people who will be in charge of planning those materials.

Generic MRP controllers require less maintenance of Customizing data, but MRP controllers that reference the users themselves will also have some advantages. For example, if ever there is a problem with a particular material, any user will be able to identify the person responsible for planning this material and contact them directly. In the latest versions of the SAP Fiori applications for DDMRP, for example, it is possible to call the MRP controller directly through Skype to expedite the supply.

> **Warning**
>
> We might have to access the MRP controller Customizing settings very frequently to create or change MRP controllers. In this case, we can open the Customizing transaction for changes in the productive system by following the procedure outlined in SAP Note 388936.

Special Procurement

The next step under the **Maintain Master Data** section is the **Special Procurement** Customizing activity. While discussing special procurement types in master data in Chapter 3, we noted that some Customizing entries are delivered standard, but we may have to create our own custom special procurements when using stock transfer, withdrawal from alternative plant, or production in alternative plant processes.

In these cases, we need to create our custom special procurement types because we need to specify the sourcing or alternative plant. If we have stock transfers with different supplying plants, we will need to create a different special procurement type for each plant. We have shown an example of a custom special procurement type in Chapter 3, Figure 3.23, in which we determined the supplying plant for a stock transfer.

Figure 4.7 shows an additional example, in which we have created a new special procurement type (72), setting the **Issuing Plant** value to 0002 for withdrawal and selecting the **Withdra. Altern. Plant** (withdrawal from alternative plant) checkbox.

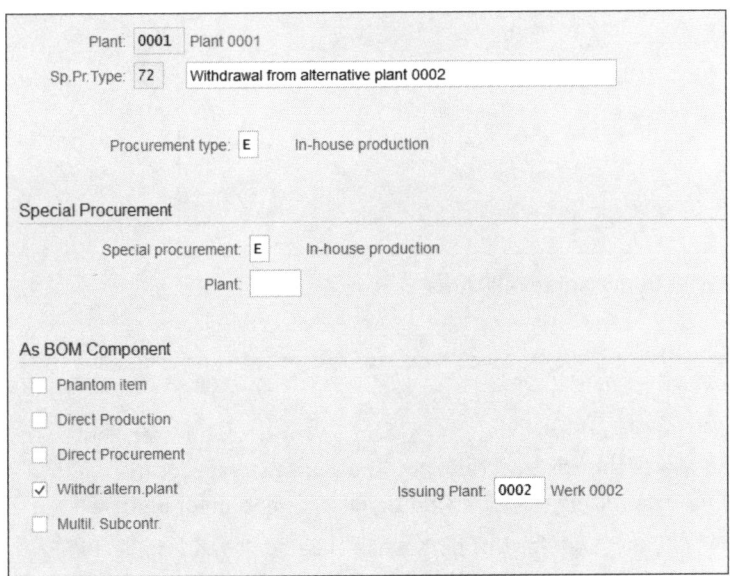

Figure 4.7 Withdrawal in Alternative Plant with the Issuing Plant

We may also have to create custom MRP types when working with storage location MRP areas. With this kind of MRP area, the storage location will be planned separately, and we can use a special procurement type to determine the source storage

4 Configuring MRP

location for an internal stock transfer. In this very specific scenario, we will use special procurement **45—Stock Transfer from Plant to MRP Area**, but the ordering plant and the supplying plant will be the same, as shown in Figure 4.8. In this special case, we will find an additional field, **Stock Transfer**, through which we can determine if MRP will generate stock transfer requisitions or stock transfer reservations.

Plant:	0001 Plant 0001
Sp.Pr.Type:	45 Stock Transfer from plant to MRP area
Procurement type:	F External procurement

Special Procurement

Special procurement:	U Stock transfer
Plant:	0001 Plant 0001
Stk Transf:	Stock Transfer Reservations from the Plant to the MRP
Add. Info for BAdI:	0001

As BOM Component

☐ Phantom item
☐ Direct Production
☐ Direct Procurement
☐ Withdr.altern.plant   Issuing Plant: [ ]
☐ Multil. Subcontr.

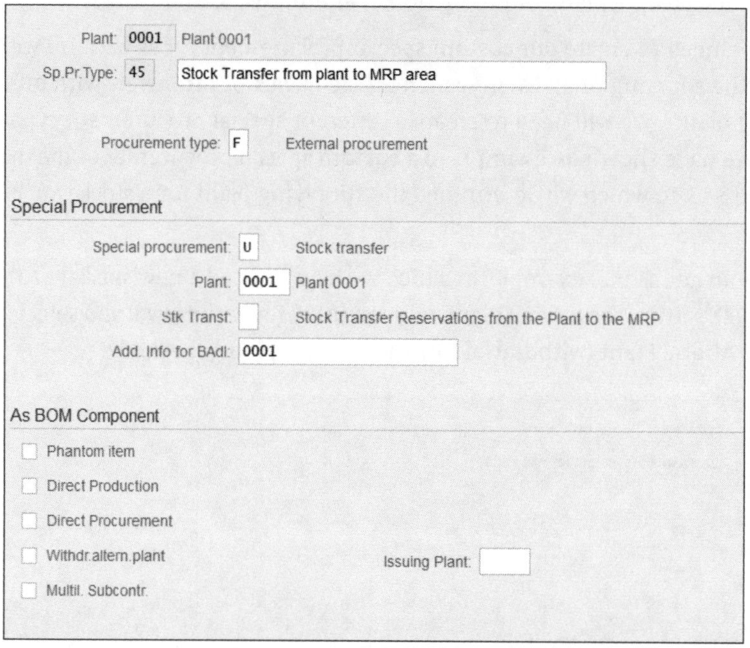

Figure 4.8 Stock Transfer from Plant to MRP Area

Note

By default, MRP will not determine the storage location for stock transfers, but we can use a BAdI to do so. In this case, we can enter the source storage location in the special procurement Customizing using the **Additional Information for BAdI** field.

You can use the `MD_EXT_SUP` BAdI for this purpose in classic MRP and the `PPH_MRP_SOURCING_BADI` ABAP-Managed Database Procedure (AMDP) BAdI for this purpose in MRP Live.

Floats

The third step of the **Maintain Master Data** section is the **Floats** activity, in which we will define the scheduling margin keys, mentioned in the previous chapter. Scheduling margin keys 000 and 001 are predelivered in Customizing, as shown in Figure 4.9, but we can create new entries with different values for the floats.

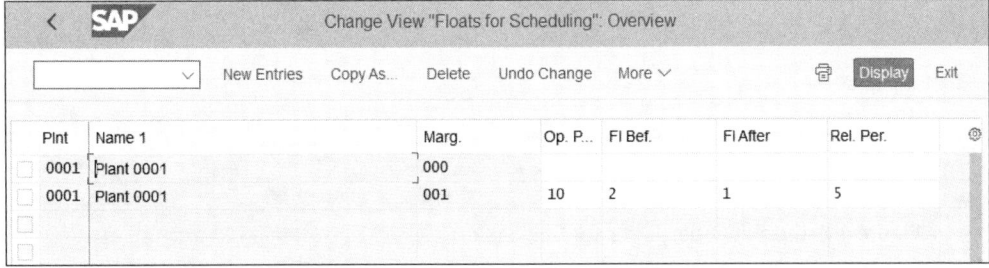

Figure 4.9 Scheduling Margin Keys in Customizing

4.1.3 Maintain Planned Orders

The section under the **Overall Plant Parameters** Customizing settings is related to planned orders (see Figure 4.10). Both of the Customizing activities found here are related to the conversion of planned orders to production/process orders or purchase requisitions.

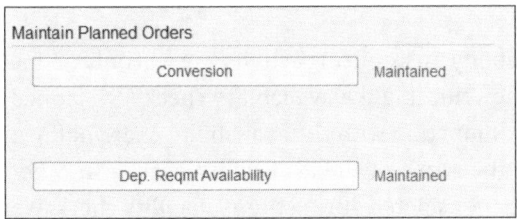

Figure 4.10 Maintain Planned Orders Section in the Overall Plant Parameters Customizing

Conversion

Under the **Conversion** activity, there will be two options to define the settings for the planned order conversion. Under the **Planned Order • Production Order** activity, we can select the default order types for the planned order conversion to production orders and process orders, as shown in Figure 4.11. The order types defined in this Customizing activity will be used when we convert planned orders with the MRP

141

transactions, such as the Stock/Requirements List, for example. In the second option, we will simply define a maximum number of planned orders to be proposed.

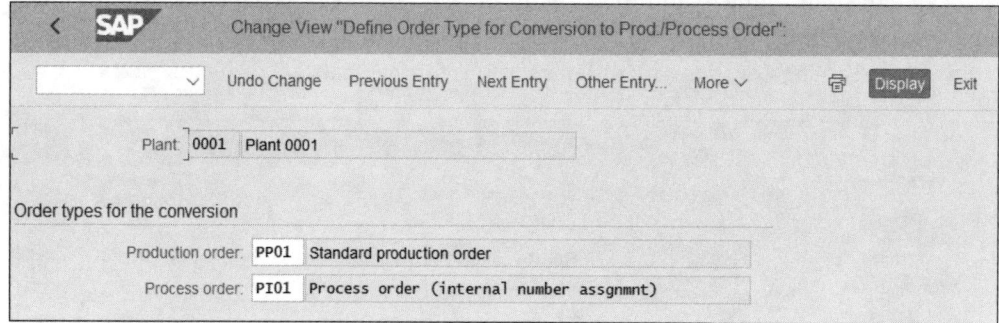

Figure 4.11 Default Order Types for Conversion

Under the **Planned Order • Purchase Requisition** activity, we will only define a limit for the number of planned orders proposed in the collective conversion of planned orders into purchase requisitions (Transaction MD15). This is basically a measure to avoid performance or memory overflow issues during the planned order conversion. The default value proposed is 500, and the maximum number allowed is 999; however, if the field is left empty, there will be no maximum number of planned orders to be converted.

Dependent Requirements Availability

In the **Dependent Requirements Availability** Customizing activity, we will only define the checking rule that will be used when running the availability check for planned orders. This checking rule is used in conjunction with the availability check defined in the material master to determine the scope of the availability check—in other words, which planning elements will be considered during the availability check. We will see the scope of check Customizing later in Section 4.5.

4.1.4 Maintain Planning Run

Let's examine the final section of the plant maintenance Customizing screen shown in Figure 4.2: **Maintain Planning Run** (see Figure 4.12).

This is the section where we will find the most important settings of the **Overall Plant Parameters** Customizing activity. Here, we will find settings to influence the BOM explosion, the detailed scheduling that happens during the MRP run, the creation of replenishment proposals for external procurement, the rescheduling check, and other settings relevant to the planning run. In the following sections, we will examine each setting in detail.

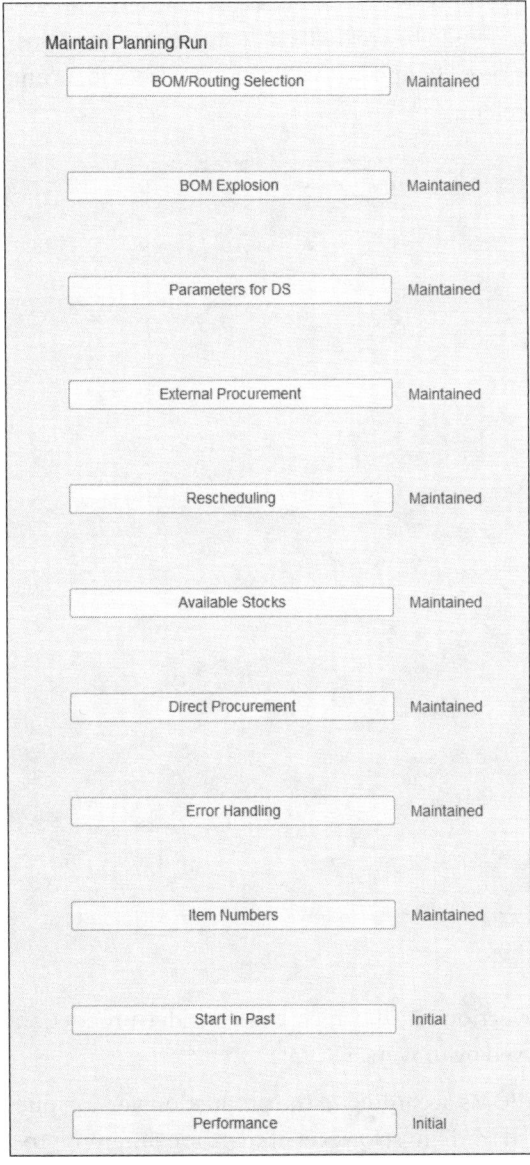

Figure 4.12 Maintain Planning Run in the Overall Plant Parameters Customizing

4 Configuring MRP

BOM/Routing Selection

BOMs are selected according to a BOM selection ID, and we will define which BOM selection ID will be used for each plant in this Customizing activity.

The BOM selection ID basically will determine which BOM usages will be considered by MRP and in which order. These IDs should be created in advance in the BOM customizing Transaction OS31 (see Figure 4.13), and we will only choose which one should be considered by MRP for the plant.

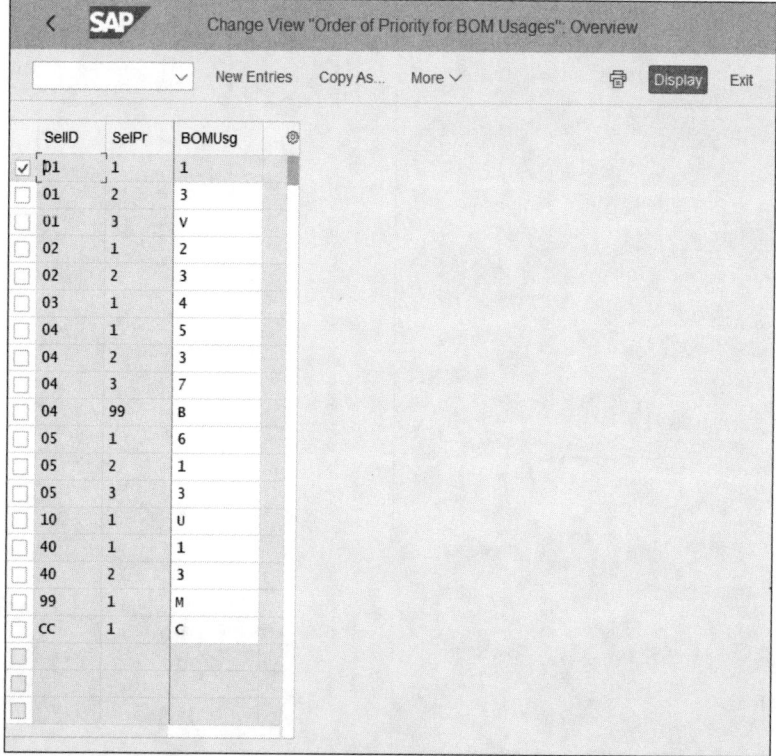

Figure 4.13 BOM Selection ID Customizing

The default option is to use BOM selection ID 01, which will consider production BOMs with the highest priority, followed by universal BOMs.

In SAP S/4HANA, MRP will select the BOMs according to the production version due to the logic implemented by simplified sourcing. However, if there are different production versions and each one references a BOM with a different usage, then MRP

4.1 Overall Plant Parameters

will select the production version according to the priority defined in the BOM **Selection ID** field.

> **Note**
>
> This Customizing activity was also affected by MRP simplifications implemented in SAP S/4HANA. In SAP ERP, we could also choose a routing selection ID, but this option is no longer available because routings will be selected by MRP according to the production version only.

BOM Explosion

Under the **BOM Explosion** Customizing activity, we have settings that will influence the dates used for the master data selection and additional settings related to the BOM explosion during the planned order creation by MRP. Figure 4.14 shows the details of these Customizing settings.

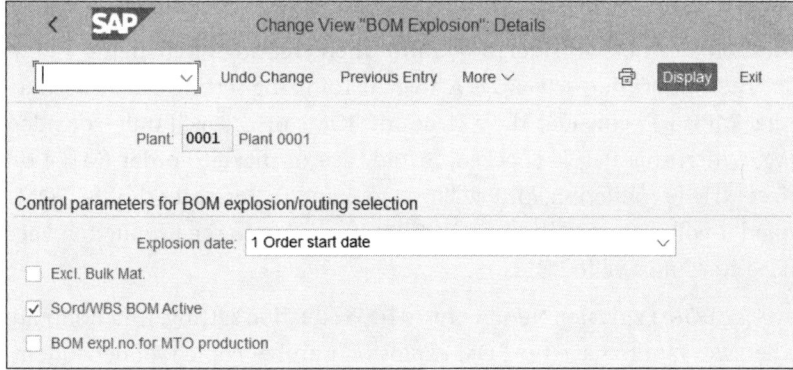

Figure 4.14 BOM Explosion Customizing

The first one is the **Explosion Date** Customizing activity, which will determine the date used for the master data determination in MRP:

- **Order Start Date**: Master data will be read on the planned order start date.
- **Order Finish Date**: Master data will be read on the planned order finish date.
- **BOM Explosion Number/Order Start Date**: The SAP S/4HANA system will first check for the existence of a BOM explosion number and try to read the master data according to the BOM explosion number date. If no BOM explosion number is found, then master data will be read on the planned order start date.

- **BOM Explosion Number/Order Finish Date**: The SAP S/4HANA system will first check for the existence of a BOM explosion number and try to read the master data according to the BOM explosion number date. If no BOM explosion number is found, master data will be read on the planned order finish date.

> **Note**
>
> We will talk more about BOM explosion numbers in Chapter 8 when we discuss advanced MRP features.

When the **Exclude Bulk Materials** flag is checked, MRP will not create a dependent requirement for bulk materials during the BOM explosion. In this case, those bulk materials will not be displayed in the planned order components list and an entry will not be created for those items in table RESB. This setting can be useful when there are too many components for the planned order, which leads to performance issues during the MRP run.

We discussed in the previous chapter that we can create sales order and WBS BOMs and that those BOMs can be considered by MRP when creating or changing a new planned order. The **Sales Order/WBS BOM Active** Customizing setting can be used to control whether MRP will consider those types of BOMs or if it will only consider material BOMs. When this flag is checked, in the case of make-to-order (MTO) or make-to-project (MTP) production, MRP will first look for a sales order or WBS BOM, respectively, and it will try to read a material BOM according to the production version only if it cannot find a valid BOM.

At last, we have the **BOM Explosion Number for MTO Production** setting, which should be checked when we want to have the BOM explosion number copied for dependent receipt elements that are linked to the sales order special stock. This setting is also valid for MTP production and receipt elements under the project/WBS special stock.

Parameters for Detailed Scheduling

We noted earlier that the in-house production time defined in the material master can be used to calculate the planned order basic dates and that the routing operation duration can be used to calculate the planned order production dates in a process called *detailed scheduling*.

Under the **Parameters for Detailed Scheduling** Customizing activity, we will find all the settings that can be used to influence the detailed scheduling during the MRP run.

As shown in Figure 4.15, we have the option to define different detailed scheduling parameters for each combination of plant, planned order type, and production scheduler supervisor. We can also create generic entries that are valid for all the planned order types and production scheduler supervisors by using the asterisk (*) character. In this Customizing activity, we can also create different detailed scheduling parameters for each specific LTP scenario so that MRP and LTP can have independent detailed scheduling settings.

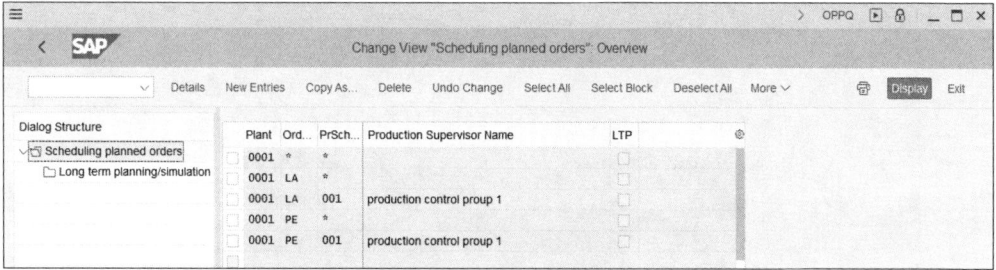

Figure 4.15 Scheduling Parameters for Planned Orders

In the detail screen of the **Scheduling Parameters** Customizing activity (see Figure 4.16), you will notice some differences if comparing SAP S/4HANA with SAP ERP. In SAP ERP, we would have independent settings for detailed scheduling, rate-based scheduling, and rough-cut scheduling, with a different routing selection ID for each scheduling level. In SAP S/4HANA, we will only have the detailed scheduling, and the routing will be selected according to the production version only. If we are using repetitive manufacturing and we want to select a rate routing, for example, we will simply create a production version with reference to the rate routing, and it will be considered by MRP during lead-time scheduling.

> **Note**
>
> See SAP Note 2380568 (SAP S/4HANA Simplification Item: Rate and Rough-Cut Planning) for details about the simplification item that changed the scheduling parameters Customizing.

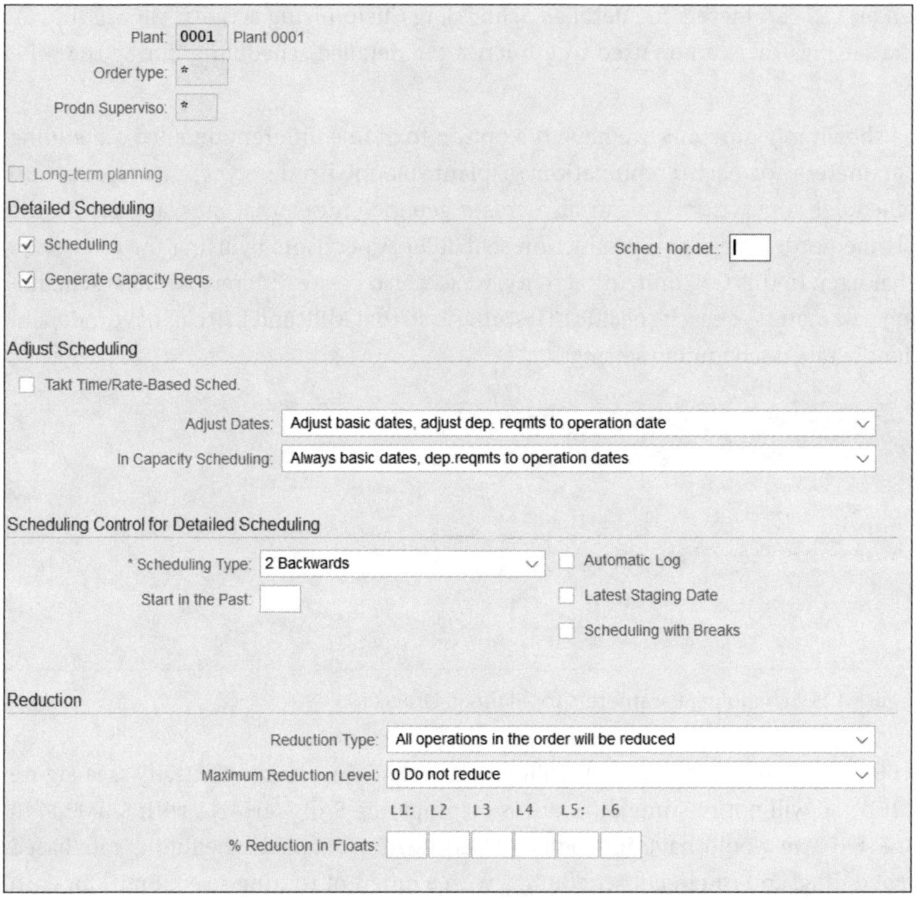

4 Configuring MRP

Figure 4.16 Details of the Scheduling Parameters Customizing

If we want to run detailed scheduling during MRP and want to use capacity leveling for planned orders, we need to ensure that the **Scheduling** and **Generate Capacity Requirements** checkboxes are set for the plant/planned order type/supervisor.

We can also define a scheduling horizon for detailed scheduling (the **Sched. Hor. Det.** field) to limit the detailed scheduling so that it is executed just for planned orders within this horizon. When we are using very complex routings, especially with variant configuration, MRP may have to spend a lot of time reading the routing and scheduling planned orders. In this case, it might be a good idea to limit the detailed scheduling within a shorter horizon in order to avoid performance problems during

MRP. This horizon will depend on the product's lead time; we should ensure that it includes all the planned orders that we expect to see in the capacity management transactions and SAP Fiori applications.

Another important setting that we can find during the under this Customizing activity is **Scheduling Type**. During the MRP run, SAP S/4HANA will first calculate the planned order basic start and finish dates using the in-house production time defined in the material master, considering the shortage date as the planned order finish date and then using backward scheduling to calculate the basic start date. Once the basic dates are calculated, detailed scheduling is executed to calculate the production dates—and this is where the scheduling type defined in Customizing will be used.

The following scheduling types are the most frequently used during the MRP run:

- If **Backward Scheduling** is selected, MRP will consider the basic finish date as the production finish date and will calculate the production start date using the routing.
- If **Forward Scheduling** is selected, MRP will consider the basic start date as the production start date and will calculate the production finish date using the routing.

As a best practice, we suggest that you keep the in-house production date in the material master as close as possible to the total duration of the routing operations in order to avoid differences between the basic dates and the production dates. Another way to avoid those differences is to use the **Adjust Dates** setting by selecting one of the options where the basic dates will be adjusted. In this case, whenever there is a difference between the in-house production time and the routing duration, the basic dates will be automatically adjusted by MRP to match the basic finish date.

> **Note**
>
> In general, only the planned order basic start date will be adjusted by MRP. The basic finish date will be only adjusted by MRP under a very specific scenario, in which the basic finish date initially calculated with the in-house production time was after the requirement date, in order to avoid the planned order starting in the past. In this specific case only, if the production start date is earlier than the basic finish date, the basic finish date will be adjusted to match the production date.

External Procurement

The **External Procurement** Customizing activity brings plant-level settings related specifically to replenishment proposals created for external procurement. Figure 4.17 shows the settings and details of this Customizing activity.

The **Purchasing Processing Time** setting is a buffer of working days considered when scheduling a replenishment proposal with external procurement. It should represent the time that the purchasing department will take to process a purchase requisition and generate a purchase order. The value maintained here will be considered for all the purchase requisitions created by MRP for the entire plant. It will affect the delivery date calculation, so we need to ensure that a realistic value is used here. In our example, we used a purchasing process time of one day.

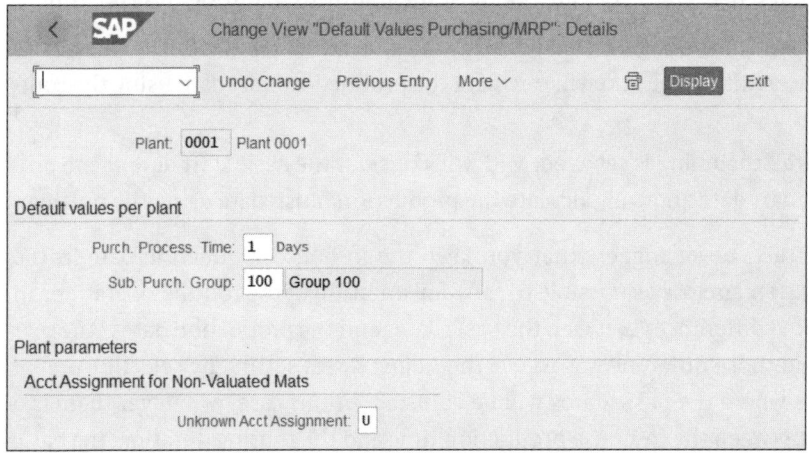

Figure 4.17 External Procurement Customizing Settings

The purchasing group is generally defined for a material in the **Purchasing** tab of the material master and is considered by MRP when generating purchase requisitions. If the **Purchasing Group** field is empty in the material master, then MRP will read the **Substitute Purchasing Group** value defined in the **External Procurement** Customizing activity. We can also define a default account assignment for purchase requisitions created for nonvaluated materials in the **Unknown Account Assignment** field.

In this Customizing activity, we have another impact of the simplified sourcing logic implemented in SAP S/4HANA. In SAP ERP, we would be able to choose here if the planned delivery time considered when scheduling an externally procured replenishment proposal would come from the material master or from the info record/

scheduling agreement. In SAP S/4HANA, this setting is no longer available because MRP will always consider the planned delivery time from the info record or scheduling agreement, as they are relevant for automatic sourcing. This is because they are generally more accurate than the generic value defined in the material master.

In SAP ERP, we could define in this Customizing activity the creation indicator for schedule lines, which allows us to choose if schedule lines should be generated or not for materials belonging to this MRP group. This setting is no longer available because in SAP S/4HANA, MRP will always create schedule lines if there is an MRP-relevant scheduling agreement.

Rescheduling

The rescheduling check happens during the MRP run or during the evaluation of the MRP results. In this process, MRP will check for fixed MRP elements in the future that could cover a requirement. If MRP finds a fixed MRP element within the rescheduling check, then it will generate an exception message suggesting that the MRP controller reschedule the MRP element instead of generating a new replenishment proposal.

In the Customizing activity **Rescheduling**, we can define the horizon considered in the rescheduling check and which firm elements will be considered by MRP. Figure 4.18 shows the details of this Customizing activity.

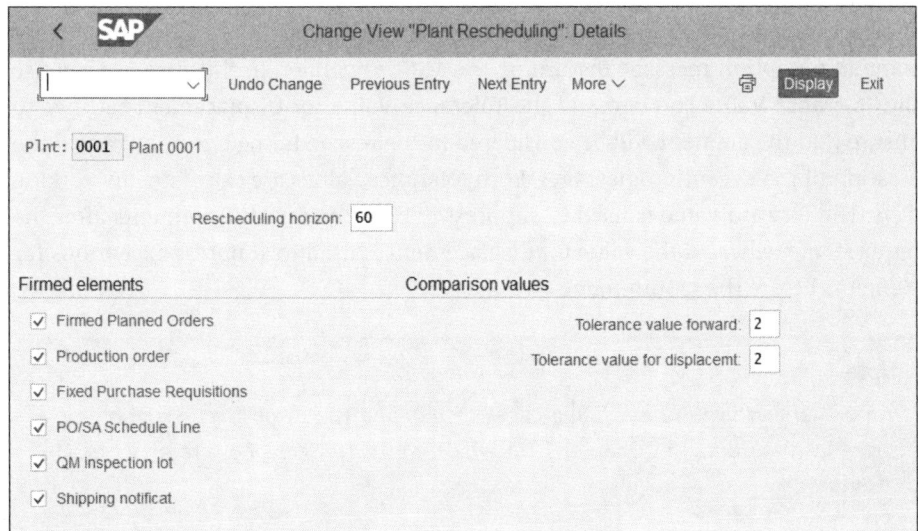

Figure 4.18 Rescheduling Customizing

The **Rescheduling Horizon** field is a value in working days, and it defines the period for which MRP will look for fixed elements in the future to cover a shortage. The calculation of the rescheduling horizon only starts at the end of the replenishment lead time.

> **Example**
>
> Consider a rescheduling horizon of 60 working days, as shown in Figure 4.18. If we have a shortage on January 10, MRP will look for firm replenishment elements in the following 60 working days to cover this shortage. If a production order is found on February 1, MRP will not create a new planned order to cover the shortage on January 10 and will suggest that the MRP controller change the dates of the existing production order to cover the shortage.

Besides the rescheduling horizon, we can define which specific MRP elements will be included in the rescheduling check in this Customizing activity. Considering the previous example, if we do not want MRP to propose the date changes in the production order, we can uncheck the **Production Order** flag in Customizing. This way, MRP would still create a new planned order to cover the shortage, even though there is a production order within the rescheduling horizon.

In some situations, usually when the replenishment proposal is too close to the shortage date, we do not want MRP to create a new planned order, but we also do not want an exception message disturbing the MRP controller. In this case, we can use the **Tolerance Value Forward** and the **Tolerance Value for Displacement** settings to ensure that the element will be considered in the rescheduling check, but avoid the creation of the exception messages. Both tolerance values are calculated in working days. The forward value is used to suppress exceptions for MRP elements after the requirement, whereas the value for displacement is used to suppress exceptions for elements before the requirement.

> **Note**
>
> We will analyze the rescheduling check results and the respective exception messages in more detail in Chapter 5, in which we will discuss how to analyze MRP results.

Available Stocks

As we have shown, MRP considers the available stocks during the net requirements calculation in order to determine when there is a shortage. This available stock is generally unrestricted stock, but it can also include additional stock types, such as those represented by the following checkboxes:

- **Stock in Transfer**: This checkbox is for the stock that is being transferred. In a two-step stock transfer, we first post a goods issue when the material leaves the supplying plant and then post a second goods issue when it reaches the delivery plant. Between those movements, it is considered stock in transfer.
- **Blocked Stock**: This checkbox is for stock that we have intentionally blocked—perhaps for quality purposes, for example. A special goods movement is posted to move a certain quantity to blocked stock.
- **Restricted Use Stock**: When we are working with batches, there is a special restricted use batch status. This checkbox can be used, for example, when a whole batch has quality issues.

Under the **Available Stocks** Customizing activity, we can determine which of these stock types will be considered available during the MRP net requirements calculation by setting the respective flags, as shown in Figure 4.19. Once we uncheck one flag, the corresponding stock type will not be considered available during the MRP evaluation transactions, so it won't appear in the Stock/Requirements List, for example.

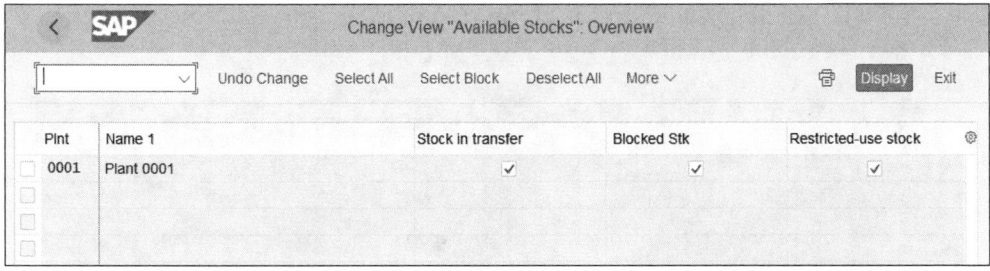

Figure 4.19 Available Stocks Customizing

Direct Procurement

When working with the special procurement type direct procurement or with nonstock items as BOM components, we have the option to define when the purchase requisition for directly procured components will be created in the **Default Values for Direct Procurement** Customizing activity, shown in Figure 4.20.

4 Configuring MRP

We can use the **Direct Procurement/Production** field to define if the purchase requisition will be created by MRP or only upon the conversion of the parent planned order to production order. In addition, we can choose a default value for the account assignment of purchase requisitions created with direct procurement. The default value is **U** (unknown), but it can be changed in this Customizing activity.

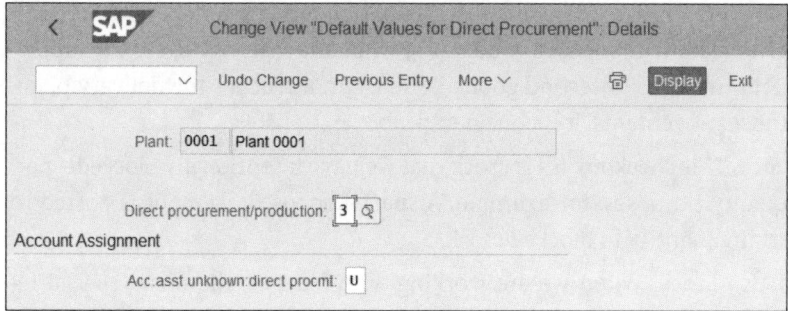

Figure 4.20 Default Values for Direct Procurement

Error Handling

In the **Error Handling** Customizing activity, we can find settings to prevent or handle possible errors during the MRP run.

The first setting is **Maximum Number of Proposals per Date**, shown in Figure 4.21. To avoid memory consumption problems or even performance problems during the MRP run, it is important to limit the number of replenishment proposals created in the same day.

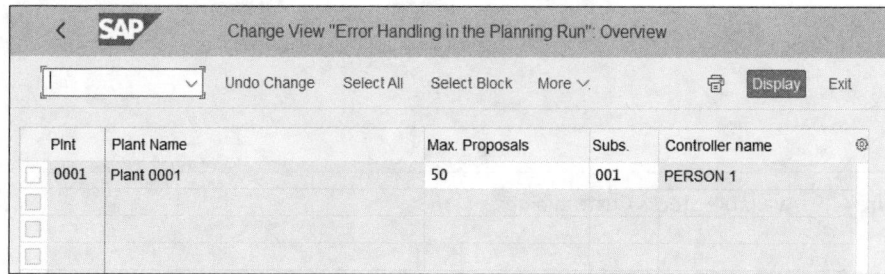

Figure 4.21 Error Handling in Planning Run

Example

In some scenarios, we may have to define a very small fixed lot sized for a material, such as 1, for example. In those cases, if a large requirement is created for this material, MRP will have to create hundreds of planned orders to cover this requirement, impacting the MRP performance and leading to memory consumption issues. We can use the **Maximum Number of Proposals per Date** setting to limit the number of orders created, avoiding this kind of problem.

When the maximum number of proposals per day that was determined in Customizing is reached, the planning run for this material will be terminated and we will see an error message in the Display MRP Master Data Issues app when using MRP Live or in the MRP List when using classic MRP.

In this Customizing activity, we can also determine a substitute MRP controller (the **Subs.** and **Controller Name** columns), which will be used only when MRP cannot determine an MRP controller for a material. This situation does not happen frequently in the system and should only be observed in the event of inconsistent master data.

Item Numbers

MRP can generate purchase requisitions for external procurement and stock transfer reservations when a special procurement type is used. Those purchase requisitions and stock transfer reservations created by MRP will only contain one item, and we can define in Customizing what item number will be used by MRP, as shown in Figure 4.22.

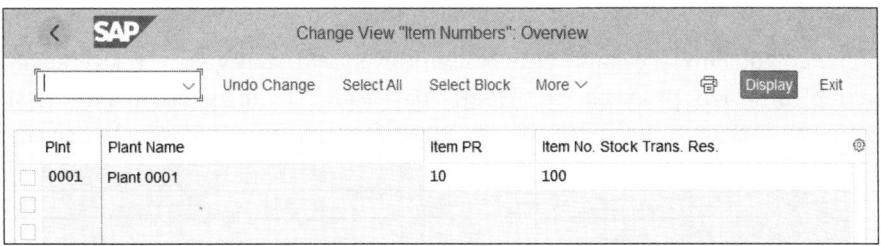

Figure 4.22 Item Numbers Customizing

The default values used for MRP are 10 for purchase requisitions and 100 for stock transfer reservations, and we will only change those values if we want to differentiate requisitions and reservations generated by MRP from the ones created manually.

Start in Past

When MRP is generating new replenishment proposals, it will generally consider the shortage date as the basic finish date, and it will calculate the basic start date using the in-house production time or the planned delivery time. Sometimes, the basic start date calculated by MRP may lie in the past, which means that there will not be enough time to produce or purchase the component.

Using the **Start in Past** Customizing setting, we can control whether MRP will allow a start in the past. If this flag is unchecked in Customizing, MRP will automatically switch to today scheduling when the basic start date is calculated in the past. *Today scheduling* means that the system will consider the planning date as the basic start date and it will use forward scheduling to recalculate the basic finish date.

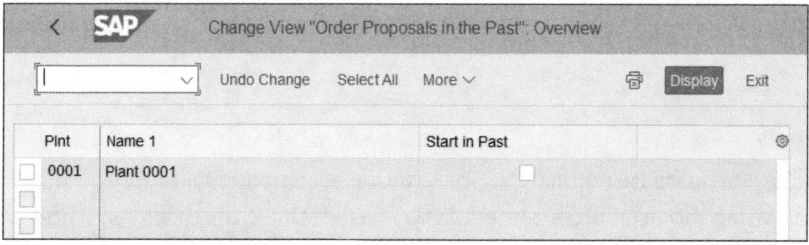

Figure 4.23 Start in Past Customizing

Allowing the start in the past is usually not a best practice because it will lead to replenishment proposals with unrealistic dates that cannot actually be met.

When we do not allow the start in the past, however, MRP may generate several different replenishment proposals on the same day, leading to an excessive number of rescheduling exception messages. Allowing the start in the past is usually an alternative to avoid this situation.

Performance

In the **Performance** Customizing activity, we can find another simplification implemented in SAP S/4HANA. In SAP ERP, we had the option to define here if MRP Lists would be stored in the transparent table MDTB or aggregated in table MDTC.

When storing the information in table MDTB, we could directly read this information in custom programs or queries. However, this was not a good option for performance. The aggregated table approach was faster, but data could not be directly read.

In SAP S/4HANA, the MRP List information will be only stored in table MDTB because we do not improve performance by aggregating the information when using an SAP HANA database. Therefore, the Customizing activity to define the aggregation of MRP Lists was removed from SAP S/4HANA.

> **Note**
> Because MRP Live will not generate MRP Lists, it does not save any information in those tables. Only when we run classic MRP is the information stored in the MRP List.

In this Customizing activity, we can still find the option to activate the BOM **Buffering** setting (see Figure 4.24) in order to improve the performance when exploding BOMs during the MRP run.

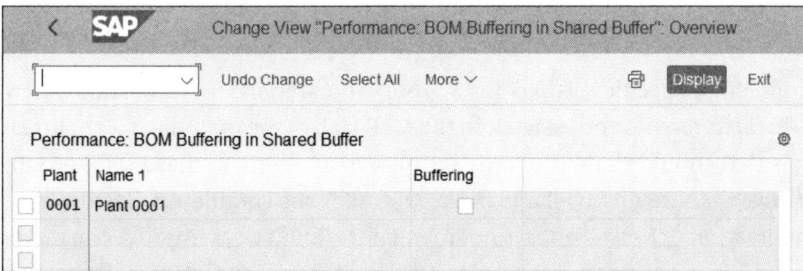

Figure 4.24 BOM Buffering

When we activate this setting in Customizing, we activate the cross-transactional buffering of the processed BOMs. This means that MRP will no longer access the database to read the most frequently used BOMs and will read that information directly from the shared memory buffer.

This setting can generally improve the MRP performance if the same BOM is used several times to generate planned orders during the MRP run or if the same material is frequently planned during the day.

4 Configuring MRP

> **Warning**
> SAP does not recommend frequent changes into this indicator because the BOM timestamps in the buffer might become inconsistent. If it is necessary to switch this indicator off and on again, we should run program RMMDBOM1 to delete the BOMs from the buffer.

4.2 MRP Group

In the previous section, we analyzed all the MRP customizing settings that can be defined at the plant level. On the same plant, however, we may have a variety of different planning scenarios and groups of materials that may require different settings. For example, the rescheduling horizon for materials manufactured internally may be different than the rescheduling horizon of components purchased because we do not depend on the supplier to adjust the dates of a production order. Figure 4.25 shows an overview of the Customizing activities available in the MRP group Customizing.

If we want to define specific settings for a group of materials, we can create a new MRP group in Customizing and assign it in the **MRP 1** tab of the material master for all the materials that should share the same settings. In addition, we have MRP-group-specific settings that are not available in the **Overall Plant Parameters** Customizing activity. The creation of MRP groups is not mandatory, but it does improve the material master maintenance process and gives us more flexibility when defining the MRP Customizing settings.

> **Tip**
> Usually we need to assign the MRP group to the material master for the desired materials. However, if the MRP group key matches the product type key, this MRP group will be automatically considered by MRP. For example, if we create the FERT MRP group in Customizing, MRP will use it for all the FERT materials for which there is no MRP group assigned in the material master.

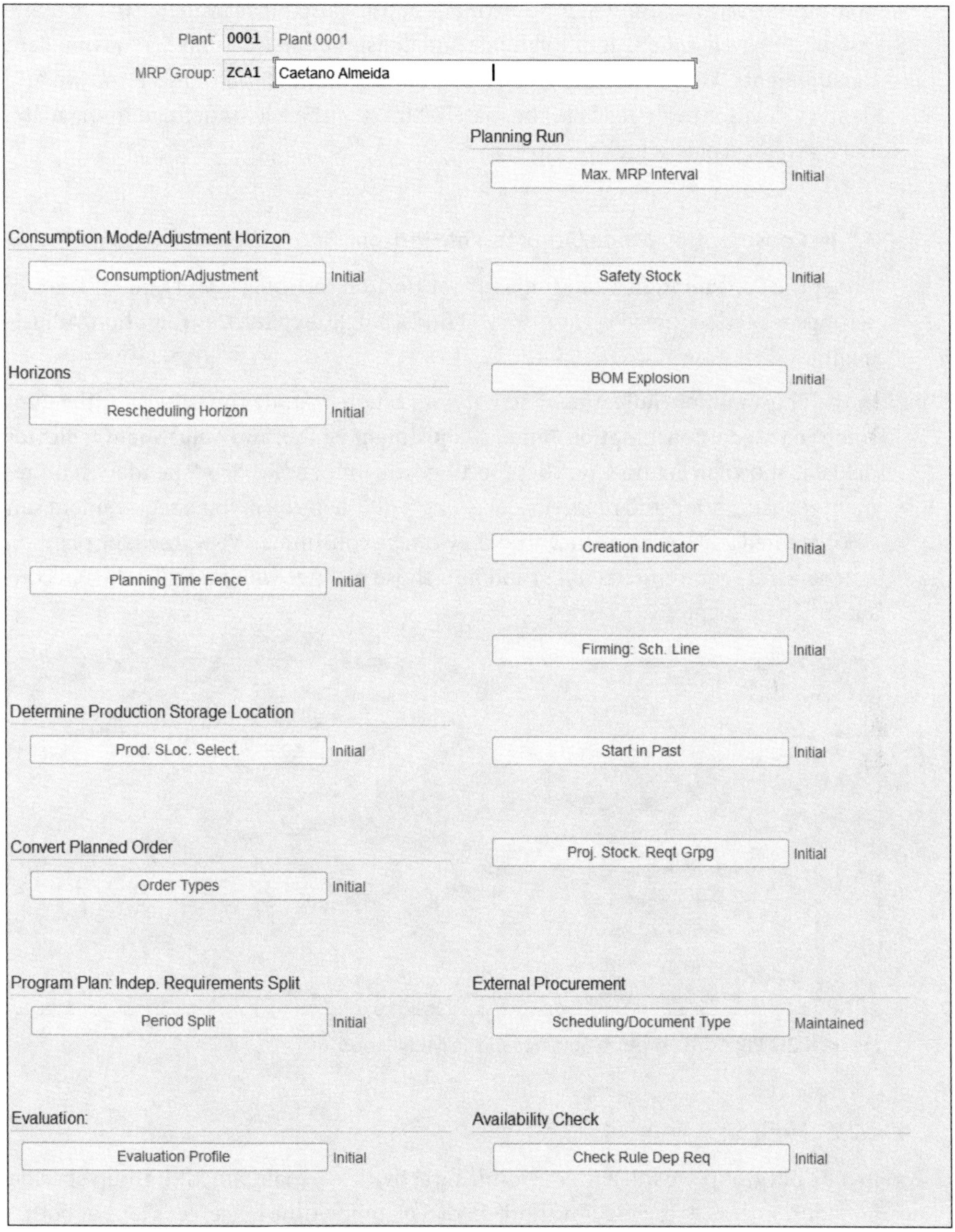

4.2 MRP Group

Plant: 0001 Plant 0001
MRP Group: ZCA1 Caetano Almeida

Planning Run

| Max. MRP Interval | Initial |

Consumption Mode/Adjustment Horizon

| Consumption/Adjustment | Initial |

| Safety Stock | Initial |

Horizons

| Rescheduling Horizon | Initial |

| BOM Explosion | Initial |

| Creation Indicator | Initial |

| Planning Time Fence | Initial |

| Firming: Sch. Line | Initial |

Determine Production Storage Location

| Prod. SLoc. Select. | Initial |

| Start in Past | Initial |

Convert Planned Order

| Proj. Stock. Reqt Grpg | Initial |

| Order Types | Initial |

Program Plan: Indep. Requirements Split

External Procurement

| Period Split | Initial |

| Scheduling/Document Type | Maintained |

Evaluation:

Availability Check

| Evaluation Profile | Initial |

| Check Rule Dep Req | Initial |

Figure 4.25 MRP Group Customizing

Some of the settings defined for the MRP group are also fields available in the material master, such as **Consumption Mode** and **Consumption Horizons for Independent Requirements**. When we assign an MRP group to the material master and we also define values for those fields in the material master, the values defined in the material master will have a higher priority.

4.2.1 Consumption Mode/Adjustment Horizon

Under the **Consumption Mode/Adjustment Horizon** section, we will find MRP group settings related to the PIRs. Here, we will find a single activity: **Consumption/Adjustment**.

In the **Consumption/Adjustment** activity, we can determine the values for the **Consumption Mode**, **Consumption Periods**, **Adjustment Period**, and **Adjustment Indicator** fields, as shown in Figure 4.26. These settings will influence the independent requirements consumption and reduction, defining if PIRs before or after a requirement can be consumed and the horizon within they can be consumed. We will see the planned independent requirements (PIRs) and how those settings will influence the PIR consumption in Chapter 9.

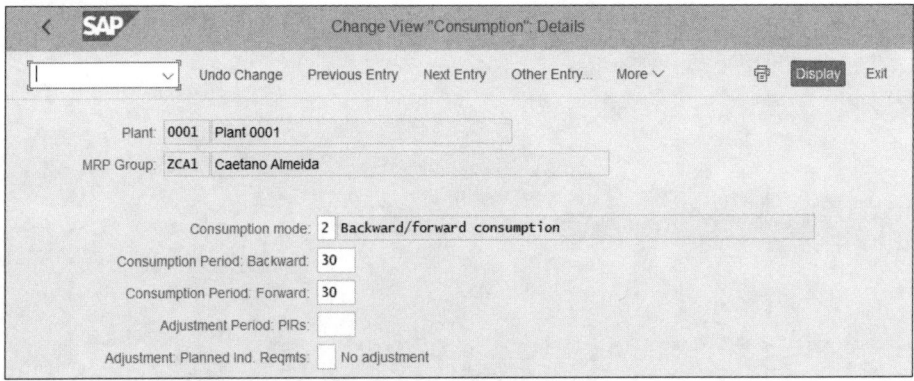

Figure 4.26 PIR Consumption Settings in the MRP Group

4.2.2 Horizons

In the MRP group, we will have Customizing activities to maintain MRP group-specific horizons, such as a rescheduling horizon or a planning time fence. Let's look at both.

Rescheduling per MRP Group

We discussed in the previous section that we can define a rescheduling horizon, tolerance values, and which specific planning elements will be considered during the rescheduling check in the **Overall Plant Parameters** Customizing activity.

At the MRP group level, we can define a different rescheduling horizon and tolerance values, but the option to select which elements will be considered during the rescheduling check is not available here, as shown in Figure 4.27.

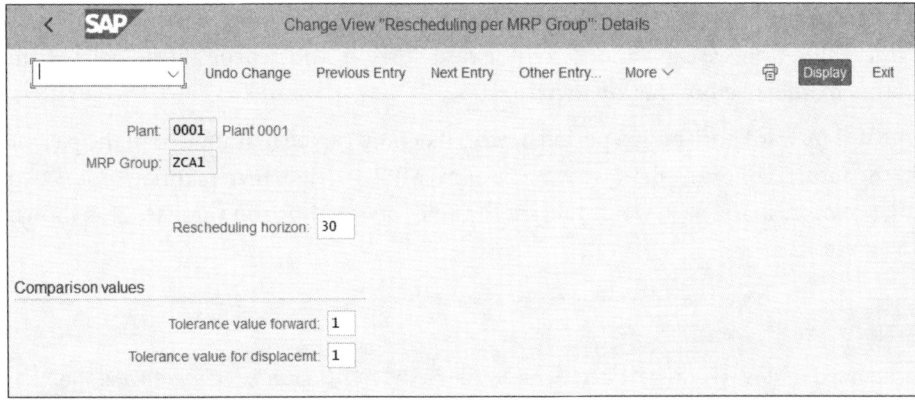

Figure 4.27 Rescheduling per MRP Group

Time Fence

When discussing the MRP types in Chapter 3, we noted that some MRP types will have a firming type, which allows planned orders to be automatically firmed within a predefined period called a time fence. We have the option to set the time fence directly in the material master, but we can also set a planning time fence (**Pl. Time Fence**) setting at the MRP group level, as shown in Figure 4.28.

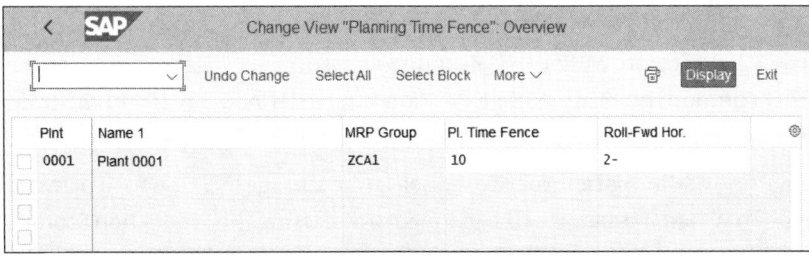

Figure 4.28 Planning Time Fence Customizing

The time fence maintained in the material master will always have a higher priority, which means that MRP will only consider the MRP group time fence when that field is empty in the material master. It will only be considered by materials for which an MRP with firming has been set.

One of the problems that may happen when we are using a time fence to automatically firm planned orders is that our planned orders will not be touched by MRP when they are within the time fence because they are firmed. In a capacity overload situation, this means we might not be able to convert all the planned orders to production orders, and those planned orders might be accumulated in the past. To avoid this kind of situation, we can define a roll-forward horizon. MRP will be able to delete firm planned orders before this given period.

The roll-forward horizon is a period of workdays and can be maintained in the past or in the future. For example, if we want to allow MRP to delete firm planned orders two days or more in the past, we should set the **Roll-Forward Horizon** value to -2, as shown in Figure 4.28.

> **Note**
> Planned orders will only be deleted if in the MRP type Customizing we have defined the **Delete Firm Planned Orders** option. (Those orders will only be deleted if they are no longer necessary.)

4.2.3 Determine Production Storage Location

In the MRP group Customizing, we have the option to define which logic will be used to determine the production storage location for the planned order components under the **Production Storage Location Selection** Customizing activity.

Production Storage Location Selection

During the BOM explosion, MRP can determine an issuing storage location for the planned order components. This storage location can be defined directly in the BOM item and will be copied to the planned order.

However, there are additional alternatives to select the storage location for a planned order component when it is blank in the planned order. Using the **Production Storage Location Selection** setting, we can choose one of the following strategies to select the component storage location:

1. MRP will check if the storage location is defined in the component material master only.
2. MRP will use the issue storage location defined in the assembly production version. If it is empty, MRP will use the assembly production storage location defined in the material master.
3. If no storage location has been defined for the component, MRP will first use strategy 1 and then use strategy 2.
4. If no storage location has been found for the assembly, MRP will first use strategy 2 and then use strategy 1.

4.2.4 Convert Planned Order

We can also determine default values for the order types at the MRP group level in the **Conversion** Customizing activity.

Conversion

Under the **Conversion** Customizing activity, we can define default order types for the conversion of planned orders to production or process orders. This is similar to the **Conversion** Customizing activity that was available in the **Overall Plant Parameters** Customizing options and was discussed in Section 4.1. However, the order types maintained at the MRP group level will have a higher priority than the settings maintained at the planned order level.

4.2.5 Program Plan: Independent Requirements Split

Besides the settings related to the PIR consumption and adjustment, we can also determine specific settings for the independent requirements split at the MRP group level under the **Period Split** Customizing activity.

Period Split

When working with PIRs, the values are usually created in monthly buckets for the materials. However, these values can be split into weekly or even daily buckets in order to smooth out production and allow MRP to generate more planned orders with a smaller quantity, instead of a single planned order for the whole month.

This automatic split can be carried out automatically when we are creating PIRs using a reference, such as the SOP planning. In the **Period Split** Customizing activity, we will

4 Configuring MRP

define how exactly this period will be split. In this Customizing activity, we will select a period split and define the number of weeks that should be split into days and the number of weeks that should be split into weekly requirements.

> **Note**
> The period split defined in this Customizing activity should be previously created in the customizing Transaction OMPH.

4.2.6 Evaluation

The MRP group also offers settings related to the evaluation of the MRP results, in the **Evaluation Profile** Customizing activity. We will discuss this activity in Chapter 5.

4.2.7 Planning Run

Most of the MRP group settings are related to the MRP planning run. In the following sections, we will go over each planning-run-related setting in detail.

Maximum MRP Interval

Materials will be selected to be planned by MRP according to the planning file entries, and the planning file entry will be updated for a material whenever there is a planning relevant change for this material. However, there are situations in which we want a material to be planned regularly by MRP despite missing planning file updates. In this kind of situation, we can use the **Maximum MRP Interval** setting in the MRP group to define that a material will be planned at regular intervals, as shown in Figure 4.29.

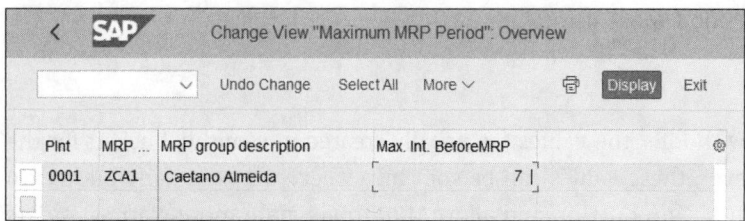

Figure 4.29 Maximum MRP Interval

This setting is generally used with classic MRP if we need to generate purchase requisitions in the opening period only. For example, if a planned order was generated outside the opening period and there was no MRP-relevant change for this material until it reached the opening period, this material would not be planned again by MRP and the planned order would not be replaced by a requisition.

Another usage of this setting is when we are working with MRP Lists in classic MRP and we want to ensure that they are updated at regular intervals. As noted earlier in this chapter, some goods movements may not mark the planning file if they are posted with a reference, so the MRP List may show a sales order or a reservation that is no longer relevant to MRP.

Using a maximum MRP interval, we can ensure that this material will be planned at regular intervals, planned orders will be replaced by requisitions when they reach the opening period, and the MRP List will be constantly updated.

> **Note**
> The maximum MRP interval will be only considered for materials for which the **Plan Regularly** setting is checked in the MRP type.

Safety Stock

In Chapter 3, we discussed how to define a safety stock in the material master and how this safety stock is considered by MRP during the planning run. In addition, we have seen that a share of this safety stock can be considered by MRP as available in order to avoid the creation of a new replenishment proposal just to cover a small part of the safety stock, reducing the procurement costs and only generating a new replenishment proposal when there is a relevant shortage.

This share of the safety stock available for planning is defined at the MRP group level under the **Safety Stock Availability** Customizing activity, shown in Figure 4.30. The number defined in this Customizing activity is a percentage. If the shortage quantity is below this percentage of the safety stock defined for the material, a new replenishment proposal will not be created.

4 Configuring MRP

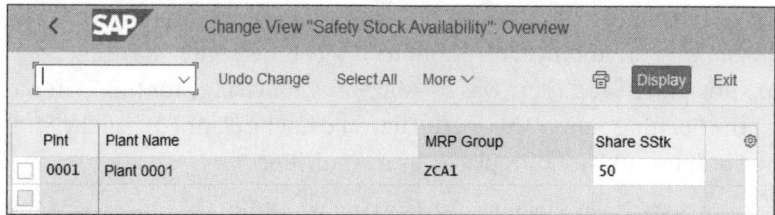

Figure 4.30 Share of Safety Stock Available for Planning

BOM Explosion

Under the **BOM Explosion** Customizing activity, we can choose if we want to keep the same settings defined at the plant level for the **Explosion Date** and **Exclude Bulk Materials** settings. We can choose the same options available for the **BOM Explosion** settings at the plant level, and these settings will have a higher priority—or we can explicitly choose to consider the setting at the plant level, as shown in Figure 4.31.

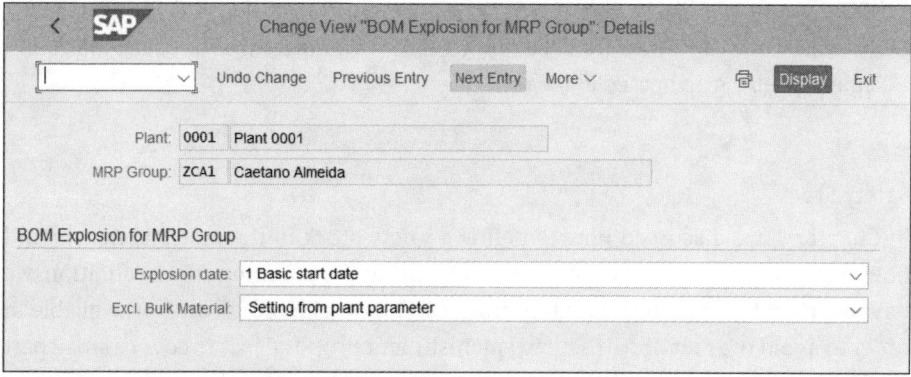

Figure 4.31 BOM Explosion for MRP Group

Creation Indicators

When we are scheduling the classic MRP planning run, we have the option to select the creation indicators and to choose if we want MRP to create planned orders or purchase requisitions for externally procured materials, if MRP should create MRP Lists, and if MRP should create schedule lines or not. The creation indicators defined in the MRP selection screen are relevant for all the materials planned during that planning run, but we might have different settings for particular sets of materials. In this case, we can define different creation indicators at the MRP group level, and they will be considered by MRP when planning materials belonging to this MRP group.

Under the **MRP Creation Indicators** Customizing activity, we can define default values for the **Create Purchase Requisitions**, **Create MRP List**, and **Schedule Lines** indicators, as shown in Figure 4.32.

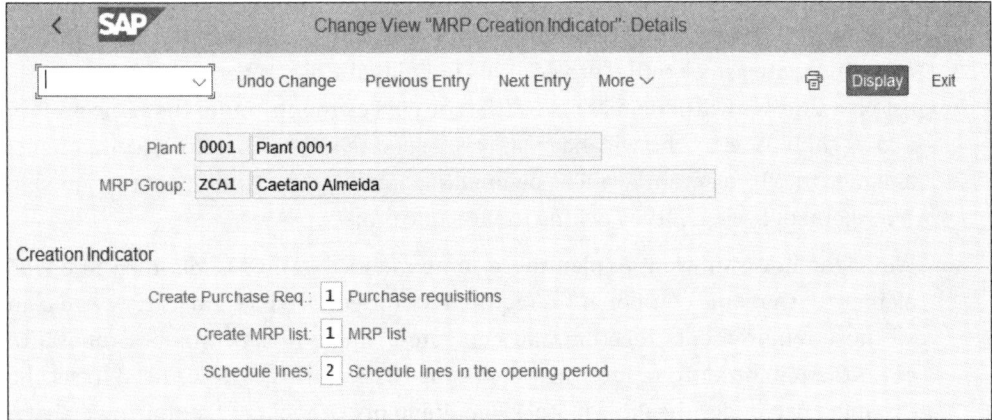

Figure 4.32 MRP Creation Indicators Customizing

> **Note**
> These indicators are considered by classic MRP only. MRP Live will not create MRP Lists and will create purchase requisitions and schedule lines by default. Also, this setting will be only relevant in the total planning transactions, such as Transactions MD01 and MD40 or when running MRP as a background job. In the single-item MRP transactions, such as Transaction MD02 or MD03, the creation indicators entered in the selection screen will still be considered.

Firming: Schedule Lines

The **Firming: Schedule Lines** Customizing activity provides a checkbox to define when the schedule lines will be considered firmed by MRP. Using this setting, we can ensure that only schedule lines that were already transmitted to the vendor will be considered firmed by MRP.

Start in the Past

This is the same **Start in the Past** setting available in the **Overall Plant Parameters** Customizing area. Here, we can choose if materials using this MRP group will follow the value defined at the plant level or if they will always allow or never allow the start of a replenishment proposal in the past.

Project Stock Requirements Grouping

MRP supports planning under different types of individual stocks, such as the sales order individual stock or the project/WBS individual stock. When working with project planning, we will generally have different WBS elements under the same project, and each WBS element will have its own special stock. Therefore, components assigned to WBS element A will be planned separately from components assigned to WBS element B, even if they belong to the same project.

We might, however, want to plan those components together, under the same WBS element. If the same component is required for different WBS elements, we can plan all those requirements together and generate a single replenishment proposal to cover them in order to reduce the purchasing costs. In this case, we need to set the **Grouping** flag under the **Project Stock Requirements Grouping** Customizing activity, as shown in Figure 4.33, in order to activate this feature and allow MRP to group requirements from different WBS elements belonging to the same project.

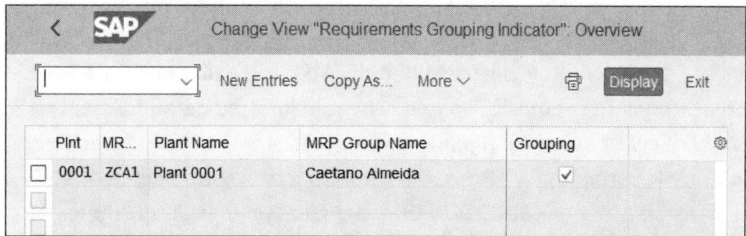

Figure 4.33 Requirements Grouping for Project Stock

> **Note**
> Besides this setting at the MRP group level, there are additional settings required at the project level, such as the activation of the automatic requirement group in the project definition and the selection of the grouping WBS elements at the WBS element level.

4.2.8 External Procurement

We can maintain settings related to the creation of replenishment proposals with external procurement in the **External Procurement Scheduling/Document Type** Customizing activity.

External Procurement Scheduling/Document Type

In SAP ERP, we could choose if an externally procured replenishment proposal would be scheduled with the planned delivery time from the material master or if the planned delivery time maintained in the info record or in the scheduling agreement would be considered. That system behavior was controlled by a Customizing setting under this Customizing activity, but this behavior was changed in SAP S/4HANA. Now, a replenishment proposal will be automatically scheduled with the planned delivery time maintained for the info record or agreement. The planned delivery time from the material master will be only considered if a source of supply could not be selected for the replenishment proposal or if the planned delivery time in the selected source of supply is empty.

What we can *still* do in this Customizing activity is to select the document types that will be used by MRP to generate different purchase requisition types. Here, we will be able to choose the purchase requisition types used for standard requisitions, subcontracting requisitions, or stock transfer requisitions. In the example shown in Figure 4.34, we have defined a custom purchase requisition type to be used in a subcontracting scenario, so MRP will always generate purchase requisitions of type ZNB for materials assigned to this MRP group and with a subcontracting special procurement type.

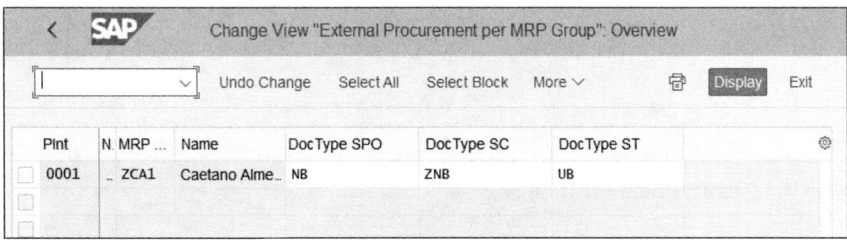

Figure 4.34 External Procurement Document Types Customizing

4.2.9 Availability Check

Finally, the MRP group also offers settings related to the planned order availability check, as you can see in the **Checking Rule for Dependent Requirements** Customizing activity.

Checking Rule for Dependent Requirements

This Customizing activity is similar to the **Dependent Requirement Availability** activity, which is available under the **Overall Plant Parameters** section. Here, we can select which checking rule will be used during the planned order availability check.

However, as shown in Figure 4.35, there is an additional **Activate Full Confirmation Logic** flag here. When this flag is not checked, the availability check will confirm the planned order components' available quantity proportional to the component with the lowest confirmed quantity. If this flag is checked, however, the confirmed quantity of each component is determined independently, so we can confirm the full available quantity of each component even if there are components for which we could not determine a confirmed available quantity.

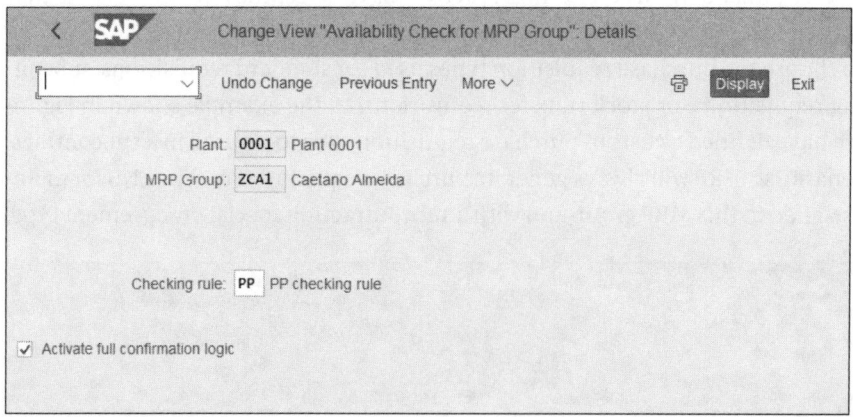

Figure 4.35 Availability Check Customizing

4.3 MRP Type

We discussed the standard MRP types in detail in Chapter 3, and those MRP types will cover most of our business requirements. However, there are some Customizing settings behind the MRP types that can be changed to influence the MRP behavior.

Whenever we need to change any setting in the MRP types, we should copy one of the existing standard MRP types and change the desired settings, generating a custom MRP type.

The transaction to change the MRP type Customizing is Transaction OMDQ. When we enter this transaction, we will see a list of the existing MRP types. When we access the details screen of the MRP type, we will see all the settings that can be changed for the MRP type, as shown in Figure 4.36.

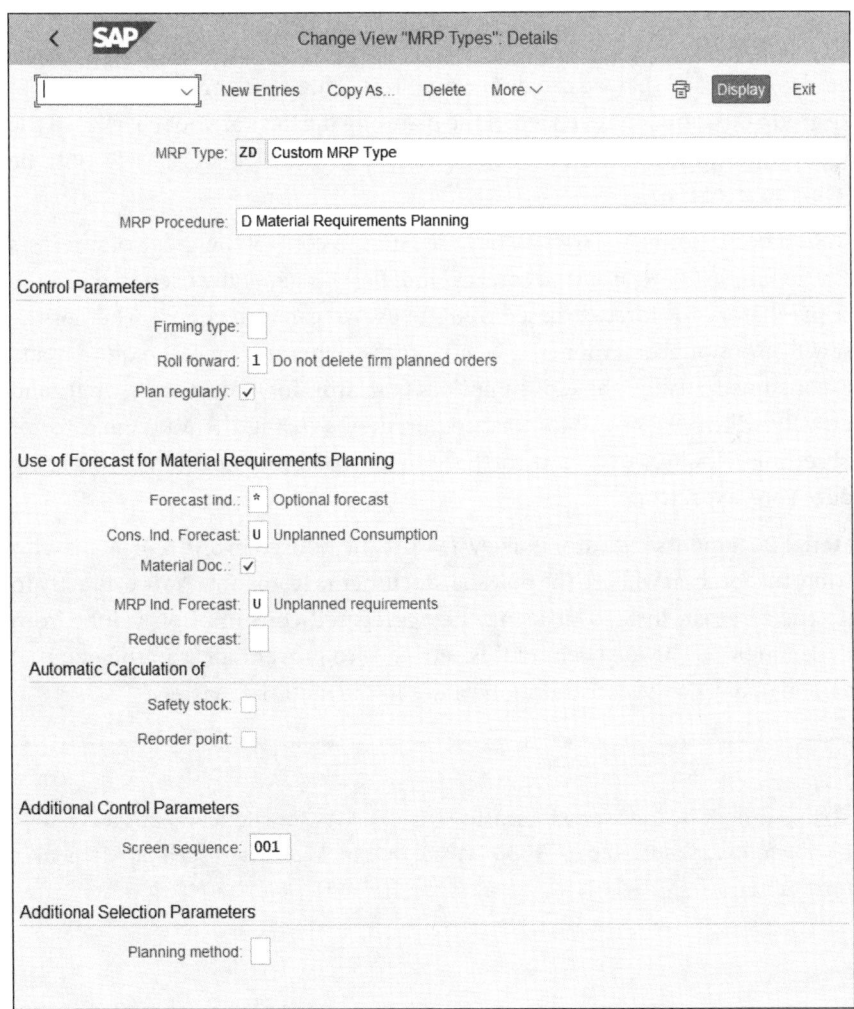

Figure 4.36 MRP Type Customizing

We discussed the **Firming Type** setting in detail in the previous chapter; this setting usually doesn't need to be changed because SAP offers MRP types for each of the existing firming types.

Earlier in the chapter, we described how to define a roll-forward horizon at the MRP group level and noted that MRP can delete planned orders before this horizon. To activate the deletion of planned orders, we need to set the **Roll Forward** setting to the **Delete Firm Planned Orders** value in the MRP type Customizing. This way, we can have two levels of control for the deletion of planned orders: the MRP group and the MRP type.

We have also discussed that we can define an interval for regular MRP executions in the MRP group Customizing, even when the planning file flags are not checked. If the **Plan Regularly** setting is checked in the MRP type, then a material will only be planned in those intervals.

In the MRP type Customizing, we also have settings to control the usage of forecasts by MRP. The forecast indicator (the **Forecast Ind.** field) is generally used to make the forecast mandatory for forecast-based MRP types. We can also choose whether the forecast will be optional or if there will be no forecast, whether forecast requirements will be consumed (using the **Consumption Indicator for Forecast** setting), and whether MRP will consider the forecast requirements (using the **MRP Indicator of Forecast** setting). Finally, we can control the reduction of forecast requirements using the **Reduce Forecast** setting.

The **Material Documents** indicator is a new feature introduced in SAP S/4HANA. With this setting, the forecast will use the material documents from table MATDOC directly to calculate the forecast, instead of using the aggregated consumption values from tables MVER and DVER. The idea behind this setting is to prevent locks in the material master when updating the consumption values in the material master.

> **Note**
>
> This setting cannot be used for a forecast with period P. More details about this feature can be found in SAP Note 1929000 (MP38: Material Forecast based on Material Documents).

In the MRP type Customizing, we can also define the automatic calculation of the reorder point or the MRP type, setting the **Safety Stock** and **Reorder Point** flags, respectively. These flags are set, for example, for the standard MRP type V2, as explained in the previous chapter.

In the MRP evaluation transactions, such as the Stock/Requirements List, in the header details section, we can find several tabs with additional information about the material and the MRP-related settings. Depending on the MRP type, a different sequence of screens and different fields can be displayed, and we will control which screens will be shown using the **Screen Sequence** setting. For example, for a material with a reorder point MRP type, it makes sense to show information related to the reorder point, but this field is not relevant for a material with a deterministic MRP type.

> **Note**
> The **Screen Sequence** setting must be previously defined in the customizing Transaction OMIO. We can choose from among the standard screens available for program SAPLM61K or we can create custom screens for this program and select them.

The **Planning Method** indicator is only used for materials planned externally, and it will not affect the MRP logic. It is generally used by MRP type X0 or similar MRP types.

If we select an MRP procedure with a reorder point MRP type, we will see additional fields that are only relevant if we are using the reorder point logic. We noted in Chapter 3 that the standard MRP type VB will not consider external requirements and that MRP type V1 can consider customer requirements within the replenishment lead time. We can control how these external requirements will be considered by a reorder point MRP type using the **Include External Requirements** setting. Besides the options already mentioned, we can create a custom MRP type that will consider external requirements in the total horizon. We also have settings to select additional MRP elements to be considered as external requirements, as shown in Figure 4.37.

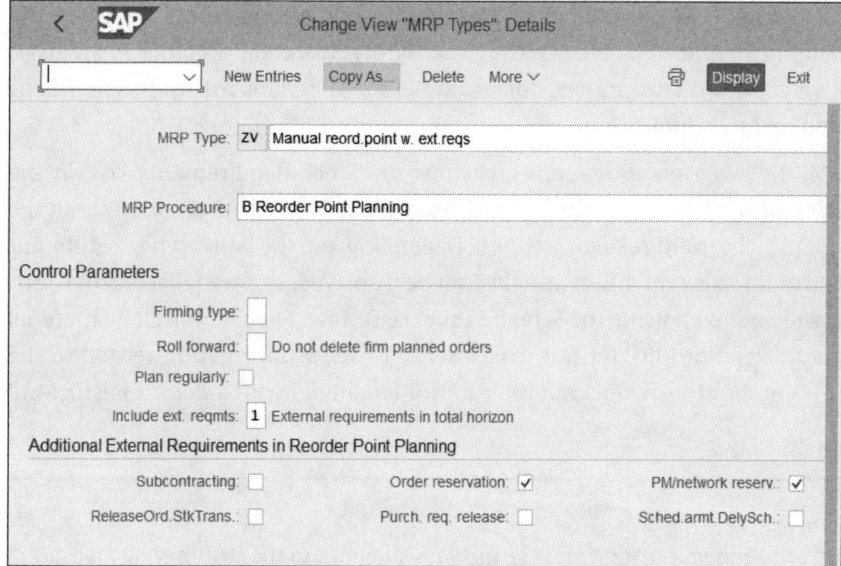

Figure 4.37 MRP Type Customizing for a Reorder Point MRP Procedure

4.4 Lot-Sizing Procedure

We discussed how to use the standard lot-sizing procedures in the previous chapter and the effects of additional material master settings in the calculation of the replenishment proposal quantities. Very frequently, however, we need to create a custom lot-sizing procedure to make changes to the standard lot-sizing procedure settings.

To create or change a lot-sizing procedure, we use customizing Transaction OMI4. When we enter this transaction, which is shown in Figure 4.38, we can choose the **MRP Lot Size** button (to define the general lot size settings) or the **Storage Costs Indicator** button (which is used for the optimum lot-sizing procedures).

We can find the most important settings under the **MRP Lot Size** section, shown in Figure 4.39. The first setting that we can change in our custom lot-sizing procedure is the **Last Lot Exact** flag, which was mentioned in the previous chapter. We can use this setting when we want to use a fixed lot-sizing procedure so that the replenishment proposals will always be created with a fixed quantity, but we want to have the last replenishment proposal created with the exact quantity. This can avoid an unnecessary remaining quantity in stock.

4.4 Lot-Sizing Procedure

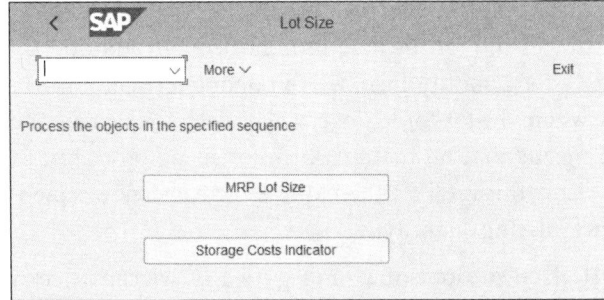

Figure 4.38 Lot Size Customizing

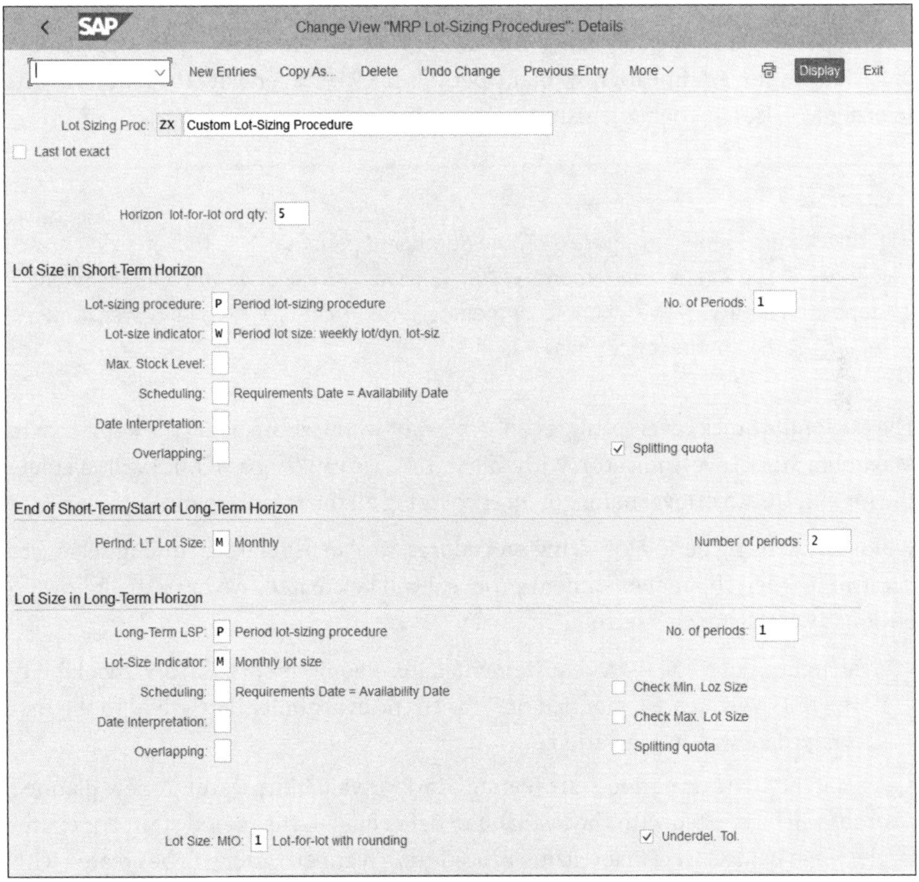

Figure 4.39 MRP Lot-Sizing Procedure Customizing

In the lot-sizing procedure Customizing, we have the option to define different lot-sizing procedures for the short-term and for the long-term horizon. In addition, by using the **Horizon: Lot-for-Lot Order Quantity** field, we can define a small horizon before the short-term horizon, where the lot-for-lot logic will be used to calculate the replenishment proposal. This means that no matter which lot-sizing procedure is selected, if there is a shortage within this interval, then MRP will create a new replenishment proposal with the exact missing quantity.

In the **Lot Size in Short-Term Horizon** section shown in Figure 4.39, we can select a combination of the **Lot-Sizing Procedure** and **Lot-size Indicator** fields that will be used within the short-term horizon. We will choose static, period, or optimum lot-sizing procedures, discussed in Chapter 3.

When choosing a **Period Lot-Sizing** indicator (P), we will also need to set the **Number of Periods** value to define for how many periods MRP will aggregate the requirements in order to calculate the replenishment proposal quantity.

> **Example**
>
> In the example shown in Figure 4.39, the number of periods is 1, so the lot-sizing procedure will aggregate requirements within one week to calculate the replenishment proposal quantity. If we want to aggregate requirements within two weeks, we should set the number of periods to 2.

The **Maximum Stock Level** setting is only relevant when we are using the **Replenish to Maximum Stock Level** indicator. With this setting, we can choose if MRP will calculate the maximum stock level before or after covering all the requirements.

When we are using period lot-sizing procedures, we can use the **Scheduling** setting to determine when the replenishment proposal will be created. We have the following options available for this setting:

- Availability date equal to requirement date (**Requirements Date = Availability Date**): MRP will create a planned order with the availability date equal to the first shortage date within the period.
- Availability date at period start (**Period Start = Availability Date**): A new planned order will be created with the availability date equal to the period start. For example, when using a weekly lot-sizing procedure, a planned order will be created with the availability date on the first day of the week.

- Availability date at period end (**Period End = Availability Date**): A new planned order will be created with the availability date equal to the period end.
- Start date at period start (**Period Start = Start Date / Period End = Availability Date**): MRP will create a planned order with the start date equal to the period start.
- Planned order start date at period start and availability date at period end (**Period Start = Start Date**): With this setting, MRP will schedule the planned order to match the period start and finish, and the in-house processing time in the material master record will be ignored.

When we are using a goods receipt processing time in our material, we will have a delivery date and an availability date. The delivery date is the date on which the actual goods receipt happens, while the availability date is when the material is available to be used (in other words, the delivery date plus the goods receipt processing time). With the **Date Interpretation** indicator, we can control if a period lot-sizing procedure will consider the availability date or the actual delivery date in the scheduling calculation.

The **Overlapping** indicator can be used to avoid the creation of several planned orders on the same date if we are using, for example, a fixed lot-sizing procedure or a maximum lot size. MRP will use the value defined in the **Takt-Time** field of the material master to set an interval between the different planned orders created to cover the same shortage. We can define in Customizing that this overlapping will be forward or backward.

The **Splitting Quota** setting is relevant when we are using quota arrangement and we want to split the quantity of each shortage between the different sources of supply according to the shortage quantities. The effects of this setting in the MRP results were explained in detail in Chapter 3.

As mentioned earlier in this section, we can have different lot-sizing logic for the short-term horizon and for the long-term horizon. The **End of Short-Term/Start of Long-Term Horizon** section will define the duration of the short-term horizon. Here, we need to enter the period indicator (the **PerInd** field) and for how many periods the short-term horizon should last.

Under the **Lot-Size in Long-Term Horizon** section, we have basically the same options available for the short-term horizon. In addition, we use the **Check Minimum Lot Size** and **Check Maximum Lot Size** flags to determine if the minimum or the maximum lot size will be considered in the long-term horizon, respectively.

> **Note**
> The idea behind different lot-sizing procedures for the short-term and for the long-term horizon is usually to minimize the number of replenishment proposals generated in the long term, reducing the noise for the MRP controller because we will not need such detailed planning in the long-term horizon.

When we are working with MTO or MTP scenarios, we will usually procure the exact missing quantity to avoid a remaining quantity assigned to the sales order stock or to the project stock. Therefore, the standard behavior is to use the lot-for-lot logic, despite the lot sizing for MTO and MTP. However, this is not always the case, and we might have to use a lot-sizing procedure to procure additional quantities even for MTO and MTP. In this case, we can use the **Lot Size: MTO** field to determine whether MTO and MTP will use a lot-for-lot logic with rounding or if the same lot-sizing procedure selected for the short-term horizon will be used.

Finally, another important setting for the MTO scenario is the **Underdelivery Tolerance** flag. This setting was part of the Discrete Industries and Mill Products industry solution in SAP ERP and it is now available by default in SAP S/4HANA. When this flag is checked, MRP will not generate a new replenishment proposal if the sales order stock plus replenishment proposals are within the underdelivery tolerance defined in the sales order. This setting will be considered not only for the sales order, but also for the lower-level elements assigned to the sales order special stock.

4.5 Availability Check

The availability check is a feature used to determine whether the components of a planned order will be available and to determine a committed date and committed quantity for a planned order.

Earlier in this chapter, we described several Customizing activities in which we need to enact a checking rule, either for dependent requirements or for backorder processing. This checking rule will be used in combination with the availability check maintained in the **MRP 3** tab of the material master to determine the scope of the availability check. It is in the scope of the availability check, in which we will define which stocks can be considered available and which requirements or future receipts can also be considered in the availability check.

The availability check Customizing for planned orders can be accessed directly in Transaction OPPJ. Here we can create a new checking rule, determine the check, and assign a checking rule to the plant or to the MRP group.

When we select the **Determine the Check** option, we will be able to choose a specific checking rule and availability check combination and define specific **Availability Check** settings. Figure 4.40 shows the details of this Customizing activity, with the following sections:

- Under the **Stocks** section, we can determine which stock types are considered available, such as safety stock, stock in transfer, or blocked stock.

- In the **Future Supply** section, we can determine which types of receipts in the future will be considered available, such as purchase requisitions, purchase orders, shipping notifications, planned orders, or production orders.

- The **Delayed Supply** section allows us to determine if supply elements in the past will be considered or not and if a message should be displayed to the user to confirm delayed supplies.

- Under the **Requirements** section, we will determine which additional requirements should be considered during the calculation of the availability check.

- The **Replenishment Lead Time** checkbox allows us to determine if the availability should be confirmed at the end of the replenishment lead time, if it cannot be confirmed with existing stocks and future receipts.

- In the **Special Scenarios** section, we can determine whether the availability check will be restricted to the storage location and if it will consider subcontracting stock and requirements.

- In the **Missing Parts Processing** section, we need to enter a period in the future in which the system will check for a goods receipt that is missing parts. A workflow can be used to trigger an email whenever a goods receipt is posted to the MRP controller for a missing part within this period.

> **Note**
> These settings will be only considered when we run the availability check, for example, for a planned order. They will not affect the MRP results or the information displayed in the Stock/Requirements List.

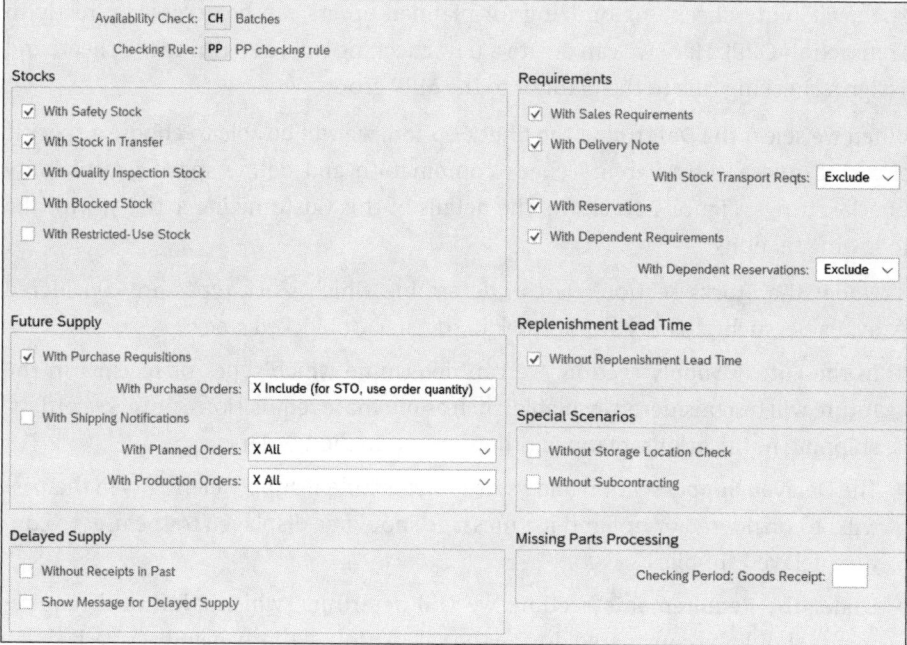

Figure 4.40 Scope of the Availability Check

4.6 MRP Areas

MRP areas were already available in SAP ERP, but their usage became mandatory in SAP S/4HANA so that users could segregate the subcontractor stock for the plant and either plan a storage location separately or exclude it from MRP. Therefore, during a migration to SAP S/4HANA or during a new implementation, we will need to create MRP areas in Customizing.

An *MRP area* is basically an organizational unit that is planned independently by MRP. The Customizing transaction to create or change MRP areas is Transaction OMIZ. There are three types of MRP areas:

- Plant (01): The plant MRP area is created automatically by the system and we cannot change it in Customizing. It is a 1:1 relationship, where each MRP area will refer to one specific plant.
- Storage location (02): It needs to be created manually when we need to plan a storage location separately. A storage location MRP area may refer to one or more

storage locations under the same plant. A storage location, however, can only belong to a single MRP area.

- Subcontractor (03): The subcontractor MRP area represents a vendor involved in the subcontracting scenario. It requires a 1:1 assignment, where each MRP area will refer to a single vendor a vendor can only belong to one MRP area.

In SAP ERP, we had to first activate the usage of MRP areas in Customizing and then to convert the planning file entries. These steps are no longer necessary in SAP S/4HANA because MRP areas are already active by default, so we can directly create MRP areas in Transaction OMIZ.

When we first enter the MRP areas Customizing, we will see all the plant MRP areas already created. If there are storage location or subcontracting MRP areas created, they will also appear in the **MRP Area Overview** screen, as shown in Figure 4.41.

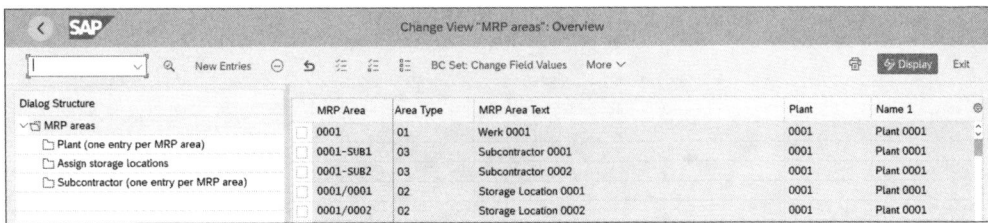

Figure 4.41 MRP Areas Overview

By clicking the **New Entries** button, we will jump into a new screen, where we will set the MRP area name, description, MRP area type, and plant in the corresponding fields. Figure 4.42 shows the details of the creation of a new storage location MRP area, with MRP area type 02.

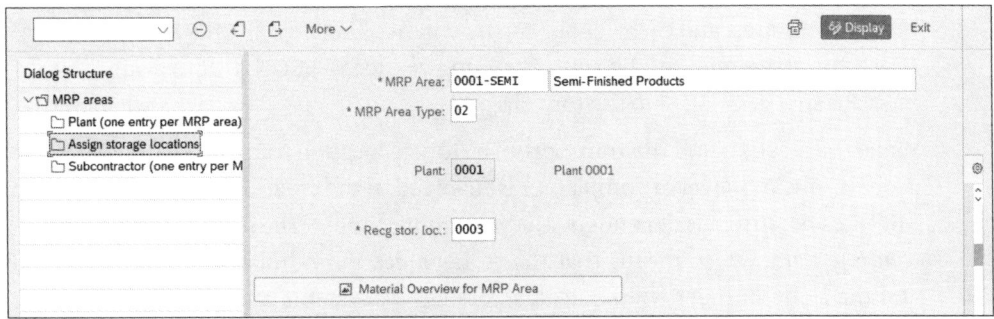

Figure 4.42 Creation of a New Storage Location MRP Area

4 Configuring MRP

After confirming the data input, a new field will appear on the screen: **Receiving Storage Location**. This would be the storage location where the components will be received into the MRP area; it needs to be one of the storage locations belonging to this MRP area. This assignment will be automatically created when we enter the receiving storage location.

If we need to include additional storage locations in our MRP area, we can select the **Assign Storage Locations** option in the menu located on the left side of the screen. Figure 4.43 shows the assignment of multiple storage locations to the MRP area.

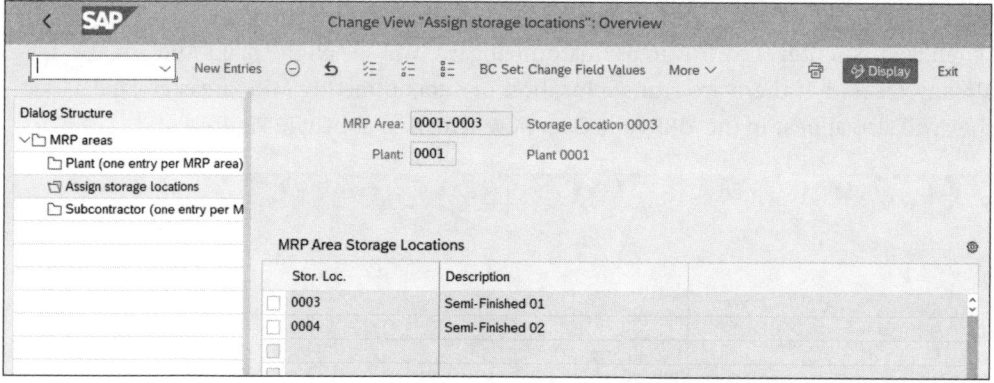

Figure 4.43 Assignment of Multiple Storage Locations to the MRP Area

If we are creating a subcontracting MRP area, the process is almost the same. The main differences are that we won't see the field to define the storage location, as shown in Figure 4.44, and that we will need to select the **Subcontractor** option from the left-hand menu in order to assign a vendor to the subcontracting MRP area.

As discussed earlier, we can only assign a single subcontracting vendor to the subcontracting MRP area, and each vendor can be only assigned to one MRP area. Figure 4.45 shows the assignment of the subcontracting vendor SUBCON_001 to a subcontracting MRP area 0001-SUB1 in Customizing.

While the creation and the transport of a storage location MRP area is a very simple process, an extra level of complexity is involved in the creation of a subcontracting MRP area because it is dependent on the vendor number. The storage location is *customizing data*, which means that the storage location number will be transported and the same number will be used across all the systems and clients. The vendor number, however, is *master data*, which means that the vendor number can be different across different systems and clients.

4.6 MRP Areas

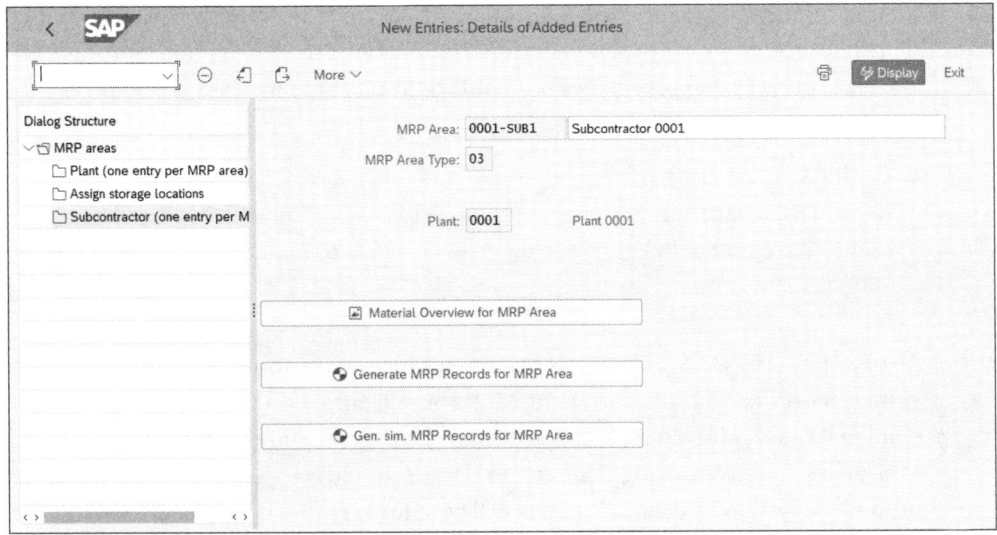

Figure 4.44 Creation of a Subcontracting MRP Area

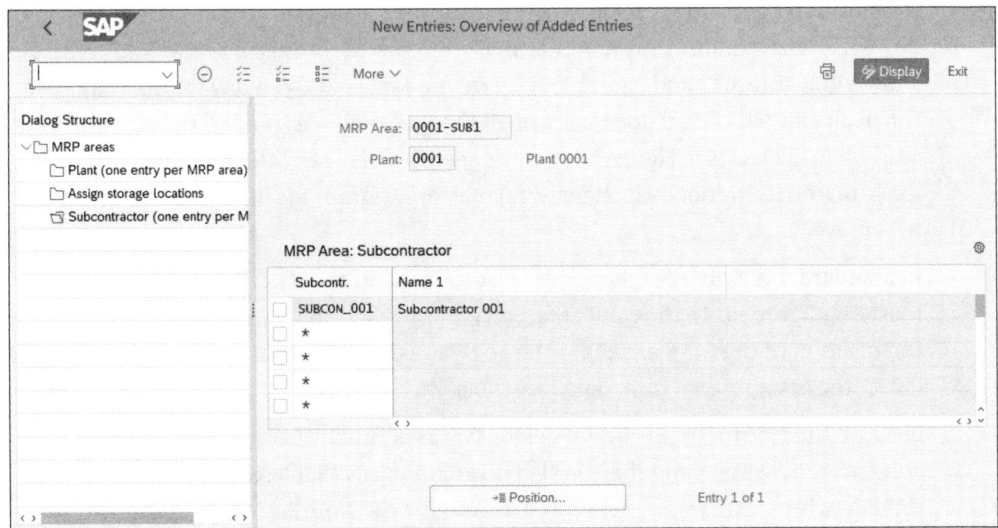

Figure 4.45 Subcontracting Vendor Assignment to the MRP Area

If we transport subcontracting MRP areas to a different system, we usually need to adjust the vendor number manually. To adjust the settings in the productive system, we would need to open this Customizing transaction to changes in the productive system by changing the customizing objects to **Current Settings**. This is a procedure usually executed by the system administrator; SAP Note 317650 (Transporting MRP Areas between Systems) provides more information about it.

> **Warning**
>
> We can only adjust the vendor number in Customizing if the MRP area was not yet assigned to any material, so the adjustment should happen just after the MRP areas transport.

As of SAP S/4HANA 1909, SAP has delivered separate Customizing transactions for storage locations and subcontracting MRP areas. Transaction OMIZA will only access storage location MRP areas, and Transaction OMIZB will only access subcontracting MRP areas. The customizing Transaction OMIZB should be opened for changes in the productive system by default, so users will be able to create a new MRP area whenever a new vendor is created in the system.

Besides the creation of new MRP areas in Customizing, there are some situations in which we might want to delete MRP areas from Customizing. This is only possible, however, when there is no material master assignment made to the MRP area. As shown in Figure 4.42 and Figure 4.44, there is a **Material Overview for MRP Area** button available, which will open a list of all the materials assigned to this specific MRP area when clicked (see Figure 4.46). If we need to delete an MRP area, we can use this list of materials to check which material master assignments of the MRP area we need to remove.

In standard SAP S/4HANA, however, we can only set the deletion flag for a material master assignment to the MRP area. Setting the deletion flag is not enough to allow the deletion of the MRP area. In order to delete the MRP area, we need to physically delete the assignments from database table MDMA.

Because the feature to physically delete this assignment from the table is not available in SAP S/4HANA and there is also no archiving available, SAP offers report YMR-PAREO, which can be implemented through SAP Note 54544 (Reorganization of Materials in MRP Areas) to delete the MRP area assignment. This report will delete all the MRP area assignments for which the deletion indicator has been already set. After the deletion of all the assignments for a specific MRP area, we can proceed with the deletion of the Customizing entry.

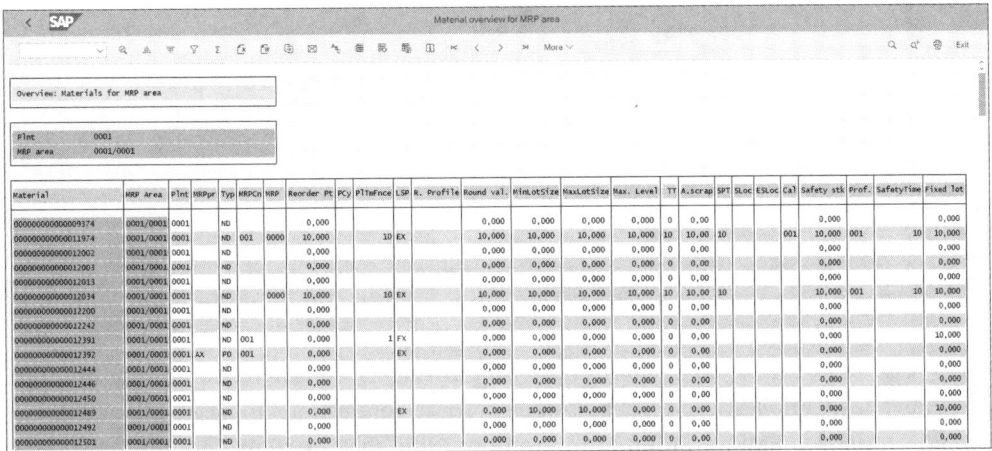

Figure 4.46 Material Overview for MRP Area

> **Tip**
> Report RMMDDIBE can be used initially to set the deletion flag for the material master assignments, and report YMRPAREO can be used in a subsequent step to physically delete the entries from table MDMA.

4.7 Parallel Processing

If we are using classic MRP, we can activate parallel processing to improve the MRP performance. With *parallel processing*, MRP splits the planning run into small packages of materials that can be processed in parallel. We can create several sessions in the same server, use different work processes under the same server, or trigger sessions in a different server by means of an RFC connection.

The activation of parallel processing in the planning run is simple: we just need to check the **Parallel Processing** flag in the MRP selection screen. However, before we can use this setting, we need to define the settings for parallel processing in Customizing.

This Customizing activity can be accessed through Transaction OMIQ. There, we just have to select the destinations (servers) for parallel processing and define the number of sessions allowed for each server, as shown in Figure 4.47.

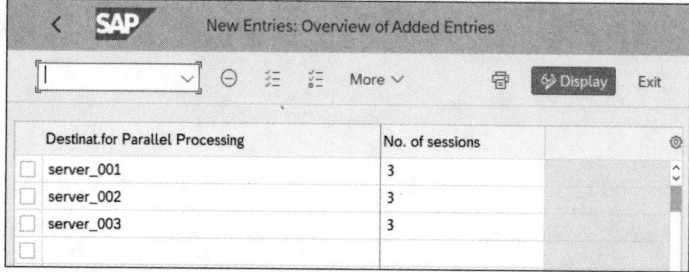

Figure 4.47 Destinations for Parallel Processing in Customizing

Before we can select the entries, we need to ensure that there are RFC connections available for each server to be selected. These connections must be maintained in Transaction SM59 as internal connections. Note that SAP S/4HANA does not allow the selection of a server group, and we need to define the individual servers as the destinations for parallel processing.

For technical reasons, each individual package is processed as a dialog process, so we need to ensure that the number of sessions does not exceed the number of dialog processes available in the server.

> **Warning**
>
> If we set a very high level of parallel processing, we might be consuming too many system resources. Therefore, we suggest that you discuss the parallel processing settings with your system admin before defining the servers and the number of sessions to be used.

An inconsistency in the parallel processing Customizing is a very common cause for terminations during the MRP run. If MRP cannot find the destination for parallel processing, a short dump may be triggered, and the planning run can be terminated. If this happens, we can check if the servers defined in Customizing for parallel processing are all up and running by comparing against instances available in Transaction SM51. In addition, in case the servers available in the system changes, we need to come back to Customizing and adjust the settings.

Very often, the servers defined in the development system are not the same as those defined in the quality or productive system. Therefore, just like the subcontracting MRP areas, we may have to adjust the Customizing settings in the productive system after the Customizing entries transport. We can also set this Customizing activity to **Current Settings**, as explained in SAP Note 187253 (OMIQ: Not Possible to Maintain Destinations).

4.8 Summary

In this chapter, we have gone through all the basic MRP-related Customizing settings for overall plant parameters, the MRP group, the MRP type, the lot-sizing procedure, and the MRP areas. These settings should be reviewed in a newly created system, whenever we are creating a new plant for which MRP should be executed, or when we need to improve and optimize the MRP run. After implementing these Customizing settings in a system, we should be able to execute MRP in an SAP S/4HANA system and have new replenishment proposals to cover the shortages. Therefore, we will cover the MRP execution in the following chapter, including both classic MRP and MRP Live, as well as the different transactions and the SAP Fiori applications available in SAP S/4HANA to run MRP.

We will see the additional Customizing settings related to the MRP evaluation in Chapter 6 and advanced MRP settings in Chapter 8.

Chapter 5
Running MRP

In this chapter, we will discuss the different options available in SAP S/4HANA to run classic MRP and MRP Live. We will go through the different transactions and SAP Fiori applications to run MRP and to schedule the MRP execution as a background job.

Now that you have learned how to create the basic MRP master data and how to configure MRP in an SAP S/4HANA system, we are ready to trigger MRP execution in order to plan materials.

SAP S/4HANA offers MRP Live, which executes an in-memory planning run on SAP HANA, but it also offers the option to keep using the classic MRP transactions to execute the planning run purely in ABAP. We'll begin this chapter by identifying the main differences between classic MRP and MRP Live and discussing when we should choose one or the other (Section 5.1). Then we will dive into executing MRP operations with classic MRP in Section 5.2 and MRP Live in Section 5.3. We will also discuss all the planning parameters that we can choose in the MRP planning run and all the transactions that we can use to run MRP. Finally, we will walk through the integration between MRP Live and Production Planning and Detailed Scheduling (PP/DS) functionality in SAP S/4HANA, through which we can plan advanced planning materials using MRP Live, in Section 5.4.

5.1 MRP Live versus Classic MRP

SAP S/4HANA offers two different options to execute MRP: classic MRP and MRP Live. To understand when to use classic MRP versus MRP Live, we need to understand a little bit about MRP design and the differences between the options.

Because it needs to run a large data selection from the database and to execute complex algorithms to calculate shortages and create replenishment elements, MRP is usually a performance-intensive application.

In SAP ERP, the database was usually a performance bottleneck for the MRP execution because too many MRP elements had to be selected from the database and processed by ABAP code. MRP was originally designed with logic by which, for each material to be planned, the planning elements were selected individually from the database; each planning element selected was postprocessed by ABAP source code, which would check if it was a valid element for MRP. For example, MRP would first select planned orders, and then each planned order would be validated by ABAP source code. Then MRP would select production orders, and each order would be validated. Then it would select purchase requisitions, and so on, until it finished reading and validating all the planning elements.

When SAP launched SAP HANA, a powerful in-memory and columnar database, it was clear that MRP performance could be improved by it. But though this traditional MRP logic worked fine for many years in SAP ERP, it did not take advantage of SAP HANA's internal parallelism, meaning that running MRP on an SAP HANA database would not result in major performance gains. To extract the best of the SAP HANA resources and tune the MRP performance, the underlying logic of MRP had to be completely redesigned.

The first performance improvement delivered by SAP was to redesign the data selection from the database during the MRP run. Instead of selecting the MRP records one by one, MRP optimized for an SAP HANA database would trigger the whole data selection at once and allow the SAP HANA internal parallelism to work its magic. In a second step, ABAP code would postprocess and validate all the planning elements selected from the database, and the rest of the MRP logic would remain the same.

This change improved the MRP performance, but it was restricted to the data selection. There was still room for improving the overall MRP performance through the power of the SAP HANA database. Therefore, MRP Live was created, pushing the MRP logic into the SAP HANA database and allowing an in-memory planning run, which was much faster than classic MRP.

> **Note**
>
> In SAP ERP on SAP HANA, the performance optimizations for classic MRP and the new MRP Live should be activated by a business function. In SAP S/4HANA, however, the performance optimizations for MRP are active by default.

The new MRP Live is executed in a different transaction, which means that we can choose whether we want use classic MRP or MRP Live for planning. It also brings some simplifications and changes when compared with classic MRP, so if we need to choose which one to use, it is important to understand those differences.

One of the simplifications with the most impact is related to MRP Lists. When MRP was created many years ago, it used the concept of the MRP List: a static report that provides a screenshot of the MRP results for each material. The MRP results were saved into a single table, which could be easily and quickly accessed by the user after the MRP run.

SAP S/4HANA offers the new MRP Live and the SAP Fiori applications of the MRP Cockpit, which means faster MRP and a new user interface to evaluate the MRP results. In addition, the performance was improved in the classic MRP transactions, such as the Stock/Requirements List, which means that the user can work always with live data, instead of analyzing a screenshot of the past MRP run. With all those new features, the MRP List became obsolete, so when we run MRP Live in the new transaction, Transaction MD01N, the MRP List will no longer be generated during the planning run.

MRP Lists were traditionally saved into table MDKP, MDTB, or MDTC, and those tables were commonly used for the creation of custom reports based on the MRP results. Those reports will not work when using MRP Live because they will no longer be updated.

> **Tip**
>
> SAP recommends function module MD_MDPSX_READ_API to be used in custom reports to read the information previously read from the MRP List tables.

Another simplification that affects MRP Live is related to creation indicators, which allow us to choose whether it should create planned orders, purchase requisitions, or delivery schedules for materials procured externally. As mentioned in Chapter 4, MRP Live will not use creation indicators. MRP Live also does not offer the option to create purchase requisitions only within the opening period defined in the scheduling margin key.

MRP Live will always create purchase requisitions for materials procured externally, or it can create schedule lines when a valid scheduling agreement is selected as a source of supply. If the creation of planned orders for materials procured externally is still required during the MRP Live planning run, we can use the ABAP-Managed Database Procedures (AMDP) BAdI PPH_MRP_SOURCING_BADI => SOS_DET_ADJUST to change the MRP element to be generated during the planning run.

The last major difference between MRP Live and classic MRP is related to the BAdIs available to implement any custom code. While classic MRP is almost entirely written in ABAP, the new MRP Live logic was pushed down into the SAP HANA layer, meaning that it is almost entirely executed with SAP HANA stored procedures. This change allowed for a performance improvement, but classic MRP BAdIs that were previously executed in ABAP will no longer be called in MRP Live. This means that any custom logic written in ABAP-based BAdIs will have to be translated into the new AMDP BAdIs provided by SAP in MRP Live. In Chapter 14, we will offer a list of the old ABAP BAdIs and the respective AMDP BAdIs that can be used in their place in MRP Live.

> **Tip**
>
> If it is not possible to translate a BAdI into its respective AMDP BAdI, we can use Transaction MD_MRP_FORCE_CLASSIC to force a material to still be planned in ABAP, even when using the new MRP Live transaction, Transaction MD01N. If we force too many materials to be planned in ABAP, however, we may not see any performance improvement when using MRP Live, so it is always advisable to use the new AMDP BAdIs.

One additional feature of MRP Live is the possibility to plan PP/DS advanced planning materials when PP/DS is used in SAP S/4HANA system. We can combine PP/DS and the MRP planning run in a single job, reducing the effort of synchronizing different jobs for materials planning. This feature is not available in classic MRP; it is a major improvement delivered for MRP Live. We will talk a little bit about PP/DS in more detail later in Section 5.4.

Finally, MRP performance is also a major difference between MRP Live and classic MRP. MRP Live was developed to improve MRP overall performance because the planning run can take hours to be executed. However, note that though MRP Live is much faster than classic MRP when planning large sets and very complex materials (e.g., materials with complex BOMs), classic MRP can still be faster when planning a few simple materials.

These critical differences are key when deciding whether to use the new MRP Live or classic MRP, but they are also important for defining a migration strategy to SAP S/4HANA. For example, companies that currently rely heavily on MRP Lists or on custom reports based on MRP Lists will have to carefully plan steps to migrate to MRP Live by adapting the custom code.

Another thing to consider is that it is possible to adopt MRP Live gradually, rather than abandoning classic MRP and exclusively using MRP Live all at once. For example, we can adopt a hybrid approach: use MRP Live for planning large sets of materials and taking advantage of the performance improvement, but keep using classic MRP for single-item planning, in which we can see the results before saving and for which classic MRP performance might still be better.

However, a note of caution here: before defining any migration strategy or choosing between MRP Live and classic MRP, always keep in mind that MRP Live has been defined by SAP as the target architecture and that classic MRP is now considered part of the SAP S/4HANA Compatibility Pack, which means that new features and improvements will mostly focus on MRP Live, rather than classic MRP.

In the following sections, we will cover all the MRP control parameters, the options available for running MRP, and additional differences between classic MRP and MRP Live that will impact this chapter. For more information, refer to the following SAP Notes:

- SAP Note 2268085 (S4TWL—MRP Live on SAP HANA—MD01N)
- SAP Note 2640393 (Differences between T-Code MD01N and Classic MRP T-Codes MD01/MD02/MD03)

5.2 Classic MRP

Let's begin by examining classic MRP, as run in SAP S/4HANA.

Although there is now just a single transaction to execute the new MRP Live, we still use multiple transactions to execute classic MRP, depending on the planning run scope. For example, we have a transaction to plan a single material, a transaction to plan a material and all its components, a transaction for a total planning run, and so on. All these transactions have very similar designs and share the same control parameters.

In this section, we will discuss how to use each of these transactions and will start going through the parameters that control the MRP execution and the planning run results.

5   Running MRP

5.2.1   Control Parameters

Different transactions can be used to execute classic MRP, depending on the desired scope of materials to be planned. In all those transactions, however, we will find the **MRP Control Parameters** settings, which we can use to define how the MRP run should behave. Figure 5.1 shows the **MRP Control Parameters** section that we can find in the classic MRP transactions.

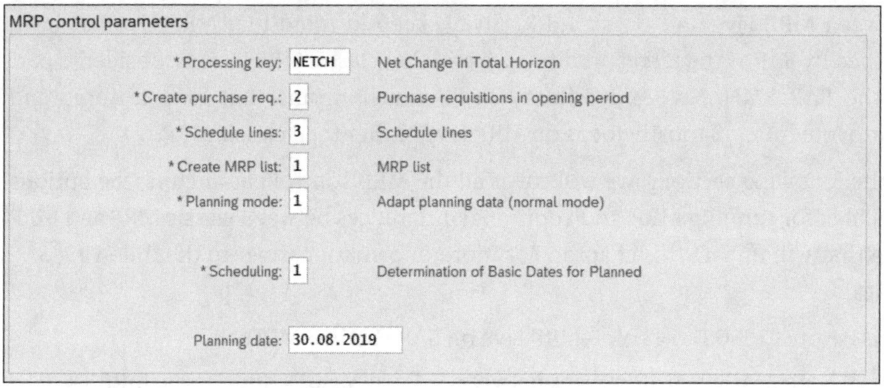

```
MRP control parameters
                * Processing key:  NETCH      Net Change in Total Horizon
            * Create purchase req.: 2         Purchase requisitions in opening period
                * Schedule lines:   3         Schedule lines
                * Create MRP list:  1         MRP list
                * Planning mode:    1         Adapt planning data (normal mode)

                    * Scheduling:   1         Determination of Basic Dates for Planned

                    Planning date:  30.08.2019
```

Figure 5.1 Classic MRP Control Parameters

The first setting available is **Processing Key**, which is used in the total planning run when we are planning one or more plants and which defines the materials to be selected for planning. The following processing keys are available in SAP S/4HANA:

- Net change in total planning (**NETCH**): When this processing key is used, MRP will select the materials to be planned according to the planning file entries. This means that if there was an MRP-relevant change for this material since the last time it was planned by MRP, the **NETCH** flag will be marked in the planning file, and this material will be selected for planning. Otherwise, if there was no change since the last planning run, this material will not be planned again if the **NETCH** key is used.

- Regenerative planning (**NEUPL**): This processing key is used when we want to plan all the materials with a valid planning file, even if there was no change since the last time they were planned. Using this processing key usually increases the planning run duration because we will be planning a large set of materials, but it is a good practice to do a regenerative planning run periodically (once a week, for example).

> **Note**
>
> In the previous releases, SAP ERP offered an additional processing key through which we could select only materials with an MRP-relevant change within the planning horizon to be planned by MRP.
>
> This processing key was a measure to restrict the number of materials to be planned even more, targeting a reduction in the planning run duration. This processing key is no longer available in SAP S/4HANA due to a simplification enacted because MRP Live drastically improved MRP performance when planning large sets of materials.

The **Create Purchase Requisitions**, **Schedule Lines**, and **Create MRP List** control indicators are known as the *creation indicators*. We mentioned these settings in Chapter 4 because default values can be defined in the MRP group Customizing. In a total planning run, the values defined for these fields will only be used if the creation indicators were not defined in the MRP group, whereas in the single-item planning transactions, the values defined in the MRP group will not be considered.

The **Create Purchase Requisitions** indicator is considered for materials with external procurement only and will define if MRP should create purchase requisitions for the total horizon, purchase requisitions within the opening period (as defined in the scheduling margin key), and planned orders outside the opening period or planned orders for the total horizon.

A very similar logic lies behind the **Schedule Lines** indicator. Whenever a valid scheduling agreement is found with a valid source of supply, this indicator will control whether MRP should create schedule lines for the total horizon or for the opening period, or if schedule lines should not be created at all.

The **Create MRP List** indicator allows us to choose if MRP will always create an MRP List, if it will be created only in the case of exception messages, or if it should not be created at all.

The **Planning Mode** field defines the reusability of the unfirmed replenishment elements created in the previous planning runs. Three planning modes are available in classic MRP:

- **1—Adapt Planning Data (Normal Mode)**: With planning mode 1, MRP will reuse existing planning proposals whenever possible. For example, if a planned order was created to cover a requirement in a previous planning run and there was no change in the date or quantity, this planned order will not be touched by MRP. If there was only a minor change—in the quantity, for example—then MRP will adapt this planned order to the changes.

- **2—Re-explode BOM and Routing**: With planning mode 2, MRP always will force a new BOM and routing explosion for existing replenishment proposals, even when it is not necessary, but it will keep the same planned order number.
- **3—Delete and Recreate Planning Data**: Planning mode 3 will always force the deletion and the recreation of all the existing unfirmed replenishment proposals.

In general, we just need to use planning mode 1 for a daily planning run because the BOM and routing re-explosion or the deletion and recreation of planned orders will have a negative effect on MRP performance. Planning mode 3 is not even recommended by SAP to be used on a regular basis in a productive system because it drastically increases the MRP runtime and the number range will be quickly consumed.

In fact, we do not even need to use planning mode 2 on a regular basis. Whenever there is a master data change that will require BOM re-explosion or the deletion and recreation of planned orders for a specific material, the **Explode BOM** or **Reset [Procurement] Proposals** flags will be checked in the planning file (see Figure 5.2). With those flags checked, the BOM will be re-exploded and the replenishment proposals will be deleted and recreated even with planning mode 1.

Plan. file entries

Material: S4HANA_FERT_001
Plnt: 0001

No. of entries: 4
NETCH plnng file ent: 3
NETPL plnng file ent: 3

Current data from 30.08.2019 At 04:51 Tim

R	Cde	Material	MRP Area	MPS ind.	NChge plng	NChgePHor.	ResetProps	ExplodeBOM	Planning date
B	000	S4HANA_FERT_001	0001	☐	X	X	X	X	
B	000	S4HANA_FERT_001	0001/0001	☐					
B	000	S4HANA_FERT_001	0001/0002	☐	X	X			
B	000	S4HANA_FERT_001	0001/0003	☐	X	X	X	X	

Figure 5.2 The Reset [Procurement] Proposals and Explode BOM Flags in the Planning File

Planning mode 2 may be required in the case of changes in the routing because the planning file entries will not be updated in this case and the routing will not be read again with planning mode 1. Because the routing is generally not critical for MRP planning and changes in the routing are usually not frequent, we can schedule a weekly MRP run with planning mode 2 on the weekend, just to ensure that all the routings are updated.

Planning mode 3 may only be required in a productive system if we transport Customizing changes that will affect the existing replenishment proposals and we want to ensure that they will be updated with the new settings.

The **Scheduling** parameter (see Figure 5.1) controls whether only the basic dates of the planned order dates will be determined according to the in-house production time or if lead-time scheduling will be executed; where the routing will be exploded; and if the production dates will be calculated according the routing operation dates. Capacity requirements will be generated only if we are using lead-time scheduling, so we need to use it if we want to run capacity leveling for planned orders.

Finally, we can determine the **Planning Date** for the MRP run. A different planning date is generally used when we are working with materials with time-phased MRP and we want to plan them ahead of the actual planning date. Also, if we use a planning date in the future, this planning date will be considered as the current date if today scheduling is executed during the planning run.

Now that we have covered the main settings for MRP control parameters that are common to the classic MRP transactions, let's go through the different transactions available to execute classic MRP.

5.2.2 Single-Item/Single-Level Planning

The simplest MRP execution is the single-item/single-level execution (Transaction MD03), in which we will plan a single material. When we use this transaction, MRP will plan a material and generate dependent requirements for the planned order components, but the components themselves will not be planned.

This transaction is useful if we want to replan a specific material if changes have been made since the last planning run or if we want to troubleshoot any issue that might have happened during the planning run. Despite the MRP control parameters, we also have to enter the material to be planned and the plant or MRP area to be planned, as shown in Figure 5.3. We cannot plan multiple materials or the same material in multiple plants or MRP areas using this transaction.

One additional setting that we have in Transaction MD03 is the **Display Results Prior to Saving** flag. When this flag is checked, MRP will be executed for the material, but we will be able to evaluate the MRP results before they are saved, as shown in Figure 5.4. We can even take actions, such as creating additional replenishment proposals or manually setting the firm date, before saving the MRP results.

5   Running MRP

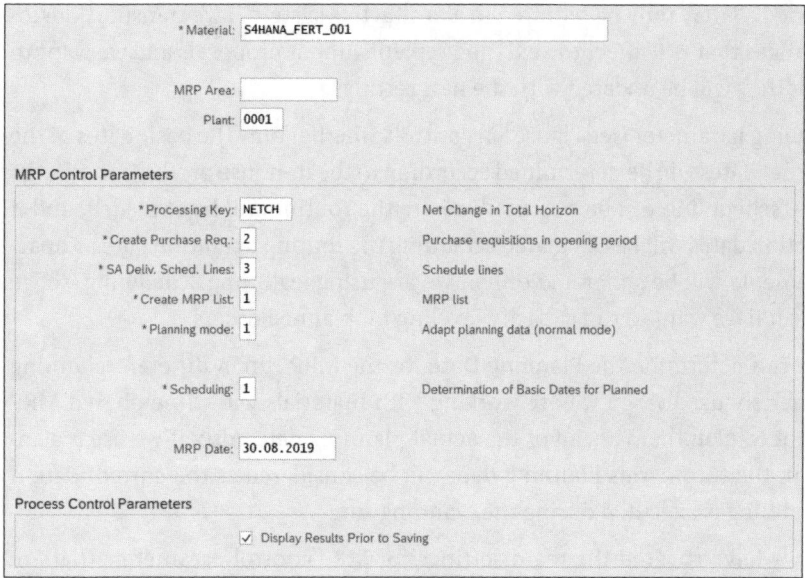

Figure 5.3 Single-Item/Single-Level Transaction

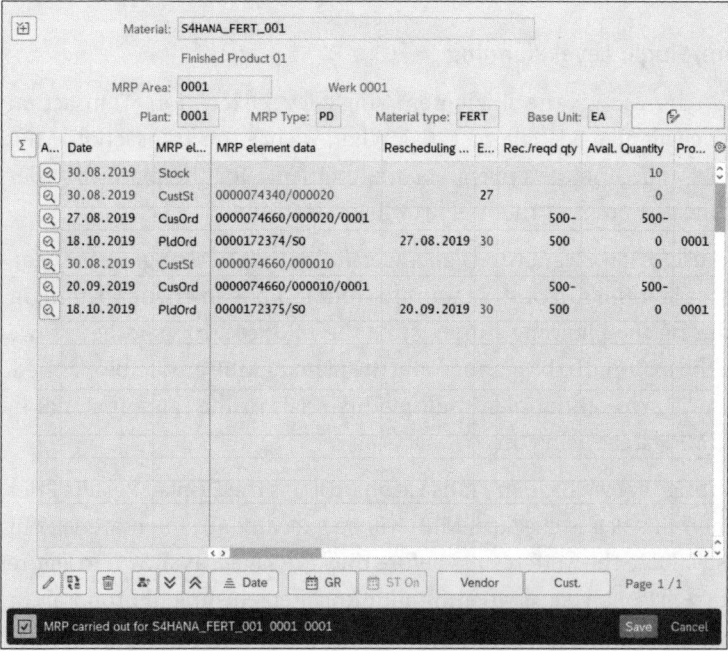

Figure 5.4 MRP Planning Results before Saving

5.2.3 Single-Item/Multilevel Planning

While the single-item/single-level transaction is useful for planning an individual material, we might need to plan an individual material and also plan the components together to avoid any possible shortages. For this purpose, we can use the single-item/multilevel transaction, Transaction MD02.

When we use this transaction, we will select one specific material and plant or MRP area to be planned. During the planning run, if there are planned orders, the BOM will be exploded, dependent requirements will be generated for the components, and these components will also be planned. Planning will be *multilevel*, which means that all the levels of components for which there is a dependent requirement will be planned, until we reach the raw material level. If there is a stock transfer involved, planning will also continue in the supplying plant.

As shown in Figure 5.5, the selection screen is very similar to the single-item/single-level transaction, but we do have some additional process control parameters and an additional section called **Scope of Planning**. In this section, we can find the **Product Group** setting, which is used when we want to plan an entire product group and its components.

> **Note**
> A product group is a master data element, generally used in sales and operations planning. It is used to combine different materials that will be planned together.

By default, only components for which a dependent requirement was created or changed during the planning run will planned again in Transaction MD02. If we want to force those materials to be planned, we can check the **Also Plan Unchanged Components** flag in the selection screen.

Similar to the single-item/single-level transaction, we have the **Display Results Prior to Saving** flag, by which we can evaluate the MRP results before saving. Because we may have many materials being planned, we will see the results one by one. After we save each material, we will see a pop-up asking what to do next (see Figure 5.6). We can simply continue the planning run (the **Plan Up Until Stopping Point** radio button), execute MRP until the last level without stopping (the **Proceed without Stopping** radio button), cancel the planning run (the **Cancel Planning Run** radio button), or determine a new stopping point (the **Determine New Breakpoint** button).

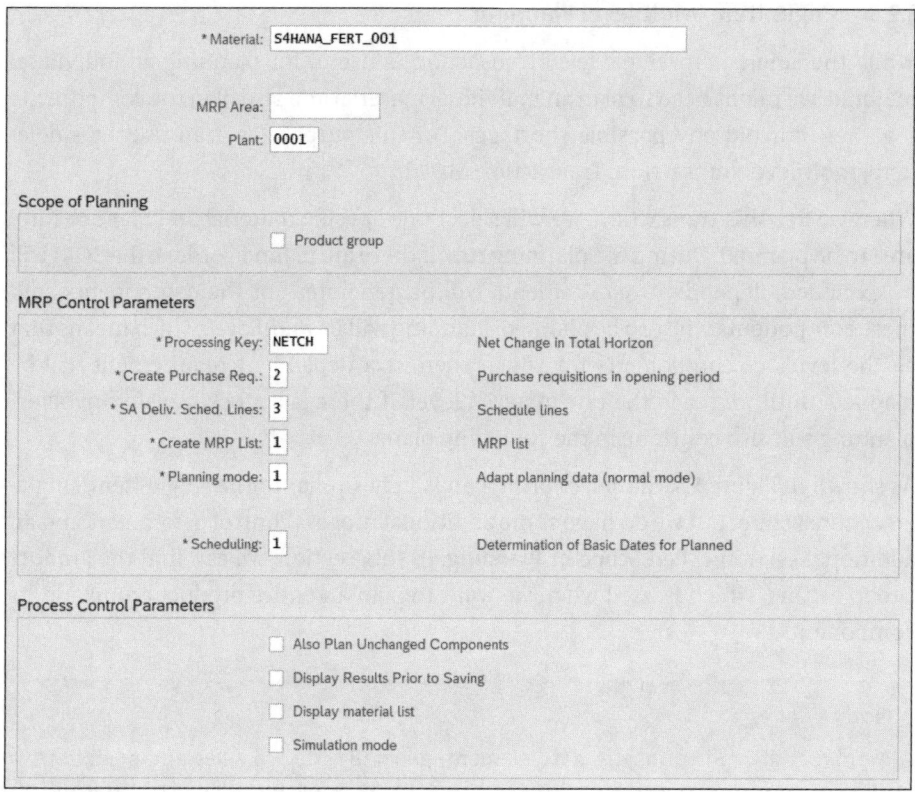

Figure 5.5 Single-Item Multilevel Transaction

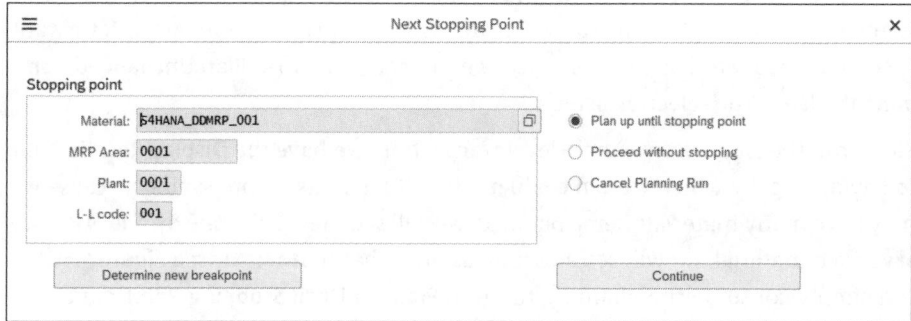

Figure 5.6 Pop-up Triggered after Saving Results

5.2 Classic MRP

> **Warning**
>
> Components with a consumption-based MRP type will not be planned in the single-item/multilevel MRP transaction. The component will also not be planned if the low-level code is smaller than or equal to the parent low-level code. This check prevents a recursive BOM structure from causing an endless loop in the MRP planning.

Once the MRP run is finished, we will see a results screen like the one in Figure 5.7, showing the MRP run statistics—including, for example, how many materials were planned, how many materials had exceptions, database statistics, runtime statistics, and the ranking of materials with the highest runtime.

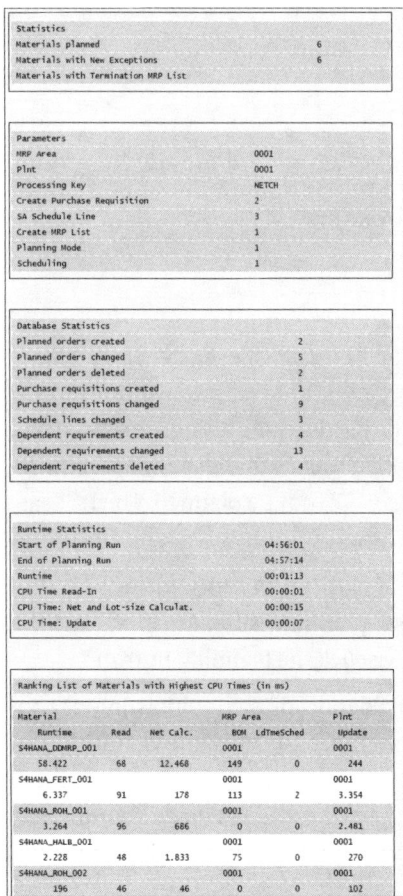

Figure 5.7 Single-Item/Multilevel Results Screen

5 Running MRP

If the **Display Material List** flag is also checked, we will see the **Materials** button in the upper-left corner of the results screen. By clicking this button, we can see a detailed list of the materials planned, including exceptions and stock days' supply for each material. Figure 5.8 shows the details of the material list after the single-item/multilevel MRP run.

Finally, if we just want to analyze the multilevel MRP results without saving, we can set the **Simulation Mode** flag. In this case, the **Display Material List** flag will be set automatically by the system and we will branch directly into the material list, where we will be able to evaluate the MRP results. We can still choose to save the MRP results after evaluating, even in simulation mode.

Valid from date	Material	Ext. Manuf	MRP Area	Material description	MRPCa	N	1	2	3	4	5	6	7	8	StckDS	1st RDS	2nd R	Plan...	BUn	Safe...	Reord...	MTyp	PT	SP	A...	MR...	MT Cde
	S4HANA_FERT_001		0001	Finished Product 01	ZCA	✓							2		4,0-	4,0-	4,0-	10	EA	0	0	FERT	E			ZCA1	PD 000
	S4HANA_DDMRP_001		0001	Demand Driven MRP	ZCA	✓		1				1	4		999,9-	1,0-	1,0-	0	EA	99	209	FERT	E				D1 001
	S4HANA_HALB_001		0001	Finished Product 01	ZCA	✓						1	4		999,9-	187,9-	187,9-	8	EA	10	50	HALB	E				D1 002
	S4HANA_ROH_001		0001	Raw Material 01	ZCA	✓			2				4		33,0-	1,0-	1,0-	0	EA	0	0	ROH	F				PD 003
	S4HANA_ROH_002		0001	Raw Material 02	ZCA	✓							4		2,0-	2,0-	2,0-	80	EA	29	0	ROH	F				PD 003
	S4HANA_ROH_003		0001	Raw Material 03	ZCA	✓		1					4		124,0-	124,0-	124,0-	0	KG	0	0	ROH	F				PD 003

Figure 5.8 Material List after Single-Item/Multilevel MRP Run

5.2.4 Single-Item Interactive Planning

While the single-item/single-level and the single-item/multilevel transactions are very well-known and frequently used, there is an additional interactive transaction for single-item planning. Transaction MD43 can be used to plan a single material or a product group. This transaction is single-level, which means that dependent requirements will be created for the components, but they will not be planned. The transaction selection screen is shown in Figure 5.9.

The main difference between this transaction and the previously discussed MRP transactions is that we will evaluate the current planning situation first, but the actual planning run will only be triggered when we click the **Planning** button.

After we trigger the planning run, we can still see details of the replenishment proposals created by MRP, for example, and make changes to dates and quantities, to react to exception messages or to resolve problems (see Figure 5.10). When a rescheduling exception message is triggered, we can simply click the **Reschedule Order** button next to the end date, and the proposed rescheduling date will be automatically adopted to this replenishment proposal.

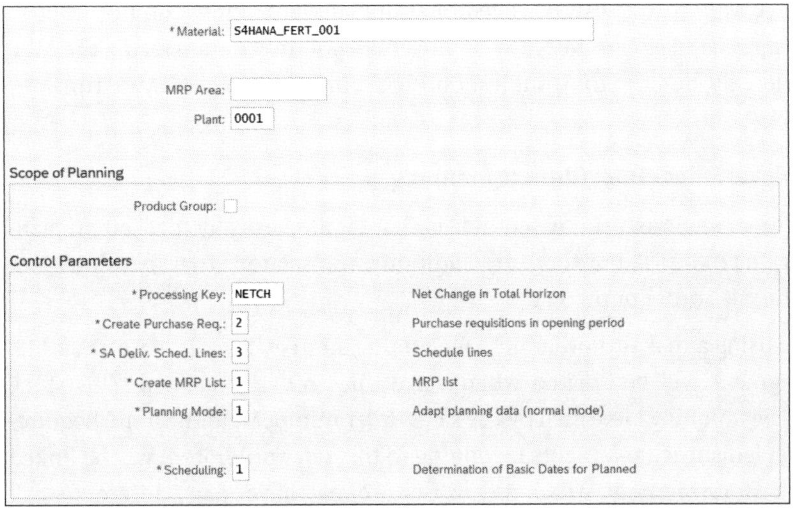

5.2 Classic MRP

Figure 5.9 Single-Item Interactive Planning

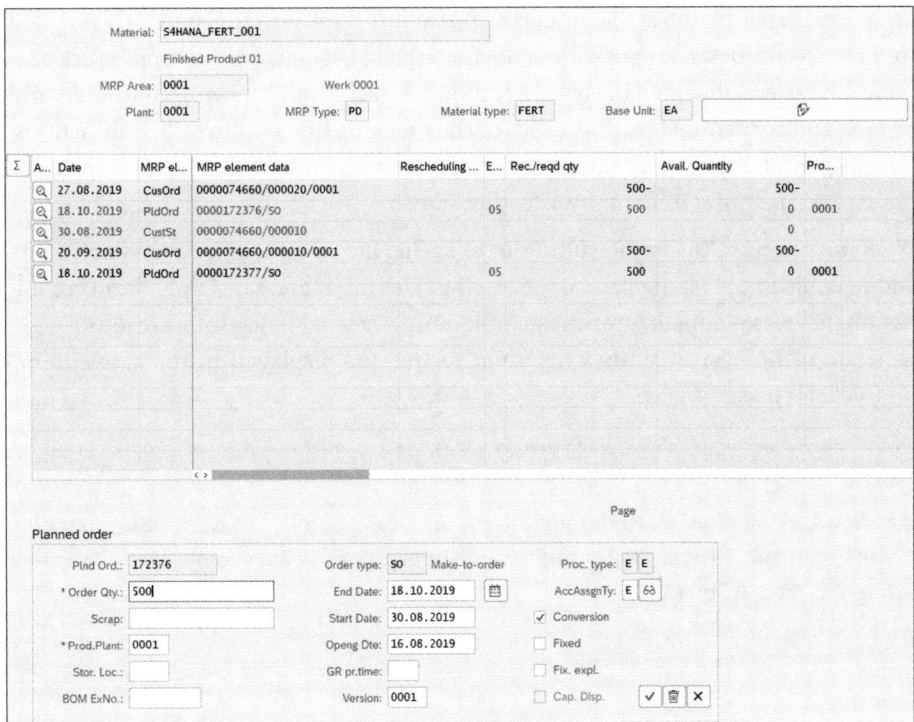

Figure 5.10 Details of the Planned Order in the Interactive Planning

The interactive MRP results can be saved or simply discarded if we do not want to keep the changes. Transaction MD43 is very useful—not only for analyzing the MRP results individually, but also for troubleshooting problems during the MRP run.

5.2.5 Multilevel Sales Order/Project Planning

The transactions previously discussed in this chapter are basically focused on planning one specific material, but there are additional transactions that focus on planning a specific sales order or project.

When we are using a make-to-order (MTO) planning strategy for our material, a special stock segment will be created whenever a sales order is created. This stock segment will be uniquely identified by the sales order number and the item. Requirements and replenishment elements belonging to this sales order item will be linked to this special stock segment, which means that we may have many different stock segments being planned separately for the same material, each one related to a different sales order item.

In this case, Transaction MD50 offers the possibility to plan all the materials assigned to this special stock segment—and *only* materials assigned to this special stock segment. The selection screen in Figure 5.11 shows the same MRP control parameters and process control parameters discussed for the previous single-item MRP transactions, but instead of entering a material and plant combination, we enter just the sales order and sales order item in the selection screen.

When we select the **Display Results Prior to Saving** flag, we will only see requirements and replenishment elements assigned to the sales order and sales order item combination that was planned. After the planning run, we will branch into a results screen with the planning run statistics, similar to the one displayed in the single-item/multilevel transaction.

> **Note**
> Each sales order may have different items, and each item will have its own special stock segment. Different items of the same sales order will have to be planned separately in Transaction MD50.

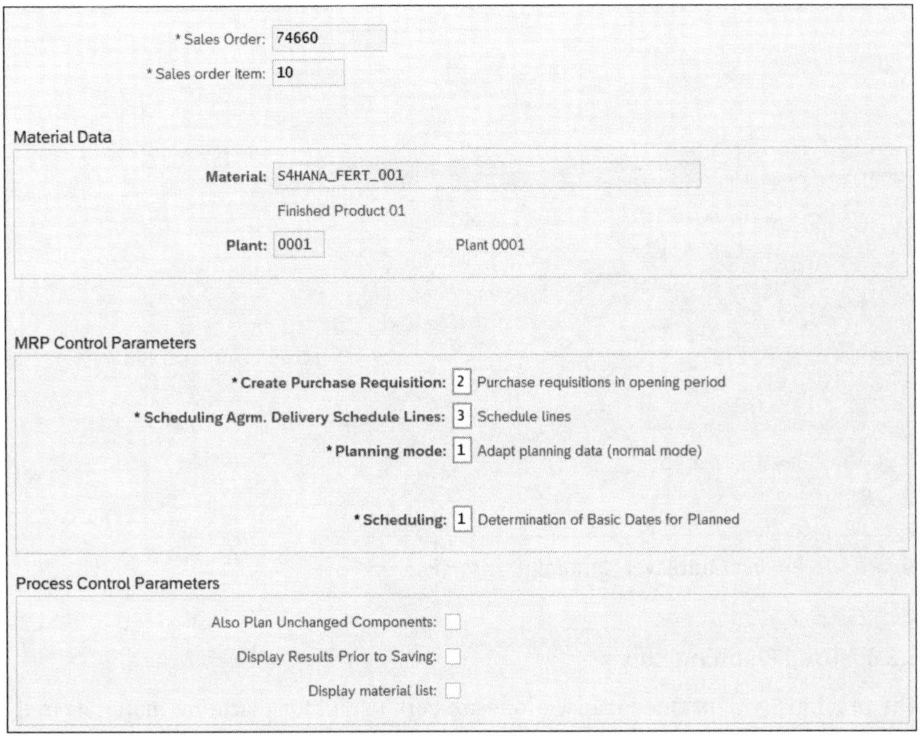

Figure 5.11 Make-to-Order Multilevel Planning

Similar to the make-to-order (MTO) strategy, the make-to-project (MTP) planning strategy entails requirements and replenishment elements that may be linked to the project or to the WBS special stock. The transaction to plan a project or WBS element special stock is Transaction MD51. The selection screen is shown in Figure 5.12.

We can trigger the MRP run after filling either the **Project Definition** or **WBS Element** fields in the selection screen. If the **With Hierarchy** flag is selected, the entire WBS hierarchy will be considered during the planning run, rather than just the WBS element entered on the selection screen.

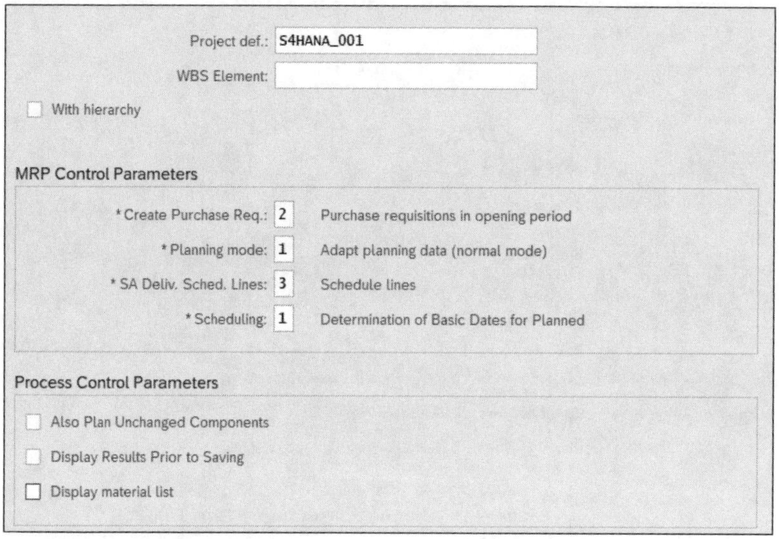

5 Running MRP

[Form screenshot showing:]

```
              Project def.:  S4HANA_001
            WBS Element:  
  ☐ With hierarchy

MRP Control Parameters
      * Create Purchase Req.:  2    Purchase requisitions in opening period
            * Planning mode:  1    Adapt planning data (normal mode)
      * SA Deliv. Sched. Lines:  3    Schedule lines
               * Scheduling:  1    Determination of Basic Dates for Planned

Process Control Parameters
  ☐ Also Plan Unchanged Components
  ☐ Display Results Prior to Saving
  ☐ Display material list
```

Figure 5.12 Project Multilevel Planning Transaction

5.2.6 Total Planning Run

The previously mentioned transactions are very useful for planning materials individually, but they are mostly used in exceptional situations. For example, if we know that there was a new sales order create for a material and this material needs to be planned immediately to start the procurement of the components, then we can run a single-item/multilevel planning run. However, we will not plan all the materials individually every day.

Most companies schedule a periodic total planning MRP run to be executed in the background, usually during the night. In the total planning run, we can plan an entire plant or plan multiple plants and MRP areas using a scope of planning. Depending on the processing key selected for the planning run, MRP can plan only those materials for which a change happened since the last planning run or all the materials with a valid MRP type.

> **Note**
>
> A *scope of planning* defines a sequence of plants or MRP areas that should be planned during an MRP total planning run. The scope of planning has to be created previously in the customizing Transaction OM0E.

If we want to manually trigger a total planning run, we can do it directly in Transaction MD01. In the selection screen shown in Figure 5.13, we enter either one plant or the desired scope of planning. Besides the MRP control parameters and the process control parameters already discussed in this chapter, we have an additional flag called **Parallel Processing**. When this flag is checked, MRP will try to split the planning run into small packages and distribute it among the different servers defined in Customizing, as shown previously in Chapter 4. Remember that parallel processing improves MRP performance—and it is mandatory to use it when planning with a scope of planning.

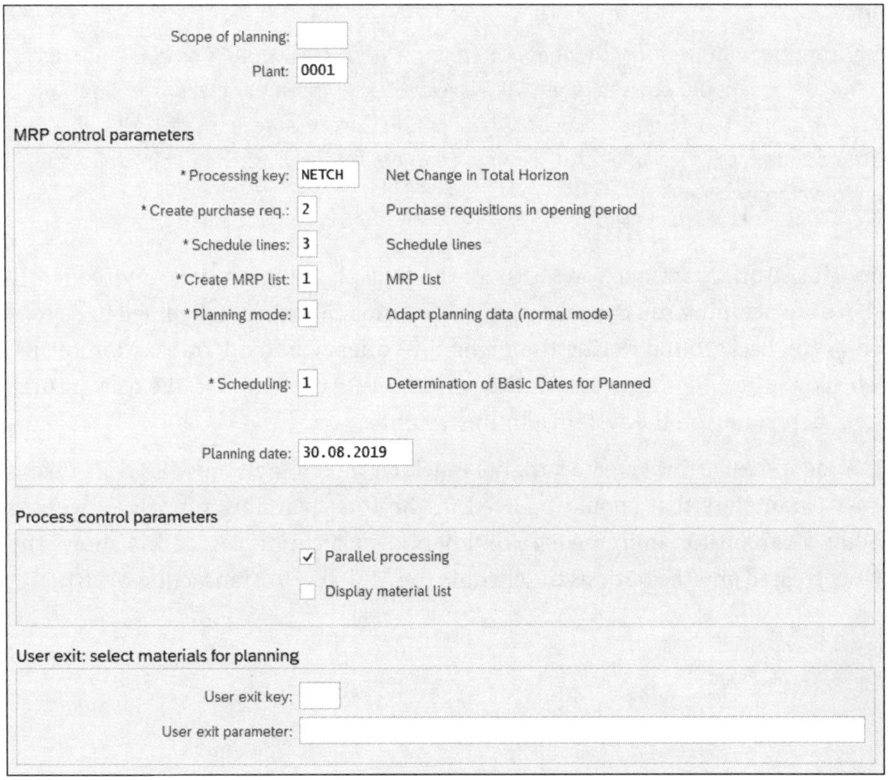

Figure 5.13 Total Planning Run in Transaction MD01

A total planning run would generally select for planning all the materials under a plant or the selected scope of planning, depending on the planning file entries. However, there are situations in which we want to restrict the planning for a selected group of materials—for example, for a specific MRP controller or for a specific MRP group. It is not possible in the standard classic MRP to select a small set of materials for planning, but SAP offers a user exit through which we can implement our own logic to select the materials to be planned on a total planning run. The **User Exit Key** and **User Exit Parameter** fields are used in this case to determine which logic will be used, and the input parameters for the custom code are implemented in this exit.

Before we can start using those fields, we need to create the user exit key in customizing Transaction OMIX and create our own implementation of enhancement M61X0001.

> **Tip**
>
> There are two different components of enhancement M61X0001. Component `EXIT_SAPMM61X_001` should be used when MRP is executed without parallel processing, and `EXIT_SAPLM61C_001` should be used when parallel processing is used. SAP delivers sample code for `EXIT_SAPMM61X_001`, which can be used as a starting point for a custom development.

Although SAP offers Transaction MD01 for the total planning run, it is not frequently used. A total planning run can take a long time, and it is usually scheduled to be executed in the background during the night. SAP offers standard Transaction MDBT, which allows the end user to schedule a periodic MRP execution in the background, without depending on the system administrator.

In Transaction MDBT, we create variants in which we enter all the MRP control and process parameters that should be used in the total planning run. Later, we will schedule a variant for an immediate or a periodic execution. Figure 5.14 shows the variants created and the options to schedule the MRP run in Transaction MDBT.

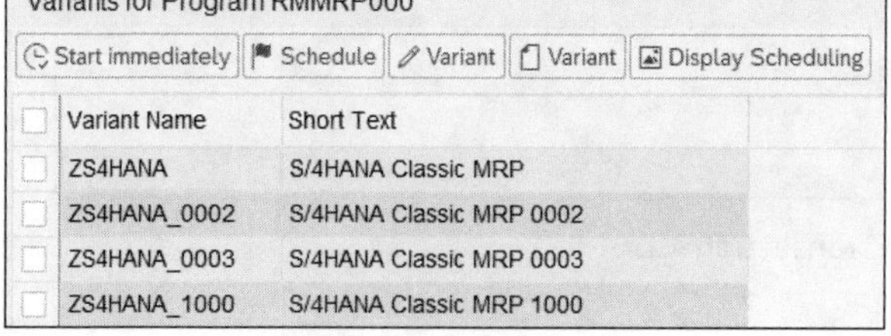

Variants for Program RMMRP000	
ⓒ Start immediately | ▶ Schedule | ✎ Variant | ⬜ Variant | ▣ Display Scheduling	
Variant Name	Short Text
ZS4HANA	S/4HANA Classic MRP
ZS4HANA_0002	S/4HANA Classic MRP 0002
ZS4HANA_0003	S/4HANA Classic MRP 0003
ZS4HANA_1000	S/4HANA Classic MRP 1000

Figure 5.14 Variants for the Total Planning Run

Alternatively, we can schedule a periodic MRP execution with the manual creation of a background job for program RMMRP000 in Transaction SM36. This transaction is often used when we need to run additional programs before or after MRP—such as the conversion of planned orders or purchase requisitions, for example.

> **Tip**
> Transaction SM37 shows the background jobs currently scheduled and already finished. We can check the status of the MRP planning run and the MRP statistics in this transaction.

5.2.7 Master Production Scheduling

Recall from Chapters 2 and 3 that there are different MRP types. Some MRP types have a special MRP procedure called *master production scheduling* (MPS); materials that use this kind of MRP type are planned separately in a different set of transactions.

Although they are different sets of transactions, the concept behind the MPS transactions and their design is very similar to the MRP transactions. For each MRP transaction, we have an equivalent MPS transaction. We have the following transactions for the MPS execution:

- Single-item/single-level can be executed with Transaction MD42.
- Single-item/multilevel can be executed with Transaction MD41.
- The total planning run is triggered with Transaction MD40 or scheduled for a background execution in Transaction MDBS or with program RMMPS000.

For most of these transactions, we will have exactly the same MRP control parameters and process control parameters that we find in the respective MRP transactions (such as Transactions M03, MD02, and MD01). The only exception is the total planning run, where we can find an additional parameter called **Process MRP Materials** in the MPS transactions, as shown in Figure 5.15. When this flag is checked, the MPS planning run will process not only materials with an MPS MRP type, but also materials using MRP.

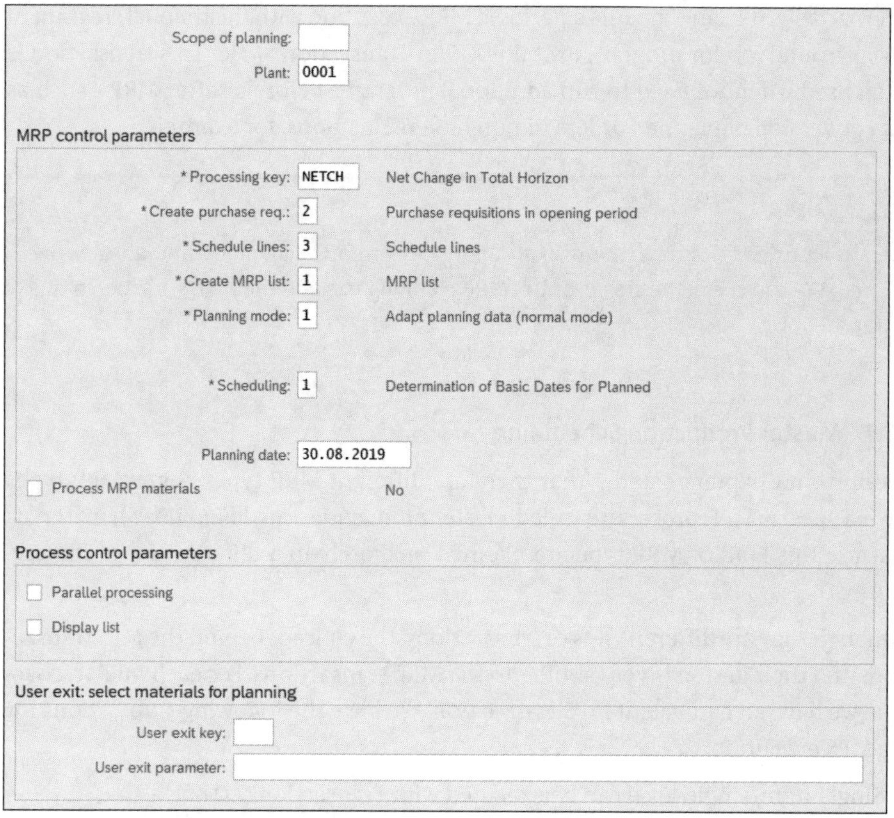

5 Running MRP

Scope of planning:	
Plant:	0001

MRP control parameters

* Processing key:	NETCH	Net Change in Total Horizon
* Create purchase req.:	2	Purchase requisitions in opening period
* Schedule lines:	3	Schedule lines
* Create MRP list:	1	MRP list
* Planning mode:	1	Adapt planning data (normal mode)
* Scheduling:	1	Determination of Basic Dates for Planned
Planning date:	30.08.2019	
☐ Process MRP materials		No

Process control parameters

☐ Parallel processing
☐ Display list

User exit: select materials for planning

User exit key:	
User exit parameter:	

Figure 5.15 MPS Total Planning Run

We should consider, however, that the idea behind using MPS is to have a separate planning run for the most important materials so that we can evaluate the MPS results or even run capacity leveling before MRP. Therefore, it is usually not recommended to run MPS on a daily basis if you are also including MRP materials.

In this chapter, we have discussed the options available in SAP S/4HANA to run classic MRP, which is still available as part of SAP S/4HANA. However, SAP considers classic MRP to be no longer strategic; it is part of the SAP S/4HANA Compatibility Pack. If we are migrating from SAP ERP to SAP S/4HANA, we can keep using classic MRP for some time, in order to accelerate adoption and reduce migration costs. In the long term and for a new SAP S/4HANA implementation, however, we should consider MRP Live as the go-to solution for materials planning. Let's examine MRP Live operations now.

5.3 MRP Live

As discussed earlier, MRP Live offers several benefits, such as performance improvements when planning large sets of materials, a new transaction with flexible selection criteria, and the possibility to also plan PP/DS advanced planning materials.

In this section, we will explore the options available for the MRP Live execution both in SAP GUI and in SAP Fiori, and we will examine the changes in the control parameters implemented in MRP Live. We will start by talking about the MRP dispatcher, which determines how each material will be planned during the MRP Live execution.

5.3.1 MRP Dispatcher

With MRP Live, most of the MRP logic that was previously executed in ABAP was translated into SAP HANA stored procedures to take advantage of the SAP HANA internal parallelization and allow MRP to plan several materials at the same time. However, there still some restrictions or material master settings that will require a material to be planned in ABAP. For example, materials using a forecast will still have to be planned in ABAP, with the classic MRP logic.

But we do not need to plan a separate planning run for those materials when we are using MRP Live. The MRP dispatcher is nothing but logic introduced in MRP Live that will automatically identify those restrictions and trigger the planning run in ABAP for the affected materials. The MRP results should still be the same; in fact, the end user generally will not notice any difference between a material that was planned in SAP HANA and a material that was planned in ABAP. The MRP dispatcher is basically logic executed within the MRP Live planning run, so we do not need to take any action related to the dispatcher.

There are also some situations where we might want to force a specific material to be planned in ABAP—for example, if an ABAP-based BAdI should be executed for this material. In this case, we can run Transaction MD_FORCE_MRP_CLASSIC to force a specific material to always be planned in ABAP.

The MRP dispatcher is also responsible for identifying if a material is using PP/DS advanced planning and will trigger the planning run with the heuristic defined in the material master, instead of using the MRP logic for planning. Figure 5.16 illustrates the logic behind the MRP dispatcher, where we can see that for each low-level code, it will select which materials can be planned in SAP HANA, which materials should be planned in ABAP because of a restriction, and which materials have the **Advanced Planning** flag checked and should be planned with a PP/DS heuristic.

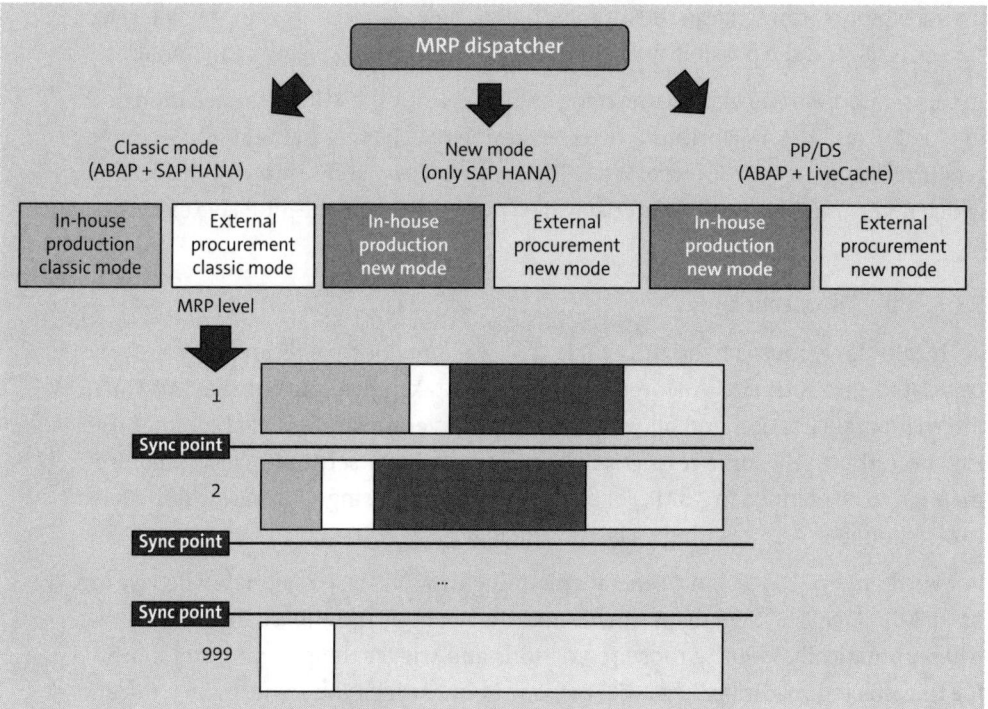

Figure 5.16 MRP Dispatcher

5.3.2 MRP Live Control Parameters

When SAP S/4HANA was introduced, the idea was to simplify transactions and business process, and MRP Live was created based on this premise. Therefore, all the settings and control parameters that would add an extra level of complexity without a clear gain for the business were simplified.

In classic MRP we can choose, for example, to create planned orders or purchase requisitions for externally procured materials. If planned orders are created for externally procured materials, we first need to convert those orders to purchase requisitions and later convert the purchase requisitions to purchase orders. This means that there are two levels of conversion, without a clear business advantage to justify it.

Therefore, this logic was simplified in MRP Live, and purchase requisitions will be directly created for materials procured externally. With this new logic, the creation indicator for purchase requisitions is no longer needed in MRP Live; notice its absence from Figure 5.17. The same logic was applied for the creation indicator for schedule lines; now MRP Live will create schedule lines by default whenever a scheduling agreement is found as a valid source of supply.

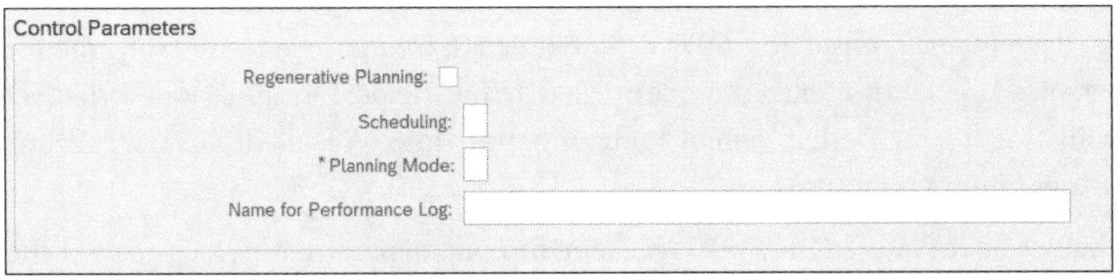

Control Parameters	
Regenerative Planning:	☐
Scheduling:	
*Planning Mode:	
Name for Performance Log:	

Figure 5.17 MRP Live Control Parameters

Remember that MRP Live will no longer generate MRP Lists; because the performance improvements in MRP will allow for more frequent MRP executions, we no longer have to evaluate the MRP results based on past and outdated data. Therefore, we do not have a creation indicator for MRP Lists in the MRP Live transaction.

While classic MRP offers the processing key, through which we can select the materials to be included in the planning run, this option was simplified in MRP Live. By default, MRP Live will execute a net change planning run, selecting for planning all those materials for which the planning file entry is marked, according to the selection criteria. If we want to force all the materials to be selected for planning, despite the planning file entry, we need to check the **Regenerative Planning** flag in Transaction MD01N.

The **Scheduling** indicator is similar to classic MRP, where we can control if basic dates scheduling or lead-time scheduling will be carried out for planned orders procured internally.

The **Planning Mode** setting in MRP Live, however, only allows planning mode **1—Adapt Planning Data** or planning mode **3—Delete and Recreate Planning Data**. In addition, if we are using planning mode 1 with MRP Live, existing replenishment proposals will be only reused if there are no changes. For any change in the quantity or dates, an existing (and unfirmed) planned order or purchase requisition will be deleted and recreated. This change in the planning mode design was introduced because it is faster in SAP HANA to delete and recreate a planned order than to update an existing planned order.

> **Tip**
>
> If we want to influence the reusability of replenishment proposals with planning mode 1, we can create a custom implementation of the PPH_MRP_REUSE_BADI AMDP BAdI.

During the MRP Live execution, a performance log will be generated, which can be later analyzed with Transaction MD_MRP_PERFLOG. Using the additional **Name for Performance Log** parameter, we can define a title for the performance log so that we can easily find it later, perhaps when analyzing those logs. We will discuss the performance logs later in Chapter 13.

Now that we have covered the MRP Live–specific control parameters, let's go over the options available to run MRP Live in SAP GUI and in the SAP Fiori launchpad.

5.3.3 Running MRP Live in SAP GUI

Whereas there were many different transactions available to run classic MRP, a single transaction runs MRP Live in SAP S/4HANA. However, the new transaction, Transaction MD01N, provides many more options and additional selection criteria, so we actually have more flexibility to choose which materials will be planned with MRP Live.

As shown in Figure 5.18, the **Planning Scope** section in Transaction MD01N brings several additional fields that will allow us to define exactly which materials will be planned. For example, in MRP Live we can select for planning multiple plants, materials, product groups, or MRP controllers—all in the same transaction.

Similarly, MRP Live does not need to process MRP and MPS materials in different transactions because Transaction MD01N is capable of planning both MRP and MPS materials. We can use the **Material Scope** field to choose whether we want to plan all the materials, only MRP materials, or only MPS materials.

> **Note**
>
> A scope of planning is not required in MRP Live because we can manually select all the plants to be planned. If we are working with MRP areas, MRP Live will always plan all the existing MRP areas for the materials included in the planning scope.

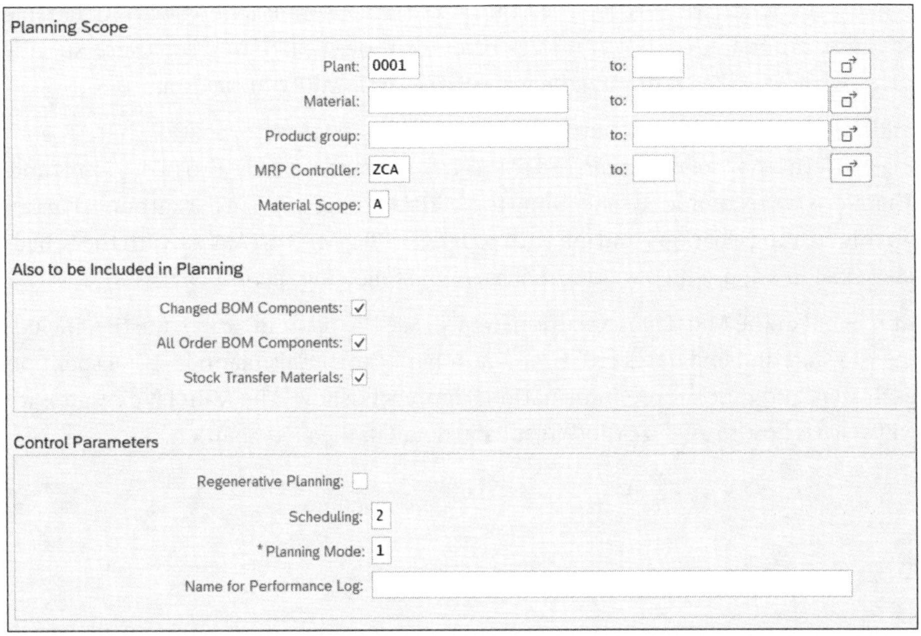

Figure 5.18 Selection Screen in Transaction MD01N

We can use a few additional parameters to include the components of the selected materials in the planning run. If the **Changed BOM Components** flag is marked, then all the components for which a dependent requirement was created or changed will be included in the planning run. If we check the **All Order BOM Components** flag, then even components that were not changed will be included in the planning run. We can use those flags to simulate Transaction MD02 and run a multilevel planning run, with the advantage that we can do it for multiple items.

The **Stock Transfer Materials** flag is used to define if materials with stock transfers being generated by MRP will also be planned in the supplying plant. If this flag is checked, then those materials will be planned in the supplying plant, even if the plant is not included in the planning scope.

> **Tip**
> While Transaction MD01N brings additional fields for selection in the planning scope, we might still want to include more fields in the selection screen. For this purpose, we can create a custom implementation of the MRP_DISPATCHER_BADI BAdI, which allows the extension of the selection screen in Transaction MD01N.

5 Running MRP

While Transaction MD01N replaced most classic MRP transactions with its flexible selection criteria, it cannot run sales order or project planning. For those specific cases, we need to keep running the respective classic MRP transactions.

MRP Live execution is generally much faster than classic MRP execution, but depending on the number of materials and plants to be planned, it may also take a long time. Therefore, we recommend scheduling the MRP Live execution in background. We can do this creating a background job with program PPH_MRP_START or with the Schedule MRP Runs app, which we will analyze in the following section.

At the end of the MRP Live execution, we will see the planning run statistics, including the start and end dates and times, number of materials planned, time spent on each step, and much more information. Figure 5.19 shows the MRP Live results; we will discuss how to analyze those results in detail in the next chapter.

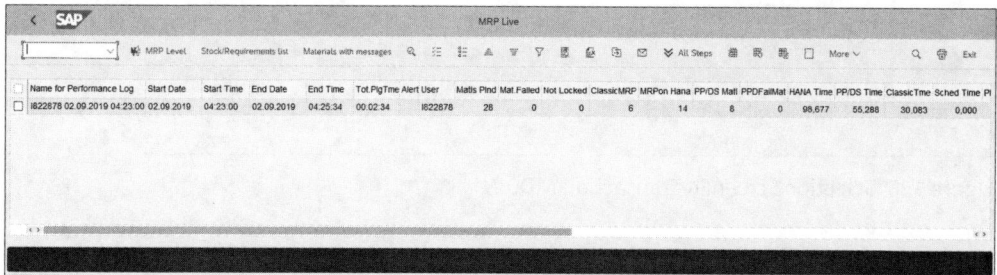

Figure 5.19 MRP Live Results

5.3.4 SAP Fiori

One significant benefit of implementing SAP S/4HANA is the availability of its new SAP Fiori user interface, which offers additional options to run MRP with SAP Fiori. In the SAP Fiori launchpad, we can schedule the MRP Live planning run and can control the previous planning runs using the Schedule MRP Runs app, shown in Figure 5.20.

Figure 5.20 The Schedule MRP Runs App Tile

When we first enter this application, we will see a list of the scheduled, finished, or failed MRP Live runs. By clicking the arrow in the last column (see Figure 5.21), we can see the details of the job variant, including the MRP control parameters and selection criteria.

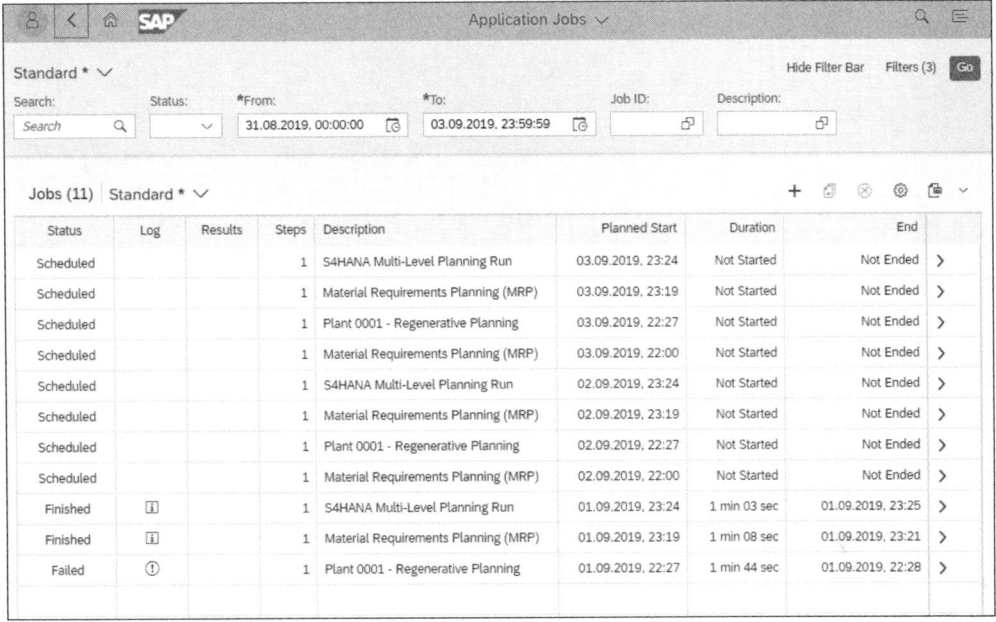

Figure 5.21 List of MRP Live Jobs Scheduled, Finished, and Failed

In the upper-right corner, a menu bar contains buttons to schedule a new MRP Live execution, copy an existing schedule, or cancel an execution that is still in process.

For the finished and failed MRP Live executions, we will see green and red icons, respectively, in the **Log** column. Clicking one will open the detailed log of the MRP Live execution, as shown in Figure 5.22. This screen shows the message type, description, and time stamp of each execution.

To schedule a new MRP Live execution, we need to click the icon with the plus sign at the upper-right corner of the initial screen, shown in Figure 5.21. We also have the option to create a new job by copying an existing one and using the same control parameters and selection criteria.

5   Running MRP

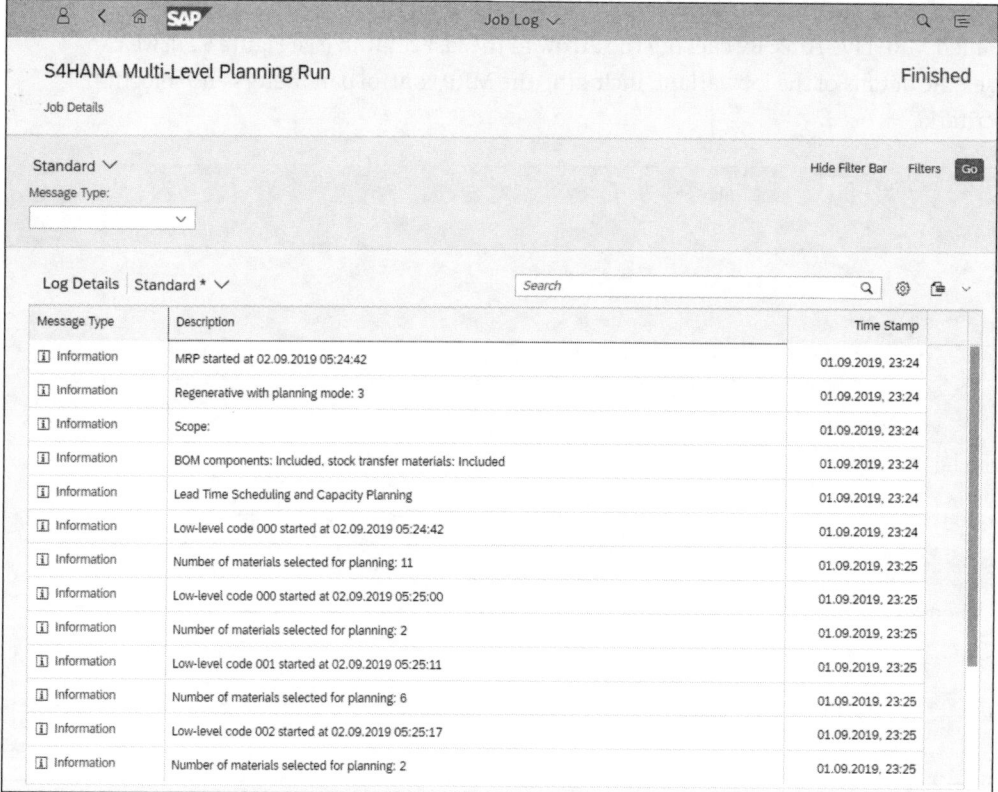

Figure 5.22 MRP Live Job Log

> **Tip**
>
> We can create job templates that will help us when we need to schedule many different MRP runs by clicking the **Template** button in the lower-right corner (see Figure 5.23). For example, if we want to schedule separate planning runs for the different plants under the same company, we can create a job template with the default control parameters and just change the plant when creating the job.

5.3 MRP Live

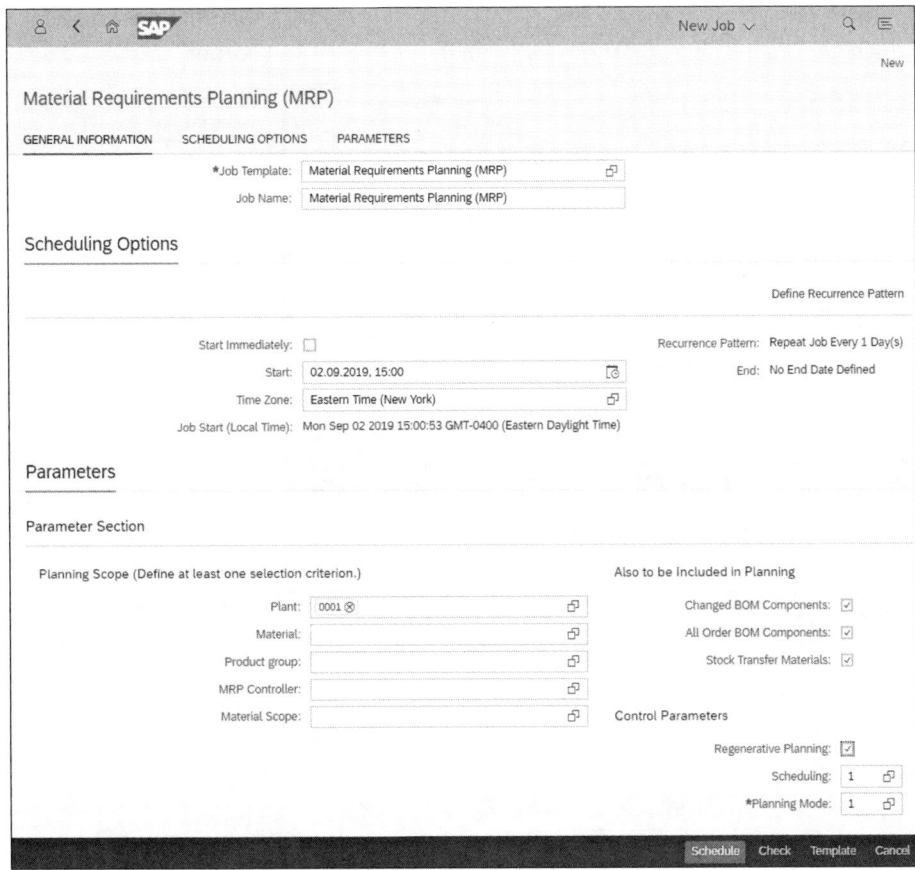

Figure 5.23 Scheduling a New MRP Run

When creating a new job with this SAP Fiori application, the selection fields and the control parameters available are the same as those available in the SAP GUI transaction, Transaction MD01N. We can check the **Start Immediately** flag to trigger the MRP run immediately or choose a date and time to schedule the execution in the future. In the Schedule MRP Runs app, we can also schedule a periodic background execution by selecting the **Define Recurrence Pattern** option and choosing the recurrence of the MRP periodic execution in the pop-up, as shown in Figure 5.24.

The Schedule MRP Runs app is not the only option available to trigger the MRP run from the SAP Fiori launchpad. In the SAP Fiori applications of the MRP Cockpit, we can immediately trigger the MRP run for the material being processed by selecting the **Start MRP Run** button. Figure 5.25 shows the Manage Material Coverage app, which offers a button to start the MRP run in the lower-right corner.

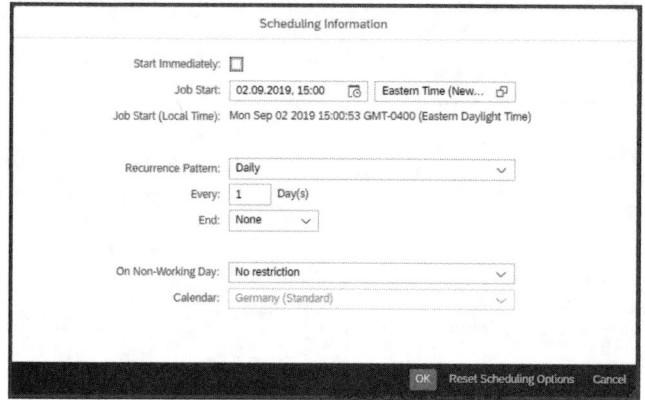

Figure 5.24 MRP Recurrence Pattern

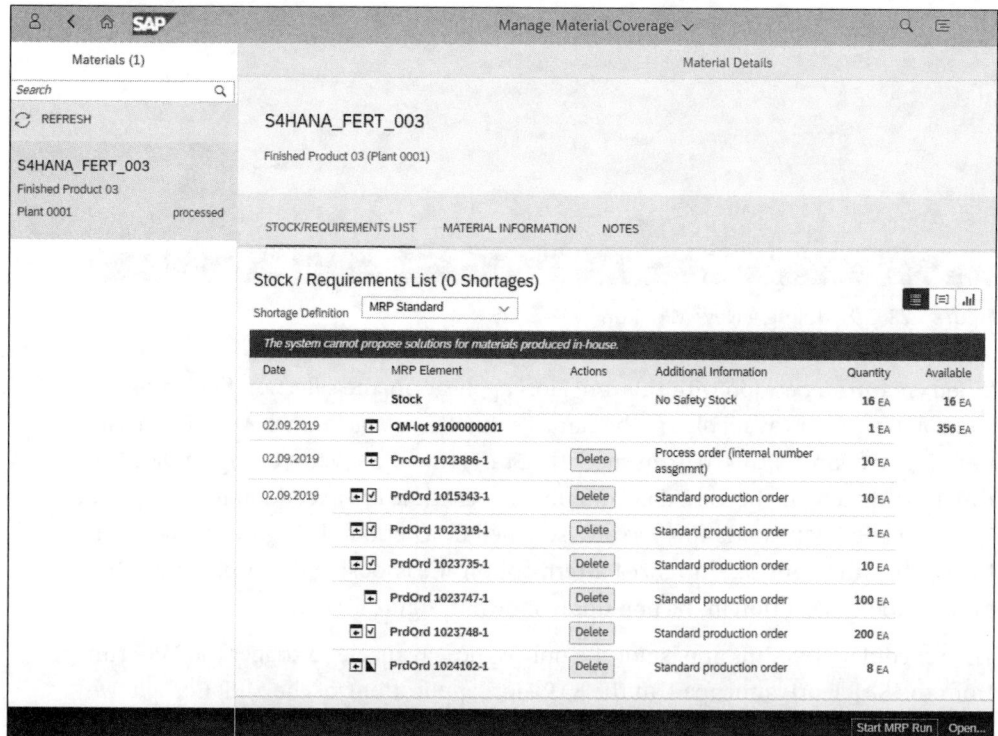

Figure 5.25 Starting the MRP Run from the Manage Material Coverage App

When we trigger the MRP run from an MRP Cockpit application, single-item/single-level planning will be executed. The following MRP control parameters will be hard-coded on this planning run:

- **MRP Regenerative Planning**: Unchecked
- **Include BOM Components in Planning**: Unchecked
- **Include Stock Transfer Materials in Planning**: Unchecked
- **Planning mode**: 1 (Adapt Planning Data)
- **Material Scope for MRP**: A (All)
- **Date for Planning**: Current date
- **Scheduling of Planned Orders**: 1 (Determination of Basic Dates)

SAP provides SAP Note 2482315 (Parameters of the MRP Run when Called from the MRP Apps) with a modification that can be implemented, allowing us to choose different parameters for the planning run.

5.4 Planning PP/DS Materials in MRP Live (One MRP Run)

While MRP is capable of planning the most common scenarios, some companies may require advanced planning scenarios, such as taking the batch shelf life into consideration during the planning run or considering capacity restrictions during the materials planning run.

Those features were not available in SAP ERP because these complex algorithms would consume a lot of the system resources, such as database and CPU. Instead, we could find those features and much more in another system called SAP Advanced Planning and Optimization (SAP APO), which ran on a special database called LiveCache that was developed especially to support the processing of these complex algorithms. Companies using SAP APO would run a separate planning run in a tool called Production Planning and Detailed Scheduling (PP/DS), and the results would be integrated into SAP ERP.

Now, SAP S/4HANA runs on top of the SAP HANA database, which is very powerful and can support the kind of complex planning algorithms previously executed by PP/DS in SAP APO. Therefore, SAP took the opportunity to redesign this architecture. As of SAP S/4HANA 1610, LiveCache was moved into the SAP HANA database and PP/DS was brought into the SAP S/4HANA core, bringing advanced planning features not supported by MRP to the new suite.

> **Note**
>
> Although SAP APO can still be used and integrated with SAP S/4HANA, SAP plans to discontinue it in the future. While PP/DS was brought into the SAP S/4HANA core, additional SAP APO features (e.g., those for demand planning) were moved into a cloud solution called SAP IBP, as mentioned in Chapter 1.

Although PP/DS is a separate feature that requires special configuration and master data, we can plan both MRP and PP/DS advanced planning materials in the MRP Live transaction (Transaction MD01N) or in the Schedule MRP Runs app. Because we do not need to synchronize different background jobs for materials planning using MRP and PP/DS, administration is simpler.

PP/DS materials will be planned in MRP Live with the default heuristic and planning parameters defined in the **Advanced Planning** tab of the material master. We should always use an MRP type with procedure X, such as the standard MRP type X0.

For consistent MRP results, we need to ensure that whenever a semifinished product is planned with advanced planning, the parent should also be planned with PP/DS advanced planning. This is necessary because PP/DS uses the LiveCache database, and we need to ensure that all the dependent requirements are within LiveCache.

Figure 5.26 shows the supported product structures for planning PP/DS advanced planning materials in MRP Live. Besides the scenario in which a semifinished material and its parent are planned with advanced planning, we can also see a material planned with MRP under a parent planned with advanced planning and a structure in which all the materials are planned with MRP only.

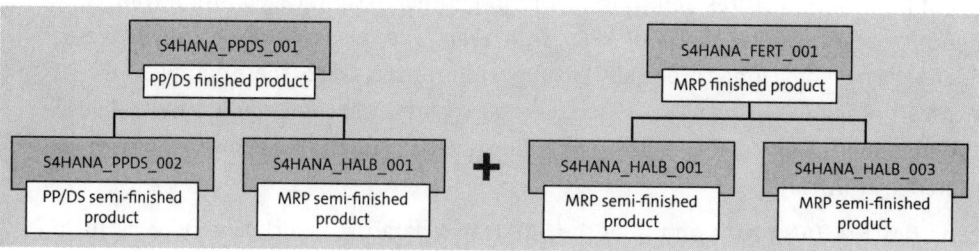

Figure 5.26 Supported Product Structures when Planning PP/DS Materials in MRP Live

5.5 Summary

> **Tip**
>
> There is no option in the standard system to plan only the PP/DS materials or to exclude the PP/DS materials from the planning run. However, we can create an implementation of the MRP_DISPATCHER_BADI BAdI to bring additional selection fields into the MRP Live selection screen. We can add, for example, the MRP type as a selection criterion and filter for materials with MRP type X0.

During the planning run, for each low-level code, PP/DS materials will be planned first, followed by materials planned with MRP Live on SAP HANA, followed by classic MRP materials. Figure 5.27 shows the MRP Live planning run log, which lists the different steps of the planning run, including the advanced planning steps.

MRP Live Performance Log per Low-Level Code for I822878 02.09.2019 21:

Cde Step	Matl f.Plg	Matls Plnd	Mat Failed	Start Date	Start Time	Elapsed	ConsTime	Time Mast.	Time Docs	Time Calc.	Time Upd.	Time PRUpd	Time PLAF	Time PLAFd	Time SchdL	Time Q.Qty
000 Advanced Plng	5	5	0		00:00:00	00:00:00	22.374	0,000	0,000	0,000	0,000	0,000	0,000	0,000	0,000	0,000
000 Preparation	0	0	0	02.09.2019	21:57:46	00:00:03	3,000	0,000	0,000	0,000	0,000	0,000	0,000	0,000	0,000	0,000
000 MRP Live on HANA	5	5	0	02.09.2019	21:57:46	00:00:28	29.164	0,716	2,353	18,761	3,204	0,918	1,414	0,161	0,354	0,005
000 Classic MRP	4	4	0	02.09.2019	21:58:06	00:00:07	7,330	0,000	1,123	5.228	0,557	0,000	0,000	0,000	0,000	0,000
001 Advanced Plng	2	2	0		00:00:00	00:00:00	9.505	0,000	0,000	0,000	0,000	0,000	0,000	0,000	0,000	0,000
001 MRP Live on HANA	2	2	0	02.09.2019	21:58:24	00:00:11	11,782	0,338	1,240	7,482	0,616	0,153	0,204	0,075	0,090	0,002
001 Preparation	0	0	0	02.09.2019	21:58:24	00:00:00	0,000	0,000	0,000	0,000	0,000	0,000	0,000	0,000	0,000	0,000
002 Advanced Plng	2	2	0		00:00:00	00:00:00	6,139	0,000	0,000	0,000	0,000	0,000	0,000	0,000	0,000	0,000
002 Preparation	0	0	0	02.09.2019	21:58:34	00:00:01	1,000	0,000	0,000	0,000	0,000	0,000	0,000	0,000	0,000	0,000
002 MRP Live on HANA	1	1	0	02.09.2019	21:58:35	00:00:06	6,174	0,314	1,119	2,814	0,325	0,091	0,051	0,049	0,063	0,002
003 MRP Live on HANA	4	4	0	02.09.2019	21:58:41	00:00:20	20.616	0,335	1,173	14,023	1,906	1,411	0,062	0,076	0,109	0,003
003 Preparation	0	0	0	02.09.2019	21:58:41	00:00:00	0,000	0,000	0,000	0,000	0,000	0,000	0,000	0,000	0,000	0,000
003 Postprocessing	0	0	0	02.09.2019	21:59:00	00:00:01	1,052	0,000	0,000	0,000	0,000	0,000	0,000	0,000	0,000	0,000
003 Classic MRP	2	2	0	02.09.2019	21:59:01	00:00:04	4,159	0,000	2,723	0,710	0,544	0,000	0,000	0,000	0,000	0,000
999 MRP Live on HANA	2	2	0	02.09.2019	21:59:04	00:00:11	11,665	0,336	1,370	7,105	0,458	0,129	0,061	0,071	0,095	0,002
999 Preparation	0	0	0	02.09.2019	21:59:04	00:00:00	0,000	0,000	0,000	0,000	0,000	0,000	0,000	0,000	0,000	0,000

Figure 5.27 MRP Live Performance Log per Low-Level Code

5.5 Summary

In this chapter on the execution of MRP in SAP S/4HANA, we began by examining the major differences between MRP Live and classic MRP and discussed when to use each one. We then reviewed the different transactions and SAP Fiori applications that we can use to trigger the classic MRP and the MRP Live planning runs.

Remember that because classic MRP has been defined by SAP as nonstrategic and part of the SAP S/4HANA Compatibility Pack scope, MRP Live will be the focal point for future innovations. You can consider classic MRP for a transition period, but in the long term, we recommend that you use MRP Live as the main tool for materials planning.

In the following chapter, we will discuss how to evaluate the MRP results using both the SAP GUI transactions and the new SAP Fiori applications of the MRP Cockpit available in SAP S/4HANA.

Chapter 6
Evaluating the MRP Results

After the MRP execution, the MRP results should be evaluated. This chapter explains how to evaluate the MRP results using both SAP GUI and the SAP Fiori applications of the MRP Cockpit in SAP S/4HANA.

We discussed in the previous chapter how to trigger the MRP planning run in different transactions and in the SAP Fiori launchpad, and how to generate replenishment proposals to cover any existing material shortage. But because MRP is a computer program, it has some limitations, and we should not simply adopt the MRP results. Some situations and conflicts simply cannot be resolved by an algorithm and require human intervention. Therefore, MRP results should be carefully evaluated by the MRP controller to resolve conflicts and exceptional situations.

In this chapter, we will go through the MRP transactions and SAP Fiori applications for evaluating MRP results. But before we can start analyzing the MRP evaluation transactions, we need to discuss the concept of MRP exception messages and their influence on the MRP results evaluation—so we will do so in Section 6.1. In Section 6.2 through Section 6.8, we will cover the evaluation transactions in the SAP GUI (such as the Stock/Requirements List and the order report), and Section 6.9 will cover the SAP Fiori applications of the MRP Cockpit. Most of the transactions and applications covered here can be used with both classic MRP and MRP Live, but we will discuss the exceptions throughout the chapter.

6.1 Exception Messages

In the previous chapters, we have shown many screenshots from the Stock/Requirements List, and we have discussed the MRP results several times. However, we intentionally avoided covering the exception messages that are generated during the MRP run until now.

6   Evaluating the MRP Results

When MRP is executed, it will try to generate replenishment proposals to cover existing material shortages. In some situations, there might be a conflict or an error that will not allow MRP to generate the ideal replenishment proposal or a situation in which MRP needs to bring attention to a specific replenishment proposal. Whenever this kind of situation arises, MRP will generate an *exception message*, which can be viewed in the MRP evaluation transactions. Figure 6.1 shows the column for exception messages in the Stock/Requirements List.

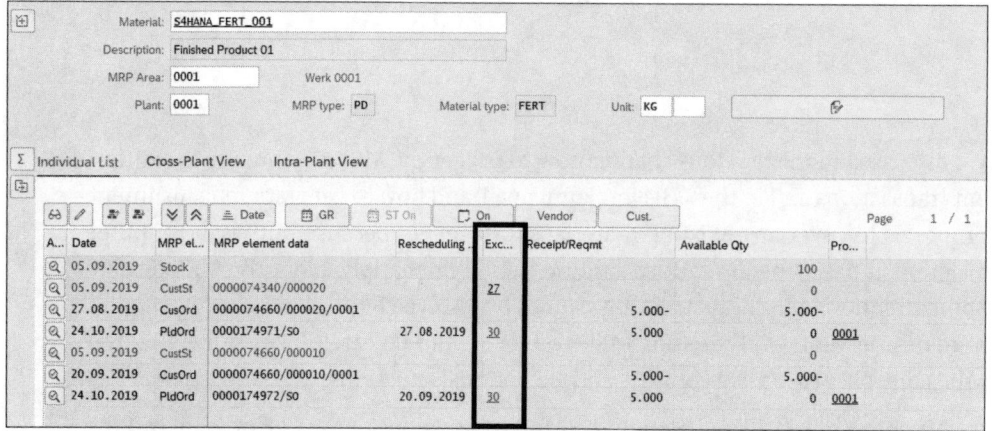

Figure 6.1 Exception Messages in the Stock/Requirements List

The different exception messages are distributed among selection groups, as indicated in Table 6.1.

Selection Group	Exception Message Number	Exception Message
1: New; opening date in the past	69	Recursive BOM components possible
	02	New, and opening date in the past
	05	Opening date in the past
2: New; start date in the past	03	New, and start date in the past

Table 6.1 Exception Messages in Selection Groups

Selection Group	Exception Message Number	Exception Message
	06	Start date in the past
	63	Production start date before order start
3: New; finish date in the past	04	New, and finish date in the past
	07	Finish date in the past
	64	Production finish after order finish
4: General messages	01	Newly created order proposal
	42	Order proposal has been changed
	44	Order proposal re-exploded
	46	Order proposal has been manually changed
	61	Scheduling: Customizing inconsistent
	62	Scheduling: Master data inconsistent
	80	Reference to retail promotion
	82	Item is blocked
5: Exception during BOM explosion	50	No BOM exists
	52	No BOM selected
	53	No BOM explosion due to missing config.
	55	Phantom assembly not exploded

Table 6.1 Exception Messages in Selection Groups (Cont.)

Selection Group	Exception Message Number	Exception Message
6: Exception during availability check	25	Excess stock
	26	Excess in individual segment
	27	Excess stock applied to superseding material
	27	Underdelivery intolerance
	40	Coverage not provided by master plan
	56	Shortage in the planning time fence
	57	Discontinued material partly replaced by follow-up
	58	Uncovered requirement after effective-out date
	59	Receipt after effective-out date
	60	Discontinued receipt applied to superseding material
	70	Max. release quantity quota exceeded
	96	Stock fallen below safety stock level
7: Exception during rescheduling	10	Reschedule in
	15	Reschedule out
	20	Cancel process
	30	Plan process according to schedule
8: Terminations	98	Abnormal end of materials planning

Table 6.1 Exception Messages in Selection Groups (Cont.)

We cannot create new selection groups because the MRP evaluation transactions are designed to show exactly eight groups—but we can change the description of each group in the customizing Transaction OMOL. Only exception group 8 cannot be changed: it is used for critical exception messages, which lead to termination of the MRP run.

Besides the selection groups, there are Customizing settings for each specific exception message in Transaction OMD3, as shown in Figure 6.2. If we click the **Information** icon close to the exception message key, we can find more information about each exception message and learn why it is triggered.

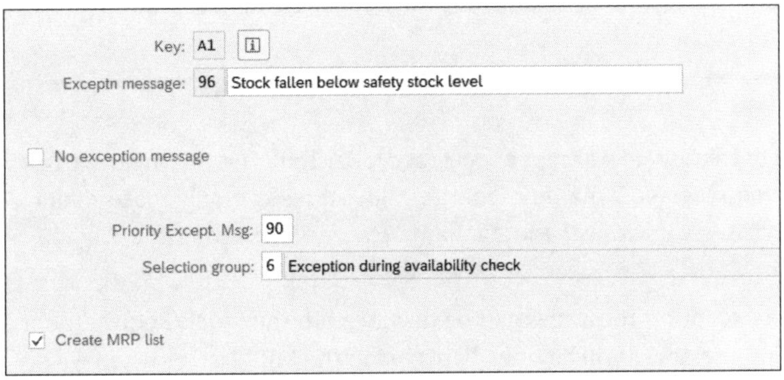

Figure 6.2 Exception Message Customizing

In Customizing, we can change an exception message long text or completely avoid having the exception message displayed by marking the **No Exception Message** checkbox. Most companies, however, will use the standard exception messages delivered by SAP. By default, MRP evaluations will only show one exception message per MRP element, as shown in Figure 6.1. If more than one exception message is triggered for an MRP element, then the exception with the highest priority will be displayed. We can define this priority in the **Priority Exception Message** field. We can find additional exception messages for an MRP element in the **Additional Data for MRP Element** pop-up shown in Figure 6.3.

We can also assign an exception message to a different group by changing the value in the **Selection Group** field, but we need to choose one of the existing groups because it is not possible to create new groups in Customizing.

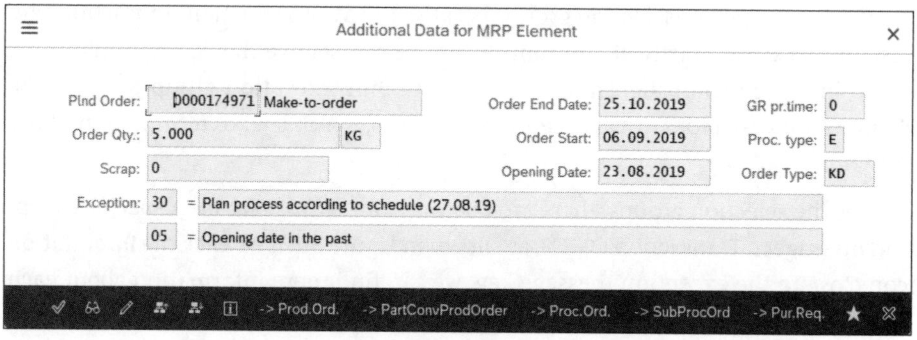

6 Evaluating the MRP Results

Figure 6.3 Exception Messages in the Additional Data for MRP Element Pop-up

> **Note**
>
> It is not possible to create a new exception message in Customizing. The logic to trigger each exception message is hard-coded into MRP, so we can only make minor changes. In most cases, we will keep the standard-delivered SAP settings.

While most of the exception messages can be displayed in the Stock/Requirements List, a few exception messages will be only displayed in the MRP List, or when we display the MRP results in the single-item planning transactions, for example. That is mostly because some exception messages can only be triggered during the actual MRP run, and the Stock/Requirements List will show the exceptions when reading the planning elements from the database.

The best example is exception message **01—Newly Created Order Proposal**, which can only be triggered during the actual MRP run. We cannot, therefore, compare the exception messages between the Stock/Requirements List and the MRP List and expect to see the same results.

For more information about exception messages, refer to SAP Note 550441 (FAQ: Exception Messages in Material Requirements Planning).

6.2 Rescheduling Checks

Exception messages from selection group 7 are triggered during a specific step of the MRP run called the *rescheduling check*. To evaluate the MRP results, we need to understand what the rescheduling check is and how it can affect the MRP results.

6.2 Rescheduling Checks

We noted earlier that different replenishment elements can be considered during the MRP run and that those MRP elements can be firmed or unfirmed. *Firmed planning elements* include production orders, purchase orders, or planned orders, as well as purchase requisitions with the firming indicator. *Unfirmed planning elements* include planned orders, purchase requisitions, or scheduling lines, as long as the firming indicator is not set (or they are not within the firm horizon).

Whenever MRP finds a shortage and there is an unfirmed planning element in the future, it can simply delete or change this planning element, in order to cover the shortage in the correct date. If the planning element in the future is firmed, however, then MRP cannot change it to cover the shortage. This is where the rescheduling check comes into the picture.

As shown in Chapter 4, we can define a rescheduling horizon and select which MRP elements will be considered during the rescheduling check. Whenever a shortage is identified, there are two possibilities:

- A firm receipt element is found within the rescheduling horizon. MRP will not create a new replenishment proposal; it will trigger exception message **10 — Reschedule In** and propose a rescheduling date to match the shortage date.
- A firm receipt element cannot be found within the rescheduling horizon. In this case, a new replenishment element is created to cover the shortage.

Figure 6.4 illustrates the first scenario, wherein a firm receipt element is found within the rescheduling horizon. For a shortage on 09.09.2019, MRP found a production order within the rescheduling horizon and triggered exception message 10, suggesting that the planner reprogram this order to cover the shortage.

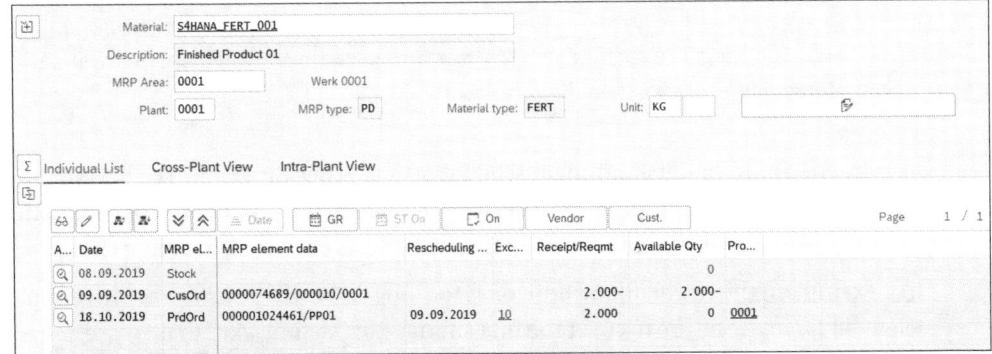

Figure 6.4 Firm Receipt Element within the Rescheduling Horizon

On the other hand, Figure 6.5 shows an example wherein the existing firm receipt element date had been changed and is now outside the rescheduling horizon. In this case, MRP created a new replenishment element to cover the shortage, and because the firm receipt element was not required to cover any shortage, MRP triggered exception message **20—Cancel Process**, suggesting that the planner cancel this irrelevant replenishment proposal.

During the MRP run, the rescheduling check is executed before the actual materials planning; this way, MRP can avoid creating additional replenishment proposals when a firm receipt element already exists. The rescheduling check is carried out for the entire time axis, but the rescheduling horizon will be counted from each shortage date.

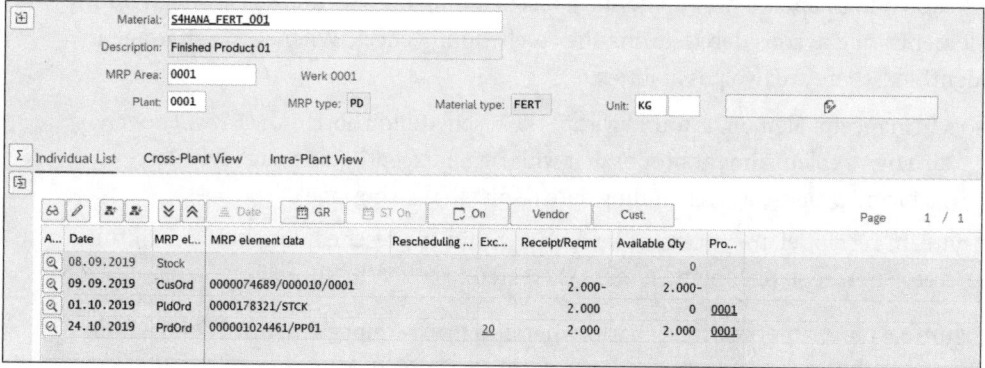

Figure 6.5 Firm Receipt Element outside the Rescheduling Horizon

> **Note**
>
> In the customizing Transaction OMDW, we can select which firm elements will be considered during the rescheduling check.

It is important to understand the rescheduling logic check in detail, so that we can interpret the MRP results properly. Users will very frequently describe problems with the MRP results that are nothing more than the effects of the rescheduling check.

For example, if the rescheduling horizon is too long, MRP may consider a firm receipt element far in the future to cover the first shortage in the time axis. In this case, users might get the impression that MRP is not generating replenishment proposals to cover the shortage, but the problem is just a long rescheduling horizon. A short rescheduling horizon may also bring problems because MRP may generate too many new replenishment proposals when there are firm receipt elements that could cover the requirement.

The rescheduling check is carried out not only during the MRP run, but also when the planning elements are read from the database in the MRP evaluation transactions. The rescheduling exception messages may be different in both cases because in the MRP evaluation transactions, we are not carrying out the whole MRP planning logic—we are simply reading the planning elements from the database. The lot-sizing calculation, for example, is not carried out in the MRP evaluation transactions, so there might be different exception messages in those transactions, especially when using different a lot-sizing option, such as a period or fixed lot size.

When a firm receipt is before the shortage date, we will see the rescheduling exception message **15—Reschedule Out** for the firm receipt element. This suggests that the planner delay the start to avoid the product sitting in stock when it is not yet required. Figure 6.6 shows an example of such a scenario in which exception **15— Reschedule Out** is triggered.

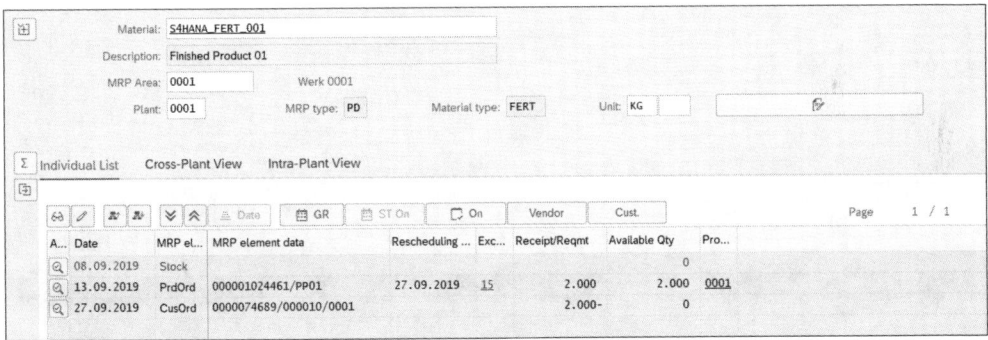

Figure 6.6 Firm Receipt Element before the Shortage

> **Tip**
> You might want to have the firm receipt element considered during the rescheduling check, but we recommend that you avoid the exception messages, especially if it is close to the shortage date. In this case, we can define the tolerance values in the customizing Transaction OMDW, as discussed in Chapter 4.

6   Evaluating the MRP Results

When we do not allow the start in the past, MRP will try to first calculate the planned order dates using backward scheduling. If the calculated start date is in the past, it will change to today scheduling, considering the current date as the start date and running forward scheduling to calculate the finish date. In this case, it will trigger the rescheduling exception message **30—Plan Process According to Schedule** for the newly created replenishment elements.

While we can see the exception messages in the MRP evaluation transactions, such as the Stock/Requirements List, the SAP Fiori applications of the MRP Cockpit were designed without the concept of exception messages. In earlier SAP S/4HANA releases, we did not have the visibility of rescheduling proposals in MRP-related SAP Fiori applications. As of on-premise SAP S/4HANA 1909, however, a new column was introduced in the MRP applications, bringing this visibility to the rescheduling proposals and even allowing the planner to adopt the rescheduling proposal.

Figure 6.7 shows the new **Rescheduling** column, where we can see a button with an arrow for the MRP elements that need to be rescheduled. If we scroll over this button, we will see the rescheduling date; if we click the button, we will be able to change the replenishment proposal date.

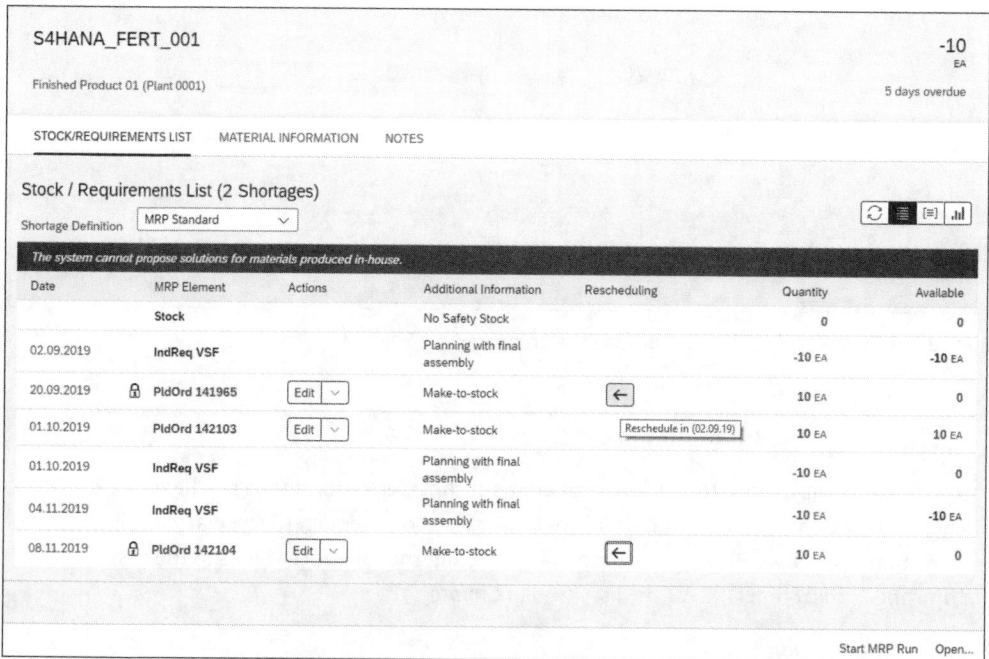

Figure 6.7 Rescheduling Proposals in the Check Material Coverage App

SAP S/4HANA also offers a new feature called *situation handling*, which can be used in different areas to focus users' attention on specific situations that should be reviewed. As of SAP S/4HANA 1909, there is a specific scenario in which a customer can be notified about the rescheduling exception messages already mentioned in this section. We will walk through how to use this feature when we discuss the SAP Fiori applications of the MRP Cockpit in Section 6.9.

> **Tip**
>
> For more information about the rescheduling check, refer to the following SAP notes:
>
> - SAP Note 25388 (MD01, MD02, MD03: Rescheduling Proposals: Documentation)
> - SAP Note 550302 (FAQ: Rescheduling Check)

6.3 The Stock/Requirements List

SAP S/4HANA's new SAP Fiori user interface offers many new applications that can be used to monitor and manage the MRP results. However, the "old" Transaction MD04 is still important and is widely considered the most complete point of entry to analyze the MRP results. For this reason, we will start learning how to analyze the MRP results using this transaction.

Transaction MD04 was originally developed for the SAP GUI in the earlier SAP ERP releases, but in SAP S/4HANA it also can be accessed through the SAP Fiori launchpad. For an MRP controller who needs to analyze the MRP results on a daily basis, the Stock/Requirements List is usually the main point of entry. There are two ways to access this transaction:

- Individual access, through which we will focus on a single material
- Collective access, through which we use broader selection criteria and select multiple materials

> **Note**
>
> Data selection in the Stock/Requirements List was also changed in SAP S/4HANA. For performance improvement, the data selection logic executed in ABAP was pushed down into the SAP HANA layer, which means that ABAP BAdIs that were called during data selection will be no longer called. The `MD_CHANGE_MRP_DATA` BAdI, for

example, was frequently used to manipulate the MRP elements and will not be called any longer in SAP S/4HANA. Existing implementations should be replaced with the MD_ADD_ELEMENTS BAdI, which is called *after* the data selection.

Let's start with individual access, which is the simplest way to access the Stock/Requirements List.

6.3.1 Individual Access

Individual access to the Stock/Requirement List happens through Transaction MD04 in the SAP GUI or through clicking the **Monitor Stock/Requirements List** tile in the SAP Fiori launchpad.

In the initial screen shown in Figure 6.8, we have the option to enter the material and the plant or the MRP area as selection criteria. We also can set the **With Filter** flag, which adds more fields in which we can select filters for the planning elements. We also have the option to jump into collective access from here, which will be discussed later.

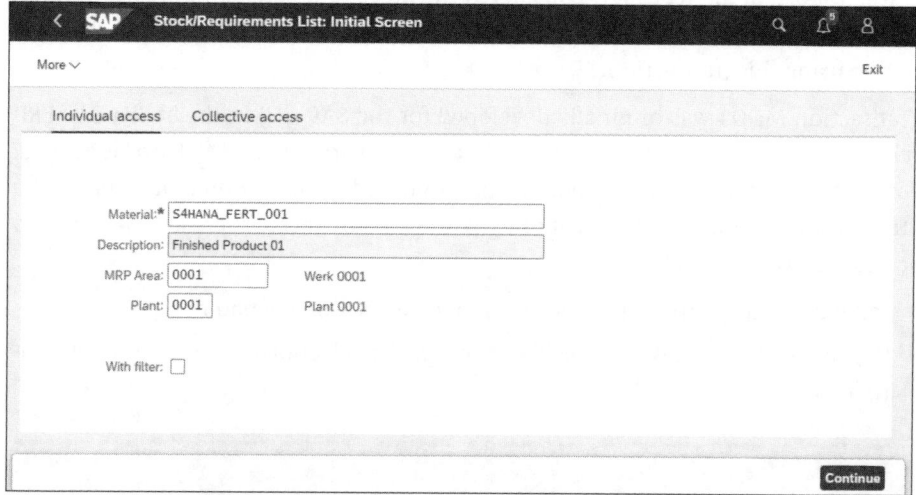

Figure 6.8 Stock/Requirements List in the SAP Fiori Launchpad

When we click the **Continue** button, we will access the actual Stock/Requirement List, showing a list of the MRP-relevant planning elements for the selected material and plant/MRP area combination. Planning elements will be sorted by date, with columns that show the **Date, MRP Element, MRP Element Data, Rescheduling Date, Exception Message, Receipt/Requirement Quantity**, and **Available Quantity** data. Additional columns will be automatically displayed if necessary. For example, Figure 6.9 shows a column for the production version because here we have planned orders with production versions.

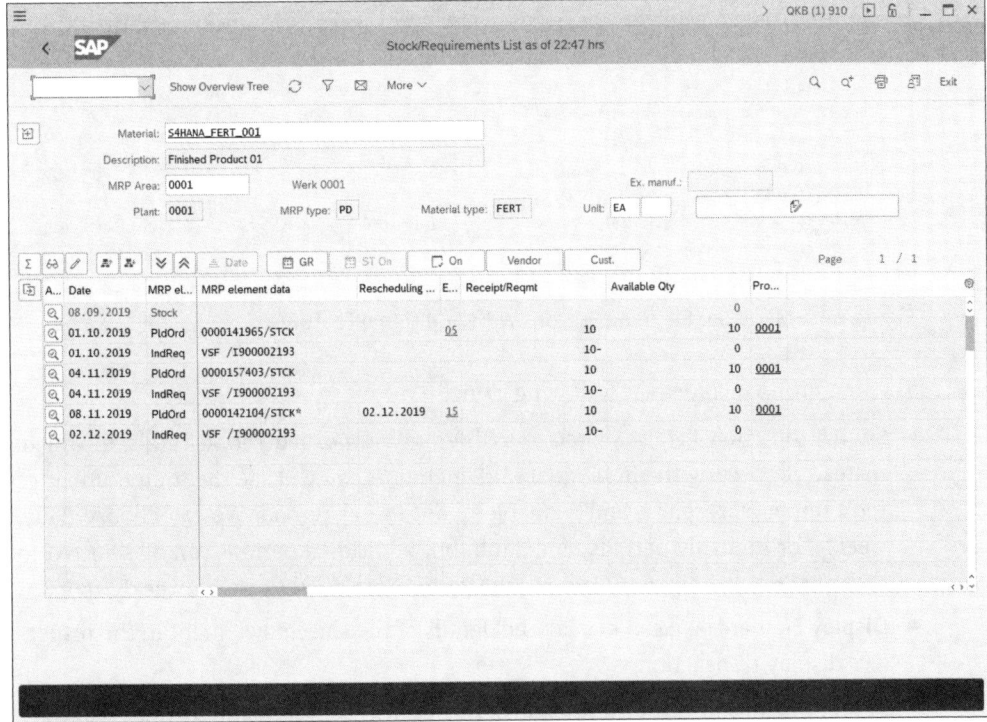

Figure 6.9 Individual Access of the Stock/Requirements List

> **Tip**
> Look carefully at Figure 6.9: the line dividing the **MRP Element** and **MRP Element Data** columns is thicker than the other columns. If we drag this line to the right, we will find additional columns that are hidden by default, such as the **Start/Release Date** and the **Opening Date** columns.

The menu bar highlighted in Figure 6.10 offers additional features that can influence the display of the MRP elements in the Stock/Requirements List.

6   Evaluating the MRP Results

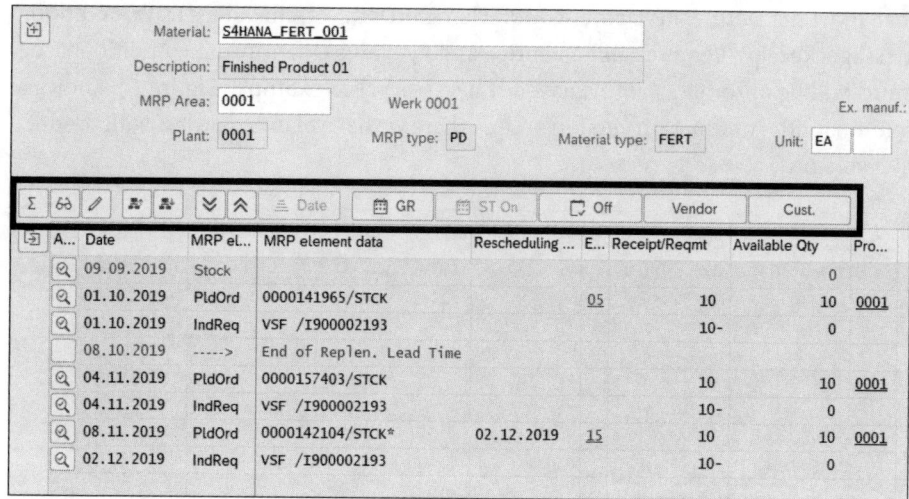

Figure 6.10 Menu Bar Showing Buttons with Additional Features

The first group includes the following icons:

- **Switch to Period Totals**: Switch to a different view called **Period Totals**, in which, instead of viewing the individual MRP elements, we will see the total number of requirements, receipts, and available quantity per period. We can choose daily, weekly, or monthly periods by default, but additional periods can be selected in the user settings. Figure 6.11 shows the **Period Totals** screen with a weekly split.
- **Display Element**: We can display the details of the selected element in the respective display transaction.
- **Change Element**: We can change the selected MRP element in the respective change transaction.

The next group of buttons in the menu bar allows us to see which requirements are pegged to a specific MRP receipt element or which receipt element is pegged to a requirement.

In the sequence, we have another group of three icons, through which we can choose if we want to display requirements individually or group requirements on the same date. The third button in this group allows us to sort individual stocks by the first requirement date when we are working with make-to-order (MTO) or make-to-project (MTP) production, for example.

6.3 The Stock/Requirements List

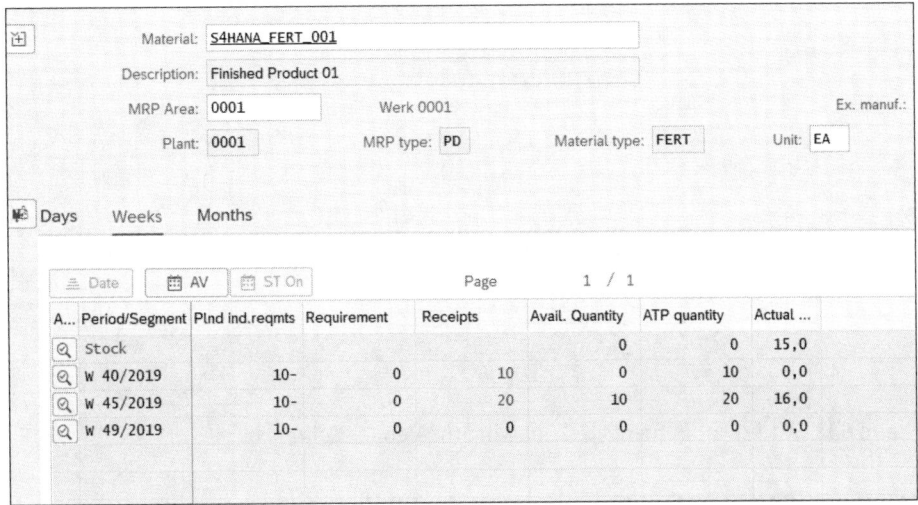

Figure 6.11 Period Totals with Weekly Split

The last group of buttons offers the following features:

- **Display at Goods Receipt/Availability Date**: If we are using a goods receipt processing time, we can choose to show the replenishment elements by the goods receipt date or the availability date.
- **Switch On/Off Safety Time**: When a safety time is defined in the material master, the requirement date will be brought forward in the Stock/Requirements List. Using this button, we can switch the safety time off and see the actual requirement date.
- **Show Total Replenishment Lead Time**: The total replenishment lead time is based on the in-house production time for materials procured internally or on the planned delivery time for purchased materials, plus the goods receipt processing time or purchasing processing time. By clicking this button, we can show an additional line: **End of Replenishment Lead Time**. This line is shown in Figure 6.10.
- **Show Vendor**: If there are replenishment elements with an associated vendor, we can show an additional column with the vendor number and the vendor name. In the purchase requisition in Figure 6.12, the vendor info is shown.
- **Show Customer**: For sales orders or deliveries, we can show additional columns with the customer number and customer name by clicking this button.

239

6   Evaluating the MRP Results

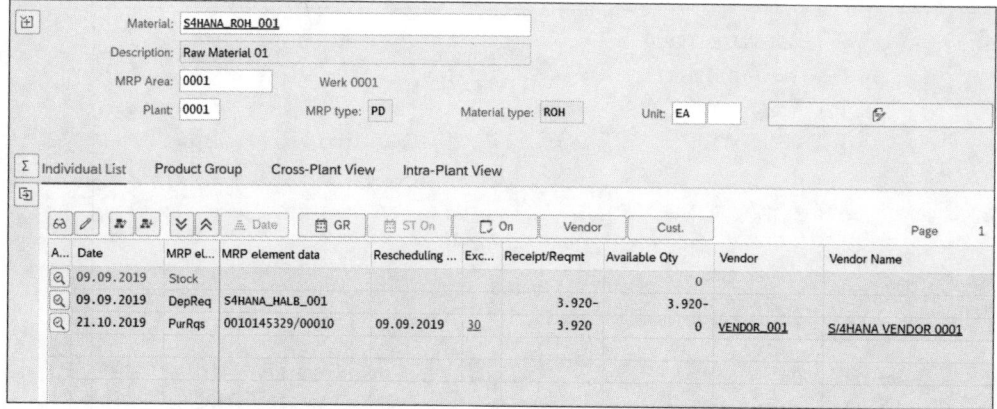

Figure 6.12 Stock/Requirements List Showing the Vendor Columns

SAP Note 94145 (MD04: Explanation Note for Displaying Columns) offers technical information about the display of columns in the Stock/Requirements List.

> **Tip**
>
> The `MD_ADD_COL_EZPS` BAdI allows custom screens to be included in the MRP evaluation transactions. We can fill up to three custom columns and show or hide them dynamically.

Besides the information related to the receipt and requirement elements, we can also display an additional subscreen called **Header Details**, in which we will see the material related information and master data settings. Figure 6.13 shows this subscreen, including a button to collapse or display it in the upper-left corner.

As we discussed in Chapter 4, the screen sequence shown in the **Header Details** area is tied to the MRP type defined for the material. We assign a different screen sequence in the MRP type Customizing. Screen sequences should be previously created in the customizing Transaction OMIO, and we can even create our own custom screens to show additional information in the **Header Details** section.

As discussed in Chapter 3, there are MRP types with a firming type, for which we can consider a firm period that will be defined by the time fence maintained in the material master. In the Stock/Requirements List, we have the possibility to manually add a firming date that will be considered by MRP even if MRP does not have a firming type set in Customizing. This firming date can be defined in the **Edit • Set Firming**

6.3 The Stock/Requirements List

Date menu option. We should see an additional blue line between the MRP elements showing the **Firming Date**, as shown in Figure 6.14.

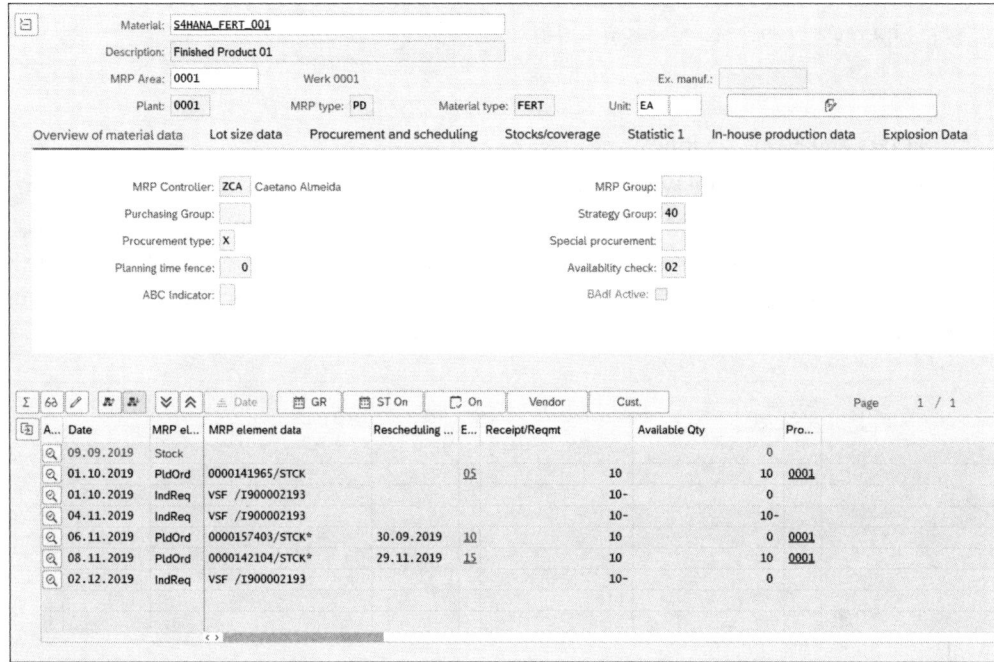

Figure 6.13 Header Details Subscreen

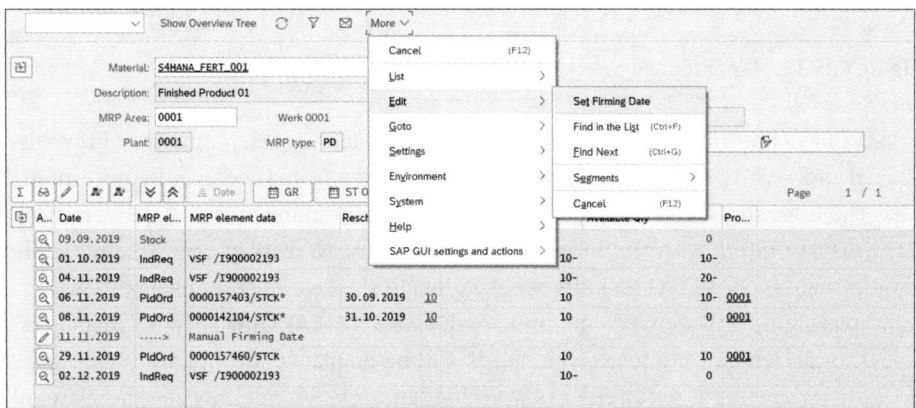

Figure 6.14 Manual Firming Date in the Stock/Requirements List

6   Evaluating the MRP Results

> **Tip**
> In the **Settings** • **User Settings** menu, we can define default values at the user level for most of the settings discussed in this chapter.

Filters and Selection Rules

Figure 6.8 showed the **With Filter** flag that can be selected when accessing the Stock/Requirements List. Whenever we access the Stock/Requirements List with this flag checked, we will see additional two additional fields: **Display Filter** and **Selection Rule**, as shown in Figure 6.15. We can also choose the **Settings** • **Filter On** menu option from the Stock/Requirements List results screen to add those fields.

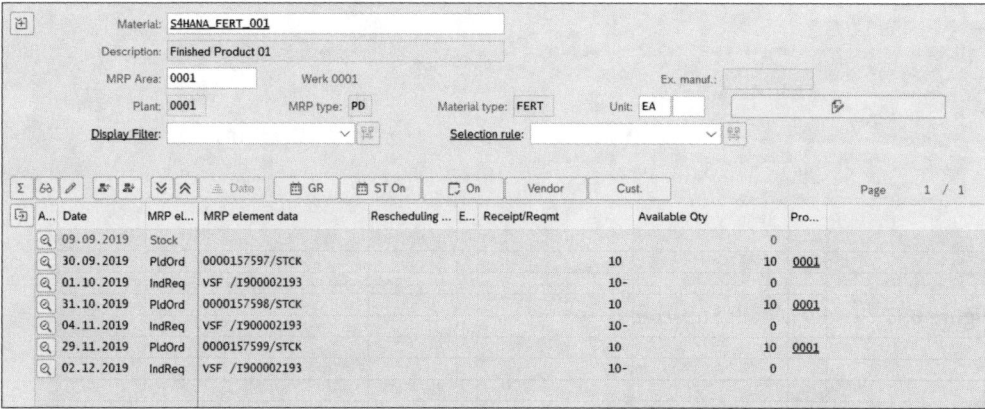

Figure 6.15 Display Filter and Selection Rule in the Stock/Requirements List

The **Display Filter** field can be used to select which planning elements should be displayed and which planning elements should be hidden from the Stock/Requirements List. The filter should be created in Customizing beforehand, but SAP delivers standard display filters with the most common options: to display only receipts, only requirements, only MTO, or only what is inside the replenishment lead time, for example. Figure 6.16 shows an example of the standard **SAP Only Receipts** display filter, through which only receipt elements will be displayed. Compared with Figure 6.15, the independent requirements were hidden. Here we can only see the planned orders.

6.3 The Stock/Requirements List

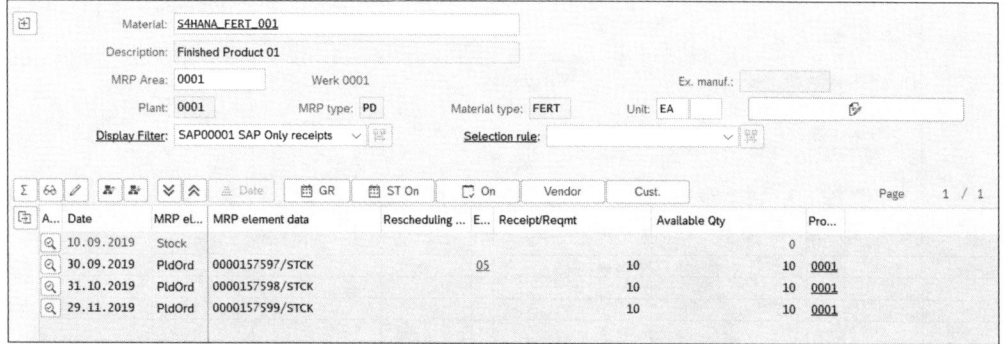

Figure 6.16 The SAP Only Receipts Display Filter

One important remark about the display filter is that the planning elements can be hidden, but they will still be considered when the **Available Quantity** value is calculated. As shown in Figure 6.16, even though we have three planned orders of 10 EA, the available quantity is not 30 EA at the end of the time axis because the requirements are hidden—but they were still counted for the calculation.

A new display filter can be created in customizing Transaction OM0J; Figure 6.17 shows the details. We have the following tabs available in the display filter Customizing:

- **MRP Elements**: In this tab, we can select which types of MRP elements will be considered or not. For each MRP element, we can choose the **Display** or **Do Not Display** options.
- **Segments**: Besides the planning elements, we can also choose if we want to display specific planning segments, such as the MTO or MTP individual stocks, for example.
- **Display Horizon**: We can choose to restrict the display of the MRP elements within a specific time horizon. We can predefine this time horizon in Customizing or define it directly in the Stock/Requirements List.
- **Additional Selections**: Additional fields can be used to restrict the selection, such as the **Customer**, **Vendor**, **Supplying/Receiving Plant**, **Storage Location**, and **Production Version**. The restriction can be predefined in Customizing, or we can choose fields directly in the Stock/Requirements List when this filter is selected. If we choose a filter with a restriction per production version, for example, only planning elements with the specified production version will be selected.

243

6   Evaluating the MRP Results

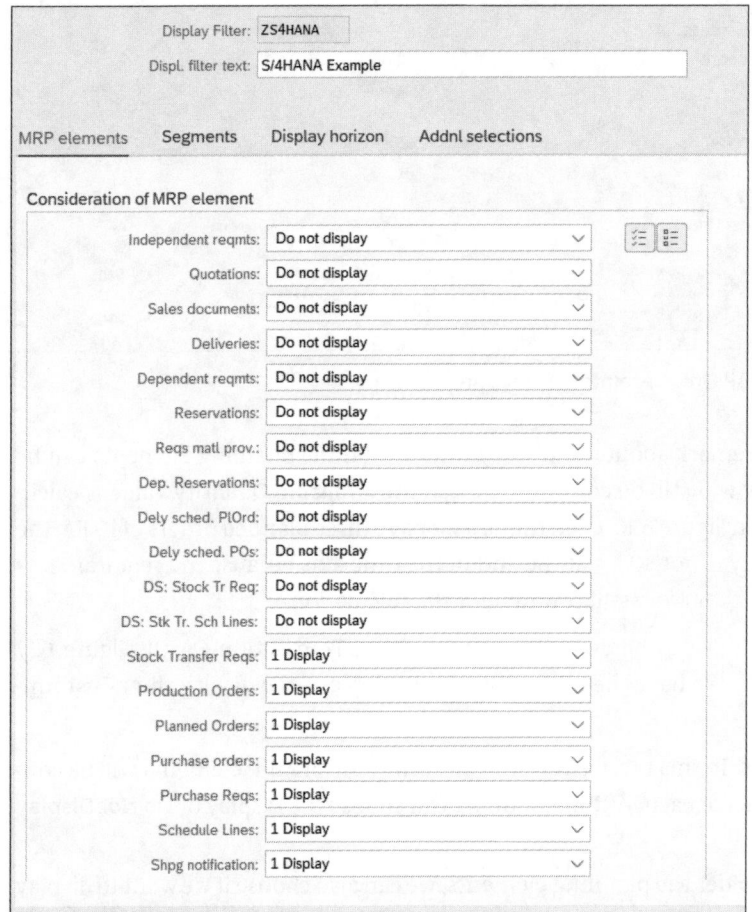

Figure 6.17 Display Filter in Customizing

Similar to the display filter, we have the option to restrict the selection with a selection rule. The main difference between these options is that whereas the display filter will only hide the planning elements, with a selection rule we can also avoid having them influence the available quantity calculation.

We also have SAP's standard-delivered selection rules; Figure 6.18 shows an example of the **SAP Only Receipts** selection rule. Compared with the Stock/Requirements List from Figure 6.16 (in which we used the **SAP Only Receipts** display filter), the Stock/Requirements List in this figure differs primarily in the available quantity because the requirements were not included in the calculation when using a selection rule in Figure 6.18.

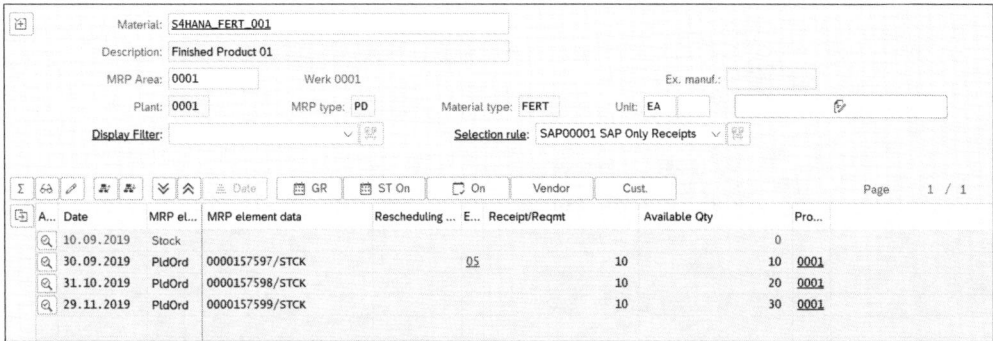

Figure 6.18 The SAP Only Receipts Selection Rule

Custom selection rules can be created in customizing Transaction OMOI; Figure 6.19 shows the details of this customizing transaction. Here, we will find the **MRP Elements**, **Stock**, and **Selection Horizon** tabs.

Under the **MRP Elements** tab, we can define how each MRP element will be considered in the Stock/Requirements List, with the following options:

- **Do Not Consider**: The MRP element is not displayed and is not used to calculate the quantity available or the ranges of coverage.
- **Display**: The element is displayed, but it will not affect the available quantity calculation.
- **Display Availability Relevance**: The element is displayed, and it is considered for the available quantity calculation.
- **As in the Standard System**: The MRP element will not be affected by the selection rule, and the standard logic used in the Stock/Requirements List for this element will be used.

In the **Stock** tab, we can choose which particular stock types will be considered available, such as the unrestricted stock, blocked stock, restricted-use stock, stock in transfer, or safety stock.

Finally, in the **Selection Horizon** tab, we can restrict the interval for which the planning elements will be selected.

6   Evaluating the MRP Results

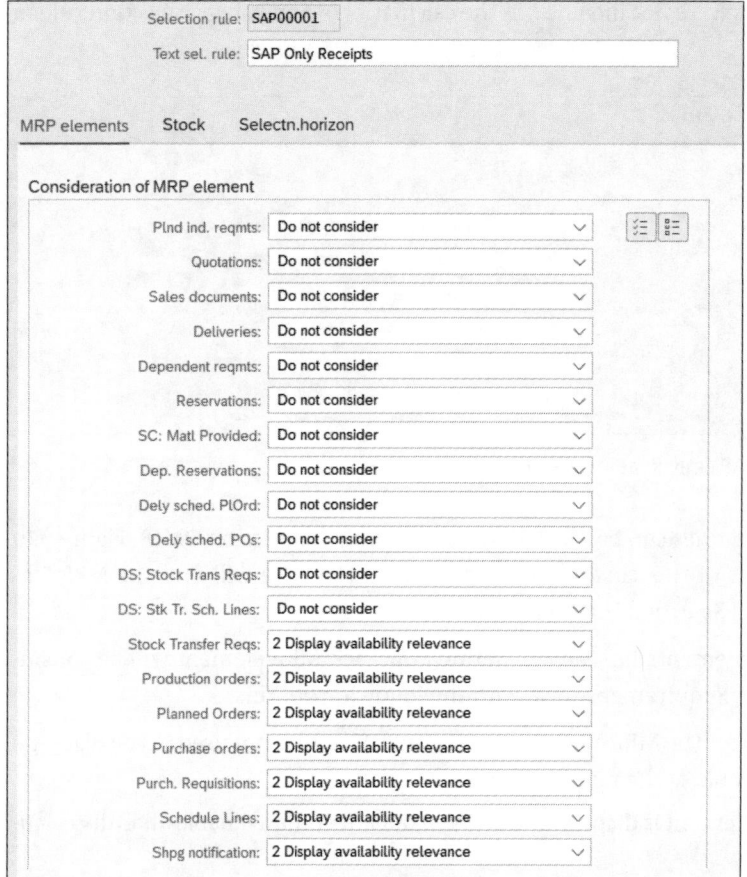

Figure 6.19 Selection Rule Customizing

Grouping

When using the individual access of the Stock/Requirement List, we will enter a material and a plant or MRP area. Inside the transaction, however, we see additional tabs with an integrated view called **Material Grouping**, showing different materials, plants, or MRP areas. The following material grouping standard options are available:

- **APO Supersession Chains**: This option is displayed when the material is part of an SAP APO *supersession chain* (a feature that allows products to replace each other) and shows the MRP elements of all the supersession members.

- **Product Groups**: This is displayed when the material is part of a product group; it shows the MRP elements of all the product group members.

- **Cross-Plant View**: This tab will be displayed when a material exists in different plants; it shows the existing MRP elements for this material on all the plants.
- **Intra-Plant View**: Under this tab, we can see information from all the MRP areas relevant for this material.

The first step to see those additional tabs is to activate the material grouping in Customizing. We can access this through IMG menu path **Production • Material Requirements Planning • Evaluation • Display Material Groupings**. In this Customizing activity, we will simply activate the tabs we want to see in the Stock/Requirements List by checking the respective flags. Figure 6.20 shows the details of this Customizing activity.

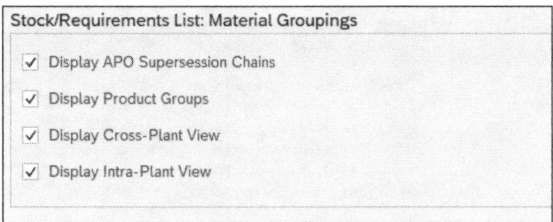

Figure 6.20 Material Grouping Customizing

> **Note**
> The **Intra-Plant** view was introduced in SAP S/4HANA 1809, so this tab will not be available in earlier releases.

Once we set the **Material Grouping** flags in Customizing, we will see the respective tabs in the Stock/Requirements List. Those tabs, by default, will only be shown when they are relevant for a specific material. For example, the **Product Group** tab will only be displayed when the material is part of a product group, and the **Cross-Plant View** tab will be only shown when a material exists in multiple plants. In the Stock/Requirements List **User Settings** menu, however, we can define which tabs should always be displayed, even if they are not relevant for a material, so long as they are active in Customizing.

Figure 6.21 shows the details of the **Product Group** tab, where we can see receipts and requirements of multiple materials belonging to the same product group. We can observe in this figure that there are additional tabs to indicate to which material, plant, and MRP area each planning element belongs.

6 Evaluating the MRP Results

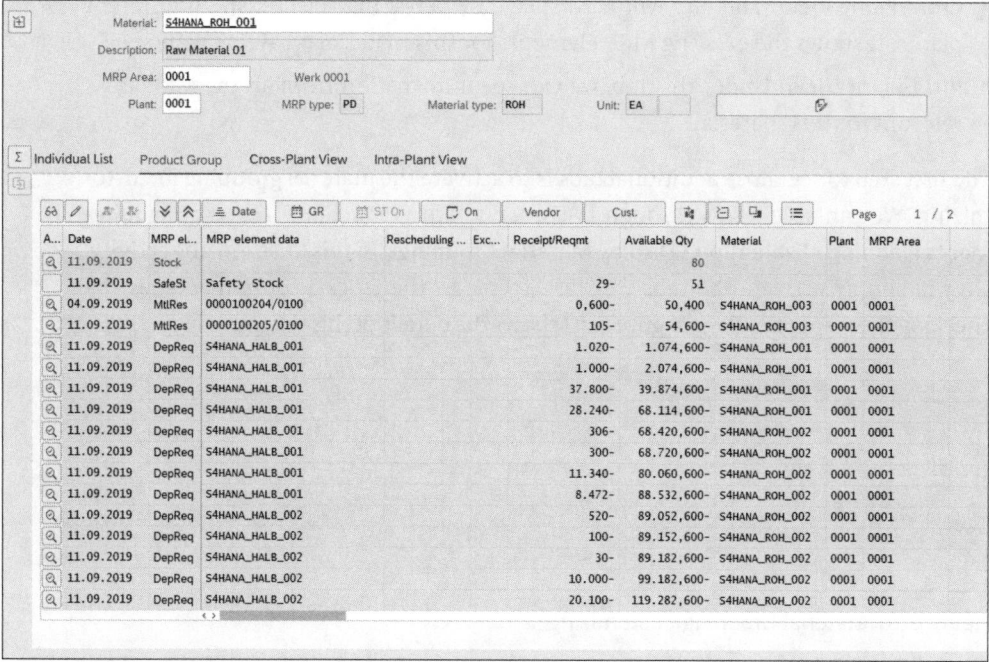

Figure 6.21 Product Group Tab in the Stock/Requirements List

> **Warning**
>
> For material groupings involving different materials, such as the product group, the selection will be restricted to materials with the same unit of measure or with a unit of measure convertible to the unit of measure of the accessed material.

In the **Cross-Plant** view, we can see MRP elements for the same material in multiple plants in a single screen. This view is especially relevant for materials involved in a stock transfer scenario, in which a material needs to be moved from one plant to another. If desired, we can choose to hide the stock transfers in this view by checking the **No Stock Transfers in Cross-Plant View** flag, which can be found in the **User Settings** menu.

SAP S/4HANA introduced several simplifications, including the mandatory usage of MRP areas for subcontracting and for planning at the storage location level. While using MRP areas is a much more complete solution compared to the previous approach, in the first SAP S/4HANA releases users missed having a complete overview

6.3 The Stock/Requirements List

of the Stock/Requirements List, including all the subcontractors and storage locations planned separately, as they used to have in SAP ERP. For this reason, SAP introduced the new **Intra-Plant** view in SAP S/4HANA 1809, which provides an overview of all the MRP areas relevant for a material within a plant.

Figure 6.22 shows the default display of the **Intra-Plant** view, where we can see all the MRP elements under the different MRP areas assigned to the selected material. We have the additional **MRP Area** column here, identifying to which MRP area each planning element belongs.

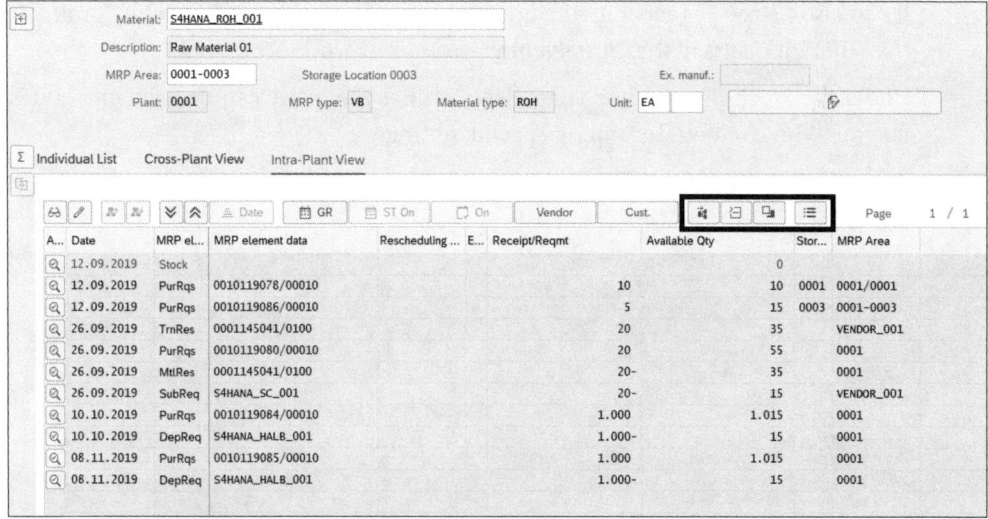

Figure 6.22 Intra-Plant View in the Stock/Requirements List

There are additional buttons in the **Material Grouping** tab, highlighted in Figure 6.22, that can be used to change the display of the Stock/Requirements List in those tabs. The first button is **Switch On/Off Aggregation**, which controls the calculation of the available quantity. If the aggregation is switched off, we will see separate stock lines for each product group, plant, or MRP area, and the available quantity will be calculated for each individual segment, even though the planning elements are still displayed together.

The second button is **Hide/Show Internal Stock Transfers**. When working with MRP areas, we can have stock transfers moving the stock to the different plants or MRP areas, and we might not want to see those stock transfers when displaying everything in a single screen.

6 Evaluating the MRP Results

The **Separate MRP Areas** button was introduced in SAP S/4HANA 1809 with the **Intra-Plant** view. When selecting this option, we will see all the MRP areas in the same screen, but they will be completely separated. With this option, we can have a display that is closer to the old SAP ERP features that were simplified in SAP S/4HANA (storage location planned separately and subcontracting without MRP area). As shown in Figure 6.23, each blue line represents an individual MRP area; the planning elements below this line are assigned to this MRP area. We will have a complete separation of the stocks and the planning elements of each MRP area, but they will still be displayed in a single screen. Although this setting was originally created for MRP areas, it can also be used to separate the different materials of the same product group or the different plants in the **Cross-Plant** view.

Under the Stock/Requirements List **User Settings** menu, we can save default values for these three material grouping-specific settings.

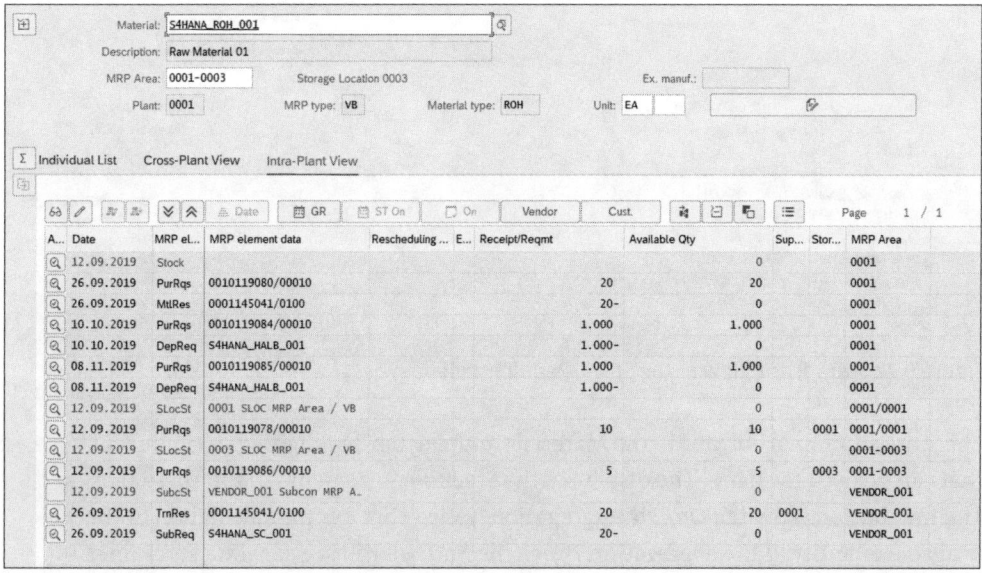

Figure 6.23 Intra-Plant View with Separated MRP Areas

The last button highlighted in Figure 6.22 is the **List of Materials** button, which opens a pop-up screen listing the materials, plants, or MRP areas belonging to the material grouping.

6.3 The Stock/Requirements List

Besides the standard options to create material groupings in the Stock/Requirements List, we also have the option to create our own custom groupings. This can be done with a custom implementation of the MD_CREATE_GROUPING BAdI.

Navigation Profiles

The Stock/Requirements List is a central point of entry for the MRP controller, who, after evaluating the MRP results, might need to perform additional actions, such as replanning a particular material or creating an additional planned order.

We can call additional transactions and perform actions without leaving Transaction MD04 by using a navigation profile. With a navigation profile, additional icons will be displayed in the Stock/Requirements List menu, each one allowing a different transaction call.

We can select a navigation profile under the **General Settings** tab of the **User Settings** menu (see Figure 6.24), which can be accessed through the **Settings • User Settings** menu selection. We can also directly assign the navigation profile and access the assigned transactions through the **Environment • Navigation Profile** menu selection.

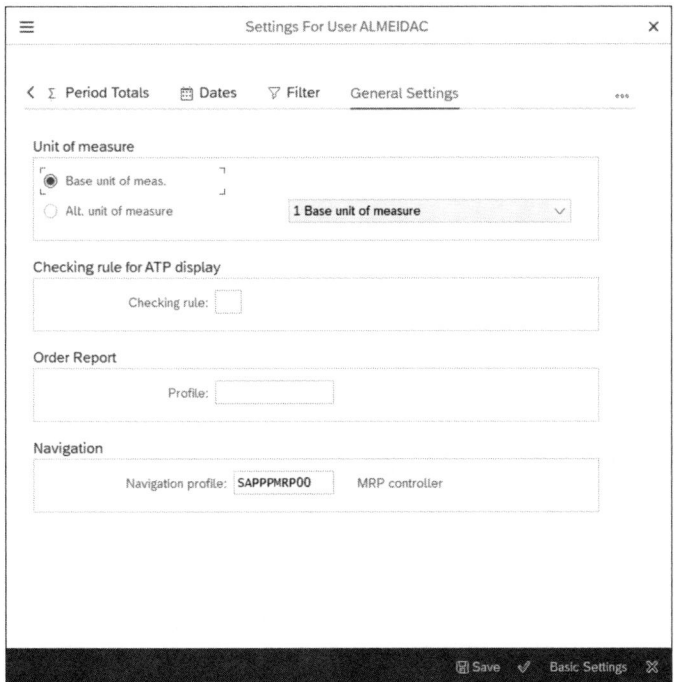

Figure 6.24 Navigation Profile in the User Settings Menu

6   Evaluating the MRP Results

When a navigation profile is assigned to the user, icons for the transaction calls will be displayed in the Stock/Requirements List menu, and the user will be able to navigate to each of these transactions, coming back to the Stock/Requirements List after processing. Figure 6.25 shows an example using the standard navigation profile SAP0000000, which offers a collection of examples with different transactions calls.

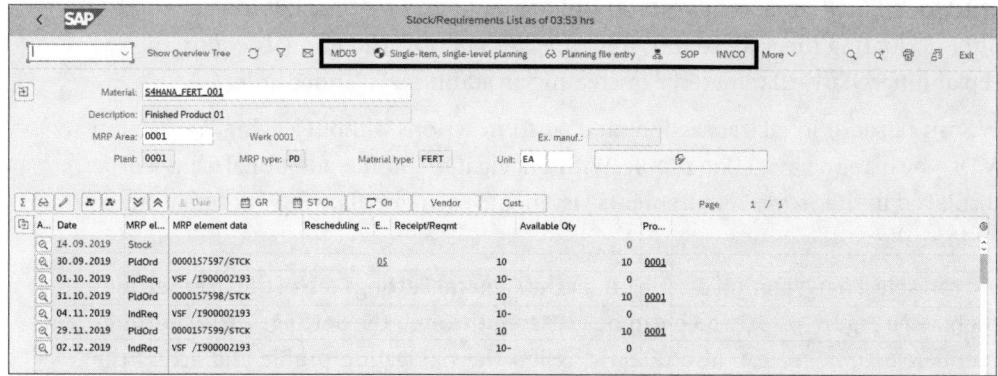

Figure 6.25 Navigation Profile Transactions in the Menu

The navigation profile can also bring in icons to trigger transaction calls specific to each MRP element. These icons will be displayed when we select the details of the MRP element by double-clicking a line or selecting the magnifying glass. Figure 6.26 shows the details of the navigation profile transaction calls for a production order.

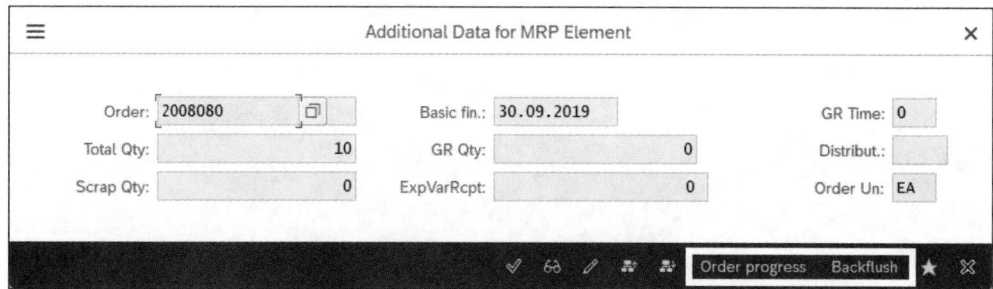

Figure 6.26 Element Details with the Navigation Profile Transaction Calls

A custom navigation profile can be created in Transaction OMOK, and we can use the collection of transaction call examples provided by navigation profile SAP0000000 to create our own navigation profile. We can assign, for example, custom transactions or even calls to SAP APO transactions. Figure 6.27 shows the details of this

Customizing transaction. As shown, there are settings for **General Transaction Calls**, which will be displayed in the menu, and for **Transaction Calls per MRP Element**, which are called from the MRP element details.

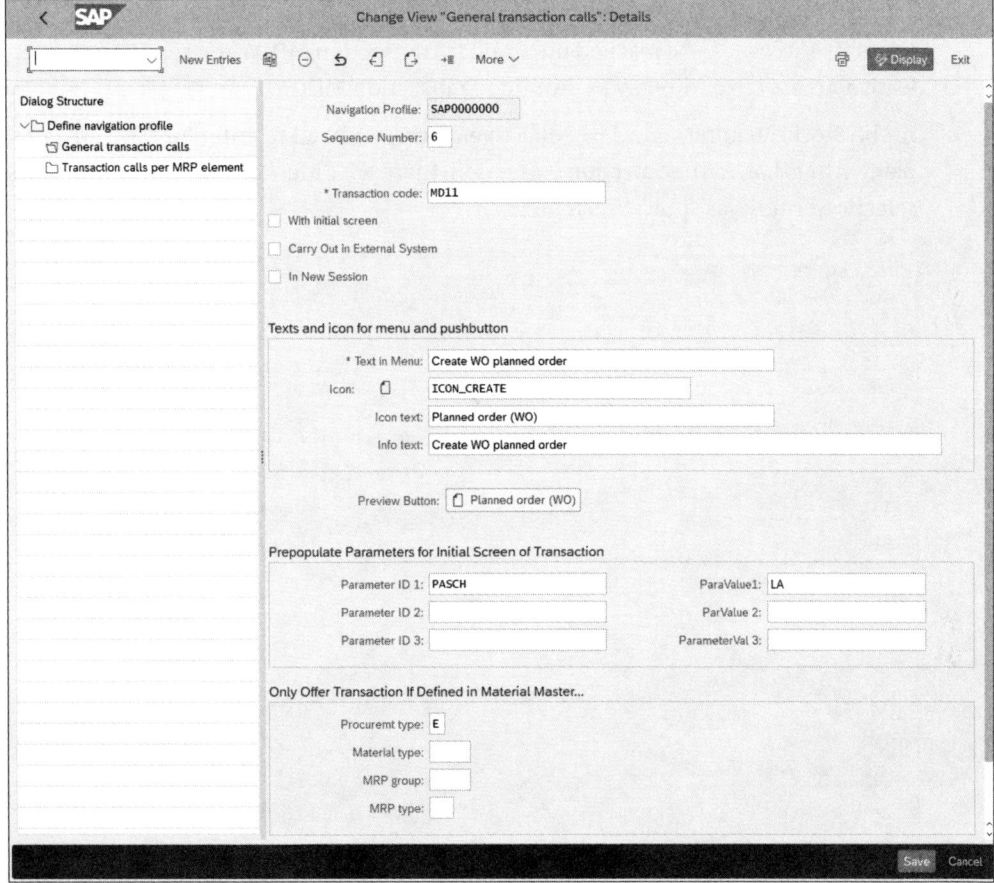

Figure 6.27 Navigation Profile Customizing

In this Customizing screen, we will be able to define whether the transaction's first screen will be skipped; whether it will be called in a new session; details of the pushbutton, including its icon and text; parameters to be populated in the initial screen; and options to restrict the transaction call when specific material master settings are used.

6.3.2 Collective Access

Besides offering individual access for analyzing the MRP results for a single material, the Stock/Requirements List also provides for collective access, through which we can analyze the MRP results for a group of materials.

Collective access can be reached by running Transaction MD04 and selecting the **Collective Access** tab or directly by running Transaction MD07.

In the Stock/Requirements List collective access, we need to enter an MRP area or a plant. After that, in the **Selection By** section, there are different options to be used as selection criteria, as shown in Figure 6.28.

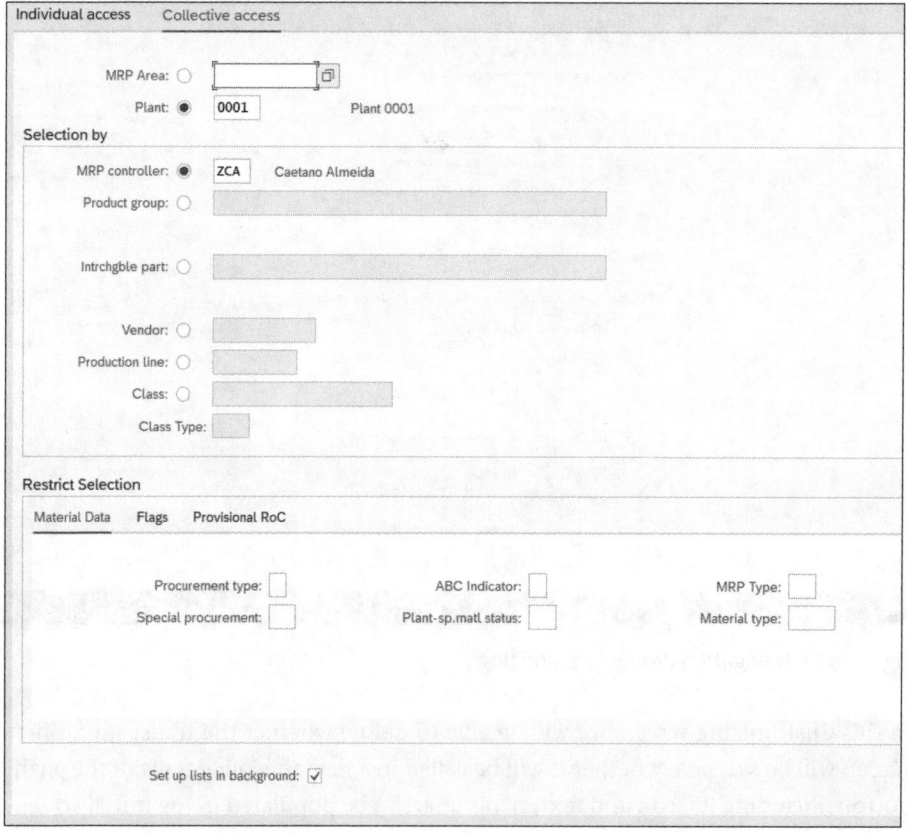

Figure 6.28 Collective Access of the Stock/Requirements List

The most commonly used selection criterion in the collective access is the **MRP Controller** radio button, which is used to list all the materials assigned to a specific planner. The idea behind the MRP controller concept is to use it as a material aggregator so that the planner can easily access all the materials they are responsible for.

When selecting some of these options, like the **Vendor** or the **Production Line** radio buttons, additional fields will be shown so that we can restrict the selection. For example, we could choose to select materials with planned orders, purchase requisitions, or scheduling agreements for a vendor.

Under the **Restrict Selection** section, we have additional fields that can be used to restrict the selection even more. We can, for example, filter based on the **Plant-Specific Material Status** value to avoid the selection of obsolete materials, which would allow the planner to focus on what is really important.

By checking the **Set Up Lists in Background** flag, the system will build the Stock/Requirements List for each of the selected materials in background so that it can summarize the exception messages for each material, calculate the stock days' supply, and show traffic lights for each line, pointing the planner to which materials are in a critical situation and should be taken care of first. A large selection may lead to performance issues if we check the **Set Up Lists in Background** box because the time will be more or less the total time taken to build the Stock/Requirements List for each of these materials.

We can also use filters or selection rules in the collective access of the Stock/Requirements List. By selecting the **With Filter** flag, additional fields will be shown, through which we will be able to enter a display filter or selection rule.

> **Tip**
> If the MRP controller needs to access a large selection of materials in the Stock/Requirements List collective access, we can activate parallel processing for power users in Transaction OM0N. Parallel processing will improve the performance of this transaction because different servers will be used to read data in parallel. As a general rule, the system admin must be contacted before activating parallel processing because it will consume additional system resources.

Although the selection criteria available in the collective entry of the Stock/Requirements List is very flexible, it has some limitations. For example, we cannot use multiple selection or range selection for the available fields, which limits the selection to a single MRP controller or a single product group. Also, we need to choose if we want to base our selection on the product group, vendor, or production line, for example; it is not possible to mix different selection criteria.

6   Evaluating the MRP Results

For this reason, SAP provides the standard report RMMD07NEW, which was delivered as an example of a user-specific entrance to the collective display Transaction MD07 for Stock/Requirements Lists for one or more plants.

As shown in Figure 6.29, report RMMD07NEW provides multiple and range selection for the selection fields, and we do not need to choose if we want to select based on the **MRP Controller**, **Vendor**, **Production Line**, or **Product Group** values.

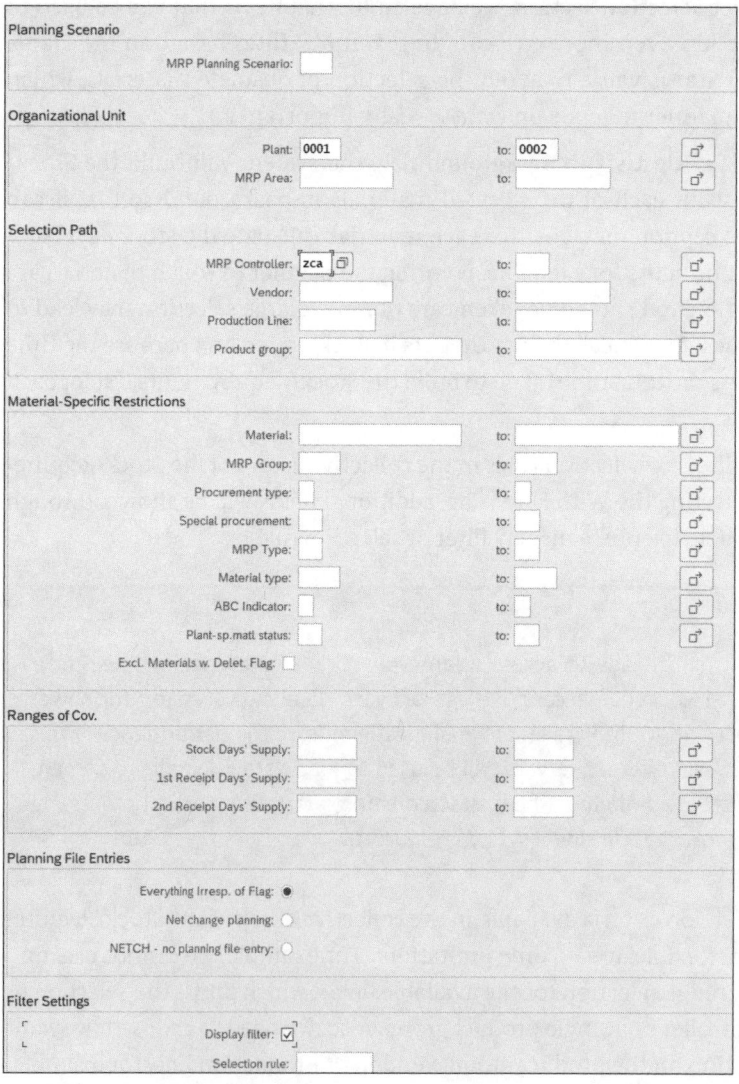

Figure 6.29 Report RMMD07NEW Selection Screen

6.3 The Stock/Requirements List

All those fields are open to be used as selection criteria by default, without any prior selection. We will also filter the results using the same restrictions available in Transaction MD07.

As already mentioned, the report was delivered by SAP to be used as a template for custom development, so we can enhance it, including adding fields as selection criteria, or we can simply create a transaction to call this report as it is delivered by SAP.

Once we run the collective access of the Stock/Requirements List, through either Transaction MD07 or report RMMD07NEW, we will reach the same results screen with a list of materials. If the **Set Up Lists in Background** flag was checked in the selection screen, we will see traffic lights, the stock days' supply, and information about the number of exception messages triggered. Figure 6.30 shows an example of the material list.

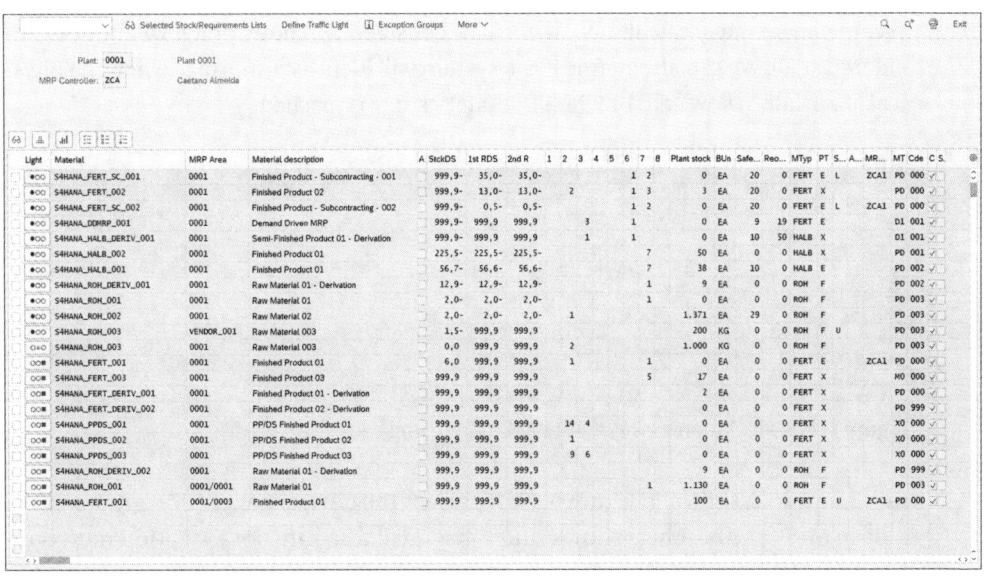

Figure 6.30 Stock/Requirements List: Material List

The **Days' Supply**, **First Receipt Days' Supply**, and **Second Receipt Days' Supply** columns are very important: they are used to define the traffic lights and to sort the MRP elements. These fields are also known as *range of coverage data*.

The **Days' Supply** value represents the number of days for which the on-hand stock can cover the actual requirements. For example, a stock days' supply of 5 means that the existing stock will cover the requirements for five days, or that the first shortage

257

will be in five days, without taking into consideration existing replenishment elements. If the stock days' supply is 999.9, then there will be no shortage and the existing stock can cover all the requirements. A negative stock days' supply means that there is a shortage in the past; if the value is -999.9, then the existing stock will never be enough to cover the requirements.

The **First Receipt Days' Supply** and **Second Receipt Days' Supply** values also represent how many days the stock will last, but they can also include receipt elements predefined in Customizing. The logic used is the same as that used by stock days' supply, but it will include some receipt elements.

The Customizing transaction to select which receipt elements can be included in the first receipt days' supply and second receipt days' supply calculation is Transaction OMIL, which is shown in Figure 6.31. Here, for each type of receipt element, we can select if it will be included only in the first receipt days' supply or only in the second receipt days' supply calculation, if it will be considered in both, or if it will not be considered at all. We can also define if the system will identify a shortage when the physical stock falls below zero or when the safety stock is reached.

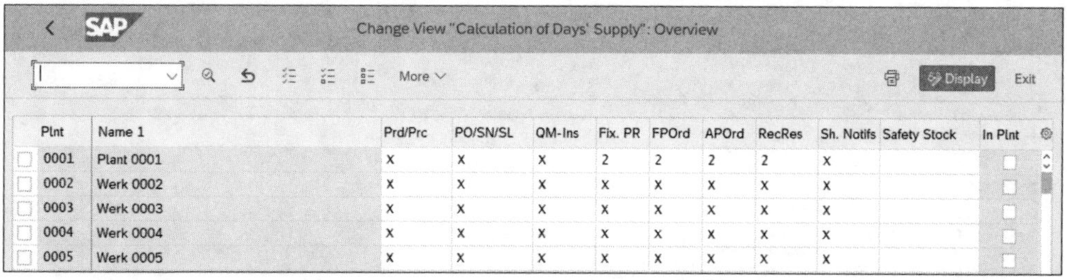

Figure 6.31 Calculation of Days' Supply Customizing

Columns 1 to 8, shown in Figure 6.30, represent the different exception groups available in MRP. The numbers shown under those columns are not exception messages, but the total number of exceptions in each group that were triggered for a specific material.

If we select the **Define Traffic Lights** button, we will see a pop-up showing how the traffic lights colors are determined. As we can see in Figure 6.32, the traffic lights will depend on the **Stock Days' Supply**, **First Receipt Days' Supply**, **Second Receipt Days' Supply**, and **Exception Groups** fields. We can define thresholds for the days' supply, determining, for example, that the yellow traffic light should be shown for a minimum value of the stock days' supply or that it will be shown when rescheduling exception messages are triggered. These changes can be saved individually for each user.

6.3 The Stock/Requirements List

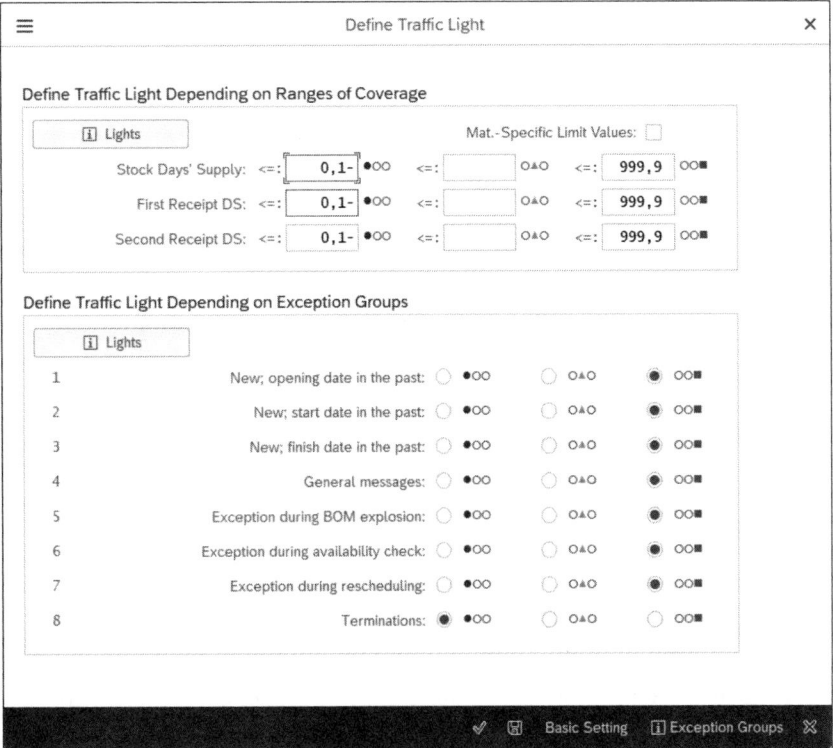

Figure 6.32 The Define Traffic Light Pop-up

In Chapter 4, we discussed the **Evaluation Profile** Customizing activity available for the plant and for the MRP group. The *evaluation profile* can be created in customizing Transaction OMOO and it allows us to set default values for the definition of the traffic lights based on the **Range of Coverage** fields. Figure 6.33 shows the evaluation profile Customizing in the Stock/Requirements List. The profile is assigned to the plant or MRP group. Once we select the **Material Specific Limit Values** flag in this pop-up, those values will be used in the collective access of the Stock/Requirements List.

> **Tip**
> We can use the MD_SET_TRAFFIC_LIGHTS_DS BAdI to define material-specific values that will have a higher priority than the values defined in the evaluation profile. The **Modified by BAdI** indicator will be shown in the pop-up when these values were changed by the BAdI.

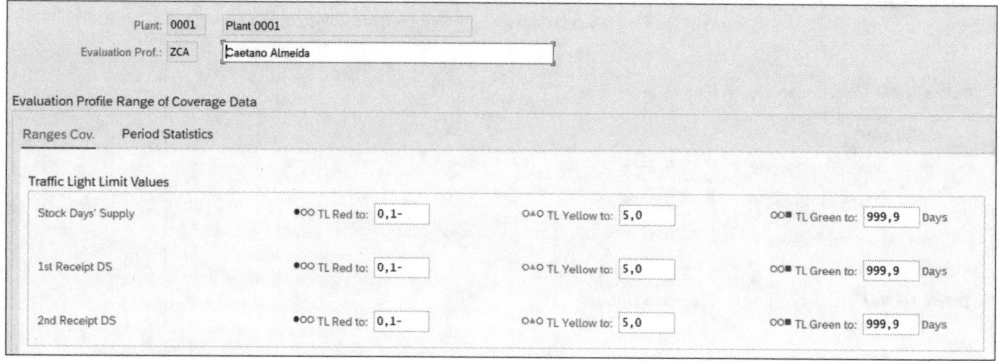

Figure 6.33 Evaluation Profile

By double-clicking a specific line, we will move to the individual access of the Stock/Requirement List, where we will be able to resolve any issues and adjust the planning results for each material.

> **Tip**
>
> The **Already Accessed** column will be flagged automatically after we see the individual Stock/Requirements List for a material. It is useful for informing the planner which materials have been already processed.

6.4 MRP List

In the past, the MRP List was very useful when hardware limitations negatively affected the Stock/Requirements List performance. With the current hardware available and with the power of SAP HANA, it is no longer necessary to work with outdated data saved into a table, so the planner can always work with live data. The new SAP Fiori applications of the MRP Cockpit offer a newly redesigned user interface, so the MRP List has become an obsolete tool in SAP S/4HANA. In fact, now MRP Live will not even generate the MRP List. The design of the MRP List transactions is very similar to the Stock/Requirements List, with the main difference that whereas the Stock/Requirements List is built dynamically whenever we access it, the MRP List is stored into a table and shows a screenshot of the last MRP run. For this reason, we will simply provide an overview of the MRP List features in this book.

In SAP S/4HANA, the MRP List will be only available if we decide to keep using classic MRP. As we have discussed before, this not considered a target solution by SAP and we should not rely on classic MRP in the long term. The main advantage of the MRP List is that data will be saved into a table so that it can be read by custom reports or any other application.

The transaction to access the MRP List is Transaction MD05. We will have both individual and collective access for the MRP List, just as we have for the Stock/Requirements List. Collective access may also happen through Transaction MD06.

> **Note**
>
> MRP will only store one MRP List per material. It will refer to the last execution of classic MRP.

If we compare the MRP List with the Stock/Requirements List, the only noticeable difference is the processing indicator (a check and slash icon), shown in Figure 6.34. The processing indicator is manually checked by the planner in the MRP List, indicating that this MRP List was already evaluated. If, for example, MRP runs again and does not plan this material, a new MRP List will not be created and the planner will know that this material was already evaluated previously.

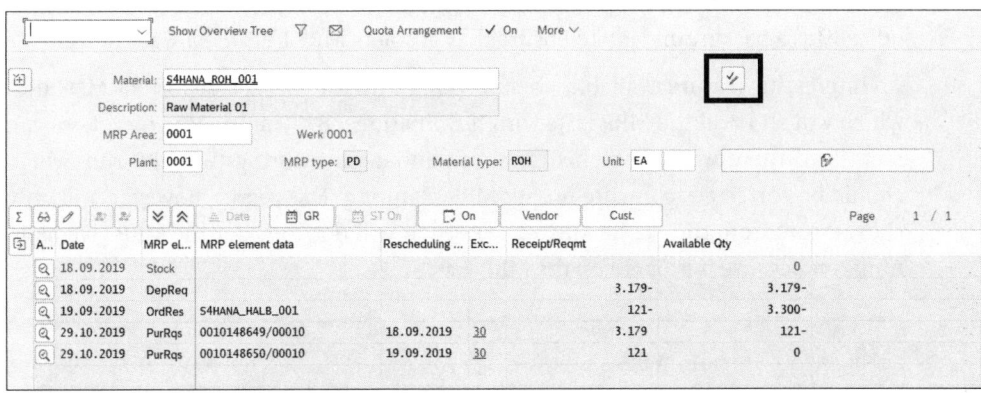

Figure 6.34 Processing Indicator in the MRP List

Collective access will be also very similar to the Stock/Requirements List collective access, but we will have additional selection criteria, such as the MRP List date or the processing indicator.

6   Evaluating the MRP Results

In the collective access results screen, shown in Figure 6.35, we will find an additional column for the processing indicator, plus the **New Exceptions** column, in which a checkbox will appear if new exceptions were triggered for a material during the last MRP run.

Light	Material	MRP Area	Material description	CI	N1	2	3	4	5	6	7	8	StckDS	1st RDS	2nd R	MRP date	Plan...	BUn	Safe...	Reo...	MTyp	PT	SP	A...	MR...	MT Cde
●○○	S4HANA_DDMRP_001	0001	Demand Driven MRP		1					1	4		999,9-	14,0-	14,0-	30.08.2019	0	EA	99	209	FERT	E				D1 001
●○○	S4HANA_FERT_002	0001	Finished Product 02			2				1	2		999,9-	15,9-	15,9-	28.08.2019	3	EA	20	0	FERT	X				PD 000
●○○	S4HANA_FERT_SC_001	0001	Finished Product - Subcontracting - 001		1					1	2		999,9-	44,0-	44,0-	19.07.2019	0	EA	20	0	FERT	F	L		ZCA1	PD 000
●○○	S4HANA_HALB_001	0001	Finished Product 01							1	4		999,9-	56,9-	56,9-	11.09.2019	8	EA	10	0	HALB	E				PD 002
●○○	S4HANA_HALB_002	0001	Finished Product 01								6		225,5-	225,5-	225,5-	11.09.2019	50	EA	0	0	HALB	X				PD 001
●○○	S4HANA_HALB_DERIV_001	0001	Semi-Finished Product 01 - Derivation							1	1		999,9-	112,0-	112,0-	08.04.2019	0	EA	10	50	HALB	X				D1 001
●○○	S4HANA_ROH_001	0001	Raw Material 01								2		1,0-	1,0-	1,0-	18.09.2019	0	EA	0	0	ROH	F				PD 003
●○○	S4HANA_ROH_002	0001	Raw Material 02			1					1		6,0-	6,0-	6,0-	11.09.2019	80	EA	29	0	ROH	F				PD 003
●○○	S4HANA_ROH_003	0001	Raw Material 003			1					2		137,0-	137,0-	137,0-	11.09.2019	0	KG	0	0	ROH	F				PD 003
●○○	S4HANA_ROH_DERIV_001	0001	Raw Material 01 - Derivation								1		111,9-	111,9-	111,9-	08.04.2019	9	EA	0	0	ROH	F				PD 002
●○○	S4HANA_ROH_003	0001/ASTRI	Raw Material 003								1		137,0-	137,0-	137,0-	08.04.2019	0	KG	0	0	ROH	F	U			PD 999
○○■	S4HANA_FERT_003	0001	Finished Product 03								8		999,9	999,9	999,9	29.08.2019	16	EA	0	0	FERT	X				M0 000
○○■	S4HANA_PPDS_002	0001	PP/DS Finished Product 02			2							999,9	999,9	999,9	29.08.2019	0	EA	0	0	FERT	X				X0 000
○○■	S4HANA_HALB_002	0001/ASTRI	Finished Product 01										999,9	999,9	999,9	08.04.2019	0	EA	0	0	HALB	F	U			PD 001

Figure 6.35 MRP List Collective Access

If we decide to work with classic MRP and use the MRP List, one best practice is to periodically delete old and obsolete MRP Lists so that they will not disturb the planner. For example, if a material became obsolete and is no longer relevant for MRP, this material will not be planned again, and the MRP List can be deleted manually in Transaction MD08 or with program RMMDKP01. This program can be executed periodically as a background job to ensure that obsolete MRP Lists are always deleted.

An interesting feature available when working with MRP Lists is report RMMDERRO, which will show all the MRP Lists with terminations. By running this report, we can identify if there were problems for specific materials during the MRP run, which should be corrected to ensure proper MRP planning. This report, however, will only show errors from the classic MRP execution; it will not consider the MRP Live planning run because it is based on the MRP List.

> **Tip**
>
> The MD_MRP_LIST BAdI is triggered when the MRP List is created. It allows further actions to be triggered, such as sending an email to the MRP controller when a specific exception message is triggered or saving the MRP List into an additional table.

6.5 Information and Settings for Materials in MRP on SAP HANA

We have noted that MRP Live will not generate the MRP List and that report RMMDERRO will not show any errors coming from the MRP List, but this does not mean that we do not have any information about the results of the MRP run.

Transaction MD_MRP_FORCE_CLASSIC in the SAP GUI, shown in Figure 6.36, will provide a list of materials planned by MRP Live. It shows where the material was planned (in SAP HANA, ABAP, or PP/DS), whether there was any warning or error during the planning run, and the dates of the planning run.

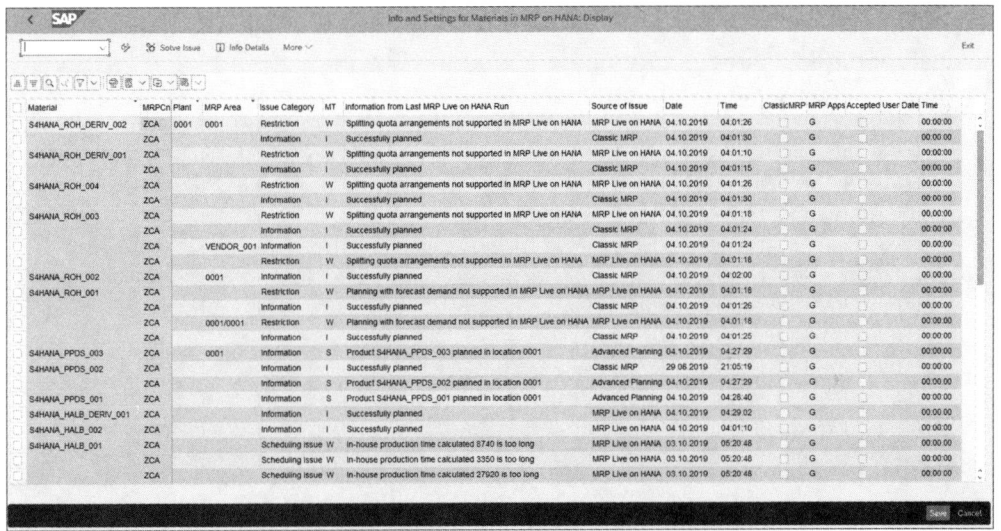

Figure 6.36 Transaction MD_MRP_FORCE_CLASSIC

For materials with issues, we can click the **Solve Issue** button and try to resolve the problem, in order to avoid a further impact in the following MRP runs. For example, if a material was planned with classic MRP because of a material master setting, we can click this button and be redirected to the material master to resolve the issue.

As mentioned in Chapter 5, we can also use this application to force a material to always be planned with ABAP using the classic MRP logic, instead of being planned on the SAP HANA layer. This feature can be used, for example, if we want to ensure that an ABAP BAdI will be always executed for a specific material. This transaction can also be used to prevent a specific material from being displayed in the SAP Fiori applications in the MRP Cockpit, as we will discuss in Section 6.9.

6.6 Order Report

Besides the evaluations available for one material or for multiple materials, we also have the option to see a multilevel evaluation of a planning element. This can be done in the order report, Transaction MD4C. The order report can be triggered for the following MRP elements, each of which has its own tab in Figure 6.37:

- Sales order
- Project
- WBS element
- Production/process order
- Network
- Planned order

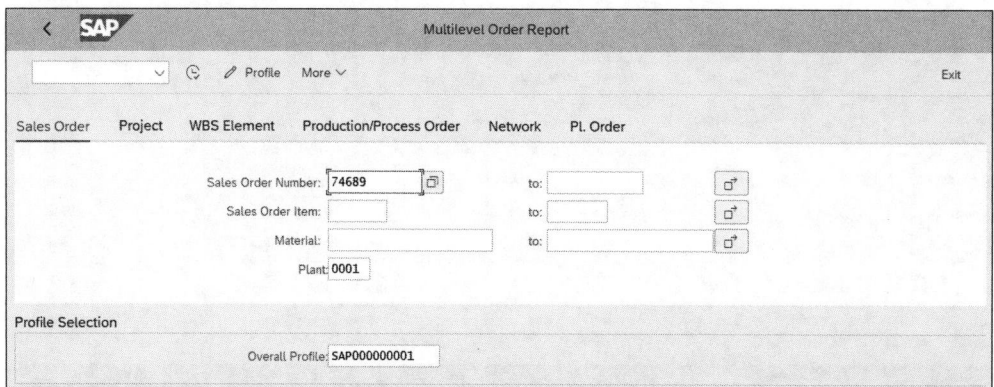

Figure 6.37 Order Report Selection Screen

If the order report is triggered for a sales order, SAP S/4HANA will try to identify a receipt element that can cover the sales order requirement and explode its BOM, building the hierarchy tree until reaching the raw material level.

When the order report is triggered for a project or WBS element, SAP S/4HANA will try to read all the requirements linked to the project or WBS stock and then build the hierarchy for those requirements.

If the element is a production, process, or planned order, then the BOM is exploded and the hierarchy is built based on the reservations or dependent requirements. Figure 6.38 shows the order report results screen, where we can see the hierarchy, starting with a sales order and then showing each receipt and requirement, level by level. This structure will be based on the current planning situation—in other words, the Stock/Requirements List.

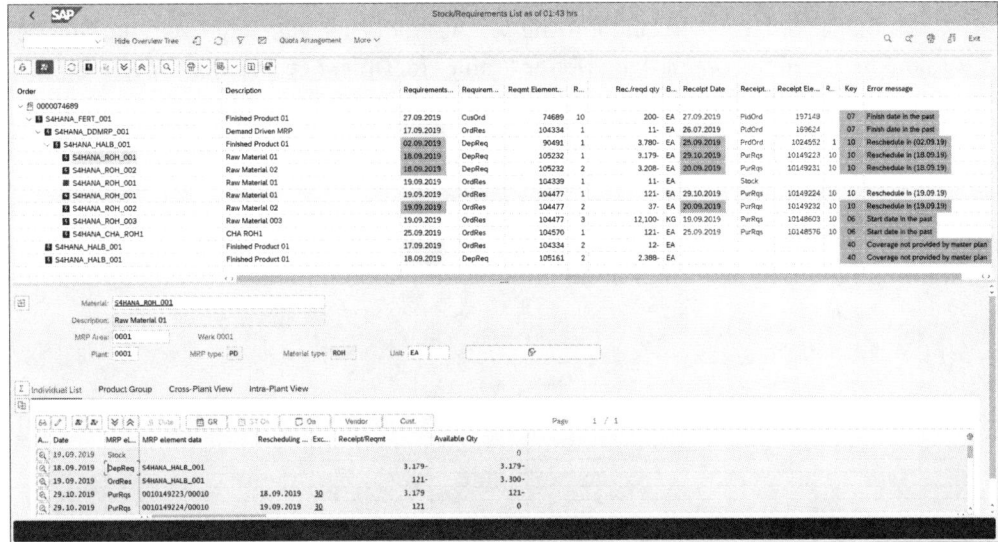

Figure 6.38 Order Report

For each line, we can see exception messages (highlighted in red) and columns for the requirement and receipt dates (highlighted whenever there is a delay). An icon at the beginning of each line shows if there is a problem (red icon) or if everything is fine for this requirement (green light).

If we double-click any line, the respective Stock/Requirements List will be displayed in the lower section of the screen, as shown in Figure 6.38. We can identify the requirement considered in the order report because it will be highlighted in blue.

> **Note**
>
> The pegging information is not stored anywhere after the MRP run, and there is no 1:1 relationship between requirements and receipts. The order report is built dynamically by reading the Stock/Requirements List for each of the involved components. Due to the amount of data processed, performance problems may arise for products with very complex product structures. The parallel import can be activated for users in customizing Transaction OM0N, mentioned earlier.

6 Evaluating the MRP Results

In the order report selection screen (see Figure 6.37), there is an **Overall Profile** field and a button to change the profile. This profile contains parameters that can be used to control how the report is built and to influence the order report display. A custom profile can be created in Customizing, via the **Production Planning · Material Requirements Planning · Evaluation · Define Profiles for Order Report** path.

In the profile shown in Figure 6.39, we can control, for example, whether to explode all the levels up to the raw material level, or whether to limit the number of levels to be exploded.

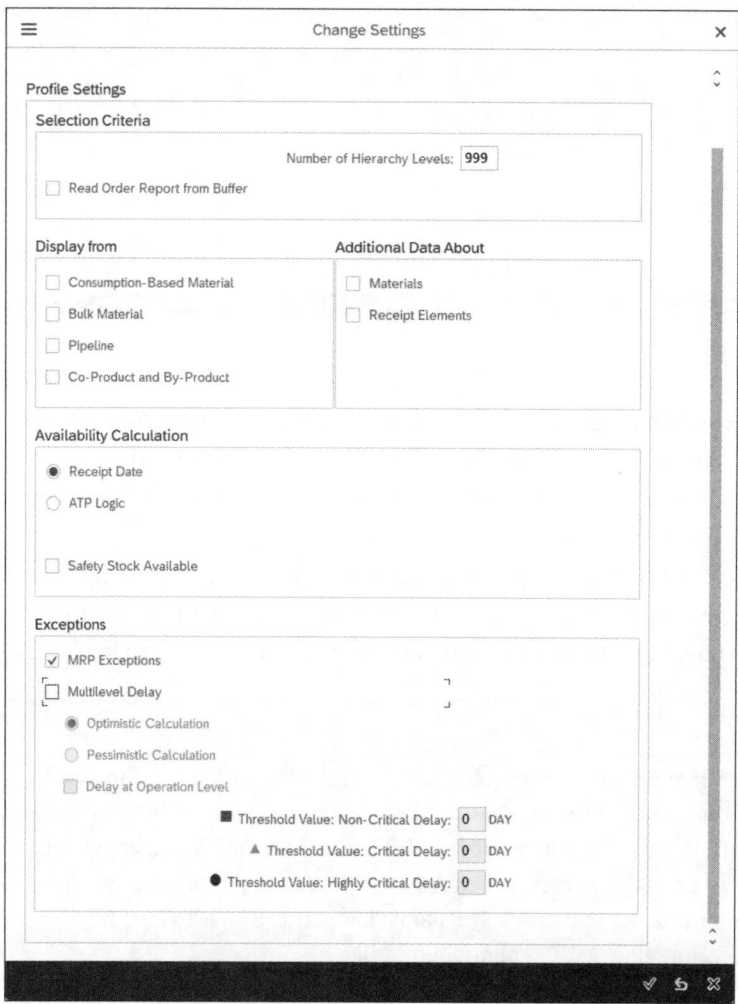

Figure 6.39 Order Report Overall Profile

This can be done with the **Number of Hierarchy Levels** setting and is particularly important for materials with complex product structures, in which we may find performance issues. The **Read Order Report from Buffers** setting can also be used to improve the performance because the Stock/Requirements List can be read from the memory buffer if it has already been accessed.

By default, materials with a consumption-based MRP type (such as reorder point), bulk materials, pipeline materials, and coproducts are not considered in the order report. We can display those materials by checking the respective flags in the overall profile. We can also define in the profile if the receipt date or the available-to-promise logic will be used to determine the availability and if the safety stock will be considered as available or not.

Finally, we can determine if the MRP exception messages will be displayed using the **MRP Exceptions** checkbox, and whether a multilevel delay will be calculated for which we can define thresholds for noncritical, critical, or highly critical delays.

> **Tip**
>
> The order report was completely redesigned in SAP ERP 5.0 when the new ABAP List Viewer layout was introduced. This new layout will only show one receipt, so if you want to see all the requirements assigned to a single receipt, you can access the old layout by assigning the `MTOLD` user parameter with a value of X to the user's own data.

Besides being run with Transaction MD4C, the order report can also be triggered directly from the Stock/Requirements List. We can do so by selecting a specific MRP element and then clicking the **Order Report** button in the pop-up window, as highlighted in Figure 6.40.

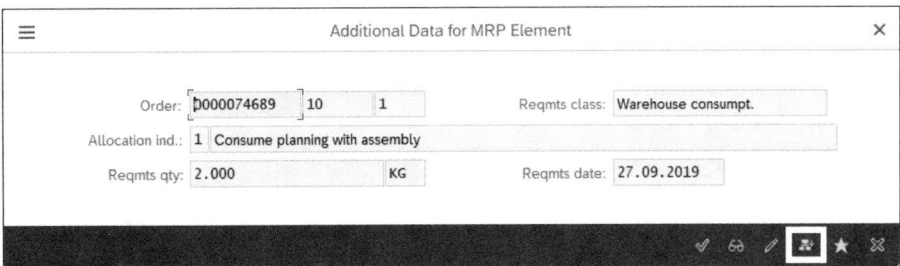

Figure 6.40 Order Report for an MRP Element in the Stock/Requirements List

SAP Note 772012 (Redesign of Transaction MD4C for ECC 5.0) talks about the changes introduced in SAP ERP 5.0 and provides more details about the order report. See also SAP Note 550038 (FAQ: Order Report/Order Tree) for frequently asked questions about the order report.

6.7 Pegged Requirements

Whereas the order report finds all the receipts assigned to the requirements on a multilevel, top-down pegging overview, we can also run a bottom-up pegging analysis to find which requirements are assigned to a given receipt element. We can determine the pegged requirements using Transaction MD09, as shown in Figure 6.41.

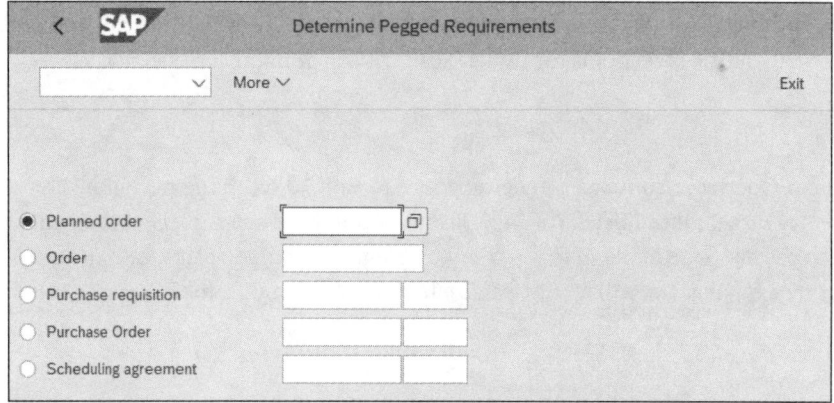

Figure 6.41 Determining Pegged Requirements in Transaction MD09

Pegged requirements can be determined for receipt elements such as the following:

- Planned orders
- Production or process orders
- Purchase requisitions
- Purchase orders
- Scheduling agreements

Starting with the receipt element, SAP S/4HANA will try to find the pegged requirement and build the pegging structure level by level, until it reaches the finished product.

Figure 6.42 shows the results screen of Transaction MD09. In the **Pegged Requirements** section, we will see the finished product requirement to which the receipt element is pegged. The **Route from Source Requirements to MRP Element** section will only be shown if we click the **Order Route** button (highlighted in Figure 6.42); it shows the pegged requirements level by level. In this example, we have triggered the determination of the pegged requirements for a raw material purchase requisition, so we can see the pegged requirements for a semifinished product until reaching the finished product level.

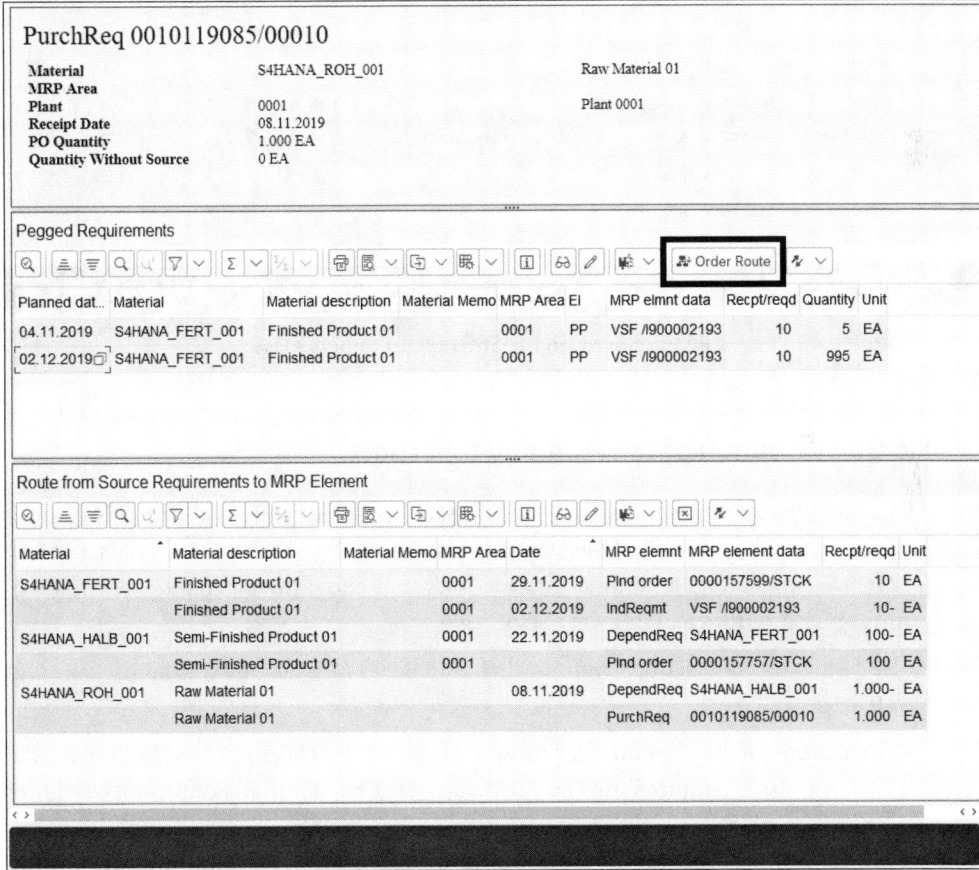

Figure 6.42 Pegged Requirements for Purchase Requisition

We can also trigger the determination of the pegged requirements for an MRP element directly in the Stock/Requirements List. This can be done by clicking the **Pegged Requirements** button, highlighted in Figure 6.43. In the Stock/Requirements List, we can determine the pegged requirements for *any* MRP element, not only for the receipt elements available as selection criteria in Transaction MD09. In Figure 6.43, for example, the pop-up shows the details of a dependent requirement, yet we still have the option to determine the pegged requirements.

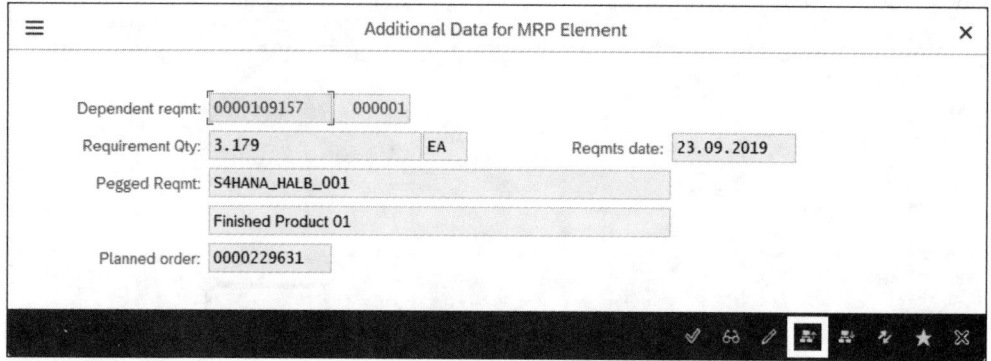

Figure 6.43 Pegged Requirements in the Stock/Requirements List

6.8 Evaluation of the Planning Situation

The Stock/Requirements List and the transactions already discussed in this chapter will provide all the details of the planning results for one or several materials. But SAP S/4HANA also offers additional transactions that allow the evaluation of the planning situation from a high-level perspective.

The following transactions were available in SAP ERP and can still be used in SAP S/4HANA:

- Evaluation of the Planning Situation (Transaction MD44): Based on the actual data, like the Stock/Requirements List, this shows the total number of receipts, requirements, available quantity, and ATP quantity per period.
- Evaluation of the Planning Result (Transaction MD45): Similar to Transaction MD44, but based on the MRP Lists.
- Evaluation of the Planning Result per MRP Controller (Transaction MD46): This is a collective entry for Transaction MD45, in which we can select all the materials

belonging to an MRP controller. A list of materials will be shown, with the respective exception messages. When selecting a material, we will see the planning situation details.

- Evaluation of Product Group Planning (Transaction MD47): This is based in actual data, like Transaction MD44, but it aggregates information from all the materials belonging to the same MRP group.
- Cross-Plant Evaluation (Transaction MD48): Also based in the actual data, this shows the planning situation for a single material across different plants.

The overall design of these transactions is similar, with the main difference being the criteria on the selection screens. For example, in Transaction MD44, we need to enter a material and plant combination, as shown in Figure 6.44. The only transaction with a different design is Transaction MD46, in which we will first see a list of materials before jumping into the details.

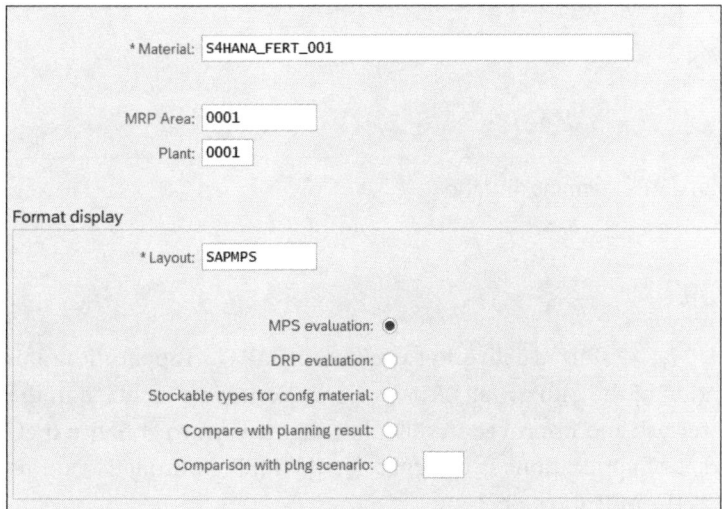

Figure 6.44 Evaluation of the Planning Situation Selection Screen

In the selection screen, we also have options to select the format display and can choose a layout or evaluation type. SAP S/4HANA offers the standard SAPMPS and SAPSOP layouts with predefined settings. When we enter the actual evaluation, we will find a **Definition of Evaluation Profile** button (see Figure 6.45), which explains which MRP elements are considered by each layout.

Besides the layout, we can also set additional display options in the selection screen. We can, for example, compare the planning situation with the planning result or with an LTP planning scenario.

Figure 6.45 shows an evaluation of the planning situation using the SAPMPS layout and the MPS evaluation. The total **Receipts** and **Issues** values are grouped into monthly buckets; we can also see an overview of the available quantity.

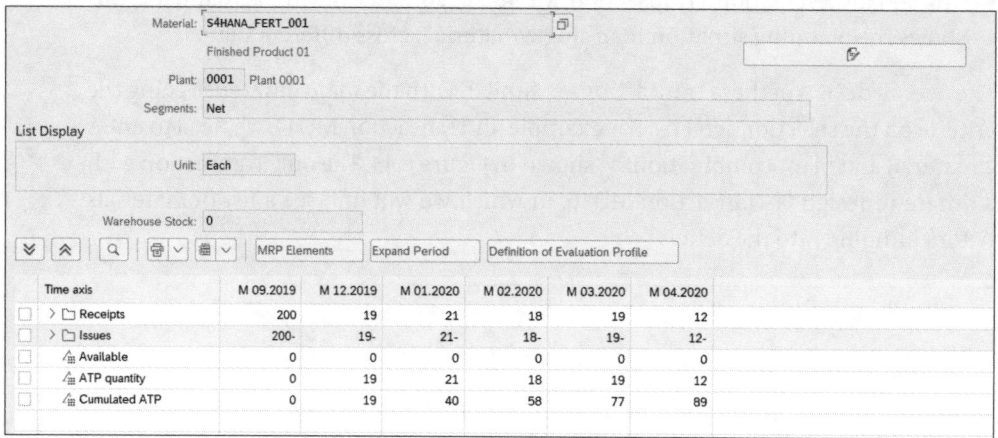

Figure 6.45 Evaluation of the Planning Situation

6.9 MRP Cockpit

As of SAP ERP 6.0 EHP 7, SAP started delivering a new set of SAP Fiori applications tailored for the evaluation of the MRP results. These applications were included in the first SAP S/4HANA release and improved in the following releases to enhance their look and feel. This set of applications is designed for the MRP controller's various tasks and is known as the MRP Cockpit.

Within the MRP Cockpit, the most-used SAP Fiori applications are Monitor Material Coverage and Manage Material Coverage, which will give us a general overview of the planning situation, just like the Stock/Requirements List. Specialized applications such as Monitor External Requirements and Manage External Requirements (focused on sales order requirements), Monitor Internal Requirements and Manage Internal Requirements (focused on order reservations), and Monitor Production and Process Orders and Manage Production and Process Orders (focused on the order itself) are also part of the MRP Cockpit. There are also applications to display MRP issues, display MRP key figures, and detect MRP situations.

In this section, we will discuss how to access the SAP Fiori applications of the MRP Cockpit. Before we go through the MRP Cockpit applications, though, we need to discuss the concept of and the settings behind shortage, on which those applications are based.

6.9.1 Shortage

The main idea of MRP applications is to alert the MRP controller when the projected available quantity will not be able to cover the requirements; this is considered a *shortage*.

The shortage calculation is based on a shortage definition in which we select which MRP elements will be considered in the calculation. SAP S/4HANA provides standard shortage definitions with predefined settings and sets supply and demand elements that will be used to calculate the shortage quantity. We can, however, create custom shortage definitions in Customizing to define our own settings and sets of supply and demand elements to be considered in the calculation.

The Customizing for the SAP Fiori applications in the MRP Cockpit can be accessed in SPRO menu path **Production** · **Material Requirements Planning** · **Apps for Material Requirements Planning** · **General Settings**. The first step to create a new shortage definition is to access the **Supply and Demand Profiles** Customizing activity, where we will select which elements will belong to supply and demand groups. Supply elements will be grouped as stock, execution supplies, ordered supplies, and planned supplies. Demand elements will be grouped as negative stock, execution demands, order demands, and planned demands.

In general, we do not need to create or change those profiles, but if we have to change them, the best way to do so is by copying the SAP standard profiles and then implementing the desired changes. Figure 6.46 shows the details of this Customizing activity, with supply profile SAP00000001 and its assigned receipt elements.

After creating the supply and demand profiles, we can proceed with the creation of the actual material shortage profile in the **Define Material Shortage Profiles** Customizing activity. In this Customizing activity, we will assign the previously created supply and demand profiles and select additional settings, such as the **Evaluation Horizon** setting to define the horizon for which the shortage will be evaluated, the **Past Data** setting to define if requirements in the past will be moved to today or

6 Evaluating the MRP Results

remain in the past, and the **Threshold** setting to define if a shortage is considered when the stock falls below the safety stock or below zero. There are additional settings that are app-specific: the **Demand Driven** setting is used to control whether the profile can be used in the DDMRP applications, and the **Check Components** flag needs to be set in the profile used in the Monitor Production Orders or Monitor Process Orders app.

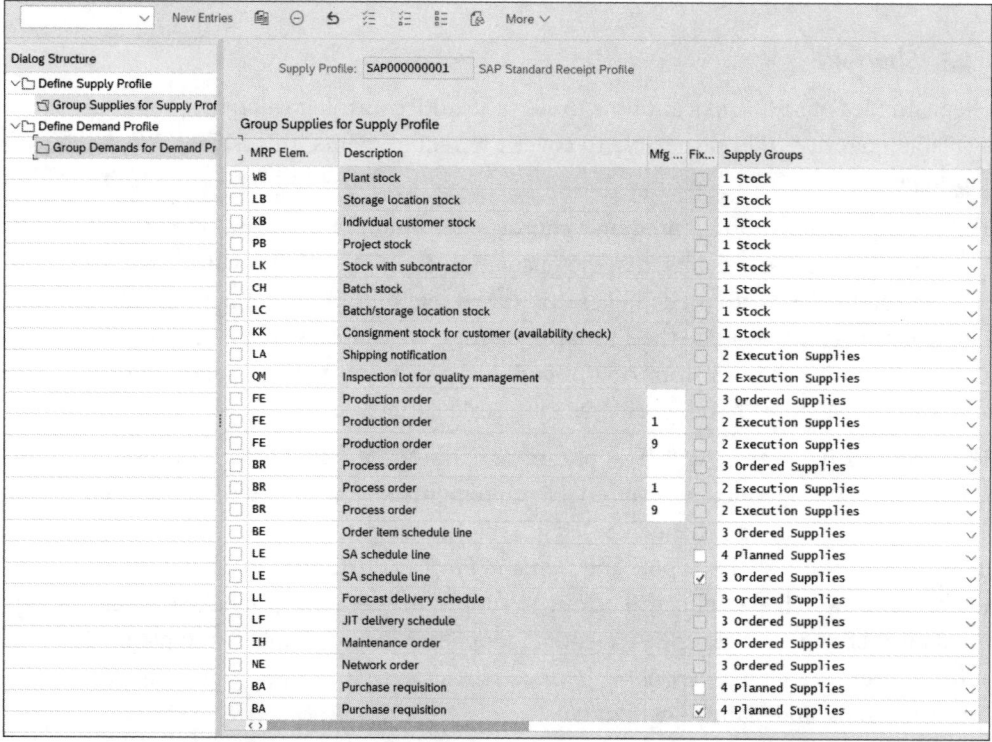

Figure 6.46 Supply and Demand Profiles

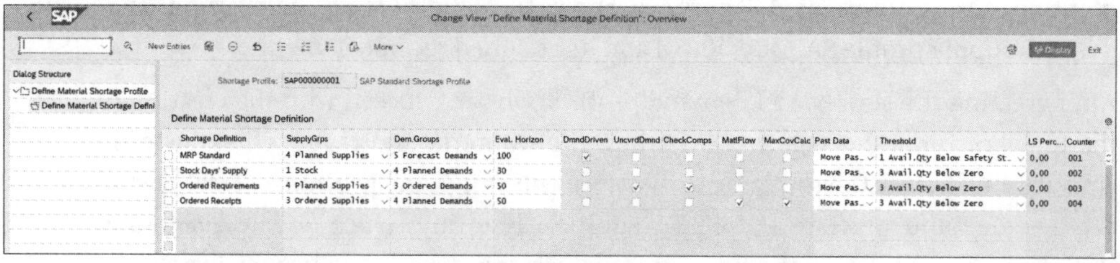

Figure 6.47 Material Shortage Profile Customizing

After the material shortage profile creation, we need to assign it to specific users in the **Assign Material Shortage Profile to User** Customizing activity.

> **Note**
> Customizing changes will only be adopted in the MRP Cockpit applications once the cache is updated, which usually happens the following day. We can manually trigger the cache update using report PPH_MRP_SET_CACHE.

6.9.2 Accessing SAP Fiori Applications for MRP

The SAP Fiori applications for MRP can be accessed through the SAP Fiori launchpad directly in the browser, either with the URL provided by the system administrator or by logging into the SAP Fiori system and running Transaction /UI2/FLP.

When we access the SAP Fiori launchpad in the web browser, we will see different tiles, each one representing a different SAP Fiori application. Each user may have access to a different group of applications, depending on their assigned roles. The MRP Cockpit applications can be accessed by adding the following roles to the user:

- SAP_BR_MATL_PLNR_EXT_PROC (Material Planner—External Procurement)
- SAP_BR_PRODN_PLNR (Production Planner)

> **Tip**
> If we want to know details about a specific SAP Fiori application, including its associated roles, detailed information lives in the SAP Fiori Library at *https://fioriappslibrary.hana.ondemand.com*.

SAP Fiori applications will be grouped in the SAP Fiori launchpad according to the business processes they belong to. MRP applications are grouped into different tabs, such as **Demand Forecasting and Material Data Planning**, **External Procurement**, **Production Planning and Execution**, and **Demand-Driven Replenishment**. Figure 6.48 shows the details of the **Demand Forecasting and Material Data Planning** group, which contains several apps: Maintain PIRs, Monitor Material Coverage (Net Segments), Monitor Material Coverage (Net/Individual Segments), Check Material Coverage, and more.

When accessing an MRP Cockpit application, we will be prompted to choose an area of responsibility with one or more plant and MRP controller combinations. Materials

6 Evaluating the MRP Results

that are displayed in the application are selected according to the area of responsibility assigned to the user. Figure 6.49 shows the details of the **Area of Responsibility** assignment screen; the area of responsibility defined here will be valid for all the MRP Cockpit applications. If we want to change it later, we need to access one of the MRP applications and then go to the **App Settings** menu.

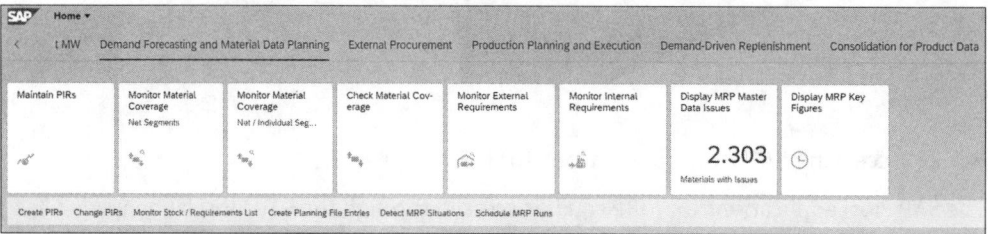

Figure 6.48 MRP Cockpit Applications in the SAP Fiori Launchpad

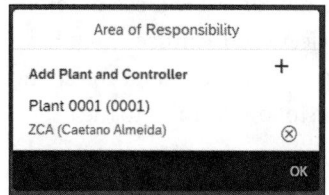

Figure 6.49 Area of Responsibility

If we want to hide a specific material to be displayed in the MRP Cockpit applications, we can use Transaction MD_MRP_FORCE_CLASSIC. This transaction provides a column where we can specify if a material should not be displayed in the MRP applications, as shown in Figure 6.50. If we decide to hide a material from the MRP applications in a specific plant, this change will be valid for all the MRP areas.

Figure 6.50 Transaction MD_MRP_FORCE_CLASSIC

6.9.3 Monitor and Manage Material Coverage

Now that we have clarified the concept of shortage and the Customizing settings behind it, we can discuss how each of the MRP Cockpit applications work. We will start with the Monitor Material Coverage and Manage Material Coverage applications, which are similar to the Stock/Requirements List.

When we access these applications, we will see a list of the materials belonging to the user's area of responsibility, sorted according to the date of the first shortage, as shown in Figure 6.51. For each material, we will see a different line for each MRP area, plus additional information, such as the **Shortage Date** and the **Shortage Quantity** values. We can open the filter bar and include additional fields to limit the number of materials to be displayed; we can also choose a different shortage definition. It is also possible to include additional fields by clicking the cogwheel button.

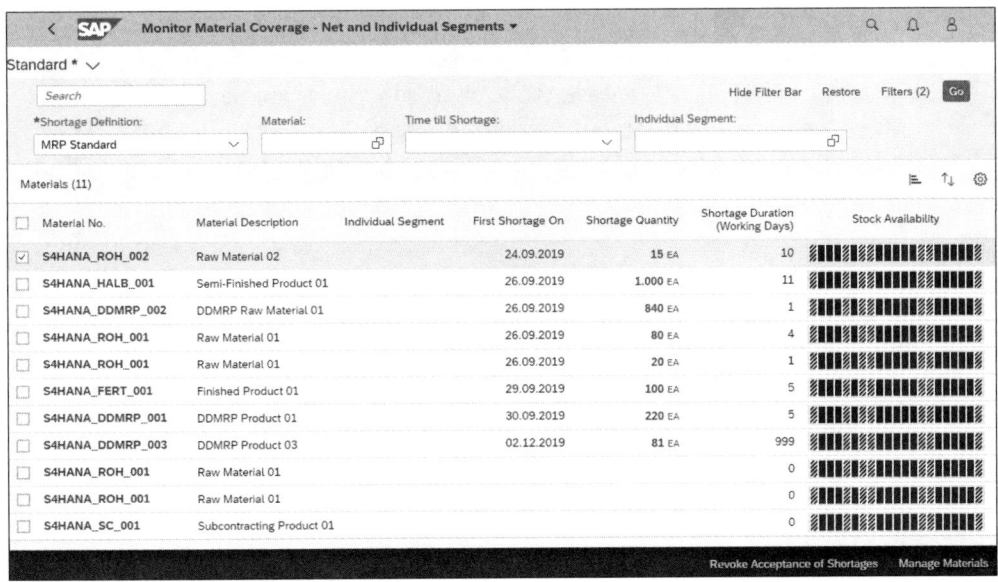

Figure 6.51 The Monitor Material Coverage App

On the right side of the list, we find the **Stock Availability** column, which graphically represents the material availability and the shortages over time. By clicking the **Configure Chart** button, we can choose if the horizon will be defined in days or weeks and the total number of periods, as shown in Figure 6.52.

6   Evaluating the MRP Results

Figure 6.52 Chart Settings

> **Note**
>
> In the first SAP S/4HANA release, this application was not capable of showing shortages in individual segments (sales order and project). As of SAP S/4HANA 1610, a new version was delivered that made it possible to monitor shortages in the individual segments.

After defining all the filters and the chart settings, we can save the settings in a view and use it as the default when accessing the application. It is even possible to create a new tile for the application using a specific view.

By selecting one or more materials in the Monitor Material Coverage app and clicking the **Manage Materials** button, we will open the Manage Material Coverage app. As shown in Figure 6.53, this is where we can see the individual Stock/Requirements List for each material.

In this application, we have an overview of receipts and requirements, very similar to the display of Transaction MD04. By clicking an MRP element, we can see the details of this MRP element in a pop-up (see Figure 6.54) and take actions such as editing the MRP element, changing dates or quantities, opening a specific application, or showing the document info. In this pop-up, we can also see the MRP controller details, including the phone number; we can even directly contact the MRP controller using Skype.

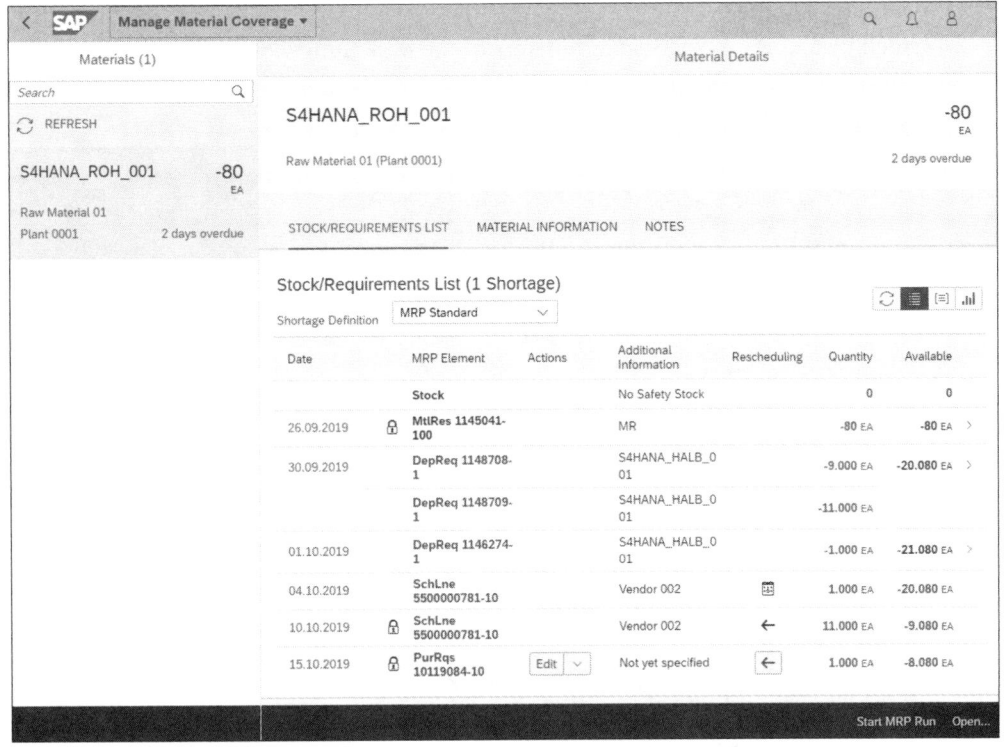

Figure 6.53 The Manage Material Coverage App

> **Note**
> We can also access Manage Material Coverage directly from the SAP Fiori launchpad without going through the Monitor Material Coverage app. In this case, we will be prompted to select the material and plant combination once we access the application.

Besides the Stock/Requirements List, there are two other tabs: the **Material Information** tab stores additional information about the material, and the **Notes** tab is for logging notes relevant for this material.

In the lower-right corner, we find the **Start MRP Run** button, which triggers MRP Live execution for this material, and the **Open** button, which allows us to open the actual Stock/Requirements List (Transaction MD04) or the material info. As discussed in Chapter 5, a single-item, single-level planning run will be executed with hard-coded planning parameters, but these parameters can be changed with a modification provided by SAP Note 2482315 (Parameters of the MRP Run when Called from the MRP Apps).

Figure 6.54 Pop-up with MRP Element Details

In this SAP Fiori application, we do not have information about general exception messages, but as of SAP S/4HANA 1909, there *is* a column showing information about rescheduling messages. For MRP elements such as purchase requisitions, a left-facing arrow button is shown; we can click this button to automatically adopt the rescheduling proposal. For other MRP elements, such as delivery schedules or planned orders, a calendar icon is shown. We can see additional information by positioning the mouse over this button.

In the upper-right corner, two icons allow us to change the Stock/Requirements List display. Besides the default display, we also have an **Aggregated Table** view (the grid icon) and a **Chart** view (the bar chart icon).

For requirements that are causing a shortage, the system highlights the available quantity in red. For materials that are externally procured, we can solve the shortage by selecting the line. The system will automatically show proposals for the different sources of supply available for the material. We can simulate each different source of supply and analyze the best options to cover the shortage. Figure 6.55 shows the material shortage resolution using the chart view, with a graphical overview of the stock availability for each source of supply.

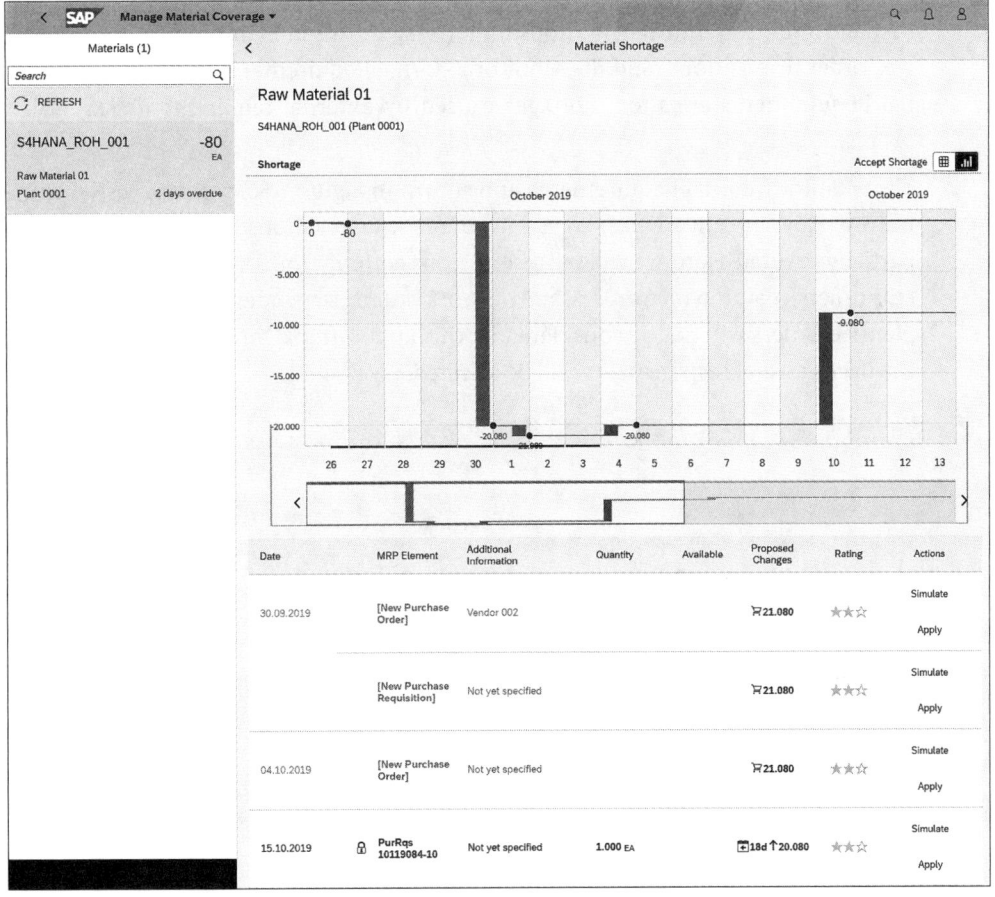

Figure 6.55 Material Shortage Resolution with Chart View

If none of the solutions proposed by the system is actually feasible, we can simply click the **Accept Shortage** button and the shortage will no longer be considered for this material. This means it will go to the bottom of the list in the Monitor Material Shortages app, and the shortage will be greyed out instead of highlighted in red in the chart.

6.9.4 Monitor and Manage Internal Requirements

Whereas Monitor Material Shortages and Manage Material Shortages are generic applications that can be used for any kind of material shortage, there are two sets of applications for specific types of shortages: the Monitor Internal Requirements and Manage Internal Requirements apps for shortages caused by internal requirements (i.e., order reservations) and the Monitor External Requirements and Manage External Requirements apps for shortages caused by external requirements (e.g., sales orders).

The Monitor Internal Requirements app shown in Figure 6.56 can be accessed from the SAP Fiori launchpad and shows a list of order reservations that are uncovered or partially covered. Here, we will see reservations coming from production orders, process orders, maintenance orders, and network orders. Dependent requirements from planned orders will not be considered by this application. Only orders belonging to the user's area of responsibility will be selected.

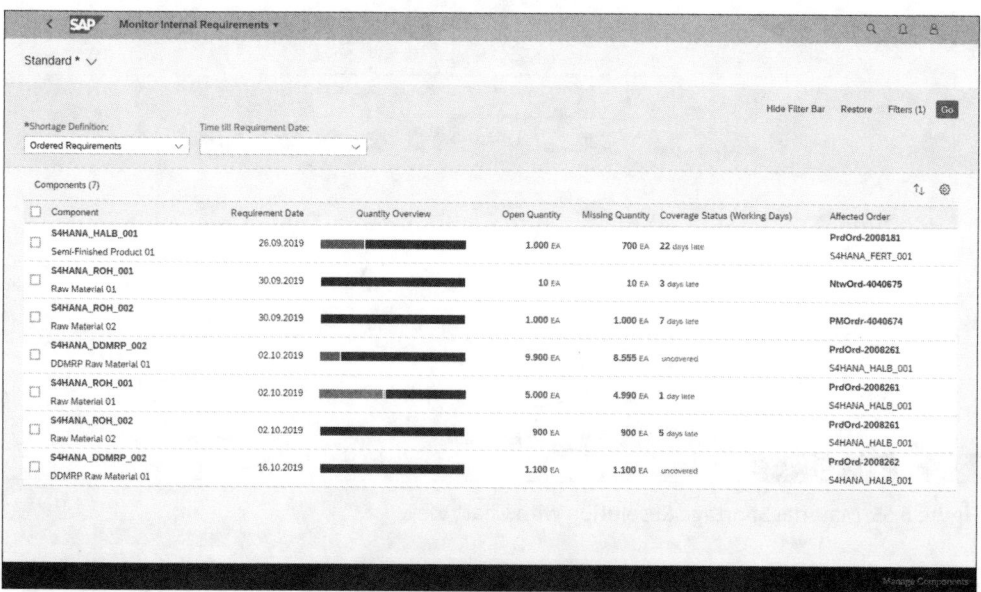

Figure 6.56 The Monitor Internal Requirements App

Each record shown in this app will represent a different reservation that cannot be covered with the projected stock. These reservations are sorted according to the **Requirement Date** column, and we can also see **Open Quantity**, **Missing Quantity**, **Coverage Status**, and **Affected Order** values in their corresponding columns.

A graphical representation of the **Quantity Overview** value is shown for each line: green represents the covered quantity, red represents the uncovered quantity, and grey represents the issued quantity.

In this application, we also have the shortage definition and can define filters, save views, and select the columns to be displayed. Only the shortage definition with the **Uncovered Demand** and **Check Components** flags set in Customizing can be selected in this application.

> **Tip**
>
> We can limit the number of reservations to be displayed in this application using the **Time till Requirement Date** filter. We might not want to take action on shortages that are far in the future because MRP will have time to plan the coverage accordingly.

By selecting one or more lines and clicking the **Manage Components** button, we will jump into the Manage Internal Requirements app shown in Figure 6.57 and will see the immediately see the Stock/Requirement List.

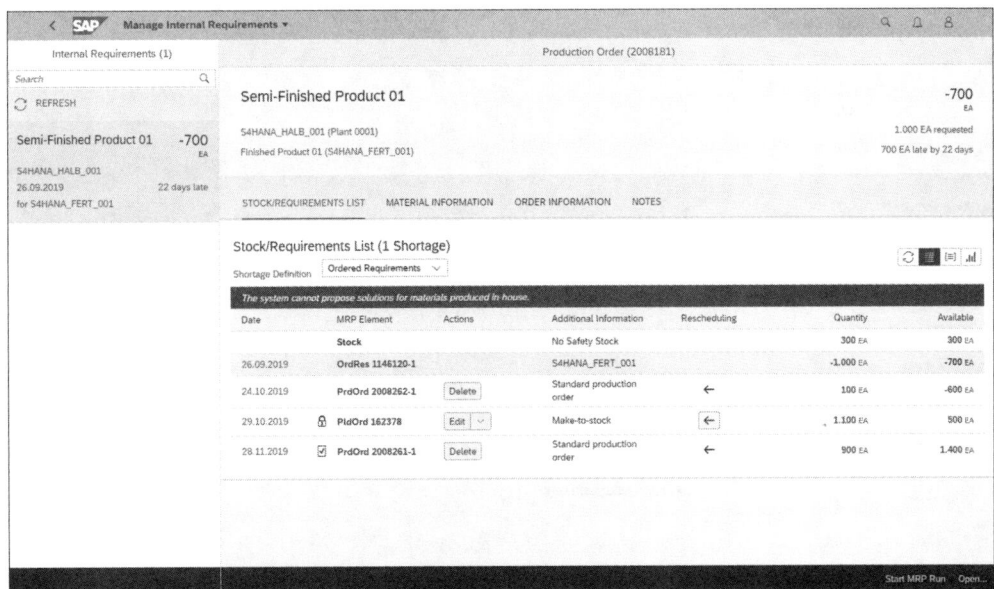

Figure 6.57 The Manage Internal Requirements App

6   Evaluating the MRP Results

This application is very similar to the Manage Material Shortages app shown in the previous section; the main differences are that we will see the production order number on top of the screen, the selected reservation will be highlighted in the Stock/Requirements List, and we have an additional **Order Information** tab for information about the order.

6.9.5   Monitor and Manage External Requirements

For managing external requirements (i.e., requirements coming from sales orders), we also have the specialized Monitor External Requirements and Manage External Requirements apps. These applications are very similar to the ones for monitoring and managing internal requirements that we discussed in the previous section, but the main difference is that they will focus on sales orders instead of reservations.

We can also access these applications directly through the SAP Fiori launchpad. We will immediately see a list of sales order requirements that are leading to a shortage, per the shortage definition.

As shown in Figure 6.58, sales orders will be sorted according to the **Requirement Date** column, and there will be columns showing the **Open Quantity**, **Missing Quantity**, and **Coverage Status** values.

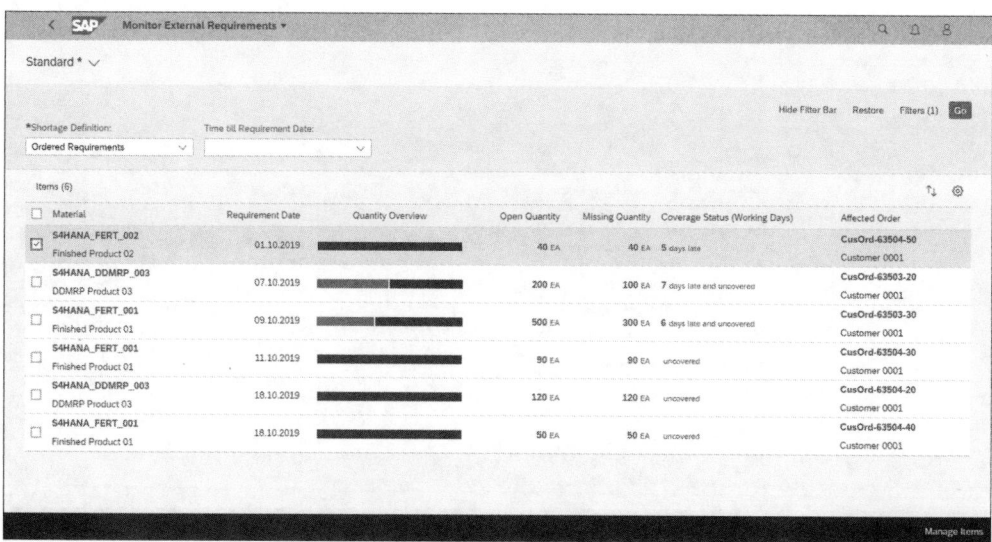

Figure 6.58   The Monitor External Requirements App

In the **Quantity Overview** column, there is a graphical representation of the quantity, similar to the Monitor Internal Shortages app. Additional features already mentioned for the other applications, such as adding new columns, changing the filters, or saving the views, are also available in this application.

By selecting a line and clicking the **Manage Items** button, we will open the Manage External Requirements app, where the Stock/Requirements List will be displayed. Here we have information about the sales order, such as the sales order number, item, and customer, as shown in Figure 6.59.

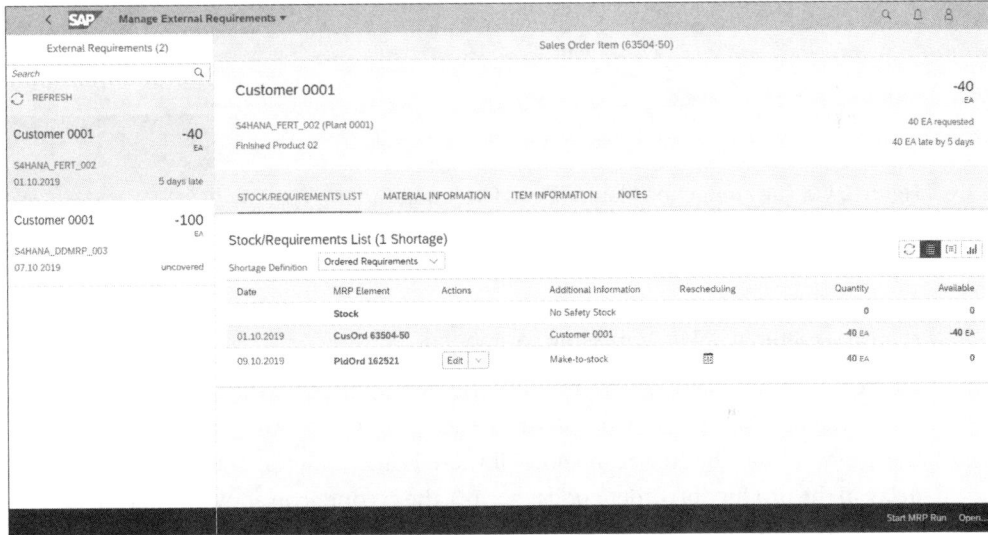

Figure 6.59 The Manage External Requirements App

An additional **Item Information** tab will show the sales order item details, such as customer information, dates, and quantity. From here, we can also trigger the MRP run or open the info page with details about the material or the sales order document.

6.9.6 Monitor and Manage Production or Process Orders

The Monitor Production Orders and Monitor Process Orders apps can be found under the **Production Planning and Execution** group in the SAP Fiori launchpad (see Figure 6.60), but they are still considered part of the MRP Cockpit. These applications are focused on production and process orders, respectively—not on the shortage, like the applications previously discussed, but on delays for the order receipt, missing components, and delayed order milestones.

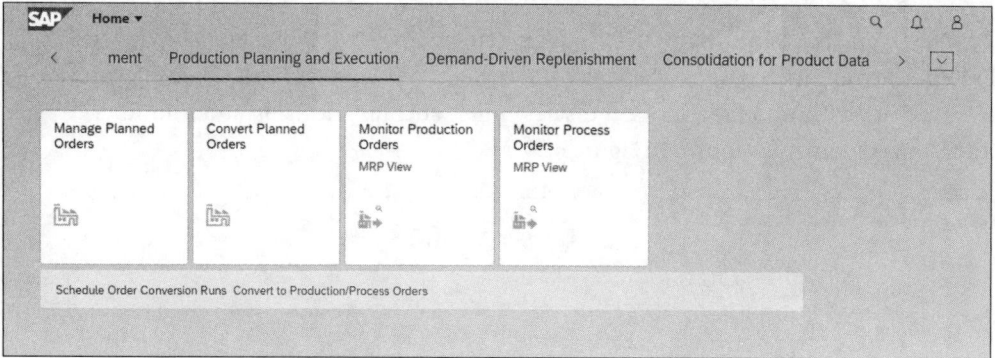

Figure 6.60 The Production Planning and Execution Group

When entering one of these applications, we will see a list of production or process orders belonging to the user's area of responsibility for which we have a problem, such as a material delay or missing components.

Figure 6.61 shows the Monitor Production Orders app, where we will have three icons in the first column, showing the status of each production order, highlighted in red if there is an issue. The first icon shows if there is any material delay (i.e., if there is a delay in the production order goods receipt), the second icon shows if there are missing components, and the last one shows if there are delays in the order milestones (i.e., if there is a delay in releasing or in the operation confirmation dates). Besides these icons, we have information about the order start, end, quantity, status, and delays.

By selecting the orders and clicking the **Manage Orders** button in the bottom right, we will see the **Stock/Requirements List** pane (see Figure 6.62), as for the other MRP Cockpit applications. If there are problems in the header material goods receipt, with the components, and with the order milestones, then we will also see icons that will be highlighted in red. We also have additional icons showing the material information and order information.

6.9 MRP Cockpit

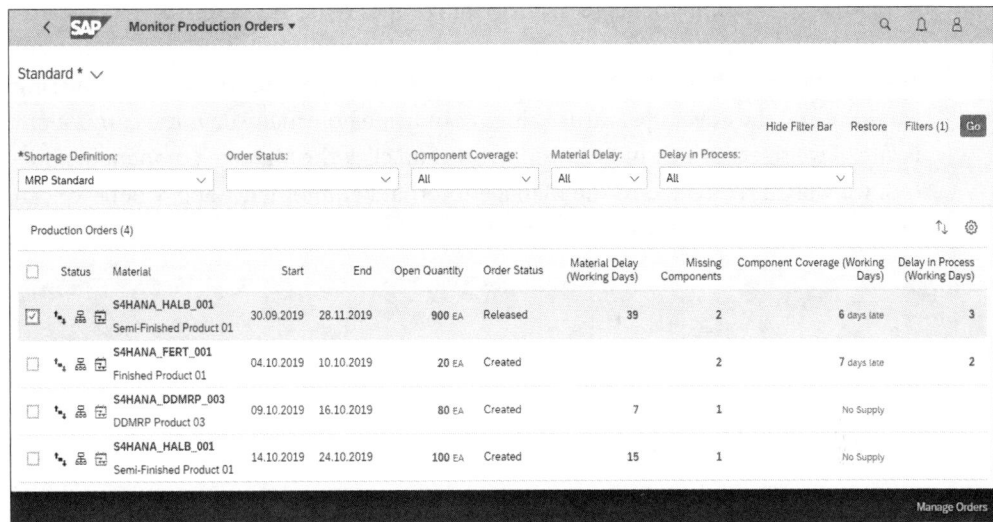

Figure 6.61 The Monitor Production Orders App

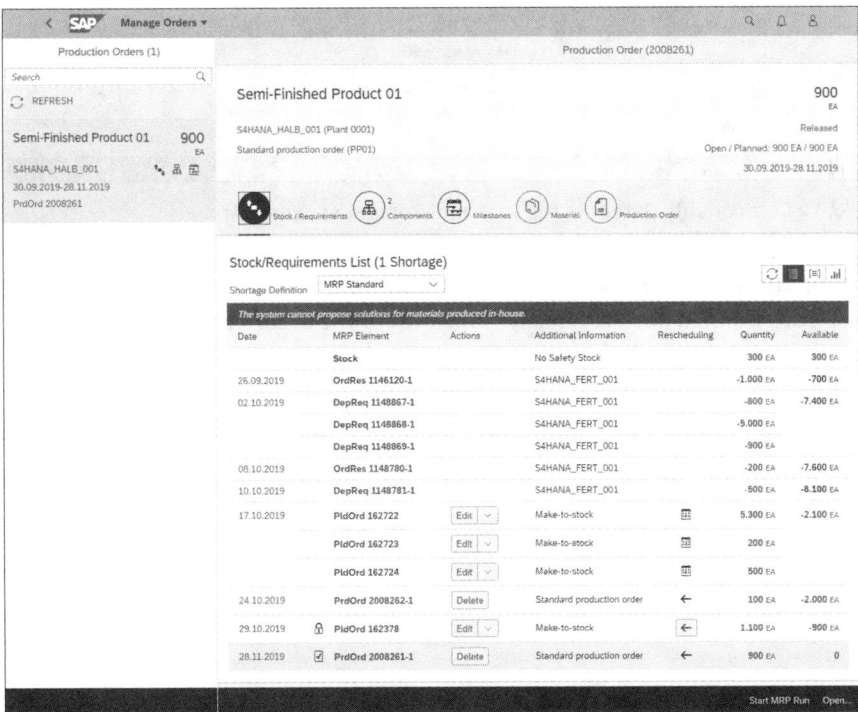

Figure 6.62 The Manage Production Orders App

6 Evaluating the MRP Results

If we select the **Components** icon, a list of components will be displayed, and the **Quantity Overview** column will offer a graphical representation of the component availability, as shown in Figure 6.63. We can also see a column showing the **Missing Quantity** and the **Coverage Status** values to indicate how many days the component is late. If we select one or more components and click the **Manage Components** button, we will be redirected to the Manage Internal Requirements app, where we can take actions to resolve the component shortage.

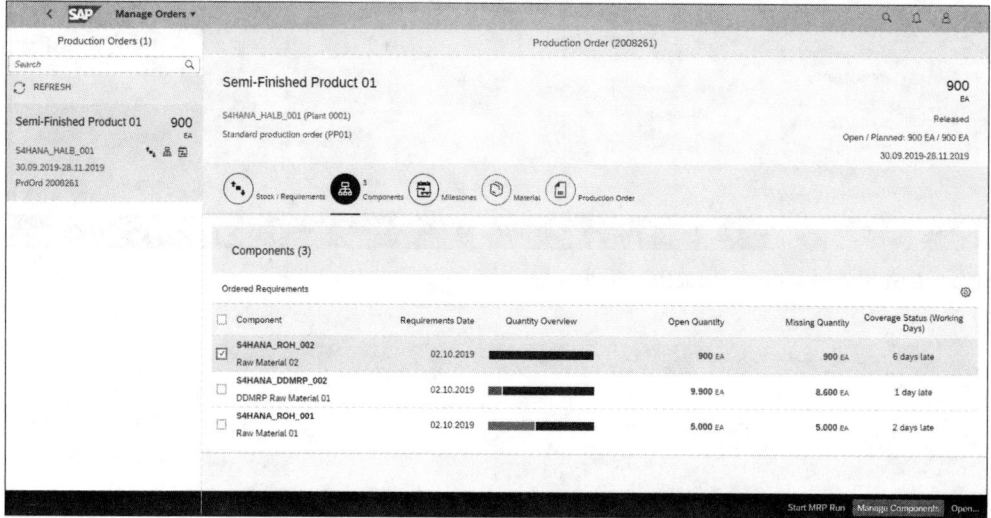

Figure 6.63 Components Details in the Manage Production Orders App

By clicking the **Milestones** button, we will see an overview of the order milestones, including the planned and actual dates and a list of the order operations (see Figure 6.64). The order operations will show the open quantity, the order status, and, as of SAP S/4HANA 1909, an overview of the work center utilization.

6.9 MRP Cockpit

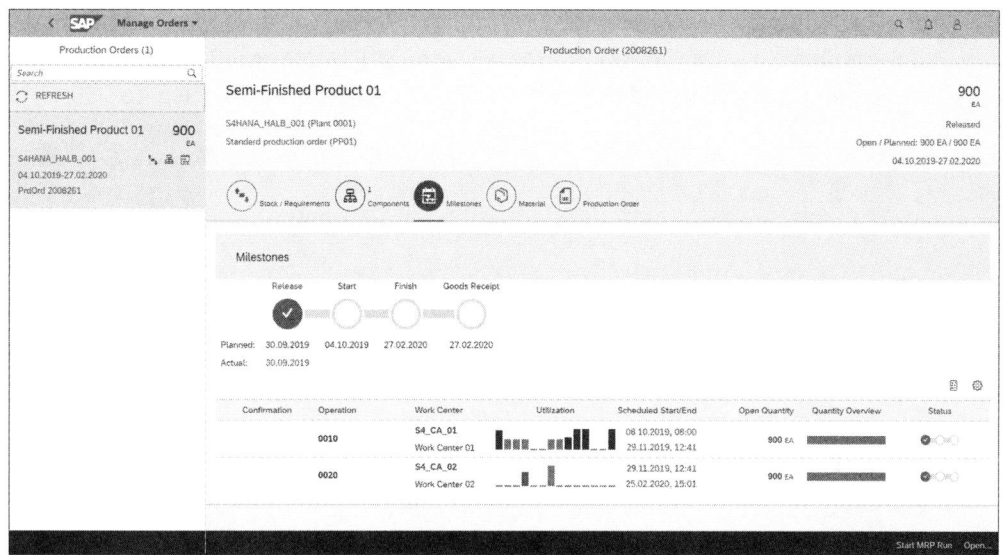

Figure 6.64 Production Order Milestones

6.9.7 Display MRP Master Data Issues

SAP S/4HANA no longer includes the MRP List, but as of release 1809, it offers the new Display MRP Master Data Issues app. The application can be accessed through the SAP Fiori launchpad; its tile will highlight the total number of issues detected during the MRP run, as shown in Figure 6.65.

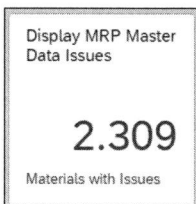

Figure 6.65 The Display MRP Master Data Issues Tile

When we enter this application, a list of the materials that were previously planned by MRP will be shown. By default, all the planned materials will be shown, even those which were successfully planned. If we only want to focus on materials with actual issues, we can use the **Category** field to filter.

289

6 Evaluating the MRP Results

The application will show a description of the issue, the category, whether the material was planned in classic MRP or in MRP Live on SAP HANA, whether it was accepted or not, who accepted it, and the creation date and time, as shown in Figure 6.66.

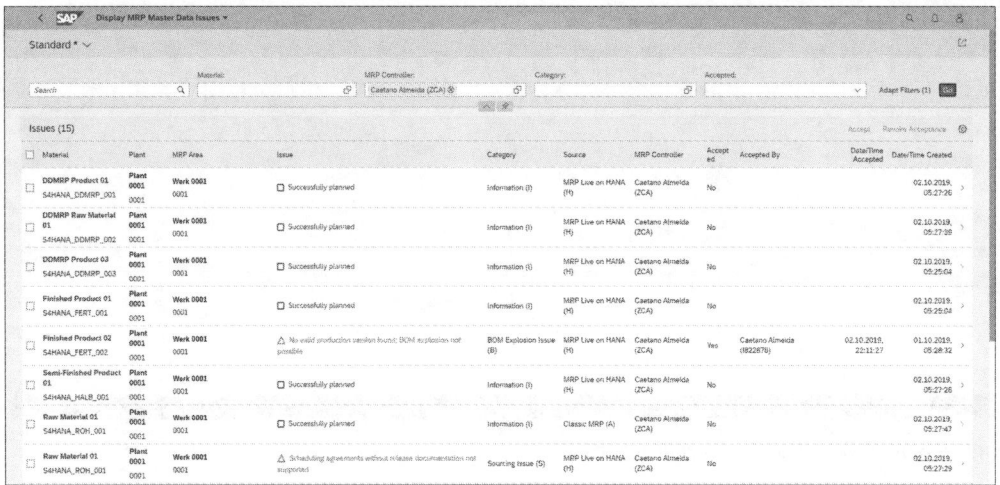

Figure 6.66 The Display MRP Master Data Issues App

> **Warning**
>
> This application will not limit the selection based on the area of responsibility. If we want to limit the selection by MRP controller, we need to add it as a filter and save a standard view for the user.

If we select a material with an actual issue, we can click the **Accept** button to let the system know that we are aware of this issue and will take care of it. If an issue is accepted, the total number of materials with issues shown in the SAP Fiori application tile will be reduced. We can also click the arrow at the end of the line to see additional information about the issue, such as the error message ID and number, for example.

6.9.8 Manage Change Requests

The MRP Cockpit applications allow us to make changes to the dates and quantities of replenishment proposals created by MRP. For replenishment proposals created for externally procured materials, we may not simply make the changes in a purchase order because we will depend on the vendor acknowledgement.

The MRP Cockpit applications offer a new process by which we can request the changes in purchase order dates or quantities and manage those change requests. To activate this feature, we access any of the MRP Cockpit applications and open the **User** menu, choosing the **MRP Settings** option. Here, we will have the option to activate the **Change Requests** setting, as shown in Figure 6.67.

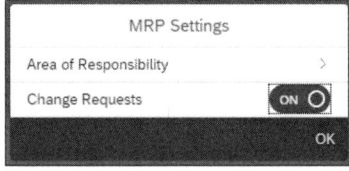

Figure 6.67 Activation of Change Requests on MRP Settings

After we activate the change requests, whenever we make a change to an existing purchase order through the MRP Cockpit applications, we will have the option to make the change immediately, to request the change immediately, or to request a change to be processed later, as shown in Figure 6.68.

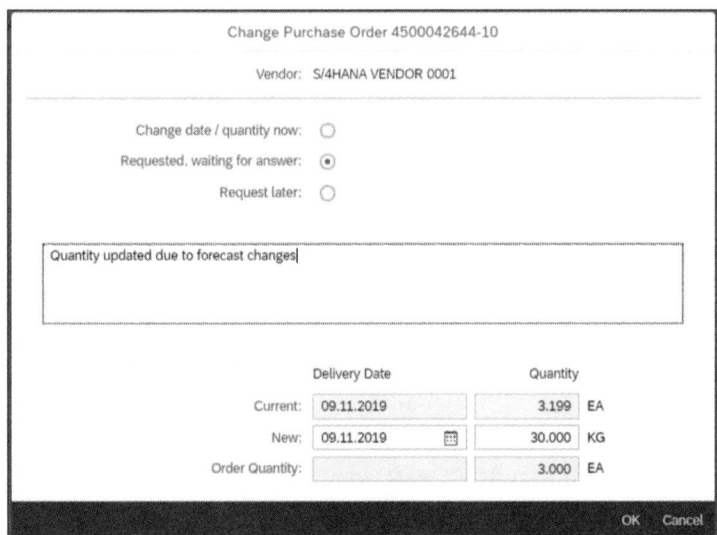

Figure 6.68 Creation of Change Request when Changing a Purchase Order

After the creation of the change request, we can use the four SAP Fiori applications shown in Figure 6.69 for managing all change requests, new change requests, requested change requests, and answered change requests. The application tiles will also show the total number of requests at each stage, with the exception of the application that shows all the requests.

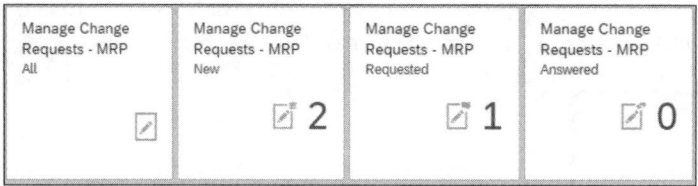

Figure 6.69 SAP Fiori Applications for Managing Change Requests

The designs of those applications are very similar, and in all of them we will have tabs showing the change requests at the different stages. The only difference between them is that we will open directly on the pertinent tab for each application. Figure 6.70 shows the application to manage change requests with a list of new change requests.

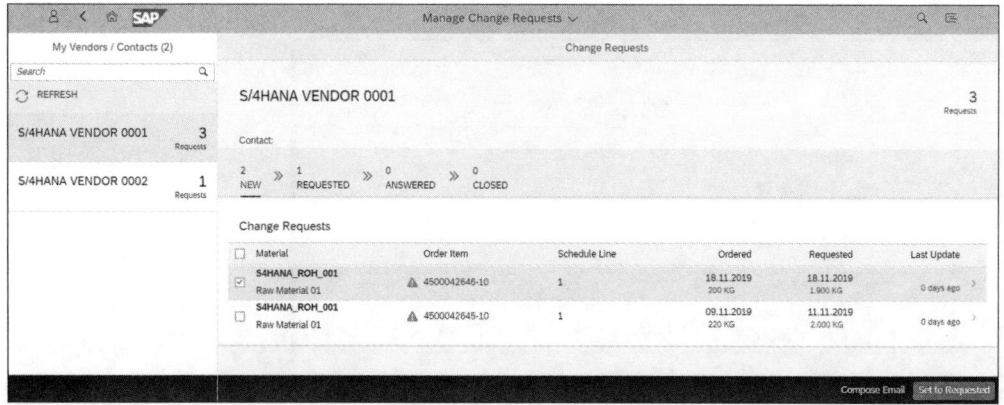

Figure 6.70 New Change Requests

For the new change requests, we have the option to send an email to the supplier requesting the change and then to set it to a requested status. For the pending change requests, we can select one of the requests and choose if it was accepted, rejected, or if the vendor came back with a new proposal, as shown in Figure 6.71. Here, the requested changes can be applied to the purchase order or simply discarded.

6.9 MRP Cockpit

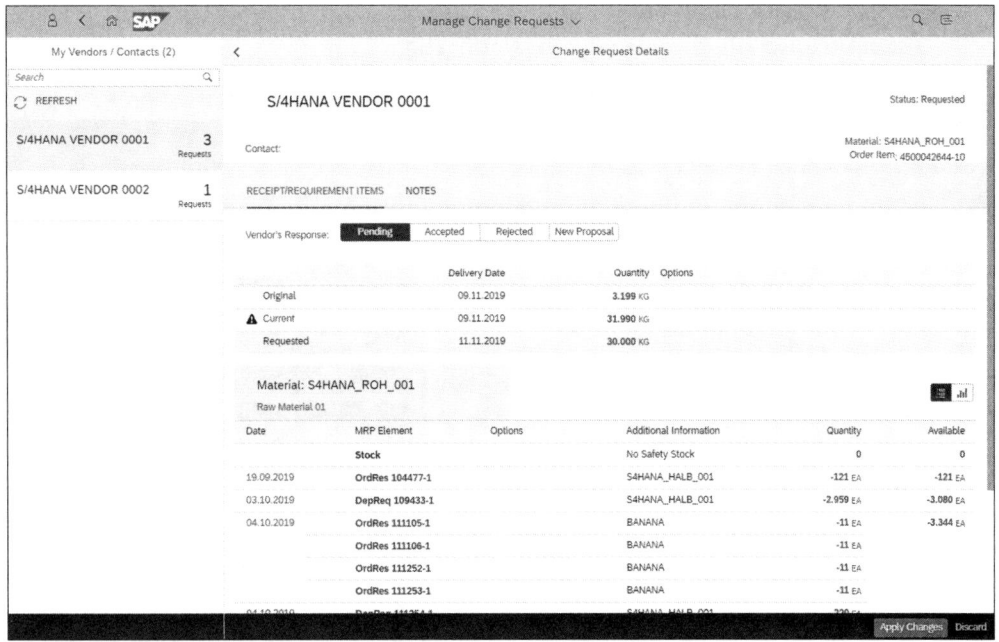

Figure 6.71 Pending Change Requests

Tip

Report PPMRP_CHANGE_REQUEST_DELETE can be used to delete the applied or discarded change requests. It should be executed periodically to avoid performance issues in the Manage Change Requests apps.

6.9.9 Detect MRP Situations

SAP S/4HANA 1909 includes a new cross-application feature called *situation handling*, used to direct users' attention to important situations in which they need to take action. For example, if a stock transfer was created to bring an important product from another plant, then situation handling can be used to inform the inventory planner if it becomes overdue.

Whenever a situation is identified, the **Notifications** icon (a bell) will be highlighted; when clicked, it will show a list of the pending situations. It is also possible to see an overview of all the existing situations in the My Situations app, which displays the number of situations on its tile. Figure 6.72 shows the SAP Fiori application tile and a list of situations displayed under the **Notifications** icon.

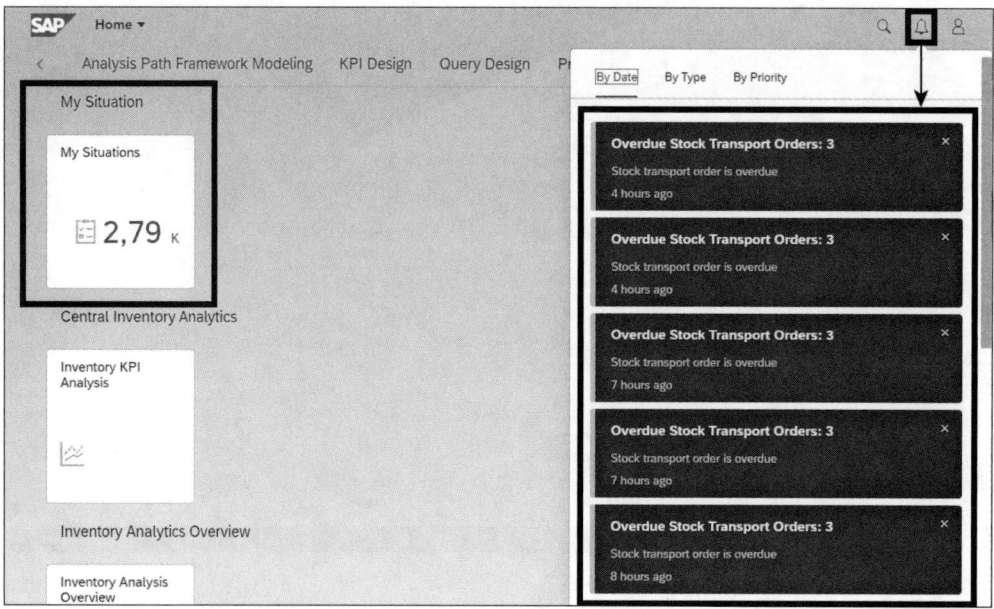

Figure 6.72 Situation Handling in the SAP Fiori Launchpad

Situation handling is a framework that can be used in many different applications, from notifying users about sales quotations about to expire or invoices that were skipped for payment advice. We also have a situation handling scenario in MRP, wherein the planner will be informed about rescheduling exception messages for the selected materials.

The following MRP exceptions can be identified in this situation handling MRP scenario:

- Excess stock
- Cancel process

To enable the situation handling for MRP exception messages, we need to set it up in the system. Part of the setup is MRP-specific and part is related to the situation handling framework, with activities typically performed by the system administrator.

On the MRP side, we must schedule periodic execution of a background job that will detect the MRP exception messages for the MRP materials. This background job can be set up with the Detect MRP Situations app.

This application will be used to schedule and manage a background job that will provide the inputs for the situation handling framework. In the initial screen, we will see the list of the scheduled and finished jobs; we also have options to create, copy, or delete the jobs—similar to the other SAP Fiori applications used to manage background jobs, such as the application used to schedule MRP runs.

When scheduling a new background job, we need to provide the scheduling options and the parameters that will be used to select for which materials we want to detect situations. We can use the material, MRP area, MRP controller, or the plant as a selection criterion, as shown in Figure 6.73.

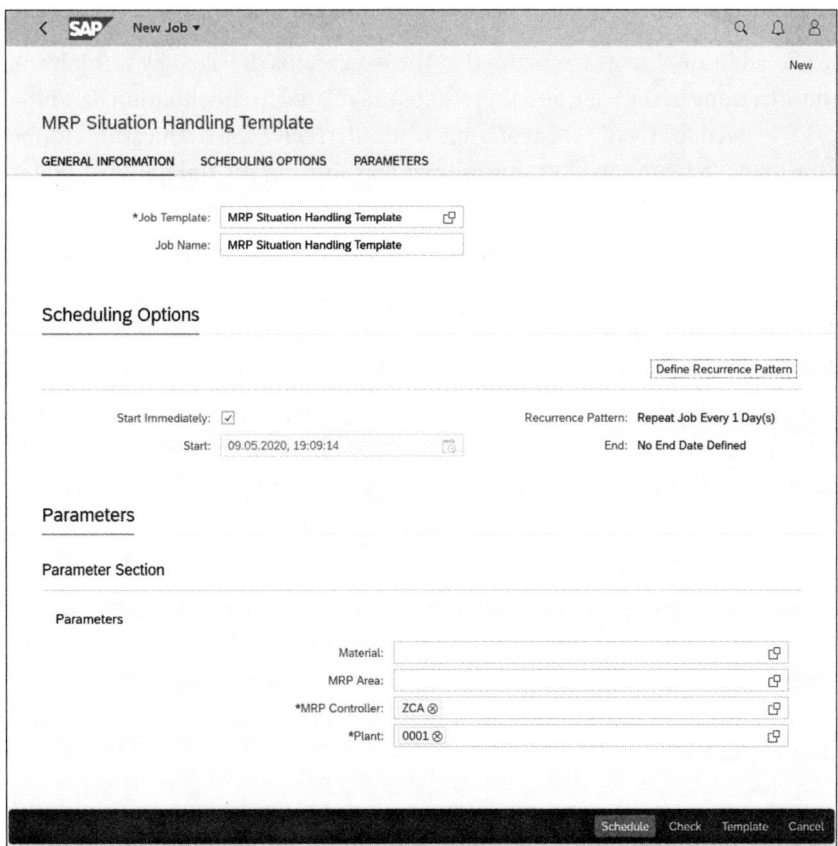

Figure 6.73 The Detect MRP Situations App

6 Evaluating the MRP Results

After the job execution, we will be able to see the job log, showing a list of exception messages detected for each material, as shown in Figure 6.74.

Material	Plnt	MRP Area	MRPCn	El	MRP elemnt	MRP No.	MRP itm	Sche	MRP segment	Planning segment	MRP Situation	Exception Message	Rec./reqd.qty	BUn	Matl Group
S4HANA_FERT_001	0001	0001	ZCA	PA	Plnd order	179665	000000	0000	20	00000643300000100000	CAN	Cancel process	40,000	EA	000000001
S4HANA_FERT_001	0001	0001	ZCA	PA	Plnd order	182121	000000	0000	20	00000643300000100000	CAN	Excess in individual segment —> 60,000	100,000	EA	000000001
S4HANA_FERT_002	0001	0001	ZCA	PA	Plnd order	179195	000000	0000	02		CAN	Cancel process	600,000	EA	000000001
S4HANA_ROH_001	0001	0001	ZCA	BA	PurchReq	10124463	000010	0000	02		CAN	Excess stock —> 500,000	600,000	EA	000000001
S4HANA_ROH_001	0001	0001	ZCA	BA	PurchReq	10124464	000010	0000	02		CAN	Excess stock —> 500,000	600,000	EA	000000001
S4HANA_ROH_001	0001	0001	ZCA	BA	PurchReq	10124465	000010	0000	02		CAN	Excess stock —> 500,000	600,000	EA	000000001
S4HANA_ROH_001	0001	0001	ZCA	BA	PurchReq	10124466	000010	0000	02		CAN	Excess stock —> 500,000	600,000	EA	000000001

Figure 6.74 Exceptions Detected during Job Execution

There are two additional steps to ensure that the exceptions detected by this job will become notifications to the user, and these steps are related to the situation handling framework. We need to create a team of users who will receive the notifications (done through the Manage Teams and Responsibilities app) and use the standard templates to create a situation type (done through the Manage Situation Types app).

Because running those applications is not responsibility of the MRP planner, they are not included in the roles mentioned earlier in this chapter. Users will get access to those applications with the SAP_BR_BPC_EXPERT (Configuration Expert—Business Process Configuration) role.

We will use the Manage Teams and Responsibilities app to create a team of users who will receive the notification. We will choose type PPMRP, which is delivered by SAP, and the responsibility definitions will be automatically determined. To use this team, we need to ensure that the **Ready to Use** status is selected.

The responsibility definition comprises the selection criteria that will be used to determine for which group of materials this team will receive exceptions. In the example shown in Figure 6.75, we filter by the **MRP Controller** value, so all team members will receive notifications related to the materials assigned to a specific MRP controller. It is also necessary to define a team owner and the team members who will receive the notifications.

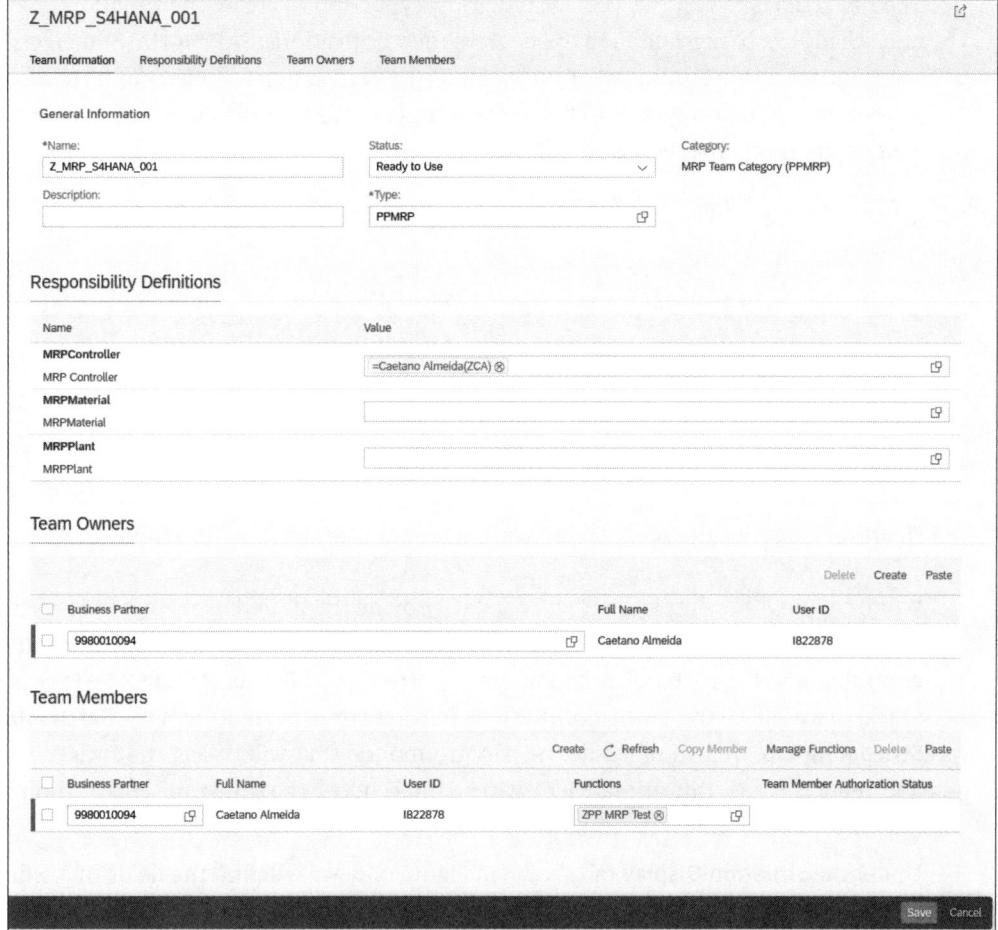

Figure 6.75 The Manage Teams and Responsibilities App

> **Note**
> The team owner and the team members must be business partners linked to an SAP user. The following business partner roles can be used:
> - Employee (BUP003)
> - Service Provider (BBP005)
> - Freelancer (BBP010)

6 Evaluating the MRP Results

The final step is to run the Manage Situation Types app to create the situation type and schedule a background job to generate the notifications. SAP S/4HANA delivers the standard SAP_PP_MRP_MATERIAL_EXCEPTION situation template for us to create our own situation type. We choose the template and click the **Copy** button to create our situation type, as shown in Figure 6.76.

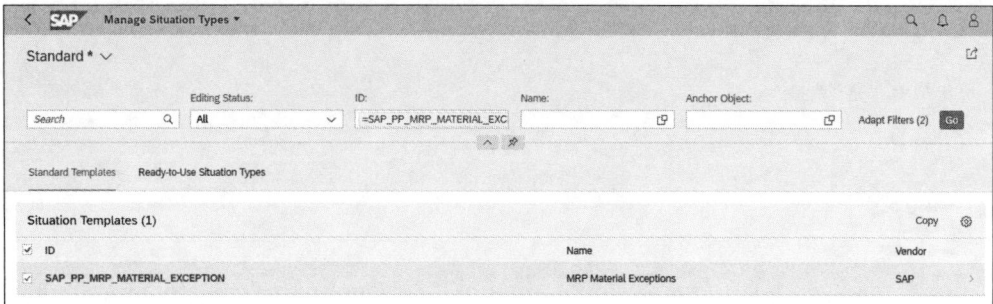

Figure 6.76 Copying the Situation Template in the Manage Situation Types App

When copying the template, we will need to provide the ID and use filters to restrict the notifications. In the example shown in Figure 6.77, we have filtered using the MRP controller and the material situation types **CAN—Cancel Proposal** and **EXC—Excess Stock**, so we will be triggering notifications for these exceptions. Under the **Batch Job Scheduling** tab, we will schedule the background job that will collect the situations and generate the notifications. Here, we can only choose the time zone and the hour for which the job will be scheduled every day.

Under the **Situation Display** tab shown in Figure 6.78, we will find the fields that will determine how a notification will be displayed in the SAP Fiori launchpad. Those fields are prepopulated by the situation template, but we can change the description to change the notification display.

> **Tip**
> If we do not want to see a new notification for the same exception message whenever the job runs, we need to uncheck the **Resend Notifications** flag.

6.9 MRP Cockpit

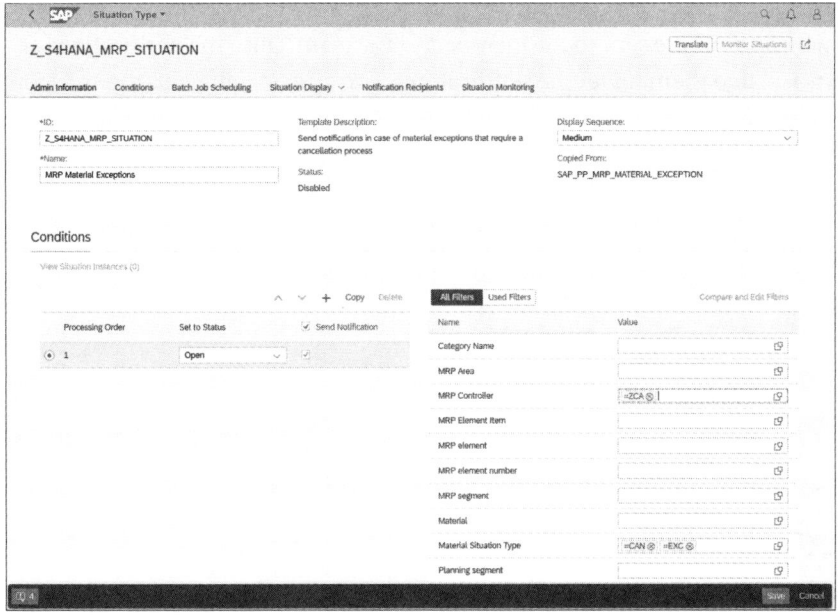

Figure 6.77 Creating a Situation Type

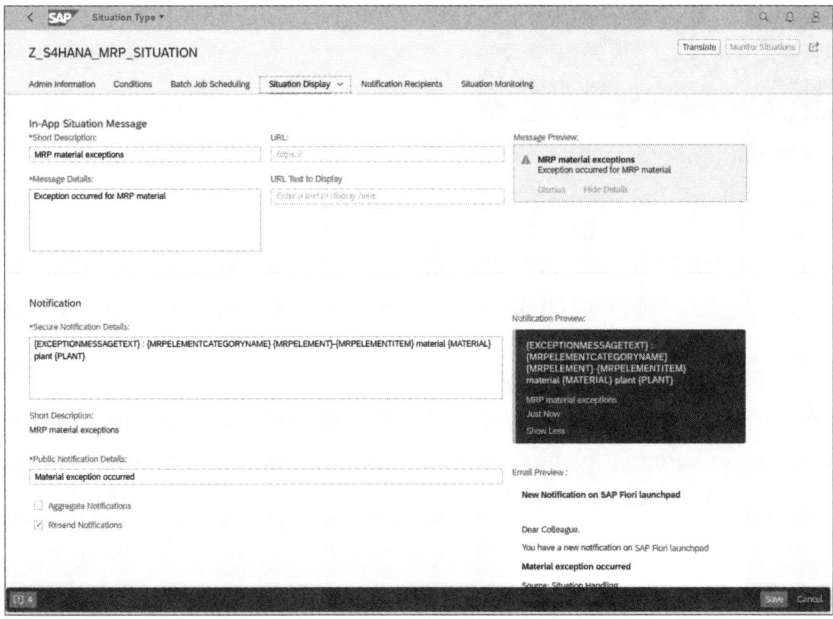

Figure 6.78 Situation Display

299

After enabling the situation type, we will only need to wait until the job is executed and the notifications are sent to the members of the team. Once the notifications are sent, users will find them under the **Notifications** icon after logging into the SAP Fiori launchpad, as shown in Figure 6.79.

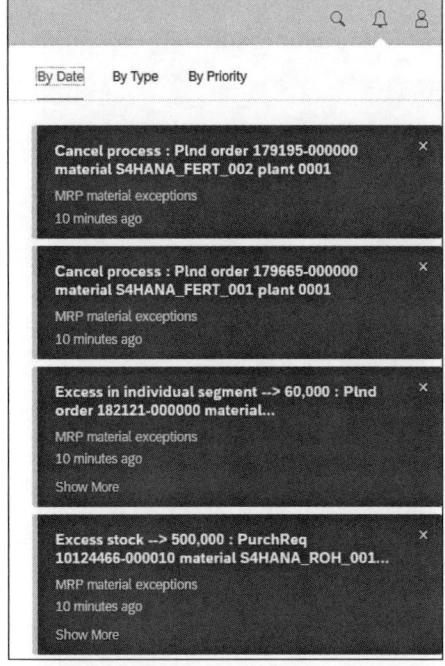

Figure 6.79 Notifications for MRP Exception Messages

By selecting one of these notifications, we will be redirected to the Manage Material Coverage app, in which the planner will be able to take actions to prevent this exception from causing any issues, as shown in Figure 6.80. For example, if the exception message is **Cancel Process**, the planner can verify that there really is no requirement for this replenishment proposal and can proceed with the order cancellation.

Using SAP S/4HANA's situation handling feature for MRP exception messages is an excellent way to ensure that planners stay informed of important exceptions that could potentially cause problems, such as excess stock or even a material shortage.

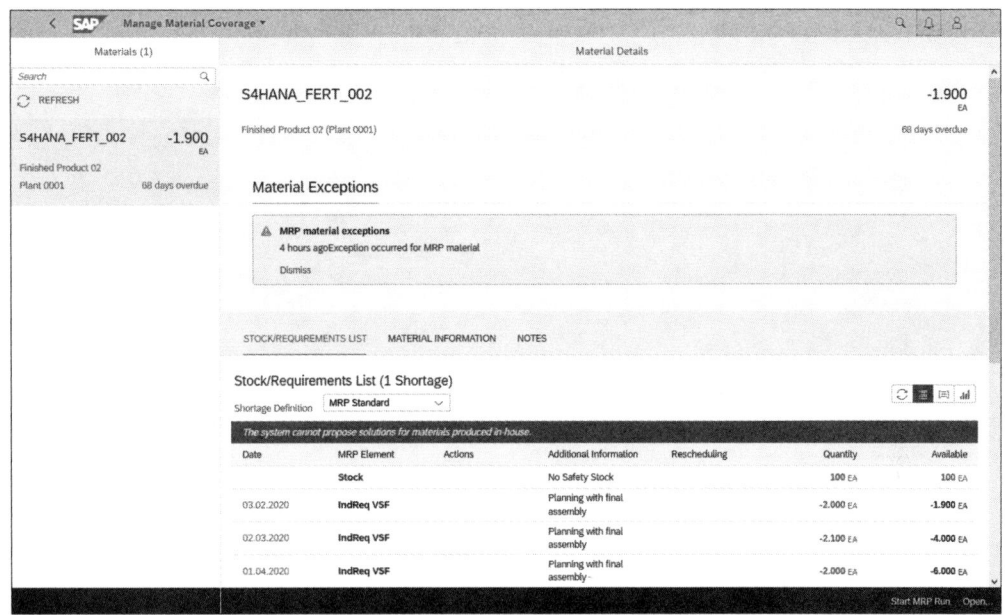

Figure 6.80 Material Exceptions in the Manage Material Coverage App

6.10 Summary

When MRP runs overnight, it resolves most of our material shortages, but it cannot always resolve very complex situations. Therefore, one of the main tasks of a materials planner is to evaluate the MRP results after the execution.

In this chapter, we introduced the concepts of exception messages and the rescheduling check, both very important for proper MRP results evaluation. After that, we discussed the MRP evaluation transactions that can be used in SAP GUI, including some improvements delivered in SAP S/4HANA, and we finished the chapter by going through the SAP Fiori applications of the MRP Cockpit.

As part of the evaluation of the MRP results, the planner may have to change some of the planned orders created by MRP, perhaps rescheduling to a different date or changing the order quantity. In the following chapter, we will learn about the planned orders and how to make those changes.

Chapter 7
Managing Planned Orders

The output of MRP will be new replenishment proposals, created to cover shortages and avoid understock situations. In this chapter, we will go through the planned orders, the main replenishment proposals generated by MRP.

When we execute MRP, our expectation is that the system will identify any potential material shortages and generate replenishment proposals to stop these shortages from happening. The most commonly generated replenishment proposals are planned orders for materials procured internally and purchase requisitions for materials procured externally.

In this chapter, we will go through all the details of the planned order and the main transactions that can be used to process a planned order. We will learn the basic transactions to create, change, and check the component availability of planned orders and to convert planned orders into production orders or purchase requisitions.

> **Note**
> The purchase requisition is an object that belongs to purchasing rather than materials planning, and there is extensive and complex Customizing behind it. In this MRP book, we will focus exclusively on the planned order.

7.1 Planned Orders

When MRP finds a shortage for a material, it will generate a replenishment proposal to cover this shortage. For materials procured internally, the replenishment proposal is a planning object called a *planned order*. The planned order will later be used in repetitive manufacturing or converted to a production or process order.

If we are using classic MRP, we also have the option to let MRP generate planned orders for materials procured externally; those planned orders should later be converted to purchase requisitions.

A planned order is merely a planning object that is deleted from the database after the conversion or the backflush, so there is no archiving object for planned orders. Planned orders are generally created by MRP during the planning run, but they also can be created manually, in Transaction MD11, if we expect a future receipt to come on a given date.

There are different planned order profiles available in the SAP S/4HANA system, but the profile for a given order is automatically determined by MRP when it is created. The profile will be determined based on the procurement type, special procurement type, and account assignment. For example, if MRP created a regular planned order for a material procured internally, the order profile will be LA; if a similar planned order is assigned to the sales order special stock (account assignment E), the order profile will be KD. Table 7.1 shows the list of standard planned order profiles and the respective procurement types, special procurement types, and account assignments.

Order Profile	Description	Procurement Type	Special Procurement Type	Account Assignment
KB	Standard purchase order	F	K	
KD	Individual customer order	E	E	E
LA	Stock order	E	E	
LB	Standard purchase order	F	L	
LBE	Standard purchase order	F	L	E
NB	Standard purchase order	F		
NBE	Standard purchase order	F		E
PR	Project order	E	E	Q
UL	Standard purchase order	F	U	

Table 7.1 Standard Planned Order Profiles

If we are creating a planned order manually, we need to enter the profile manually during the order creation. Depending on the profile selected, different fields may be available for input during the planned order creation. For example, if we select the order profile NB, which is used for externally procured planned orders, we will have an additional **Source of Supply** tab, where we can select a vendor, a scheduling agreement, or a contract as the source of supply. This tab will not be displayed for a planned order with order profile LA.

The profile may also be automatically redetermined during the manual planned order creation, depending on the data entered in Transaction MD11. For example, if we try to create a planned order with order profile LA, but we add an account assignment to a sales order, then SAP S/4HANA will automatically change the order profile to KD, since there is no account assignment on order profile LA.

Figure 7.1 shows the creation of a new planned order in Transaction MD11. When creating a new planned order, we need to set the **Material**, **MRP Area**, **Order Quantity**, and **Basic End Date** values. The **Basic Start Date** value will be calculated automatically using the in-house production time defined in the material master. SAP S/4HANA will also automatically try to determine a production version (because it is mandatory for the BOM explosion) and storage location.

> **Note**
> When a planned order is manually created, the **Firming Indicator** will be set automatically by the system. This indicator will prevent the planned order from being deleted or changed by a future MRP run. The firming indicator will also be set automatically with any manual change to a planned order created by MRP. If we want to also firm the planned order components, we can check the **Firming Indicator for Components**, which will also prevent the BOM from being re-exploded by MRP.

The storage location is automatically determined when a planned order is created. If a planned order is procured internally, the system will first check if the **Receiving Storage Location** setting has been defined in the production version and try to use this storage location. If the **Receiving Storage Location** is empty in the production version, then it will be read from the production storage location in the material master. If the planned order is procured externally, then the storage location will come from the **Storage Loc. for EP** (storage location for external procurement) field of the material master.

7   Managing Planned Orders

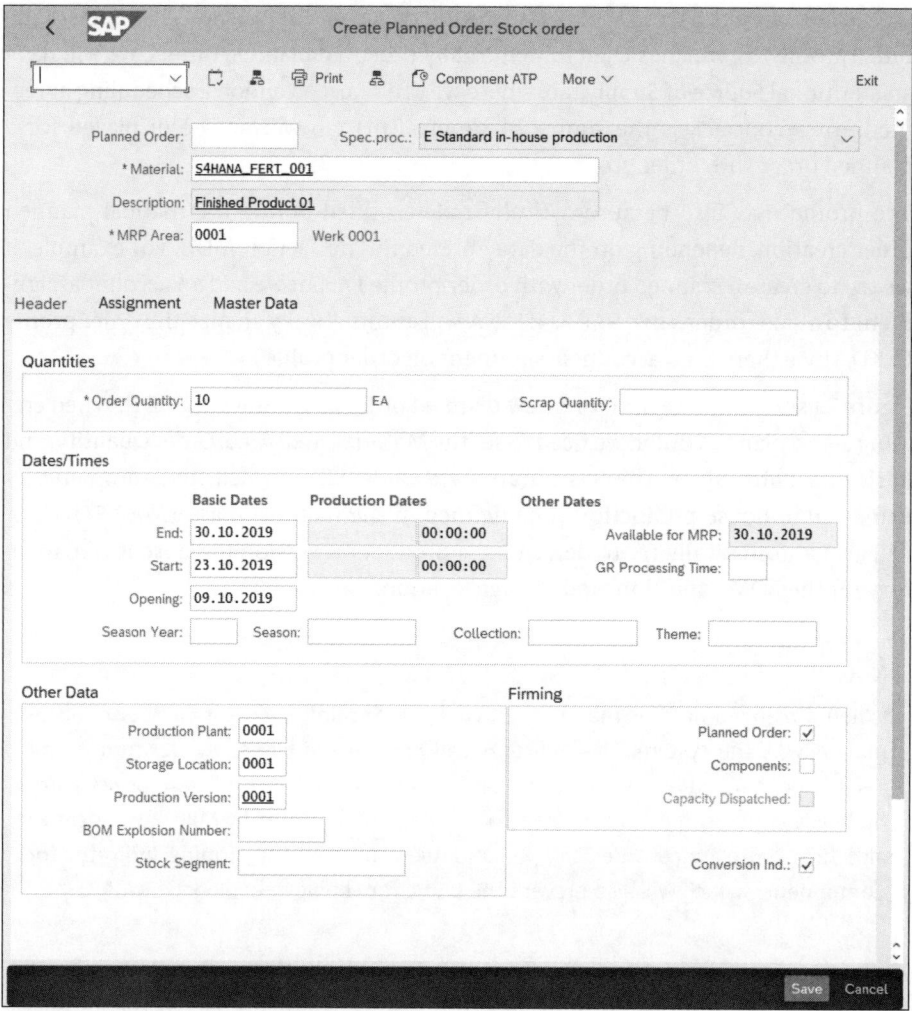

Figure 7.1 In-House Production Planned Order Creation in Transaction MD11

Lead-time scheduling will not be executed automatically for a planned order created manually. If we want to read the routing, generate capacity requirements, and calculate the production dates based on the routing operations, then we need to manually trigger lead-time scheduling by clicking the first icon in the menu shown in Figure 7.1. After we schedule the planned order, a new **Detailed Scheduling** tab will be displayed as shown in Figure 7.2; here we will see the planned order operations details, including dates and capacity requirements.

7.1 Planned Orders

> **Note**
> A planned order that went through capacity leveling and had an operation dispatched to a work center will automatically receive the **Capacity Dispatched** flag.

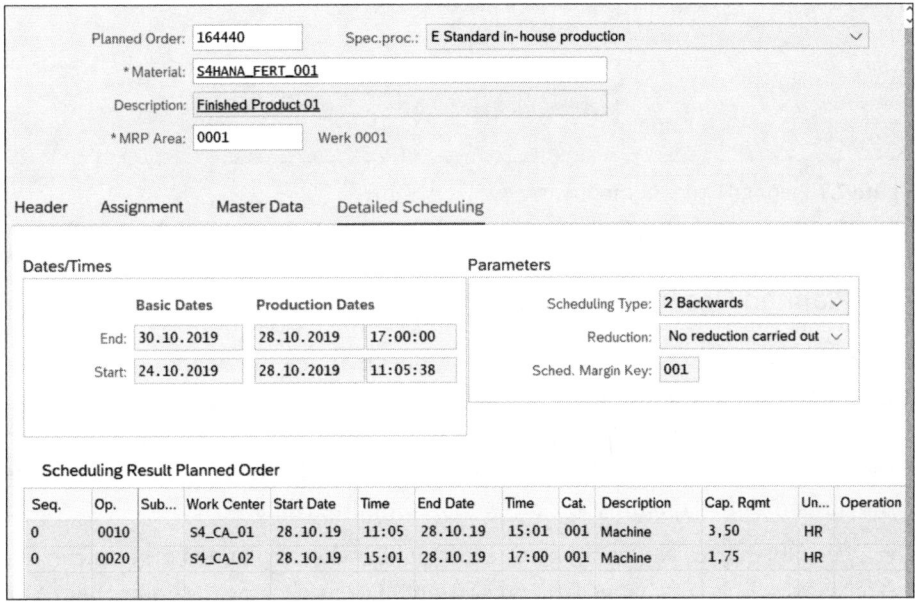

Figure 7.2 Detailed Scheduling in the Planned Order

In the menu, we can also see two different buttons for which the icon is a BOM structure. The first one will simply show the component overview, which is the list of planned order components. The second button will force a new BOM explosion, so the components might be updated if there was any change to the BOM.

Figure 7.3 shows the **Planned Order Component Overview** screen, which is displayed when any of the buttons mentioned previously are clicked. The **Collective Entry** and **Detailed Entry** buttons will allow the insertion of new components, collectively and individually.

The storage location for the components is also determined automatically when a planned order is created, and it can come from the BOM, from the **Production Storage Location** field in the material master, or from the production version's issuing storage location. We noted in Chapter 4 that we can influence the logic to select the issuing storage location in the MRP group Customizing.

307

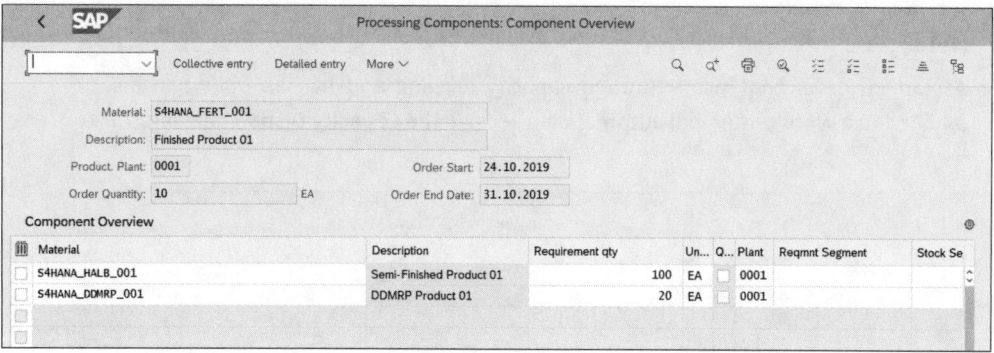

Figure 7.3 Planned Order Components

7.2 Planned Order Availability Check

After the creation of a planned order for a product manufactured internally, it is very important to know whether all the components are available to start the production. The *planned order availability check* tells us if the all the components are available or if there are missing parts. If all the components are available, the system will determine the committed quantity and an overall committed date.

The availability check can be triggered individually when a planned order is created in Transaction MD11 or changed in Transaction MD12 by clicking the **Component ATP** button shown in Figure 7.1. The check will be executed for the planned order according to the settings defined in the scope of availability check Customizing, discussed in Chapter 4.

Figure 7.4 shows the results of the availability check for a planned order; in this example, one of the components is not available, so an overall committed date could not be determined.

We can also run a collective availability check for several planned orders in Transaction MDVP. In this transaction, we can select multiple planned orders and run a collective availability check. Figure 7.5 shows the selection screen for this transaction, with fields like **Planned Order**, **Plant**, **MRP Controller**, **Production Supervisor**, and **Material**, plus date-based selection. We also have options to consider only planned orders with capacity dispatched, consider only planned orders relevant to production (repetitive manufacturing planned orders), or exclude assembly orders.

7.2 Planned Order Availability Check

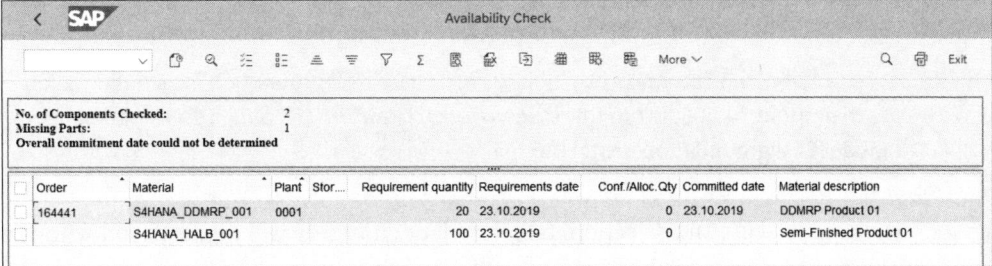

Figure 7.4 Availability Check Results for Planned Order Components

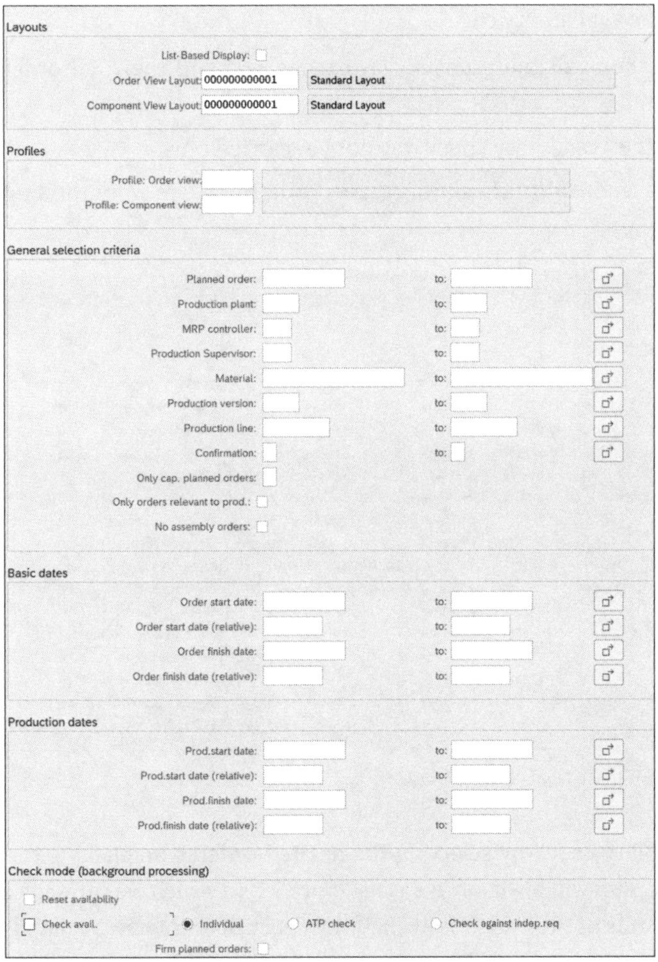

Figure 7.5 Selection Screen in Transaction MDVP

7   Managing Planned Orders

> **Tip**
> We can also run the mass availability check as a background job, scheduling a job with program RLD05000. In this case, we need to inform the parameters in the **Check Mode (Background Processing)** box.

When we execute the selection, a list of planned orders will be displayed with the results of the last availability check, including the **Confirmation Factor** (the percentage of the total order quantity that could be committed), **Committed Date**, and **Committed Quantity** values. A traffic light is shown in the first column of Figure 7.6 and it indicates the results of the availability check:

- A green light means the availability check was carried out and the total order quantity was committed.
- A yellow light means the availability check was not yet carried out.
- A red light means the availability check was carried out, but there were missing components.

A	Plnd Ord.	RC	CFc	%	DDf	Order Qty.	Comm. qty	Unit	Order Start	Ord.Finish	Commitment	A	TA...	Material	Material Description	PIPI	SLoc
■	161743	100	%	0		15	15	EA	24.09.2019	09.10.2019	09.10.2019	3	1	S4HANA_DDMRP_001	DDMRP Product 01	0001	
▲	162521	0	%			40	0	EA	01.10.2019	09.10.2019				S4HANA_FERT_002	Finished Product 02	0001	
●	161980	3	%	13		2.684	85	EA		16.10.2019	05.11.2019	2	1	S4HANA_DDMRP_001	DDMRP Product 01	0001	
■	162849	100	%	0		260	260	EA	04.10.2019	18.10.2019	18.10.2019	3	1	S4HANA_DDMRP_003	DDMRP Product 03	0001	
●	164670	0	%	999		5.500	0	EA	09.10.2019	23.10.2019	99.99.9999	1	1	S4HANA_HALB_001	Semi-Finished Product 01	0001	
●	164671	0	%	999		500	0	EA		23.10.2019	99.99.9999	1	1	S4HANA_HALB_001	Semi-Finished Product 01	0001	
●	164677	0	%	8		100	0	EA		23.10.2019	05.11.2019	1	1	S4HANA_HALB_001	Semi-Finished Product 01	0001	
●	164638	7	%	10		580	40	EA		16.10.2019	30.10.2019	2	1	S4HANA_FERT_001	Finished Product 01	0001	
●	164720	0	%	9		90	0	EA	10.10.2019	17.10.2019	30.10.2019	1	1	S4HANA_FERT_001	Finished Product 01	0001	0003
●	164721	0	%	9		50	0	EA		17.10.2019	30.10.2019	1	1	S4HANA_FERT_001	Finished Product 01	0001	0003
●	162378	0	%	999		1.100	0	EA	15.10.2019	29.10.2019	99.99.9999	1	1	S4HANA_HALB_001	Semi-Finished Product 01	0001	
●	164676	0	%	4		20	0	EA		29.10.2019	05.11.2019	1	1	S4HANA_DDMRP_001	DDMRP Product 01	0001	
▲	164552	0	%			50	0	EA	17.10.2019	31.10.2019				S4HANA_DDMRP_001	DDMRP Product 01	0001	
●	164438	0	%	4		10	0	EA	23.10.2019	30.10.2019	06.11.2019	1	1	S4HANA_FERT_001	Finished Product 01	0001	
▲	164551	0	%			50	0	EA	24.10.2019	31.10.2019				S4HANA_FERT_001	Finished Product 01	0001	0003

Figure 7.6 Collective Availability Check: Order View

We trigger a new availability check by selecting the desired orders and clicking the **Check Order** button. A pop-up will be displayed (see Figure 7.7) in which we can select if we want to reset the results of the previous availability check or run a new availability check. If we click the **Mode** button, additional options will be displayed: we will be able to select if we want to firm the planned orders for which the availability check is carried out, if we want to run an individual availability check according to the settings defined in each material check, if it should be an ATP check for all the materials, or if it should be carried out against planning.

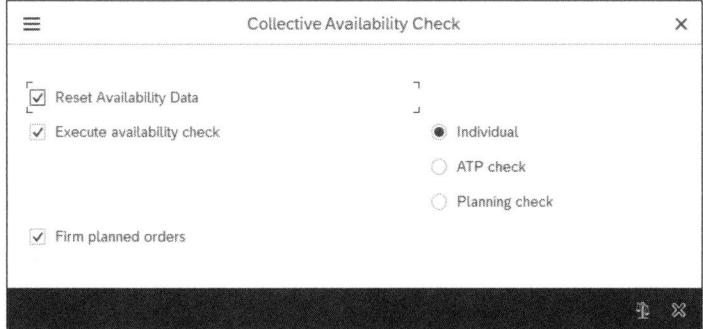

Figure 7.7 Pop-up with Collective Availability Check Settings

> **Note**
> Collective availability checks can also be carried out for planned orders using Transaction COHV. We will discuss this transaction later, in Section 7.4.

7.3 Planned Order Conversion

When a planned order reaches the opening period, it means that it is time to convert it to a production order or process order for materials procured internally or to a purchase requisition for materials procured externally. In general, all the planned orders will be converted; the only exceptions are repetitive manufacturing planned orders.

There are different transactions to covert a planned order and ways to convert it. We can run an individual conversion to convert a single planned order or a collective conversion to convert several planned orders. We can also convert the whole planned order quantity or run only a partial conversion, converting part of the planned order but keeping the remaining quantity as a planned order.

The easiest way to convert a planned order to a production order, process order, or purchase requisition is through the Stock/Requirements List. We can simply double-click a planned order, and the **Convert Planned Order to Production Order** (ProdOrd) button,

7 Managing Planned Orders

Convert Planned Order to Production Order (Partial Quantity) (PartConvProdOrd) button, **Convert Planned Order to Process Order** (ProcOrd) button, **Convert Planned Order to Process Order (Partial Quantity)** (SubProcOrd.) button, and **Convert Planned Order to Purchase Requisition** (PurReq) button will be displayed, as shown in Figure 7.8.

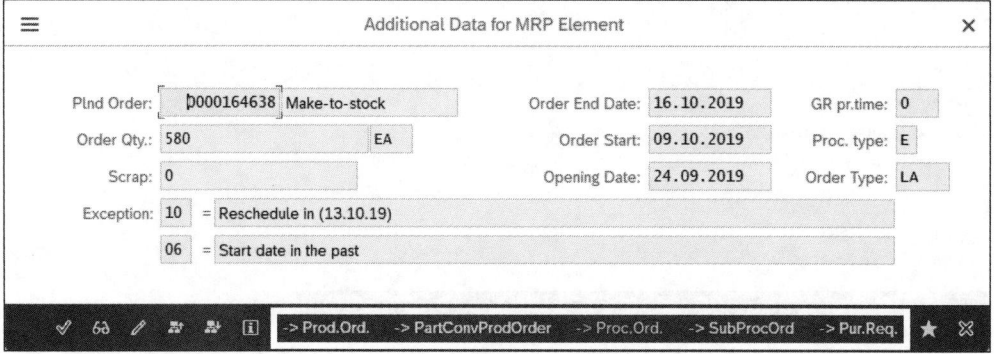

Figure 7.8 Planned Order Conversion in the Stock/Requirements List

The same kind of individual conversion can be done in the SAP Fiori launchpad using the MRP Cockpit applications. For every planned order, a dropdown menu will displayed from which we can choose the **Conversion** option to start the conversion, as shown in Figure 7.9.

> **Note**
>
> As seen in Chapter 4, we can define default production and process order types for the planned order conversion at the plant and MRP group levels. These order types will be automatically selected when we trigger the planned order conversion.

The individual conversion of planned orders for materials procured internally is also possible directly through Transaction CO40 when we are converting to production orders, and through Transaction COR7 when we are converting to process orders. In this transaction, however, we need to know the planned order number in advance because we need to enter it on the initial screen.

The Convert Planned Orders app shown in Figure 7.10 allows for the mass conversion of planned orders. Here, all the planned orders belonging to the user's area of responsibility will be selected, and we can trigger the conversion by choosing the desired option in the dropdown menu at the end of each line. In this application, we can also trigger a collective conversion for production orders, process orders, or purchase requisitions, but the conversion will be executed in the respective SAP GUI transaction.

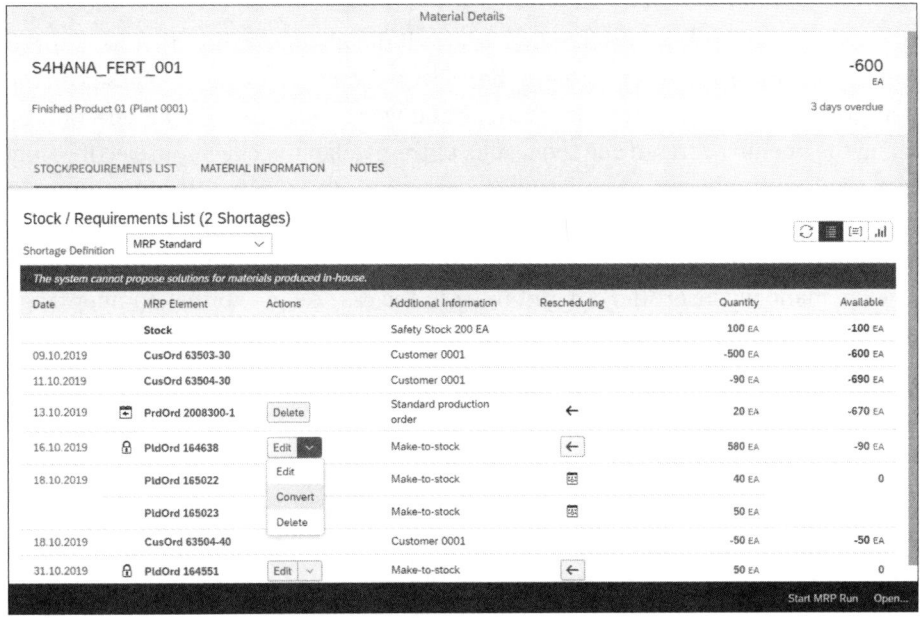

Figure 7.9 Converting a Planned Order in the Manage Material Coverage App

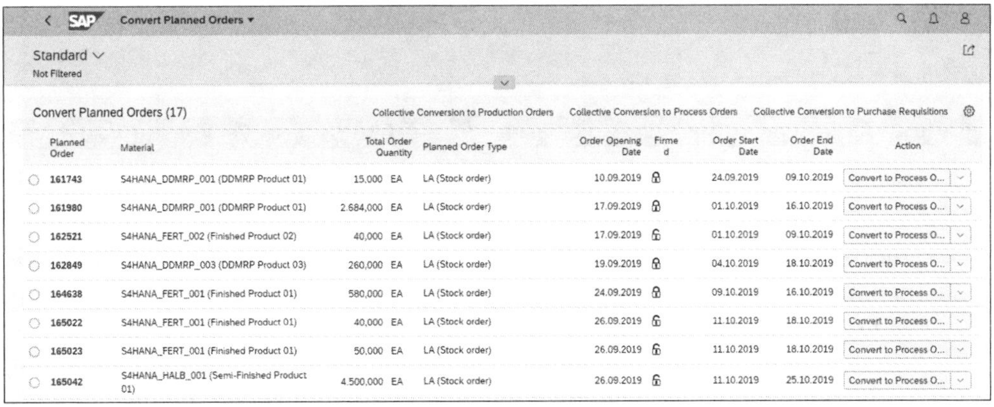

Figure 7.10 The Convert Planned Orders App

There are also many ways to trigger a collective conversion of planned orders. Transaction CO41, for example, can be used in the SAP GUI to run a collective conversion of planned orders to production orders; Transaction COR8 can run the collective conversion to process orders. The design of both transactions is very similar, and the main difference is really the order that will be generated after the conversion.

In those transactions, we need to first select all the planned orders that we want to process using the criteria available in the selection screen. We can select based on the plant or the MRP controller, for example, and we can also restrict the selection by using the opening dates, using the results of the availability check, or selecting only planned orders with capacities dispatched or firmed. After we run the selection, a list of planned orders will be displayed, and we can choose exactly which orders to convert. Here we can change the quantity to run a partial conversion, change the dates, or even manually insert the order number in the case of an external number range assignment. Figure 7.11 shows the collective conversion in Transaction CO41.

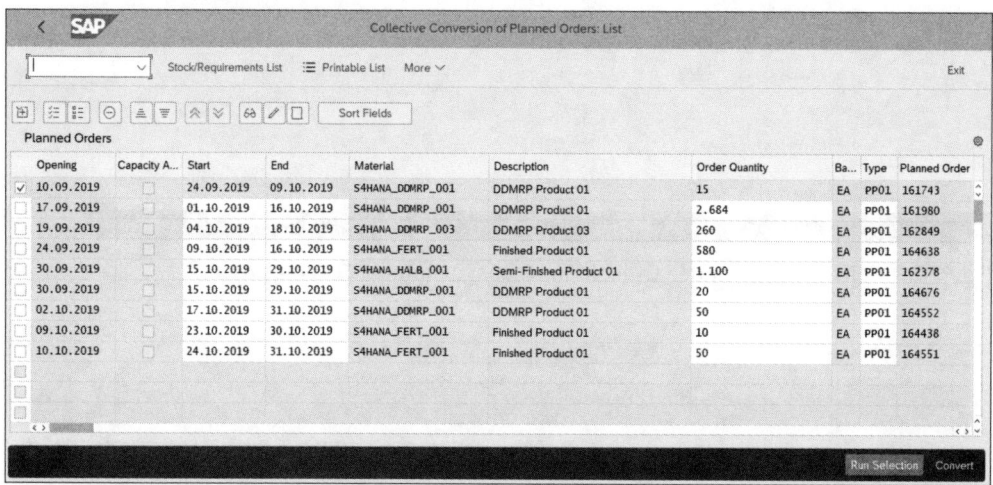

Figure 7.11 Collective Conversion of Planned Orders in Transaction CO41

The conversion of planned orders can also be automated, and we can schedule a background job to run the conversion periodically. Reports PPBICO40 and PPBICOR8 can be used to convert planned orders to production and process orders, respectively. These reports are merely simplified versions of Transactions CO41 and COR8 that can be executed in the background. It is common to use the opening date as a selection criterion so that we automatically run the conversion of all the planned orders that reached the opening period, as defined in the material scheduling margin key.

> **Note**
> If we trigger a collective conversion of planned orders to production or process orders in the Convert Planned Orders app, then Transactions CO41 and COR8 will be called in the SAP Fiori launchpad.

With MRP Live, the conversion of planned orders to purchase requisitions is no longer a necessary step, but companies that decide to keep using classic MRP or that have enhanced MRP Live to generate planned orders for materials procured externally will also have to run the conversion of planned orders to purchase requisitions.

As we noted earlier in this section, the conversion can also be done directly through the Stock/Requirements List or through SAP Fiori applications. If we are running the conversion using SAP GUI transactions, there are additional transactions that can be used. The individual conversion to purchase requisitions is triggered through Transaction MD14; we simply need to enter the planned order number in the initial screen. This will open a detailed screen, where we will be able define the requisition number and change the quantity, dates, and additional settings in the purchase requisition to be generated, as shown in Figure 7.12. We can also change the source of supply manually or run a new source of supply determination by clicking the **Assign Source of Supply** button. If there are several sources available for this material, a pop-up window will be displayed to choose the desired source of supply.

We can use Transaction MD15 to run a collective conversion of planned orders to purchase requisitions. We will be able to search planned orders for a material, MRP controller, or WBS element, and we can restrict the selection—for example, by the **Opening Date** or **Procurement Type** field. In the initial screen, we can also define default parameters for the requisitions to be generated.

A list of planned orders will be shown, from which we can select the ones to be converted to purchase requisitions (see Figure 7.13). Here, we can change the planned order before the conversion, check the pegged requirements, and run the conversion. The conversion can be done either online if we click the **Convert Online** button or in the background if we click the **Do Not Convert Online** button. If we choose the online conversion, the behavior will be similar to Transaction MD14, where we can see the same screen shown in Figure 7.12 and change some of the fields before the conversion if necessary. If we are converting a large set of planned orders, however, it is preferable not to convert online so that the system will convert all the orders in the background instead.

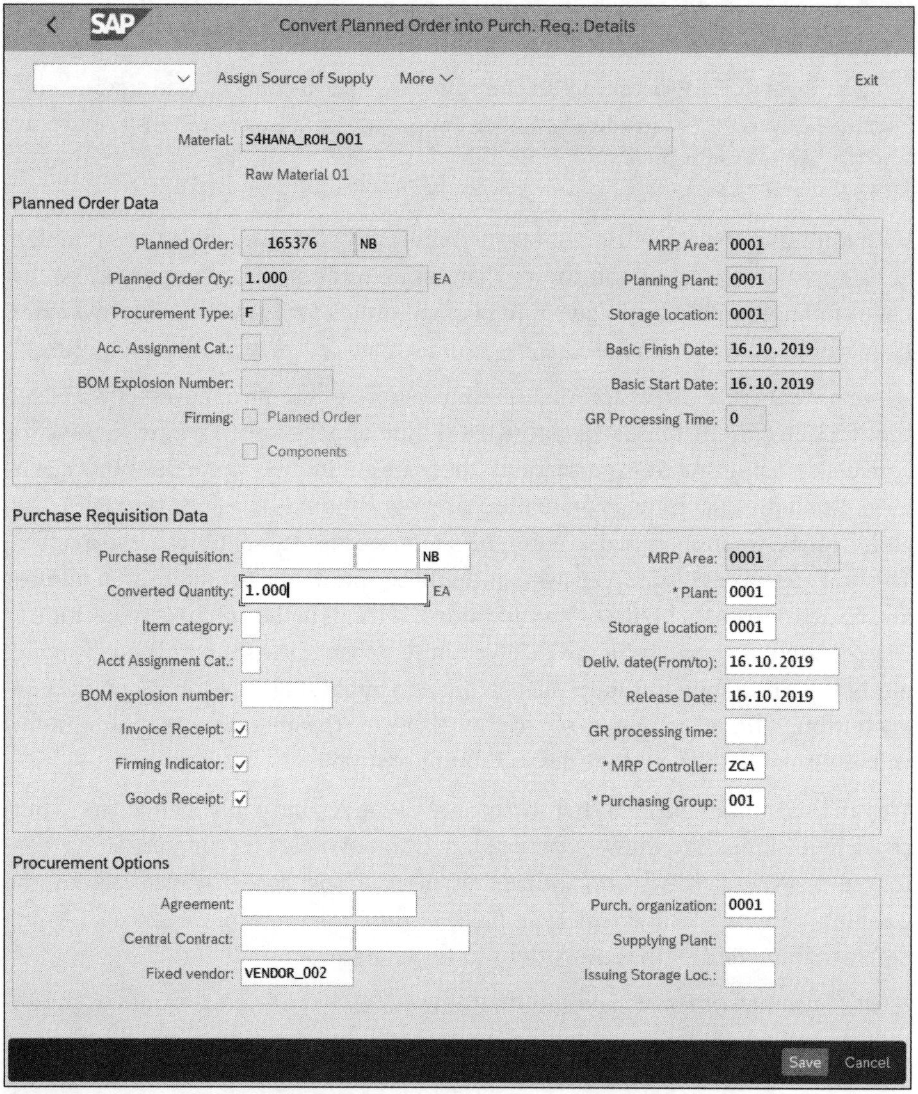

Figure 7.12 Conversion of Planned Order to Purchase Requisition

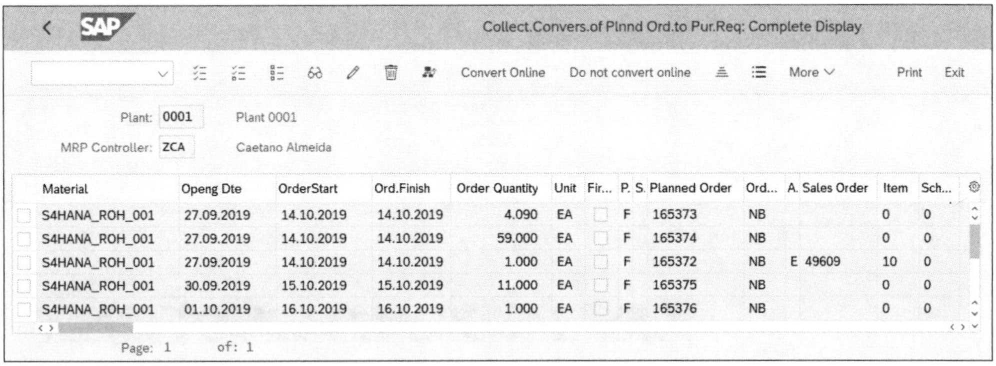

7.4 Additional Options for Mass Processing

[Figure showing SAP screen: Collect.Convers.of Plnnd Ord.to Pur.Req: Complete Display, with plant 0001, MRP Controller ZCA Caetano Almeida, and a list of S4HANA_ROH_001 materials]

Figure 7.13 Collective Conversion of Planned Orders to Requisitions

The conversion of planned orders to purchase requisitions can also run as a periodic background job through report RMCVPLRQ in order to avoid manual work. We can create a background job manually with this report, but SAP also provides Transaction MDUM to schedule jobs and manage the scheduled jobs for the background conversion of planned orders.

7.4 Additional Options for Mass Processing

We have discussed some mass processing functionality in this chapter, such as the mass availability check in Transaction MDVP or the mass conversion of planned orders, but there are additional features available for mass processing of planned orders.

For example, we can use Transaction MD16 to get a list of planned orders per MRP controller, material, production version, line from production version, or WBS element. Figure 7.14 shows an example of the selection by MRP controller, which can still be restricted by the date.

A list of planned orders will be displayed, as shown in Figure 7.15, and we can even take some actions, such as running a planned order conversion or deleting unnecessary planned orders. We can also trigger the pegged requirements or the order report from a specific planned order from the list.

317

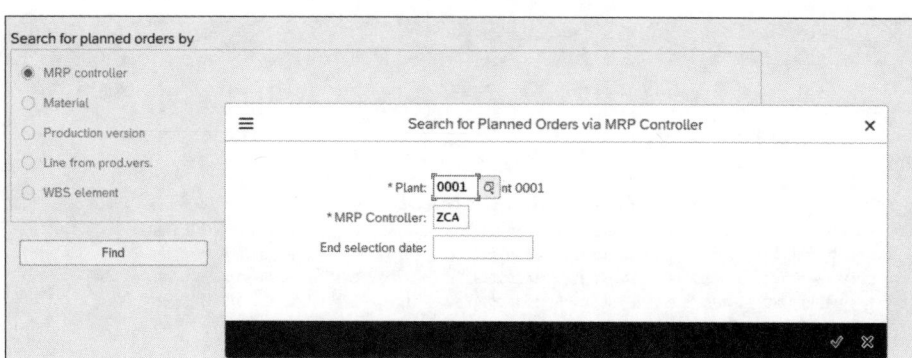

Figure 7.14 Search for Planned Orders in Transaction MD16

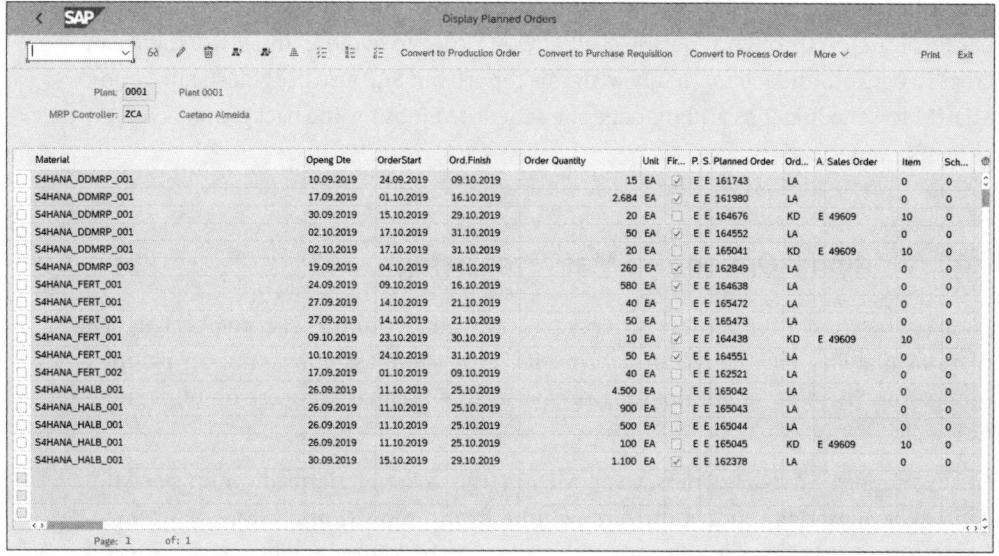

Figure 7.15 Display Planned Orders

Besides the planned order-specific transactions, the production order information system and mass processing transactions can also be used to process planned orders. The following transactions are available to process planned orders:

- Transaction COOIS and Transaction COOISPI: These transactions will provide a list of planned orders for discrete manufacturing and process manufacturing, respectively.

7.4 Additional Options for Mass Processing

- Transaction COHV and Transaction COHVPI: These transactions can be used for mass processing of production orders or process orders and will also include some specific mass processing options for planned orders.
- Transaction COMAC: This transaction can be used to run a mass availability check for production orders and can also include planned orders.

The design of these transactions is virtually the same: they are all different versions of the standard report PPIO_ENTRY. When using these transactions, checkboxes in the selection screen will denote if we want to work with production/process orders, with planned orders, or with both, as highlighted in Figure 7.16.

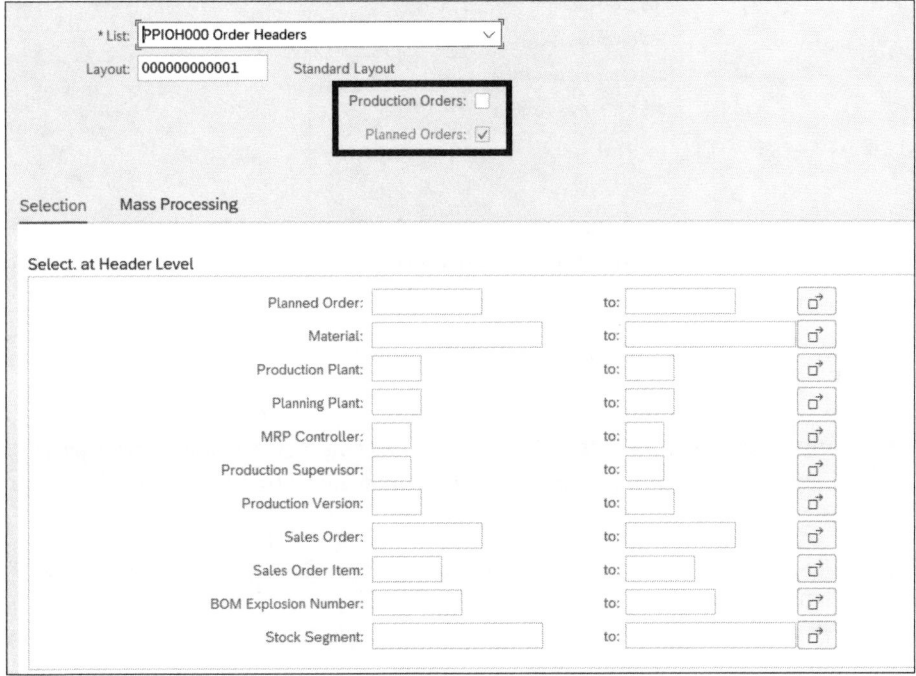

Figure 7.16 Planned Order Selection in Transaction COHV

If we are working with mass processing in Transaction COHV, we will be able to select the **Mass Processing** function in the **Mass Processing** tab of the selection screen (see Figure 7.17) or later in the results list.

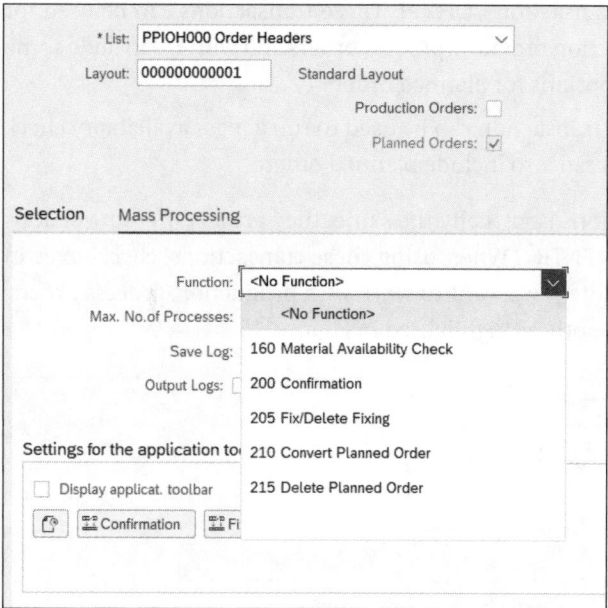

Figure 7.17 Mass Processing Function in Transaction COHV

> **Tip**
> Some mass processing functions are specific for planned orders and will be displayed if we are working with planned orders only. The only mass processing function available for both planned and production orders is the availability check.

When we execute the transaction, a list of planned orders (and production/process orders, depending on the selection criteria) will be displayed. If we are running Transaction COHV, COHVPI, or COMAC, a mass processing function can be executed when we click the **Mass Processing** button highlighted in Figure 7.18. Here we can see the results of a processing execution for a set of planned orders. The **Message Type** column will show an icon with the mass processing result; by double-clicking it, we access the details of any message triggered. We can also see an overview of the logs by selecting the **Mass Processing • Logs of Last MP** menu option.

7.5 Summary

	Order	Material	Ic...	Order Type	MRP ctrlr	Pr.Superv.	Plant	Target Q...	Unit	Bsc start	Basic fin. date	Type	Sys.Status	Version	Material description
✓	161743	S4HANA_DDMRP_001		LA	ZCA		0001	15	EA	24.09.2019	09.10.2019			0001	DDMRP Product 01
✓	161980			LA	ZCA			2.684	EA	01.10.2019	16.10.2019			0001	DDMRP Product 01
✓	164676			KD	ZCA			20	EA	15.10.2019	29.10.2019			0001	DDMRP Product 01
✓	164552			LA	ZCA			50	EA	17.10.2019	31.10.2019			0001	DDMRP Product 01
✓	165041			KD	ZCA			20	EA		31.10.2019			0001	DDMRP Product 01
✓	162849	S4HANA_DDMRP_003		LA	ZCA			260	EA	04.10.2019	18.10.2019			0001	DDMRP Product 03
✓	164638	S4HANA_FERT_001		LA	ZCA			580	EA	09.10.2019	16.10.2019			0001	Finished Product 01
	165472			LA	ZCA			40	EA	14.10.2019	21.10.2019			0001	Finished Product 01
	165473			LA	ZCA			50	EA		21.10.2019			0001	Finished Product 01
	164438			KD	ZCA			10	EA	23.10.2019	30.10.2019			0001	Finished Product 01
	164551			LA	ZCA			50	EA	24.10.2019	31.10.2019			0001	Finished Product 01
	162521	S4HANA_FERT_002		LA	ZCA			40	EA	01.10.2019	09.10.2019				Finished Product 02
	165042	S4HANA_HALB_001		LA	ZCA			4.500	EA	11.10.2019	25.10.2019			0001	Semi-Finished Product 01
	165043			LA	ZCA			900	EA		25.10.2019			0001	Semi-Finished Product 01
	165044			LA	ZCA			500	EA		25.10.2019			0001	Semi-Finished Product 01
	165045			KD	ZCA			100	EA		25.10.2019			0001	Semi-Finished Product 01
	162378			LA	ZCA			1.100	EA	15.10.2019	29.10.2019			0001	Semi-Finished Product 01

Figure 7.18 Mass Processing in Transaction COHV

7.5 Summary

As we have shown in this chapter, the planned order is the main MRP planning object. It will be created by MRP when a shortage is identified, and it also can be created manually by the planner to identify a future planned receipt. The MRP controller will work daily to create and adjust planned orders in order to ensure that the production plan is feasible and that a smooth conversion to a production or process order will occur.

In this chapter, we described the basic processing of a planned order, starting with the planned order profiles and going through the creation of a new planned order and all its underlying details, such as the scheduling and the BOM explosion. We have also discussed the functions available for the planned order, such as the availability check and conversion. We finished the chapter with a look at additional mass processing features.

So far, we have covered MRP basic steps and scenarios, such as managing basic master data, running MRP, and evaluating the results. We are now ready to explore some advanced MRP features, like subcontracting planning, planning calendars, range of coverage profiles, and BOM explosion numbers. We will also cover parts interchangeability, which was used only for industry solutions in SAP originally, but is available for everyone now in SAP S/4HANA.

Chapter 8
Advanced MRP Features

In this chapter, we will go beyond the MRP basics to discuss some advanced MRP features and scenarios, including the subcontracting scenario, planning calendars, BOM explosion number, parts interchangeability, and range of coverage profiles.

We have reached Chapter 8 of this book, and now we leave behind the MRP basic master data and settings. It is time to explore more advanced features and planning scenarios that can be used to achieve better results using MRP. In this chapter, we will analyze the following advanced MRP features and scenarios:

- Subcontracting planning in Section 8.1
- Planning calendars in Section 8.2
- BOM explosion date using a BOM explosion number in Section 8.3
- Interchangeable parts planning using a manufacturer part number (MPN) MRP set in Section 8.4
- Range of coverage profiles for creating dynamic safety stock in Section 8.5

We will start with subcontracting because it is a feature very frequently used in manufacturing and because the simplifications implemented in SAP S/4HANA introduced several changes in this area.

8.1 Subcontracting Planning

Subcontracting is a special procurement situation in which we need to send components to an external supplier (subcontractor), who will perform the manufacturing activity and then return a finished or semifinished product. In a subcontracting process, MRP will generate purchase requisitions (or schedule lines) with item category L (Subcontracting) and components.

8   Advanced MRP Features

Figure 8.1 shows a subcontracting purchase requisition generated by MRP. Two things are highlighted here: the item category and the buttons to explode the BOM and see the requisition components. MRP will automatically explode the subcontracting requisition BOM, generating subcontracting requirements for those components.

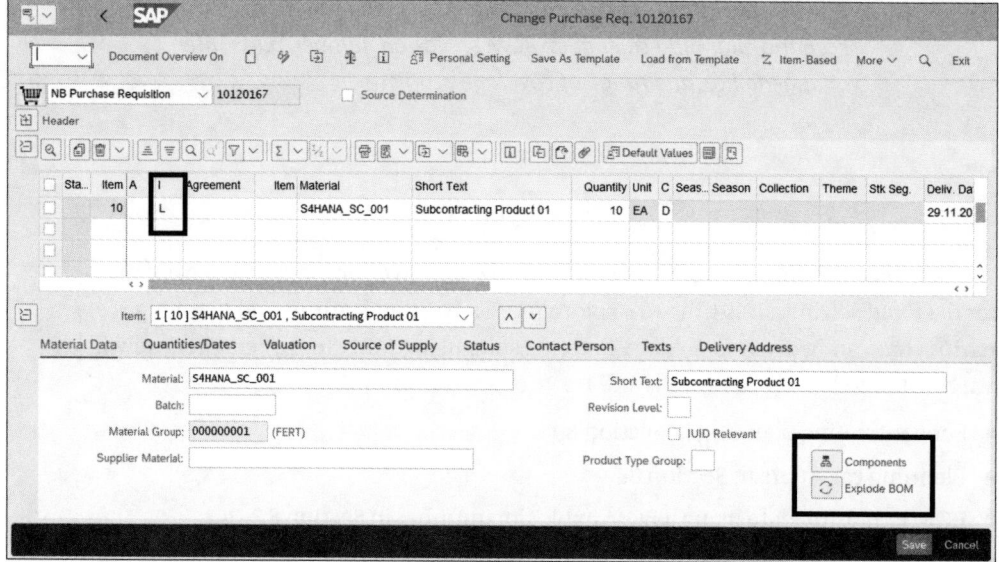

Figure 8.1 Subcontracting Purchase Requisition

A basic subcontracting process will require the following master data in SAP S/4HANA:

- A BOM that lists the components that should be sent to the subcontractor
- A production version with a reference to the BOM (a reference to the routing is not necessary because it is not used in the subcontracting process)
- A source of supply, which can be a subcontracting info record with the **Automatic Sourcing** flag checked, a contract, or a scheduling agreement with item category L

When we compare the subcontracting planning in SAP ERP to SAP S/4HANA, we note two major differences related to the simplifications implemented in SAP S/4HANA. The first is that SAP S/4HANA requires a production version to execute the BOM explosion in subcontracting purchase requisitions, while this was not necessary in SAP ERP. This means that during an SAP S/4HANA implementation, we also need to consider the creation of production versions for subcontracting materials.

> **Tip**
> In a scenario in which we have multiple subcontractors for the same product, each subcontractor may require a different BOM. We can create a different production version for each subcontractor, and we can enter which production version should be used by MRP in the subcontracting info record.

The second simplification is related to the subcontracting planning itself and the different ways to implement it. SAP ERP provided three options to implement the subcontracting scenario:

- There is no separation between the plant and the subcontractor stock from a planning perspective (logic implemented with the MD_SUBCONT_LOGIC BAdI).
- There is partial separation between the plant and the subcontractor stock using special subcontractor planning segments, in which the plant and the subcontractor stock would be separated, and uncovered subcontracting requirements in the subcontractor stock would be planned at the plant level.
- There is complete separation between the plant and the subcontractor using MRP areas, in which we can choose specific planning parameters (MRP type, lot sizing, procurement type, etc.) for each material at the subcontracting MRP area level, defining how uncovered subcontracting requirements will be replenished (assignment of the MRP area to the material is required).

SAP S/4HANA simplified subcontracting planning, allowing only the following two options:

- No separation between the plant and the subcontractor stock from a planning perspective. No BAdI is required, and this option is used whenever an MRP area does not exist for the vendor.
- Complete separation between the plant and the subcontractor stock using MRP areas. Assignment of the MRP area to the material master is no longer required, and it is enough to create the subcontracting MRP area in Customizing so that it is considered by MRP.

This means that in SAP S/4HANA, we will no longer have the partial separation using the subcontractor planning segments, which was the solution most commonly used for subcontracting planning in SAP ERP. The recommended solution in SAP S/4HANA is to use MRP areas because it allows more flexibility in the assignment of the MRP area to the material, allowing us to define a different MRP type or a lot-sizing procedure for each subcontractor.

The usage of MRP areas allows, for example, MRP planning of third-party subcontracting, wherein we can purchase the components and request the delivery directly to the subcontractor. It would also allow for multilevel subcontracting, wherein one subcontractor manufactures a semifinished product and delivers it directly to another subcontractor in order to continue the manufacturing process for the product.

> **Note**
>
> The MRP area assignment is usually only necessary at the component level because it is the component that will be provided to the vendor, and it is for the component that we will have subcontracting requirements.

From an MRP planning evaluation perspective, if there is no MRP area available for the vendor involved in the subcontracting process, we will see all the subcontracting requirements at the plant level. The stock provided to the subcontractor will be added to the stock available at the plant.

Figure 8.2 shows an example of a material that is a component of a subcontracting purchase requisition and for which an MRP area has not been created.

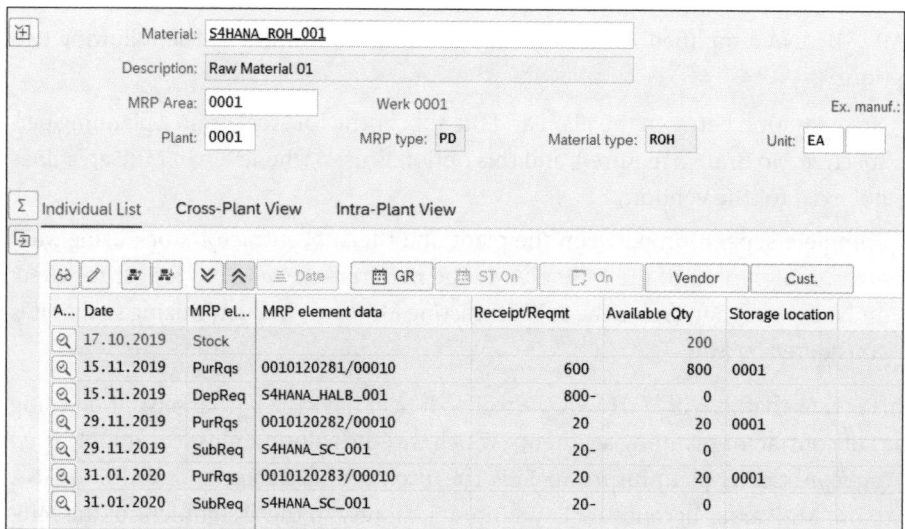

Figure 8.2 Subcontracting Requirements at Plant Level

As shown in this figure, dependent requirements from planned orders (**DepReq**) and subcontracting requirements (**SubReq**) are shown together at the plant level. Everything will be planned together; MRP will neither create stock transfers to move the stock from the plant to the subcontractor nor plan a delivery directly to the subcontractor. Depending on the lot-sizing procedure selected, the same purchase requisition may replenish a subcontracting requirement and a dependent requirement.

When we create the subcontracting MRP area for the vendor involved in the subcontracting process, all the subcontracting requirements will be automatically redirected to the MRP area, and MRP should plan them separately. Figure 8.3 shows the same example from the previous figure, but now an MRP area has been created in Customizing for the subcontractor VENDOR_002, and we are accessing the Stock/Requirements List using this MRP area. As shown in the **Intra-Plant View** tab, now there is a separation between the plant stock and the subcontractor stock (represented by the blue line). Subcontracting requirements are shown under the subcontractor and will not generate a new replenishment proposal because the stock provided to the vendor is enough to cover the requirements. On the other hand, at the plant level, we will have only 100 EA available, so MRP has to generate a replenishment proposal with a higher quantity to cover the existing dependent requirement.

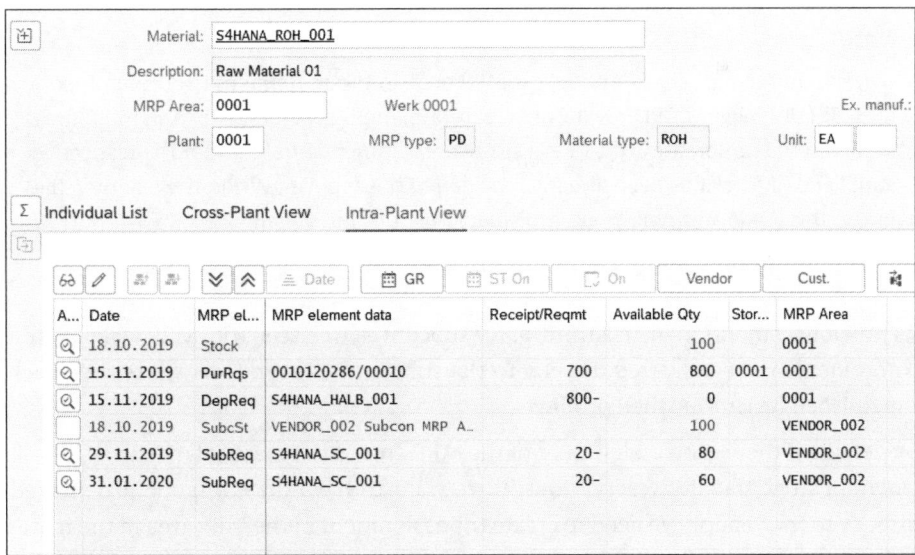

Figure 8.3 Subcontracting Requirements at the MRP Area Level

> **Note**
>
> Figure 8.3 shows both the plant stock and the subcontracting MRP area because we are using the **Intra-Plant** view. If we opened the **Individual List** tab instead, we would only see what is under the plant or under the MRP area, depending on how we access the Stock/Requirements List.

If we simply create the subcontracting MRP area in Customizing but we do not assign it to the material master, MRP will try to simulate the same logic used in the old SAP ERP subcontracting logic, which has been simplified. This means it will use a lot-for-lot procedure to calculate the lot size and will generate stock transfer reservations to bring the missing components from the plant. If we want to use different logic, then we need to create an assignment of the MRP area to the component. In this case, we can define settings such as a different MRP type, a lot-sizing procedure, or a special procurement type at the MRP area level.

Additional details about the subcontracting simplification in SAP S/4HANA can be found in SAP Note 2227532 (SAP S/4HANA Simplification Item: LOGISTICS_PP-MRP—Subcontracting).

> **Note**
>
> If we do not assign a subcontracting MRP area to the material master, then report PPH_SETUP_MRPRECORDS will only create a planning file entry for this MRP area and material combination if there is a subcontracting requirement for the respective supplier or if stock has been already provided to the supplier. Without a planning file entry, this MRP area will not be displayed in the **Intra-Plant** view of the Stock/Requirements List.

As previously mentioned, in a third-party subcontracting scenario, MRP will plan the components to be delivered directly to the subcontractor, and we will receive back the finished or semifinished product.

By default, if there is no assignment of the MRP area to the material master, MRP will generate stock transfer reservations. If we want to have the component delivered directly to the vendor, we need to create the assignment of the MRP area in the material master and set the special procurement to **20—External Procurement** (as shown in Chapter 3) or something similar. When MRP creates a purchase requisition to be delivered directly to the subcontractor, note that the **SC Supplier** flag will be checked; we will find the vendor from the MRP area in the **Supplier** field, as shown in Figure 8.4.

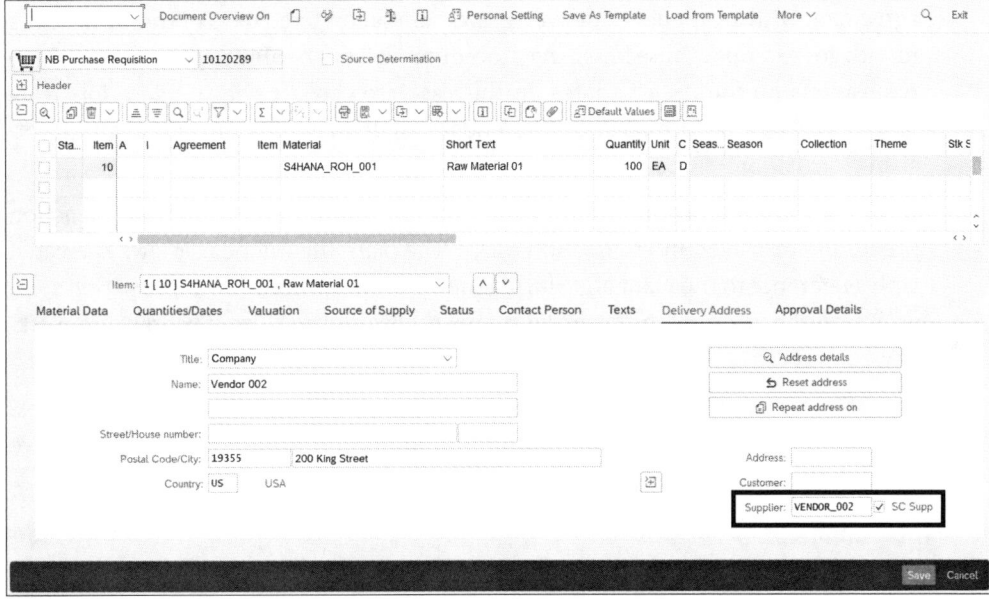

Figure 8.4 SC Supplier in Purchase Requisition

> **Tip**
>
> If we want to have a schedule line generated in a third-party subcontracting scenario, the **SC Vendor** flag must be checked, and the supplier must be set in the scheduling agreement. Those fields can be accessed in the scheduling agreement transactions (such as Transaction ME31 or ME32) via menu path **Item • More Functions • Delivery Address**.

8.2 Planning Calendar

While discussing the MRP master data in Chapter 3, we mentioned the period lot-sizing procedures and the time-phased MRP types; we have also mentioned that a planning calendar can be used in those cases. In this section, we will cover how to create a planning calendar and how it affects MRP planning results.

In the lot-sizing procedures delivered by SAP, we have a weekly lot-sizing procedure (in which the period starts at the beginning of the week) or a monthly lot-sizing procedure (in which the period starts at the beginning of the month). If we have an agreement with a supplier to deliver a raw material on fixed days of the week or the month, for example, those lot-sizing procedures will not be able to generate purchase requisitions on the desired dates. In this case, we can use the standard lot-sizing procedure PK and create a planning calendar that defines a custom period for the lot-sizing calculation.

A new planning calendar can be created in Transaction MD25, changed in Transaction MD26, and displayed in Transaction MD27. The planning calendar is always created with a reference to the plant and, during the creation, we need to select a period split: weeks (weekdays), months (weekdays), months (workdays), years (workdays), workdays, or weekdays.

Let's say, for example, that our supplier will have deliveries scheduled for every Tuesday and every Thursday. In this case, we would select a weekly period split, and we would select on which weekdays the period should start, as shown in Figure 8.5.

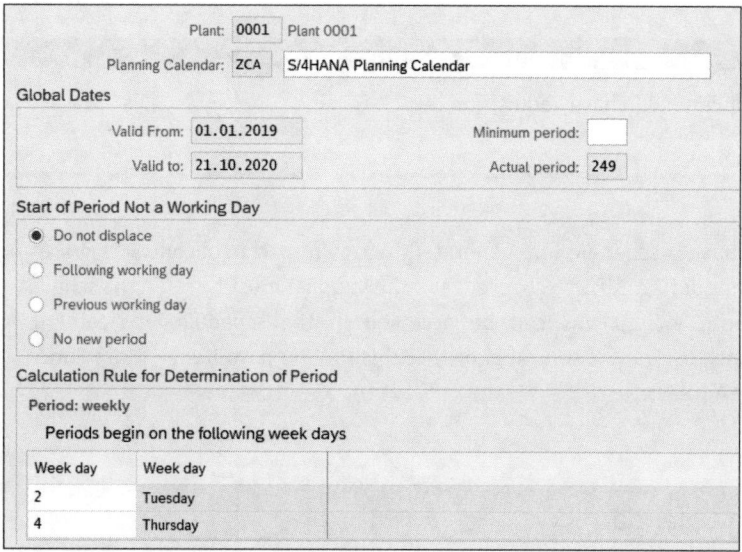

Figure 8.5 Planning Calendar Creation

We also need to select here what will happen if the start of the period falls on a non-working day: we can move the start to the previous day or the following day, or even choose not to start a new period.

8.2 Planning Calendar

Once the planning calendar details have been defined, the system will generate the new periods and we will see a list of the calculated periods, as shown in Figure 8.6. In this example, we can observe that the periods calculated will always start on a Tuesday or Thursday, as we defined in the planning calendar rule. On this screen, we can also make manual adjustments to the periods calculated by the system, and we can firm/fix the periods to avoid having a new period calculation make any changes to the firmed periods.

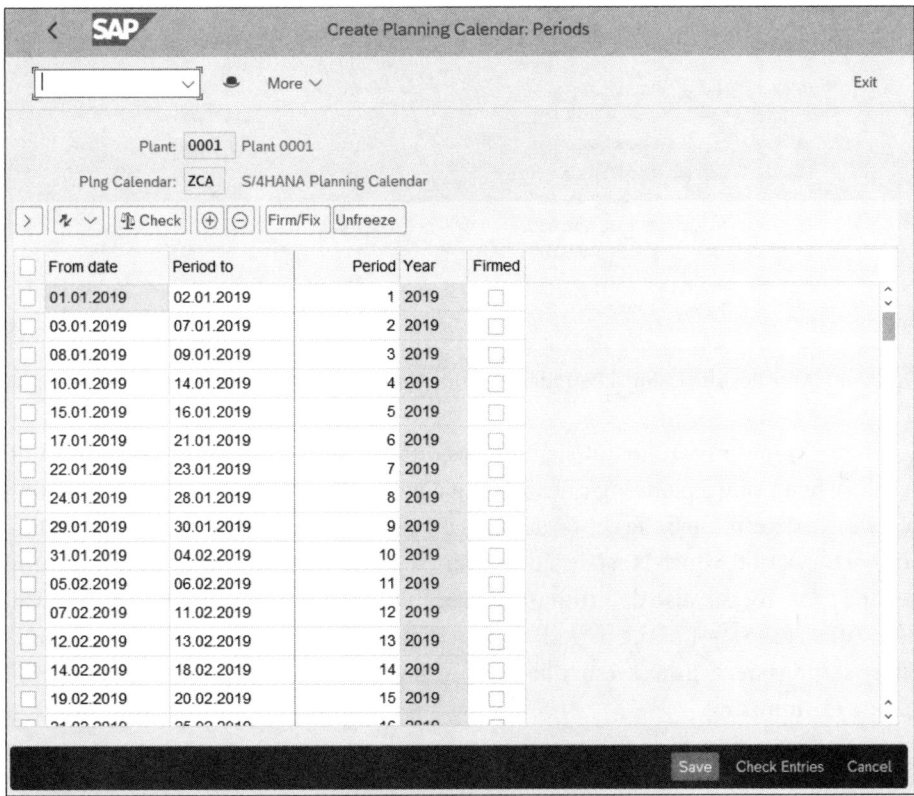

Figure 8.6 Periods Calculated for a New Planning Calendar

Figure 8.7 shows the MRP results when using a period lot-sizing procedure and the planning calendar created in the previous example. In this case, MRP will group all the requirements within a given period, and the actual replenishment proposals to cover the shortages will always fall on a Tuesday or Thursday.

331

8 Advanced MRP Features

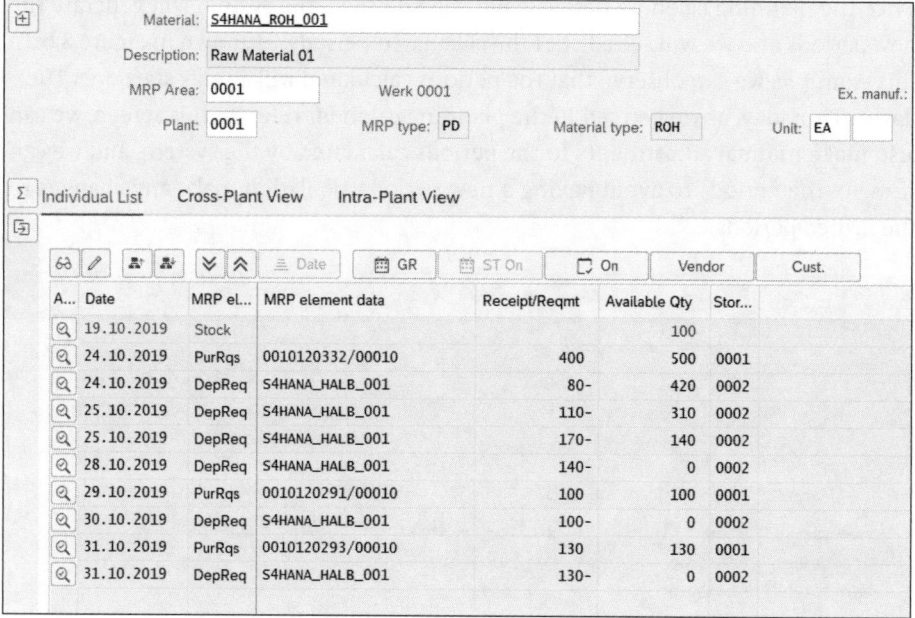

Figure 8.7 MRP Results Using a Period Lot-Sizing Procedure with a Planning Calendar

There are some important lot-sizing procedure settings that will affect the MRP results when using a planning calendar and a period lot-sizing procedure. For example, we can determine if the actual delivery date or the availability date will fall at the start of the period, which is especially relevant when we are using a goods receipt processing time. We can also determine, for example, if the replenishment proposal will be created at the start of the period, on the shortage date, or at the end of the period. These settings were discussed in Chapter 3 when we went through the lot-sizing procedure Customizing.

> **Note**
>
> The standard lot-sizing procedure PK will consider the availability date as the shortage date, so replenishment proposals will not necessarily be created on Tuesday or Thursday with our planning calendar. In this example, we have changed the **Scheduling** setting in the lot-sizing procedure to ensure that replenishment proposals will fall at the start of the period.

8.3 BOM Explosion Number

When we are working with complex assemblies in which the multilevel BOM may have many levels, we might want to have more control over the BOM explosion date to ensure that we are exploding the correct BOMs on all levels during the MRP run. We discussed in Chapter 4 that we can determine in Customizing if the BOM will be exploded on the order start or finish date, and we can also determine whether a BOM explosion number will be considered or not. The BOM explosion number is the feature that allows us to determine a fixed key date for the BOM explosion, which is transferred for all the BOM levels.

A BOM explosion number is created and changed in Transaction MDSP, shown in Figure 8.8. Here, we only *have* to enter the **BOM Explosion Number** and **Fixed Key Date** values, but we can also set the plant or a material number if we want to restrict the BOM explosion number usage for a specific plant or material.

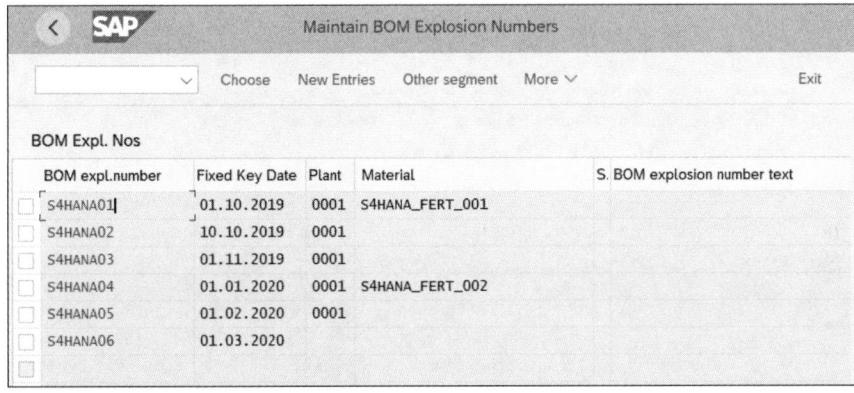

Figure 8.8 BOM Explosion Numbers in Transaction MDSP

> **Note**
> It is also possible to define a different explosion date for specific subcomponents under a given BOM explosion number. We can do so by selecting the **Maintain New Key Assignments** menu option.

The BOM explosion number can be entered directly in the sales order item or in the planned independent requirements, and it will be considered by MRP when generating the planned orders that will cover those requirements. Alternatively, the BOM

8   Advanced MRP Features

explosion number can be manually entered directly into the planned order (see Figure 8.9). The BOM explosion number will be propagated to the lower-level materials through the planned order-dependent requirements, and the planned orders created to cover those dependent requirements will also have a reference to the BOM explosion number. All these planned orders created with a reference to the BOM explosion number will use the same fixed key date to read the BOM.

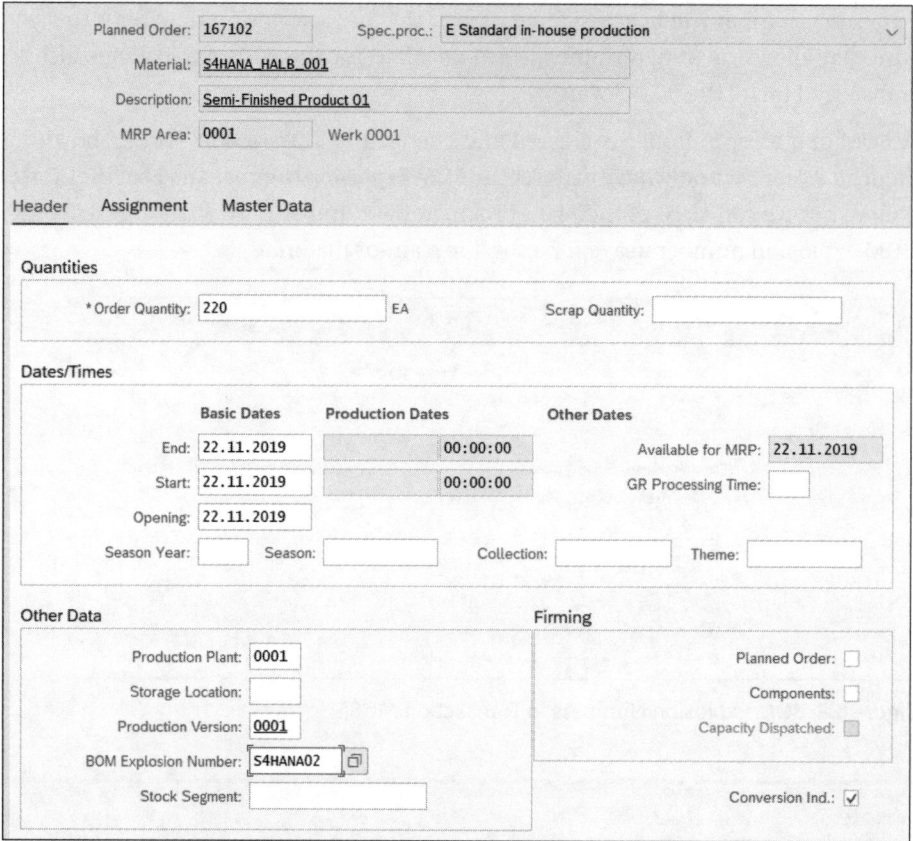

Figure 8.9 BOM Explosion Number in the Planned Order

The **BOM Explosion Number** column will be displayed in the Stock/Requirements List, showing the BOM explosion number for the MRP elements, whenever it is available. Figure 8.10 shows the Stock/Requirements List, where we can see a BOM explosion number for different dependent requirements and for the planned orders that are covering those requirements.

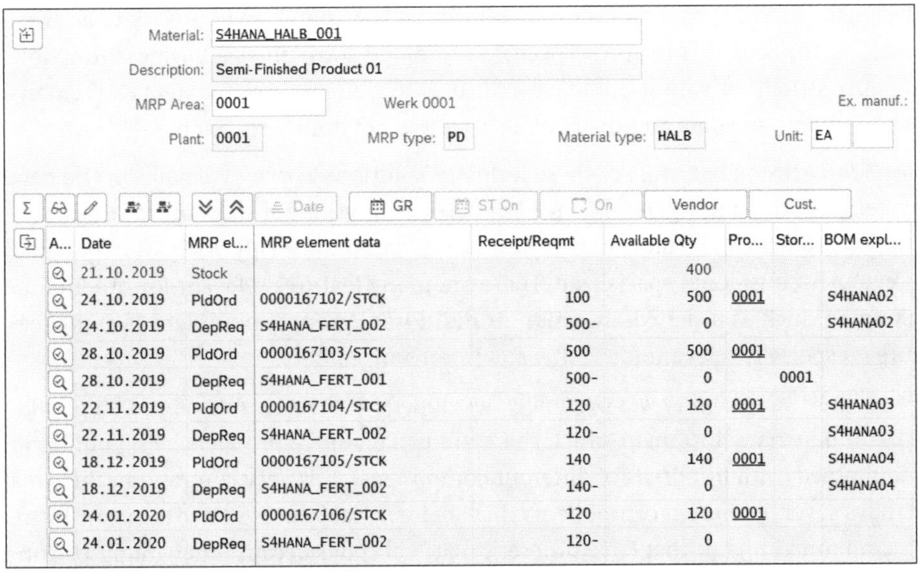
Material: S4HANA_HALB_001
Description: Semi-Finished Product 01
MRP Area: 0001 Werk 0001 Ex. manuf.:
Plant: 0001 MRP type: PD Material type: HALB Unit: EA

A...	Date	MRP el...	MRP element data	Receipt/Reqmt	Available Qty	Pro...	Stor...	BOM expl...
	21.10.2019	Stock			400			
	24.10.2019	PldOrd	0000167102/STCK	100	500	0001		S4HANA02
	24.10.2019	DepReq	S4HANA_FERT_002	500-	0			S4HANA02
	28.10.2019	PldOrd	0000167103/STCK	500	500	0001		
	28.10.2019	DepReq	S4HANA_FERT_001	500-	0		0001	
	22.11.2019	PldOrd	0000167104/STCK	120	120	0001		S4HANA03
	22.11.2019	DepReq	S4HANA_FERT_002	120-	0			S4HANA03
	18.12.2019	PldOrd	0000167105/STCK	140	140	0001		S4HANA04
	18.12.2019	DepReq	S4HANA_FERT_002	140-	0			S4HANA04
	24.01.2020	PldOrd	0000167106/STCK	120	120	0001		
	24.01.2020	DepReq	S4HANA_FERT_002	120-	0			

Figure 8.10 BOM Explosion Number in the Stock/Requirements List

A conflict may arise when there are two or more different requirements with different BOM explosion numbers and, due to the lot-sizing procedure, a single planned order should be created to cover them. This scenario is possible even when using a lot-for-lot procedure because MRP creates a single planned order to cover requirements in the same day. When this kind of conflict arises, MRP will use the BOM explosion number from the first requirement to create the planned order because we can only have a reference to one BOM explosion number per planned order.

> **Note**
>
> In the customizing Transaction OPPQ, we can restrict the usage of BOM explosion numbers for MTO scenarios only. In this case, a BOM explosion number would not be considered during the creation of MTS planned orders. See details about this setting in Chapter 4.

8.4 Parts Interchangeability

SAP ERP supported many different industries, and because some features were designed specifically for an industry solution, it was therefore necessary to activate those features by turning on a specific switch and sometimes a business function. Because switch activation would have far-reaching effects in the system (e.g., changing programs and data dictionary objects), it was not done very often.

SAP S/4HANA makes most of these industry solutions active by default in the core system, so we do not generally need to activate anything if we want to use one of these features. The result is that organizations can more easily access functionality previously considered specialized. There are many features relevant for production planning, such as order combination or multi-item production orders, but one feature is especially relevant for MRP: parts interchangeability.

Parts interchangeability was originally developed for the Aerospace and Defense (IS-ADEC) industry solution, in which there are usually huge products being built and maintained, with hundreds of different components. It is very common in this area to have several different components that are identical (i.e., they have the same form, fit, and function) but that have different material codes because they might be supplied by different vendors. In this particular case, they will have different manufacturer part numbers (MPNs).

With this feature, these components can be planned together by MRP so that MRP will not create a replenishment proposal for a component if there is enough stock of another material with the same form, fit, and function.

8.4.1 Creating an MPN-MRP Set

The first step to use the parts interchangeability functionality is to create a form-fit-function (FFF) class material. This can be done in Transaction MM01, in which we create materials. We should use the standard material type FFFC. This material type only has the **Basic Data 1** and **Basic Data 2** tabs, and the most important setting for this type of material is the **Manufacturer Part Profile** setting. Figure 8.11 shows a FFFC material and the manufacturer part profile (the **Mfr. Part Profile** field) in the **Basic Data 1** tab.

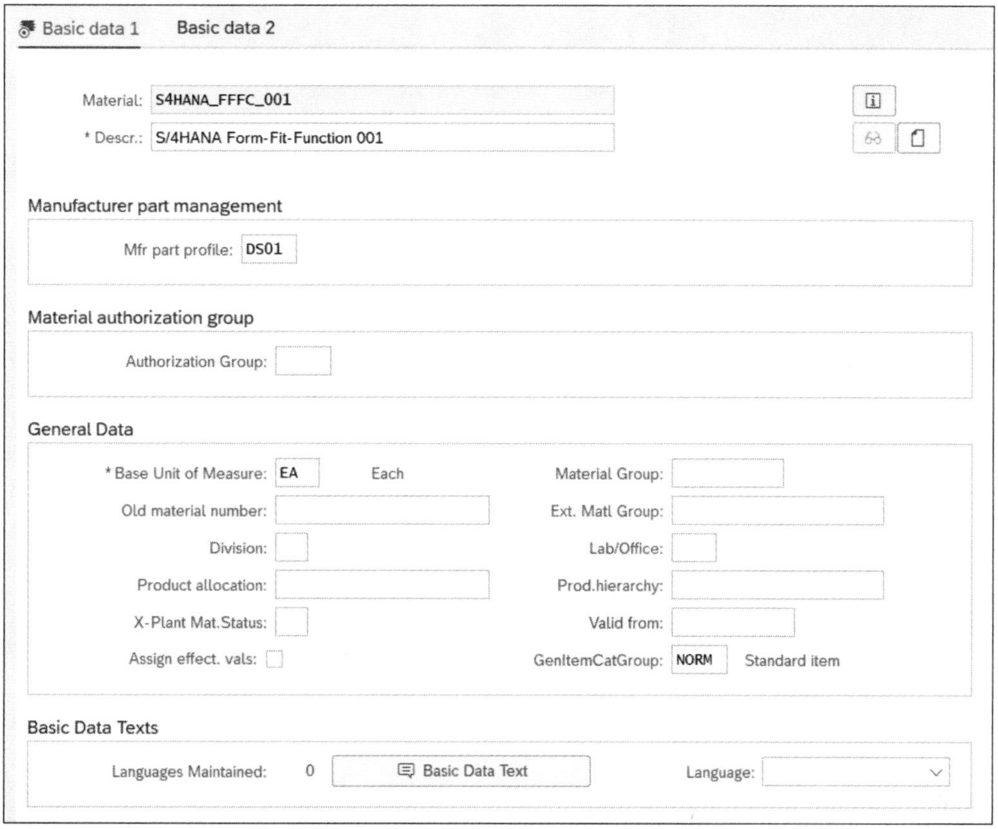

Figure 8.11 Form-Fit-Function Class Material

> **Note**
> SAP delivers standard manufacturer part profiles, but we can also create a custom profile in the customizing Transaction OMPN. Here, it is important to define it as an *inventory-based manufacturer part* so that lower-level parts are inventory-managed and can be planned by MRP.

After the creation of the FFF class, we need to create an MPN-MRP set, in which we will define which components can replace each other and can be planned together by MRP. We can create an MPN-MRP set in Transaction PIC01, in which we will first enter the FFF class, then select which materials can be interchangeable, and then click the **Full Interchangeability** button highlighted in Figure 8.12.

Figure 8.12 Creation of an MPN-MRP Set in Transaction PIC01

We will then add the components to the FFF class, as shown in Figure 8.13. After that, it is time to create the actual MPN-MRP sets by clicking the **MPN-MRP Sets** button highlighted in Figure 8.13.

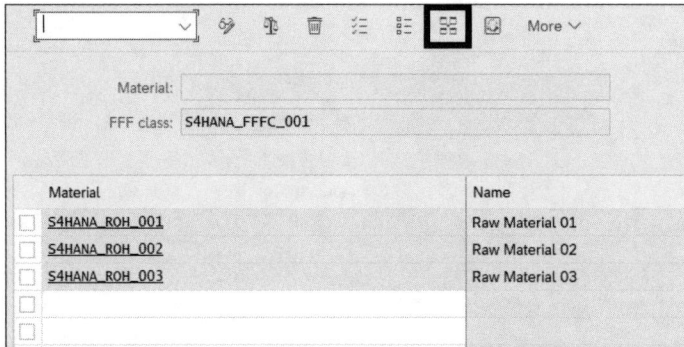

Figure 8.13 Maintenance of Full Interchangeabilities

To create a new set, we need to define the MPN-MRP set name and select the set components and the plant/MRP area in which they will interchangeable. Materials belonging to the same MPN-MRP set will be interchangeable from an MRP perspective. We can have multiple MPN-MRP sets under the same class, but the following rules apply when creating a new set:

- Each MPN-MRP set needs one (and only one) leading part. When a shortage is identified by MRP for the MPN-MRP set, a replenishment proposal will be created for the leading part.
- There must be no overlapping of parts in the MPN-MRP sets. This means that each part may only belong to a single MPN-MRP set in a plant/MRP area combination.
- A part may belong to different MPN-MRP sets, so long as the MRP area is not the same.

- If the parts should be interchangeable in different plants, we need to create different entries for the same material in each plant. The interchangeability, however, is not cross-plant.

Figure 8.14 shows the MPN-MRP set components, where we can see in the **Leading Part** column that the first line has been selected as the leading part.

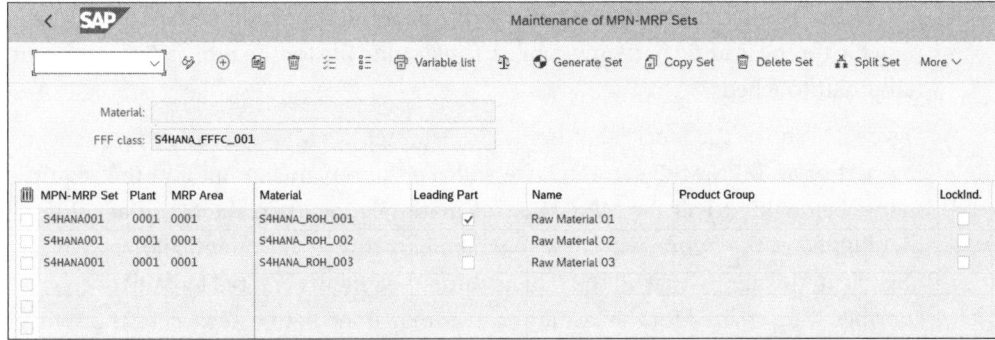

Figure 8.14 Maintaining MPN-MRP Sets

In the menu, we can also find some actions to be performed with a set, such as the options to generate, copy, or split an MPN-MRP set. We also have the option to automatically generate a product group with the MPN-MRP set that can be used in different MRP transactions to process all the components of the same set together.

> **Note**
> If we click the **Generate Set** button, the system will automatically generate a new MPN-MRP set with all the interchangeable parts belonging to the class. If we use this option and select an MPN-MRP set that already exists, the system will add the parts belonging to the FFF class that are not yet part of an MPN-MRP set.

8.4.2 Planning an MPN-MRP Set

For materials that are part of an MPN-MRP set, we only need to run MRP for the leading part because all the interchangeable parts will be planned together when the leading part is planned.

If we are planning a nonleading part using a classic MRP single-item transaction, for example, then an error message will be triggered to inform the user that only the leading part should be planned. When planning the leading part, the net requirements calculation will sum up the stock of all the parts and consider requirements and replenishment elements of all the parts when identifying a shortage. When a shortage is identified, a new replenishment proposal will be created for the leading part.

The update of the planning file will also follow the same logic, and we will see that any MRP-relevant change for an interchangeable part will trigger an update of the planning file for the leading part only, while the planning file for the nonleading parts will remain untouched.

Figure 8.15 shows the Stock/Requirements List after the MRP execution for the leading part of an MPN-MRP set. Here, we will see the replenishment and the requirements belonging to all the MPN-MRP set materials together; the **Material** column, highlighted in the figure, will show to which part this requirement belongs. We can observe in this figure that all the replenishment elements created by MRP to cover a shortage were created for the leading part, as explained before. If we click the **Switch Off MPN MRP Total** button highlighted in Figure 8.15, then only the stock, receipts, and requirements of the selected part will be shown.

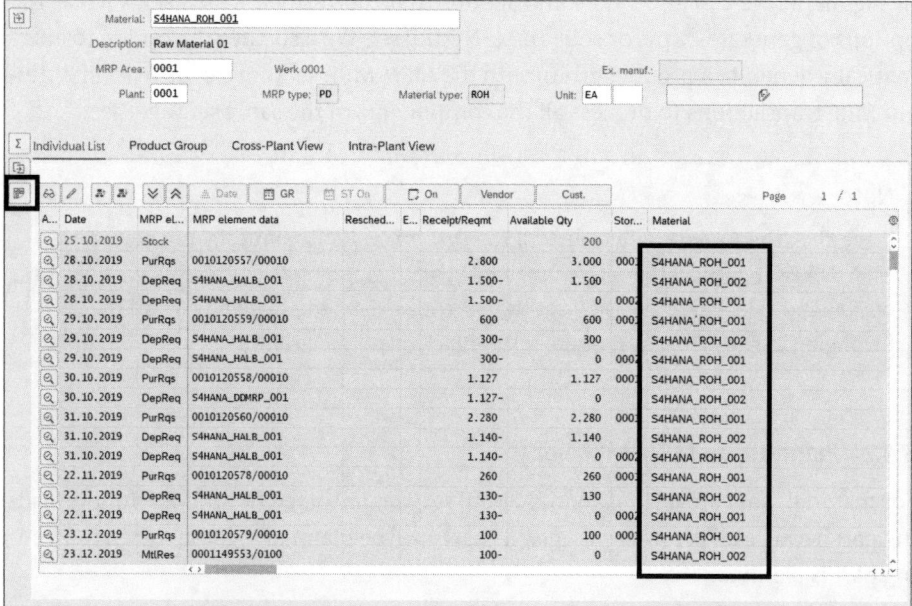

Figure 8.15 Stock/Requirements List

8.5 Range of Coverage Profile (Dynamic Safety Stock)

Safety stock can be manually defined in the material master, as we noted in Chapter 3, and MRP will consider it as an additional requirement during the net requirements calculation, trying to keep the stock level above the safety stock. This safety stock from the material master, however, is fixed and does not take into account the variability caused by seasonal changes in material consumption patterns, for example. That means it could conceivably be too high for the period of the year when the material consumption is lower or possibly not high enough in the season of peak consumption.

An alternative in this case is to let the system calculate the safety stock dynamically, based on the projected daily average consumption of a material. This can be achieved with the usage of a range of coverage profile in the material master. In the range of coverage profile Customizing, we will define a target range of coverage in days to represent how many days our safety stock should last. This target range of coverage will be multiplied by the average daily requirements, and this additional quantity will be considered when supplying our material.

A range of coverage profile is created in customizing Transaction OMIA. Each profile will belong to a specific plant. The first thing we define when we are creating a profile is the **Period Indicator** value that will be used during the calculation; we can choose a monthly period, weekly period, or a period according to the planning calendar. After that, we will define the **Number of Periods** and the **Type of Period Length** values in working days, calendar days, or standard days. If we are using standard days, we need to also set the number of days for the period.

Figure 8.16 shows an example of a range of coverage profile in which we are using a period of weeks, two periods, and calendar days. In this example, the system would read all the requirements within a period of two weeks and divide it by the total number of calendar days in these two weeks.

After defining the periods in Customizing, we need to set the actual range of coverage. We have the option to define three different periods, and for each period, we can define a different range of coverage, including a minimum, a target, and a maximum range of coverage. Those values are entered in days, and the system will multiply them by the average daily requirements to calculate the minimum safety stock, the target safety stock, and the maximum safety stock.

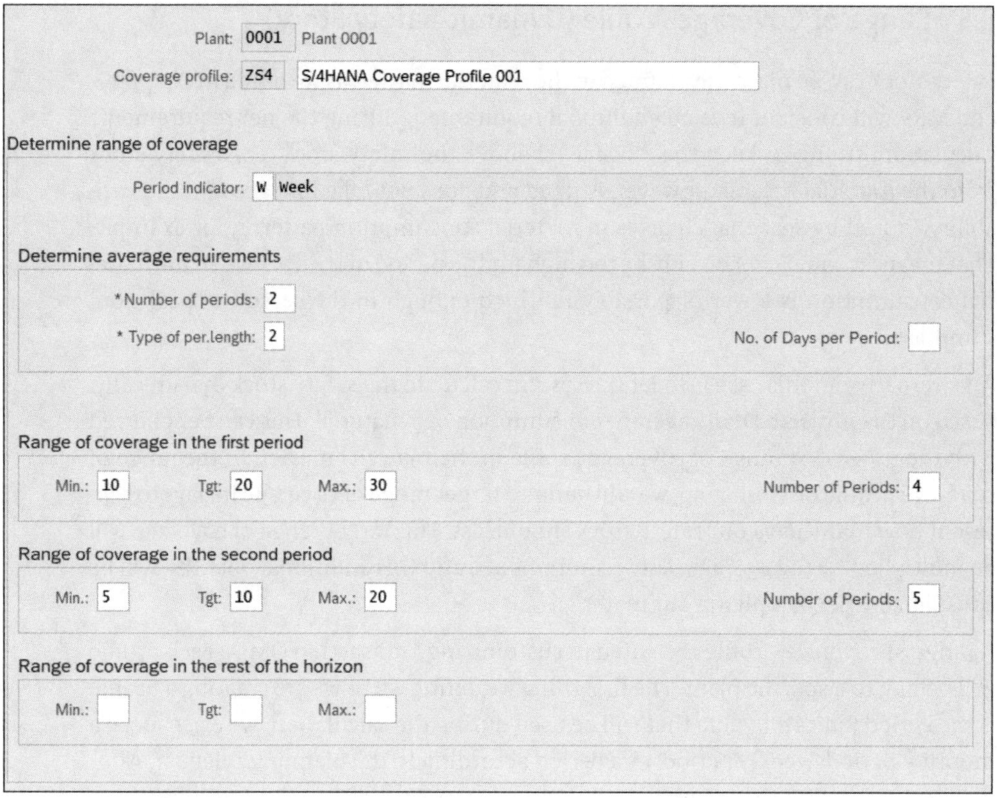

8 Advanced MRP Features

Figure 8.16 Range of Coverage Profile

Now that we have covered the Customizing behind the range of coverage, let's analyze an example using the range of coverage profile shown in Figure 8.16. In this example, we will use a lot size EX with a lot-for-lot procedure and MRP type PD for our material to simplify the calculation.

Figure 8.17 shows the Stock/Requirements List for our material after the MRP run, where we can analyze the MRP results. The figure shows that on 04.11.2019, the dependent requirement of 400 EA leads to a shortage of 300 EA. Because we are using lot-sizing procedure EX, the quantity calculated for the replenishment proposal would 300 EA, which would be the shortage quantity. However, due to the range of coverage profile assigned to this material, MRP added a dynamic safety stock of 1,000 to the replenishment proposal quantity, so the total quantity is actually 1,300 EA.

8.5 Range of Coverage Profile (Dynamic Safety Stock)

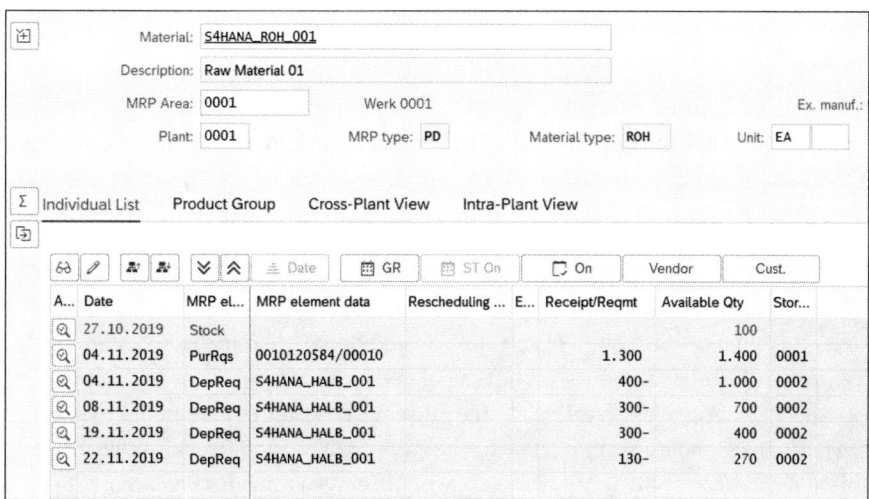

Figure 8.17 MRP Results for a Material with a Range of Coverage Profile

To understand how system calculated a dynamic safety stock of 1,000, we can switch to the period totals view to get more details about the situation on 04.11.2019.

In the period totals view, as shown in Figure 8.18, we can see that the average **Daily Requirements** value calculated for 04.11.2019 is 50 EA.

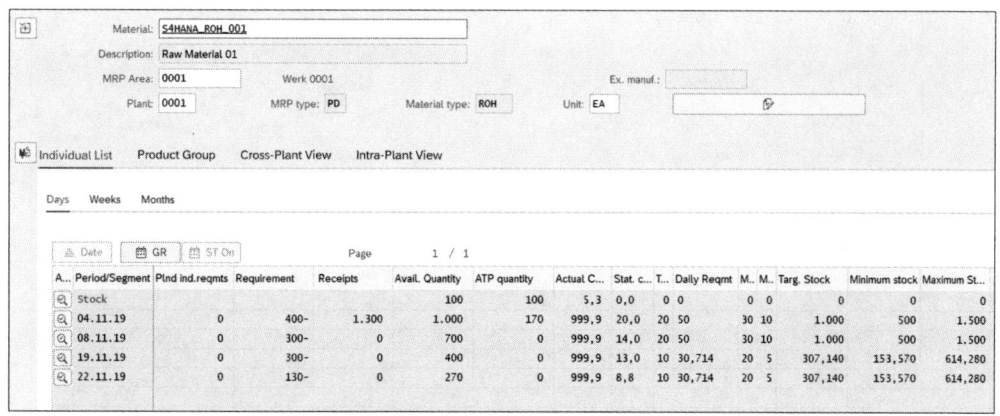

Figure 8.18 Period Totals View Showing Target Stock

Considering that we have defined the weeks period indicator for our profile and that the number of periods is two, MRP added together the requirements within those two weeks (400 for 04.11 and 300 for 08.11) to get the total requirements of 700 EA.

343

8 Advanced MRP Features

This value was divided by 14 (the number of calendar days within two weeks) to get the average daily requirements of 50 EA on 04.11.2019.

Because we have defined a target range of coverage of 20 days in our range of coverage profile, MRP will multiply this value by the average daily requirements of 50 EA to get to the target safety stock of 1,000 EA, which is also shown in Figure 8.18. Similar logic will be used to calculate the minimum and maximum stock.

> **Note**
>
> Because it is usually not desired to calculate an additional quantity for requirements in the past, a dynamic safety stock is not calculated for those requirements. This way, we avoid calculating excessive stock in the current period for requirements that are in the past. The standard system behavior, however, can be modified with the implementation of SAP Note 407035 (MOD: Range of Coverage Profile for Requirements in the Past).

Figure 8.19 shows another example of the same material using the same settings and the same range of coverage profile as in Figure 8.16, showing that the minimum safety stock was used by MRP.

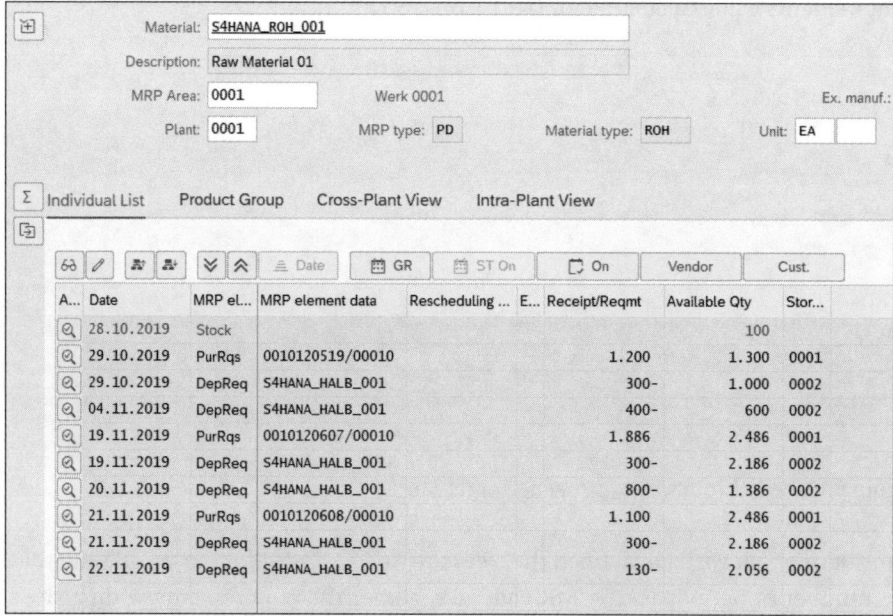

Figure 8.19 New Requisition Created when Minimum Safety Stock Is Reached

8.5 Range of Coverage Profile (Dynamic Safety Stock)

This figure shows that the dependent requirement of 300 EA on 19.11.2019 would not cause an actual shortage for our material, but MRP still created a new replenishment proposal on that date.

If we switch to the period totals view once again (see Figure 8.20), we will see that a minimum safety stock of 1,092.860 was calculated for our material for 19.11.2019, and because the available quantity is below the minimum safety stock, MRP generated a new replenishment proposal. Because the requirement did not actually lead to a shortage situation, the total replenishment proposal is just enough to ensure that the available quantity will match the target safety stock of 2,185.720.

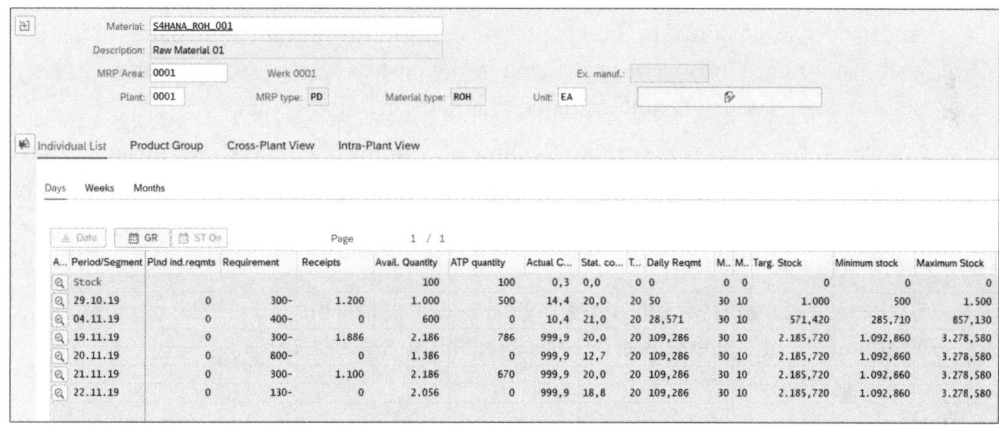

Figure 8.20 Period Totals View Showing the Minimum Safety Stock

These examples show that the range of coverage profile is a powerful tool to avoid shortages and, at the same time, avoid the safety stock fluctuating according to the actual demand for a material. This will simplify the master data maintenance because we will not need to calculate a safety stock for the each material: we will simply enter how many days of requirements we expect MRP to cover.

SAP Note 217144 (Range of Coverage Calc. w/Range of Coverage Profile) brings additional technical information about the range of coverage profile's usage and its effects in the MRP calculation.

8.6 Summary

At the beginning of this book, we focused on the MRP basics, but this chapter focused on more advanced features that can be used to improve the MRP results.

We started the chapter by explaining how to implement the subcontracting process, with a special focus on the changes introduced by the SAP S/4HANA simplifications in subcontracting planning. We discussed the usage of MRP areas and advanced subcontracting planning scenarios, such as third-party subcontracting. In this chapter, we also discussed how to create a planning calendar and a BOM explosion number, how those features can be used, and how they will affect the MRP results.

Another topic explained in this chapter was the interchangeability of parts—a feature that is not new, but that was restricted in the past to systems with specific industry solutions activated. It is now available by default in SAP S/4HANA.

We closed the chapter by explaining how we can use a range of coverage profile to create a dynamic safety stock for our products, allowing the system to automatically calculate a safety stock that will vary according to the product demand and the average daily requirements.

In the next chapter, we will step away from MRP a little bit and discuss demand management and the planning strategies available in SAP S/4HANA.

Chapter 9
Demand Management

This chapter will cover demand management, which is used to translate a forecast into an actual MRP requirement. We will cover the main planning strategies used in demand management, its configuration, the consumption and reduction of independent requirements, and the alternatives to generate a demand plan in SAP S/4HANA.

The overall concept of MRP is based on top-down planning: we first plan our finished products, driving dependent requirements to the lower-level materials until reaching the raw material level. In the case of a make-to-order (MTO) scenario, sales orders will act as requirements for the finished products, but in the case of make-to-stock (MTS) production, we need to have a forecast as an input for MRP so that we can plan the production and the purchase of components. Sometimes, even in MTO production, we need to have a forecast as an input for MRP so that we can buy the components and produce some semifinished products before the actual creation of a sales order, in order to reduce the lead time to deliver the product to the customer.

This kind of sales forecast is usually based on the past sales history and can be generated using different tools. SAP S/4HANA still offers the old sales and operations planning (S&OP), which was used very often in SAP ERP, but it is part of the SAP S/4HANA compatibility scope and thus cannot be considered as a long-term solution. As an alternative, SAP offers SAP Integrated Business Planning (SAP IBP), a powerful cloud solution that can be also used to generate a sales forecast. In other cases, companies may use a third-party or custom solution to generate this forecast.

No matter what solution is used to generate the sales forecast, *demand management* is the tool used to translate this forecast into planned independent requirements (PIRs), which can be considered inputs for MRP and which can drive the planning of finished products and lower-level components.

This chapter starts by explaining what demand management is and its basic concepts, like independent requirements consumption and reduction in Section 9.1. We will then go through the standard planning strategies and discuss how to use them in

SAP S/4HANA in Section 9.2, and walk through the main demand management transactions and SAP Fiori applications in Section 9.3. We will close the chapter with an examination of demand management configuration, including planning strategies, strategy groups, requirement types, and requirement classes in Section 9.4.

9.1 What Is Demand Management?

Demand management is the component that we will use to create a demand plan. The demand plan consists of independent requirements divided into periodic buckets; those requirements will be one of the main inputs for the MRP net requirements calculation.

Each independent requirement will have a date, a quantity, and a requirement type. The requirement type is derived from the planning strategy assigned to the material master, and the planning strategy will determine the MRP behavior when covering the requirements. SAP S/4HANA offers several different standard planning strategies, and they can be used for both MTO and MTS scenarios. The independent requirements are generally created for the finished products, but specific planning strategies have to be used when planning at the component level. We will go through the main planning strategies later in this chapter, but first we will discuss the basics behind demand management.

To start using demand management, we first need to define some settings in the material master. We start with the **Strategy Group** setting, defining a group of planning strategies that we can use for this material, and the consumption parameters (the consumption mode, the forward consumption period, and the backward consumption period). All those settings are shown in Figure 9.1 and will be explained in this chapter. Depending on the planning strategy used, we may need to define additional settings, such as the **Mixed MRP** or **Planning Material** settings.

The strategy group contains a main planning strategy and additional secondary strategies. For example, if we have a material that is generally produced to stock, but under special circumstances can be produced for a specific sales order, then we can create a strategy group in which the main planning strategy is an MTS strategy and there is a secondary MTO planning strategy. SAP delivers standard planning strategies and strategy groups, and we will discuss the main planning strategies (and the Customizing behind planning strategies and strategy groups) in this chapter in detail.

9.1 What Is Demand Management?

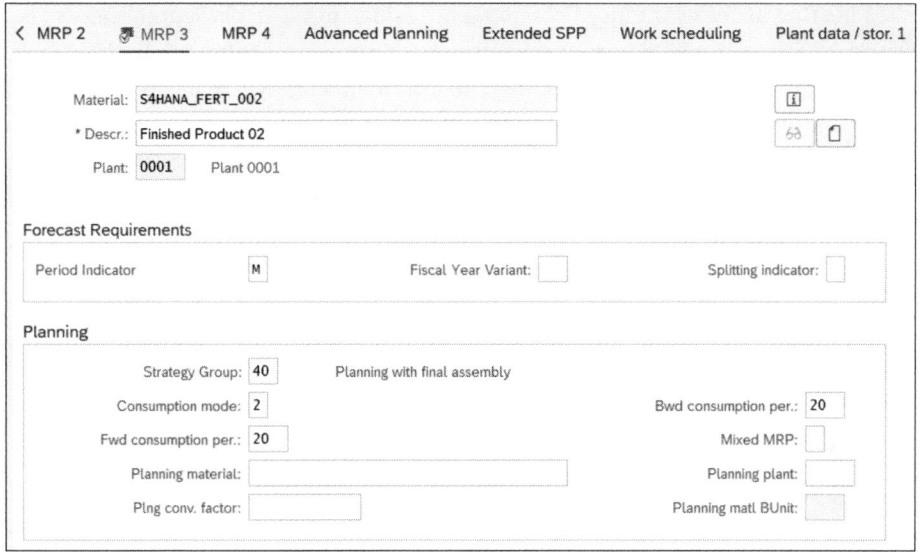

Figure 9.1 Demand Management Settings in the Material Master

After defining those settings in the material master, we will be able to create PIRs for our material. There are different options to create PIRs in SAP S/4HANA, which we will discuss later in this chapter, but the most common option is Transaction MD61 in the SAP GUI.

Figure 9.2 shows the PIR planning table, which lists the PIRs in monthly buckets. Here, there are two different versions, but the **Active** flag is checked for one, and only the PIRs from that version will be relevant to MRP.

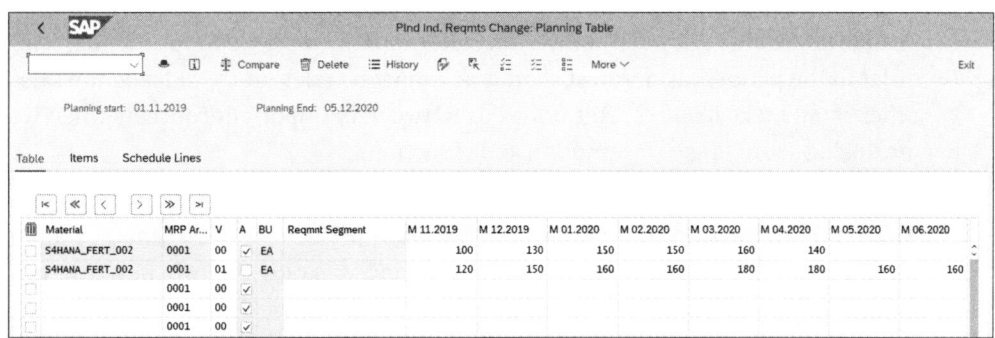

Figure 9.2 PIRs in Transaction MD61

The PIRs that are relevant for MRP should be visible in the Stock/Requirements List. Figure 9.3 shows the PIRs from the active version shown in Figure 9.2. In this figure, note that all the PIRs shown in the Stock/Requirements List will match the quantities of the PIRs in planning table, with the exception of the PIR from December. For this PIR, the planned quantity was 130, but only 90 is shown in the Stock/Requirements List. That is because there is a sales order within the PIR consumption horizon maintained in the material master, so this sales order is actually consuming the PIR to avoid a duplication of requirements.

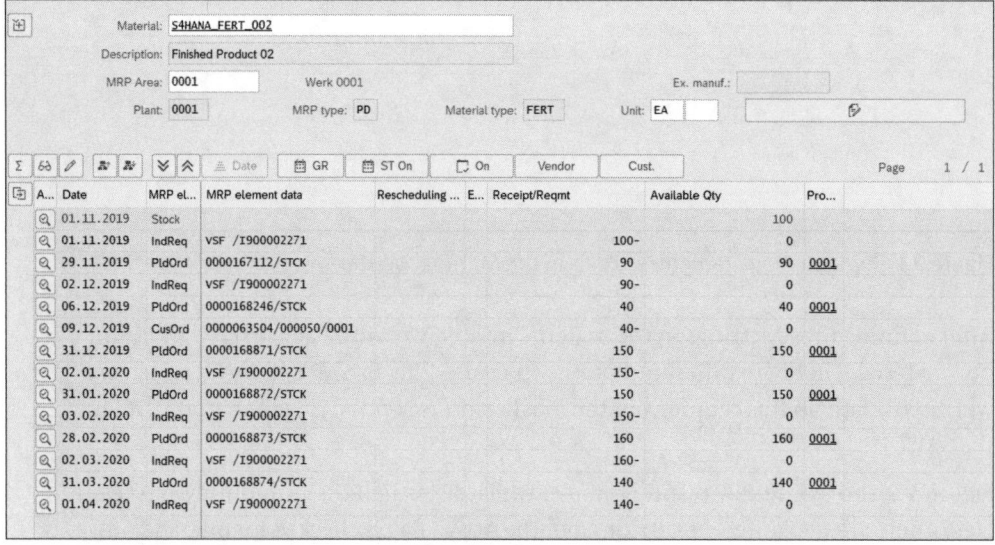

Figure 9.3 PIRs in the Stock/Requirements List

The idea is that the PIR will be only a *forecast*; therefore, once we have an actual sales order in the period, this forecast should no longer be relevant to MRP and the sales order should take its place. This brings us to two very important concepts when we are talking about PIRs: consumption and reduction.

PIR *consumption* happens when we create a sales order or another requirement within the backward or the forward consumption period; this requirement should replace this forecast. The consumption is dynamic, meaning that whenever we run MRP or call the Stock/Requirements List, the system will check which requirements are within the consumption period and consume those PIRs. In the case of a PIR consumption, MRP will subtract the requirement quantity from the PIR quantity before the net requirements calculation or before showing it in the Stock/Requirements

List. The PIR quantity, however, will not be changed in the database; we will still see the total PIR quantity when we open it in the demand management transactions. If we cancel a sales order that was consuming a PIR, for example, it will be no longer relevant for consumption, and we will see the original PIR quantity in the Stock/Requirements List.

PIR *reduction* happens when we post a goods movement, such as a goods issue for a delivery, within the consumption horizon. If this goods movement is relevant for PIR reduction, then the PIR quantity should be adjusted and will then be physically changed in the database tables. This means that the change will be permanent, and it will be reflected in the demand management transactions. The PIR quantity may be restored if we post a cancellation for the goods movement.

> **Note**
>
> If there are no values maintained for the consumption periods in the material master, then the system will check if there are values maintained in the MRP group Customizing. If there are no values in the material master or in the MRP group, the system will use consumption mode 1 (backward consumption only) and a backward consumption period of 999 days.
>
> This means that the PIR consumption may still happen, even if we leave the consumption periods empty.

To have a PIR consumption when a requirement is created or a PIR reduction when a goods movement is posted, the system will check if there is a PIR within the consumption period. The consumption period is defined by the backward and forward consumption periods; these values are in workdays, which can be maintained in the material master. Depending on the consumption mode, the system may check for PIRs in the future (within the forward consumption period), in the past (within the backward consumption period), or in both the future and the past.

The following options are available to select for the consumption mode:

- **1—Backward Consumption Only**: The system will only look for PIRs in the past, within the backward consumption period.
- **2—Backward/Forward Consumption**: The system will first look for PIRs within the backward consumption period, then, if there is no PIR in the past or if all the PIRs were already consumed, it will try to find PIRs within the forward consumption period.

- **3—Forward Consumption Only**: The system will only look for PIRs in the future, within the forward consumption period.
- **4—Forward/Backward Consumption**: Similar to consumption mode 2, but the system will first look for PIRs within the forward consumption period and then look for PIRs within the backward consumption period.
- **5—Period-Specific Consumption**: This is a new consumption mode introduced in SAP S/4HANA that allows the PIR consumption to be restricted within a given period. We can use this consumption mode, for example, if we are using PIRs with monthly buckets and we want to restrict the PIR consumption within the current month. In this case, the consumption periods will not be in calculated in days, but according to the PIR periods.

Now that we have defined core concepts for demand management, let's move into the planning strategies. These planning strategies will define how the PIRs will be interpreted by MRP and will influence the MRP results.

9.2 Planning Strategies

In the previous section, we discussed the basics of PIRs, including the creation of PIRs, how they are shown in the Stock/Requirements List, and how they are consumed. However, depending on which planning strategy we choose, we may have a different result in the MRP run. In this section, we will analyze the different planning strategies available in SAP S/4HANA, starting with the simplest and commonly used planning strategies and moving to the most elaborate and complex strategies.

Before going thorough each planning strategy, let's discuss how they work. Each planning strategy consists of a requirement type for independent requirements and a requirements type for customer requirements. Figure 9.4 shows the Customizing behind planning strategy 40 (planning with final assembly), where we can see the details of the mentioned requirement types.

The requirement type for independent requirements is defined when we create a PIR. Usually, this requirement type is automatically derived from the planning strategy assigned to the material master when we create a PIR, but we have the possibility to change the requirement type or to manually select a requirement type if there is no strategy defined for the material master.

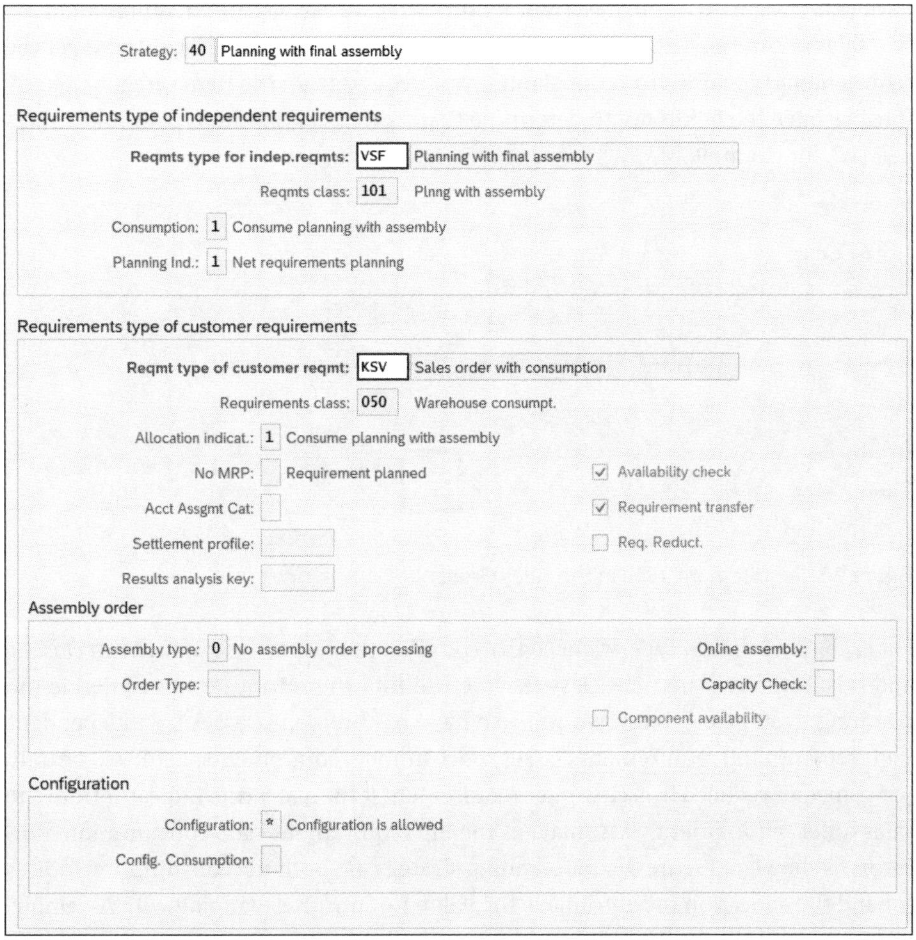

Strategy:	40	Planning with final assembly		

Requirements type of independent requirements

Reqmts type for indep.reqmts:	VSF	Planning with final assembly	
Reqmts class:	101	Plnng with assembly	
Consumption:	1	Consume planning with assembly	
Planning Ind.:	1	Net requirements planning	

Requirements type of customer requirements

Reqmt type of customer reqmt:	KSV	Sales order with consumption	
Requirements class:	050	Warehouse consumpt.	
Allocation indicat.:	1	Consume planning with assembly	
No MRP:		Requirement planned	☑ Availability check
Acct Assgmt Cat:			☑ Requirement transfer
Settlement profile:			☐ Req. Reduct.
Results analysis key:			

Assembly order

Assembly type:	0	No assembly order processing	Online assembly:
Order Type:			Capacity Check:
		☐ Component availability	

Configuration

Configuration:	*	Configuration is allowed
Config. Consumption:		

Figure 9.4 Planning Strategy Customizing

The requirement type for customer requirements comes from the sales orders and usually is also derived automatically from the planning strategy. If we have defined a strategy group with different planning strategies, we will be able to select the requirement types related to those strategies during the sales order creation. Figure 9.5 shows the **Requirement Type** column in the **Procurement** tab of the sales order.

9 Demand Management

In the sales order Customizing (Transaction OVZI), we can also tie a requirement type to a sales order item category, and we can choose if the system should try to get the requirement type first from the planning strategy or from the item category. Therefore, we have the flexibility to determine that a given sales order type would always be MTO, for example.

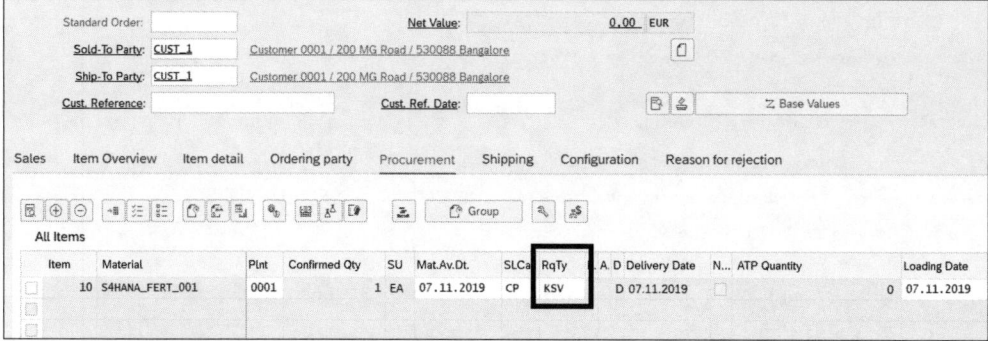

Figure 9.5 Requirement Type in the Sales Order

For each requirement type, we need to determine the respective *requirement classes*, and it is in the requirement class that we will find the settings that will define the planning strategy behavior. We will also have requirement classes for independent requirements and requirement classes for customer requirements. A PIR will be only consumed or reduced by a customer requirement if the allocation indicator from the sales order requirement class matches the PIR requirement class consumption indicator. As shown in Figure 9.4, for planning strategy 40, both the consumption indicator and the allocation indicator have the value **1—Consume Planning with Assembly**, which means that the planning strategy settings are correct and the PIR consumption will happen.

> **Warning**
>
> Although we can change the settings behind the requirement classes and, technically, can even create a new planning strategy, this is usually not recommended. The standard code behind demand management was tailored for the standard planning strategies, and even a minor change in Customizing may lead to problems in consumption and reduction. Therefore, we should try to stick with the standard planning strategies as much as possible.

9.2.1 Planning with Final Assembly (Strategy 40)

Planning strategy 40, planning with final assembly, is perhaps the most widely used planning strategy within SAP ERP. This is basically an MTS strategy, in which MRP will generate planned orders to cover the PIRs if they cannot be covered by existing stock or planned receipts. Sales requirements will consume the PIRs, but MRP can also react to any sales requirement that exceeds the PIR quantity or that cannot consume any PIR.

This strategy will also act as a "fake" MTO strategy because it will react to sales requirements when there is no PIR and the sales orders cannot be covered with stocks or planned receipts.

This strategy is widely used due to its flexibility and simplicity. To use this strategy, we simply need to define strategy group 40 in the material master and set the consumption parameters either from the material master or from the MRP group Customizing. An example of the settings used for this strategy was shown in Figure 9.1.

We showed an example of the planning results using planning strategy 40 in Figure 9.3. As shown there, the PIR requirement type appears in the Stock/Requirements List under the **MRP Element Data** column. MRP considered the available stock to cover PIRs, and the PIR from December was partially consumed by a sales order.

The same example is shown again in Figure 9.6, but now the sales order quantity was increased, and it exceeds the quantity of the PIR for the month of December. Here, the PIR quantity for December is totally consumed and, due to the limits established by the consumption periods, there is no other PIR to be consumed. In this case, MRP reacts to the sales order requirement, generating a planned order to cover the total requirement, not only the quantity covered by the PIR. This exemplifies the flexibility of this planning strategy as MRP will react to both PIRs and additional sales order requirements.

9 Demand Management

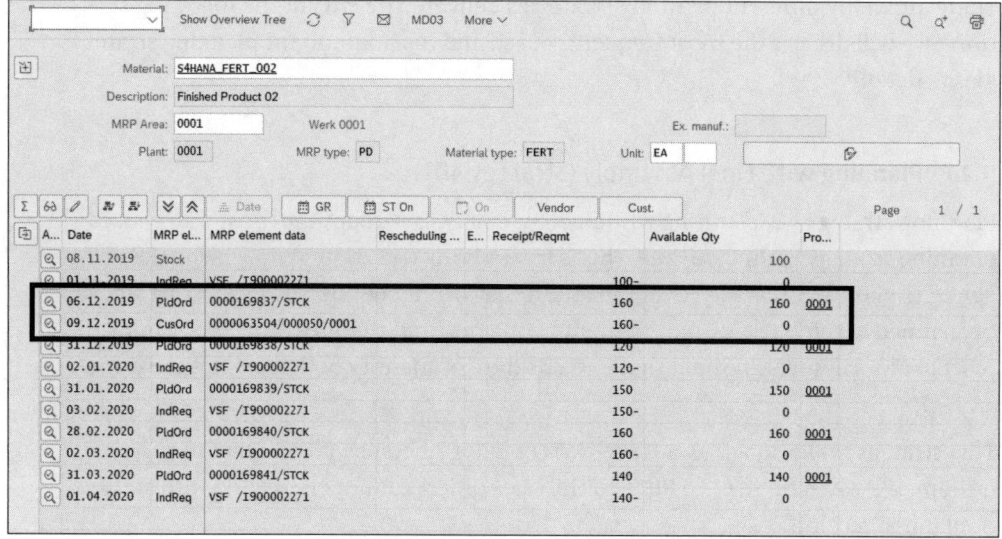

Figure 9.6 MRP Reacts to Sales Order when Using Planning Strategy 40

9.2.2 Net Requirements Planning (Strategy 10)

Planning strategy 10, net requirements planning, is useful when we need to produce our material to stock based on the demand plan and we do not want any noise introduced by sales orders. With this planning strategy, MRP will react to PIRs, but it will not consider sales order requirements.

This planning strategy is very often used for products with a seasonal demand or a lot of demand variability, where the demand needs to be smoothed. We will also frequently see this planning strategy used with repetitive manufacturing, in which it is used for cheap products that are produced in bulk.

With this planning strategy, sales orders will be displayed in the Stock/Requirements List, but they will not be relevant to MRP. This means that they will not be included in the net requirements calculation and they will not affect the calculation of the available quantity. Moreover, with this planning strategy there is no PIR consumption, as the sales orders will not be relevant to MRP and we want to stick to the demand plan. We will only observe the PIR reduction when we post a goods issue and consume the stock to a sales order delivery.

This strategy includes the existing stock in the net requirements calculation, and MRP will not generate a new planned order if the PIRs can be covered by the stock.

9.2 Planning Strategies

> **Warning**
> With this planning strategy, the consumption mode is not relevant and the oldest PIR is always reduced first. If we want to reduce PIRs according to consumption mode, SAP Note 71804 proposes a modification that can change the standard logic.

To use this planning strategy, we simply need to define standard strategy group 10 in the material master and set the consumption periods either from the material master or from the MRP group Customizing. The PIR requirement type used is LSF, and the sales order requirement type is KSL.

Figure 9.7 shows an example of the MRP results when using planning strategy 10, in which MRP only created planned orders to cover the PIRs. We can see sales order requirements in the Stock/Requirements List, but they will not affect the available quantity because they are not relevant for the MRP calculation. We can also observe in this figure that the first PIR is completely covered by the existing stock and that a planned order was not generated by MRP to cover this PIR.

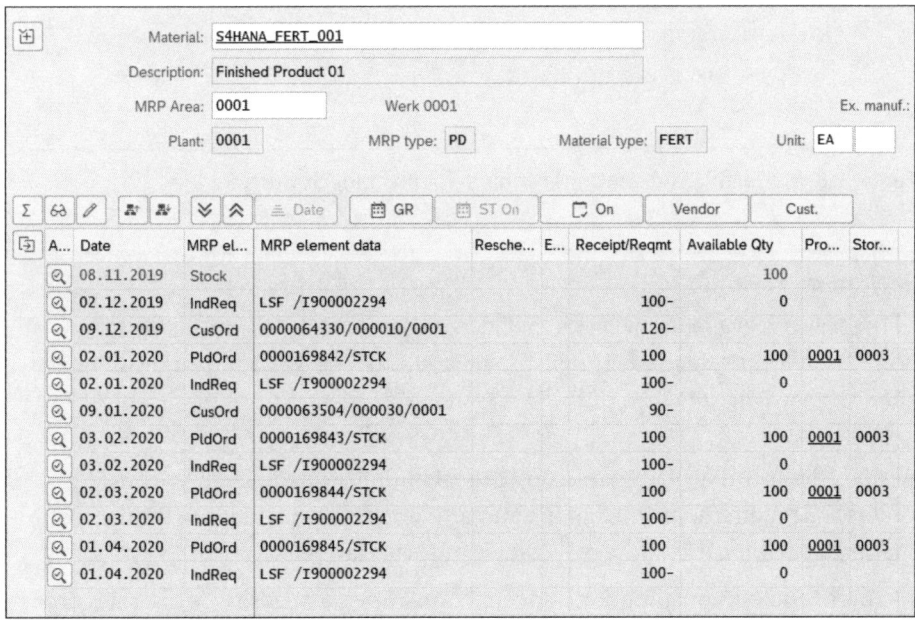

Figure 9.7 Net Requirements Planning PIRs

9.2.3 Gross Requirements Planning (Strategy 11)

Planning strategy 11, gross requirements planning, is similar to planning strategy 10: we will only consider the PIRs, and the sales orders will not be relevant to MRP and will not consume PIRs. The main difference between the planning strategies is that strategy 11 will not consider the on-hand stock to cover PIRs.

Gross requirements planning is used in situations in which the production lines cannot stop (e.g., in the steel industry, where furnaces cannot be turned off), so we need to follow the demand plan without taking into consideration the current stock situation. The production plan needs to ensure that production is always happening, no matter what is already on stock.

To use this planning strategy, we need to define strategy group 11 in the material master, and we also need to set the **Mixed MRP** field to **2—Gross Requirements Planning** in the **MRP 3** tab, as shown in Figure 9.8.

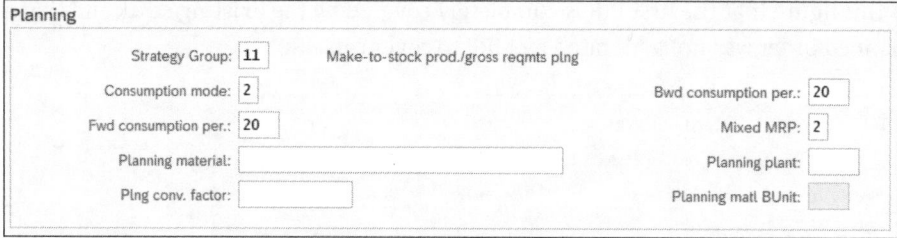

Figure 9.8 Material Master Settings Required for Planning Strategy 11

> **Warning**
>
> The **Mixed MRP** setting generally should not be used, unless it is required for a specific planning strategy. An incorrect value in this field may lead to inconsistent and incorrect MRP results.

Besides the fact that materials using this planning strategy will not consider sales orders as a requirement and that the on-hand stock is not included in the net requirements calculation, this strategy has additional special characteristics:

- There is no PIR consumption and reduction during a goods issue to a sales order.
- This is the only planning strategy in which the PIR reduction will happen upon goods receipt for a production/process order, repetitive manufacturing planned order, or purchase order.

- PIRs and procurement elements will remain in a separated stock segment called *gross requirements planning*. All the requirements that are not relevant for MRP and the stock will remain separated from the PIRs.

Figure 9.9 shows the Stock/Requirements List for a material using gross requirements planning, showing the special stock segment containing all the PIRs and the receipts that are relevant to PIR reduction, such as planned orders and production orders.

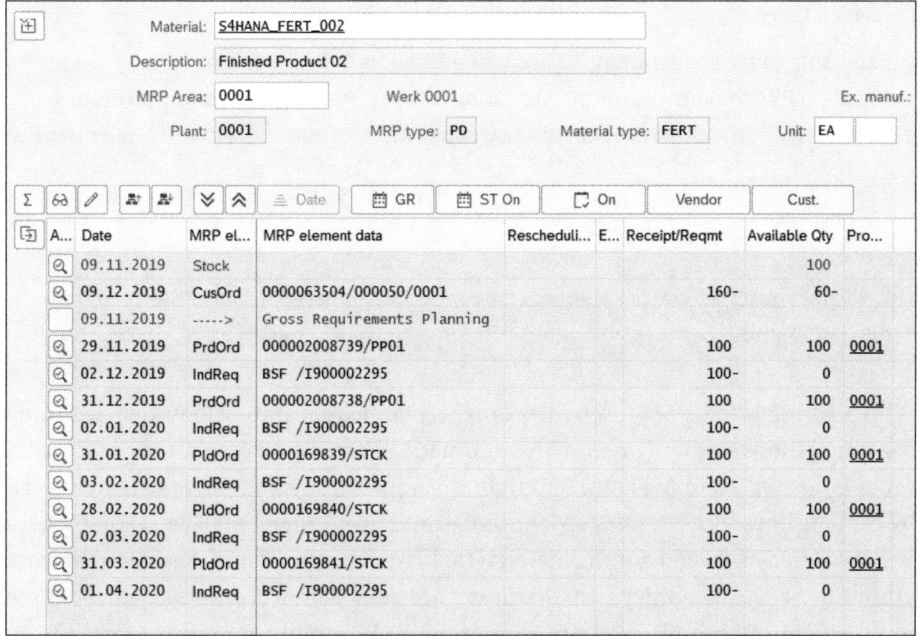

Figure 9.9 Gross Requirements Planning in the Stock/Requirements List

For this planning strategy, the requirement type for independent requirements is BSF, and the requirement type for customer requirements is KSL.

9.2.4 Make-to-Order Production (Strategy 20)

So far, we have discussed planning strategies used for MTS production, but SAP also offers planning strategies for MTO production.

9   Demand Management

The classic example is planning strategy 20, MTO production. This strategy is identified by the complete absence of PIRs: we will not plan the production to stock, as we will only start the procurement after we receive an actual sales order.

This strategy is generally used for very expensive products that we cannot afford to produce to stock, for products that can quickly become obsolete, or those that are specially manufactured for a customer. If needed, we can use this planning strategy for a finished product and combine it with a planning strategy to plan at the component level in order to ensure that we will have the components in stock to reduce the total lead time.

When using planning strategy 20, we will not create PIRs for the finished product, so there is no PIR consumption or reduction. To use it, we only need to maintain strategy group 20 in the material master; the consumption parameters will have no influence.

> **Note**
> Planning strategy 25, make-to-order for configurable material, is a variation of planning strategy 20, in which a variant configuration will be used in an MTO scenario.

With planning strategy 20, each sales order is planned separately in its own planning segment. These stock segments are automatically created when a new MTO sales order is created. Note in Figure 9.10 that those special stock segments are identified by the blue lines with the sales order number and sales order item. Even though there is stock already available for the material in this example, it is not considered for covering the MTO sales orders; MRP still creates new planned orders to cover these requirements. Those planned orders created by MRP will have an account assignment to the sales order number and sales order item, so once they are converted to production orders, the goods receipt will be posted to this sales order special stock.

> **Tip**
> The components of a planned order that is under the sales order special stock can also be planned within the special stock. If we define the **Individual/Collective** field in the material master (the **MRP 4** tab) as **1—Individual Requirements Only**, it will be planned under the sales order special stock.

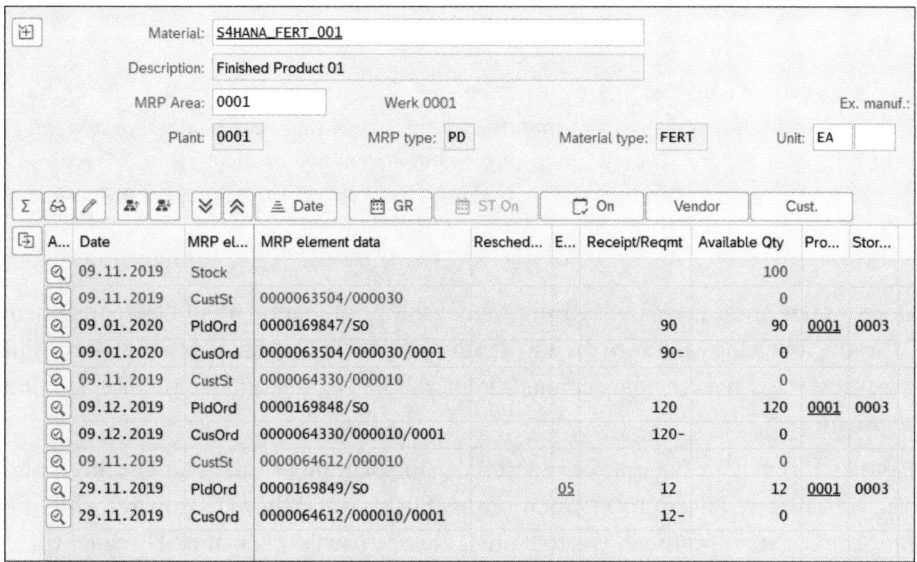

Figure 9.10 Sales Orders with Strategy 20 in the Stock/Requirements List

9.2.5 Planning without Final Assembly (Strategies 50 and 52)

In some situations, we want to use finished product PIRs to procure components ahead of time, but we want to delay the final assembly of the product until the actual receipt of a sales order. In this case, we can use planning strategies 50 and 52 to ensure that we will have all the components available when the sales order is created, reducing the total lead time.

Strategies 50 and 52 are very similar, allowing the planning of the components and delaying the final assembly until the receipt of a sales order. The main difference between them is that with strategy 50, once a sales order is received, it will be treated as MTO, whereas for strategy 52, the sales orders will be treated as MTS. To use these planning strategies, we simply need to set the respective strategy group in the material master and create PIRs for the finished product.

When analyzing the results of MRP, we will see a special planning segment called *preplanning*, holding all the PIRs and the planned orders created by MRP to cover those requirements. Those planned orders that were created within the preplanning segment have the special type VP; they are only created so that the BOM can be exploded and dependent requirements can be passed to the components.

9   Demand Management

> **Note**
>
> The special VP planned orders cannot be used for procurement, so they cannot be converted or used for repetitive manufacturing backflush. These planned orders can only be changed by MRP, so we cannot manually change or delete them. The only way to delete a VP planned order is to delete the PIR and run MRP for the material again.

Once a sales order is created within the consumption period, the PIR is consumed. After the following MRP run, the VP planned order will be adjusted to match the PIR quantity, and a new regular planned order will be created outside the **Preplanning** segment.

Figure 9.11 shows an example of a material using planning strategy 52. For this material, we have five PIRs of 100 EA in monthly buckets, and they are shown within the preplanning stock segment. The first PIR is already partially consumed because there is a sales order of 80 EA within the consumption period, so the PIR quantity displayed in the Stock/Requirements List is only the remaining quantity of 20 EA.

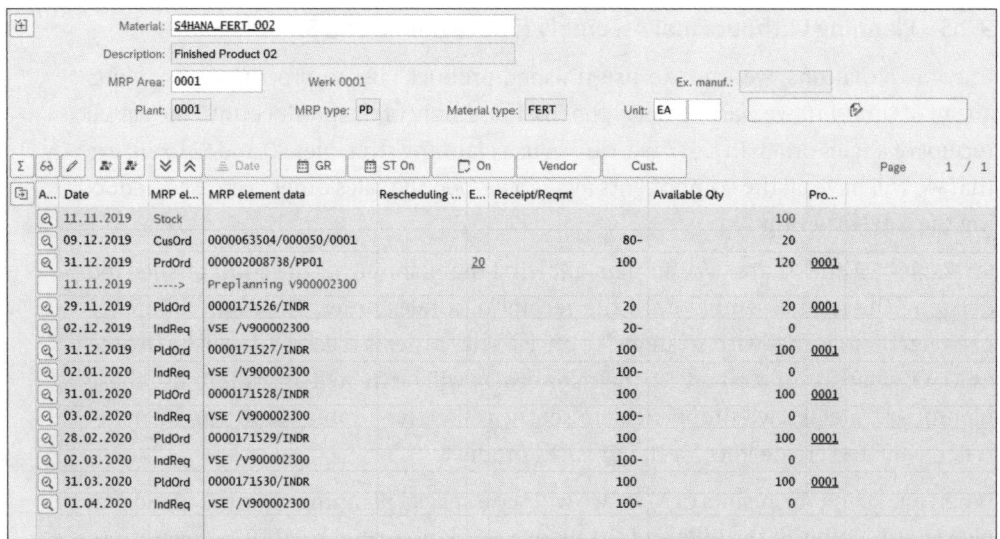

Figure 9.11 Preplanning Stock Segment in the Stock/Requirements List

The sales order that consumed the PIR is shown without the preplanning stock segment, just like the actual replenishment elements, like the production order shown in the figure. In this example, we are using planning strategy 52, so there is no account assignment, and the sales order remains in collective stock. When planning strategy 50 is used, there will be an account assignment to the sales order special stock, and the sales order will remain under the individual sales order stock.

> **Note**
>
> If necessary, semifinished products can also remain in the preplanning stock segment until the receipt of a sales order. We will use the individual/collective setting from the material master, mentioned earlier, to control if a component will be within the individual preplanning stock or will remain in collective stock.

For planning strategy 50, the requirement type for independent requirements is VSE and the requirement type for customer requirements is KEV. For planning strategy 52, the requirement types for independent and customer requirements are VSE and KSVS, respectively.

9.2.6 Planning with a Planning Material (Strategies 60 and 63)

In the previous section, we noted that we can use planning strategies 50 and 52 to delay the final assembly of a product until the receipt of an actual sales order. With these strategies, we will need to create PIRs for each of the finished products, and the components will be procured in advance.

In a scenario in which we have one or more components that are shared by different finished products, we can use planning strategies 60 or 63, for which we will use a planning material. Those strategies are similar to the planning without final assembly strategies, 50 and 52, but the difference is that the PIRs will be created for a separate material that will be the planning material. Procurement will be started for the planning material components, and once a sales order is received for the finished product, the PIRs are consumed and the components will be already in stock because they were procured in advance.

A classic example of planning with a planning material is a scenario in which we can sell an expensive product in many different colors. Each color of the product can be a different material number in SAP S/4HANA, but they will all have the same component—that is, the unpainted product. We will use the planning material to ensure that we have enough of the unpainted product in stock, but we will only start the painting operation after receiving a sales order.

These planning strategies can be also used if we can sell a product in different packages. We can delay the packaging until the receipt of a sales order and use the planning material to ensure that we have enough product in stock to quickly pack it and fulfill the sales orders.

Similarly to planning strategies 50 and 52, the main difference between planning strategies 60 and 63 is that the first one will generate sales orders with an account assignment to the sales order individual stock (MTO), while the second one will generate MTS sales orders.

In the material master of the planning material, we only need to define strategy group 60 or 63 and the consumption parameters. In the material master of the finished products that will be sold, we need to define the strategy group and set the planning material, the planning material plant, and a conversion factor to be used in the case of different units of measure.

Figure 9.12 shows the required settings for the finished product; note here that we do not need to define the consumption parameters, which will come from the planning material. Here, there might be several finished products with components in common, referencing the same planning material.

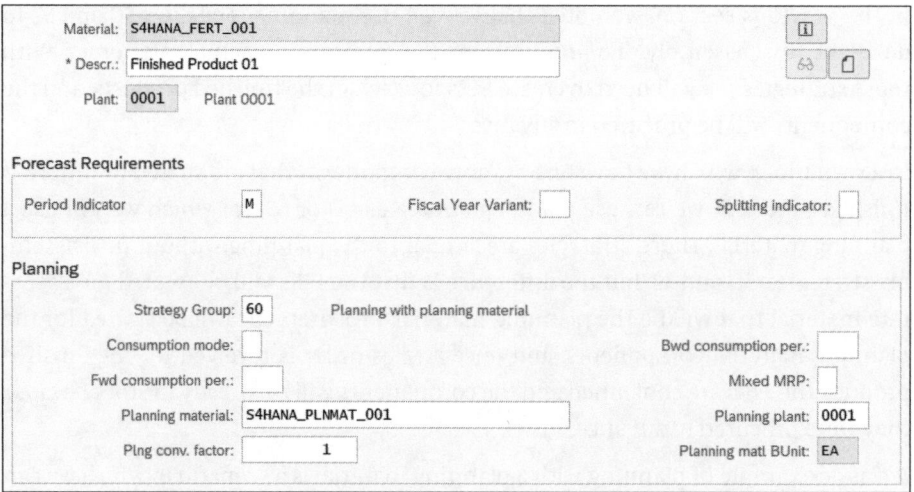

Figure 9.12 Material Master Settings for Planning Strategy 60

9.2 Planning Strategies

> **Note**
> Because we can define that the planning material can be in a different plant, this planning strategy can be used as a cross-plant planning without final assembly.

If we open the Stock/Requirements List for the planning material, we should only see the independent requirements and the planned order under the preplanning stock segment, as shown in Figure 9.13. Planned orders will also have the order type VP, which means that they are not convertible or manually changeable, and they will be used only to pass the demand to the components.

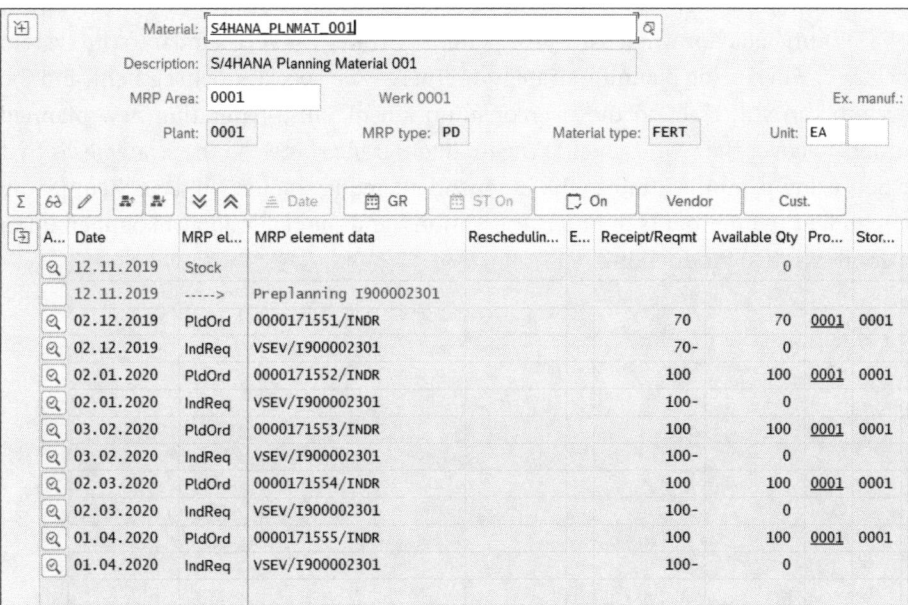

Figure 9.13 Planning Material in the Stock Requirements List

The requirement type for independent requirements is VSEV for both planning strategies 60 and 63. The requirement type for customer requirements for planning strategy 60 is KEVV and for planning strategy 63 is KSVV.

9.2.7 Planning at Assembly Level (Strategies 70, 74, and 59)

SAP S/4HANA offers several planning strategies in which we can trigger the procurement of components using PIRs.

For example, with planning strategy 70, planning at assembly level, we can create a forecast and procure a specific component to stock based on this forecast. Planning strategy 70 is used when, due to the business nature, it is easier to generate a stable forecast at the component level than at the finished product level. This strategy is very often combined with an MTO or assembly-to-order strategy at the finished product level, so we can have the component available in stock to react quickly to customer requirements, making us ready for the final assembly once a sales order is received.

This planning strategy requires the strategy group 70 to be selected in the material master, the consumption parameters to be set, and the **Mixed MRP** field should be set to **1—Subassembly Planning with Final Assembly**.

The system behavior when using this planning strategy is very similar to the system behavior when using planning strategy 40: there is no special stock segment, and the system can still react to the overconsumption of PIRs, generating new planned orders to cover the requirements. The main difference between the strategies is that when using planning strategy 70, independent requirements will be consumed by dependent requirements or order reservations, and the reduction will happen upon a goods issue to production.

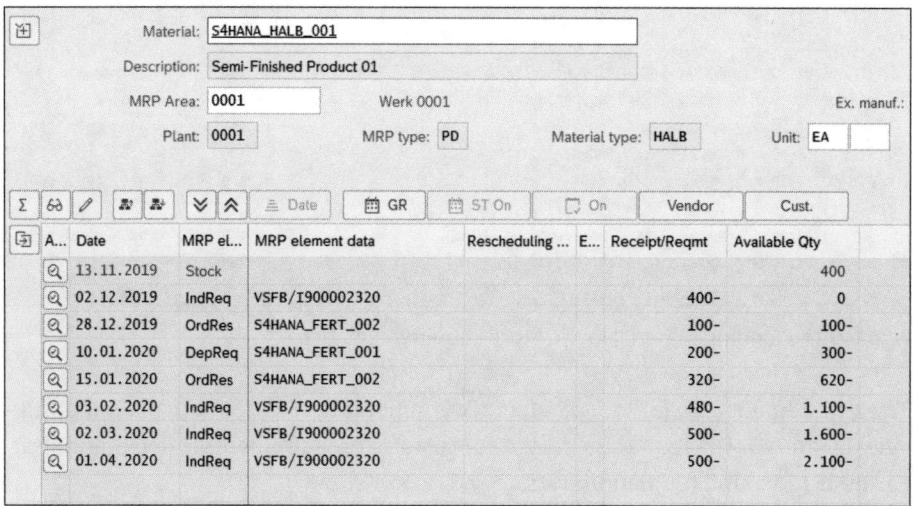

Figure 9.14 Independent Requirements at Subassembly Level

Besides planning strategy 70, SAP S/4HANA also offers planning strategy 74, planning without final assembly at assembly level, and planning strategy 59, planning at phantom assembly level, to be used for planning at component level.

Planning strategy 74 is very similar to planning strategies 50 and 52: we will have independent requirements created in the preplanning stock segment and VP planned orders generated by MRP to cover those PIRs. The main difference is that when using planning strategy 74, independent requirements will be consumed by dependent requirements or order reservations.

With planning strategy 59, we will create independent requirements for a specific phantom assembly so that all the components can be procured based on a forecast created for this phantom assembly. With this strategy, PIRs will be reduced upon goods issue to a production order, so backflush is mandatory because all the components should be consumed at the same time.

9.2.8 Assembly-to-Order (Strategies 81 through 86)

Assembly-to-order (ATO) is a special case of MTO production in which, instead of using MRP to generate a planned order to cover the sales order requirement, we will generate a replenishment element directly from the sales order. This replenishment element can be a production order, a process order, a repetitive manufacturing planned order, an SAP Project System network order, or a service order.

With ATO, there will be a link between the sales order and the procurement element. There are two different procedures for ATO:

- Static assembly: There is a hard 1:1 link between the sales order item and the procurement element.
- Dynamic assembly: There is a loose link between the sales order item and the procurement element, so quantities and dates can be split.

One of the greatest advantages of using ATO is that because a production order can be generated during the sales order creation, we can run an availability check for the production order components and a capacity availability check on the work centers, so we will know exactly when the order can be fulfilled. Another advantage is that because there is a link between the sales order and the procurement element, changes in the sales orders, such as a change in the date or quantity, will be immediately reflected in the procurement element.

Like in the MTO strategy, an ATO sales order will have an account assignment to the sales order special stock, and the respective procurement element also will be linked to the sales order special stock.

The following standard planning strategies are available in SAP S/4HANA for ATO:

- 81 (assembly processing with planned orders)
- 82 (assembly processing with production orders)
- 83 (assembly processing with networks)
- 84 (service orders)
- 85 (assembly processing with network/project)
- 86 (assembly processing with process orders)

9.3 Creating a Demand Plan

Now that we have discussed the basics of demand management and the main planning strategies, it is time to discuss how to create a demand plan in SAP S/4HANA.

As noted earlier in this chapter, using Transaction MD61 is the simplest way to generate a demand plan. Using this transaction, we can manually input the quantities for each bucket, split the quantities in different periods, and copy or even compare the requirements.

Figure 9.2 showed an example of a requirements plan created using this transaction, with two different PIR versions: one active and one inactive. We can have many different versions for the same material because we can have optimistic, realistic, or pessimist forecast scenarios.

Instead of creating the forecast plan separated by materials, we can also create a *requirements plan*, in which we will process the demand for several materials on the same screen. We can see a more detailed view of each material by switching to the **Schedule Lines** tab, as shown in Figure 9.15. In the details screen, we can assign a production version or a BOM explosion number for the individual PIR, and these values will be considered by MRP. For example, if we assign a production version to a PIR, then MRP will use this production version when generating a planned order to cover this PIR. These columns are greyed out by default, but we can open them for input in the **Settings** menu.

9.3 Creating a Demand Plan

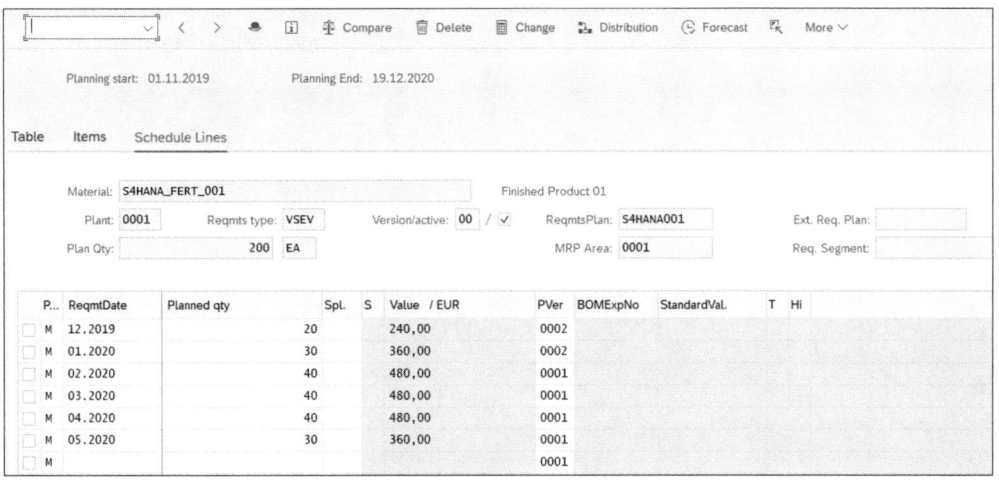

Figure 9.15 Schedule Lines Details in Demand Management

> **Tip**
> Using Transaction MD61, we can also see the history of changes for a PIR, but the PIR reduction will not be shown. However, history during the PIR reduction can be activated in customizing Transaction OMP4. PIR reduction history will always appear under the user ABBAU-, which is an internal identification, not the user who actually posted the goods movement.

Within this transaction, we can also copy the PIRs from a reference, such as sales and operations planning or a forecast created for this material in the material master. This can be done through the **Edit · Copy Requirements** menu option.

Besides the traditional way to create and change PIRs in the SAP GUI transactions, SAP S/4HANA also offers the possibility to manage a demand plan in SAP Fiori. In the earlier SAP S/4HANA releases, an SAP Fiori application called Manage PIRs was available in the SAP Fiori launchpad for the maintenance of PIRs. However, as of SAP S/4HANA 1909, PIR maintenance was redesigned, and this SAP Fiori application was replaced by the new Maintain PIRs app.

When entering this application, we see a list of materials with KPIs related to the PIRs, as shown in Figure 9.16. Here, we see key figures: the accuracy in the current period, the accuracy in the last week, and the accuracy in the last month, where the accuracy is the percentage of PIRs consumed/reduced by an actual demand.

369

9   Demand Management

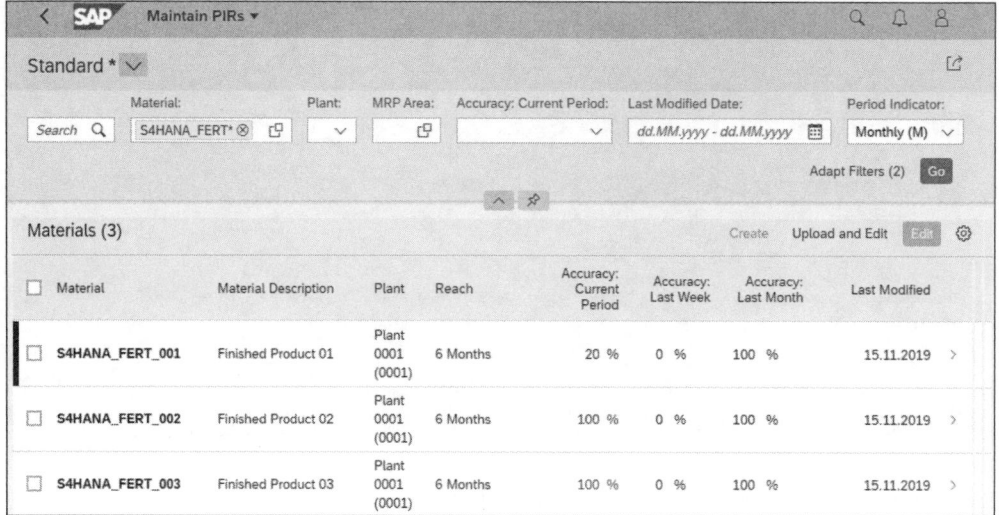

Figure 9.16 The Maintain PIRs App

When selecting one or more materials, we have the **Edit** option, which moves us to a screen where we can change the PIRs, or the **Upload and Edit** option, through which we can upload a CSV file with the PIR quantities and then change the uploaded values. If we choose the option to upload a file, a pop-up screen will appear in which we can choose the file to be uploaded (see Figure 9.17). This option to upload PIRs is a major benefit of this new SAP Fiori application. It was not present in the previous application, and there is no simple feature to upload PIRs in SAP GUI.

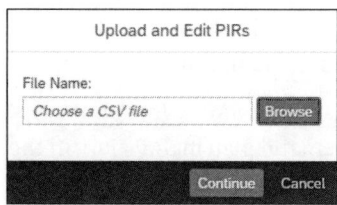

Figure 9.17 Uploading and Editing PIRs

After the file upload, or if we simply choose the **Edit** option, we will move into a new screen in which we can change the existing or the newly uploaded PIR quantities. As shown in Figure 9.18, this screen will be very similar to Transaction MD62 in SAP GUI, in which we have different materials and PIR quantities in the period buckets.

In the upper-right corner, we have the **Mass Maintenance** option, in which we can set a value for a given period for all the materials displayed, and the **Download to Spreadsheet** option, through which the demand plan can be downloaded as a CSV file. This CSV file can be used as a model for uploading PIRs as shown earlier.

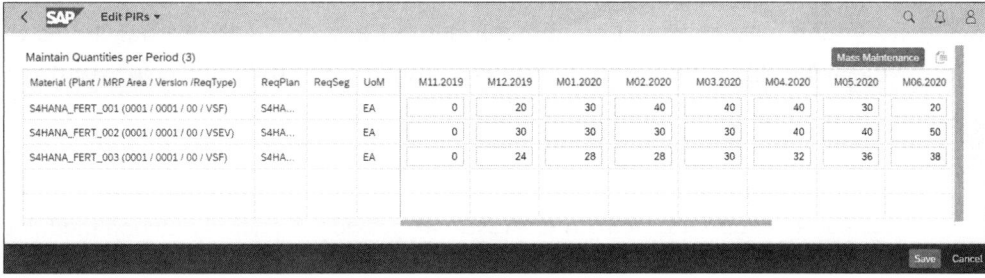

Figure 9.18 Editing PIRs in the Maintain PIRs App

PIRs can also be created based on a material forecast. We discussed forecast-based MRP types in Chapter 3, but we can use the same forecasts as inputs to generate demand plans. Transaction MD70 can be used to copy a forecast and automatically generate a demand plan based on this forecast; we can even schedule a periodic background job to automatically copy the material forecast into PIRs. This can be done with the manual creation of a background job using program RM60FORC, but SAP S/4HANA also offers the Schedule Copying Total Forecast Runs app, which can be used to manage a job through the SAP Fiori launchpad.

> **Warning**
> The forecast will be only copied when the MRP type assigned to the material has the **Consumption Indicator for Forecasting** setting equal to **G—Total Consumption**. If we are copying the forecast to PIRs, it does not make sense to include forecast requirements in the MRP calculation, so we also need to adjust the **MRP Indicator for Forecasting** accordingly in the MRP type Customizing.

Although SAP offers these standard features to create PIRs in the system, in many cases they are not used. Very often companies will use an external system to generate a forecast, and the forecast results will be uploaded directly into demand management.

In the past, most companies used the S&OP feature that is available within SAP ERP. It was able to read the past consumption and generate a demand plan using different forecast algorithms. This forecast could be then automatically transferred to demand management, either manually or automatically, through a background job. This is still available in SAP S/4HANA, but it is considered an interim solution and is part of the compatibility scope.

SAP now offers SAP IBP, a cloud solution with the same forecast capabilities and much more. The results of a forecast generated in SAP IBP can be transferred to demand management to serve as an input to MRP. In both traditional S&OP with SAP S/4HANA and SAP IBP, we can run rough-cut capacity planning to check if we will have enough resources to fulfill the planned demand.

Besides the standard solutions provided by SAP, we can also integrate a forecast generated by an external system. In this case, SAP provides standard function modules called BAPIs that can be called by an external system to generate a forecast in SAP S/4HANA. To create PIRs, we can use the standard BAPI_REQUIREMENTS_CREATE and BAPI_REQUIREMENTS_CHANGE BAPIs to create and change PIRs, respectively.

There are also situations in which the demand plan will not come from a forecast generated internally, but will be provided directly by a customer. This is very common, for example, in the automotive industry, in which the automaker will provide a forecast to its suppliers that can be used as an input for demand management. In this case, the same BAPIs can be used to generate the forecast within SAP S/4HANA.

After the creation of the demand plan, we can use Transaction MD73 to show the results, including the assignment to requirements that are consuming the PIRs and the withdrawal quantity. Figure 9.19 shows the independent requirements with the assigned customer requirements in Transaction MD73.

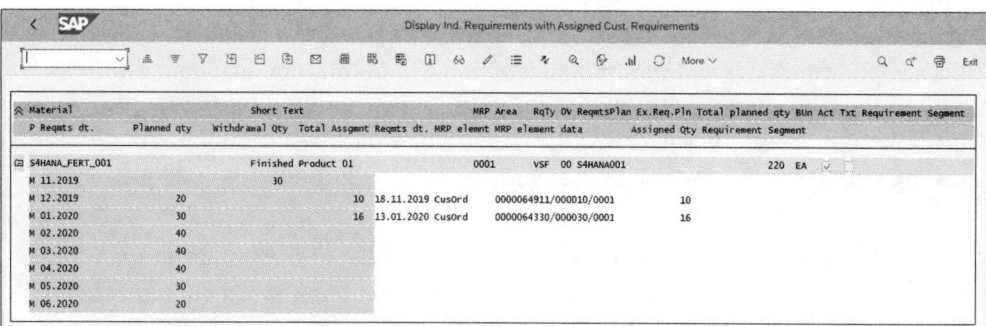

Figure 9.19 Total Requirements in Transaction MD73

9.3.1 Splitting Independent Requirements

A forecast often will be created in monthly buckets, so our demand plan also usually will be created first in monthly buckets, with the PIRs being created on the first day of the month. However, from a production execution perspective, it may not be useful to have a production order with the total quantity for all the finished products at the beginning of the month.

To avoid this situation, we can split the PIRs into weekly or daily buckets manually using Transaction MD67 or automatically by running program RM60ROLL, which is the program behind the transaction.

To run the staggered period split, we need to first create a period split in the customizing Transaction OMPH. Here, we will define the following settings:

- The number of weeks that should be split into daily buckets
- The number of weeks that should be split into weekly buckets
- Distribution keys for splitting the weeks and the months

The distribution key will define how the split quantities will be distributed over time, and SAP delivers the standard distribution key GLEI for an equal distribution.

When running the staggered period split in Transaction MD67, we will reference the desired period split and select the PIRs to be split based on the plant, MRP area, material, MRP controller, requirement type, or version. We can also add a selection period, considering the start and end date of the PIRs to be selected. We can also run the split in simulation mode so that we can check the results before saving the changes in the database.

9.3.2 PIR Reorganization

Besides the creation of the demand plan, it is a best practice to periodically run a PIR reorganization to clean out old PIRs that were not reduced by actual sales orders.

The PIR reorganization is executed in three different steps, by the respective transactions and programs:

1. Transaction MD74 (program RM60RR20): The quantity of all the selected PIRs will be adjusted to match the quantity of requirements consuming the PIR. If there is no requirement consuming a PIR, the quantity will be set to zero.
2. Transaction MD75 (program RM60RR30): PIRs that have a zero quantity will be physically deleted.

3. Transaction MD76 (program RM60RR40): The PIR history will be deleted, and the PIR header will be deleted if there are no longer PIRs.

> **Tip**
> It is a good practice to schedule a periodic background job with these programs in order to delete old independent requirements.

SAP S/4HANA also offers the Schedule PIR Reorganizing Runs app, which can be used to schedule and manage periodic PIR reorganization. This SAP Fiori application provides job templates to adjust requirements, delete old PIR records, and delete history and PIRs, which will be similar to the actions carried out by the transactions and programs previously mentioned.

9.4 Configuring Demand Management

As mentioned earlier, SAP delivers several standard planning strategies for the respective requirement types and requirement classes.

Although there are customizing transactions behind the requirements and planning strategies, major changes to this Customizing are not recommended, and it is not likely that we will create a new planning strategy in Customizing by mixing two or more strategies because the standard logic is hard-coded in the programs. Nevertheless, it is important to know how this Customizing works so that we can troubleshoot or make minor changes to the strategy, especially in the sales order requirements class and type, if necessary, and create a custom strategy.

The first step in demand management Customizing is the requirement class for independent requirements Customizing in Transaction OMPO. As shown in Figure 9.20, we have requirement classes for the most important strategies, such as planning with final assembly (40), planning without final assembly (50 and 52), and gross requirements planning (11). In this Customizing activity, there are settings that will define the planning segment that will be used by a PIR or the PIR consumption logic.

The second step in demand management Customizing is the assignment of a requirement class to a requirement type in the customizing Transaction OMP1. This is important because in the planning strategy Customizing, we will refer to the requirement type, not to the requirement class.

ReqC	Description	PI	Consu...	C	CCon	Red	Cat
100	Make-to-stock prod.	1					1
101	Plnng with assembly	1	1				1
102	Gross reqmts plnning	2					1
103	Plnng w/o assembly	3	2				1
104	Planning plng mat.	3	3				1
105	Assembly planning	1	1				1
106	Plng phantom assemb.	3	2				1
107	Plng assy w/o fn.ass	3	2				1

Figure 9.20 PIR Requirement Class Customizing

In customizing Transaction OVZG, we have settings related to the requirement class for customer requirements. Usually, if changes are required in a planning strategy, they are most likely related to this requirement class rather than to the PIR's requirement class. Some settings that we can change here are the **No MRP** field (to make a sales requirement not relevant to MRP) or the **Automatic Planning** field (to trigger MRP automatically after the sales order creation for an MTO sales order). We can also define here an order type for an ATO strategy or the usage of order change management (OCM). Figure 9.21 shows the settings for requirement class 050, which is related to requirement type KSV and used by planning strategy 40.

Requirement classes created in this Customizing activity will be assigned to the requirement types in customizing Transaction OVZH. Also in Transaction OVZI, we can assign a requirement type to a sales order item category and we can define if the requirement type will be derived first from the material master planning strategy or from the item category.

If we need to create a new strategy, the requirement type for independent requirements and the requirement type for customer requirements will be combined together in customizing Transaction OPPS, generating a new planning strategy. This Customizing was shown earlier in Figure 9.4.

If the creation of a new planning strategy is not common, the creation of a strategy group is often required. With the creation of a strategy group, we can define a main strategy to be used by a material, plus additional alternative strategies. During the sales order creation, users will be able to select the alternative strategies requirement types so that procurement is triggered using the alternative strategy logic. Figure 9.22 shows an example of a custom strategy group where the main strategy is **40—Planning with Final Assembly** and the alternatives are **20—Make-to-Order Production** and **81—Assembly Processing with Planned Orders**.

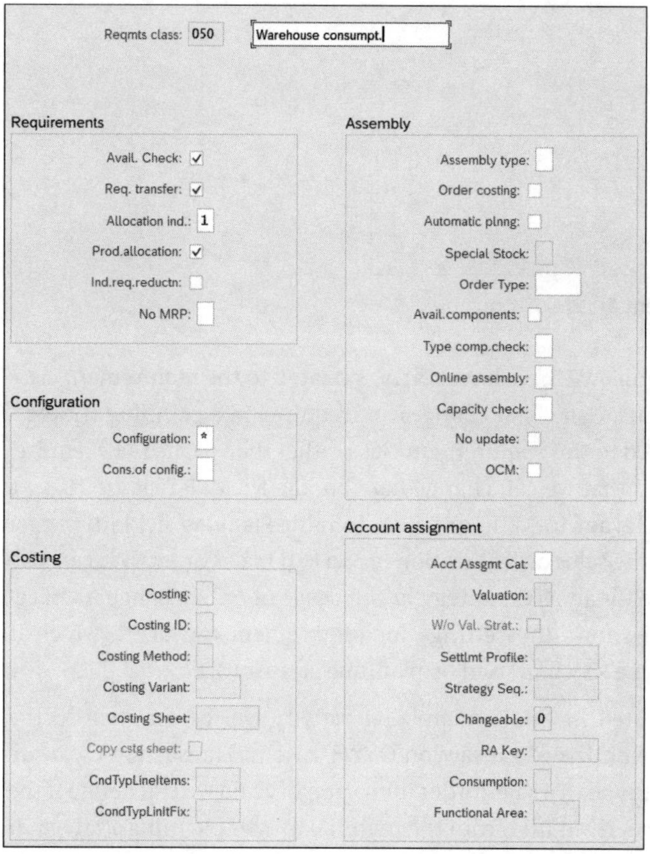

9 Demand Management

Figure 9.21 Requirement Class Customizing

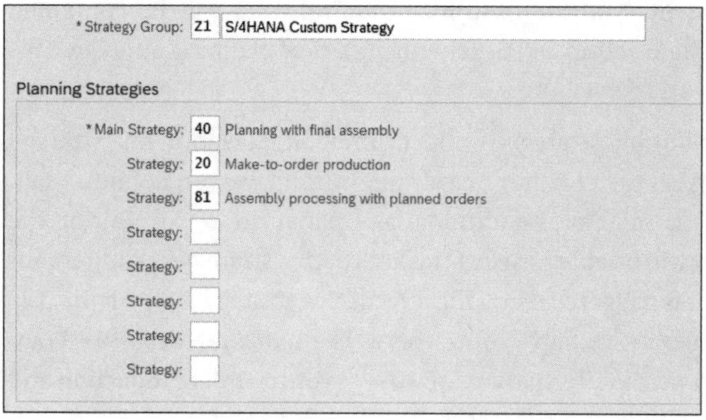

Figure 9.22 Strategy Group Customizing

Another Customizing setting that might affect the PIR reduction can be found at the material movement level, in customizing Transaction OMJJ. In this Customizing activity, we will find the **Independent Requirements Reduction** flag, which will define if a given movement will reduce PIRs or not. This setting is not required, however, for goods movements that will be posted through a sales order delivery, such as goods movement 601. In this case, the logic to determine if the PIR should be reduced is derived internally, and it is not required to check this setting in the movement type.

Besides those settings related to the planning strategy, requirement class, and requirement type, there is also the assignment of the planning strategy. We have Customizing activities to define default consumption values and the period of adjustment to PIRs. These settings were shown in Chapter 3.

9.5 Summary

In this chapter, we stepped away from MRP a bit in order to discuss the basics of demand management. We have described how the PIRs are created through different transactions and SAP Fiori applications and how they can come from other sources, such as a material forecast, S&OP, SAP IBP, or even an external system.

We also took a deep dive into the main planning strategies available in SAP S/4HANA and discussed the effects of each strategy on the MRP results. We have also discussed the difference between PIR consumption and PIR reduction, which is a very important concept in demand management, and the basics of housekeeping with PIR reorganization.

Finally, we went through the demand management Customizing, discussing when and how to make changes in the requirement classes and requirement types in order to create a new strategy and strategy group.

In the next chapter, we will discuss demand-driven MRP, a new concept and one of the major innovations implemented in SAP S/4HANA.

Chapter 10
Demand-Driven MRP

Demand-driven MRP is one of the major innovations introduced in SAP S/4HANA. It allows the system to automatically classify products and to calculate buffer levels based on this product classification and past consumption. We will discuss demand-driven MRP and how to use it in SAP S/4HANA in this chapter.

Over the years since the MRP planning method was designed in the 1950s, there has been a gradual evolution, but the original concept remains the same. We use customer requirements or a forecast as the input for the MRP calculation of finished products, and the BOM explosion generates dependent requirements for input into the MRP calculation on the lower-level components. This logic was implemented in the first releases of SAP ERP and has seen some incremental improvements since then, but core logic of the original concept did not change.

However, supply chain experts, Chad Smith and Carol Ptak recently proposed a new concept called *demand-driven MRP* (DDMRP), which tries to improve and correct some imperfections in the MRP logic that may lead to problems in the current world. Together, they have created the Demand Driven Institute, which defines DDMRP strategies and best practices.

In this chapter, we will discuss what DDMRP is and why it was created in Section 10.1, and how it can be implemented in SAP S/4HANA in Section 10.2. We will then go through the DDMRP execution in Section 10.3. We close the chapter in Section 10.4 by talking about the APIs provided for possible integration with SAP IBP.

10.1 What Is DDMRP?

Traditional MRP has been around for decades and is a great tool for planning, but it is not a perfect planning system. According to DDMRP's creators, the traditional deterministic MRP leads to the following problems:

- MRP is generally based on a forecast, and a forecast always has an inherent level of inaccuracy. The more detailed a forecast, the less accurate it is.
- MRP logic often leads to something called the *bullwhip effect*, in which distortions occur when propagating the demand to the lower-level products and noise may occur in opposite direction.
- A small change in the demand for a higher-level product leads to severe exceptions for the lower-level products in the supply chain.
- Inventory may quickly and cyclically move from a position where there is a shortage to a position where there is excess stock. We may have a lot of stock for a product that we do not need and a shortage for the product that we actually do need.

Aiming to avoid those problems, they have proposed DDMRP, which tries to create a flow by establishing material buffers strategically positioned within the supply chain. These material buffers should absorb any demand variability, decoupling the component from the higher-level product.

> **Note**
>
> The Demand Driven Institute uses the term *product* to refer to what is known as a *material* in the SAP terminology. The DDMRP applications in SAP S/4HANA will also use the term *product*, but they are actually referring to the material master.

Figure 10.1 illustrates a product and its complete structure, including semifinished products and raw materials. Decoupling points were defined, and the buffers were positioned at those points to create independence between the higher-level and lower-level products.

By inserting these buffers in the decoupling points, we will be also decoupling the lead time. This means that the time that we will take to manufacture a product will no longer be the total replenishment time, but only the lead time to reach the next buffer. We will call this a *decoupled lead time*. It becomes possible because, in theory, we will have enough stock to cover the demand in the buffer, so we will not need to wait for procurement of all components.

When we talk about a buffer, this is nothing more than a stock buffer, which will be used to absorb the demand. This stock buffer will be automatically calculated by the system and will consist of three parts: the top of the green zone will represent the maximum stock level, the top of the yellow zone will represent the reorder point, and the top of the red zone will represent the safety stock.

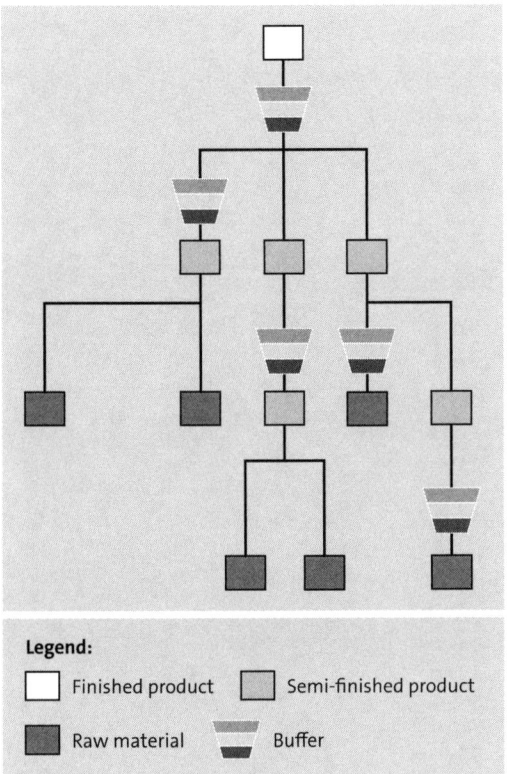

Figure 10.1 DDMRP Decoupling Point Buffers

10.1.1 Buffer Calculation

Before going deeper into the calculation of these zones, we need to understand that, according to the DDMRP principles, our products will first be classified according to the usage value (ABC classification), lead time (EFG classification), BOM usage (PQR classification), and variability (XYZ classification).

Depending on the results of the variability and the lead time classification, SAP S/4HANA will determine a variability factor and a lead time factor. Both of these factors are predetermined in a buffer profile and are used to calculate the buffer. Figure 10.2 shows the standard buffer profile delivered by SAP, which can be found in the Buffer Profile Maintenance app. If necessary, a new buffer profile can be created with adjusted factors, and a different buffer profile can be assigned to each plant.

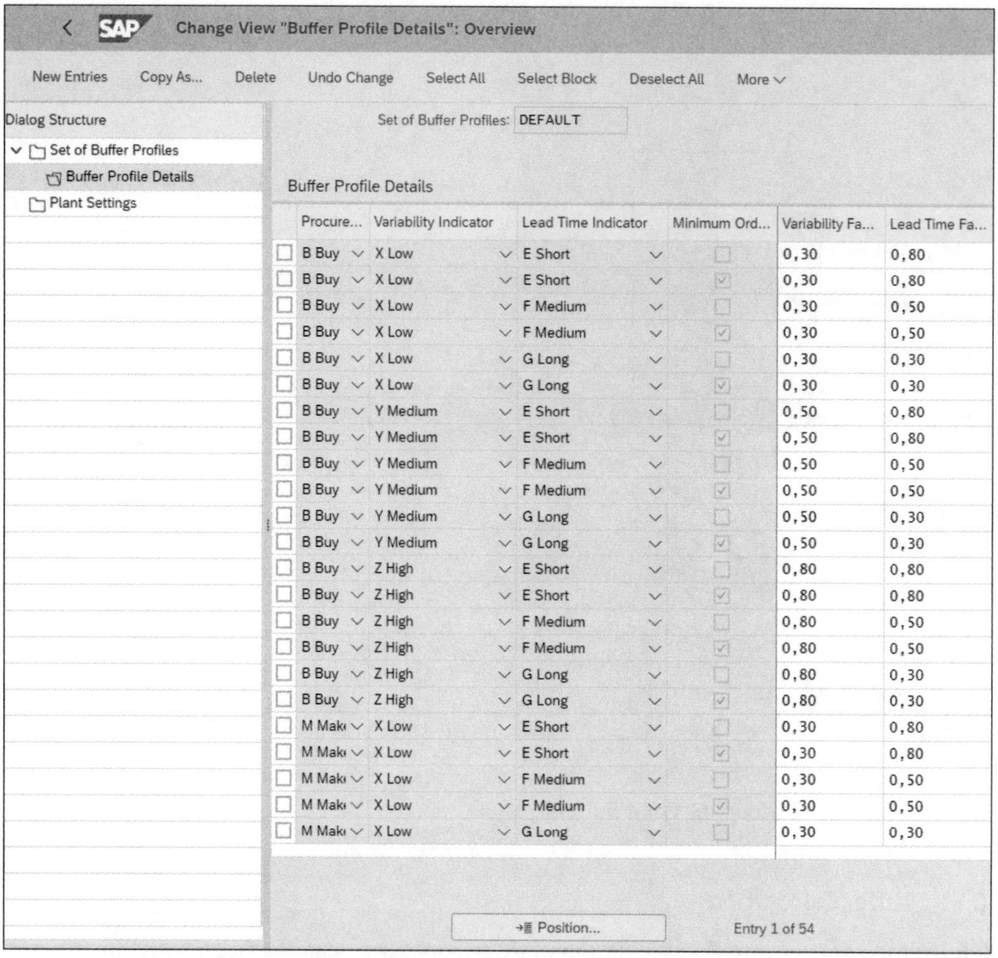

Procure...	Variability Indicator	Lead Time Indicator	Minimum Ord...	Variability Fa...	Lead Time Fa...
B Buy	X Low	E Short	☐	0,30	0,80
B Buy	X Low	E Short	☑	0,30	0,80
B Buy	X Low	F Medium	☐	0,30	0,50
B Buy	X Low	F Medium	☑	0,30	0,50
B Buy	X Low	G Long	☐	0,30	0,30
B Buy	X Low	G Long	☑	0,30	0,30
B Buy	Y Medium	E Short	☐	0,50	0,80
B Buy	Y Medium	E Short	☑	0,50	0,80
B Buy	Y Medium	F Medium	☐	0,50	0,50
B Buy	Y Medium	F Medium	☑	0,50	0,50
B Buy	Y Medium	G Long	☐	0,50	0,30
B Buy	Y Medium	G Long	☑	0,50	0,30
B Buy	Z High	E Short	☐	0,80	0,80
B Buy	Z High	E Short	☑	0,80	0,80
B Buy	Z High	F Medium	☐	0,80	0,50
B Buy	Z High	F Medium	☑	0,80	0,50
B Buy	Z High	G Long	☐	0,80	0,30
B Buy	Z High	G Long	☑	0,80	0,30
M Mak	X Low	E Short	☐	0,30	0,80
M Mak	X Low	E Short	☑	0,30	0,80
M Mak	X Low	F Medium	☐	0,30	0,50
M Mak	X Low	F Medium	☑	0,30	0,50
M Mak	X Low	G Long	☐	0,30	0,30

Figure 10.2 Default Buffer Profile Delivered by SAP

> **Example**
>
> Considering the default buffer profile for a material purchased externally with a medium variability indicator and a short lead time, as shown in Figure 10.2, the variability factor will be 0.50 and the lead time factor will be 0.80.

With our product classified and the variability and lead time factors determined, we can move on to the buffer calculation. We have seen that there are three different zones in the buffer, and the first zone to be calculated will be the *yellow zone*. This calculation will be the basic formula generally recommended for the reorder point calculation, or the average daily usage multiplied by the lead time. Note that this calculation uses the decoupled lead time, not the total replenishment lead time.

After the calculation of the yellow zone, we can find the value for the *red zone*, which is dependent on the value previously calculated. The red zone is divided into two different parts: the red base and the red safety. The *red base* will be the value previously calculated for the yellow zone multiplied by the lead time factor, while the *red safety* will be the red base multiplied by the lead time factor. Both values should be added together to get the red zone, which is basically the safety stock.

The calculation of the *green zone* will be based on the maximum value of the following:

- Yellow zone multiplied by the lead time factor
- Minimum order quantity
- Average daily usage multiplied by the cycle time

Figure 10.3 illustrates the calculated buffers and the formulas that are used to calculate each zone. This logic was implemented in SAP S/4HANA 1709, and in Section 10.2.3 we will walk through an example of this calculation in the system.

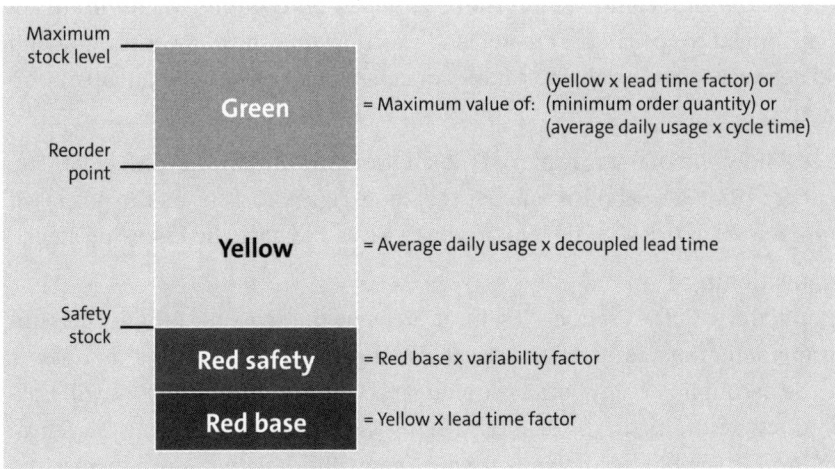

Figure 10.3 Buffers and Formulas to Calculate Each Zone

10.1.2 The DDMRP Process

The Demand Driven Institute defines five sequential steps for DDMRP implementation and execution:

1. Strategic inventory positioning
2. Buffer level profiles and levels
3. Dynamic adjustments
4. Demand-driven planning
5. Visible and collaborative execution

The first component is basically the buffer positioning, or defining where a decoupling point buffer should be positioned, as shown in Figure 10.1. The second and the third components are related to the buffer calculation. While the second component is the buffer calculation itself, the third is a buffer adjustment for foreseen events, such as a marketing event, a product discontinuation, or a market change. These three components are more related to the DDMRP implementation itself, even though the buffer should be periodically recalculated in order to match changes in the average daily usage.

The fourth component is the MRP planning run, which will check if stocks and receipt elements are enough to cover the buffer and trigger replenishment proposals if necessary. The fifth and last component is the collaborative execution, which will ensure that replenishment proposals are created and executed on time to meet the demand and avoid delays. Both components can be considered part of the DDMRP operation and execution.

All these DDMRP components are part of the solution implemented in SAP S/4HANA, and we can find SAP Fiori applications for each one. Figure 10.4 shows the proposed DDMRP process from in SAP S/4HANA, in which we would have the following steps:

1. **Buffer positioning**
   This step starts with the product classification using the Schedule Product Classification app. After the classification, we can use the Buffer Positioning app to select where the decoupling point buffers should be positioned, and finally we will classify products according to the lead time using the Schedule Lead Time Classification of Products app. Alternatively, we can manually classify the products using the Mass Maintenance of Products (DD) app.

2. **Buffer sizing**
   This is the step in which the actual buffer calculation will be executed with the

Schedule Buffer Proposal Calculation app. The calculated buffers can be reviewed using the Manage Buffer Levels app.

3. **Replenishment planning**

    The Replenishment Planning by Planning Priority app will be used to evaluate which products are below the reorder point.

4. **Replenishment execution**

    With the Replenishment Execution by On-Hand Status app, we can check for which products the on-hand stock cannot cover the buffer and expedite the supply.

5. **Analytics**

    This is the last step of the process. With the Planned Overview app, we can find DDMRP-related KPIs in order to take actions and avoid problems.

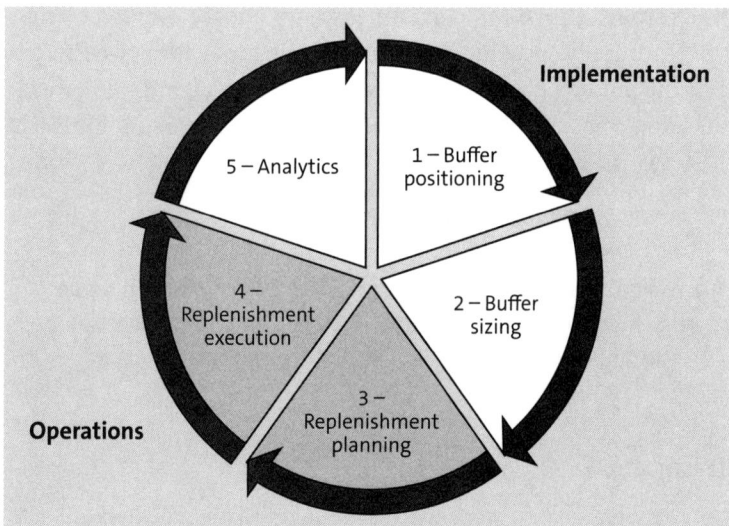

Figure 10.4 DDMRP Process Flow in SAP S/4HANA

This process will not be finished after the last steps: we always need to be reevaluating the situation and recalculating the buffers due to constant market changes. A buffer that was positioned six months ago may no longer be needed due to changes in the lead time, for example. In addition, because the buffer calculation is based on the average daily usage, it is wise to periodically recalculate the buffer because the product average daily usage is always variable.

Now that we have discussed the logic behind DDMRP and the basic process flow in SAP S/4HANA, we can go deeper into the DDMRP solution implemented in SAP S/4HANA.

10.2 Setting Up DDMRP

In this section, we will go through the SAP Fiori applications mentioned in the previous section and we will walk through how to implement DDMRP in SAP S/4HANA with a practical example.

As we noted in the previous section, some SAP Fiori applications for DDMRP implementation need to be executed when we want to start using DDMRP for a product, whereas operational SAP Fiori applications for DDMRP are used on a daily basis. In this section, we will go through the DDMRP implementation, and we will start by classifying our products. Technically speaking, buffer positioning may take place before the classification, but the product classification is an important factor to be considered when we are deciding where a buffer should be positioned, so we should always start with the product classification.

> **Note**
> Because the product classification will help identify where a buffer should be positioned, we recommend that you classify all the products that may potentially be planned with the DDMRP logic.

10.2.1 Product Classification

Product classification happens in two steps, both scheduled to be executed in background jobs.

The first step is to run the Schedule Product Classification (DD) app, in which we will classify our products according to the usage value (classification ABC), BOM usage (classification PQR), and variability (classification XYZ). This classification is scheduled to be executed in background. When we enter this application, we will immediately find a list of the background jobs scheduled or already finished, as shown in Figure 10.5. Here, we have the option to check the logs of the previously finished background jobs by double-clicking the icon in the **Log** column or to schedule a new job by clicking the button with the plus icon.

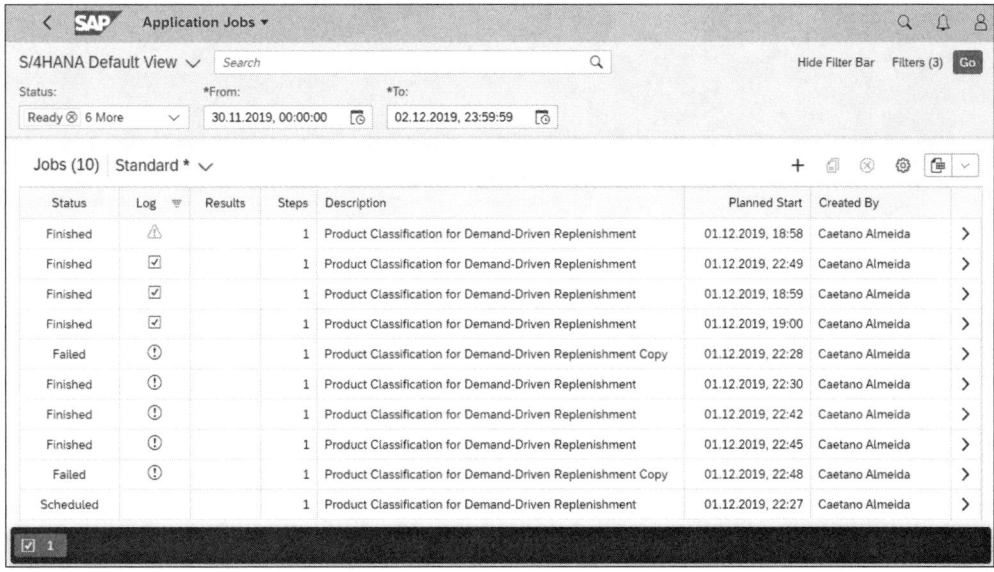

Figure 10.5 Product Classification Jobs

When scheduling a new job, we need to first define the scheduling options that will set the job start date and the recurrence pattern. Following the scheduling, we need to define the **Selection Criteria** settings that will be used to select which products will be classified in the job.

In the example shown in Figure 10.6, we are using the **MRP Controller** value as a selection criterion, so we will classify all the products assigned to this specific MRP controller. Another important parameter included in the selection criteria is the **Number of Days (Past)** value. This will represent the number of days in the past for which the system will look for goods movements in order to calculate the average daily usage. In our example, the **Number of Days (Past)** value is 30, so the system will look for goods issues in the past 30 days to determine the average daily usage.

Below the **Selection Criteria** section, we will define the thresholds for the value, BOM usage, and variability classifications. For each one, we need to enter what is considered a high, medium, or low value within our company.

10 Demand-Driven MRP

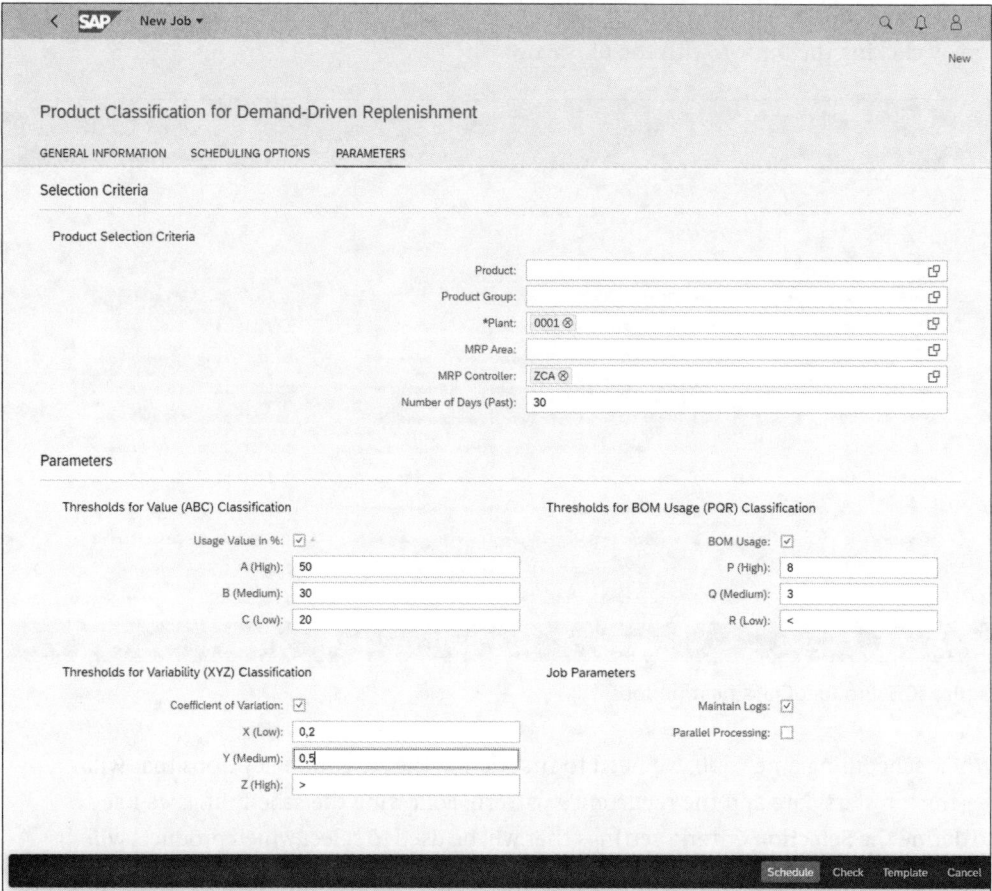

Figure 10.6 Product Classification

The **Value (ABC) Classification** setting will be used to define if a product belongs to the group of products with the largest goods issue value (classification A), to the intermediate group with a medium goods issue value (classification B), or to the group of products with the lowest goods issue value (classification C). SAP S/4HANA will calculate the total goods issue value of these products within the interval defined in the selection criteria, sort materials according to this value, and then define to which group each product belongs, according to the percentages defined in these thresholds. This means that our input for these thresholds will be a percentage, and the sum of the three values should be 100%.

> **Note**
>
> SAP S/4HANA will calculate the total goods issue value within the period, which means that both the material price and the number of issues will be considered. This means that a material with a high price but without too many goods issues may have the same classification as a material with a low price and a high number of goods issues.

The **BOM Usage (PQR) Classification** setting is used to determine if a material is used in a high number of BOMs (classification P), if it is used in a medium number of BOMs (classification Q), or if it is used in a low number of BOMs (classification R). The value defined for each threshold is basically the total number of material BOMs in which a product is used, and it will be classified accordingly.

The **Variability (XYZ) Classification** setting will classify products according to the demand variability. Products with the classification X will have a low variability, products with classification Y will have medium variability, and products with classification Z will have high variability. The total sum of sales orders overdue, sales orders due on the current date, and order spikes is considered the actual demand. With the mean and standard deviation of the actual demand, a coefficient of variation is calculated. This coefficient is used as the threshold for variability: the higher the coefficient, the higher the variability.

After the first step of product classification, we will have the information to position the decoupling buffers for our products. To position those buffers, we may consider the results of the previous classification to determine if a product is a good candidate for a buffer. The product classification, however, is not the only factor to be considered: there are external factors, and the planner can also use his own experience to determine when a buffer is necessary. There are some situations in which a buffer may be a good option:

- A semifinished product is classified as P because it is used in too many BOMs. Because it is a key component and it is used to produce many products, it might be a good idea to position a buffer for this product, avoiding stock-outs that might have far-reaching effects.

- The source of supply of a given component purchased externally is not reliable, and there are too many delayed deliveries. In this case, adding a buffer would mean that the demand for this product would be absorbed by the safety stock if there is a delay.

- An important product has a long lead time to be produced, so any late demand arriving would mean a long delay.
- In case of an MTO scenario, a customer cannot wait for the whole total replenishment lead time to have the product delivered. In this case, adding a buffer to strategically selected components will reduce the lead time, as the demand for this customer will be absorbed by the buffer.

When we say that we will *position a buffer* for a product, it means that we will select a demand-driven MRP type, such as the standard MRP type D1. We also recommend using the standard lot-sizing procedure H1 so that MRP can correctly replenish up to the maximum stock level. Technically, these settings can be made directly in the material master, but SAP also offers the Buffer Positioning app, which was specially developed for this purpose. When entering this application, we can use the filters to select which products we will process, and those products will be listed with their respective classifications and further details, such as the lead time and the decoupled lead time. This information can be used to help determine whether a buffer should be positioned or not.

We can buffer or unbuffer a product directly from the initial screen of the Buffer Positioning app by clicking the **Buffer** or **Unbuffer** button, as shown in Figure 10.7.

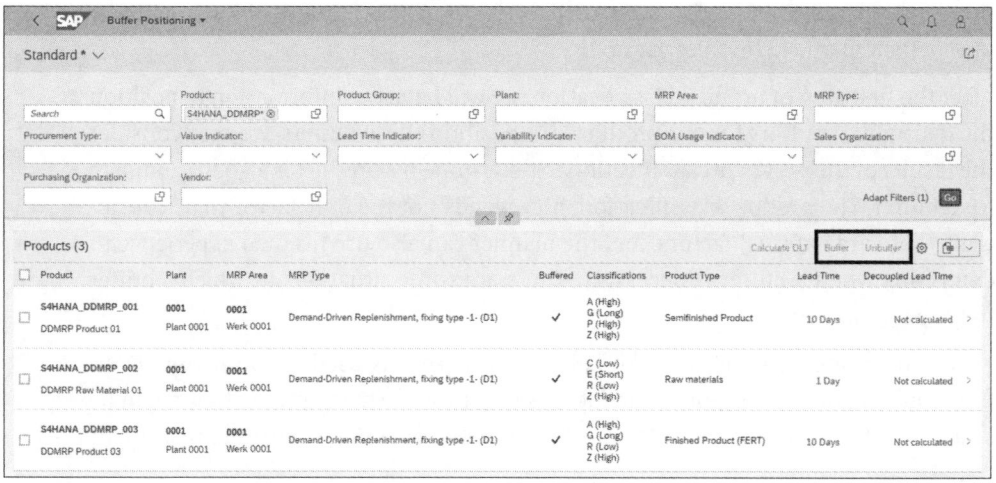

Figure 10.7 The Buffer Positioning App

If we select one of these options, a pop-up will be displayed, in which we should select the new MRP type, the new lot-sizing procedure, and additional DDMRP-related material master settings. Any changes made here will be saved directly in the material master. It is also possible from the initial screen to trigger the decoupled lead time calculation for one or more products.

Before deciding whether a buffer should be positioned for a specific product or not, we can select a specific product and jump into the **Buffer Analysis** screen, where we will have more information to support the decision (see Figure 10.8). We will find all the information related to the **Upstream** and **Downstream** values here. In this situation, *upstream* refers to product components, for which we can see the longest path or the whole BOM. *Downstream* refers to product parents, for which we will find all the BOMs in which a product is used.

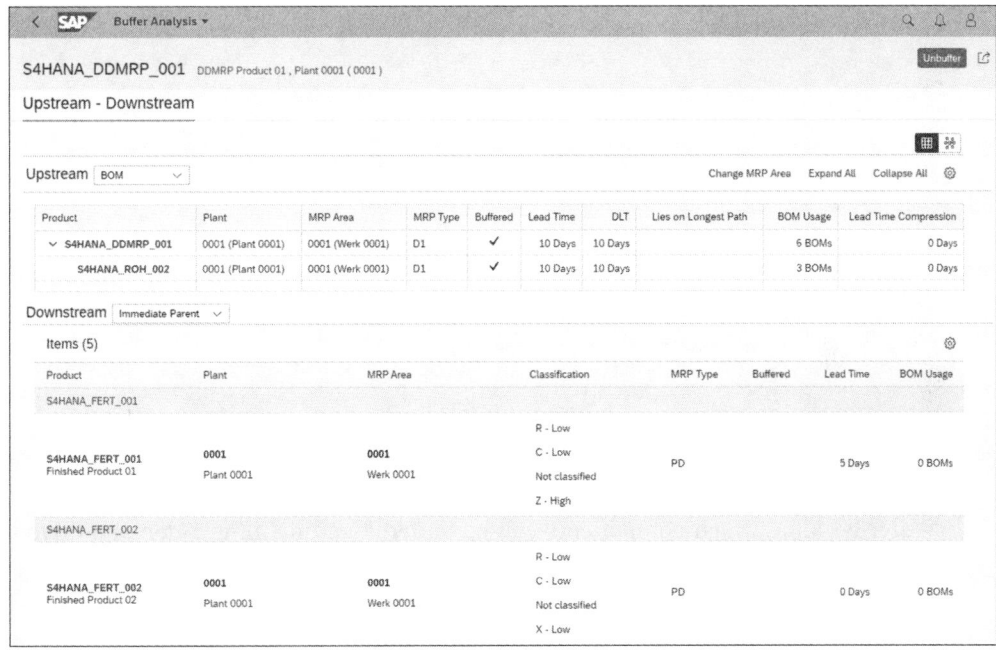

Figure 10.8 Buffer Analysis in the Buffer Positioning App

If we are analyzing a product with too many levels of components, we can switch to the **Network Graph** view, where we will find a graphical representation of the upstream and downstream and multiple display options. We can show, for example, just the longest path, the product flow, or the entire BOM and BOM usage. We also have different options to highlight specific products in the network, such as buffered products, products under an area of responsibility, products selected as favorites, or products in one of the product classifications.

The example in Figure 10.9 shows the whole BOM of a product. The BOM components are highlighted in red, yellow, or green, depending on the BOM usage. When selecting a product, we will have additional options, such as collapsing or expanding the components, adding the product as a favorite, or showing the details of the product.

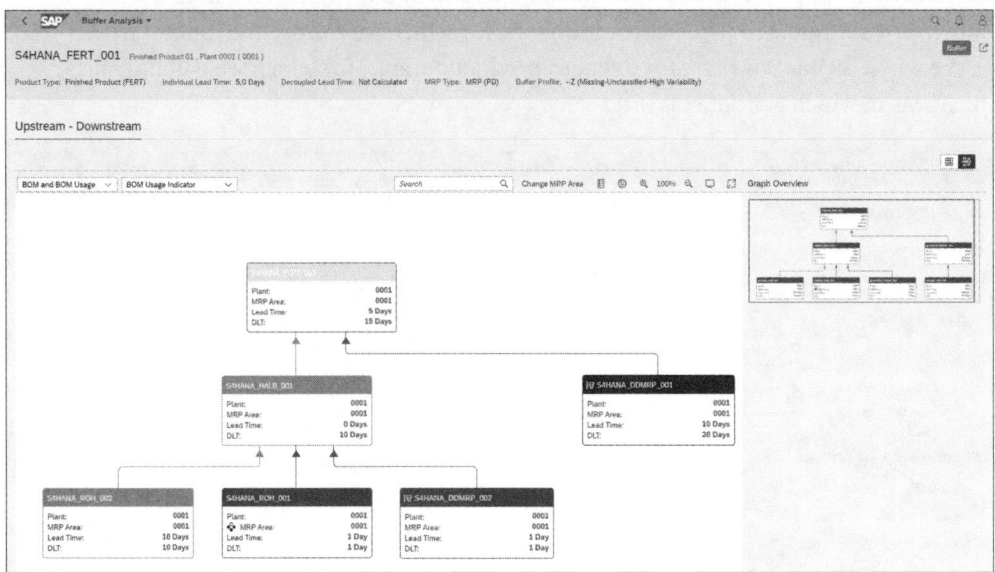

Figure 10.9 Network Graph View of the Upstream and Downstream

After deciding which components will be buffered and defining a demand-driven MRP type for those products, it is time for the third step of our DDMRP setup: the classification of products according to the lead time in the Schedule Lead Time of Products (DD) app. In this application, we will classify our products according to the lead time (EFG) classification. Just like the Schedule Product Classification application, the initial screen of this application will show an overview of the jobs already completed, in process, or scheduled. On this screen, we will be able to create a new job, copy an existing job, or check the results of the finished jobs.

For the creation of a new lead time classification job, we will define the selection criteria, such as the **Product**, **Product Group**, **Plant**, and other fields, as shown in Figure 10.10. The thresholds defined here will be only for the EFG classification, but we will be able to define different thresholds depending on the procurement type. The following options are available:

- **DLT Threshold for Make**: This will be considered for products manufactured internally—that is, products with procurement type E.
- **DLT Threshold for Buy**: This is used for products procured externally—that is, with procurement type F.
- **DLT Threshold for Transfer**: This is used for products with a stock transfer special procurement type, which are supplied by means of a stock transfer from another plant.

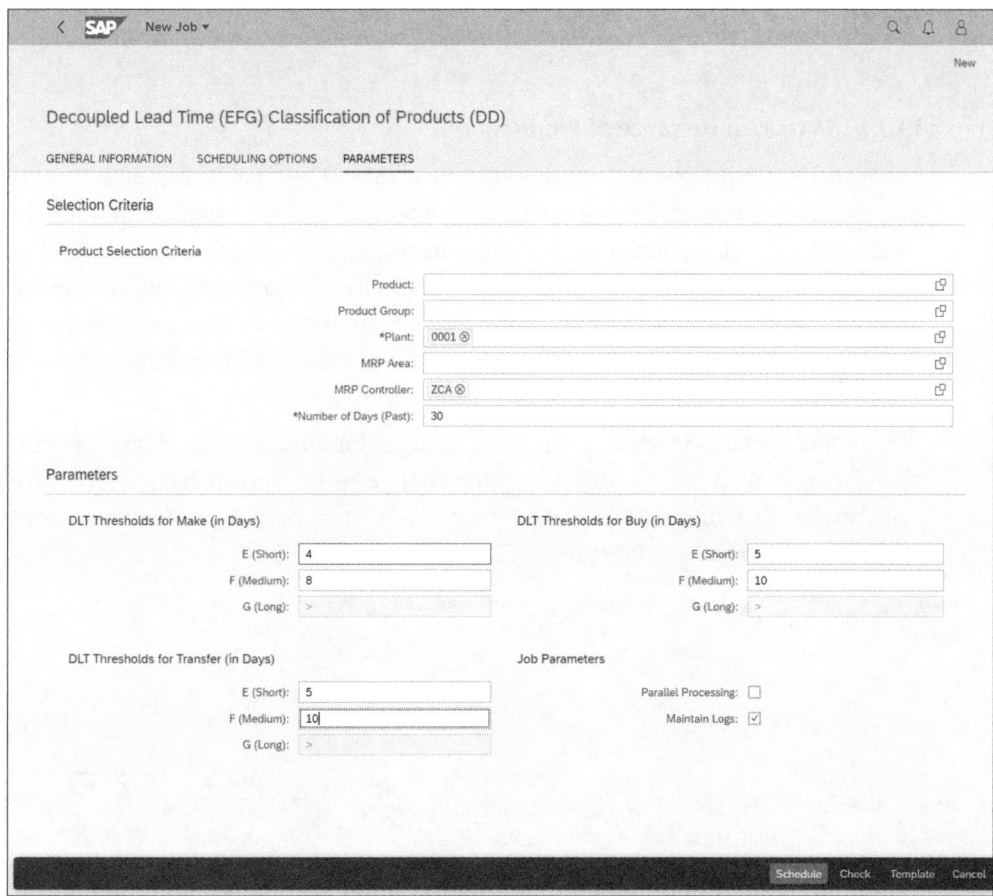

Figure 10.10 Decoupled Lead Time (EFG) Classification of Products (DD)

In these thresholds, we will define how many days are considered a short, medium, or long lead time for products manufactured, purchased, or transferred. This differentiation of thresholds depending on the procurement type happens because the lead time to manufacture a product may be very different from the lead time to buy the components.

> **Example**
> For a company based in North America that purchases most of its components from Asia, a lead time of 10 days for a purchased part may be short. However, if the in-house production is generally short, 10 days may be a long lead time for products manufactured internally.

10.2.2 Mass Maintenance of Products

There are situations, however, in which products cannot be classified because there is not enough information in the system. For example, in a new implementation, in which we lack information about the past consumption of products, we cannot classify a product according to the value or the variability. The same happens during the introduction of a new product, in which case we will not have enough information available to classify the product. In this case, we can use the Mass Maintenance of Products (DD) app to manually set the product classification.

Within this application, we can run mass changes for any of the product classifications by selecting products and clicking the **Change** button shown in Figure 10.11. We can also change additional DDMRP-related fields, such as **MRP Type**, **Maximum Stock Level**, **Reorder Point**, or **Safety Stock**.

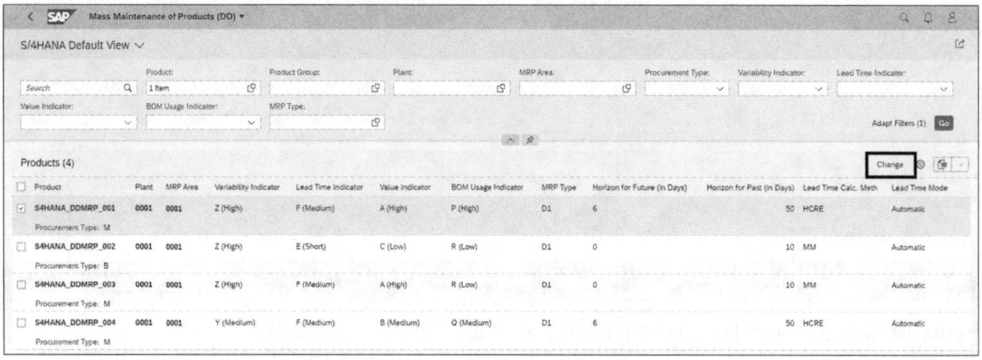

Figure 10.11 The Mass Maintenance of Prod]ucts (DD) App

10.2 Setting Up DDMRP

> **Note**
>
> For products recently created, we may not have an average daily usage because there is no past historical consumption data. In this case, the maximum stock level, the reorder point, and the safety stock can be manually defined in the Mass Maintenance of Products app.

Figure 10.12 shows the pop-up screen that will be displayed to implement the mass changes once we click the **Change** button. Here, we will select which fields should be changed and for which fields we want to keep the existing values. In the example shown in this figure, we are manually defining values for the **Variability Indicator** and the **Value Indicator** dropdowns because they cannot be calculated automatically without enough goods issues posted in the past.

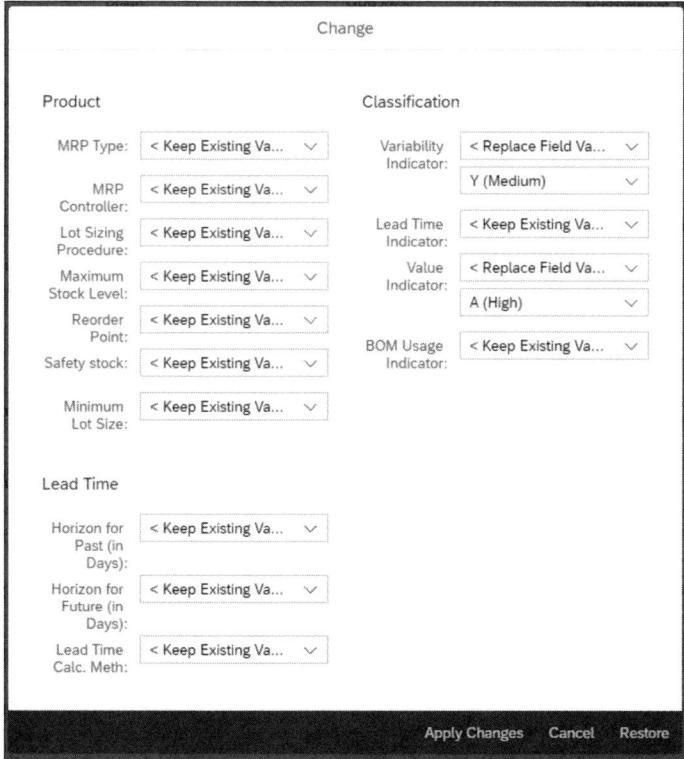

Figure 10.12 Mass Changes of DDMRP-Related Fields and Classifications

10 Demand-Driven MRP

Within this application, we can also define the **Lead Time Calculation Method**, **Horizon for Past**, and **Horizon for Future** settings. By default, SAP S/4HANA will calculate the lead time based on the values defined in the material master, but there are different methods available in which the lead time will be calculated based on confirmed production orders. These fields will define the method and the number of days used by the system to find confirmed production orders and calculate the lead time.

10.2.3 Buffer Proposal Calculation

The last step in DDMRP implementation is the actual buffer calculation, which can be scheduled as a background job using the Schedule Buffer Proposal Calculation app.

On the initial screen, we have the options to manage the already scheduled and finished jobs and to schedule a new background job execution. The selection screen provides the scheduling parameters and allows us to select which products should be included in the buffer calculation, as shown in Figure 10.13.

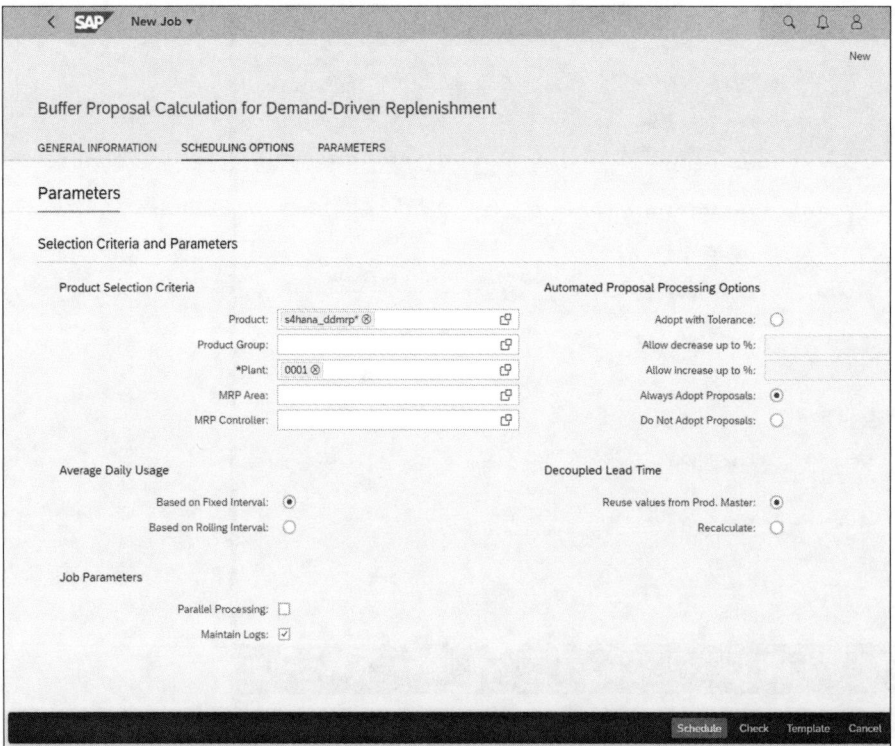

Figure 10.13 Buffer Proposal Calculation Selection Screen

We also have the option to choose if the buffer will be adopted only if the new value is within a tolerance interval, if it will be always adopted, or if it will never be adopted. If we choose the options to adopt with tolerance or not adopt, we need to review the calculated buffer later in the Manage Buffer Levels app.

We can also choose whether the average daily usage will be calculated based on a fixed interval or on a rolling interval and if the decoupled lead time will come from the material master values or if it will be recalculated.

> **Note**
>
> As of SAP S/4HANA 1909, we can use planned independent requirements (PIRs) to project an average daily usage in the future and allow the system to also calculate a projected buffer for the future.
>
> This is especially relevant, for example, if we know in advance if there will be an event that might affect the product consumption, such as a marketing campaign or a seasonal increase in the demand. The horizon in the future for which the system will look for PIRs can be defined in the Mass Maintenance of Products (DD) app.

For jobs already completed, we will see a flag on the initial screen under the **Log** column, which will show the status of the background job execution. If we double-click this flag, we will see the log details, including any warning or error messages that may prevent the buffer calculation. Figure 10.14 shows the logs of a buffer proposal calculation, in which the buffer could not be calculated for two products because there was no average daily usage. As mentioned earlier, the whole DDMRP buffer calculation is based on the average daily usage; therefore, without an average daily usage, no buffer can be calculated.

The calculated buffer levels can be reviewed in the Manage Buffer Levels app. When entering this application, we will see a list of products and the respective buffer levels calculated by the system, including a graphical representation of the historic and projected buffer levels and the average daily usage (see Figure 10.15). If we chose the option to adopt the buffer with a tolerance or not automatically adopt the buffer, we may have to decide if the new buffer level will be adopted or not for those products. We can filter only those products for which the buffer should be reviewed using the **Proposal Status** field.

10   Demand-Driven MRP

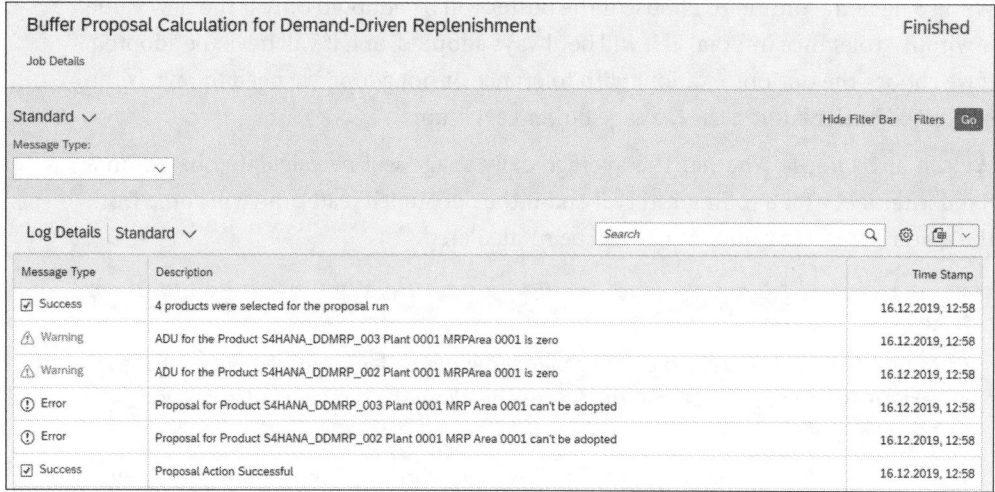

Figure 10.14 Buffer Proposal Calculation Log

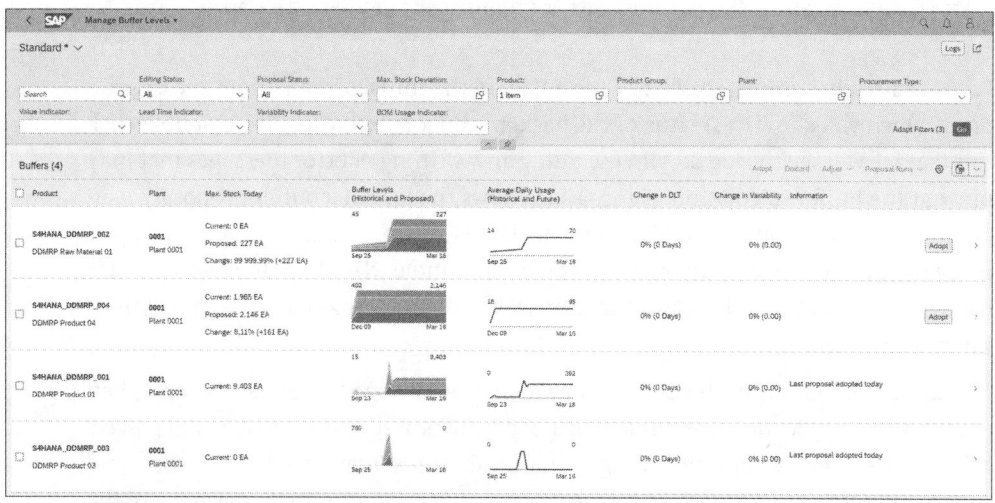

Figure 10.15 The Manage Buffer Levels App

When selecting a specific DDMRP product in this application, we will drill down into a more detailed view of the buffer, average daily usage, and decoupled lead time graphical representation, as shown in Figure 10.16. Here, there are several improvements delivered in SAP S/4HANA 1909—such as, for example, different views available for the buffer chart.

10.2 Setting Up DDMRP

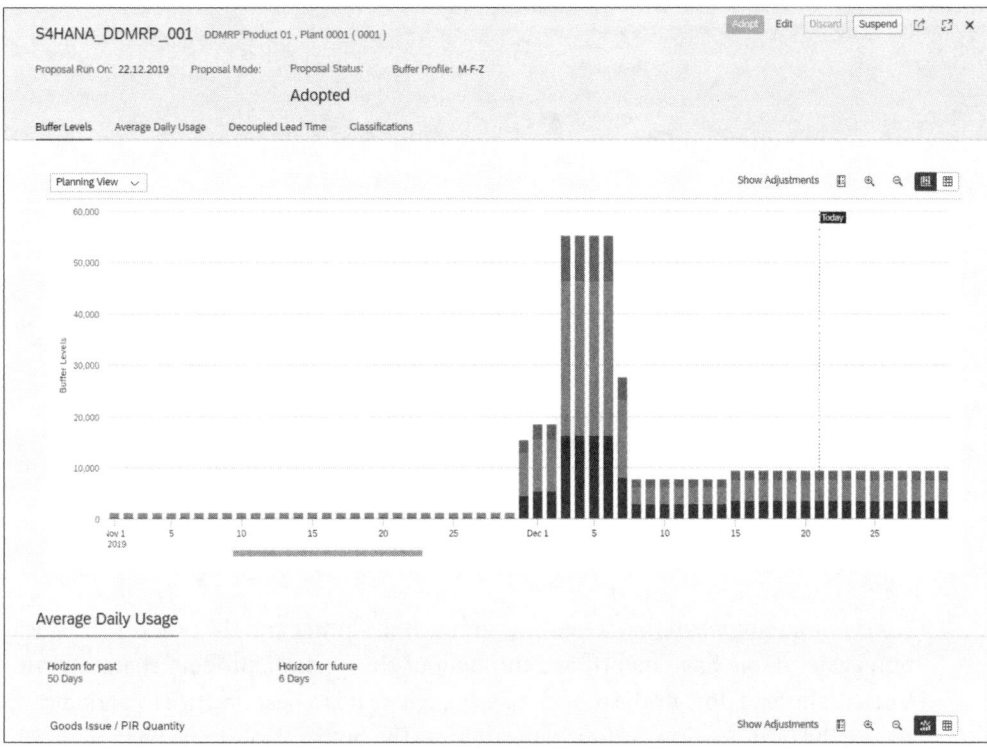

Figure 10.16 Graphical Representation of Buffers in the Manage Buffer Levels App

As of SAP S/4HANA 1909, we can also switch to edit mode and make manual adjustments in the calculated buffer level by adding an adjustment factor for each zone. The value originally calculated for each zone will be multiplied by this factor within the period defined for this buffer adjustment. After entering edit mode, we can select the **Show Adjustments** option to see all the existing zone adjustments per period. We will have the option to add a new adjustment or to delete an existing one.

Figure 10.17 shows an example in which an adjustment was created from December 23 to December 31, with a factor of 2.00 for each zone. Once we add a new zone adjustment, we can click the **Simulate Changes** button to see the changes reflected in the chart.

With the buffer calculated and adopted for the DDMRP products, the DDMRP implementation is finished and we can start the DDMRP operation that will be executed by the planner daily.

10   Demand-Driven MRP

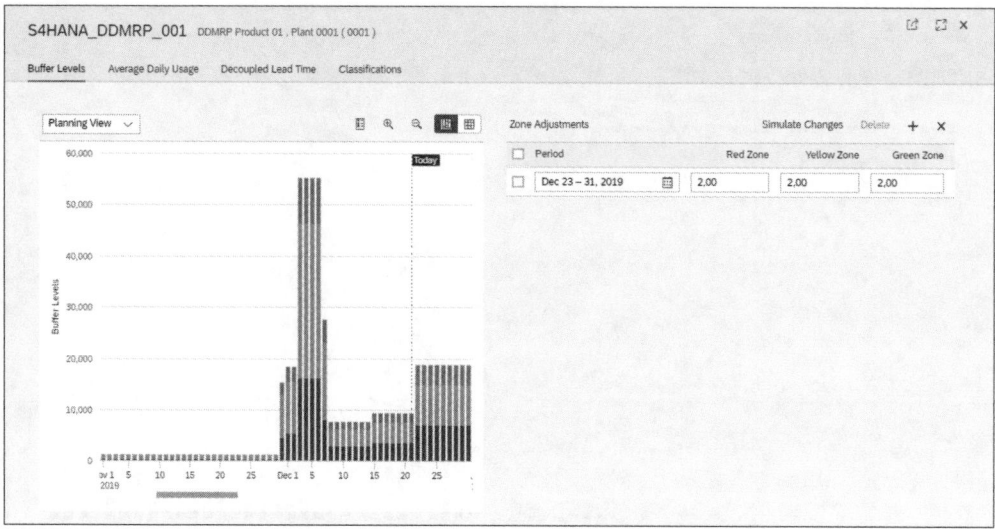

Figure 10.17 Zone Adjustment Created for the DDMRP Buffer Level

But this does not mean that we will never touch the buffer and the product classification again. As we have mentioned throughout this section, product characteristics (such as the lead time or the usage) may change, so it is a best practice to periodically review the product classifications. In addition, the buffer also should be periodically reviewed and recalculated because the average daily usage varies over time.

In the following section, we will dive into the DDMRP operation tasks and how the DDMRP replenishment planning and execution happens.

10.3   Running DDMRP

When we say that we will position a DDMRP buffer for a product, we are basically setting a demand-driven MRP type in the material master. This means that the DDMRP operation for a product will start with the actual MRP execution, so we will start this section by discussing the logic behind the demand-driven MRP types.

> **Note**
> A demand-driven MRP type can be any MRP type with MRP procedure C, like the standard MRP type D1, which will be used in the examples shown in this section.

10.3 Running DDMRP

> To achieve the correct MRP results for DDMRP, it is also important to choose a lot-sizing procedure that will replenish up to the maximum stock level after covering the requirements, so we will also use the standard lot-sizing procedure H1.

In a simple scenario, a demand-driven MRP type will act like a reorder point MRP type, wherein the yellow buffer zone will be the reorder point and the green zone will represent the maximum stock level. Figure 10.18 shows an example of the MRP results for material S4_HANA_DDMRP_004 in the Stock/Requirements List. If we expand the **Header Details** screen, we will see a **Demand-Driven Replenishment** tab, which shows the information required to interpret the MRP results. As shown in this figure, the reorder point (yellow zone) is 997, while the maximum stock (green zone) is 3,397. Because the material's on-hand stock is 0, which is below the reorder point, MRP created a new planned order of 3,397 in order to replenish up to the maximum stock level.

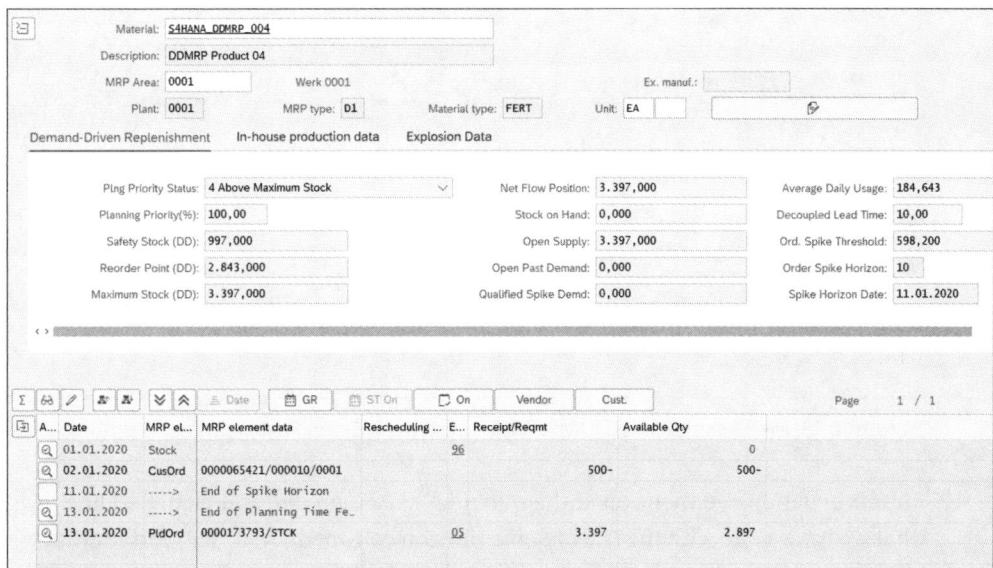

Figure 10.18 MRP Results for a DDMRP Product in a Simple Scenario

However, there are additional situations in which MRP may generate a new replenishment proposal for a DDMRP product even if the stock is not yet below the reorder point. During the MRP calculation, the system will try to calculate the net flow position, using the following equation:

On-Hand Stock + Open Supply – Open Past (Including Today's) Demand – Qualified Spike Demand

Whenever the net flow position is below the reorder point, a new replenishment proposal will be created by MRP to replenish the stock up to the maximum stock level. Figure 10.19 shows another example, in which we have an open past demand. Here, the reorder point is 905 and the on-hand stock is currently 1,000, so it is technically above the reorder point. Because the open past demand is also considered in our equation, the available quantity would be only 200, which is below the reorder point. Therefore, MRP will create a new replenishment proposal to replenish up to the maximum stock level.

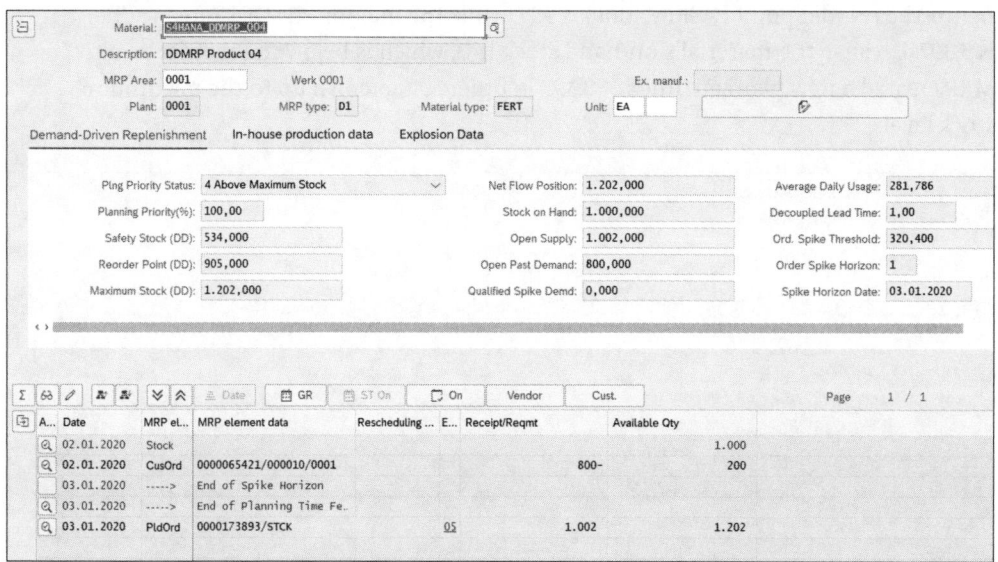

Figure 10.19 MRP Results for a DDMRP Product with an Open Past Demand

In our equation, we mentioned the *qualified spike demand*, and Figure 10.19 shows that we have a line with the **End of Spike Horizon** comment, so it is important that we define those terms for better understanding of the MRP results for a demand-driven product.

First, the *spike horizon* is a time window that starts the day after today and comprises the decoupled lead time multiplied by a factor called the *spike horizon DLT multiplier* (SHT), with the addition of an offset called the *spike horizon constant*. The idea is that DDMRP will also react to a demand within this time window in order to ensure product availability. However, MRP will not react to all the demand within the spike horizon, only to qualified demands. To be considered a qualified demand, a requirement quantity must be greater than the *spike threshold*, which is calculated by multiplying the safety stock by the spike threshold factor.

The bars in the chart shown in Figure 10.20 illustrate the different demands for a demand-driven product in the time horizon. Only those highlighted demands will be considered *qualified demands* because they are within the spike horizon and above the spike threshold.

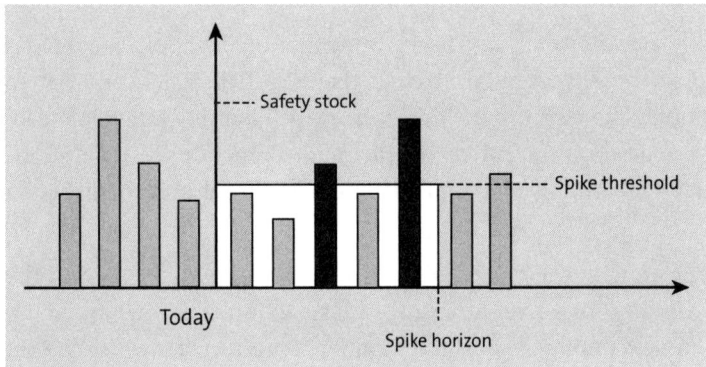

Figure 10.20 Qualified Demands within the Spike Horizon and above the Spike Threshold

Note

You can define the spike horizon DLT multiplier, the spike horizon constant, and the spike threshold factor at the plant level in the Buffer Profile Maintenance app, as shown in Figure 10.21.

Plant	Set of Buffer ...	Spike Horizon Constant	Spike Horizon DLT ...	Spike Threshold	On-Hand Aler...
	DEFAULT		1,00	0,60	0,50
0001	DEFAULT		1,00	0,60	0,50
0002	DEFAULT	1,00	1,00	0,50	0,50
0003	DEFAULT	1,00	1,00	0,60	0,50

Figure 10.21 DDMRP Settings in the Buffer Profile Maintenance App

Replenishment proposals created for a DDMRP product will always be forward-scheduled, considering today as the start date and using the decoupled lead time to calculate the finish date for both externally and internally procured products.

As shown in Figure 10.18 and Figure 10.19, in which the Stock/Requirements List for a demand-driven product is shown, we will also have a planning time fence when using a demand-driven MRP type. This *time fence* will be always equal to the decoupled lead time and will use fixing type 1 by default. This time fence exists to prevent the dates of a planned order created by MRP for a demand-driven product from being changed in the following MRP run.

The MRP run is usually executed daily as a background job, and it should ensure that there are enough replenishment proposals to cover the DDMRP buffer. In addition to the MRP run, the planner can also use the Replenishment Planning and Replenishment Execution apps to monitor the buffer coverage and take actions to avoid shortages, such as manually creating a new replenishment proposal or expediting an existing order.

Both applications will show in their tiles the total number of products within the user's area of responsibility for which he needs to take action, as shown in Figure 10.22. The **Replenishment Planning** tile the total number of products for which the net flow position is below the reorder point, whereas the **Replenishment Execution** tile shows the total number of products with on-hand stock below the safety stock margin.

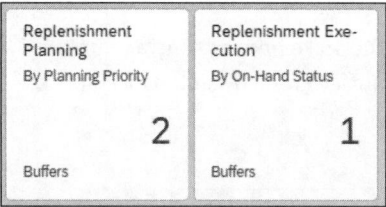

Figure 10.22 The Replenishment Planning and Replenishment Execution Tiles

When entering the Replenishment Planning app, we will see the list of products within the user's area of responsibility for which the net flow position is below the reorder point, but we can change the filter to add more planning priority statuses if we need to see additional products. All those products will be sorted according to the planning priority, which is the percentage of the buffer covered by the net flow position; we will see the lines highlighted in color, according to the respective planning priority status. Figure 10.23 shows an example, in which the first line is highlighted in red because the net flow position is below the safety stock, and the second line is highlighted in yellow because the net flow position is below the reorder point.

Note

There are five different planning priority statuses:

- Above maximum stock
- At 0 or below with demand
- Below reorder point
- Below safety stock
- Below or at maximum stock

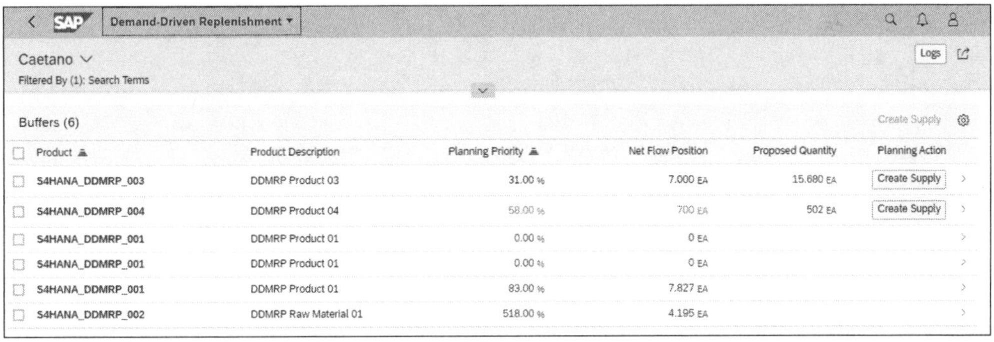
Demand-Driven Replenishment
Caetano
Filtered By (1): Search Terms
Logs
Buffers (6)
Create Supply
Product
Product Description
Planning Priority
Net Flow Position
Proposed Quantity
Planning Action
S4HANA_DDMRP_003 DDMRP Product 03 31.00 % 7.000 EA 15.680 EA Create Supply
S4HANA_DDMRP_004 DDMRP Product 04 58.00 % 700 EA 502 EA Create Supply
S4HANA_DDMRP_001 DDMRP Product 01 0.00 % 0 EA
S4HANA_DDMRP_001 DDMRP Product 01 0.00 % 0 EA
S4HANA_DDMRP_001 DDMRP Product 01 83.00 % 7.827 EA
S4HANA_DDMRP_002 DDMRP Raw Material 01 518.00 % 4.195 EA

Figure 10.23 Replenishment Planning Sorted by Planning Priority

As shown in Figure 10.23, a **Create Supply** button is displayed for those lines for which the net flow position is below the reorder point or the safety stock. When this button is clicked, SAP S/4HANA will create a new planned order to replenish this product up to the maximum stock level. The scheduling logic for this planned order will be similar to the logic used by MRP: with forward scheduling, considering today as the start date, and using the decoupled lead time to calculate the finish date.

Tip

In Figure 10.23, the same product appears many times in the list. This happens because this product is used in different MRP areas. We can either filter the selection by MRP area if we do not need to see all the MRP areas, or include the **MRP Area** column by changing the column settings if it is important to monitor all the MRP areas.

We can also select a specific line and enter a new screen on which we will find the Supply/Demand List and additional information about the product. In the Supply/Demand List, we will find information about the existing demand and replenishment elements, and we can also take actions, such as editing or deleting an existing replenishment element. Here, we can also manually create a new planned order, defining the quantity, the date, and the source of supply.

The Replenishment Planning app shown in Figure 10.24 was designed with a focus on the planning side because it is based on the comparison of the net flow position with the reorder point. Meanwhile, the Replenishment Execution by On-Hand Status app will be used to manage short-term execution. It focuses on the comparison of the on-hand stock with the safety stock.

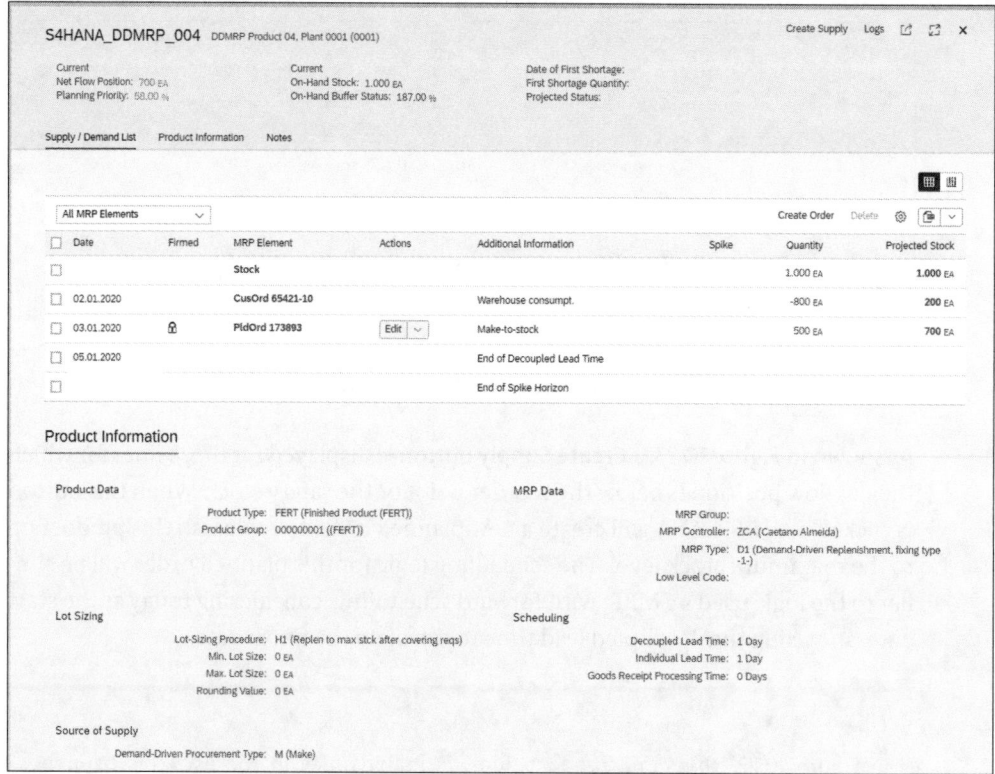

Figure 10.24 Supply/Demand List in the Replenishment Planning App

This application will show, by default, a list of products for which on-hand stock is below the safety stock (the red zone), but we can include additional products by changing the default filters. Figure 10.25 shows this list of products, where the icons in the **On-Hand Buffer Status** column highlight products with the stock below the safety stock. The exclamation point icon is shown for the first line to indicate that the stock is below the on-hand alert threshold, whereas the warning triangle icon is shown for the second line to indicate that the stock is below the safety stock, but still above this threshold.

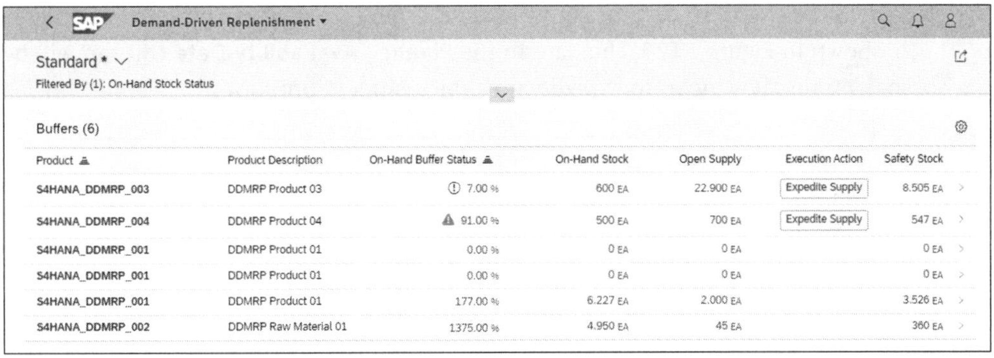

Product	Product Description	On-Hand Buffer Status	On-Hand Stock	Open Supply	Execution Action	Safety Stock
S4HANA_DDMRP_003	DDMRP Product 03	ⓘ 7.00 %	600 EA	22,900 EA	Expedite Supply	8,505 EA
S4HANA_DDMRP_004	DDMRP Product 04	⚠ 91.00 %	500 EA	700 EA	Expedite Supply	547 EA
S4HANA_DDMRP_001	DDMRP Product 01	0.00 %	0 EA	0 EA		0 EA
S4HANA_DDMRP_001	DDMRP Product 01	0.00 %	0 EA	0 EA		0 EA
S4HANA_DDMRP_001	DDMRP Product 01	177.00 %	6,227 EA	2,000 EA		3,526 EA
S4HANA_DDMRP_002	DDMRP Raw Material 01	1375.00 %	4,950 EA	45 EA		360 EA

Figure 10.25 Replenishment Planning by On-Hand Status

> **Note**
>
> The **On-Hand Alert Threshold** setting is defined as a percentage of the safety stock. This value can be set in Customizing through the Buffer Profile Maintenance app, shown in Figure 10.21.

Whenever there is an open replenishment proposal for a product for which the stock is below the safety stock, the **Expedite Supply** button will be shown in the **Execute Action** column. By clicking this button, we can change the dates of an existing replenishment element in order to ensure that the safety stock will be covered as quickly as possible, avoiding any potential product shortage.

> **Tip**
>
> By default, the Replenishment Planning app will only show the option to create a new supply, and the Replenishment Execution app will only show the option to expedite an existing supply.

10 Demand-Driven MRP

> However, in both applications we can change the column settings and include a column for the missing action. Additional columns with important information, such as the reorder point or the safety stock, can also be included.

When choosing the option to expedite supply, a pop-up screen will open in which we will see a list of the existing replenishment proposals and additional information, such as the source, the status, and the order progress (in case of production orders), as shown in Figure 10.26. The date in the **Planned Availability Date** column will be changeable, allowing us to expedite the replenishment proposal.

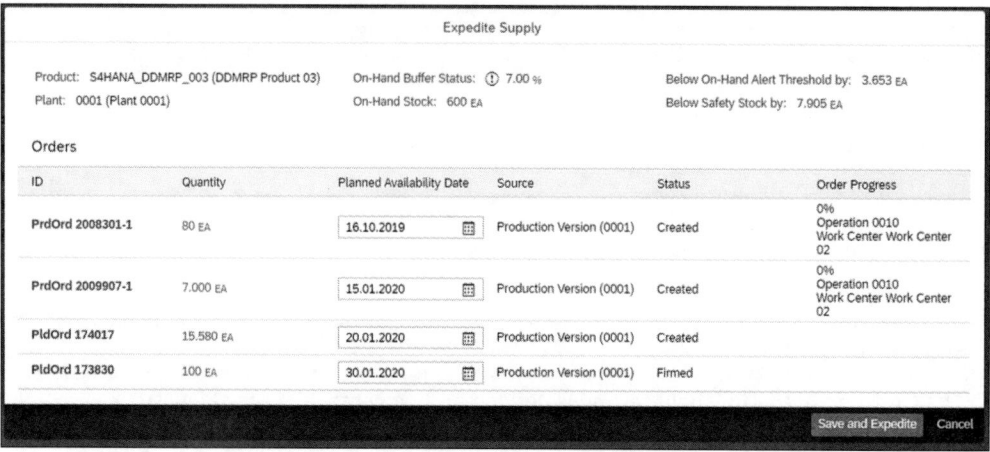

Figure 10.26 Expedite Supply Pop-up in the Replenishment Execution App

Instead of choosing the option to expedite a replenishment proposal, we can simply click one of the lines to see the Supply/Demand List and additional information about the demand-driven product, exactly as in the Replenishment Planning app shown in Figure 10.24.

Finally, we can also find the Planner Overview app in SAP S/4HANA, in which we will find an overview of the DDMRP KPIs. There are three different tiles in this application, as shown in Figure 10.27:

- **Buffer Level Management**: This tile shows the products with deviating buffers that should be approved by the planner.
- **Replenishment Planning**: Similar to the Replenishment Planning app, this tile will show products with a net flow position below the reorder point.

408

- **Replenishment Execution**: Similar to the Replenishment Execution app, this tile shows products with a stock level below the safety stock level.

Figure 10.27 Tiles of the Planner Overview App

We can also choose to break down by procurement type or by each DDMRP product classification (ABC, EFG, PQR, or XYZ). Within this application, it is also possible to click any of the bars in the charts to drill down into the application and see the respective list of products. For example, in Figure 10.27 there is one product with the **Buy** procurement type in the chart for the **Replenishment Planning** tile. If we click this bar, we will branch into the Replenishment Planning app, and this specific product will be displayed. Therefore, this application can used as a central place of entry to monitor the main DDMRP KPIs and to take actions to correct problems and deviations.

10.4 Integrating DDMRP with SAP IBP

DDMRP has been part of SAP S/4HANA since SAP S/4HANA 1709, meaning that we can run the complete, end-to-end DDMRP process in the SAP S/4HANA core. However, DDMRP is also offered by SAP as part of SAP IBP, a cloud supply chain planning solution.

As of SAP S/4HANA 1909, SAP has delivered a new set of APIs for DDMRP in SAP S/4HANA, which allows us to integrate SAP S/4HANA with the DDMRP solution in SAP IBP, or even with third-party DDMRP solutions.

The API_BUFFER_PROFILE_SRV and API_BUFFERSIZING_SRV APIs are both based on the OData protocol, and both can be consumed by external systems and interfaces. The first API can be used to read the buffer profile data, while the second can be used to read, write, and update the buffer sizing data. This API also allows additional buffer actions, such as the following:

- Adopt: The buffer calculated by the system will be adopted (accepted).
- Discard: The buffer calculated by the system will not be accepted and will be discarded.
- Suspend: The buffer calculation will be temporarily paused for a product.
- Resume: The buffer calculation that has been suspended will resume.

A possible integration scenario with SAP IBP could be created in which the buffer profile would be read by SAP IBP from SAP S/4HANA, allowing all the buffer calculations to happen on the SAP IBP side. After the buffer calculation, the calculated maximum stock levels, reorder point, and safety stock would be sent back to SAP S/4HANA. Then, all the replenishment planning and the replenishment execution could be executed by the planner in the SAP S/4HANA core, using the respective SAP Fiori applications with the addition of the Planned Overview app.

A similar integration scenario could be created with any third-party DDMRP solution, in which the buffer can be calculated externally and brought into SAP S/4HANA via API so that the operational execution can happen in the SAP S/4HANA core using native SAP Fiori applications.

Technical information about these DDMRP APIs can be found in the SAP API Hub at the following URLs:

- *https://api.sap.com/api/API_BUFFER_PROFILE_SRV/resource*
- *https://api.sap.com/api/API_BUFFERSIZING_SRV/resource*

10.5 Summary

Demand-driven MRP is one of the major innovations introduced for MRP in SAP S/4HANA, and we can find tools within SAP S/4HANA to run the end-to-end DDMRP process, from the buffer positioning to the replenishment execution.

In this chapter we went through the whole DDMRP solution, starting with the DDMRP implementation, where we learned about the product classification, buffer positioning, and buffer calculation. We then walked through the DDMRP operation, where we learned about the various SAP Fiori applications available to streamline this process. We have finished the chapter quickly discussing the options to integrate the DDMRP solution in SAP S/4HANA with SAP IBP or additional third-party solutions.

As we saw along this chapter, the DDMRP logic is not very complex and SAP S/4HANA offers a complete and intuitive solution that can be used out-of-the-box, with minimal configuration and setup. However, the DDMRP adoption by an organization is not a simple task: it breaks established concepts and completely changes the existing production planning paradigms.

With this chapter, we have finished our discussion of the *operational* MRP tools. The next two chapters will be dedicated to the *simulation* tools available in SAP S/4HANA. In the next chapter, we will cover Long-Term Planning, a simulation tool that was already available in SAP ERP. Then Chapter 12 will cover Predictive Material and Resource Planning, which was introduced in SAP S/4HANA 1909.

Chapter 11
Long-Term Planning

Long-term planning is used for mid-term and short-term simulations. With the Long-Term Planning tool, we can check if the forecasted quantities can be produced, and we can also determine the raw material quantities and provide that information to the purchasing department.

MRP is a tool mainly focused on operational planning, so the replenishment elements generated during the planning run are immediately effective. MRP generates actual purchase requisitions and planned orders that are convertible to production orders as soon as the MRP execution is finished.

Sometimes, however, the production planner wants to run simulations on the forecast provided by the sales department to ensure that the plan is feasible from a capacity or procurement point of view.

Since previous versions of SAP ERP, a tool called Long-Term Planning (LTP) could run this kind of simulation without affecting the operational data and without additional master data requirements. SAP does not consider LTP target architecture for SAP S/4HANA in the future, but it is still a relevant tool that can still be used for planning simulations.

LTP will basically take planned independent requirements (PIRs) as an input and will run a *simulative* MRP, very similar to the operational MRP. The main difference is that the output of LTP will be *simulative planned orders*, which cannot be converted to purchase requisitions or production orders, nor can they be used for repetitive manufacturing backflush.

> **Note**
>
> SAP S/4HANA 1909 introduces the first version of a tool called Predictive Material and Resource Planning (pMRP), which should replace LTP. We will discuss the pMRP capabilities in Chapter 12.

The results of long-term planning can be used for several purposes beyond production planning simulation. The first use case for the LTP tool is to validate the forecast, ensuring that there will be enough capacity in the work centers to manufacture the forecasted quantities. Because LTP runs a multilevel simulation, capacity can be verified for all the semifinished products, not only for the forecasted product. In addition, we can use the LTP results as an input for the purchasing department: by transferring the planned quantities for the raw materials to the purchasing information system, the purchasing department can negotiate a better price or contract with suppliers, knowing in advance the required quantities of raw material. The LTP results can also be transferred to inventory controlling to be used in the long-term stock evaluation, allowing a projection of the future inventory based on the forecasted quantities.

We start this chapter by discussing how to create and run an LTP scenario in Section 11.1 and Section 11.2, respectively. We will then discuss the LTP simulative planned order in Section 11.3, go through the evaluation transactions in Section 11.4, and close the chapter with the planning scenario clean-up in Section 11.5.

11.1 Creating a Long-Term Planning Scenario

Because LTP is basically a simulation tool, we have the possibility to create different simulation scenarios in order to understand how the projected forecast will affect the plant capacity, raw material consumption, and other important factors. It may be interesting, for example, to have an optimistic scenario with higher projected quantities, a realistic scenario with mid-range quantities, and a pessimistic scenario with lower projected quantities. We can validate all those scenarios and quickly switch between them, depending on the market conditions. We may also have different scenarios that vary in their planning horizons: perhaps we have a scenario with a projection for the medium term and another scenario with a projection for the long term.

To allow users to differentiate all those scenarios and evaluate them separately, LTP is based on the concept of a *planning scenario*. To run any kind of LTP evaluation, we need to first create a planning scenario in Transaction MS31.

During the planning scenario creation, shown in Figure 11.1, we have to define the specific control parameters for each scenario to define the LTP behavior for each specific scenario. We can choose from three different preconfigured scenarios in which the default settings are used for the control parameters, or we can copy the settings from any existing planning scenario. The three preconfigured scenarios are as follows:

- **Long-Term Planning**: Most of the settings are unchecked. Safety stock is used as the opening stock, and dependent requirements are created for reorder point materials.
- **Gross Long-Term Planning**: Similar to the long-term planning scenario, but the scrap calculation is deactivated, and a gross lot-sizing procedure can be selected for planning.
- **Short-Term Simulation**: Plant stock is considered as the opening stock, and existing sales orders and firmed planning elements will be considered in the simulation.

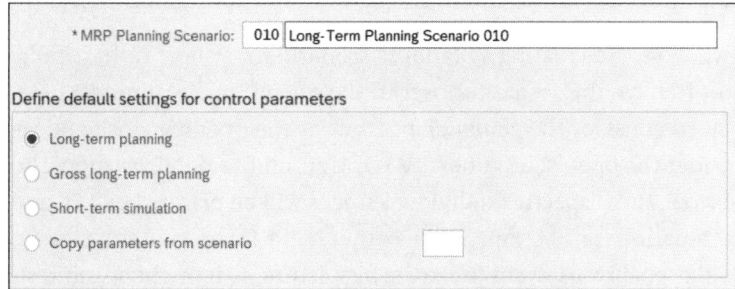

Figure 11.1 Creating Long-Term Planning Scenarios with Transaction MS31

When we select any of these options, the corresponding settings will be already checked in the planning scenario, but we still have the option to change those predefined settings. It is important to understand what each setting represents and the effects of these settings in the planning scenario.

Figure 11.2 shows the **Long-Term Planning** scenario settings, which are grouped into different sections on the screen. The **Control Parameters** section is where we will define which specific MRP features will be considered. These settings will allow us to control how close the simulation will be to the operational planning. The following settings are available:

- **Dependent Requirements for Reorder Point Materials**: When this flag is set, dependent requirements will be created for reorder point materials and they will be included in the planning run.
- **Opening Stock**: With this setting, we can control whether we should have no stock, safety stock, actual plant stock, or average plant stock as the opening stock for the materials under this scenario.

- **Consider Sales Orders**: Open sales orders may consume independent requirements, so we can choose if those sales orders will be considered or not in the long-term planning scenario.
- **Switch Off Planning Time Fence**: This setting allows us to disable the time fence on the long-term planning scenario.
- **Use Direct Production**: If this setting is not checked, LTP will not create collective planned orders, even if the respective special procurement for direct production is set in the material master.
- **Use Make-to-Order and Project Planning**: This setting controls if the special stocks for make-to-order (MTO) and make-to-project (MTP) will be considered in LTP.

As a general rule, when we are creating a planning scenario for a short-term simulation, we might want to have the scenario closer to the operational planning. Therefore, we might want to consider the actual plant stock as the opening stock and we might want to consider the open sales orders, MTO, MTP, and so on. If we choose to consider MTO and MTP, the respective individual stocks will be planned by LTP and shown in the LTP evaluation transactions. On the other hand, for a long-term simulation scenario, we will probably just want to see the big picture, so it might be interesting to avoid the consumption of our PIRs by sales orders; settings like the **Time-Fence** or **Direct Production** may be irrelevant, so we might want to disable them.

Under the **Gross Requirements Planning** section shown in Figure 11.2, we will find the **Switch Off Scrap Calculation** and **Use Gross Lot Size** settings. These are useful if we want our LTP scenario to create planned orders with the exact PIR quantity, without taking into account any scrap or any special lot-sizing procedure.

We can also choose which fixed replenishment elements will be considered in the LTP scenario in the **Receipts** section. By checking the **Include Firm Receipts** flag, we will ensure that receipts that are always considered firm by MRP—for example, production orders, purchase orders, inspection lots, or stock transfer orders—will be considered in the LTP scenario. We can also use the **Include Firm Purchase Requisitions** and **With Firm Planned Orders** flags to define if purchase requisitions and planned orders will be considered in the scenario when they are firmed.

Under the **BOM Explosion** section, we can define a different BOM selection ID to be used in the planning scenario. The **BOM Selection ID** setting is useful if we want to use a different BOM during the LTP run.

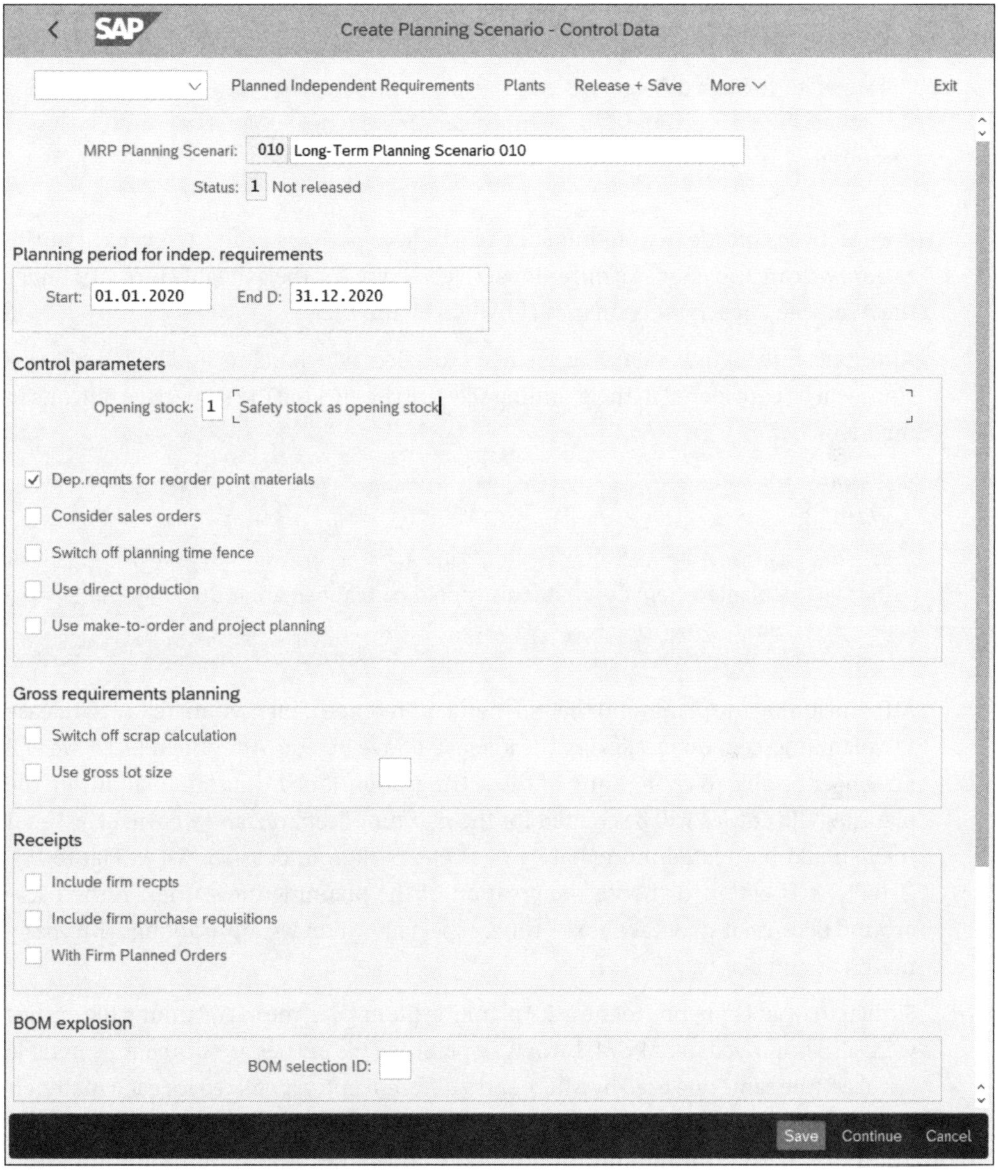

11.1 Creating a Long-Term Planning Scenario

Figure 11.2 Long-Term Planning Scenario

> **Tip**
> If we want to use a different BOM in LTP, we can create a new BOM usage for LTP in customizing Transaction OS20. Then we can create a new BOM selection ID in customizing Transaction OS31, referencing the BOM usage created.

If we want to consider a different shift schedule or perhaps a different capacity utilization, we can also choose a different active version for the available capacity under the **Available Capacity** section (not shown in Figure 11.2).

After selecting all those settings, we need to select which plants and which PIR versions will be considered in the planning scenario by clicking the respective buttons in the menu bar.

> **Warning**
> When working in a simulation that should involve stock transfers, we need to ensure that all the plants where our materials should be planned are included in the planning scenario.

After including the plants and the independent requirements, we are ready to release the planning scenario by clicking the **Release + Save** button. After the release, we will no longer be able to change any of the settings mentioned thus far. In addition, the planning file entries will be created for the planning scenario, and we will be asked if they should be created immediately or in the background, as shown in Figure 11.3. Usually, it is better to choose the creation of the planning file entries in the background because it may take some time, especially when we are working with many materials and plants.

Similar to what happened to the MRP planning file entries, the LTP planning file entries were also improved in SAP S/4HANA. LTP planning file entries are stored now in table PPH_DBVM (the same one used by MRP), and a different entry is created for each material/plant/MRP area/scenario combination. The new report PPH_SETUP_MRPRECORDS_SIMU is used to set up and check for consistencies in the LTP planning file entries; this is the report executed in a background job when we release the scenario.

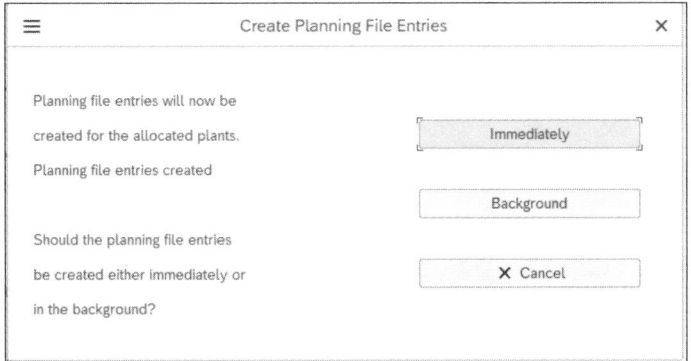

Figure 11.3 Creating Planning File Entries in LTP

Once the planning scenario has been created and released, we can execute LTP and evaluate the planning results. In the following section, we will discuss the options and the transactions available to execute LTP in an SAP S/4HANA system.

11.2 Running Long-Term Planning

The LTP execution is overall very similar to the operational MRP execution because we have similar transactions and programs to execute LTP. For most of the transactions available to execute MRP (covered in Chapter 5), we have an equivalent transaction to run LTP, and we have the same options to run a total LTP run, run a single-item/multi-level run, run a single-item/single-level run, or schedule LTP background execution. In fact, the transaction codes used to run LTP follow the same logic used for the MRP transaction codes: the main difference is that we will have an S instead of a D in the transaction code. For example, instead of Transactions MD01 and MD02, we will use Transactions MS01 and MS02, and so on.

When comparing the LTP transactions with the MRP transactions, the main difference that is immediately observed is that **Planning Scenario** is a mandatory field because every LTP execution will happen with reference to a specific planning scenario. Figure 11.4 shows the selection screen for the total LTP planning run in Transaction MS01, in which we can see that the **MRP Planning Scenario** field is mandatory.

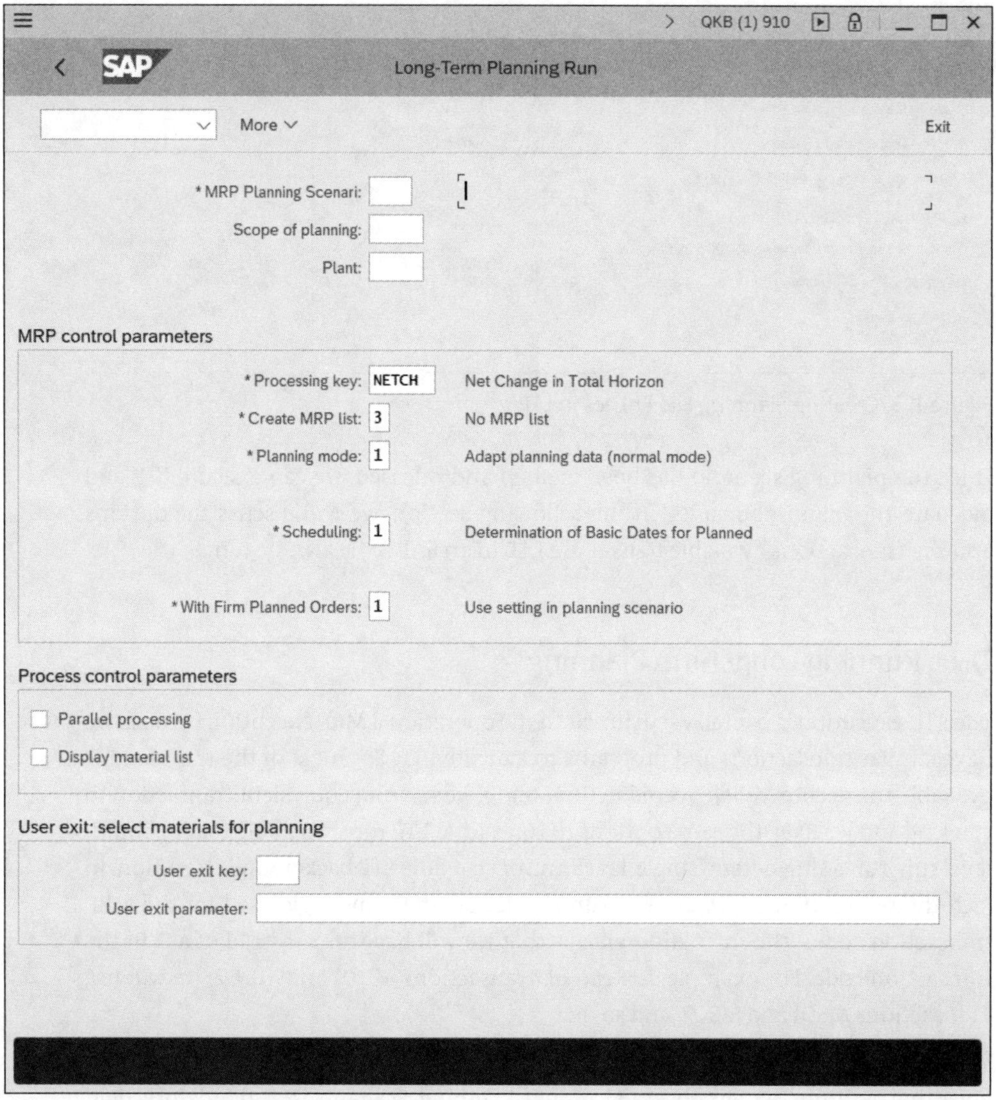

11 Long-Term Planning

Figure 11.4 Long-Term Planning Run

Another difference between the MRP and LTP transactions is that we do not have the creation indicators for purchase requisitions or scheduling agreements in LTP. That is because LTP will only generate simulative planned orders, which cannot be used for operational purposes; it cannot generate any kind of operational replenishment elements, such as purchase requisitions or scheduling agreements.

Finally, we have the **With Firm Planned Orders** field, in which we can choose whether firm planned orders from the operational MRP will be considered during LTP. Here we can choose to consider the setting defined in the planning scenario or to define a different setting for the LTP execution that will have a higher priority than the setting defined for the planning scenario.

> **Note**
> We noted in Chapter 5 that the classic MRP transactions were optimized for better performance in SAP S/4HANA and that the part of the logic where the planning elements were read was pushed down into the SAP HANA database layer. This optimization was *not* implemented in the LTP transactions: the LTP logic remains unchanged when compared to the LTP logic in SAP ERP.

Besides the already mentioned total LTP run that can be executed in Transaction MS01, we also have the following options to run LTP:

- Transaction MS02 (Single-Item, Multilevel)
- Transaction MS03 (Single-Item, Single-Level)
- Transaction MSBT (Creation and Management of Background LTP Jobs)

In addition, program RMMRP010 can be used to schedule a background total LTP run or to run LTP directly in Transaction SE38. There is no transaction equivalent to MRP Live (Transaction MD01N) to execute an in-memory LTP run.

If we have selected the option to use MTO or MTP production in the planning scenario, we also have the option to run LTP for an individual sales order or a project/WBS element. The following transactions are available:

- Transaction MS50 (Long-Term Make-to-Order Planning—Multilevel)
- Transaction MS51 (Long-Term Project Planning—Multilevel)

> **Tip**
> During a total LTP run, all materials with a valid MRP type and a planning file entry will be planned. If we are working with many different planning scenarios and a large number of materials, then the system may take a long time to plan all the scenarios.

11 Long-Term Planning

> We may exclude materials that are not relevant for the LTP simulations by setting a material status when an error message is set for LTP. A material status can be created in customizing Transaction OMS4 and assigned to the material master's **MRP 1** tab.

After the LTP run and after SAP S/4HANA has generated simulative planned orders, we will be able to evaluate the LTP results. In the following sections, we will discuss in detail the simulative planned order and the transactions that can be used for the LTP results evaluation.

11.3 Processing Simulative Planned Orders

Operational MRP can generate different replenishment elements, such as planned orders, purchase requisitions, or scheduling agreements. The LTP tool, however, will only generate simulative planned orders for materials procured internally and externally.

As we mentioned earlier in this chapter, those planned orders are not convertible to production orders or purchase requisitions, and they cannot be used for the repetitive manufacturing backflush because they are only created for simulation purposes. We can, however, copy selected simulative planned orders to the operational MRP, as we will discuss later in this section, generating a *real* planned order that *can* be further processed.

The LTP simulative planned order is very similar to the MRP planned order, with the only noticeable difference that we will find a reference to the planning scenario for which it was created in the planned order header, as shown in Figure 11.5. Transactions MS11, MS12, and MS13 are used to create, change, or display simulative planned orders, respectively.

> **Note**
>
> The simulative planned order uses the same data model used by the operational MRP planned orders, which means that it will be also saved in the same tables (PLAF, RESB, etc.).

11.3 Processing Simulative Planned Orders

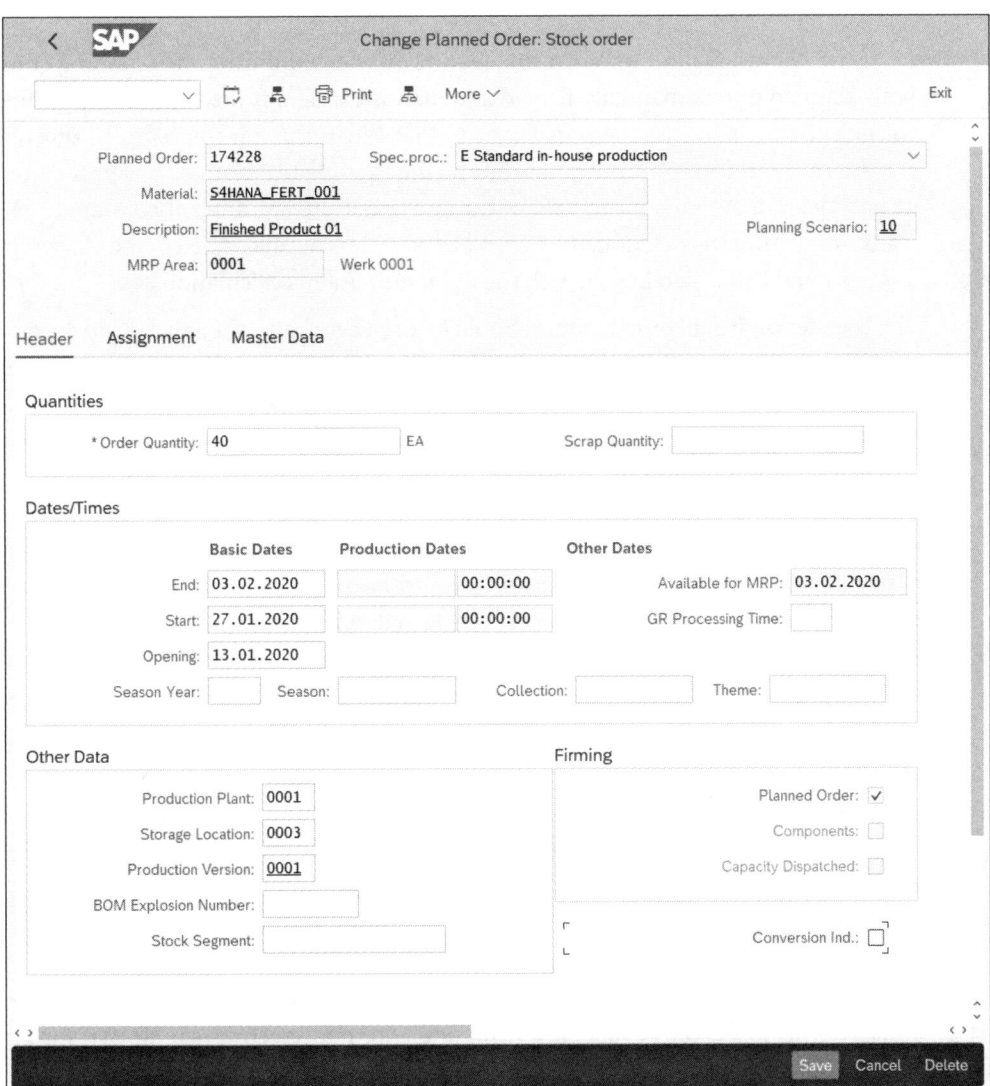

Figure 11.5 Simulative Planned Order

When processing a simulative planned order, we can take actions such as firming, scheduling, or using it for capacity analysis, for example. It is not possible to run an availability check for this kind of order, though, and the ATP-related menu button will not be displayed.

As mentioned in earlier sections, LTP offers a feature to copy firm planned orders from the operational MRP. When this feature is selected during the planning run, both planned orders manually firmed and planned orders firmed because they are within the time fence will be transferred to LTP. When the transfer happens during the LTP run, SAP S/4HANA will first delete all the existing LTP planned orders (firmed or not) that fall before the end date of the last transferred MRP planned order to be transferred. After the deletion, the firm planned orders will be copied to the planning scenario, and LTP will follow on with the net requirements calculation.

The transfer of firm planned orders should be used carefully as it may lead to excess stock in the planning scenario. Consider, for example, what would happen if a firm planned order were transferred to the planning scenario during the planning run and then we changed the planned order date to a date in the future in the planning scenario. The next LTP planning run would copy this order again from operational MRP, and it might not delete the changed order if the new date lies after the date of the last transferred order. So be aware that any changes made to the transferred orders in the planning scenario may be lost because they may be deleted in the following LTP run. Finally, when a firm planned order is transferred, only the header is copied to the planning scenario and a new BOM explosion will happen; therefore, any changes made to the components in the original planned order will not be copied to the planning scenario.

Besides the option to copy firm planned orders from the operational MRP to LTP, we also have a tool through which we can do the opposite and copy the LTP firm planned orders to the operational MRP. For example, we can generate an inactive forecast for a finished product and use it as an input for LTP, to have planned orders for all the finished product components on all levels. If we want to start the procurement for the raw material in advance, we can firm its planned orders and copy them to the operational MRP so that they can be converted later to purchase requisitions. Unfortunately, this tool is only available during single-item interactive planning (Transaction MD43), so we need to copy the planned orders for each material separately.

To copy the LTP planned orders to operational MRP, we need to trigger the interactive MRP in Transaction MD43 and then choose the **Edit** • **Copy Simulative LT Planned Orders** menu option, which is shown in Figure 11.6.

From the subsequent pop-up, we can choose from which planning scenario we are copying the firm planned orders and a date interval from which the planned orders should be copied. In Figure 11.7, the planning scenario from which we are copying is

11.3 Processing Simulative Planned Orders

10, and the date interval is 15.05.2020 to 15.01.2020. When copying those LTP planned orders, all the existing MRP planned orders that are not firmed will be deleted.

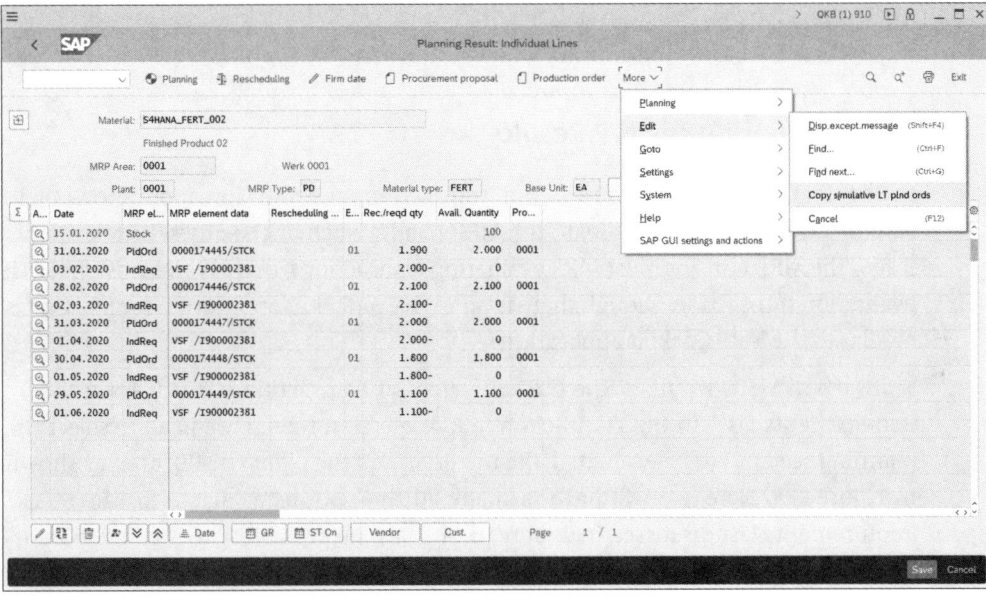

Figure 11.6 Copying Simulative Planned Orders in Transaction MD43

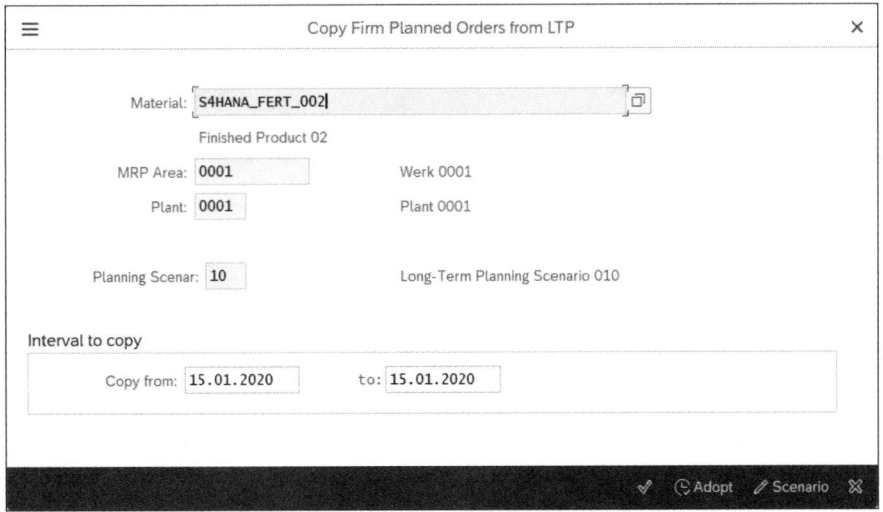

Figure 11.7 Choosing Planning Scenario and Interval to Copy Planned Orders

After copying the planned orders, it is highly recommended to trigger the MRP planning within Transaction MD43 to ensure that all the requirements are covered and that there are no shortages for the material because the previously existing planned orders were deleted.

11.4　Evaluating the LTP Results

In Chapter 6, we discussed the different transactions and SAP Fiori applications available in SAP S/4HANA to evaluate the MRP results, such as the Stock/Requirements List or the MRP List. For most MRP evaluation transactions, there is an equivalent LTP evaluation transaction, though there is no native SAP Fiori application for LTP that is similar to the MRP Cockpit applications.

Transaction MS04 would be the LTP equivalent of Transaction MD04 (i.e., the Stock/Requirements List). In the Transaction MS04 selection screen, we need to select the planning scenario to be evaluated, the material, and the plant or MRP area, as shown in Figure 11.8. Here, we will have virtually all the options available for the Stock/Requirements List discussed in Chapter 6, such as the possibility to access the transaction with a filter or selection rule, besides the collective access.

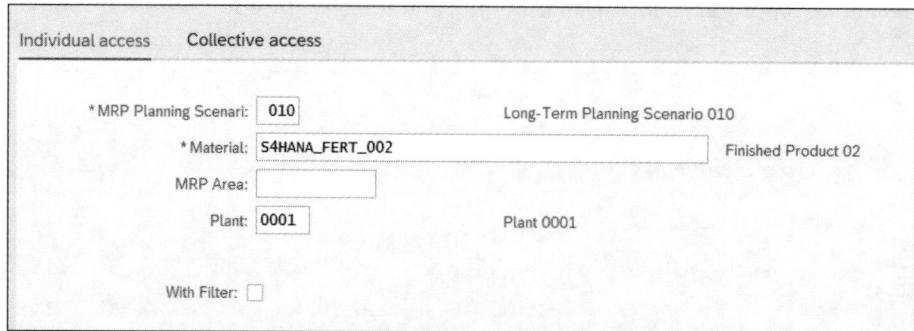

Figure 11.8 The LTP Stock/Requirements List Selection Screen

The LTP Stock/Requirements List will be almost identical to the MRP Stock/Requirements List, with the main difference that a **Scenario** field with the planning scenario number is displayed, as shown in Figure 11.9. We can use this field to switch between different planning scenarios in order to compare the LTP results for the same material.

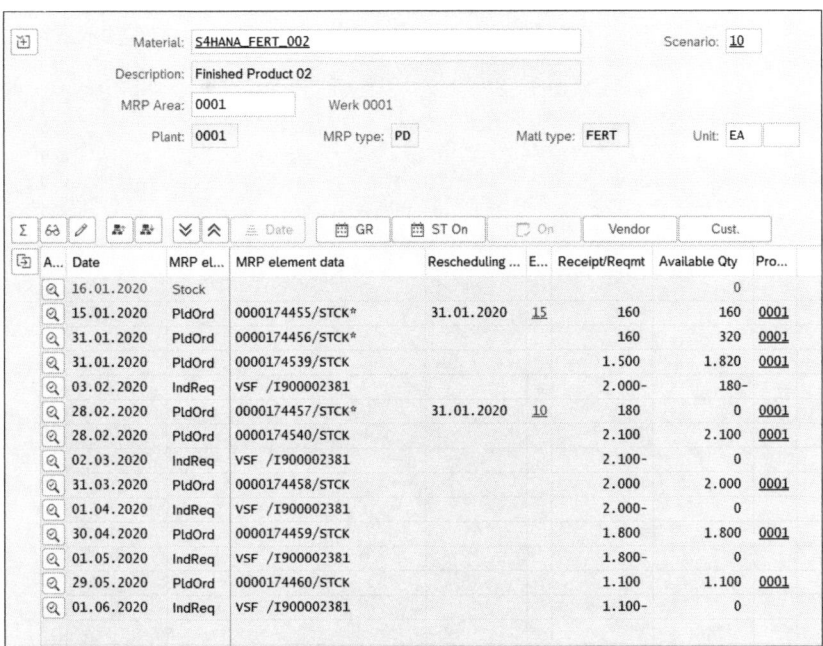

Figure 11.9 The LTP Stock/Requirements List

Another interesting option available in the LTP results is the period totals comparison with another planning scenario, in which we can compare the LTP results of different planning scenarios on a single screen. This option can be accessed through the **Goto · Comparison with Another Scenario** menu option. Figure 11.10 shows this comparison in the LTP Stock/Requirements List period totals, with two different lines for two different planning scenarios. In the **Period Totals: Comparison** table, both lines are displayed for PIRs, requirements, receipts, and the following columns.

LTP also offers the collective Stock/Requirements List, which can be accessed in Transaction MS04 through the **Collective Access** tab or directly in Transaction MS07. In the **Collective Access** tab, we will see traffic lights for each material, stock days' supply, and the total number of exception messages for each group triggered for each material. Similar to Transaction MS07, the traffic lights and the exceptions will only be shown in the overview when marking the **Set Up Lists in Background** option in the selection screen. This might lead to performance issues if too many materials are processed. Figure 11.11 shows the material list of the LTP Stock/Requirements List when using the collective access.

11 Long-Term Planning

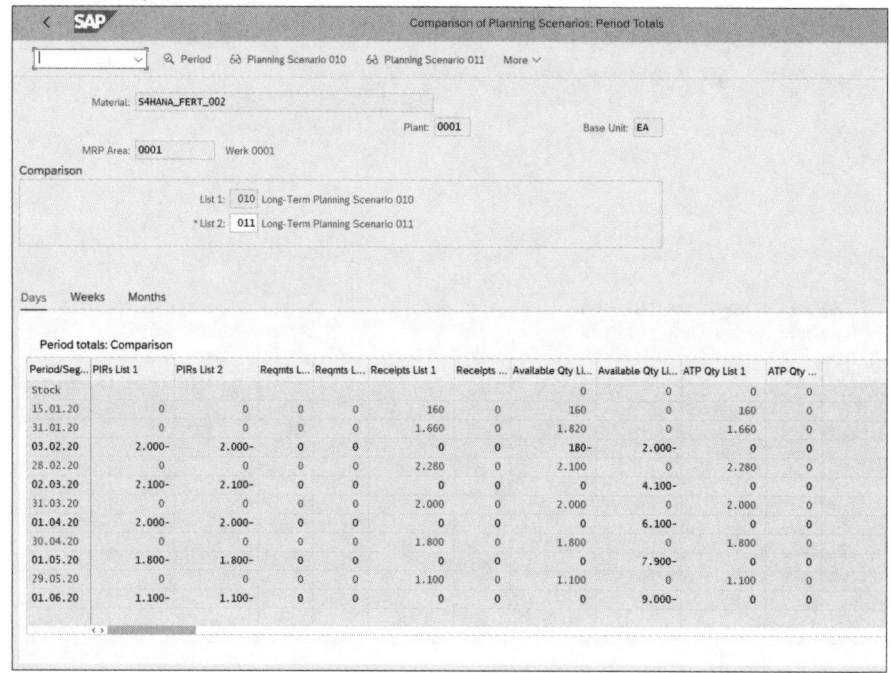

Figure 11.10 Period Totals: Scenario Comparison

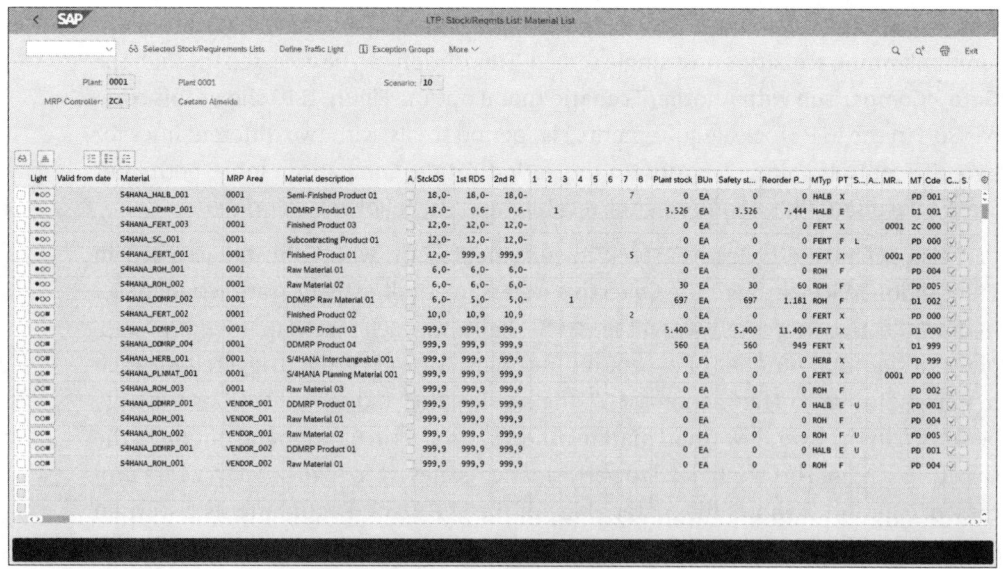

Figure 11.11 LTP Stock/Requirements List Collective Access

11.4 Evaluating the LTP Results

Besides the Stock/Requirements List, LTP also offers Transactions MS05 and MS06, which are equivalents to the MRP List transactions (Transactions MD05 and MD06). The LTP MRP List follows the same principle as the regular MRP List: the planning results are saved into a table and can be accessed later from these transactions.

Transactions MS44 and MS47 are equivalent to Transactions MD44 and MD47 and can be used for LTP evaluation based on the product group. There is no LTP equivalent transaction to the cross-plant evaluation (Transaction MD48).

> **Note**
> Because the LTP evaluation transactions are similar to the MRP evaluation transactions, we will not discuss each transaction in detail. For further information, refer to Chapter 6, in which the MRP evaluation transactions were discussed.

11.4.1 Evaluating Work Center Capacity

As discussed at the beginning of this chapter, MRP also can be used for a capacity evaluation, in order to ensure that there is enough capacity in the production work centers to manufacture the forecasted quantities.

The LTP capacity evaluation can be accessed through Transaction CM38. It will show, by default, the capacity requirements allocated to the selected work centers (the **Requirements** column), the total available capacity (the **AvailCap.** column), the percentage of the allocated capacity load (the **CapLoad** column), and the remaining available capacity (the **RemAvailCap** column). The capacity evaluation is shown in Figure 11.12, where we can see the capacity requirements for a work center on a specific planning scenario.

A prerequisite to use the LTP capacity evaluation is to set up the work centers and routings so that the capacity requirements can be calculated. In addition, lead time scheduling should be carried out for the LTP planned orders, either during the LTP planning run or manually when processing individual planned orders.

The default period of the LTP capacity evaluation is weeks, but it can be changed to months or days, for example, in the general settings. We can also select a specific period and drill down into the capacity details to show the planned orders allocated to the work center in that specific period.

11 Long-Term Planning

```
Work center    S4_CA_01        Work Center 01              Plant    0001
Capacity cat.: 001             Capacity 01
```

Week	Requirements	AvailCap.	CapLoad	RemAvailCap	Unit
03.2020	0,00	8,00	0 %	8,00	H
04.2020	0,00	48,00	0 %	48,00	H
05.2020	0,00	88,00	0 %	88,00	H
06.2020	0,00	128,00	0 %	128,00	H
07.2020	0,00	168,00	0 %	168,00	H
08.2020	32,25	208,00	16 %	175,75	H
09.2020	72,25	248,00	29 %	175,75	H
10.2020	112,25	288,00	39 %	175,75	H
11.2020	152,25	328,00	46 %	175,75	H
12.2020	216,50	368,00	59 %	151,50	H
Total >>>	216,50	368,00	59 %	151,50	H

Figure 11.12 Work Center Load for the Planning Scenario

11.4.2 Transferring the LTP Results to the Logistics Information System

The LTP results not only can be used for checking if we have enough capacity to manufacture the forecasted quantities; they also can be transferred to the purchasing information system (part of the Logistics Information System) so that the purchasing department can consider this forecast when negotiating a new contract with a supplier or even to confirm if the suppliers will be able to meet the demand.

> **Note**
>
> The Logistics Information System is considered outdated technology in SAP S/4HANA because it aggregates redundant data in InfoStructures; therefore, it is not considered target architecture by SAP. However, its transactions are still available in SAP S/4HANA 1909 and can still be used at the time of publication (summer 2020).

LTP data will be compiled and saved into InfoStructure S012 so that it can be later analyzed in the Purchasing Information System reporting transactions. The first step to use the evaluations is to set up the data in the InfoStructure via Transaction MS70. When we run this transaction, SAP S/4HANA will evaluate the existing simulative planned orders from a specific scenario and will aggregate the values into InfoStructure S012. We will need to choose the version of the InfoStructure that will be used and how the purchase order value will be calculated, as shown in Figure 11.13.

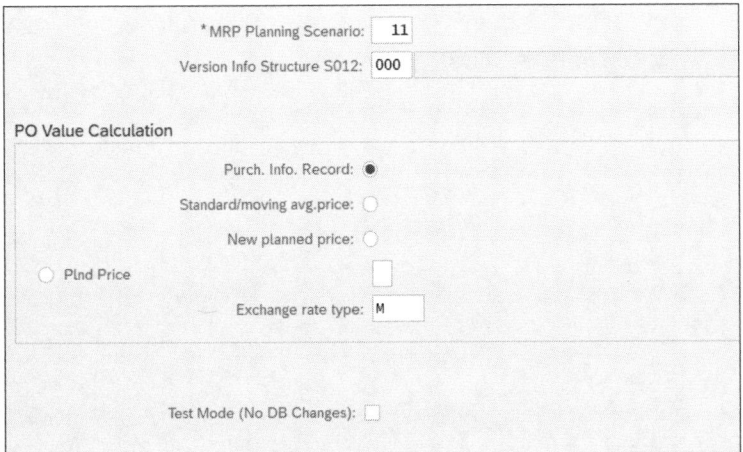

Figure 11.13 Setting Up Purchasing Data from LTP

After setting up data, we can evaluate the results using the following transactions:

- Transaction MCEC (Material Analysis)
- Transaction MCEA (Vendor Analysis)
- Transaction MCEB (Material Group Analysis)

These transactions are basically reports that will show the information aggregated into the InfoStructure, giving an overview of the values and quantities for the externally procured materials.

Figure 11.14 shows the **Long-Term Planning Material Analysis** selection screen (Transaction MCEC). Note the **Ad-hoc Evaluation** flag, which can be used to retrieve the information directly from the simulative planned orders rather than the aggregated data from the InfoStructure itself. This option is not recommended if we will evaluate many materials because the selection may then take a long time.

The results of the material analysis will be shown in the **PO Value**, **Order Quantity**, and **PO Price** columns for each material, as shown in Figure 11.15. The same key figures will be shown in the vendor analysis and in the material group analysis; the only difference will be the aggregation level. Within the transaction, we can also switch the aggregation by clicking the **Switch Drilldown** button, and we have additional options, such as to show graphics or a time series for a specific line.

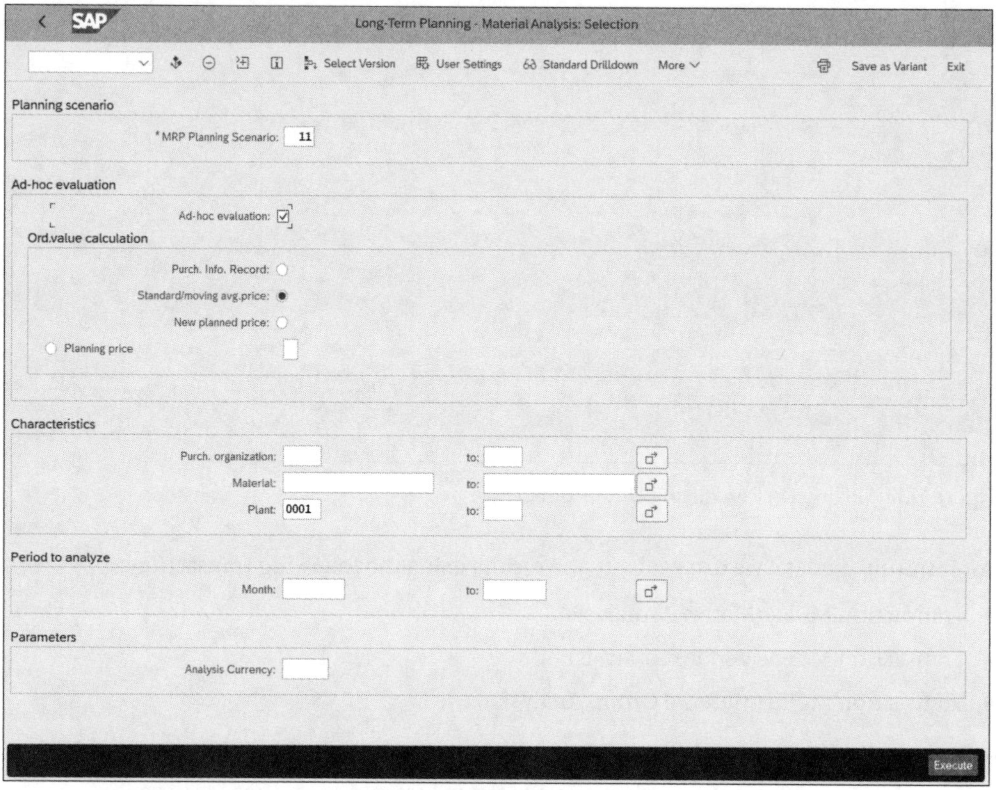

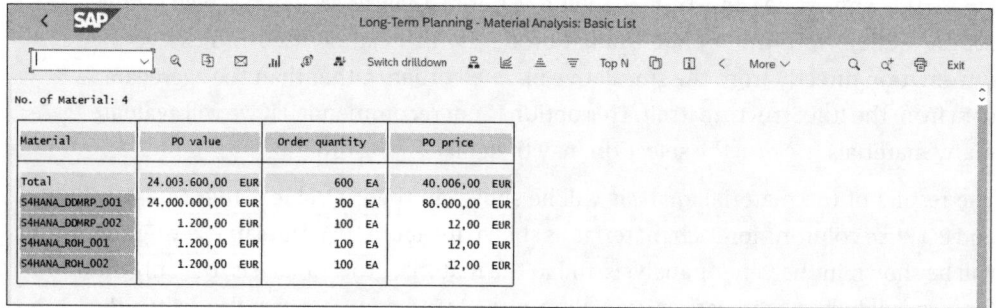

Figure 11.14 LTP Material Analysis Selection Screen

Material	PO value	Order quantity	PO price
Total	24.003.600,00 EUR	600 EA	40.006,00 EUR
S4HANA_DDMRP_001	24.000.000,00 EUR	300 EA	80.000,00 EUR
S4HANA_DDMRP_002	1.200,00 EUR	100 EA	12,00 EUR
S4HANA_ROH_001	1.200,00 EUR	100 EA	12,00 EUR
S4HANA_ROH_002	1.200,00 EUR	100 EA	12,00 EUR

Figure 11.15 LTP Material Analysis

> **Tip**
> There might be different versions of data within InfoStructure S012. We can use Transaction MS71 to copy data between those structures.

This kind of InfoStructure-based reporting for LTP is also available for inventory controlling. InfoStructure S094 aggregates data related to stock/requirements analysis, and the long-term planning scenario can be used as an input for the InfoStructure.

We can run Transaction MCB& to set up data in InfoStructure S094; in the selection screen, we will be able to choose if the LTP data will be used to build the InfoStructure by selecting the **Generate Data from Long-Term Planning?** flag, as shown in Figure 11.16. When choosing this option, we need to also choose from which planning scenario data will be selected and the info structure planning version number.

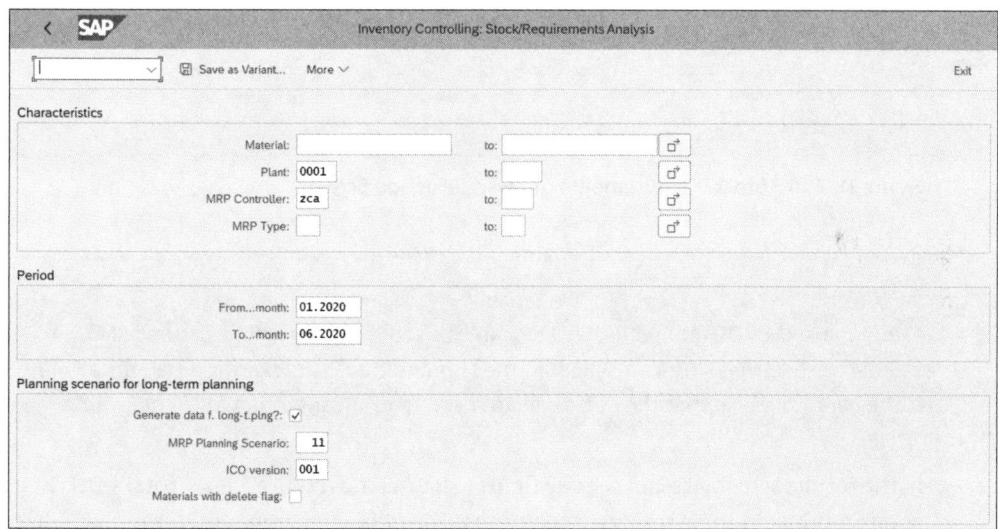

Figure 11.16 Transaction MCB& Selection Screen

After building up the InfoStructure with the LTP data, we can use Transaction MCB) to evaluate the Stock/Requirements Analysis. In the evaluation selection screen, we also have the option to run an ad-hoc evaluation (see Figure 11.17), in which data will be read directly from the LTP planned orders.

11 Long-Term Planning

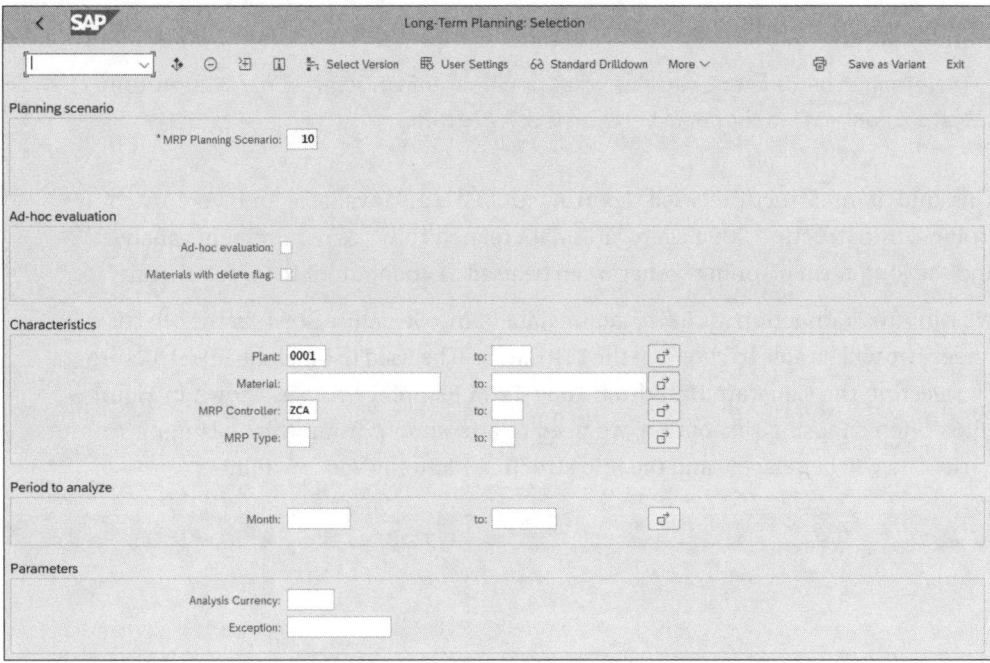

Figure 11.17 LTP Stock/Requirements Analysis Selection Screen

> **Tip**
>
> Programs RMMDEKS1 and RMCBDISP can be used to set up InfoStructures S012 and S094, respectively. We can schedule those programs to be executed periodically in the background so that the users will not need to run Transaction MS70 or MCB&.

In the results screen, we can see key figures such as the requirements, total stock, and goods receipts in their respective columns. The default aggregation is per plant, but we can switch the aggregation by clicking the **Switch Drilldown** button and choosing an aggregation per material, MRP controller, MRP type, or month. We can also include additional key figures in the report or even display a graphical representation of the results. Figure 11.18 shows the stock and requirements aggregated by material, plus the key figures mentioned previously.

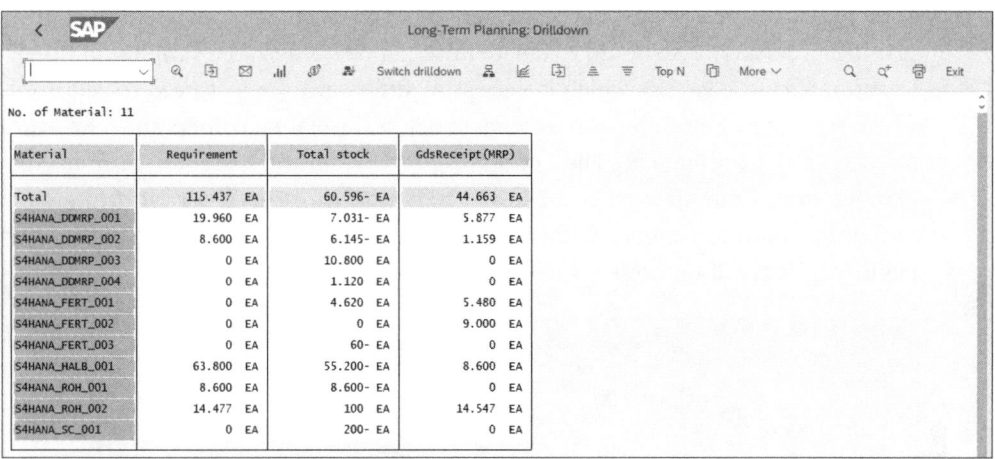

Figure 11.18 LTP Stock/Requirements Analysis

> **Note**
>
> LTP offered functionality to transfer activity type requirements to cost center accounting in SAP ERP using Transaction KSOP. This option was disabled in SAP S/4HANA: if we try to open this transaction, a pop-up screen will inform us that this function is no longer available.

11.5 Cleaning Up the Long-Term Planning Scenario

After running all the desired LTP simulations, we might want to restart the simulation from scratch or simply reuse the same planning scenario for a different simulation.

In the standard SAP S/4HANA system, there is no LTP archiving object because it is simply a simulation tool, but SAP offers options for deleting the LTP scenario-dependent data and the whole planning scenario. The deletion of dependent data can be carried out independently of the planning scenario deletion. There are different alternatives to delete the planning scenario-dependent data, and each one can be used for a different purpose.

If we are firming simulative planned orders and we are not using an MRP type with roll forward, it might occasionally be necessary to delete the old firmed planned orders because they will not be converted or backflushed like the operational MRP planned orders. If we just want to delete firm planned orders, the simplest option is to run report RMPLAF00, which is very straightforward; we just need to select for which specific planning scenario we want to delete the planned orders and if we want to activate the **Set Planning File Entries** flag so that all the materials with deleted planned orders are planned again in the next LTP run. The report also offers an option to run in test mode, as shown in Figure 11.19, which will tell us how many planned orders will be deleted before the actual deletion.

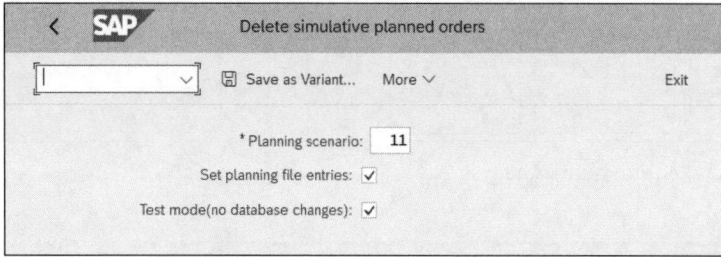

Figure 11.19 Deletion of Simulative Planned Orders with Report RMPLAF00

If we are setting manual firming dates for our materials in Transaction MS04, it will cause simulative planned orders to be automatically firmed during the LTP run. When the manual firming date is no longer required, we can use report RMMDFD00 to delete those entries so that they will no longer be relevant to LTP.

Another way to delete the planning scenario-dependent data is to run report RMPLSC00. This report will not only delete the planned orders; we can also select specific elements to be deleted by checking the **Planning File Entries**, **MRP Lists**, **Manual Firming Data**, **Data in Purchasing Info System**, **Data in Inventory Controlling**, and **Average Plant Stocks** flags in the selection screen, as shown in Figure 11.20.

Finally, we can directly delete data and the planning scenario itself when changing the planning scenario in Transaction MS32. Both options can be selected through the **Planning Scenario · Delete** menu option when changing the planning scenario, as shown in Figure 11.21.

11.5 Cleaning Up the Long-Term Planning Scenario

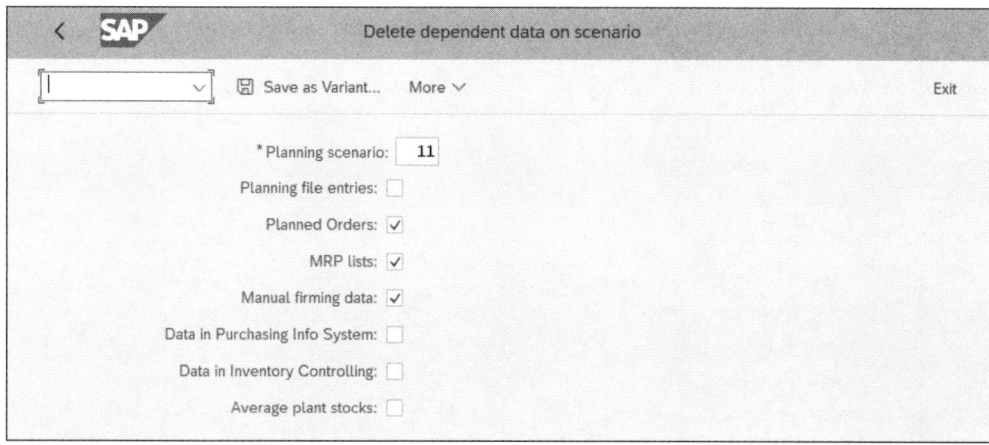

Figure 11.20 Deletion of LTP-Dependent Data with Report RMPLSC00

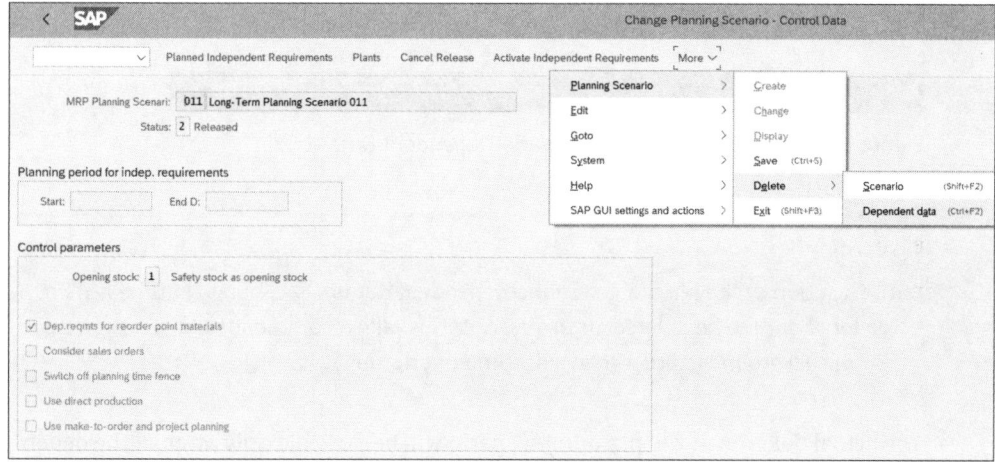

Figure 11.21 Deletion of Planning Scenario in Transaction MS32

If we choose the option to delete dependent data in Transaction MS32, then the pop-up screen shown in Figure 11.22 will appear. Here we can choose which planning elements will be deleted and whether the deletion will be executed immediately or in the background; we will only be able to mark those planning elements that actually exist for the planning scenario. In Figure 11.22, for example, the **Delete Manual Firming Data** and **Delete Average Plant Stock** fields are greyed out because these elements do not exist for the scenario chosen.

437

11 Long-Term Planning

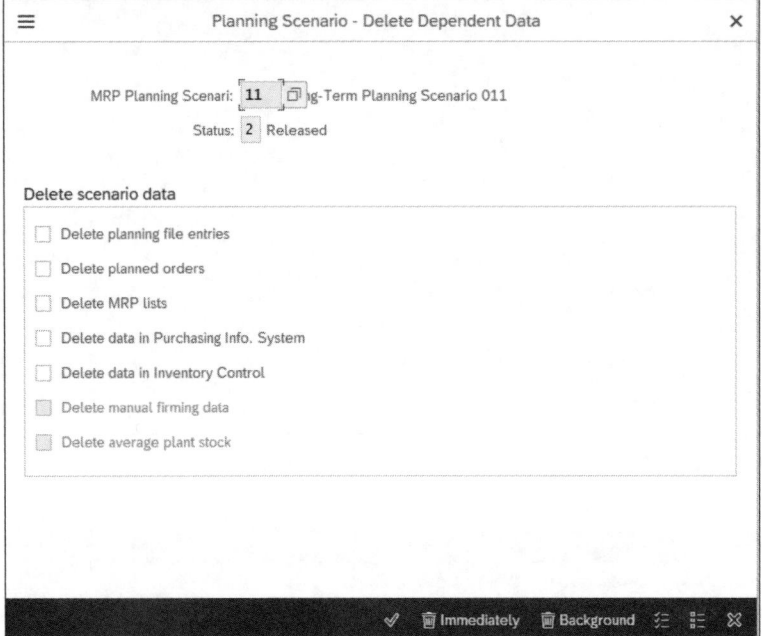

Figure 11.22 Deletion of Planning Scenario-Dependent Data

> **Warning**
> The deletion of the planning scenario-dependent data may take a long time if there is a lot of data to be deleted. In this case, it is usually recommended to run the deletion in background in order to avoid a time-out dump.

The actual deletion of the planning scenario will be possible only after all the dependent data is deleted, and it can be carried out directly in Transaction MS32, in the menu option shown in Figure 11.22. After the deletion, we can reuse the same number for the creation of a new planning scenario.

11.6 Summary

LTP is a powerful simulation tool that can be used to evaluate different planning scenarios, validate a forecast, and provide inputs for capacity requirements and the required quantities of raw material. In this chapter, we have covered how to create a new planning scenario, how to run the LTP simulation, how to evaluate the LTP results, and how to clean up data after the evaluation.

As discussed in this chapter, LTP is not the target architecture for planning simulations in SAP S/4HANA—but it is still present, and it can still be used in SAP S/4HANA 1909. The successor of LTP, Predictive Material and Resource Planning (pMRP), was first delivered in SAP S/4HANA 1909. In the next chapter, we will discuss how to use pMRP and compare it to the features presently available in LTP.

Chapter 12
Predictive Material and Resource Planning

Predictive Material and Resource Planning is a new feature introduced in SAP S/4HANA 1909 that allows the planner to simulate demand changes and check if there are capacity overloads. It uses simplified MRP logic to identify possible capacity issues.

SAP S/4HANA 1909 introduced new functionality called Predictive Material and Resource Planning (pMRP), designed provide simulation capabilities and allow a forecast to be validated according to the work center capacity. The overall concept behind pMRP is somewhat similar to LTP and can be considered an evolution of it, but without the exact same functionalities. pMRP was designed with an intuitive, SAP Fiori–based user interface, a simplified planning logic, and native use of the power of the SAP HANA database for better performance.

The main input for the pMRP simulation will be also a demand plan (represented in SAP S/4HANA by planned independent requirements [PIRs]), and the system will consider this input to run a simulated planning run that will be used to analyze the capacity under the work centers. It can also be used to determine the required quantity for a specific raw material on a simulation.

Within the pMRP simulation, users can interactively analyze the results of the simulation, taking actions to resolve a work center capacity issue, such as the following:

- Change the forecasted demand to reduce the capacity requirements in the work center
- Increase the work center available capacity to accommodate the capacity requirements for the forecasted quantities
- Preproduce a component to distribute the requirements for this component across multiple months
- Change the source of supply to use a different work center

Once finished with the simulation, it can be released to operational planning so that the quantities adjusted in the simulation can be saved into the PIRs. Because pMRP was also designed to take into consideration the new DDMRP concept, the forecasted requirements will be released by means of PIRs for components planned with a demand-driven MRP type once the simulation is released.

pMRP is mainly accessed through two SAP Fiori applications: the Schedule pMRP Simulation Creation app (in which the simulation is created) and the Process pMRP Simulations app (in which the simulation can be processed and copied). Both are accessed through the SAP Fiori launchpad, as shown in Figure 12.1. ABAP report PMRP_CREATE_ENVIRONMENT_MAT can be used as an alternative to create the simulation directly in SAP GUI, but there is no SAP GUI equivalent for *processing* the simulation, which relies on SAP Fiori graphical elements to show the work center capacity charts.

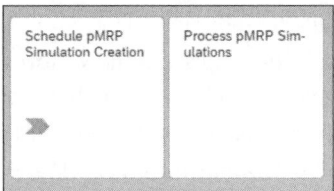

Figure 12.1 pMRP Applications in the SAP Fiori Launchpad

In the following sections, we will discuss the full pMRP process, starting with the prerequisites to run pMRP in Section 12.1, going through the creation of a new simulation in Section 12.2, covering how to process this simulation in Section 12.3, and finally discussing releasing the results to operational planning in Section 12.4.

12.1 Prerequisites to Run pMRP

From a configuration perspective, pMRP requires no specific Customizing settings before the first execution. In fact, if we look into the SAP IMG (which you can open through Transaction SPRO), we will not even find specific nodes or Customizing activities related to pMRP because there are no configuration activities for it. This means that pMRP can be used virtually out of the box, so long as we have the proper operational MRP configuration in place, such as a valid plant, MRP controllers, and so on.

From a master data perspective, to run pMRP, we will need the basic master data used by MRP for planning a material, such as the following:

- **Material master**
  Any MRP-relevant material can be used for a pMRP simulation.
- **BOM**
  A valid BOM with the BOM usage set to **1—Production** should exist for a material that will be used in a simulation.
- **Work center**
  The work center used in a simulation should have at least one capacity relevant for finite scheduling.
- **Routing**
  A valid routing should exist, and the operation in the operation in the bottleneck resource operation should be relevant for capacity planning.
- **Production version**
  At least a valid production version referring to the BOM and routing should exist. If there is more than one valid production version, we can change the source of supply during the simulation.

All the relevant master data should be created in advance, before we start to use pMRP and create the simulation version.

> **Note**
>
> Because one the main ideas behind pMRP is to allow the user to check if there is enough capacity to produce the forecasted quantities, it is very important to correctly set up the routing and the work center with the standard values and the proper formulas.

From a transactional data perspective, the main input for pMRP is a forecast plan, represented by PIRs. The planning strategy used is not relevant because it supports any requirement type and we can also use an active or an inactive PIR version. When choosing an inactive version, we will have to select which version number should be used during the simulation creation.

12.2 Creating a pMRP Simulation

When we start pMRP, the first step in the process is to create the pMRP simulation. If we compare pMRP with LTP, this step is somewhat similar to the creation of a long-term planning scenario; the difference is that the long-term planning scenario is created for a whole plant, whereas we can choose a restricted set of master data for our pMRP simulation. When we create the simulation, we select which top-level materials or work centers will be considered for pMRP.

Another difference between pMRP and LTP is that all the planning will happen during the simulation creation itself, whereas in LTP we first release the planning scenario and then execute the planning run (as many times as we want). In pMRP, we will be able to process the simulation immediately after the creation is finished and will not need to wait for a planning run.

A third difference is that whereas LTP generally runs with the same MRP type and lot-sizing procedure used by operational MRP, pMRP uses a simplified planning logic, in which all materials will use a deterministic MRP and a lot-for-lot procedure.

As mentioned in the previous section, before the creation of the simulation, we need to ensure that the relevant master data has been created. It is also important to have PIRs created: they will be the main input for the pMRP simulation. The system will plan the selected materials and determine the work center capacity requirements based on those PIRs.

> **Warning**
> When a simulation is created, master data will be copied into it, so subsequent changes to master data may not be considered.

The pMRP simulation creation is basically a background job that can be scheduled through the Schedule pMRP Simulation Creation app (see the application tile in Figure 12.1). This application can also be used to manage background jobs that are already finished, scheduled, or in process.

As shown in Figure 12.2, an icon will be shown in the **Log** column with the status of the finished background executions, and another icon is shown in the **Results** column. By clicking the icon in the **Log** column, we will jump into the job log, which will show the details of success, warning, or error messages that may have been triggered during each step of the simulation creation. Figure 12.3 shows the details of the simulation creation logs, including the success and error messages being triggered. When clicking the icon under the **Results** column, we will jump into the spool, where we will find a list of the materials and work centers selected for the simulation.

12.2 Creating a pMRP Simulation

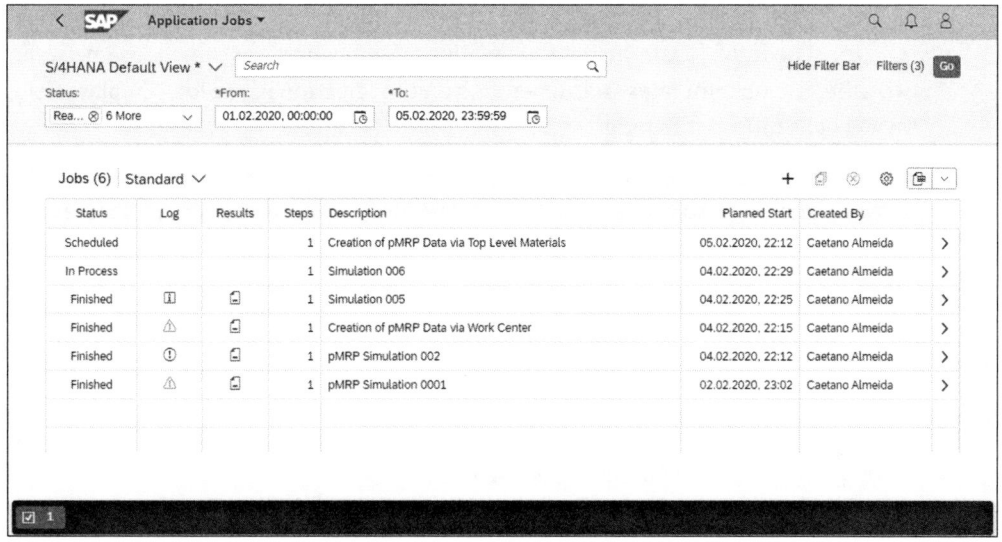

Figure 12.2 Application Jobs for pMRP Simulation Creation

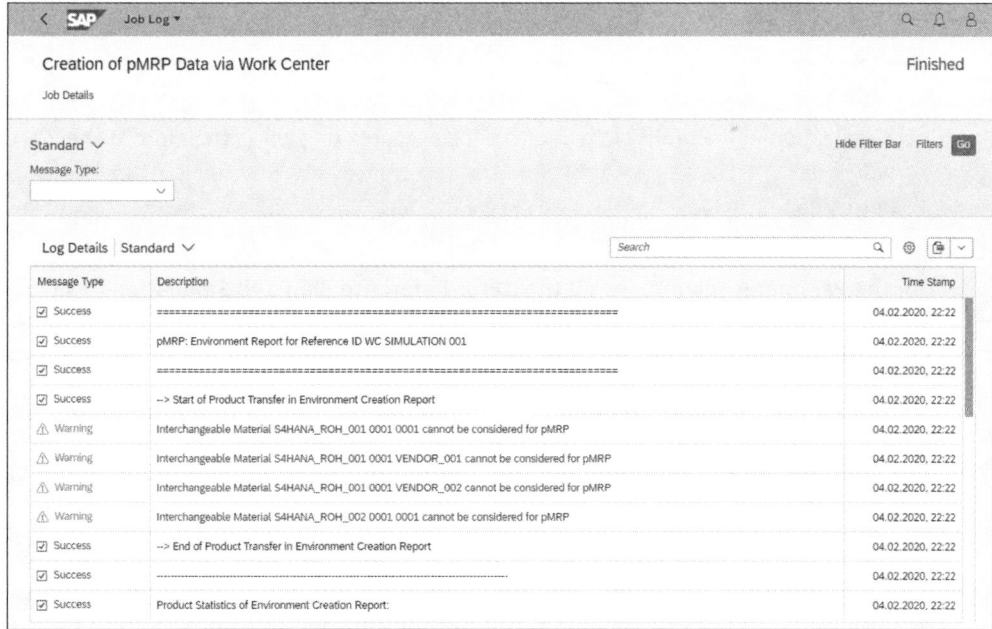

Figure 12.3 pMRP Simulation Creation Logs

We can create, copy, and delete a simulation creation (although deletion is only possible for scheduled jobs). During the creation of a new job, we can choose between two different job templates and, depending on the selection in the **Job Template** field, we will have different criteria:

- **Creation of pMRP Data via Top-Level Materials**: Object selection be based on the material master, so selection criteria will be focused on the material master information, such as material number, MRP controller, or low-level code. The system will look for PIRs for the pertinent materials and run simplified MRP to determine the required quantity for each level and the capacity allocated in the work center.
- **Creation of pMRP Data via Work Center**: Object selection is based on the work center, so the selection criteria will be focused on the work center. The system will look for capacity requirements in the selected work centers and then identify the top-level materials and the respective PIRs.

Figure 12.4 shows the creation of a new pMRP simulation based on the top-level materials and shows the job template selected. In the **Scheduling Options** section, we can define whether the job will be executed immediately or scheduled to run on a future date.

> **Note**
>
> The creation of the pMRP simulation will be executed only once; therefore, it should not be executed as a periodic job, and the **Recurrence Pattern** value is set to **Single-Run** by default.

In the **Parameter** section, we fill the **ID for Reference Plan** and **Simulation ID** fields, which are used to identify the simulation. These should be unique values; the reference ID and simulation ID cannot be the same. The ID for the reference plan will represent the set of master data selected according to the selection criteria, and new simulations can be added later under the same reference ID. Under the **Parameter** section, we also need to select the bucket category (daily, weekly, or monthly buckets) and the start and end date for the simulation.

Under the **Limits** sections, we will find fields that can be used to restrict the selection. We can use those fields to ensure that pMRP will be executed only for materials with a specific BOM, routing, or material status, or for a BOM or task list usage. The **Object Selection** section contains the fields we will use to select the materials or work centers. Depending on the job template selected, we will see material-related fields (such as the **Material**, **Plant**, **MRP Controller**, **Material Type**, or **Low-Level Code**) or work center-related fields (such as **Work Center**, **Work Center Category**, or **Person Responsible**). We can also define if we will consider stock transfers in the scenario and which plants and which work centers from those supplying plants should be considered in the simulation.

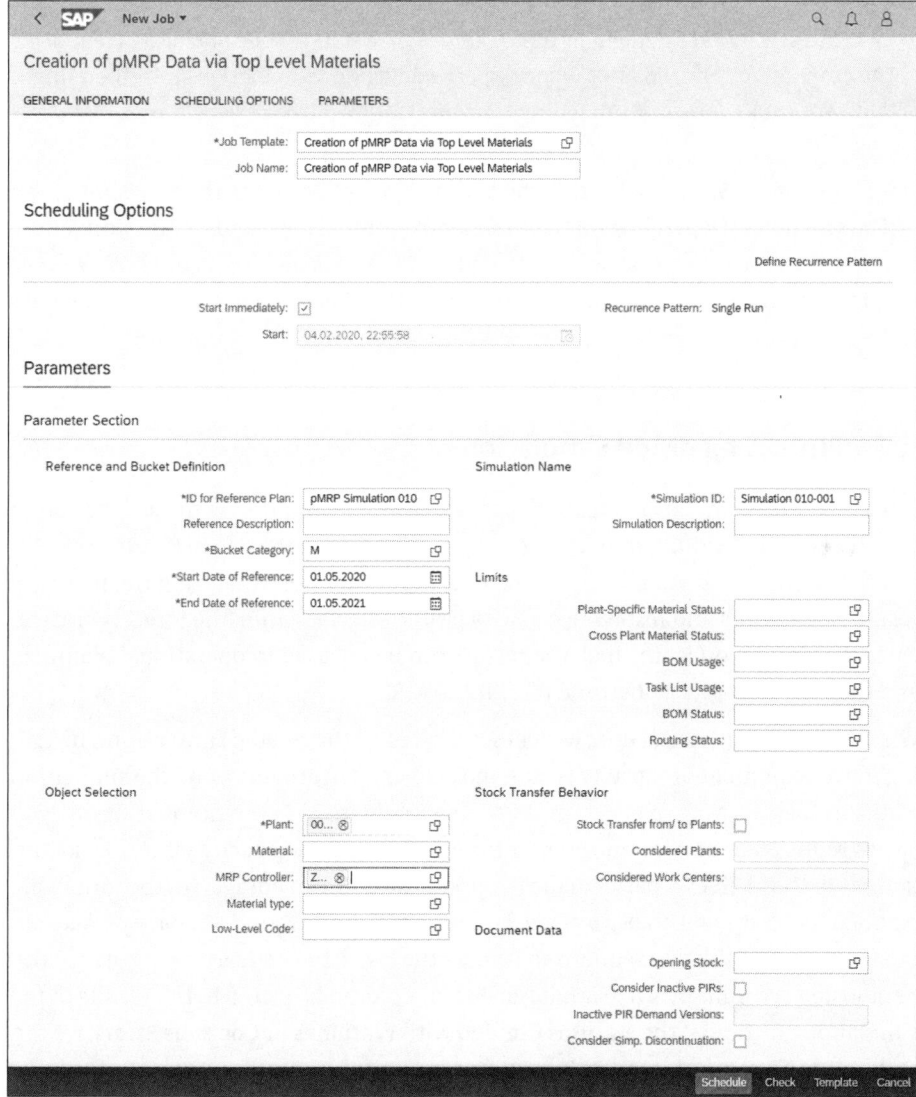

Figure 12.4 Creating pMRP Data via Top-Level Materials

Finally, under the **Document Data** section, we can choose if the opening stock will be zero, if it will be the safety stock or the actual material stock at the plant, if we will consider an inactive PIR version instead of the active version, and if the simple discontinuation will be considered.

> **Note**
>
> All those settings are defined in the reference plan during the simulation creation. They cannot be changed later when we are adding new simulations into the same reference plan.

Once we click the **Schedule** button, the background job to create the new simulation will be scheduled. Depending on the number of materials selected for the simulation, it may take some time because an actual planning run is being executed. We will see the simulation creation logs and the spool after the execution (Figure 12.2 and Figure 12.3).

12.3 Processing pMRP Simulations

After the pMRP simulation creation, users will be able to process the simulation in the Process pMRP Simulations app (the application tile was shown in Figure 12.1). This where the end users will actually work with the simulation, analyzing the planning results, identifying and resolving capacity issues, and validating the forecast created. Once the simulation is finished, the results can be released to operational planning, and then the forecast can become relevant to MRP.

When entering the transaction, we will see a list of all the created simulations, including the total number of capacity issues, the delivery performance, and the simulation status in their respective columns, as shown in Figure 12.5. The number of capacity issues represents the total number of buckets in which a capacity issue was identified, and the delivery performance represents the percentage of the originally planned forecast that can be fulfilled. For example, if you found a capacity issue and the forecast quantity was reduced to resolve the issue, the delivery performance will be adjusted accordingly. The **Simulation Status** column is related to the results of the simulation creation; if the status is **Created with Warnings** or **Contains Errors**, we can refer to the simulation creation logs shown in Figure 12.3.

12.3 Processing pMRP Simulations

Figure 12.5 The Process pMRP Simulations App

In this application, we also have the option to copy, rename, or delete an existing simulation or to override errors. When copying a simulation, it will be linked to the same reference data as the original simulation. We can also choose when copying whether to copy data from the simulation or from the reference data, as shown in Figure 12.6. If we choose the option to copy from the simulation, then changes already made to the simulation will also be copied; if we choose the option to copy from the reference data, changes made to the simulation will not be considered and the original forecast quantities from the reference data will be copied. We can also add a percentage for the **Overload Tolerance** value so that pMRP will not consider a work center overload until reaching the tolerance.

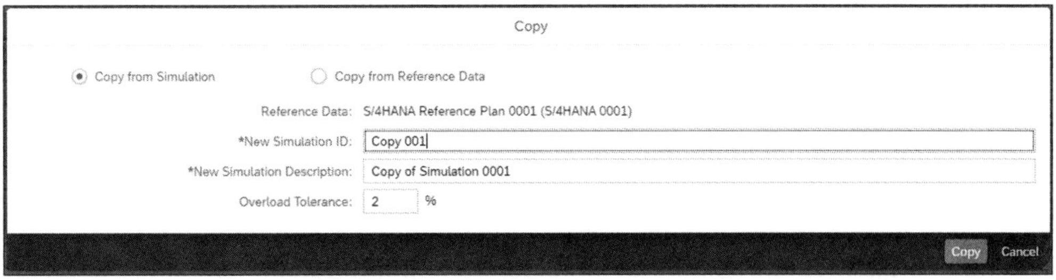

Figure 12.6 Copying a Simulation

When clicking one of the simulations, we will immediately see the **Demand Plan Simulation** screen. This screen shows the lines with the materials selected for this simulation, where each column will represent the forecast quantity for a specific bucket, as shown in Figure 12.7. Some cells are highlighted in red because there is an issue with a capacity overload in the work center: the forecasted quantities will require more time to be produced than is available with the current shift schedules in the work centers. The capacity issue may be related either to the top-level materials or to a semifinished product in the BOM's lower levels.

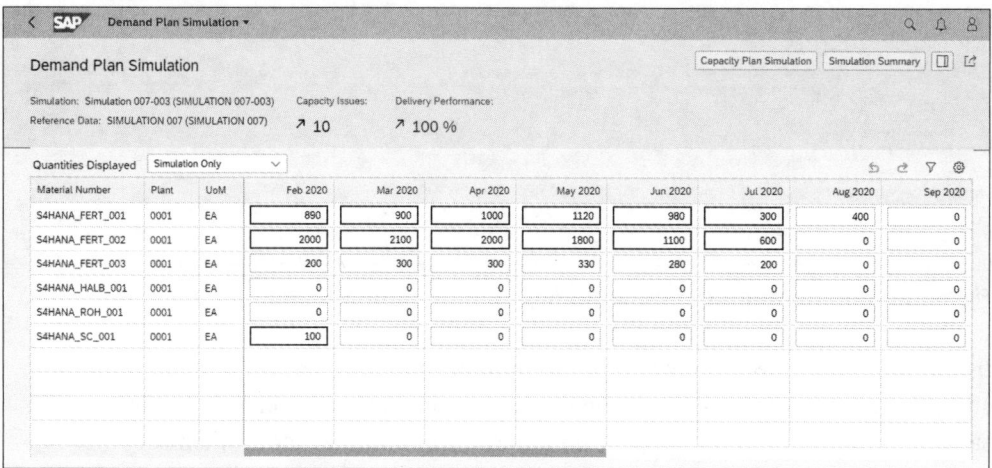

Figure 12.7 The Demand Plan Simulation Screen

We can also find in the **Demand Plan Simulation** screen the number of capacity issues and the delivery performance. The number of capacity issues will not necessarily match the number of highlighted cells; two or more cells may be highlighted due to the same capacity issue in a specific work center. In our example, the delivery performance is still **100%** because the originally forecasted quantities were not yet changed, but this number may change when we try to resolve the capacity issues caused by the forecasted quantities.

Here, we can choose from the following options for the **Quantities Displayed** dropdown:

- **Simulation Only**: We will only see the forecast quantities related to the simulation.
- **Reference/Simulation**: Two columns will be shown: the original quantity from the reference and the simulation quantities. With this option, we can compare the

12.3 Processing pMRP Simulations

changes made to the simulation with the original quantities for a better estimation of the impact of the changes over the originally forecasted quantity.

- **Delta of the Reference and Simulation**: We will see only one column containing the difference between the reference and the simulation. This view is also useful to estimate the impacts of the changes made in the simulation.

When clicking the **Capacity Plan Simulation** button, we will change to a different screen, where the focus is the work center capacity, as shown in Figure 12.8. In the upper part of the screen, we will see a list of the work centers selected for this simulation, with the total number of hours allocated and the remaining capacity of the work centers for every month. In the lower part of the screen, a chart will show a graphical overview of the work centers' possible load and the overload. In the chart bars, the green area represents the feasible load (the capacity requirements that can be fulfilled with the current work center capacity), whereas the red area represents the capacity overload that is causing the issue.

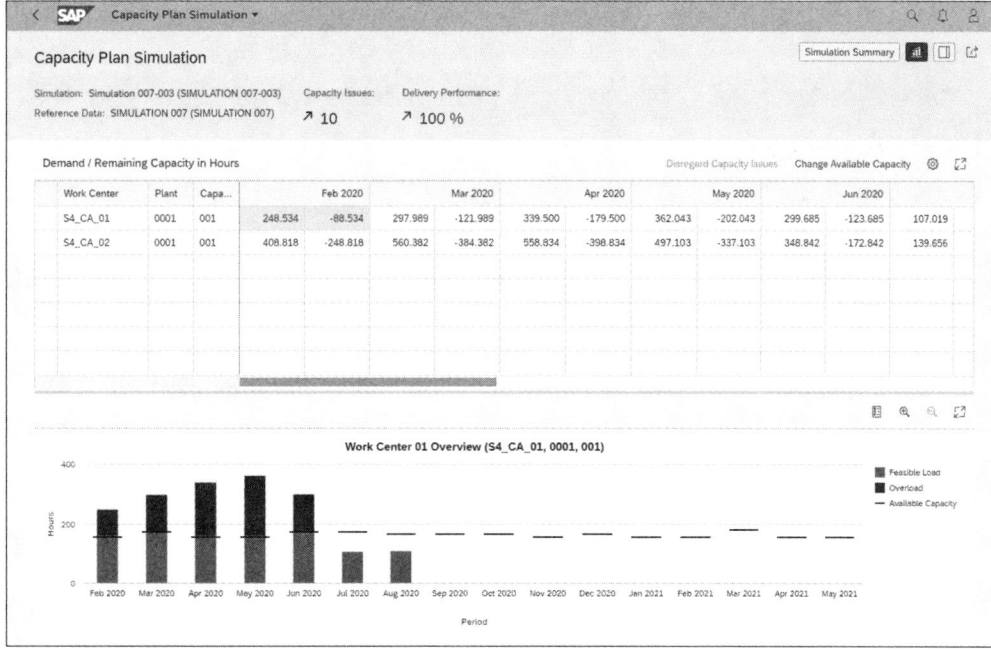

Figure 12.8 Capacity Plan Simulation

451

12 Predictive Material and Resource Planning

From the capacity plan simulation, two buttons correspond to the two alternatives for dealing with the capacity issues:

- **Disregard Capacity Issues**: pMRP will simply ignore all the existing capacity issues for the selected work center. The total number of capacity issues will be reduced, and the cells will no longer be highlighted in red.
- **Change Available Capacity**: The work center available capacity can be changed to allow a capacity overload. When choosing this option, a pop-up screen will be shown (see Figure 12.9), where we can choose months and the percentage of overload allowed. Months with a capacity issue will be highlighted in red; the system will propose a capacity utilization that can resolve the capacity issue for each month.

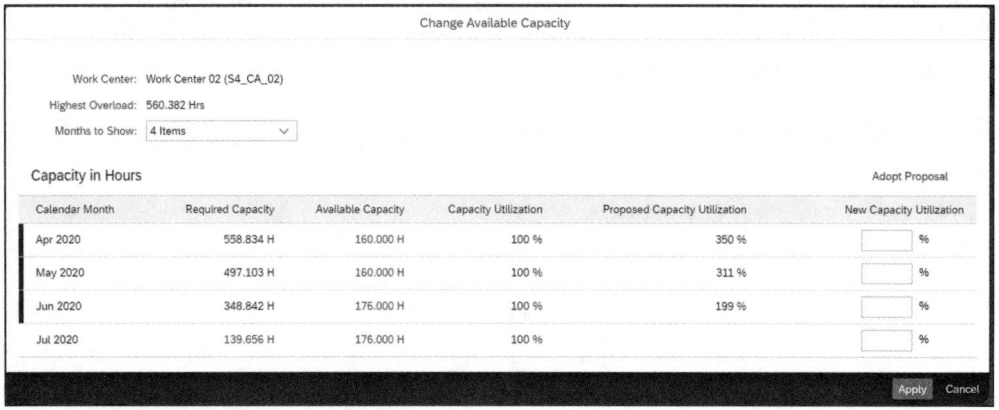

Figure 12.9 Changing Available Capacity

From both the **Capacity Plan Simulation** and the **Demand Plan Simulation** screens, we can show the Object Inspector view to display a side panel with additional information about the selected object. When using the Object Inspector from the capacity plan simulation, the inspected objects will be the work center and the capacity allocated for the selected month, and the Object Inspector will also show the top-level materials related to the capacity allocated in the work center.

If we are using the Object Inspector tool from the demand plan simulation, then the inspected objects will be the material and the quantity forecasted for the selected month. We will also see the capacity issues related to the forecast created for this specific top-level material, even if it is caused by a material in the lower BOM levels. When using the Object Inspector for the demand plan simulation, we will see a link that can be clicked to see the multilevel material simulation for the selected demand. Figure 12.10 shows the Object Inspector view for a demand plan simulation. We can also see the link to the multi-level material simulation and the link to the capacity plan simulation for the work centers with capacity issues.

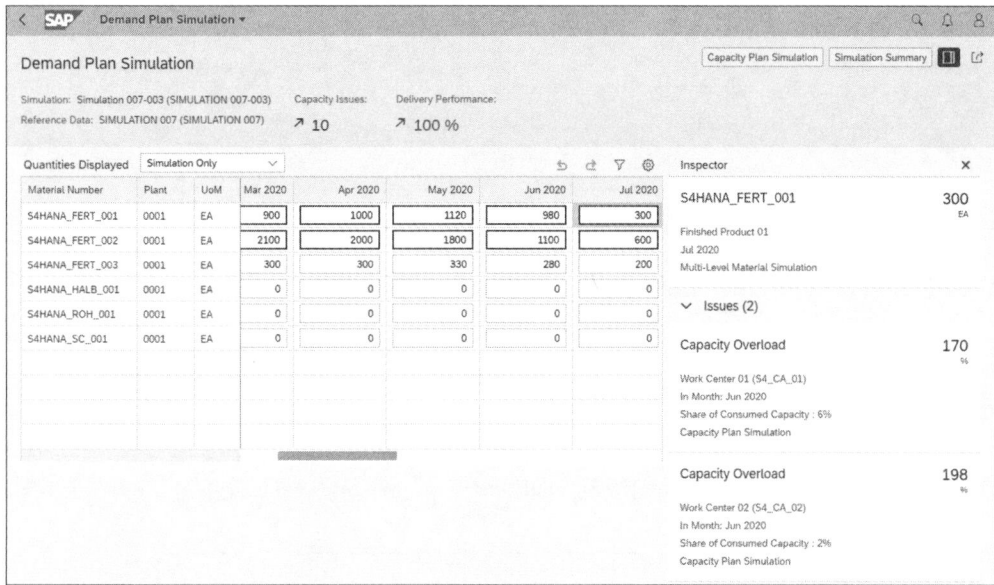

Figure 12.10 The Object Inspector View

If we click the **Multilevel Material Simulation** link, we will see the complete BOM for a specific bucket, including the details of the required and missing quantities for each material in each BOM level. We will also see the number of issues and the number of sources of supply available for each material; therefore, we will be able to identify on exactly which BOM level we have a capacity issue. Figure 12.11 shows the details of the multilevel material simulation; here, we highlighted the material with two capacity issues.

In the multilevel material simulation, we also have options to resolve the capacity issues for the top-level and lower-level materials. For materials with several sources of supply (and thus with several valid production versions), we can select the **Change Source of Supply** option, and we will be able to choose a different production version. When choosing this option, a pop-up screen will be shown (see Figure 12.12), in which we can distribute the forecasted quantity among the different production versions available for the selected material. Here we will find an overview of the available

12 Predictive Material and Resource Planning

capacity for each source of supply and a proposed distribution of the forecast quantity among the different production versions. Also, we can manually define the quantity distribution or select the **Adopt Proposal** option to automatically adopt the proposed distribution.

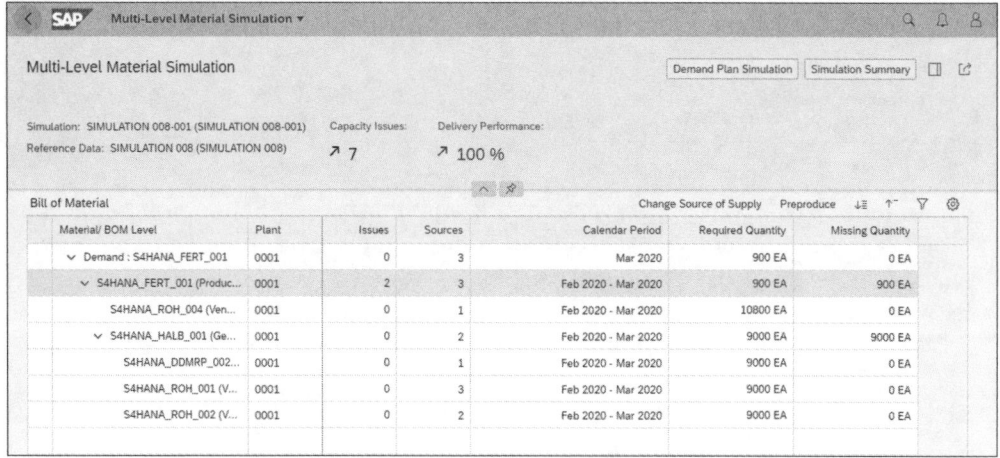

Figure 12.11 Multilevel Material Simulation

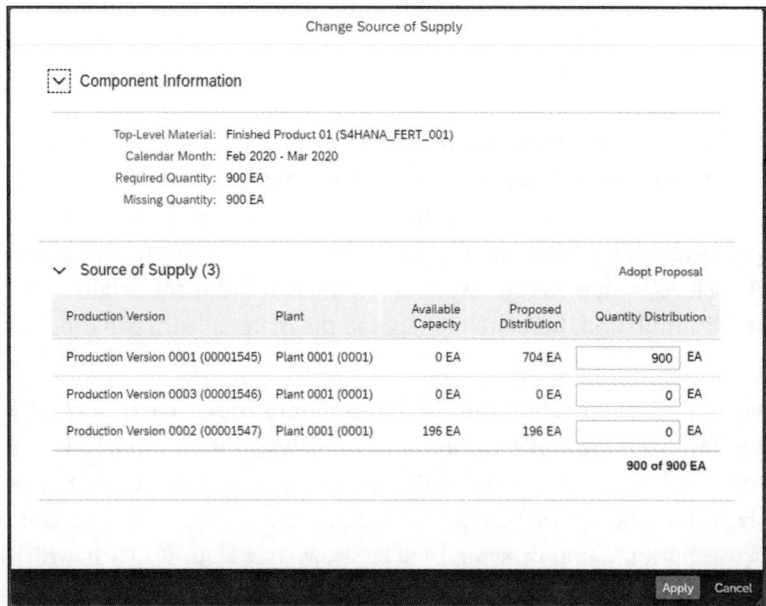

Figure 12.12 The Change Source of Supply Pop-up

Another alternative to resolve existing capacity issues is to preproduce a component—or start the production ahead of the requirement date—in order to distribute the load in the work center across multiple buckets. When selecting this option, the system will show a pop-up screen in which we can find the component information, such as the required and missing quantities, the competing top-level materials for the period, and the slots for preproduction of the component, as shown in Figure 12.13. pMRP will automatically determine and propose the buckets with available capacity and will show the **Available Capacity** and the **Proposed Distribution** values for those buckets. Again, we can manually distribute the quantities or choose the **Adopt Proposal** option to automatically adopt the proposed distribution.

Figure 12.13 Preproduction of a Component

In any of the main screens of the Process pMRP Simulations app, we can find the **Simulation Summary** button, which will provide an overview of all the changes made while processing the simulation when clicked. The following change categories will be shown:

- **Changes in Demand**
- **Changes in Capacity**
- **Preproduction**

- Changes in Source of Supply
- Unresolved Issues
- Disregarded Capacity Issues

Figure 12.14 shows the **Simulation Summary** screen, with tabs for the different change categories and the total number in each category. This table can be also exported to a spreadsheet so that the forecast changes can be further discussed and validated.

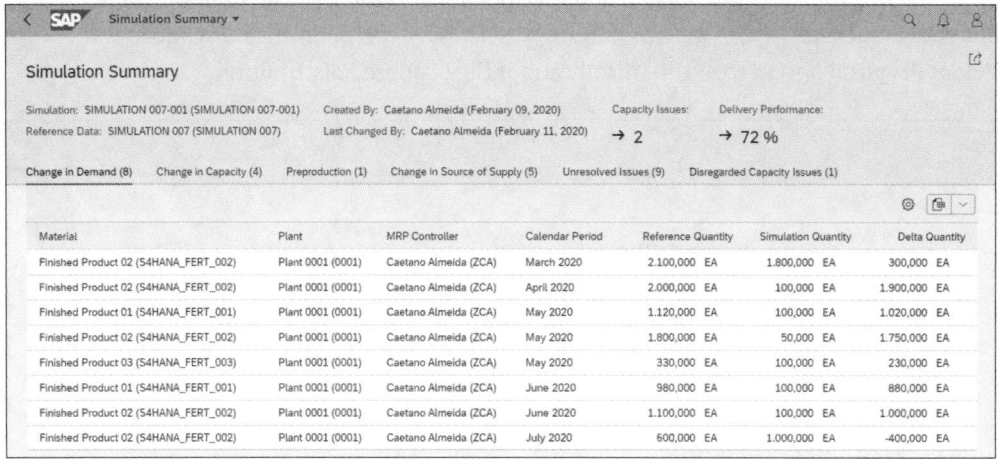

Figure 12.14 Simulation Summary

12.4 Releasing the pMRP Simulation

Once we are done with the simulation and we have identified and resolved all the capacity issues, or if we decided to disregard them, we can release the pMRP simulation.

This release is made by clicking the **Release** button in the initial screen of the Process pMRP Simulations app. When this button is clicked, the system will ask us to confirm whether the simulation should be released, as shown in Figure 12.15.

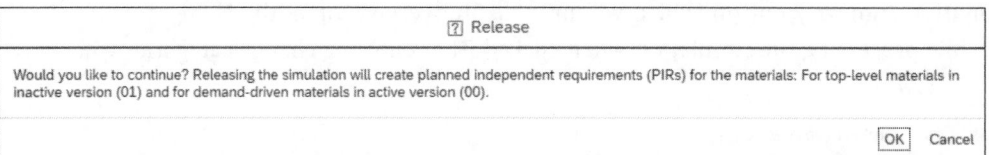

Figure 12.15 Confirming a pMRP Simulation Release

When a simulation is released, the forecast will be transferred to the top-level materials in inactive version 01, even if the simulation was created with active PIRs referenced.

As discussed in the previous chapter, as of SAP S/4HANA 1909, DDMRP can also consider PIRs for the buffer calculation, meaning that the pMRP simulation results will be an input for DDMRP. When the simulation is released, if there are DDMRP materials in the BOM's lower levels, then PIRs will be created for DDMRP materials even if there was no PIR for those materials before the simulation creation. Therefore, the buffer calculation will take into consideration any demand variability that can be anticipated by the forecast.

> **Tip**
> The inactive PIRs created by DDMRP can be copied to the active version in Transaction MD70. Alternatively, we can simply check the **Active** flag in Transaction MD62 in order to activate it.

Once the simulation release is finished, we can access the logs by clicking the **Show Log** button (see Figure 12.5). Once the simulation is finally released, the pMRP process is finished and we can start over with the creation of a new simulation.

12.5 Summary

pMRP was released in SAP S/4HANA 1909 and brings simulation capabilities that can be used to validate a forecast from a work center capacity point of view. With pMRP, we can make changes to the forecasted quantities and evaluate the results, test different sources of supply for our products, and consider the preproduction of certain critical products in order to avoid a capacity overload in a specific month.

The features introduced by pMRP can be compared with the LTP features, but as we saw in this chapter, the SAP Fiori-based user interface is much more intuitive than the old LTP transactions.

From a configuration point of view, the effort to use pMRP is minimal: it will leverage the existing MRP settings and can therefore be used virtually out of the box by companies that are already using MRP.

In this first release, we are still missing some features that are available in LTP, but further improvements should be delivered in the future. According to the roadmap published by SAP, the pMRP features delivered in this first release will still be improved and the existing SAP Fiori applications should be advanced in the next release. The long-term vision for pMRP is that it should support master data change simulations in the future.

Chapter 13
Administering MRP

MRP requires some administration and housekeeping effort to ensure that the MRP results will be consistent and that we always achieve optimal performance during MRP execution. In this chapter, we will discuss what this entails.

So far, we have discussed the MRP-related master data, the required configuration, and the transactions that we use to run and evaluate MRP. We also reviewed the main MRP-related functionalities, so we should be ready to implement and use MRP. However, after we go live with MRP in a system, some routine activities are important to ensure that the MRP results will always be consistent and that we can achieve optimal performance during the MRP run. Unforeseen problems may arise that we must troubleshoot and resolve.

In Section 13.1, we will go through the main MRP housekeeping activities, and in Section 13.2 we will cover basic troubleshooting of MRP issues, including the most common inconsistencies that we may observe in MRP transactions. Finally, in Section 13.3 we will discuss how to optimize the performance of both classic MRP and MRP Live.

13.1 Housekeeping MRP

Housekeeping activities are actions that should be performed periodically to keep the system (or the "house") clean. Together they can prevent inconsistencies, avoid excessive growth of database tables, get rid of old and irrelevant data, and so on.

In this section, we will suggest several housekeeping activities that should be performed by either system administrators or power users.

13.1.1 Keeping the Planning File Consistent

As we noted in Chapter 3, whenever an MRP type is set for a material, the planning file entry is created. Whenever this material is included as a component in a BOM, the low-level code is updated in the planning file. In an ideal world, all these planning file updates should happen smoothly, and we would always have a perfectly clean planning file. In real life, however, this is not always the case. The planning file may be updated when a component is included on a BOM, but not be decreased when the same component is deleted from the BOM, so we might end up with a planning file that is at least outdated. Besides that, we may also get inconsistencies in the planning file due to unknown circumstances.

Therefore, it is a best practice to periodically run a planning file consistency check. We do not need to run it on daily basis, but it is recommended to run the check from time to time to ensure that the planning file is consistent and thus avoid problems in the MRP run. Usually, it is enough to run the consistency check once a month, but if BOMs are updated frequently, then we can run it on a weekly basis.

In SAP ERP, a separate transaction and report were used to check the consistency of the planning file. In SAP S/4HANA, we still have a separate transaction (Transaction PPH_MDRE), but it will be used to set up a background job for report PPH_SETUP_MRPRECORDS—the same report used to create the planning file entries before we run MRP for the first time.

A good housekeeping practice is to use Transaction PPH_MDRE to schedule periodic execution of the planning file consistency check. Figure 13.1 shows the selection screen of report PPH_SETUP_MRPRECORDS, which is executed by the background job scheduled in Transaction PPH_MDRE.

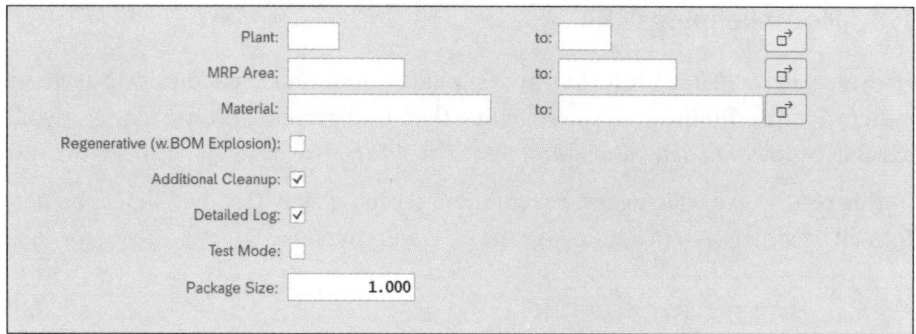

Figure 13.1 Report PPH_SETUP_MRPRECORDS

As shown, the **Additional Cleanup** flag should be selected when running a consistency check because the system will check for orphan planning file entries for which the material no longer exists.

Another recommended housekeeping activity that is related to the planning file entries is to set the MRP type to ND for a material whenever this material becomes obsolete or whenever the deletion flag or a status that prevents the MRP run is set.

The planning file entry is not deleted when the deletion flag or a status that forbids the MRP run is set, so materials will still be considered by MRP. During the planning run, the planning file is read and MRP will try to plan those materials, but when the deletion flag or the status is found, an error message is triggered, so those materials will not be planned.

This will not cause any major problem in the planning run, but if there are too many materials in this situation, it might negatively affect the MRP run performance because it leads to additional planning file entries and master data being read, without any planning activity executed for those materials.

Figure 13.2 shows the results of the MRP run: an error message was thrown for material S4HANA_ROH_003 because a material status prevents its usage in MRP. This error and the access to this material can be completely avoided if we simply set the MRP type to ND for this material. We should define a process within the organization to always set the MRP type to ND when setting the deletion flag or a status that prevents the MRP run for a material so that the planning file entry is deleted and this material is no longer included in the MRP run.

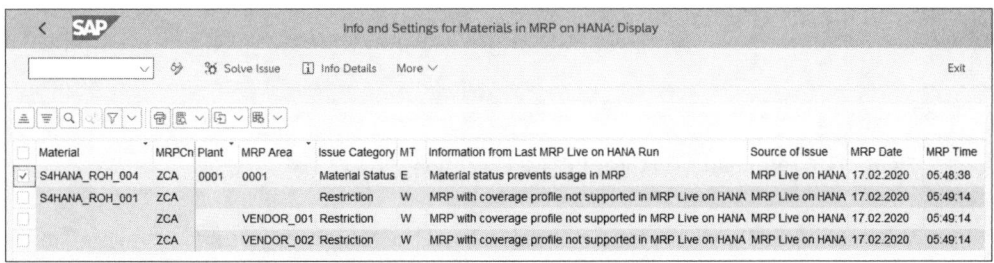

Figure 13.2 Error Triggered during the MRP Run for a Material with a Status Issue

13.1.2 Managing Background Jobs

MRP is a program essentially executed as a background job, or a series of background jobs, usually overnight. Just like any other background job, the MRP run may fail due to unforeseen circumstances. For example, we might consume all the number ranges available, or a deadlock may happen. Therefore, it is important for the power user or the system administrator to keep an eye on the MRP jobs and check for any possible termination.

We noted in Chapter 5 that the Schedule MRP Runs app can be used to schedule the MRP Live execution in the SAP Fiori launchpad. We can use this application to schedule execution, but also to check if the MRP execution was successful and if there was any termination in the background jobs.

Whenever the MRP run is terminated with an exception, the exclamation point icon will be shown in this application, as shown in Figure 13.3. After clicking the icon, we will see a detailed log that lists information about the root cause of the termination so we can prevent it from happening again.

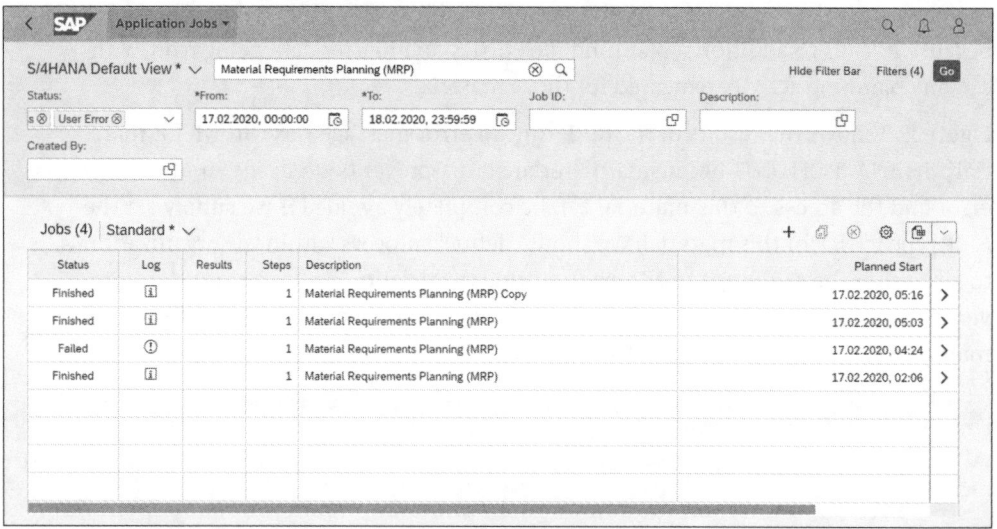

Figure 13.3 Termination in the MRP Live Execution

When using SAP GUI, we can get the details of the MRP background jobs using Transaction SM37, a transaction that is generally used by the system admin to monitor background jobs. This transaction can be used to monitor MRP Live, classic MRP, MPS, and LTP jobs: we just need to filter by the respective program in the selection screen. We can find background jobs for the following programs:

- MRP Live (program PPH_MRP_START)
- Classic MRP (program RMMRP000)

13.1 Housekeeping MRP

- MPS (program RMMPS000)
- LTP (program RMMRP010)

Transaction SM37 will show the status of the jobs scheduled for those programs, and whenever one of these background jobs fails, we will find the status **Canceled**, as shown in Figure 13.4. We can access the job details by double-clicking the job's line and accessing the job log to see what caused the job termination. Often, when an MRP background job is terminated, we can find a short dump in Transaction ST22, which may provide more details about the root cause of the termination.

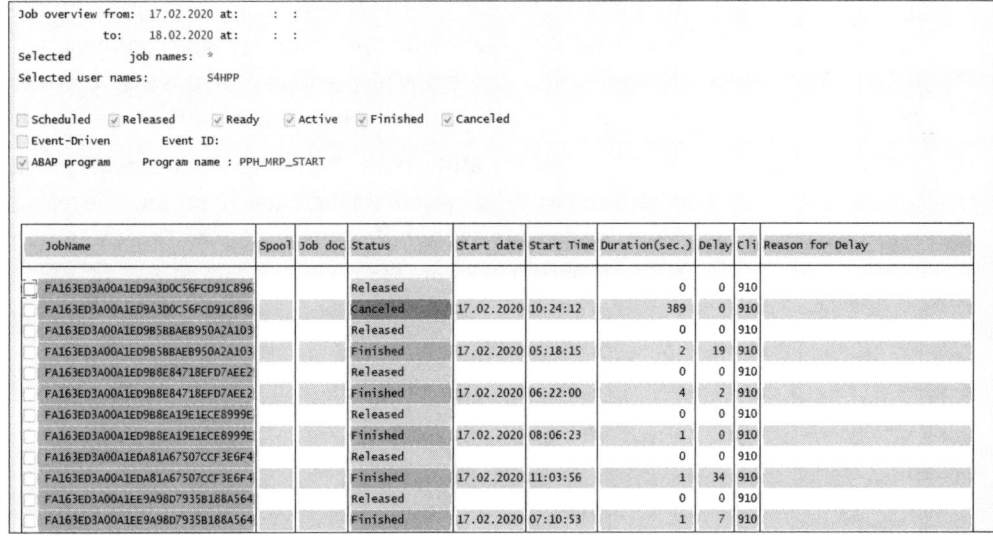

Figure 13.4 MRP Live Background Jobs

> **Tip**
> Always evaluate the MRP background jobs' total runtime to identify potential performance issues. We will see additional reports that can be used to monitor the MRP execution from a performance point of view in Section 13.3.

For classic MRP, when we check the background job details, we will find details about the material planned by accessing in the spool. For MRP Live, however, there will be no information in the spool for the background job.

463

13 Administering MRP

We noted in Chapter 6 that report RMMDERRO can be used to identify errors for specific materials when we are using classic MRP. For MRP Live, we can use Transaction MD_MRP_FORCE_CLASSIC or the Display MRP Master Data Issues app.

13.1.3 Deleting Old MRP Lists

For companies using classic MRP, another good housekeeping practice is to periodically delete the old MRP Lists using Transaction MD08 or report RMMDKP01.

Recall that the MRP List is a screenshot of the planning results taken when MRP is executed. If a material becomes obsolete, we will usually set a status that prevents the material from being planned by MRP, the deletion flag, and we also recommend setting the MRP type to ND to prevent it from being planned again. In this case, it makes no sense to keep the MRP List; we can delete those unnecessary MRP Lists.

In Transaction MD08, we can select the MRP Lists to be deleted for a specific plant, MRP area, or MRP controller, and we can also define a limit date to prevent the recent MRP Lists from being deleted and ensure we only delete the old ones. Those selection fields in Transaction MD08 are shown in Figure 13.5.

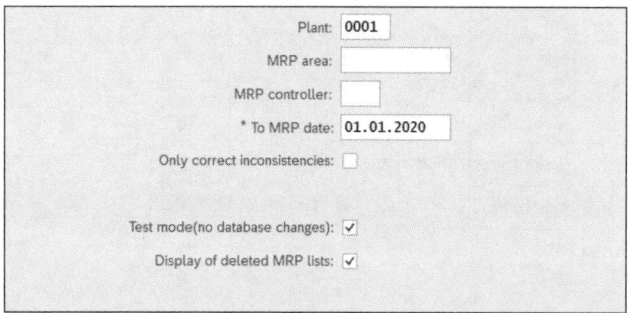

Figure 13.5 Deleting MRP Lists with Transaction MD08

13.2 Troubleshooting MRP

As we pointed out in the previous section, some problems may arise during the MRP run. The most common issues are a background job not getting completed, a material not being correctly planned, or a replenishment element not being generated as expected. We may also observe performance issues during the MRP run or inconsistencies for planning elements that may affect the MRP results, such as an already completed planning element still being displayed in the Stock/Requirements List.

464

In this section, we will cover the most common errors that arise during or after the MRP run and discuss solutions to those issues. The idea is to use this section as a troubleshooting guide for the MRP-related issues we may find in SAP S/4HANA.

13.2.1 Material Not Planned

The most common issue reported by MRP planners is that a material was not planned by MRP. In this case, we need to identify whether a material was not planned at all, if it was planned but an error occurred during the planning run, or if it was planned and a replenishment element was not generated as expected by the user.

The first check is to ensure that all the MRP background jobs finished successfully, as we explained earlier in this chapter. If there was any problem during the background MRP execution and it was *not* completed, we can check the MRP job logs and look for any short dump that may have happened during the MRP execution. If the MRP background job *was* completed, we need to find out when this material was planned for the last time and if there was any error in the planning run for this material.

When using MRP Live, we can identify if a material was planned and if an error happened when planning this material using Transaction MD_MRP_FORCE_CLASSIC. If we leave the **Only Materials with Issues** flag empty in the selection screen, this transaction will show all the materials (instead of only those with an issue during the planning run); we will then be able to tell exactly when a material was planned for the last time. We will be able to tell if the material was planned successfully, if an issue happened during the planning run, or if it was not planned by MRP. The example in Figure 13.6 shows that material S4HANA_ROH_004 was not planned because a material status prevents its usage in MRP, while other materials were planned, either in MRP Live on SAP HANA or with the classic MRP logic.

Material	MRPCn	Plant	MRP Area	Issue Category	MT	Information from Last MRP Live on HANA Run	Source of Issue	MRP Date	MRP Time
S4HANA_SC_001	ZCA	0001	0001	Information	I	Successfully planned	MRP Live on HANA	19.02.2020	05:11:57
S4HANA_ROH_006	ZCA			Information	I	Successfully planned	MRP Live on HANA	19.02.2020	17:40:32
S4HANA_ROH_005	ZCA			Information	I	Successfully planned	MRP Live on HANA	19.02.2020	05:13:22
S4HANA_ROH_004	ZCA			Material Stat..	E	Material status prevents usage in MRP	MRP Live on HANA	19.02.2020	05:12:27
S4HANA_ROH_003	ZCA			Information	I	Successfully planned	MRP Live on HANA	19.02.2020	05:12:48
S4HANA_ROH_002	ZCA			Information	I	Successfully planned	MRP Live on HANA	19.02.2020	05:13:15
	ZCA	0002	0002	Information	I	Successfully planned	Classic MRP	25.10.2019	04:32:34
S4HANA_ROH_001	ZCA	0001	0001	Restriction	W	MRP with coverage profile not supported in MRP Live on HANA	MRP Live on HANA	19.02.2020	05:12:48
	ZCA			Information	I	Successfully planned	Classic MRP	19.02.2020	05:13:04
	ZCA		0001-0003	Information	I	Successfully planned	MRP Live on HANA	18.10.2019	17:44:08

Figure 13.6 Transaction MD_MRP_FORCE_CLASSIC

If we are using classic MRP, then we should check if a material was planned or not using the MRP List. The MRP List will tell us when a material was planned for the last time and if there was any error during the planning run for this material. Considering the same example shown in Figure 13.6, if a material status prevents the MRP run, an error message will be shown in the MRP List if this material is planned in classic MRP.

If a material was not planned, either by MRP Live or classic MRP, then we should check for the following circumstances:

- If there is a valid MRP type, but no planning file entry exists for this material, then we should run a planning file consistency check so that the planning file entry is created.
- If there is a planning file entry and the planning file's **Net Change** flag is not checked, then there was no MRP-relevant change for this material since it was planned by MRP for the last time, and this material will only be included in the next regenerative planning run. Otherwise, it will be planned by a net change planning run, after any MRP-relevant change sets the **Net Change** flag in the planning file.
- If we identify that the planning situation is not updated and the **Net Change** flag is not set in the planning file, then there might be a problem in the update of the planning file. However, this is a very rare situation and we will need to check exactly which MRP-relevant changes are not updating the planning file.
- If the planning file entry is set, but the material was not planned in the last MRP run, it might be the case that the flag was set after the last MRP execution. We can check the planning file in Transaction MD21 and compare the timestamp with the last MRP run to ensure that the planning file flag was set after the last MRP run. If this is the case, this material can be planned individually, or it should be included in the following planning run.

If these steps are checked and we still cannot find an explanation for the issue, it might be the case that the material is actually being planned by MRP, but it is not triggering the expected replenishment proposals. A good option in this case is to plan this material individually and check for any problem during the MRP execution. Transaction MD43 allows us to run MRP interactively and is a good option for troubleshooting.

If we are talking about a material that is a component of another material, we need to check if dependent requirements are actually being generated by the parent material because there could be a problem with the parent BOM explosion.

If we can see the requirements, but they are not covered, it might be due to the rescheduling check. When a rescheduling horizon is too long, MRP might be considering a firm receipt that is far in the future to cover a requirement, instead of generating a new replenishment proposal to cover it. In this case, we need to carefully check for rescheduling exceptions for firm receipts in the future.

There are also situations in which there is custom code implemented on a BAdI, or even a modification in the standard MRP code that affects the MRP results. When using classic MRP, the **BAdI Active** indicator in the MRP List header details tells us if any BAdI was called with custom code during the MRP run. Otherwise, we can check if the main MRP BAdIs are implemented and if the code can be causing the issue (see Chapter 14 for more information about the MRP BAdIs).

13.2.2 Inconsistencies

MRP is a planning tool that will read data from many different sources and many different application areas. The MRP planning elements may be sales order requirements, purchase requisitions, inspection lots, or even production planning documents such as production or process orders.

There are situations in which one of these documents may become inconsistent: something may appear as MRP-relevant when it is already closed or processed or perhaps lists the wrong quantity. Often those inconsistencies are generated by custom code implemented on a user exit or BAdI, which changes the standard SAP logic to process those documents. Sometimes it is virtually impossible to find the root cause of those inconsistencies, as they only appear after the document was already processed.

In this section, we will go through the most common inconsistencies and discuss the possible root causes and solutions for those issues.

Sales Order or Delivery Requirement

The most frequently observed inconsistency in the Stock/Requirements List is related to the sales order or delivery requirements. There are cases in which a sales order or delivery was already completely processed and should be no longer relevant to MRP, but there is still a requirement in the Stock/Requirements List and it will still be relevant to MRP.

In SAP ERP, report SDRQCR21 was used to check the consistency of sales orders and delivery requirements, but this report was replaced in SAP S/4HANA by report ATP_ VBBE_CONSISTENCY. This new report is optimized for better performance in an SAP HANA database and offers additional improvements, such as a persistent log and dynamic packaging.

When running this report, it will select all the sales requirements from table VBBE and check if they are consistent. We can use the material and the plant as selection criteria, and we can run it in simulation mode to estimate the number of inconsistent entries.

The report will select all the sales requirements according to the selection criteria; if we choose the **Display Result List** option in the selection screen, we can see a list of all the selected requirements, as shown in Figure 13.7. The header shows the total inconsistent entries, and the first column of this result list will tell us if each record is consistent or not. If the **Simulation Mode** flag is not checked, then the report execution will fix inconsistent entries.

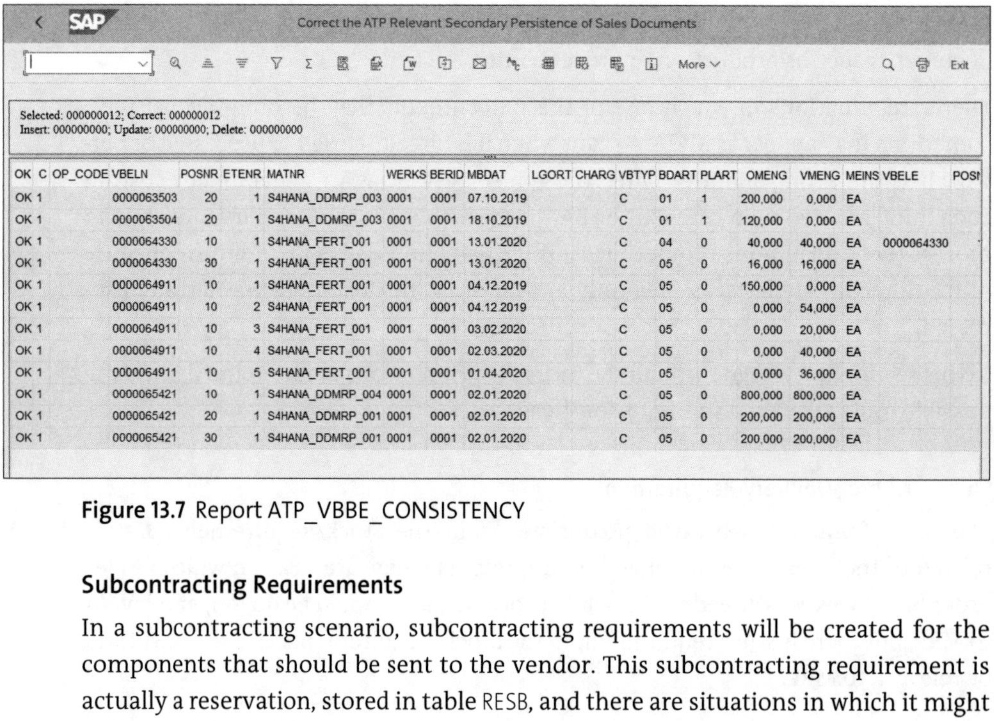

OK	C	OP_CODE	VBELN	POSNR	ETENR	MATNR	WERKS	BERID	MBDAT	LGORT	CHARG	VBTYP	BDART	PLART	OMENG	VMENG	MEINS	VBELE	POSN
OK	1		0000063503	20	1	S4HANA_DDMRP_003	0001	0001	07.10.2019			C	01	1	200,000	0,000	EA		
OK	1		0000063504	20	1	S4HANA_DDMRP_003	0001	0001	18.10.2019			C	01	1	120,000	0,000	EA		
OK	1		0000064330	10	1	S4HANA_FERT_001	0001	0001	13.01.2020			C	04	0	40,000	40,000	EA	0000064330	
OK	1		0000064330	30	1	S4HANA_FERT_001	0001	0001	13.01.2020			C	05	0	16,000	16,000	EA		
OK	1		0000064911	10	1	S4HANA_FERT_001	0001	0001	04.12.2019			C	05	0	150,000	0,000	EA		
OK	1		0000064911	10	2	S4HANA_FERT_001	0001	0001	04.12.2019			C	05	0	0,000	54,000	EA		
OK	1		0000064911	10	3	S4HANA_FERT_001	0001	0001	03.02.2020			C	05	0	0,000	20,000	EA		
OK	1		0000064911	10	4	S4HANA_FERT_001	0001	0001	02.03.2020			C	05	0	0,000	40,000	EA		
OK	1		0000064911	10	5	S4HANA_FERT_001	0001	0001	01.04.2020			C	05	0	0,000	36,000	EA		
OK	1		0000065421	10	1	S4HANA_DDMRP_004	0001	0001	02.01.2020			C	05	0	800,000	800,000	EA		
OK	1		0000065421	20	1	S4HANA_DDMRP_001	0001	0001	02.01.2020			C	05	0	200,000	200,000	EA		
OK	1		0000065421	30	1	S4HANA_DDMRP_001	0001	0001	02.01.2020			C	05	0	200,000	200,000	EA		

Figure 13.7 Report ATP_VBBE_CONSISTENCY

Subcontracting Requirements

In a subcontracting scenario, subcontracting requirements will be created for the components that should be sent to the vendor. This subcontracting requirement is actually a reservation, stored in table RESB, and there are situations in which it might become inconsistent. The SAP-provided report RM06C020 finds and corrects inconsistencies for subcontracting requirements.

According to SAP Note 115899 (Correction Report for Subcontractor Requirements), the report can be used to fix the following inconsistencies:

- A schedule line of a subcontract order or a subcontractor scheduling agreement or a subcontract requisition has no reservation number that refers to dependent requirements.
- A schedule line or a purchase requisition refers to a reservation that does not exist.
- A schedule line or a purchase requisition refers to a reservation. However, the reservation belongs to another schedule line or purchase requisition.
- A subcontracting requirement has no reference to a planned order, a subcontract requisition, a subcontract order, or a subcontractor scheduling agreement.
- A subcontracting requirement refers to an existing planned order, a nonexistent purchase requisition, or a schedule line.
- A subcontracting requirement refers to a planned order, a purchase requisition, or a schedule line that has another reservation number.
- A subcontracting requirement of a schedule line remains open though the schedule line has already been fully supplied or the item is deleted or marked as delivery completed.
- A subcontracting requirement of a purchase requisition remains open though the purchase requisition is ordered in full, deleted, or marked as completed.
- A subcontracting requirement belongs to an outline agreement requisition (and is therefore never completed).

The selection screen of report RM06C020 is shown in Figure 13.8, where the **Selected Pos/Scheduling Agreements**, **Selected Purchase Requisitions**, or **Selected Reservations** flag determines that the related document should be checked. If we keep any of those flags checked but do not enter the respective document numbers, this report will run a full scan in the respective database table, which may take a long time. By selecting the **Direct Database Update** flag, the system will not only look for inconsistencies, but also fix them.

13 Administering MRP

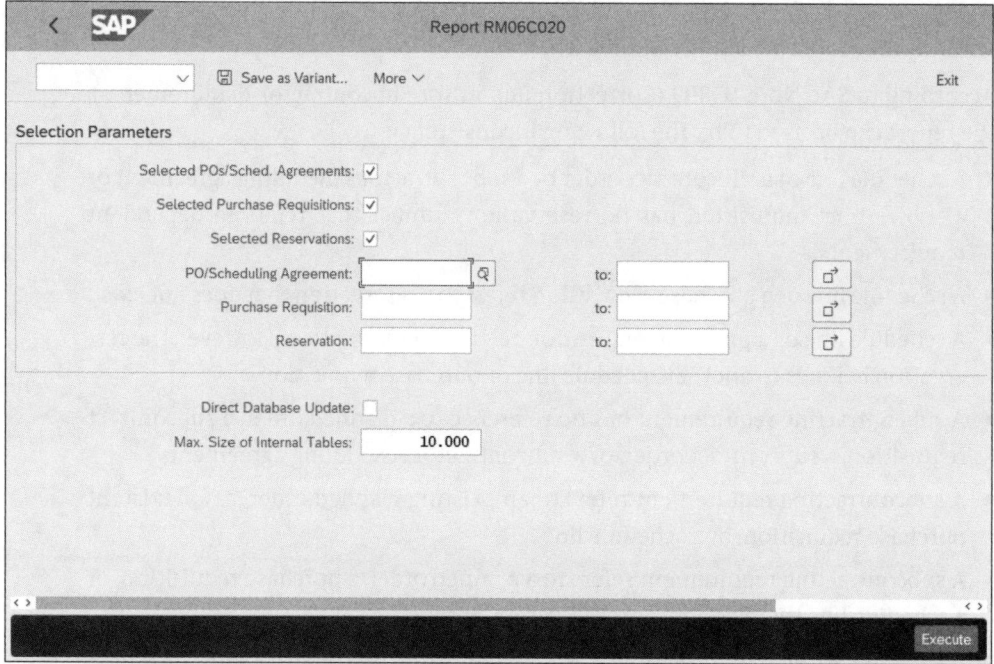

Figure 13.8 Report RM06C020 Selection Screen

> **Tip**
> Sometimes we can find an inconsistent subcontracting requirement in the Stock/Requirements List. When we try to run this report using the requisition or the purchase order number, no inconsistency is found. In those cases, we need to search for the reservation number in the Stock/Requirements List and use it as an input for the report, with the **Selected Reservations** flag checked.

Dependent Requirements

Planned order-dependent requirements can also become inconsistent sometimes. Usually, this happens when there is a problem during the planned order conversion and it is unexpectedly terminated. The planned order is then converted to a production order, but the dependent requirements are not deleted, and the result is that we will find orphaned dependent requirements that point to a planned order that no longer exists.

Another possible cause of this issue is the deletion of a planned order from a custom program with a direct database update in table `PLAF`, without the deletion of the respective dependent requirements. The planned order deletion in a custom program should be always carried out with the `BAPI_PLANNEDORDER_DELETE` BAPI to prevent this kind of inconsistency.

When a dependent requirement becomes inconsistent, we will see it in the Stock/Requirements List, but we will not be able to delete or open the parent planned order, which no longer exists.

> **Tip**
> Often this issue is related to a `COMMIT WORK` statement being incorrectly triggered from a user exit or BAdI during the conversion to production version. Therefore, if the issue is observed very frequently, custom code implemented in exits or BAdIs should be reviewed.

Although this inconsistency is very common, a report to fix it is not delivered in the SAP S/4HANA system by default. If we find this inconsistency in an SAP S/4HANA system, we should implement SAP Note 2047547 (MD04, MD05: Dependent Requirement without Planned Order), which runs the correction report ZCHECKRESB1.

We can provide the reservation number as an input parameter to the report in order to check and fix a specific requirement, or run it without the reservation number so that it checks the entire table `RESB` for inconsistencies. We can also run the report in test mode just to find the inconsistencies or without the test mode to find and fix the database inconsistencies.

Repetitive Manufacturing-Dependent Requirements

When the backflush is posted for a repetitive manufacturing planned order, the goods issue of components is also posted, and they are consumed from stock. There are situations in which this goods issue fails and the system generates a reprocessing record, identified as an NProc record in the Stock/Requirements List. This NProc record ensures that this requirement is still being considered by MRP though it is not yet processed in Transaction COGI or MF47.

This is a very common situation in repetitive manufacturing, and we usually see NProc requirements for components, but they can also become inconsistent. When a record becomes inconsistent, we will usually see error message RM887 (Changed

REM Profile Regarding Generation of Post Processing Records) when trying to process the NProc record.

When the NProc record can be found in Transaction MF47 or COGI, but it cannot be processed, this is an inconsistency that can be corrected by report ZINCON_REPROC. We will find this report in SAP Note 383141 (RM887, RM757: Collect. Note Inconsistent Postprocessing Recs), which also includes additional information about the record. When error RM887 is observed in Transaction MFBF, the report should be executed for the components, not for the parent material.

There is another possible inconsistency for NProc requirements that happens when the record cannot be found in Transaction COGI or MF47. This kind of NProc requirement is considered a lost reprocessing record, and a different report is required for fixing the issue. Report ZRMBF06 in SAP Note 95307 (Deletion Report for 'Lost' Reprocessing Records) can be used to fix this inconsistency.

Reservations

Production and maintenance order reservations may also become inconsistent and keep appearing in the Stock/Requirements List after the order is completed or the reservation deleted.

For a production order, usually the order was already deleted or completed, and a component reservation still appears in the Stock/Requirements List because the deletion indicator was not set in the table.

If the order status is **Technically Completed**, we can revoke the technical completion, save the order, and then try to set it again so that the deletion indicator can be set by the system. If it is no longer possible to revoke the technical completion, we can use report ZPSFC099, provided in SAP Note 2304812 (Order Reservations in Deleted or [Technically] Completed Orders Are Still Active), to fix the issue.

A very similar inconsistency can be observed for maintenance orders, but then the report used to fix those inconsistencies will be different. For a maintenance order, we can use report ZDELFLGINRES, provided in SAP Note 600151 (Deletion Indicator in Reservation Not Set if Status Is DLT).

Purchase Orders, Inbound Deliveries, or Shipping Notifications

This is a very broad topic: many different inconsistencies may affect purchasing documents with an incorrect quantity in the Stock/Requirements List or those that keep appearing when they are no longer relevant to MRP.

This kind of inconsistency in purchasing documents is usually related to table EKET, EKES, or EKBE; it happens because the **Quantity Reduced for MRP** field (DABMG) was not correctly updated when the document was processed. There are many different issues and inconsistencies related to this field in purchasing documents; for these, SAP Note 2044484 (Troubleshoot to EKET, EKES, EKBE Table Inconsistencies) lists these inconsistencies and the solution for each one. According to this SAP Note, the following issues can be observed in the Stock/Requirements List:

- More than one line appears for a purchasing document in the Stock/Requirements List (Transaction MD04).
- The confirmation's MRP-relevant quantity was not reduced, so MRP still calculates with it.
- The MRP element POitem is still visible in Transaction MD04 after posting inbound delivery.
- The MRP element ShpgNt is still visible in Transaction MD04 after posting goods receipt.
- There is a negative quantity in Transaction MD04 even after goods receipt is posted.
- The receipt quantity in Transaction MD04 is inconsistent from purchase order history.

Another inconsistency related to purchasing documents that might also be observed in the Stock/Requirements List is related to a purchase requisition that was already converted to a purchase order, but keeps appearing in the Stock/Requirements List and is still relevant to MRP. This inconsistency can be fixed with report RM06HL04, which is already available in SAP S/4HANA, so we do not need to implement any SAP Note to get it.

13.2.3 MRP Live Support Functions

MRP Live has a completely different architecture compared to classic MRP.

Whereas classic MRP is fully executed in ABAP and we simply type "/H" to debug the ABAP code in the case of an error, MRP Live runs mostly on the SAP HANA database layer, so it is not so easy to troubleshoot an error. MRP Live terminations will usually trigger a short dump with abort message PPH_MRP 019, which often does not provide enough information to help us identify the root cause of the issue.

13 Administering MRP

However, MRP Live has some hidden support features that can help us find the root cause and resolve problems related to MRP Live. These support functions were introduced by SAP Note 2668805 (MD01n: Support Functions for MRP Live). In the latest SAP S/4HANA releases, however, we can find these support features in the initial support package, so we do not need to implement this SAP Note.

To access the support functions, we open Transaction MD01N, type "support" in the command field (see Figure 13.9), and then press Enter. A pop-up screen displays a list of all the possible support functions available for MRP Live, as shown in Figure 13.10. Each of these buttons will trigger a different support function. We will go through these features to explain how each one can help us troubleshoot MRP Live.

The **List MRP Classes** support function shows a list of all the MRP Live classes and all the MRP Live BAdIs implemented, with the BAdIs appearing at the top of the list. This list will be useful to help us identify whether there is any custom code that may be affecting the standard MRP Live execution and causing any problems.

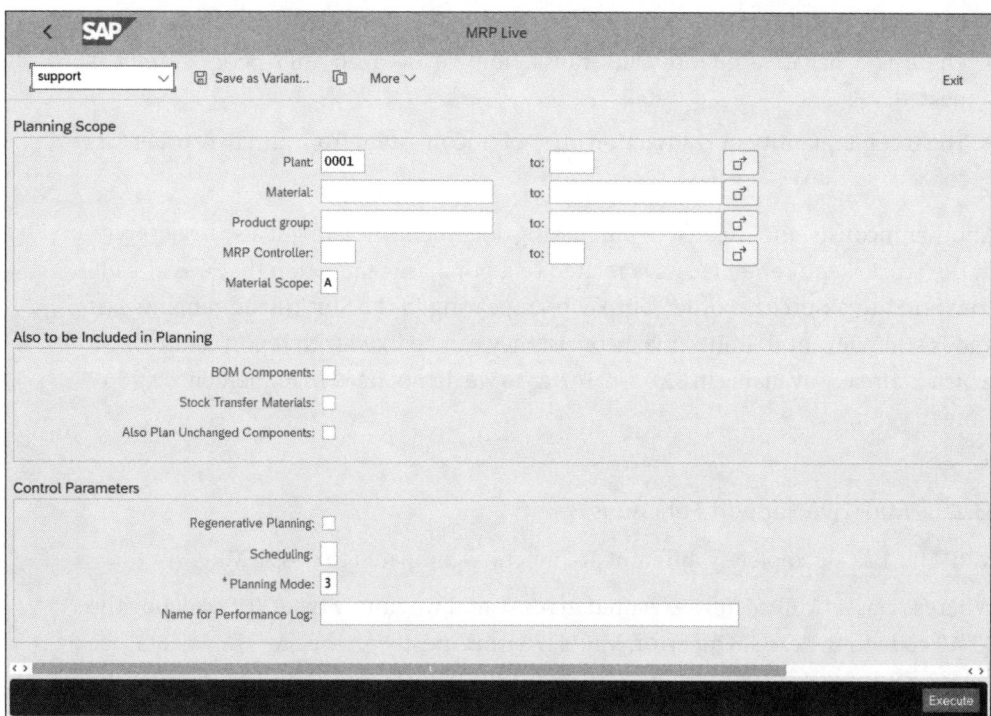

Figure 13.9 Accessing the MRP Live Support Functions

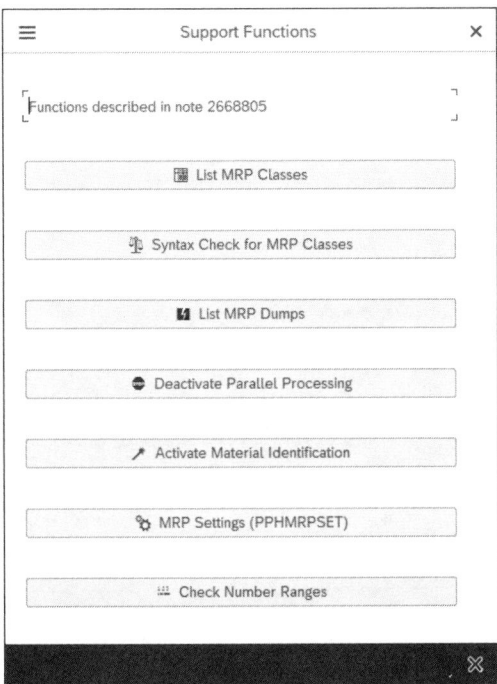

Figure 13.10 MRP Live Support Functions

The **Syntax Check for MRP Classes** support function runs a consistency check in all the MRP classes. Whenever we implement a correction SAP Note relevant for MRP Live, it may require several dependent SAP Notes; if they are not all correctly implemented, it may cause syntax errors in the MRP Live classes. A syntax error can lead to a dump during the MRP Live execution, and with this syntax check, we can identify any possible errors in the MRP Live classes. Figure 13.11 shows the results of the syntax check, where the last column shows if it was successful or if there was any error in a class.

The **List MRP Dumps** support function shows all the MRP Live–related short dumps that happened in the last two days. These dumps will be shown in Transaction ST22, where we can select a specific dump and check the details to learn what caused the dump.

13 Administering MRP

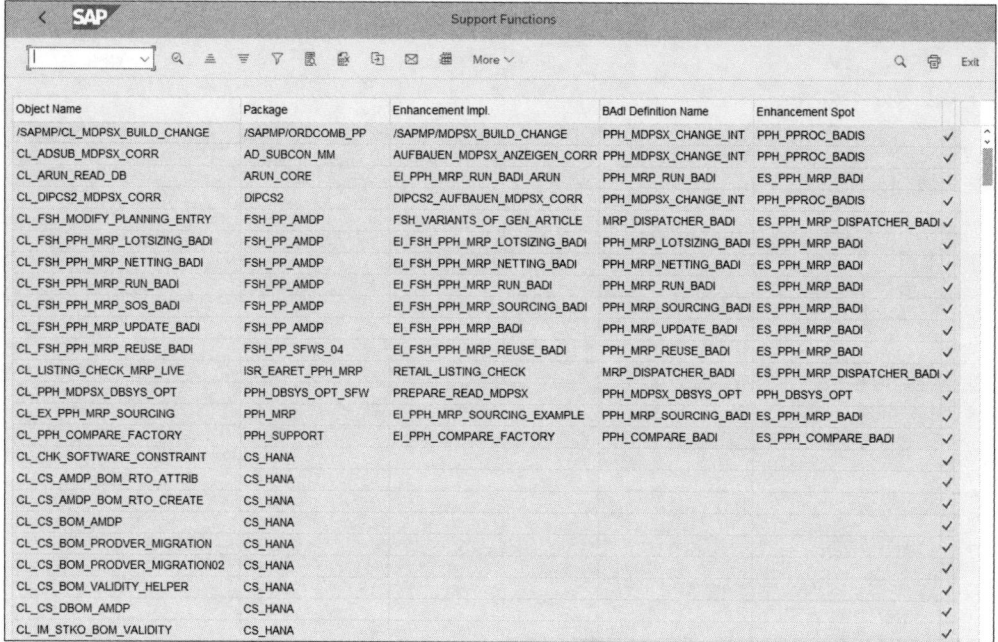

Figure 13.11 Syntax Check for MRP Classes

Often, when there is a short dump in MRP Live, we will find two short dumps happening at the same time. Usually, the first dump is a termination with runtime error MESSAGE_TYPE_X and error message PPH 019, while the second dump may be a termination with the runtime error AMDP_EXECUTION_FAILED. Both dumps are related and should be analyzed, as they provide useful information for troubleshooting. Figure 13.12 shows an example where this support function has been used and both dumps can be seen in Transaction ST22.

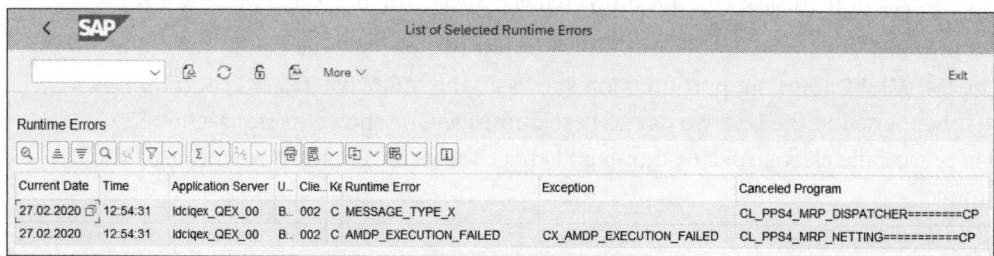

Figure 13.12 MRP Live Short Dumps in Transaction ST22

The **Deactivate Parallel Processing** support function can be used to deactivate the internal MRP Live parallelization. Even though the parallelization will improve the MRP Live performance, it makes very difficult for troubleshooting an issue using the debugger. Classic MRP offers a parameter where we can define if parallel processing will be used or not, but MRP Live uses it by default, so we should use this support function to deactivate it.

> **Tip**
> We can also deactivate the parallel processing using directly the command DEBUG in the command prompt.

Through the **Activate Material Identification** support function, MRP Live will try to identify one or more materials that will lead to a short dump. Materials that are causing the dump will be shown after the MRP Live execution, and an entry will be created for those materials in table PPHDBVMSET, with error message 227. For a background planning run, those materials should be shown also in the job log.

> **Tip**
> We can activate the material identification by typing MATERIAL_IDENTIFICATION directly in the command prompt.

The **MRP Settings (PPHMRPSET)** option will show us the contents of table PPHMRPSET, which holds the MRP technical settings. We can change technical settings, such as the size of packages for parallel processing, maximum number of locks, or CPU utilization, in order to improve MRP Live performance or prevent issues such as excessive consumption of system resources. We will go through these technical settings in more detail later in this section.

Finally, the **Check Number Ranges** support function shows an overview of the MRP Live–related number ranges. The number range consumption can lead to issues even in classic MRP, where MRP is terminated if we reach the warning percentage defined for the number range object. We will also have similar issues in MRP Live. Therefore, we can use this support function to evaluate if the number range intervals are healthy or if maintenance is required to avoid problems during MRP Live execution. Figure 13.13 shows the MRP Live–related number ranges overview that is displayed when this support function is called.

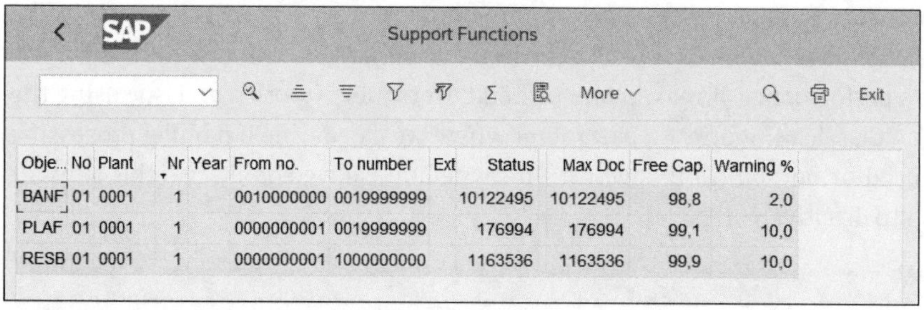

Obje...	No	Plant	Nr	Year	From no.	To number	Ext	Status	Max Doc	Free Cap.	Warning %
BANF	01	0001	1		0010000000	0019999999		10122495	10122495	98,8	2,0
PLAF	01	0001	1		0000000001	0019999999		176994	176994	99,1	10,0
RESB	01	0001	1		0000000001	1000000000		1163536	1163536	99,9	10,0

Figure 13.13 MRP Live Number Ranges Check

13.3 Improving MRP Performance

MRP is essentially executed as a background job to process large chunks of data. It usually plans a large number of materials, and for each material, it must read information from many different tables and generate replenishment elements. From a technical perspective, this results in many selects, updates, and insertions on the database tables, combined with complex algorithms that may lead to high consumption of CPU resources. From a performance point of view, this combination is usually not desirable; depending on the number and the complexity of plants and materials planned, MRP may even take hours to complete.

Classic MRP is a mature solution that has had a lot of performance tuning over the years, but usually there is still some room for performance improvement from a functional point of view. In contrast, MRP Live was designed to achieve optimal performance by taking advantage of the power of the SAP HANA database, but we can also find some ways to improve MRP Live's performance.

In this section, we will explain how to identify performance bottlenecks in both classic MRP and MRP Live, as well as how to avoid the most common mistakes that may lead to performance issues in MRP.

13.3.1 Classic MRP

Classic MRP is almost entirely executed in ABAP, which makes identifying and resolving possible performance issues a little bit easier. When a performance issue arises, however, the first thing that a system administrator or an ABAP consultant will do is run a performance trace; unfortunately, this is not always helpful when we are talking about MRP.

13.3 Improving MRP Performance

First, MRP usually has a long runtime and processes many different materials. Tracing the entire MRP execution is usually not possible and will not give us a lot of information. Further, recall that in SAP S/4HANA, the classic MRP design was changed to achieve better performance using an SAP HANA database, and the ABAP code in which the MRP elements were selected from the database was pushed down into the SAP HANA database level. Consequently, a performance trace in classic MRP will usually conclude that the system is spending too much time in the GET_MRP_ELEMENTS method of the CL_PPH_READ_CLASSIC class, in which all the MRP elements are selected from the database. This is not necessarily an issue because it really does take a lot of time to select everything from the database.

If we suspect a performance problem in the MRP execution, the first step of any investigation is to run report RMMDMONI, which shows an overview of the previous MRP runs and a lot of information that can be used to analyze the MRP performance. In addition to the planning parameters, this report shows, for example, the total MRP runtime, the number of materials planned, how much time was spent in each MRP step (read situation, calculate MRP, explode BOM, schedule lead time, and save results), whether time was spent on the execution of BAdIs, and the total number of replenishment elements created, deleted, and updated.

Figure 13.14 shows the latest MRP runs in report RMMDMONI and shows some of these fields. Many additional fields shown in the report cannot be seen in the figure.

> **Tip**
> Report RMMDMONI can be used not only for classic MRP, but also for MPS and for LTP.

With the MRP runtime and the total number of materials planned that we get from this report, we can determine the time spent by MRP to plan each material, thereby confirming whether there is an actual performance problem or if it is just a large number of materials being planned.

With all this information, we can isolate the performance problem to a specific MRP step and focus the performance improvement on this step. For example, if too much time is spent saving results, we might be generating too many planned orders and thus might consider a different lot-sizing procedure to reduce the number of orders generated. Or perhaps we are using planning mode 3, which deletes and recreates all the planned orders and in doing so negatively affects MRP performance.

13 Administering MRP

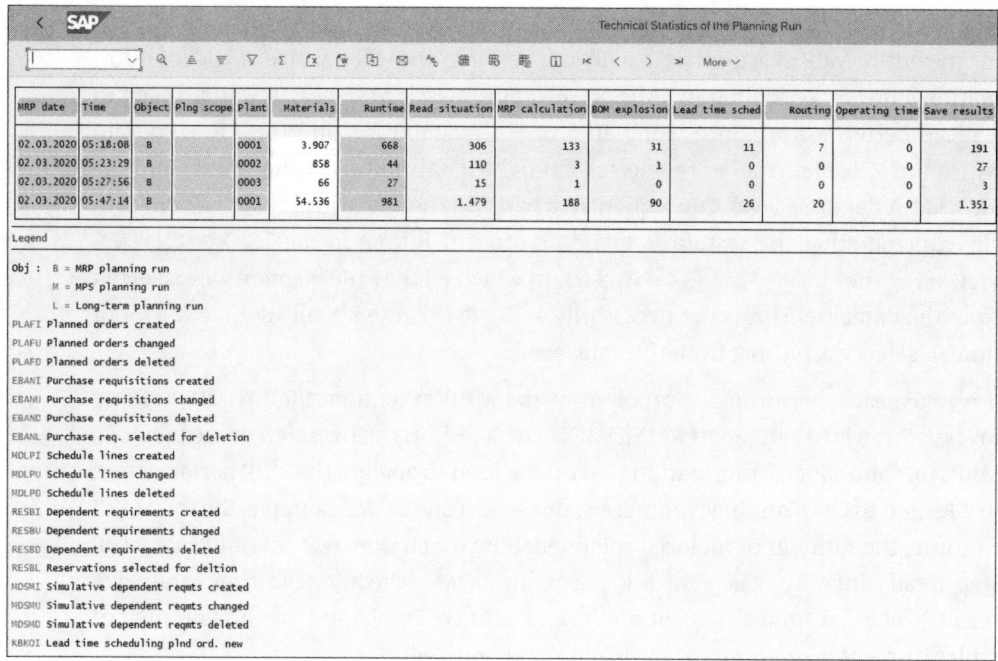

Figure 13.14 Report RMMDMONI

With this report, we can also measure the time spent by MRP to execute BAdIs, so we can have an idea of the impact of custom code on overall MRP performance.

> **Tip**
>
> Some of the MRP planning parameters, such as the planning mode or the processing key, will have an impact on MRP performance. We can use report RMMDMONI to measure the impact of each parameter on the MRP runtime and also compare the total number of materials planned and replenishment elements created, deleted, or update. For example, we can observe that the number of table RESB records deleted and created will be higher when we use planning mode 2, and this will affect the MRP performance.

But report RMMDMONI is not the only report available to help us identify performance issues in MRP. Often, a performance issue in the MRP run is caused by a few materials only, so it is important that we can identify which materials had a high runtime during the MRP run. Report RMMDPERF will provide this kind of information.

Report RMMDPERF is very similar to report RMMDMONI: it also provides the time spent in each MRP step, but the main difference is that it shows the time spent per material, not on the whole MRP run. With this information, we will be able to tell if there is a general performance issue in the MRP run or if there is a performance problem with a single material or a small group of materials only.

If we can nail down the problem to a specific material, then we can check the Stock/Requirements List to see if there are too many planning elements or if MRP needs to generate too many replenishment proposals due to the sizing procedure selected for this material. Now that we know that a specific material is causing a performance issue, we can run a single-item, single-level MRP for this material and trace the MRP execution to look for any performance issue. We should always remember that all the planning elements are read at once from the database, so we might observe in the trace that most of the time is spent in method GET_MRP_ELEMENTS of the CL_PPH_READ_CLASSIC class. The SAP HANA database administrator should be able to extract more details about each select statement and try to identify any performance bottlenecks.

Besides the already mentioned reports, the classic MRP job spool will also provide some useful information for troubleshooting performance issues in the MRP run. The job spool will show us, for example, the number of planning elements created, changed, and deleted, the ranking list of materials with the highest CPU times, and the time spent on each server (if we are using parallel processing).

Sometimes, we will identify in the spool that one of the servers is running for a longer time than the others. This means that a server is working while other servers are idle, so MRP is not utilizing the all the servers uniformly. This issue happens because MRP splits materials being planned on the same low-level code between the different servers. If a specific material or a small group of materials are taking a long time to be planned and they are all on the same package, then the server that processes this package will take a longer time to finish planning. If this is the case, we will be simply wasting time by not using all the servers uniformly.

Unfortunately, there is no solution in the standard system for this issue because MRP cannot guess which materials will take more time during the planning. But if we know in advance which materials will take a longer time (we can use report RMMDPERF to identify those materials), we can create an implementation of the MD_MRP_RUN_PARALLEL BAdI to ensure that MRP will process those materials in smaller packages and that all the servers will be kept busy during the MRP run. This BAdI allows us to define the size of the parallel processing package during the MRP run, depending on the material settings.

> **Tip**
>
> SAP delivers a sample implementation of the MD_MRP_PARALLEL BAdI that can be used as a model for a custom implementation.

By using the mentioned reports, analyzing the MRP job log, and focusing the investigation and traces on the materials with the highest runtime, we will easily find the root cause of a performance issue in classic MRP and will be able to act to improve MRP performance.

13.3.2 MRP Live

MRP Live was specially designed to optimize runtime by pushing the MRP execution into the SAP HANA database layer. However, even with MRP Live, we may observe performance issues in the MRP run or might simply want to optimize the MRP performance.

For example, as we discussed in Chapter 5, MRP Live is capable of planning most materials directly in SAP HANA, but when some specific MRP settings are used for a material, it needs to be planned with the old ABAP code—which is also used by classic MRP. (The MRP Live dispatcher is capable of automatically identifying those settings and triggers the planning in ABAP.) However, if we have too many materials being planned in ABAP, then we are not taking advantage of SAP HANA, and the MRP Live performance will not be optimal.

Therefore, the first thing that we need to do when evaluating the MRP Live performance is to check if there are too many materials being planned in classic MRP due to a restriction. We can use Transaction MD_MRP_FORCE_CLASSIC to check which materials could not be planned in SAP HANA during the MRP Live run due to a restriction. Figure 13.15 shows four materials with restrictions highlighted in Transaction MD_MRP_FORCE_CLASSIC.

Ideally, if the MRP Live performance is a major concern, we should avoid those restrictions as much as possible because we lose performance by planning too many materials with classic MRP. It is understandable that it is not always possible to remove all those restrictions; some of the settings that cause a restriction might be required, so we need to carefully evaluate case by case.

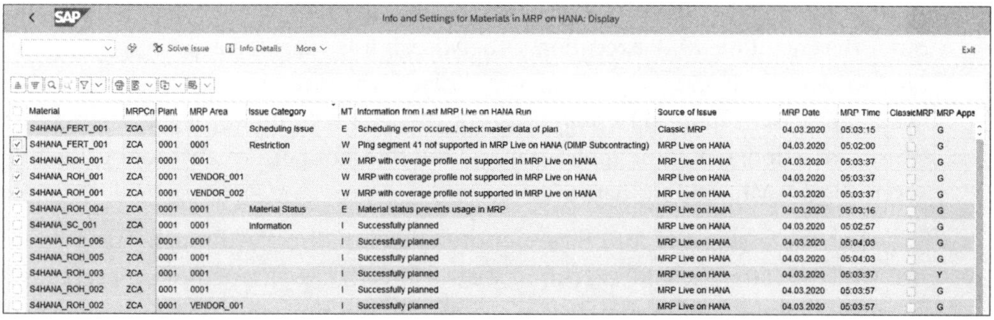

13.3 Improving MRP Performance

Figure 13.15 Restrictions in Transaction MD_MRP_FORCE_CLASSIC

If we already removed all the possible restrictions and MRP Live performance still is not optimal, we can evaluate the MRP Live results from a performance point of view. During the MRP Live execution, SAP S/4HANA will generate a performance log, which can be accessed later to evaluate possible performance issues. We can define the name of this performance log in Transaction MD01N (or in report PPH_MRP_START), using the **Name for Performance Log** field, as shown in Figure 13.16, so that we can identify it later when trying to access it.

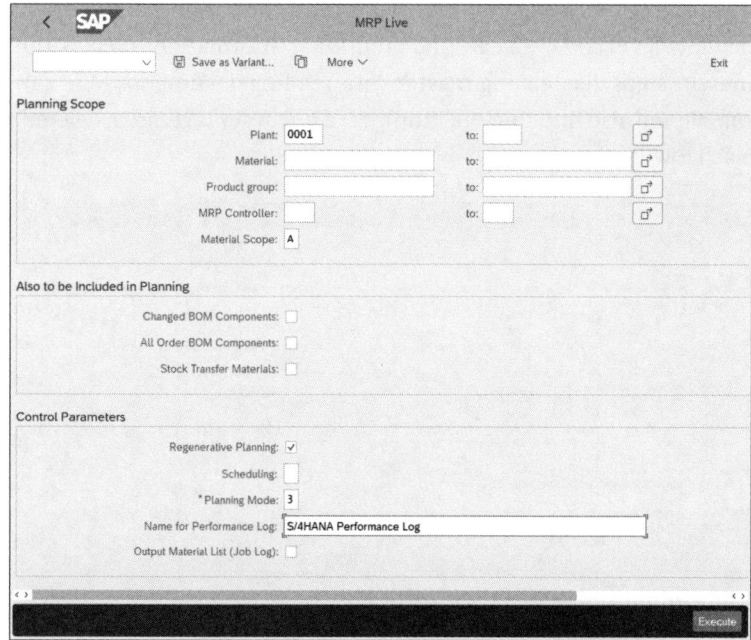

Figure 13.16 Name for Performance Log in Transaction MD01N

483

If we run MRP Live online, then the performance log will be immediately accessible after the end of the MRP execution. Otherwise, if it is executed as a background job and we want to access the performance log later, then we can use Transaction MD_MRP_PERFLOG, report PPH_MRP_PERF, or the Display MRP Key Figures app. With this transaction, report, or application, we can filter for performance logs using the user who ran MRP and the date of execution.

If we are accessing the MRP Live performance log directly through Transaction MD01N, then after the MRP execution, we will directly see a list of the low-level codes planned, the number of materials planned, and the time spent on each low-level code. For each low-level code, it is important to observe that there might be several steps, like preparation, MRP Live on SAP HANA, classic MRP, and postprocessing. In the preparation and postprocessing phases, the number of materials planned will always be zero because there is no actual materials planning. In the preparation phase, MRP will build the packages of materials that will be planned in SAP HANA or in ABAP (classic MRP), whereas the postprocessing phase is often used when MRP generates purchasing requisitions in order to complete the generated purchase requisitions.

Figure 13.17 shows the MRP Live performance log with information about all the low-level codes planned during MRP execution. Besides the number of materials and time spent on each low-level code, we can find additional information, such as the time spent on different steps like reading master data, reading documents, MRP calculation, and so on. We will also find the total number of documents created, deleted, and updated for each low-level code.

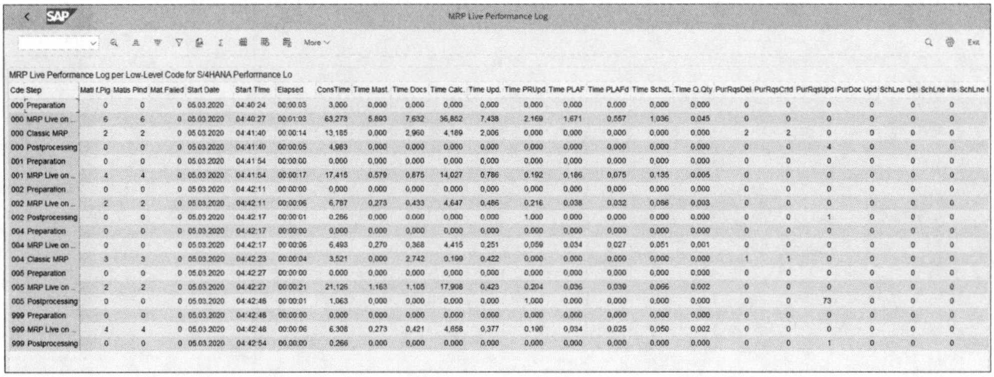

MRP Live Performance Log per Low-Level Code for S/4HANA Performance Lo

Cde Step	Matl f.Plg	Matls Plnd	Mat Failed	Start Date	Start Time	Elapsed	ConsTime	Time Mast.	Time Docs	Time Calc.	Time Upd.
000 Preparation	0	0	0	05.03.2020	04:40:24	00:00:03	3.000	0.000	0.000	0.000	0.000
000 MRP Live on ...	6	6	0	05.03.2020	04:40:27	00:01:03	63.273	5.893	7.632	36.862	7.438
000 Classic MRP	2	2	0	05.03.2020	04:41:40	00:00:14	13.185	0.000	2.960	4.189	2.006
000 Postprocessing	0	0	0	05.03.2020	04:41:40	00:00:05	4.983	0.000	0.000	0.000	0.000
001 Preparation	0	0	0	05.03.2020	04:41:54	00:00:00	0.000	0.000	0.000	0.000	0.000
001 MRP Live on ...	4	4	0	05.03.2020	04:41:54	00:00:17	17.415	0.579	0.875	14.027	0.786
002 Preparation	0	0	0	05.03.2020	04:42:11	00:00:00	0.000	0.000	0.000	0.000	0.000
002 MRP Live on ...	2	2	0	05.03.2020	04:42:11	00:00:06	6.787	0.273	0.433	4.647	0.486
002 Postprocessing	0	0	0	05.03.2020	04:42:17	00:00:01	0.286	0.000	0.000	0.000	0.000
004 Preparation	0	0	0	05.03.2020	04:42:17	00:00:00	0.000	0.000	0.000	0.000	0.000
004 MRP Live on ...	0	0	0	05.03.2020	04:42:17	00:00:06	6.493	0.270	0.368	4.415	0.251
004 Classic MRP	3	3	0	05.03.2020	04:42:23	00:00:04	3.521	0.000	2.742	0.199	0.422
005 Preparation	0	0	0	05.03.2020	04:42:27	00:00:00	0.000	0.000	0.000	0.000	0.000
005 MRP Live on ...	2	2	0	05.03.2020	04:42:27	00:00:21	21.126	1.163	1.105	17.908	0.423
005 Postprocessing	0	0	0	05.03.2020	04:42:46	00:00:01	1.063	0.000	0.000	0.000	0.000
999 Preparation	0	0	0	05.03.2020	04:42:48	00:00:00	0.000	0.000	0.000	0.000	0.000
999 MRP Live on ...	4	4	0	05.03.2020	04:42:48	00:00:06	6.308	0.273	0.421	4.658	0.377
999 Postprocessing	0	0	0	05.03.2020	04:42:54	00:00:00	0.266	0.000	0.000	0.000	0.000

Cde Step	Time PRUpd	Time PLAF	Time PLAFd	Time SchdL	Time Q.Qty	PurRqsDel	PurRqsCrtd	PurRqsUpd	PurDoc Upd	SchLne Del	SchLne Ins	SchLne U
000 Preparation	0.000	0.000	0.000	0.000	0.000	0	0	0	0	0	0	
000 MRP Live on ...	2.169	1.671	0.557	1.036	0.045	0	0	0	0	0	0	
000 Classic MRP	0.000	0.000	0.000	0.000	0.000	2	2	0	0	0	0	
000 Postprocessing	0.000	0.000	0.000	0.000	0.000	0	0	4	0	0	0	
001 Preparation	0.000	0.000	0.000	0.000	0.000	0	0	0	0	0	0	
001 MRP Live on ...	0.192	0.186	0.075	0.135	0.005	0	0	0	0	0	0	
002 Preparation	0.000	0.000	0.000	0.000	0.000	0	0	0	0	0	0	
002 MRP Live on ...	0.216	0.038	0.032	0.066	0.003	0	0	0	0	0	0	
002 Postprocessing	1.000	0.000	0.000	0.000	0.000	0	0	1	0	0	0	
004 Preparation	0.000	0.000	0.000	0.000	0.000	0	0	0	0	0	0	
004 MRP Live on ...	0.059	0.034	0.027	0.051	0.001	0	0	0	0	0	0	
004 Classic MRP	0.000	0.000	0.000	0.000	0.000	1	1	0	0	0	0	
005 Preparation	0.000	0.000	0.000	0.000	0.000	0	0	0	0	0	0	
005 MRP Live on ...	0.204	0.036	0.039	0.066	0.002	0	0	0	0	0	0	
005 Postprocessing	1.000	0.000	0.000	0.000	0.000	0	0	73	0	0	0	
999 Preparation	0.000	0.000	0.000	0.000	0.000	0	0	0	0	0	0	
999 MRP Live on ...	0.190	0.034	0.025	0.050	0.002	0	0	0	0	0	0	
999 Postprocessing	0.000	0.000	0.000	0.000	0.000	0	0	1	0	0	0	

Figure 13.17 MRP Live Performance Log

13.3 Improving MRP Performance

When analyzing the performance log, we will notice that sometimes the step in which classic MRP is executed can be faster than the MRP Live step. Recall from Chapter 5 that MRP Live was designed for optimal performance when processing large sets of materials and that classic MRP can be faster when processing a small set of materials. This can be clearly observed in the MRP Live performance log when we compare the runtime of a package with a large set of materials with that of a package with a few materials only. We can set the minimum number of materials required to send a package to be planned on SAP HANA using the MRP Live technical settings, as we will discuss later in this section.

Something that we can also observe in the performance log is that some time is spent in preparation and postprocessing for each low-level code. Because the number of low-level codes being planned has an impact on the MRP Live overall performance, checking the consistency of the planning file is always important, as mentioned earlier in this chapter, to ensure that the low-level codes are updated.

In the Display MRP Key Figures app, we will find similar information about past MRP Live runs, as well as information about any termination that happened during the MRP execution. Figure 13.18 shows the initial screen of this application, where we can select a specific MRP Live execution and drill down to see more details.

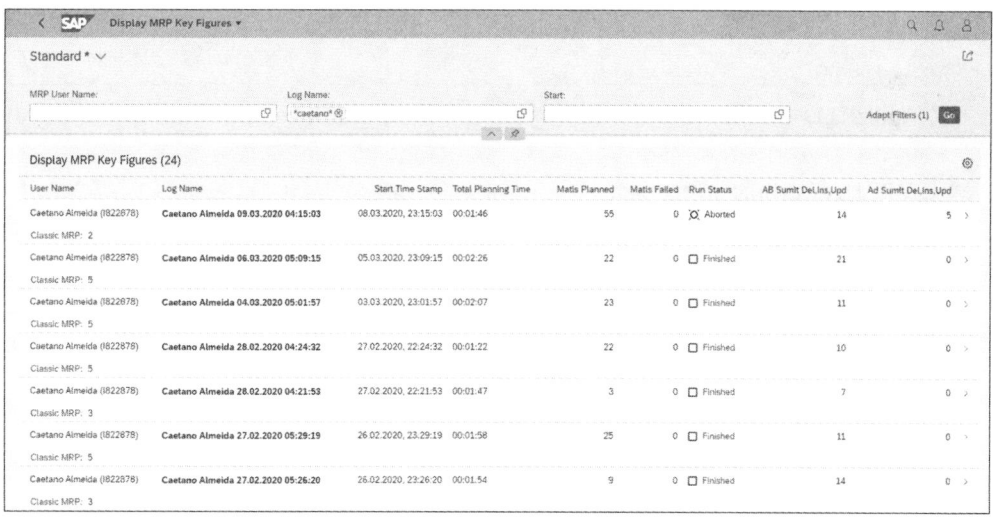

Figure 13.18 The Display MRP Key Figures App

When selecting one of the MRP Live executions, we will see details, such as the **Low-Level Code Steps** and **All MRP Live Steps** sections, as shown in Figure 13.19. We can still select each of those low-level codes or steps and drill down to see more details, such as the duration and the number of planning elements created. We also have the **Run History** tab, where we will see a graphical comparison of this MRP Live batch with past executions.

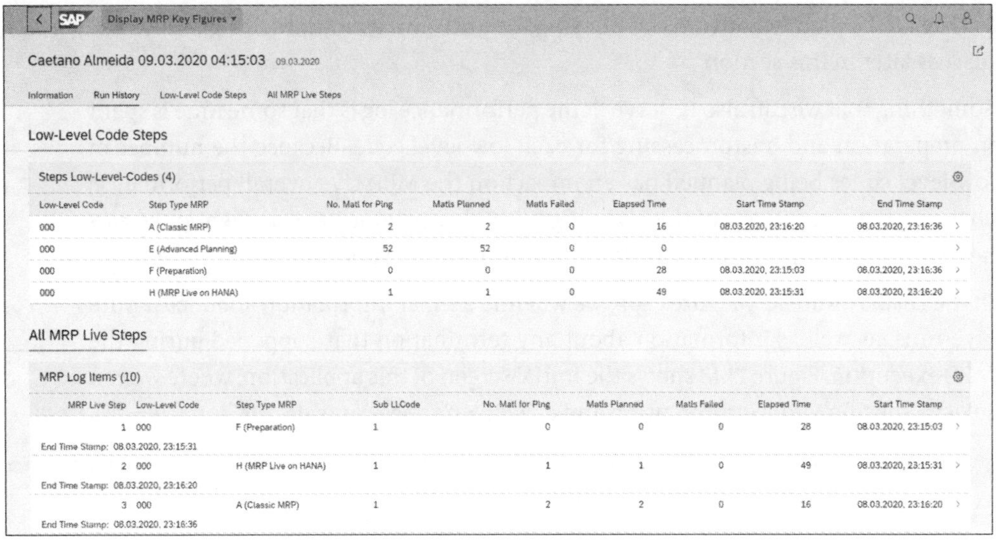

Figure 13.19 Details of the MRP Key Figures

MRP Live Technical Settings

Now that we have discussed how to analyze the MRP Live logs, we can focus on how to tune MRP Live performance by changing the technical settings. The technical settings are a set of parameters, stored in table PPHMRPSET (see Figure 13.20), that can be used to control how MRP Live will use parallelization. We have settings to control, for example, the number of parallel processes, the size of each package, and the minimum number of materials in a package to run on SAP HANA.

Earlier in this chapter, we noted that we can access the MRP Live technical settings through the support functions in Transaction MD01N. When we select this option in the MRP Live support functions, we will jump into a screen where we can change the fields of table PPHMRPSET.

13.3 Improving MRP Performance

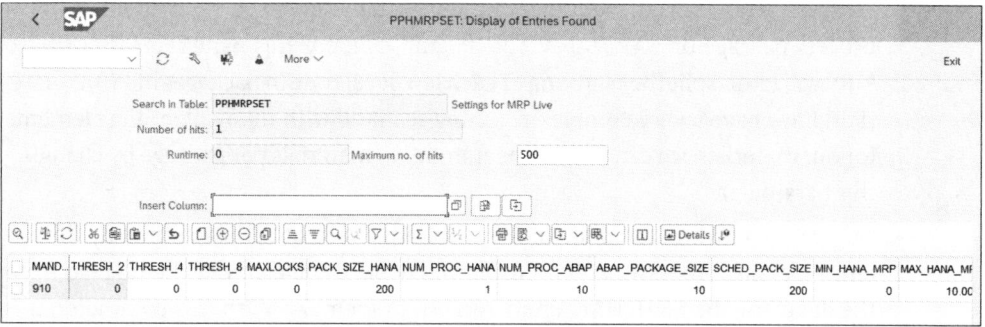

Figure 13.20 MRP Live Technical Settings in Table PPHMRPSET

In the MRP Live technical parameters, we will find settings to influence the locks, the parallelization in SAP HANA, and the parallelization in ABAP. Let's discuss each of these settings and how it will affect the MRP Live execution.

Locks

Materials being planned in each step of the MRP run should be locked by an enqueue mechanism. If there are too many concurrent locks, this mechanism will not be able to handle all of them, and this may lead to problems in the system, such as a general slowness. With the MRP Live technical settings, one parameter, MAXLOCKS, controls the maximum number of locks in MRP Live at the material level. The default value of this field is 200, which means that if MRP needs to plan more than 200 materials in the same step, it will lock at the plant level instead of generating lots of locks at the material level.

Parallelization in SAP HANA

MRP Live will use the SAP HANA internal parallelization, splitting materials to be planned in packages and processing each package in a different process. In the technical settings, we can find the following parameters to control the parallelization on SAP HANA:

- NUM_PROC_HANA: MRP Live can run several processes in SAP HANA in parallel in order to optimize the runtime. By default, the system will use eight processes, but this number can be increased if we have enough resources and we want better performance, or reduced to avoid consumption of system resources.

- PACK_SIZE_HANA: This is the target number of materials to be planned in a parallel process package on SAP HANA. The default value for this parameter is 1,000, so MRP will try to split the planning of each low-level code in packages of 1,000 materials. If we have a very complex planning scenario with many planning elements for our materials, we can reduce the number of materials per package by changing this parameter.
- MAX_HANA_MRP: When too many materials are planned at the same time by the different parallel processes and there are many planning elements being read from the database, then SAP HANA may run out of memory. With this parameter, it is possible to limit the total number of materials planned in SAP HANA at the same time. The default value for this parameter is 100,000, but it can be reduced to limit the number of materials being planned in parallel and avoid memory issues.

> **Note**
>
> The total number of materials being planned by MRP Live at the same time is basically NUM_PROC_HANA × PACK_SIZE_HANA. If this number exceeds the value of MAX_HANA_MRP, the system will reduce the number of materials per package.

When running MRP Live for the first time, it will distribute materials in packages, considering that all the packages should take the same amount of time and they should all finish together, to optimize the usage of the SAP HANA resources. However, this is not always true: some materials may take more time to be planned than other materials.

On the next MRP Live execution, however, the system will consider the results of the previous MRP Live run in order to optimize the distributions of materials into the parallel processing packages.

Parallelization in ABAP

As shown earlier in this book, some materials need to be planned in ABAP when MRP Live is executed due to certain restrictions or because we have forced execution in ABAP using Transaction MD_MRP_FORCE_CLASSIC. With the MRP Live technical settings, we can influence this parallelization—for example, by specifying the number of servers or the size of packages.

The following parameters are available to control the parallel processing in ABAP during MRP Live execution:

- `NUM_PROC_ABAP`: This parameter controls the number of parallel tasks that will be triggered in ABAP. By default, the system will use eight tasks.

- `ABAP_PACKAGE_SIZE`: This parameter controls the maximum number of materials that will be planned in a parallel process package. By default, the number is 20, but we can reduce this number when there are materials with many planning elements or complex settings, such as variant configuration.

- `MIN_HANA_MRP`: With this parameter, we can define the minimum number of materials to plan on SAP HANA. As explained earlier, SAP HANA is much faster when planning a large set of materials, but ABAP may be faster when processing a small package. The default value used by MRP Live is zero, but if we observe that small packages are taking a long time to be planned on SAP HANA, we can define a minimum value so that small packages are planned on ABAP.

- `HANA_ABAP_PARALLEL`: By default, the system will first plan on SAP HANA and then plan those materials with restrictions in ABAP. Because we do not expect to have many materials being planned in ABAP, this logic usually works fine—but if planning in ABAP is taking a long time, we can set the value X for this parameter so that planning runs in SAP HANA and in ABAP are triggered in parallel.

Parallel Processing during Postprocessing

After planning of a low-level code is finished, there is a postprocessing phase, and we can also use the following parameters to control the parallel processing in this phase:

- `PURREQ_POSTPROC_PACK_SIZE`: During the postprocessing phase, MRP Live will fill additional fields for the purchase requisitions created during the planning run on SAP HANA. To reduce the number of enqueue locks, this step is split into packages in which the default number of purchase requisitions per package is 1,000. We can use this parameter to change this field and increase or reduce the number of requisitions per package.

- `NUM_PROC_POSTPROC`: By default, MRP Live will use eight parallel tasks for the postprocessing phase, but we can increase or reduce this number by changing this parameter.

There are no optimal values for the MRP Live technical settings that will provide the best performance for all systems. SAP provides default values for each setting, which will ensure good utilization of the SAP HANA resources, optimize the parallelization, and avoid memory consumption issues. However, each system will have a different amount of resources available (memory, CPU, etc.) and a different master data constellation, so we can usually achieve better results by fine-tuning the MRP Live technical settings for better resource utilization.

There is no easy or simple way to find the optimal resources; the best way to find the perfect combination for these settings is to evaluate the MRP Live performance logs in Transaction MD_MRP_PERFLOG, identify possible points for performance improvement, make changes in the technical settings, run MRP Live, and then evaluate the performance logs again to confirm if the changes were effective or not. We may need to repeat this process several times until we find the perfect combination of parameters for our system.

> **Tip**
>
> Parameters defined in table PPHMRPSET are valid for the whole MRP execution, but under special circumstances, we might need to have different values for each low-level code.
>
> In this case, we can create an implementation of the DISPATCH_GET_PARAMETERS method of the ES_PPH_MRP_DISPATCHER_BADI enhancement spot, with specific logic for a low-level code. For example, if some finished products are very complex and take a lot of time to be planned, we might need to define a smaller package for low-level code 000.

For more information about the MRP Live technical settings, refer to SAP Note 2003405 (Technical Settings for MRP Live).

13.3.3 Frequent Causes and Solutions

Now that we have discussed how to analyze the classic MRP and MRP Live logs to identify a performance issue, we can go through the most common causes of performance issues during the MRP run.

Planning Mode

The usage of planning mode 3 will usually lead to performance issues in the MRP run. With planning mode 3, all the unfirmed planning elements will be deleted and recreated, so MRP will spend a lot of time accessing the database to delete these elements and to create them again, besides the fact that it will need to re-explode the BOM for planned orders and possibly run a new lead-time scheduling. Planning mode 2 is only available for classic MRP, and it is also bad for performance: the planned order reservations will be deleted and recreated from table RESB, and there will be several updates for the planned orders and requisitions.

We explained in Chapter 5 that planning mode 1 is usually enough for the regular planning run, so we must try to use it for the regular planning runs as much as possible.

Number of Materials Planned

MRP selects materials to be planned based on the planning file, which means that only materials that have undergone a change since the last MRP run will be planned. The regenerative MRP run (NEUPL), however, will force MRP to plan all the materials, and this usually takes much more time. Although it is recommended to have a periodic regenerative MRP run scheduled, it is not recommended to use on a daily basis because it affects the MRP performance negatively, especially if it is combined with planning mode 3 or 2.

Incorrect Lot-Sizing Settings

Too many planning elements can be created in the same day if we use a fixed or maximum lot size incorrectly. When we are using a very small lot-sizing procedure and there is a large requirement, MRP will have to generate many planned orders to cover the requirement, which usually leads to performance issues. We can define a maximum number of replenishment proposals per date in order to avoid having this problem compromise the whole MRP run. When this maximum number is reached, an error will be triggered for this material, and the planning run will continue. We should constantly monitor the MRP List and the MRP Live logs for this kind of error and review the lot-sizing policy if this situation happens, as it is a frequent cause of performance issues.

Underutilization of Parallel Processing

Parallel processing may lead to a huge performance improvement in the MRP run, but there are situations in which it is underutilized and the MRP performance is compromised. If we identify that parallel processing is not optimal in classic MRP, we can create an implementation of the MD_MRP_RUN_PARALLEL BAdI in order to control the size of the parallel processing package and ensure that all the servers will be used uniformly. In MRP Live, we can make changes to the technical settings in order to optimize the usage of resources and improve the usage of parallelization.

Materials with Restrictions in MRP Live

When we are using MRP Live, some materials will have restrictions that will force them to be planned in ABAP. Although a small number of materials with restrictions is acceptable, when there are too many materials with restrictions, MRP Live performance will be compromised because we will not be taking full advantage of the SAP HANA database during the MRP Live run. Therefore, it is always recommended to keep the number of restrictions to a minimal level in order to get optimal performance in MRP Live. If there are too many materials being planned in ABAP during the MRP Live execution, we can change the MRP Live technical settings to improve the parallelization and optimize the performance.

BOM Explosion

One of the MRP steps that usually causes performance issues is the BOM explosion, especially when there are very complex BOMs or if there are too many planned orders to be updated or created. There is a Customizing setting in Transaction OPPQ, under the **Performance** section, where we can activate BOM buffering. With this setting, BOMs that need to be accessed multiple times will be read directly from the memory shared buffer instead of being read from the database. This setting should improve performance, especially when using planning mode 2 or 3.

13.4 Summary

To ensure that MRP will continue to run consistently, we need to run some housekeeping activities, which were discussed and explained in detail in this chapter.

In addition to the housekeeping activities, we discussed troubleshooting, including the most frequent issues reported by MRP users, such as a material not being planned by MRP or an inconsistency in the planning elements affecting the MRP results. We discussed how to identify those issues and fix them to ensure that they will not affect MRP.

Finally, because MRP is a performance-intensive application, we discussed how to analyze the classic MRP and MRP Live performance logs, how to use the MRP Live technical settings to improve MRP Live performance, and causes of and solutions for the most frequent performance issues in MRP.

After reading this chapter, you should be ready to manage the MRP daily operations, to resolve basic issues that can affect the MRP run, and to optimize classic MRP and MRP Live for better performance.

Chapter 14
Enhancing MRP

This chapter explains the options available to enhance MRP in SAP S/4HANA. We will discuss the difference between classic MRP's ABAP BAdIs and MRP Live's AMDP BAdIs, as well as the main business cases for implementing each one.

The standard MRP features delivered by SAP will fit into the business processes of most companies. However, there are specific cases in which MRP should be enhanced to fulfill a very specific business requirement. SAP provides a plug-in in the source code where companies can implement their own logic in order to enhance MRP. These plug-ins are called Business Add-ins (BAdIs); several BAdIs are provided by SAP within classic MRP and MRP Live, and a standard sample implementation is provided for some of them.

Each BAdI is a specific point of the code with a specific purpose and context. There is a set of input parameters provided to the BAdI and a limited set of variables or internal tables that can be changed through the code implemented in the BAdI. Therefore, a BAdI can generally only be used for the specific purpose for which it was originally created; we cannot simply rewrite the whole MRP logic within a BAdI or use it for something completely different than it was originally created to do.

For example, consider that we want to make a planning element not relevant to MRP under very specific circumstances. In this case, there is a BAdI called just after MRP reads the planning elements from the database in both classic MRP and MRP Live. We can create a BAdI implementation to make changes in the planning elements, such as making them not relevant to MRP, but we will not be able to change the lot-sizing calculation within this particular BAdI because its scope is limited.

> **Warning**
> Although the scope of the BAdI is limited, MRP generally will not check the consistency of the changes implemented with a BAdI. Therefore, we need to be very careful

14 Enhancing MRP

> when creating a BAdI implementation so that we avoid creating any problem that will lead to inconsistent MRP results.

We can access the MRP BAdIs in Transaction SE18, where we will see, for example, if there are active implementations; which methods are available for each BAdI; which parameters are available for each method; and, if SAP delivers sample implementations, which can be used as a template for creating our own BAdI implementation.

Over the course of this book, we have mentioned the MRP BAdIs several times, whenever they could be useful, but in this specific chapter we will learn more about the existing BAdIs both for classic MRP (and the MRP evaluation transactions) in Section 14.1 and for MRP Live in Section 14.2. We will not go deeper into the technical aspects of a BAdI; the idea is to focus on the functional aspects, such as knowing which BAdI to choose and the most common reasons to create a BAdI implementation in MRP. We will close the chapter by talking about enhancements in the SAP Fiori applications for MRP in Section 14.3.

14.1 Enhancing Classic MRP

Classic MRP and the MRP evaluation transactions are mostly executed in ABAP, which means that the BAdIs called are the old ABAP-based BAdIs. We can usually identify the classic MRP BAdIs by their names: they start with MD_, such as MD_PLDORD_CHANGE.

In SAP S/4HANA, part of the logic in which data was selected from the database was pushed down into the SAP HANA layer, and some ABAP BAdIs were called in this piece of code. Those BAdIs will no longer be called during the MRP run or in the Stock/Requirements List, and any existing implementation should be replaced. The following BAdIs were affected:

- The MD_CHANGE_MRP_DATA BAdI was frequently used in SAP ERP to change the MRP elements when they are read from the database. It will no longer be called in SAP S/4HANA.
- The MD_STOCK_TRANSFER BAdI was used to change the requirement date of a stock transfer. It will no longer be called in SAP S/4HANA.
- The MD_ADAPT_DISTRIBUTION BAdI was delivered in SAP ERP to influence the start/end date and the factory calendar used for the distribution of quantities in the

MRP transactions when using a distribution key. It will no longer be called in SAP S/4HANA.

All three of these BAdIs can be replaced by the MD_ADD_ELEMENTS BAdI, which is called just after all the MRP elements are read from the database.

Besides that, the MD_SUBCONT_LOGIC BAdI was used to implement a simplified subcontracting logic, where there was no separation between the plant and the subcontractor stock. This BAdI is also no longer relevant in SAP S/4HANA, due to the simplifications in the subcontracting logic.

Let's go through the most-used BAdIs for classic MRP and the MRP evaluation transactions, starting with the most frequently used:

- The MD_ADD_ELEMENTS BAdI is called just after the planning elements are read from the database during the MRP run and in the Stock/Requirements List. As its name suggests, this BAdI can be used to add a custom MRP element, but it can be also used to change an existing MRP element that was read from the database. We can use this BAdI, for example, to make an element not relevant for MRP or to change quantities or any other field. This BAdI should be used carefully because it could completely change the MRP results. Note that changes will by only valid for MRP, and they are not going to be saved in the database.

- We can use the MD_ADD_COL_EZPS BAdI to include custom columns in the MRP evaluation. We can show additional information for each MRP element, such as custom fields or fields that are not displayed by default.

- The MD_PURREQ_CHANGE and MD_PLDORD_CHANGE BAdIs can be used to change a purchase requisition and planned order (respectively) that was created or changed by MRP. Changes will be saved in the database, so we must be very careful to avoid inconsistencies.

- The MD_MODIFY_SOURCE BAdI can be used to change the source of supply of an externally procured replenishment proposal created by MRP.

- We can use the MD_MODIFY_PRODVERS BAdI to change the production version of a planned order generated by MRP.

- Stock transfers generated by MRP will not have the issuing storage location determined, but we can create an implementation of the MD_EXT_SUP BAdI to add our own logic to determine the issuing storage location of a stock transfer.

- The MD_PIR_FLEX_CONS BAdI can be used to influence the consumption of PIRs during the MRP run and the MRP evaluation transactions.

- With the MD_MRP_PARAMETERS BAdI, we can adjust the material master settings or the MRP Customizing settings before planning a specific material.
- The MD_MRP_RUN_PARALLEL BAdI was mentioned in Chapter 13, in which we discussed classic MRP performance. We can use it to influence the size of the parallel processing package during classic MRP execution and to standardize the utilization of parallel processing.
- The MD_DISPLAY_ELEMENT BAdI allows us to change the text of an MRP element in the MRP evaluation transactions.
- The MD_PLDORD_SCHEDULING BAdI can be used to influence the scheduling parameters before lead time scheduling.
- The MD_CHANGE_CALENDAR BAdI can be used to use a different calendar for the safety time and the evaluations of the range of coverage data instead of the factory calendar.
- The MD_EXCLUDE_MATERIAL BAdI can be used to create an **Additional Selection** tab in the selection screen of Transactions MD06 and MD07, in which we can define additional selection parameters to restrict the selection.
- When using MTO or MTP production, we can use the MD_LAST_LOT_EXACT BAdI to create our own logic to determine the calculation of the last lot size under those special stocks.
- The MD_MRP_LIST BAdI is called when the MRP List is generated. Although we cannot change the MRP List itself, we can evaluate the MRP results and trigger follow-up actions. SAP delivers a sample implementation in which the MRP controller is informed by email for a specific exception message.
- As mentioned in Chapter 6, the MD_SET_TRAFFIC_LIGHTS_DS BAdI can be used to define material-specific values for the traffic lights shown in the MRP evaluation transactions.
- The MD_CREATE_GROUPING BAdI can be used to create a custom grouping of materials in the Stock/Requirements List.
- With the MD_PURREQ_REL_STRAT BAdI, we can deactivate the release strategy for purchase requisitions generated by MRP.
- We can use the MD_INTERACT_PLANNING BAdI to control whether a user is allowed to change MRP elements in the MRP results screen of Transaction MD02 or Transaction MD03.

14.1 Enhancing Classic MRP

> **Warning**
>
> MRP is a performance-intensive application, so we must be very careful with any BAdI implementation. Complex logic implemented in a BAdI may have negative effects on the MRP runtime. We can use report RMMDMONI to evaluate the time spent in the BAdI execution during the MRP run.

Whenever a BAdI is called during classic MRP execution, the **BAdI Active** indicator shown in Figure 14.1 will be checked in the **Overview of Material Data** tab of the MRP List. If a BAdI was called while reading the MRP planning elements, the indicator will be also checked in the Stock/Requirements List.

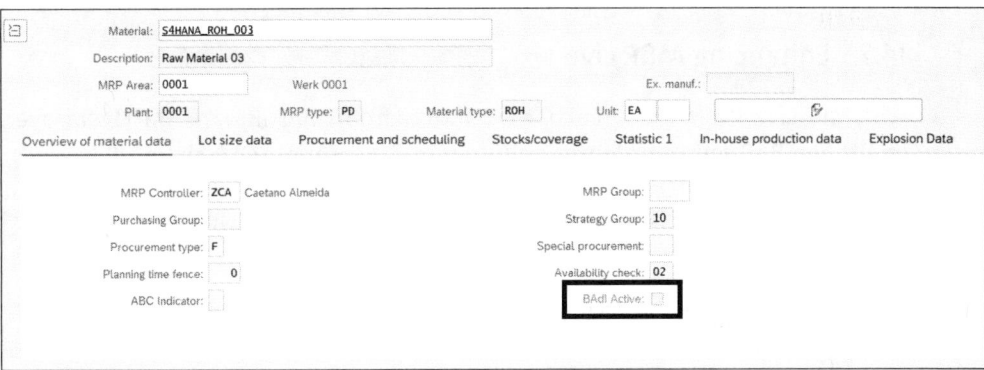

Figure 14.1 The BAdI Active Indicator

Besides the already mentioned BAdIs, classic MRP also offers an old kind of enhancement known as a *user exit*. This old concept, created even before BAdIs, allowed SAP customers to enhance the standard logic by inserting their own code in a function module rather than changing the standard SAP code. A BAdI offers many advantages over a user exit, such as the possibility to have multiple implementations (the user exit will only allow a single implementation).

We discussed in Chapter 5 that classic MRP only allows execution at the plant or material level, but we might want to split the planning of the same plant into different steps and run MRP per MRP controller or MRP group. SAP provides enhancement M61X0001, which allows us to create our own logic to select which materials will be planned. This enhancement consists of the following function modules:

- The EXIT_SAPMM61X_001 function module is called when the planning run is without parallel processing.
- The EXIT_SAPLM61C_001 function module is called when parallel processing is active during the planning run.

To use this enhancement, we will need to create the user exit parameters in customizing Transaction OMIX. These parameters will be referenced when we trigger the total MRP run in Transaction MD01 or using report RMMDMONI. The most frequent usage of this enhancement is to restrict the planning run for materials belonging to a specific MRP controller. SAP delivers sample code for the EXIT_SAPMM61X_001 function module that covers this and several additional scenarios.

14.2 Enhancing MRP Live

With MRP Live, the MRP source code was moved from ABAP into the SAP HANA layer, so all the ABAP source code was rewritten in the form of SQLScript, CDS views, or ABAP-Managed Database Procedures (AMDPs). Consequently, the ABAP BAdIs that were previously called in classic MRP will no longer be called during MRP Live execution.

For MRP Live, SAP delivered a new set of AMDP BAdIs, which are called within the SAP HANA layer. This means that if we are migrating to SAP S/4HANA, any existing ABAP BAdI will have to be migrated into the equivalent AMDP BAdI. There is no tool to automatically convert those BAdIs; the code is written in a different language, and a developer will have to rewrite the entire code.

However, the fact that we have new AMDP BAdIs in MRP Live does not mean that we have completely gotten rid of the old ABAP BAdIs. As we have discussed throughout this book, there are some restrictions that will lead to a material being planned in ABAP, so even when we are running MRP Live, we may still need to use the ABAP-based BAdIs in MRP Live. In some situations, if there are too many materials with restrictions, we may even have to implement the same logic in an ABAP BAdI and in the equivalent AMDP BAdI in order to ensure that it will be executed for all the materials.

> **Tip**
>
> If a BAdI is only needed for a few materials, we may create only an implementation of the ABAP BAdI, and then use Transaction MD_MRP_FORCE_CLASSIC to ensure that

all materials for which this BAdI is needed will be planned in ABAP. This option can have a negative influence on MRP Live performance if there are too many materials planned in ABAP.

SAP Note 2268085 (S4TWL—MRP Live on SAP HANA—MD01N) provides a list of the classic MRP BAdIs and the equivalent AMDP BAdIs, as shown in Table 14.1.

Purpose	Classic BAdI or Extension	AMDP BAdI
Subcontracting logic	MD_SUBCONT_LOGIC	PPH_MRP_RUN_BADI => MDPS_ADJUST
Reading material receipts and requirements	MD_CHANGE_MRP_DATA	PPH_MRP_RUN_BADI => MDPS_ADJUST
Scheduling of stock transfer requirements	MD_STOCK_TRANSFER	PPH_MRP_RUN_BADI => MDPS_ADJUST
User-defined MRP elements in MRP	MD_ADD_ELEMENTS	PPH_MRP_RUN_BADI => MDPS_ADJUST
PIR consumption	MD_PIR_FLEX_CONS	PPH_MRP_RUN_BADI => MDPS_ADJUST
Changing planning parameters	MD_MRP_PARAMETERS	PPH_MRP_LOTSIZING_BADI => LOT_SIZE_CALC PPH_MRP_NETTING_BADI => NET_REQ_CALC
Changing the MRP List	MD_MRP_LIST	
Changing purchase requisitions created by MRP	MD_PURREQ_CHANGE, MD_PURREQ_POST	PPH_MRP_RUN_BADI => PURREQ_BEFORE_UPDATE_ADJUST
Changing planned orders created by MRP	MD_PLDORD_CHANGE, MD_PLDORD_POST	PPH_MRP_RUN_BADI => PLANORD_BEFORE_UPDATE_ADJUST
Source of supply determination in MRP	MD_MODIFY_SOURCE, MD_MODIFY_PRODVERS, MD_EXT_SUP	PPH_MRP_SOURCING_BADI => SOS_DET_ADJUST
Package size for parallel processing	MD_MRP_RUN_PARALLEL	MRP_DISPATCHER_BADI => DISPATCH_CREATE_TASK
Material selection for MRP run	Extension M61X0001	PPH_MRP_NETTING_BADI => AT_PLANNING_FILE_ENTRIES_READ

Table 14.1 Classic BAdIs and Equivalent AMDP BAdIs

14 Enhancing MRP

Besides the AMDP BAdIs mentioned in Table 14.1, SAP introduced the following additional AMDP BAdIS for MRP Live later:

- The `PPH_MRP_READ_MASTER_BADI` BAdI can be used to change the material master data that has been read during the MRP Live run.
- The `PPH_MRP_RUN_BADI2` BAdI can be used to replan a material during the MRP Live run that has just been planned by MRP Live. This BAdI will not be usually required.

As indicated in the table, the names of the MRP Live BAdIs will usually start with PPH. AMDP BAdIs are also accessible through Transaction SE18, as shown in Figure 14.2.

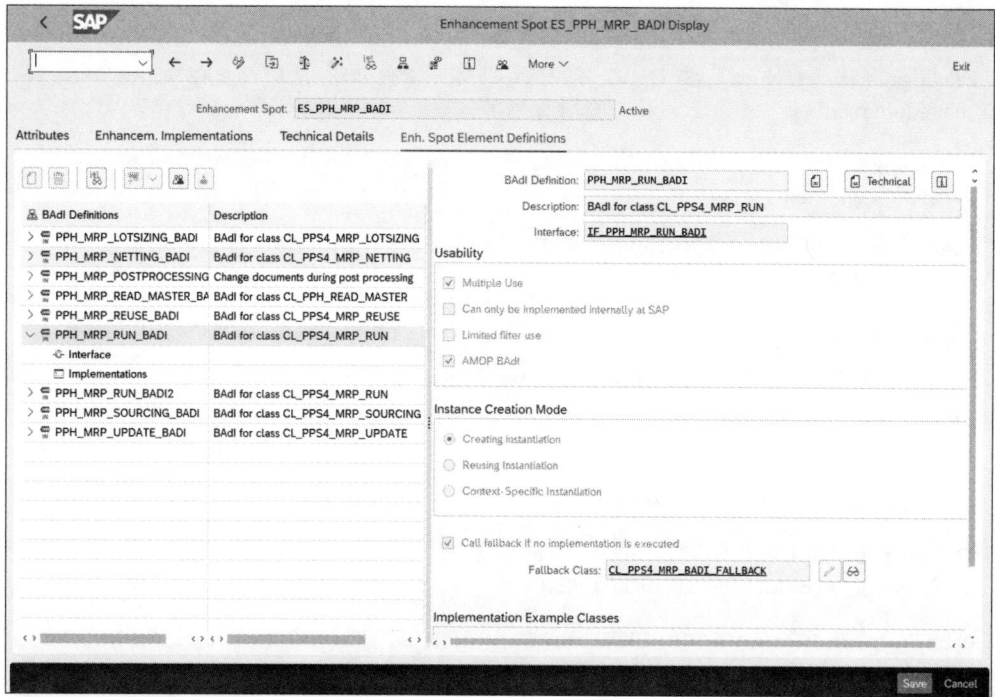

Figure 14.2 MRP Live BAdIs in Transaction SE18

MRP Live also includes a classic ABAP BAdI called in the postprocessing phase. The `PPH_MRP_POSTPROCESSING_BADI` BAdI can be used to populate customer fields and/or adapt standard fields during the MRP Live postprocessing phase.

Of the BAdIs previously mentioned, some are frequently implemented in specific MRP Live planning scenarios. For example, during a migration from SAP ERP to SAP

S/4HANA, many customers who used to run classic MRP want to keep generating planned orders for materials procured externally, which is not possible. In this case, one solution is to implement the `PPH_MRP_SOURCING_BADI` AMDP BAdI to force MRP to generate planned orders.

Another commonly implemented BAdI is `MRP_DISPATCHER_BADI`, which can be used to include additional fields in the selection screen of Transaction MD01N. Because MRP Live does not provide the MRP area as a selection parameter, we would need to create an implementation of this BAdI to plan a specific MRP area only in Transaction MD01N.

Besides the already mentioned BAdIs, method `MDPS_ADJUST` of the `PPH_MRP_RUN_BADI` BAdI is also often used. It can be used to adjust the planning elements read from the database before they are processed by MRP Live in the net requirements calculation. Additional methods of the `PPH_MRP_RUN_BADI` BAdI are also often used to adjust planned orders and purchase requisitions during the MRP run.

So far in this chapter, we have discussed the BAdIs for classic MRP and MRP Live, but we can also enhance the SAP Fiori applications of the MRP Cockpit by improving the user interface or making changes in the backend logic.

14.3 Enhancing the SAP Fiori Applications of the MRP Cockpit

Most of the MRP Cockpit applications will offer an option to extend the SAP Fiori applications in the frontend server, which usually means enhancing the user interface or adding additional fields or columns in tables. For more information about extensibility options, we can visit the SAP Fiori Library (*https://fioriappslibrary.hana.ondemand.com*), which provides more detailed information about the SAP Fiori applications for SAP S/4HANA.

When accessing any SAP Fiori application in the SAP Fiori Library, we can open the **Implementation Information** tab to find a section called **Extensibility Options**, as shown in Figure 14.3. Here, we will find all the necessary information to extend the SAP Fiori application, such as a link to a document explaining how to extend an SAP Fiori application and a link to the extensibility documentation in SAP Help for the application.

14 Enhancing MRP

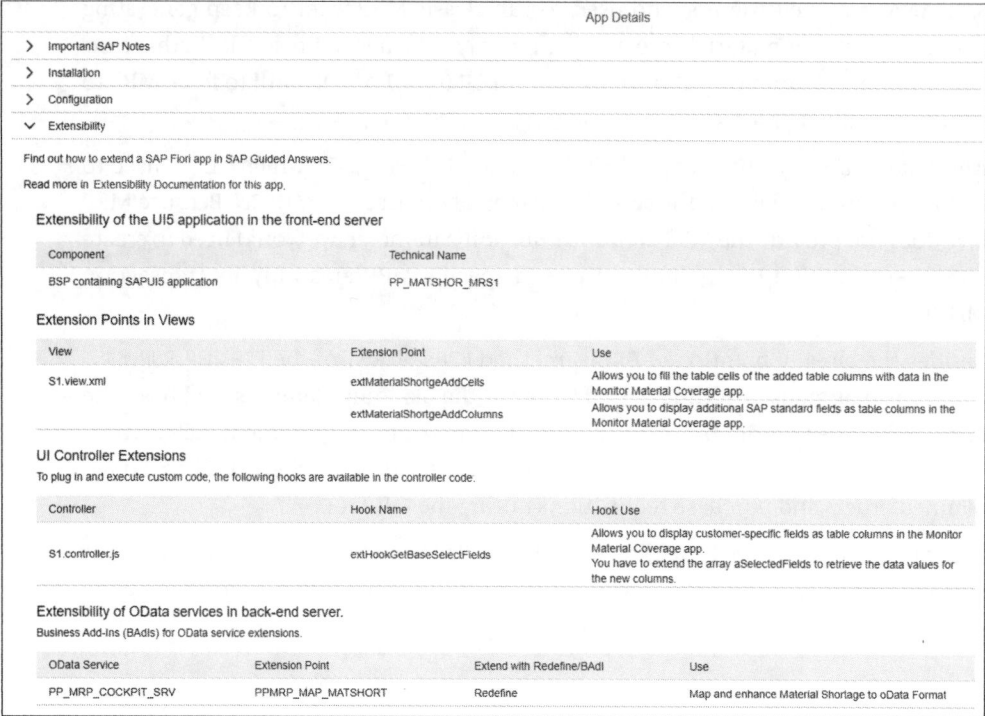

Figure 14.3 Extensibility Options in the SAP Fiori Library

We will also find here the technical name of the component and the SAP Fiori extensions available. Besides the user interface, we may also need to create enhancements on the backend side, which are also created with BAdIs, accessible through Transaction SE18. Table 14.2 shows a list of the available BAdIs for the SAP Fiori applications of the MRP Cockpit. Figure 14.4 shows these BAdIs in Transaction SE18.

BAdI	Description
PPMRP_ENHANCE_QUICKVIEW	Extensibility of Quickviews
PPMRP_ENHANCE_SDIV_DETAILS	Extensibility of Stock/Requirements and Shortage Lists
PPMRP_MAP_MATERIALORDER	Extensibility of Material Order List

Table 14.2 MRP Cockpit BAdIs

502

14.3 Enhancing the SAP Fiori Applications of the MRP Cockpit

BAdI	Description
PPMRP_MAP_MATSHORT	Extensibility of Material List
PPMRP_MAP_MFGORDCOMP	Extensibility of Manufacturing Order Components List
PPMRP_MAP_MFGORDMILESTONES	Extensibility of Manufacturing Order Milestones List
PPMRP_MAP_MFGORDOPER	Extensibility of Manufacturing Order Operations List
PPMRP_MAP_PURCHORD_ON_CREATE	Extensibility of Purchase Order Creation
PPMRP_MAP_SUPPLIERMATERIAL	Extensibility of Vendor-Specific Material List
PPMRP_MAP_UNCDEM	Extensibility of Uncovered Requirements List

Table 14.2 MRP Cockpit BAdIs (Cont.)

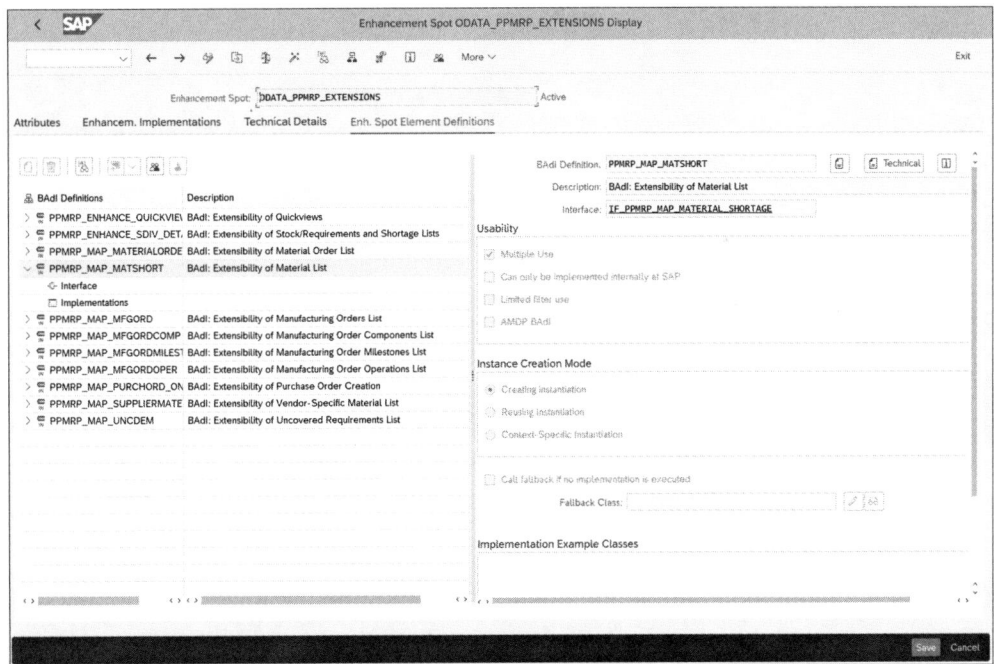

Figure 14.4 MRP Cockpit BAdIs in Transaction SE18

14.4 Summary

MRP is an application in which the standard implementation usually meets all customer requirements. However, it is also possible to enhance the standard logic to address specific business requirements.

In this chapter, we discussed how to enhance classic MRP and how to enhance MRP Live with BAdIs. We finished the chapter by talking about the extensibility options for the SAP Fiori applications of the MRP Cockpit and how to find the user interface extensions and the backend BAdIs available for each application.

Remember that we need to be very careful when implementing a BAdI in MRP because custom logic can lead to inconsistent MRP results. Complex logic implemented in an MRP BAdI may also negatively affect MRP performance by increasing the total runtime.

Chapter 15
Migrating to SAP S/4HANA

In this chapter, we will compile all the steps required for a smooth migration to SAP S/4HANA.

Over the course of this book, we have discussed the main simplifications implemented in SAP S/4HANA, and we have pointed out some of the tools that can be helpful during the migration process.

During a migration to SAP S/4HANA, we need to carefully evaluate the impact of simplifications in MRP and check if the custom code implemented in SAP ERP is still suitable for SAP S/4HANA. We should evaluate the many new features introduced in SAP S/4HANA and, ideally, replace old tools that are no longer considered target architecture by SAP.

Therefore, this chapter compiles the main migration topics that should be addressed during a migration to SAP S/4HANA. In Section 15.1, we talk about the Readiness Check, a useful tool that will help companies evaluate the impacts of a migration from SAP ERP to SAP S/4HANA. In Section 15.2, we review the simplifications implemented in SAP S/4HANA and then discuss some migration tools that can simplify the migration process. In Section 15.3, we talk about the impacts of the custom code. Finally, we close this chapter in Section 15.4 by talking about the new features available in SAP S/4HANA.

15.1 Performing Readiness Check

Evaluating the impact of the migration to SAP S/4HANA is not a simple task: there are many simplifications that might or might not have an impact on the migration, depending on the business scenarios and features that are used in SAP ERP.

SAP offers a tool for companies migrating to SAP S/4HANA called the Readiness Check. This tool will help us evaluate the readiness of the SAP ERP system for a migration to SAP S/4HANA by providing an interactive dashboard that compiles all the readiness information.

The Readiness Check offers the following features and checks:

- Simplification item check
- Activities related to simplification items
- Add-on and business function check
- SAP S/4HANA sizing simulation
- SAP Fiori recommendation
- Integration
- Business process discovery
- Custom code analysis

We will not go deeper into the Readiness Check itself because it is out of the scope of this book, but we do want to highlight here that analyzing the results of the Readiness Check is always a starting point for an SAP S/4HANA migration. It will tell us at least which simplifications will probably have an impact in that system.

Figure 15.1 shows the results of the Readiness Check with the simplification items relevant for a system in the manufacturing area. Here, some of the MRP simplifications—such as those for subcontracting, the planning file, and the planning horizon—are relevant for this system, so they should be addressed during the conversion. For each relevant simplification item, the Readiness Check will recommend an SAP Note, which provides technical information about the simplification item. A link to the relevant SAP Note will be provided directly in the Readiness Check in the **Business Impact Note** column.

Besides the simplification items, the Readiness Check will also offer additional information, such as the recommended SAP Fiori applications for each business role.

For more information about the Readiness Check, refer to SAP Note 2758146 (SAP Readiness Check 2.0 and Next-Generation SAP Business Scenario Recommendations).

15.2 Assessing Simplifications in MRP

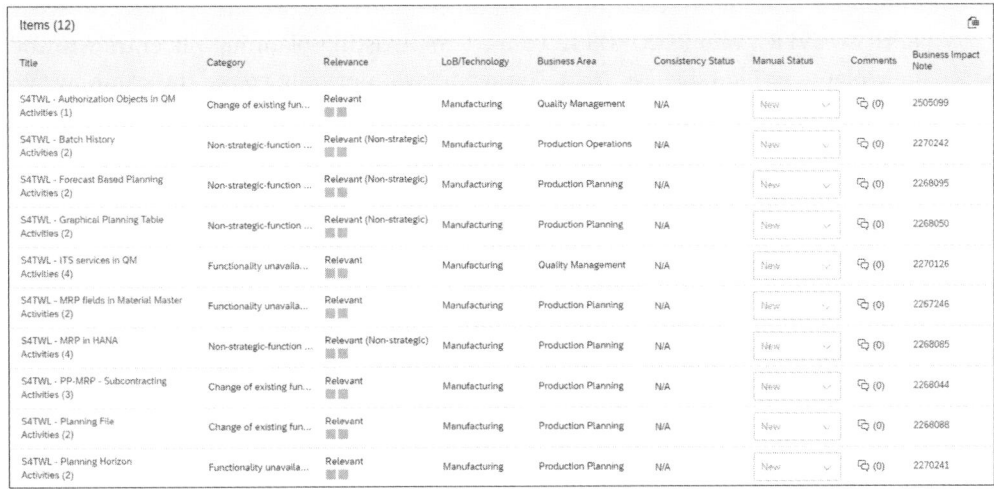

Figure 15.1 Readiness Check Results for Manufacturing

15.2 Assessing Simplifications in MRP

MRP was the target of several business scenario simplifications in SAP S/4HANA. Although these simplifications will have an impact on the migration process, there is a technical or business reason behind each one. The new planning file, for example, was implemented to achieve better performance when using an SAP HANA database, while simplified sourcing was implemented to make the sourcing model in MRP closer to the PP/DS sourcing mode because PP/DS is now embedded in the SAP S/4HANA core.

In this section, we will go through those simplifications, discuss the impact on the migration process, and learn about tools that can make this process simpler and avoid many headaches during SAP S/4HANA go-live.

15.2.1 Planning File

We noted in Chapter 3 that MRP will use the planning file to mark materials to be planned by MRP. In SAP ERP, planning file entries could be stored in table DBVM or MDVM, but SAP S/4HANA uses the new table PPH_DBVM to store the planning file entries because it is optimized for SAP HANA.

Therefore, after the system conversion to SAP S/4HANA, we should execute report PPH_CONVERT_MRPRECORDS to convert the existing planning file entries to the new planning file table PPH_DBVM. The report will not only create the planning file entries in the new table, but also set the flags in the new table according the entries in the old table.

Figure 15.2 shows the report selection screen, with **Plant**, **MRP Area**, and **Material** fields. If LTP is used in SAP ERP, then we should execute report PPH_CONVERT_MRPRECORDS_SIMU to convert the LTP planning file entries.

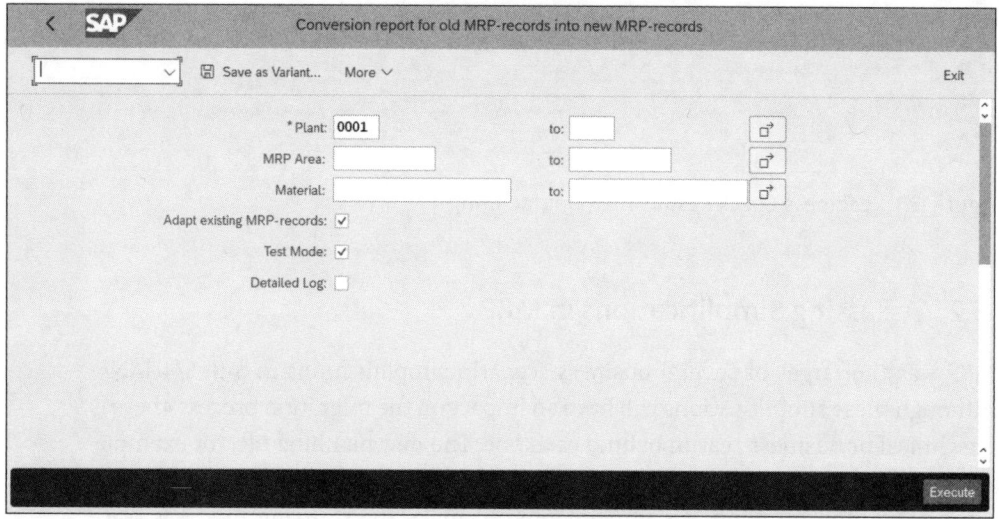

Figure 15.2 Report PPH_CONVERT_MRPRECORDS_SIMU

> **Tip**
>
> Before executing report PPH_CONVERT_MRPRECORDS, it is a good practice to run a consistency check in the planning file using report RMMDVM10.

After the report execution, a log will be shown with the total number of entries processed, as shown in Figure 15.3. More information about the planning file simplification can be found in SAP Note 2268088 (S4TWL—Planning File).

15.2 Assessing Simplifications in MRP

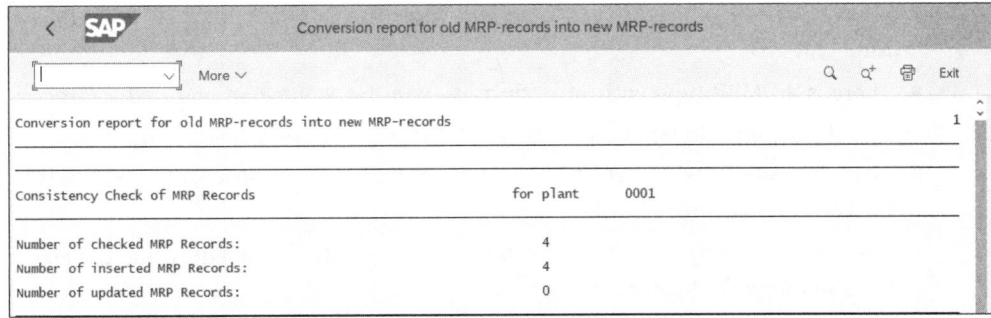

Figure 15.3 Planning File Conversion Log

15.2.2 Storage Location Planning

One of the major simplifications in SAP S/4HANA is that the usage of MRP areas is now mandatory for planning a storage location separately, for excluding a storage location for MRP, and for separating the plant stock and the stock provided to the vendor in a subcontracting scenario.

In SAP ERP, we could define that a storage location should be planned separately or excluded from MRP in the **MRP 4** tab of the material master, and it would be planned by MRP in a separated planning segment. In SAP S/4HANA, this feature no longer exists: whenever we want to plan a storage location separately or exclude it from MRP, we should create an MRP area for the storage location and assign it to the material master.

We discussed the assignment of MRP areas to the material master in Chapter 3 and the creation of MRP areas in Customizing in Chapter 4, so it should be clear by now how to create MRP areas and assign them to the material master.

To make the migration to SAP S/4HANA simpler, SAP created report MRP_AREA_STORAGE_LOC_MIGRATION, which will find materials for which a storage location was planned separately in SAP ERP, check if all the MRP areas were created in Customizing and if additional Customizing settings are in place, and then automatically convert the storage locations planned separately or excluded from MRP into MRP area assignments to the material master.

This report is executed in SAP ERP in the pre-upgrade phase, and it will check if the following Customizing settings are in place:

- MRP areas are active in Customizing.
- The planning file entries were converted from table MDVM to table DBVM.

- There is an MRP type with procedure **N—No MRP** in Customizing, like the standard MRP type ND.
- There is an MRP type with procedure **B—Reorder Point Planning** and a forecast indicator, either **No Forecast** or **Optional Forecast**, in Customizing.
- There is a lot-sizing procedure similar to EX, with a static procedure and the **Lot-for-Lot Order Quantity** lot size indicator.
- There is a lot-sizing procedure similar to FX, with a static procedure and the **Fixed Lot Size** lot size indicator.
- A special procurement exists for stock transfer where the supplying plant is the same receiving plant.
- An MRP area exists for each storage location planned separately or excluded from MRP.

If any of these settings are not in place, the report will throw an error message showing what is missing. Before we can continue with the upgrade process, we will need to fix the missing Customizing entries and then run the report again. Figure 15.4 shows the results of the execution of report MRP_AREA_STORAGE_LOC_MIGRATION.

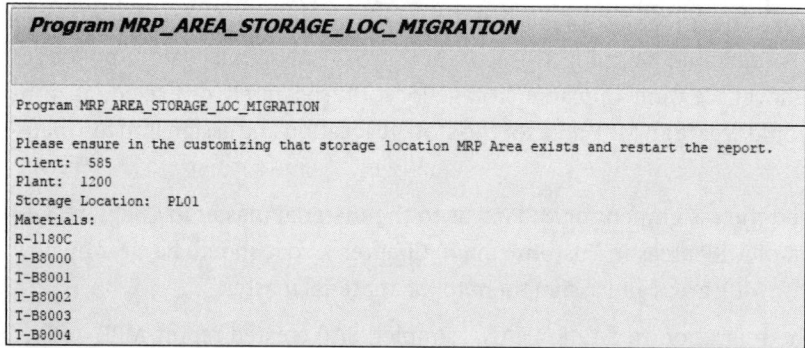

Figure 15.4 Report MRP_AREA_STORAGE_LOC_MIGRATION

Given that all these settings are in place, the report will automatically generate the MRP area assignments equivalent to the storage locations planned separately or excluded from MRP.

For materials for which a storage location was excluded from MRP, the report will create an assignment to the respective MRP area with MRP type ND so that this storage location is not planned by MRP in SAP S/4HANA.

For materials for which a storage location was planned separately, the MRP area assignment to the material master will be created with a reorder point MRP type, a fixed lot-sizing procedure, and a stock transfer special procurement. This way, we will have similar results when planning this storage location MRP area.

The following SAP Notes provide more information about this report and the storage location simplification:

- SAP Note 2469139 (Resolve Findings of Core ERP PP-MRP S/4HANA Prechecks for Storage Location Migration)
- SAP Note 2268045 (S4TWL—Storage Location MRP)

15.2.3 Subcontracting

A simplification was also implemented in the subcontracting scenario in SAP S/4HANA. As we explained in Chapter 8, to have complete separation between the plant stock and the stock provided to the subcontractor, we will have to use subcontracting MRP areas in SAP S/4HANA.

In the subcontracting planning scenario with MRP areas, however, a simplification was implemented in SAP S/4HANA that makes it no longer necessary to assign a subcontracting MRP area to the material master. In SAP S/4HANA, it is enough to have the subcontracting MRP area created in Customizing; this will be automatically considered by MRP whenever a material is involved in a subcontracting scenario.

If we are migrating to SAP S/4HANA, then we need to create the subcontracting MRP areas in Customizing if we want to separate plant stock from the stock provided to the vendor. This is not a mandatory pre-upgrade activity, and it is not necessary to run any report during the conversion process.

15.2.4 Production Versions

In SAP ERP, we could choose whether the BOM would be selected by quantity, date, or production version using the **BOM Selection Method** field in the material master. This field, however, is no longer available in SAP S/4HANA because the usage of production versions is now mandatory for the BOM explosion during the MRP run (and also for the creation of production orders).

Due to the logic implemented by simplified sourcing, the production version will be the only source of supply for in-house production, so we will need to create production versions for all the materials procured internally if they do not exist in SAP ERP.

Because the production version is mandatory for the BOM explosion in MRP, we will also have to create production versions for phantom materials and for materials with a subcontracting special procurement, where components will be provided to the vendor.

In SAP ERP, the creation of production versions was a manual step, but SAP provides report CS_BOM_PRODVER_MIGRATION02 in SAP S/4HANA to automatically generate a production version for each valid BOM. We discussed how to use this report in Chapter 3. It is important to run it after the migration to generate any missing production versions and ensure that all BOMs can be exploded during the MRP run.

For more information about this report and about this simplification, refer to the following SAP Notes:

- SAP Note 2655077 (Migration Report CS_BOM_PRODVER_MIGRATION02: Automatic Creation of Production Versions from Valid BOMs and Routings)
- SAP Note 2268069 (S4TWL—Simplified Sourcing)

15.2.5 External Procurement

In the first SAP S/4HANA release, SAP announced that the source list would no longer be considered by MRP to select a source of supply and that the new **Auto Sourcing** flag should be checked in the info record in order to have the vendor selected in a purchase requisition. With this option, however, we lacked the same validity control that we had with a source list, so SAP later changed the system behavior, making the source list relevant to MRP in SAP S/4HANA.

In the latest SAP S/4HANA releases, we can use the **Auto Sourcing** flag from the info record to make a vendor relevant for the MRP source determination, or we can keep using the source list as we were in SAP ERP. In addition, valid contract or scheduling agreements will be automatically selected by MRP as valid sources of supply, even if there is no source list.

From a migration perspective, if the source list is already used in SAP ERP, we do not need to take any action here, as it will still be considered for the source determination as a valid source of supply.

15.2.6 Total Requirements Cleanup

In SAP ERP, we could choose to see a single requirement summing up the total number of sales orders or repetitive manufacturing-dependent requirements on a single day.

For sales orders, this option was selected in the availability check assigned to the material master. Those requirements would be stored in table VBBS, rather than in table VBBE, which usually stores sales order requirements. For repetitive manufacturing-dependent requirements, the setting is made under the repetitive manufacturing profile, and the dependent requirements would be stored in table RQIT.

SAP S/4HANA no longer supports total requirements for sales orders or for planned order-dependent requirements, which means that we should perform a cleanup of total requirements before migrating to SAP S/4HANA.

Total dependent requirements are not very often used, but we can check for any entries in table RQIT. If we find any entries in this table, there is a repetitive manufacturing profile (Transaction OSP2) with the **Aggregate Requirements** setting in use. We need to ensure that this setting is removed from the repetitive manufacturing profile (see Figure 15.5) or that the profile with this setting is not being used for any material.

After making these changes, we must run MRP, re-exploding the BOMs of the planned orders for which an entry in table RQIT exists. The easiest way to do that is to run an MRP total planning run with the NEUPL key and the **Planning Mode** parameter set to **2—Re-Explode BOM and Routing**. If there are only a few materials, you may plan them individually in Transaction MD02 with the same planning mode.

The total sales requirements are stored in table VBBS. If there is any record in this table, it means that there is a checking group for the availability check with the total records per day defined in Customizing.

This availability check is set for a material in the **MRP 3** tab of the material master (Transaction MM02), and available-to-promise checking group 01 is the standard checking group delivered by SAP for total records. You may also have a custom checking group with total requirements. In this case, you must check the entries in the **Define Checking Groups** Customizing activity (Transaction OVZ2).

Here, if you find any checking group with the option **B—Totals Records per Day**, you should replace this with the value **A—Single Records**, as shown in Figure 15.6.

15   Migrating to SAP S/4HANA

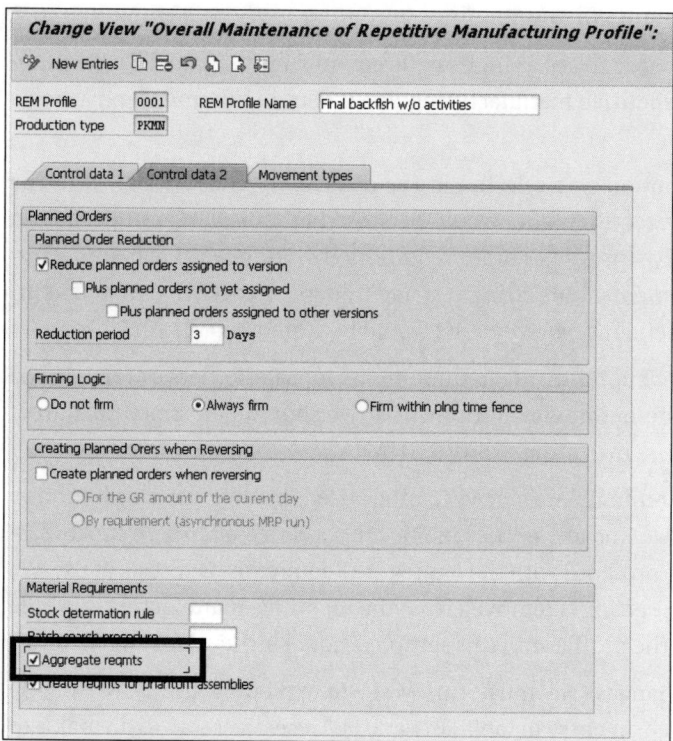

Figure 15.5 Aggregate Requirements in Repetitive Manufacturing Profile

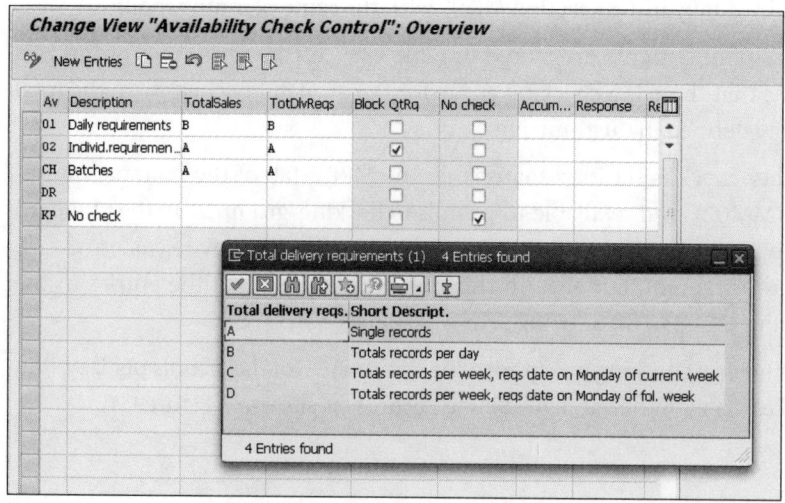

Figure 15.6 Availability Check Customizing

After making sure that the available-to-promise checking group is not used for any material and that there is no custom checking group with total records per day, you should execute report SDRQCR21 using Transaction SE38 to recreate sales orders and delivery requirements. We should no longer find any records in table VBBS after the report execution, and we are ready for SAP S/4HANA.

> **Note**
>
> Records in table VBBS will not be considered at all by MRP in SAP S/4HANA, so we might have an incorrect net requirements calculation if we follow the cleanup process.

15.3 Reviewing Custom Code

The code changes implemented in the data model and MRP source code mean that every migration to SAP S/4HANA should include a review of the custom code implemented in MRP.

First, we should review existing BAdI implementations for classic MRP: important BAdIs such as MD_CHANGE_MRP_DATA and MD_STOCK_TRANSFER will no longer be called when planning a material with classic MRP. Remember, even if we are running MRP Live, some materials may have to be planned in ABAP, so it is still important to review those BAdIs.

If we are going to use MRP Live in SAP S/4HANA, then we should completely review and convert the ABAP BAdIs implemented in classic MRP into the new AMDP BAdIs that are called in MRP Live when planning a material in SAP HANA. (Return to Chapter 14 for a list of the classic MRP BAdIs and the equivalent MRP BAdIs that can be used as a reference.)

It also is very common to have custom reports based on tables MDKP and MDTB, which are populated when classic MRP is executed and will store the MRP List data. Those tables will no longer be populated when running MRP Live because it does not generate MRP Lists, so we should adapt the custom reports to avoid reading data from those tables. The recommended solution is to use the BAPI_MATERIAL_STOCK_REQ_LIST BAPI to get the planning elements from the database, like we have for the Stock/Requirements List.

If we are already using BAPI_MATERIAL_STOCK_REQ_LIST in any custom program or if we are planning to use it in SAP S/4HANA, note that this BAPI is not automatically optimized for better performance when running on an SAP HANA database. We must call the PPH_STOCK_REQ_LISTS_PREREAD function module before the BAPI in our custom program because it is the optimized SAP HANA preread function module, which should introduce performance improvements when using this BAPI.

If there is any custom program reading information from planning file table DBVM, MDVM, or the like, they should be adapted because the planning file is now stored in a different table. We can read the planning file entries from table PPH_DBVM in SAP S/4HANA; this table can be used in our custom code.

15.4 Evaluating New MRP Features

In the previous section, we covered many simplifications that were implemented in SAP S/4HANA, but we also have many new features available for MRP. One of our tasks during the migration is to evaluate whether those new features are relevant and should replace the features previously used in SAP ERP.

Although most of the old features are still available in SAP S/4HANA, they are no longer considered target architecture by SAP. Therefore, if we really want to use SAP S/4HANA as a platform to support digital transformation, we need to seriously consider the implementation of new features like MRP Live, DDMRP, pMRP, and the MRP Cockpit.

15.4.1 MRP Live

We have seen many times in this book that we can use both classic MRP and MRP Live in SAP S/4HANA, but that only the latter is defined by SAP as the target architecture for the future.

Although migration to MRP Live has an impact, such as the changes in custom code and the fact that it no longer generates MRP Lists, for example, using MRP Live does offer some benefits.

First of all, MRP Live is faster than classic MRP, a major advantage when we talk about a background job that may take hours to be completed. Faster MRP execution means that it can be executed more frequently, resulting in always having an updated planning situation and reacting faster to material shortages.

In addition to that, for companies using PP/DS for SAP S/4HANA, MRP Live is also capable of planning materials with PP/DS heuristics. This is a great advantage for complex planning scenarios. PP/DS for SAP S/4HANA can plan materials with finite capacity or consider the batch shelf-life during the planning run, and for companies using MRP Live, both MRP and PP/DS materials can be planned together in a single planning run.

Some companies may choose to keep using classic MRP as an interim solution when they migrate to SAP S/4HANA, to reduce costs during the migration process, but they should always consider MRP Live as the long-term standard solution.

15.4.2 Demand-Driven MRP

Because the MRP Live logic generates the same results as classic MRP, but faster, deciding between MRP Live and classic MRP is usually a task for the IT department.

When we talk about DDMRP, however, it is much more a business decision than an IT-driven decision because it completely changes the existing planning paradigms. From a technical perspective, a DDMRP implementation is simple; the effort required for configuration and custom code development is minimal. From a business perspective, however, it is a huge change that involves disruption of the existing planning processes. Therefore, DDMRP can be implemented quickly during a migration to SAP S/4HANA, so long as this transition is supported (and often initiated) by the business area.

DDMRP in SAP S/4HANA can also be used with classic MRP, so moving to MRP Live solely to tap into DDMRP is not necessary.

On the other hand, if a company decides that it wants to continue with the MRP processes that are currently used in MRP, this is perfectly fine; they will still be supported in the long term in MRP.

15.4.3 Predictive Material and Resource Planning

pMRP is a new tool delivered in SAP S/4HANA 1909, and it is considered the natural successor of LTP. (In SAP S/4HANA, there was no improvement in performance or in terms of new features for LTP because it is no longer considered by SAP as the target architecture for simulations.)

A pMRP implementation should be simple and cost-effective, as there is no Customizing behind it; it is a simple and easy-to-use tool. pMRP is just in its first release. There are further improvements planned in the roadmap published by SAP, so it should be the go-to solution for materials planning simulation.

Companies relying heavily on LTP can still use it in SAP S/4HANA, but we must always keep in mind that there are no further developments planned for LTP and that pMRP is the target architecture for planning simulations in the future.

15.4.4 SAP Fiori and the MRP Cockpit

If you ask any SAP ERP user what they dislike about the system, you might hear complaints about the user interface. The SAP transactions were developed a long time ago: their fixed screen frames do not take advantage of new monitors with high resolutions, and the menus are often not exactly intuitive and user-friendly.

In addition, SAP GUI needs to be installed on each computer, which leads to additional costs for patch implementation and upgrades to new SAP GUI releases.

SAP tried to fix those issues with SAP Fiori by introducing a new web-based interface focused on improving the user experience and increasing productivity. Whereas SAP GUI needed to be accessed through a program installed on a computer, SAP Fiori is accessed directly in the browser, which means that it can run directly on a tablet or a smartphone with no prior installation.

When we talk specifically about the SAP Fiori applications of the MRP Cockpit, there are many advantages, such as increased visibility of shortages, simulations using charts, different applications focused on the different roles that need to have access to the MRP results, and much more.

The MRP planner who is already using the old Stock/Requirements List in SAP ERP will not lose anything because the Stock/Requirements List and most of the SAP GUI transactions can also be accessed directly in the SAP Fiori launchpad. In fact, the planner will actually gain mobility because they will be able to walk around the plant or the warehouse with a mobile device while they try to resolve shortages and exceptions after the MRP run.

Because some new features introduced in SAP S/4HANA, like DDMRP and pMRP, can be only accessed through their respective SAP Fiori applications, using SAP Fiori is a must for companies that want to take advantage of the innovations delivered by SAP when migrating to SAP S/4HANA.

15.5 Summary

This chapter closed this book with a list of the main topics that should be considered when planning a migration to SAP S/4HANA. It is a compilation of many simplifications and features that had been discussed throughout this book, with a special focus on the activities that should be performed during an SAP S/4HANA migration project.

As we have discussed in this chapter, a migration to SAP S/4HANA involves many more changes than an SAP ERP upgrade. We have many simplifications and many new features, plus we are switching to a new database and a new user interface. Therefore, this migration should be carefully planned in order to minimize its impact and any surprises during go-live.

Appendix A
Roadmap for MRP in SAP S/4HANA

There are many new MRP features in SAP S/4HANA, but there are still more to come. In this appendix, we will briefly discuss the roadmap for MRP in future SAP S/4HANA releases.

The first SAP S/4HANA release that included logistics functionality was delivered by SAP in November 2015. It included many new features for MRP, such as the new MRP Live functionality, built especially to work with the SAP HANA database, and the new SAP Fiori applications of the MRP Cockpit, which provided a new user interface for MRP users.

Since then, many new MRP features have been delivered in the following SAP S/4HANA releases:

- SAP S/4HANA 1610: MRP Live can now plan advanced planning materials with PP/DS heuristics.
- SAP S/4HANA 1709: This release included a set of new SAP Fiori applications to support DDMRP in SAP S/4HANA, including the material classification, buffer calculation, and a new MRP procedure.
- SAP S/4HANA 1809: New features are added to the SAP Fiori applications for DDMRP, including improvements for buffer positioning and for replenishment planning and execution. The Stock/Requirements List is also improved to better support MRP areas.
- SAP S/4HANA 1909: The new pMRP solution is released. MRP exception messages can be used in the new situation handling framework. This version also adds additional improvements for DDMRP.

Considering everything that was already delivered by SAP, we can say that in the first four logistics-inclusive SAP S/4HANA releases, we have seen more innovation for MRP than since the first release of SAP R/3. However, there is still more to come in the following releases.

A Roadmap for MRP in SAP S/4HANA

The SAP S/4HANA roadmap at *https://www.sap.com/products/roadmaps.html* lists details of the planned innovations for 2020, the product direction for 2021, and the product vision for 2021 and after.

As stated in the roadmap, SAP plans to improve the pMRP solution in 2020. The first version of pMRP released in SAP S/4HANA 1909 focused mostly on capacity planning simulations, but there are still areas where pMRP can be improved, such as for simulations for materials procured externally. As we have discussed throughout this book, LTP provides tools to estimate the required quantities for each raw material; we should expect to have the same features for pMRP in upcoming SAP S/4HANA releases.

At the time of this book's publication (summer 2020), the roadmap also states that the next release should "enable time-bucket-finite material requirements planning (MRP) for manufacturing networks with embedded production planning and detailed scheduling (PPDS)." Consequently, we expect to see an additional integration between MRP and PP/DS and additional features for finite scheduling.

Another topic where we expect improvements in 2020 is master data maintenance. The roadmap states that it should be possible in the future to automatically assign a material to an MRP area once the first goods receipt is posted for the respective storage location.

According to the product direction for 2021, we should also expect improvements for DDMRP, including scheduling capabilities and a possible integration with PP/DS.

From the user experience perspective, we have seen improvements in the MRP Cockpit applications in each SAP S/4HANA release. Through the different SAP S/4HANA releases, many improvements were delivered for the SAP Fiori applications, such as support for planning in the individual segments, a new application to show the MRP master data issues, display of rescheduling exception messages, and notifications for exception messages in the new situation handling framework. Therefore, we should still see continuous improvements for the MRP Cockpit applications, focused on better user experience and user productivity.

The product vision for 2021 and after still suggests that pMRP will be the focus for new features: the idea for the long term is that pMRP will be able to simulate the impact of master data changes on production planning. In the future, pMRP should support the simulation of changes in BOMs and routings; this would allow planners to anticipate effects on work center capacity and on the procurement of raw materials.

In summary, major simplifications were implemented in the first release, and we should not expect any new simplifications in the short-term horizon. Also, major new features such as MRP Live, DDMRP, and pMRP are already part of standard SAP S/4HANA as of release 1909. The roadmap published by SAP is now more focused on incremental improvements for the features already delivered, including improvements in the SAP Fiori applications and a focus on integration with embedded PP/DS.

Of course, we should always consider that even though the roadmap published by SAP gives a good idea of the planned innovations for future releases, there is no guarantee that the topics listed on the roadmap will become actual features in SAP S/4HANA. Future developments are subject to change by SAP, and the roadmap is not a guarantee that those features will be developed and delivered in the following releases.

Appendix B
The Author

Caetano Almeida has been working with manufacturing solutions in SAP for more than 14 years. In 2009, he joined SAP Product Support in Brazil, and since 2016, he has worked as an architect for the SAP Center of Expertise, helping SAP customers resolve complex business and technical challenges.

Caetano is also an active member of the SAP community, working to answer questions, publish blogs, and speak at SAP Inside Track events. He is the author of several SAP PRESS publications on MRP and Production Planning and Detailed Scheduling with SAP S/4HANA.

Index

A

ABAP List Viewer 267
ABAP-Managed Database Procedure
 (AMDP) 498
Actual range of coverage 341
Allocation quota arrangement 123
Area of responsibility 275, 312
Assembly scrap 85, 102
Assembly-to-order (ATO) 367
Availability check 132, 142, 178, 308
 Collective 311
 Customizing 178
 Exceptions 228
 Mass 310, 317
Availability date 176
Available stocks 153
Average daily usage 34, 383, 395, 397

B

Backflush 471
Background job 461, 462, 464, 478, 484
 Completion status 465
 Managing 295
 Schedule status 463
 Scheduling 295
 Total runtime 463
Backward consumption period 348
Backward scheduling 44, 49, 149, 234
BAdI
 MD_ADAPT_DISTRIBUTION 494
 MD_ADD_COL_EZPS 240, 495
 MD_ADD_ELEMENTS 236, 495
 MD_CHANGE_CALENDAR 496
 MD_CHANGE_MRP_DATA 235, 494, 515
 MD_CREATE_GROUPING 251, 496
 MD_DISPLAY_ELEMENT 496
 MD_EXCLUDE_MATERIAL 496
 MD_EXT_SUP 140, 495
 MD_INTERACT_PLANNING 496
 MD_LAST_LOT_EXACT 496

BAdI (Cont.)
 MD_MODIFY_PRODVERS 495
 MD_MODIFY_SOURCE 495
 MD_MRP_LIST 262, 496
 MD_MRP_PARAMETERS 496
 MD_MRP_RUN_PARALLEL 481, 491, 496
 MD_PIR_FLEX_CONS 495
 MD_PLDORD_CHANGE 495
 MD_PLDORD_SCHEDULING 496
 MD_PURREQ_CHANGE 495
 MD_PURREQ_REL_STRAT 496
 MD_SET_TRAFFIC_LIGHTS_DS 259, 496
 MD_STOCK_TRANSFER 494, 515
 MD_SUBCONT_LOGIC 325
 MRP Live 515
 MRP_DISPATCHER_BADI 215, 223, 501
 PPH_MRP_POSTPROCESSING_BADI 500
 PPH_MRP_REUSE_BADI 214
 PPH_MRP_RUN_BADI 501
 PPH_MRP_SOURCING_BADI 140, 501
 PPH_MRP_SOURCING_BADI => SOS_
  DET_ADJUST 191
 PPMRP_ENHANCE_QUICKVIEW 502
 PPMRP_ENHANCE_SDIV_DETAILS 502
 PPMRP_MAP_MATERIALORDER 502
 PPMRP_MAP_MATSHORT 503
 PPMRP_MAP_MFGORDCOMP 503
 PPMRP_MAP_MFGORDMILESTONES 503
 PPMRP_MAP_MFGORDOPER 503
 PPMRP_MAP_PURCHORD_ON_
  CREATE 503
 PPMRP_MAP_SUPPLIERMATERIAL 503
 PPMRP_MAP_UNCDEM 503
BAPI 372
 BAPI_MATERIAL_STOCK_REQ_LIST 515
Basic date 106, 197
Basic dates calculation 47
Bill of materials (BOM) 19, 31, 97, 144
 Buffering 157
 Components 100
 Creation 99
 Customizing 144

Bill of materials (BOM) (Cont.)
   Items 100
   Material BOM 98
   Multilevel BOM 104
   Multiple BOM 98
   Variant BOM 98
   Work breakdown structure (WBS) BOM 98
Blocked stock 153
BOM explosion 31, 35, 50, 51, 142, 166, 333, 379, 492
   Customizing 145, 166
   Exceptions 227
BOM explosion date 333
BOM explosion number 145, 333
   Changing 333
   Creating 333
BOM selection ID 144, 416
BOM usage (PQR classification) 144, 381, 386, 389, 409, 418
Bottom-up pegging 268
Buffer 383
Buffer action 410
Buffer calculation 34, 381, 384, 521
Buffer level 384, 397
Buffer level profile 384
Buffer positioning 384, 390
Buffer Positioning app 384, 390
Buffer Profile Maintenance app 381, 403, 407
Buffer proposal calculation 396
Buffer sizing 384
Buffer zone 34
Bulk material 92
Business Add-ins (BAdIs) 493
   Best practices 493
   Classic MRP 494, 515
   MRP Live 498
By-product 101

C

Capacity issue 441, 448, 450, 452
Capacity leveling 22, 31, 148, 307
Capacity plan simulation 452
Capacity planning 372
Capacity requirement 197, 441
CDS views 498

Change category 455
Change request 290, 292
   New 292
   Pending 293
Checking rule 136
   Customizing 136, 170
Classic MRP 24, 482
   Execution 189, 192, 193, 421
   Logic 190, 421
   Performance 478
Collective access 235, 254
Compatibility scope 193, 347
Component 50, 323
Component availability 303
Component scrap 102
Consumption horizon 351
Consumption mode 348, 351, 357
Consumption parameter 348
Consumption-based planning 33
Conversion
   Customizing 141, 163
Convert Planned Orders app 312, 315
Coproduct 102
Creation indicator 166, 191, 195, 213, 420
   Customizing 166
Cross-plant view 248
Custom code 506, 515
Customizing data 55, 182
Cycle time 383

D

Daily lot size procedure (TB) 81
   According to the planning calendar (PK) 81
   Monthly lot size (MB) 81
   Weekly lot size (WM) 81
Days' supply 257
   Customizing 258
Decoupled lead time 380, 383, 397
Decoupling point 380
Decoupling point buffer 384
Delays 286
Delivery performance 450
Delivery requirement 467
Demand Driven Institute 379

Index

Demand element 273
Demand management 21, 347
   Customizing 374
Demand plan 368, 441, 452
   Creating 368
Demand profile 273
Demand variability 380
Demand-driven MRP (DDMRP) 16, 27, 34, 74, 138, 379, 442, 517, 521
   APIs 409
   Applications 380, 384, 386
   Integration 409, 410
   Process 384
   Setup 386, 392
Dependent requirement 197, 199, 327, 347
   Inconsistency 470
Dependent requirements availability
   Customizing 142
Detailed scheduling 146, 147
   Customizing 146
Detect MRP Situations app 295
Deterministic MRP 20, 30, 35, 379
Direct procurement 86, 153
   Customizing 153
Direct production/collective order 86
Discrete manufacturing 318
Dispatcher 482
Display filters 242, 255
Display MRP Key Figures app 484, 485
Display MRP Master Data Issues app 155, 289, 464
Distribution key 51, 373
Document type
   Customizing 169
Downstream 391
Dump 475, 476
Dynamic adjustments 384
Dynamic assembly 367
Dynamic safety stock 91

E

Enhancement M61X0001 208
Error handling 154
   Customizing 154

ES_PPH_MRP_DISPATCHER_BADI
   enhancement spot 490
Evaluation profile 164, 259
   Customizing 259
Exception message 20, 35, 52, 225, 267, 300, 521
   Customizing 229
   Standard 229
Excess stock 294, 380
Explosion date 145
External material 96
External procurement 42, 112, 169, 303
   Customizing 150
External procurement scheduling
   Customizing 169
External requirement 282, 284

F

Finished product 56, 323, 347, 348, 380
Firm element 232
Firm receipt 38
Firm receipt element 233
Firming 231
   Customizing 167
   Date 240
   Type 66, 172
Fixed interval 397
Fixed lot size 491
Fixed lot-sizing procedure 79
Fixed order quantity 77
Fixed procedure 40
Fixed safety stock 91
Float 48
   After production 89
   Before production 89
   Customizing 141
Forecast 347, 350, 379, 441
Forecast indicator 172
Forecast requirement 75
Form-fit-function (FFF) class 336, 338
Forward consumption period 348
Forward scheduling 44, 149, 404
Function module 372
   EXIT_SAPLM61C_001 498

529

Function module (Cont.)
   EXIT_SAPMM61X_001 498
   MD_MDPSX_READ_API 191
   PPH_STOCK_REQ_LISTS_PREREAD 516

G

Goods issue value 388
Goods receipt processing time 46, 48, 88
Goods receipt/availability date 239
Green buffer zone 383
Gross long-term planning 415
Gross requirements planning 358, 359, 416

H

Housekeeping activities 459

I

Independent requirement 348, 373
Individual access 235
Individual stock 168
Individual stock type 168
Industry solution 336
Info record 113, 114
   Creating 113
   Maintaining 113
In-house production 46
In-house production time 197
Internal procurement 42, 96, 97, 303
Internal requirement 282
Intra-plant view 247, 327
Inventory positioning 384
Inventory-based manufacturer part 337
Item category 324
Item number 155
   Customizing 155

J

Job template 218

L

Lead time (EFG classification) 45, 381, 383, 392, 409
Lead time factor 383
Lead time scheduling 429, 496
Leading part 338
Lead-time factor 34
Lead-time offset 51, 103
Lead-time scheduling 47, 106, 197, 306
LiveCache 221
Locks 487
Long-term planning 135, 415
Long-Term Planning (LTP) 28, 413, 441, 479, 522
   Background jobs 421
   Capacity evaluation 429
   Collective access 427
   Execution 419
   Logic 421
   Material analysis 431
   Material group analysis 431
   MRP List 429
   Performance 479
   Planned order 424
   Results 430
   Stock/Requirements List 426
   Vendor analysis 431
Long-term simulation scenario 416
Lot size 50
   Customizing 175
Lot-for-lot order quantity 77
Lot-for-lot procedure 40, 328, 444
Lot-size independent cost 83
Lot-sizing procedure ... 31, 39, 76, 132, 174, 444
   Changing 174
   Creating 174
   Optimum 77
   Period 77, 81
   Standard 330, 390
   Static 77
Lot-sizing procedure EX 73

Index

Lot-sizing procedure FS 79
Low-level code 36

M

Maintain PIRs app 369
Make-to-order (MTO) 19, 21, 39, 146, 178,
  204, 238, 347, 348, 416, 496
  Scenario 23, 27
Make-to-project (MTP) 146, 178, 205, 238,
  416, 496
Make-to-stock (MTS) 19, 21, 39, 347, 348, 355
  Scenario 23
Manage Buffer Levels app 385, 397
Manage External Requirements app 272,
  284, 285
Manage Internal Requirements app 272,
  282, 288
Manage Material Coverage app 220, 272,
  277, 278, 300, 313
Manage PIRs app 369
Manage Production and Process Orders
  app 272
Manage Situation Types app 296, 298
Manage Teams and Responsibilities app 296
Manufacturer part number (MPN) 336
Manufacturer part profile 337
  Standard 337
Mass Maintenance of Products (DD) app ... 384,
  394, 397
Mass Maintenance of Products app 395
Mass processing functions 320
Master data 55, 95, 182, 289, 522
Master production scheduling (MPS) 22, 31,
  69, 209, 479
  Performance 479
Master recipe 106
Material BOM
  Changing 98
  Creating 98
  Displaying 98
Material buffer 380
Material classification 521
Material coverage 277
Material forecast 371

Material grouping 246
  Creating 251
  Custom 251
  Customizing 247
Material item 100
  Intramaterials (M) 101
  Nonstock items (N) 101
  *Plant maintenance structure
    elements (I)* 101
  Stock items (L) 100
  Variable size items (R) 101
Material master 56, 158, 348, 443, 446
  Creating 56
  Key fields 56, 90, 160
  MRP tabs 60
Material requirements planning (MRP) ... 15, 19
Material resources planning 15
Material shortage 380
Material shortage profile 274
  Creating 275
Material type 56, 336
  Standard 336
Maximum lot size 84, 125, 491
Maximum lot size quantity 41
Maximum MRP interval
  Customizing 164
Maximum quantity 125
Maximum stock level 34, 176
Method DISPATCH_GET_PARAMETERS 490
Method GET_MRP_ELEMENTS 481
Method MDPS_ADJUST 501
Migration 210, 505
Minimum lot size 84, 125
Minimum lot size quantity 41
Monitor External Requirements app 272,
  282, 284
Monitor Internal Requirements app ... 272, 282
Monitor Internal Shortages app 285
Monitor Material Coverage app 26, 272,
  277, 278
Monitor Material Shortages app 281
Monitor Process Orders app 274
Monitor Process Orders apps 285
Monitor Production and Process
  Orders app 272
Monitor Production Orders app ... 274, 285, 286

531

Index

Monthly lot size procedure (MB) 40, 81, 330
MPN-MRP set 337, 338
   Copying 339
   Generating 339
   Planning 339
MRP
   Input 20
   Logic 25
   Output 20
   Planning concept 379
   Within SAP 20
MRP area 93, 180, 325
   Assigning 326
   Creating 93
   Maintaining 94
   Subcontracting 327, 328
MRP area type 180
   Plant (O1) 180
   Storage location (O2) 180, 184
   Subcontractor (O3) 181, 184
MRP class 474
MRP Cockpit 16, 25, 219, 260, 272, 426, 501, 518, 522
MRP control parameters 193, 194, 212, 221
MRP controller 20, 137, 254, 275
   Creating 137
   Customizing 137, 138
   Titles 138
MRP dispatcher 211
MRP element 278, 495, 499
   Custom 495
MRP evaluation 136
   Custom columns 495
   Multilevel 264
MRP group 132, 158, 271
   Adjustment horizon 160
   Assign 158
   Availability check 170
   Consumption mode 160
   Customizing 159, 195
   Evaluation 164
   External procurement 169
   FERT 158
   Horizons 160
   MRP type 170
   Planned order 163

MRP group (Cont.)
   Planning run 164
   Production storage location 162
   Program plan 163
MRP List 134, 135, 260
   Changing 499
   Collective access 261
   Deleting 262, 464
   Individual access 261
   Terminations 262
MRP Live 24, 516
   Execution 189, 192, 216
   Logic 190, 213
   Performance 482
   Support functions 473
   Technical parameters 487
MRP objects 134
MRP procedure 29, 62, 521
   B—Reorder Point Planning 33
   D—Material Requirements Planning 30
   Forecast-based 69, 75
   Master production scheduling
     (MPS) 31, 69, 209
   Reorder point planning 69
   R—Time-Phased MRP 34
   S—Forecast-Based Procedure 33
   Time-phased planning 69, 75
MRP results 235
   Analysis 235
MRP type 29, 40, 62, 76, 132, 173, 460, 461, 510
   Changing 171
   Consumption-based 69, 201, 267
   Creation 62
   Custom 29, 139
   Customizing 30, 171
   Demand-driven 392, 400, 442
   Forecast-based 90, 371
   M1 69
   M2 69
   M3 69
   Master production scheduling (MPS) 69
   ND 126
   P1 .... 66, 67
   P2 .... 66, 67
   P3 67

Index

MRP type (Cont.)
  P4 67
  PD 64, 65, 81
  R1 75
  R2 75
  Reorder point 90
  Standard 29, 62, 64, 170, 390, 400
  Time-phased 329
  V1 .... 73, 173
  V2 .... 74, 173
  VB 70, 71, 73, 173
  With firming element 240
Multilevel BOM 333
Multilevel material simulation 453
Multilevel planning 199
Multilevel project planning 204
Multilevel sales order planning 204
My Situations app 293

N

Navigation profile 251
  Customizing 253
Net change 36
Net change in total planning 194
Net change planning run 36, 213
Net flow position 401
Net requirements calculation 30, 35, 37, 38,
  45, 90, 348
Network 264
NProc record 471
Number range 134, 477
  Assigning 134
  Customizing 135
  Resetting 136
  Standard 135
Number range interval 134

O

Object Inspector 452
Opening period 46, 49, 89, 311
Operation scrap 102
Operational data 413
Operational MRP 413, 419, 444

Optimal lot-sizing procedure 77
  Dynamic lot size creation (DY) 83
  Groff reorder procedure (GR) 83
  Least unit cost procedure (WI) 84
  Part period balancing (SP) 84
Optimum lot-sizing procedure 40, 83
Order finish date 145
Order report 267, 268
  Exceptions 265
Order reservation 282
Order start date 145
Overall plant parameters 132
  Environment 134
  Master data 136
  Planned orders 141
  Planning run 142

P

Parallel processing 185, 477, 488, 496, 499
  Customizing 185
Parallelization 487, 488
Parts interchangeability 336
Pegging 265
Performance 25
  Customizing 156
  Improvement 25
Performance log 485
Period lot-sizing procedure 40, 45, 77, 81,
  329, 331
  Daily lot size (TB) 81
Period split 373
  Customizing 163
Phantom assembly 51, 86
Planned delivery time 49, 88
Planned independent requirement (PIR) 21,
  38, 50, 160, 333, 347, 349, 397, 413, 441
  Changing 370
  Consumption 350, 495, 499
  Creating 349
  History of changes 369
  Reduction 351
  Reorganization 373
Planned order 141, 264, 268, 303, 495
  Availability check 308
  Changing 499

533

Planned order (Cont.)
  Component 197
  Converting 141, 142, 154, 163, 303, 311–313
  Creating 304, 305
  Date 234
  Deleting 172
Planned order (object PLAF) 134–136
Planned order profile 304
Planned receipt 38
Planner Overview app 385, 408
Planning calendar 75, 88, 329
  Creating 330
Planning calendar procedure (PK) 81
Planning date 75
Planning element 236, 495
Planning file 35, 36, 43, 126, 164, 460, 506
  Consistency check 460
Planning file entry 126, 164, 194, 418, 460, 461, 466
  Creating 126
  Updating 164
Planning horizon 506
Planning mode 195, 490
  1—Adapt Planning Data 195, 196, 213
  2—Re-explode BOM and Routing 196
  3—Delete and Recreate Planning Data 196, 213
Planning priority status 405
Planning result 270
Planning run scope 193
Planning scenario 414, 427, 443, 511
  Creating 414
  Dependent data 435
  Preconfigured 414
  Releasing 418, 444
Planning segment 243, 361
Planning situation 202, 270
Planning strategy 39, 348, 352
  10, net requirements planning 356
  11, gross requirements planning 358
  20, MTO production 360
  25, make-to-order for configurable material 360
  40, planning with final assembly 352, 355, 366

Planning strategy (Cont.)
  50, planning without final assembly 361, 363
  52, planning without final assembly 361, 363
  59, planning at assembly level 365
  60, planning with a planning material 363
  63, planning with a planning material 363
  70, planning at assembly level 365
  74, planning at assembly level 365
  81, assembly processing with planned orders 368
  82, assembly processing with production orders 368
  83, assembly processing with networks 368
  84, service orders 368
  85, assembly processing with network/project 368
  86, assembly processing with process orders 368
  Standard 374
Planning table 349
Plant 132
  Capacity 414
  Customizing 133
  Maintaining 133
Predictive Material and Resource Planning (pMRP) 16, 28, 413, 441, 517, 521, 522
  Background job 444
  Concept 441
  Creating 443
  Customizing 442
  Process 442
  Releasing 456
Process manufacturing 318
Process order 268, 285, 303, 319
Process pMRP Simulations app 442, 448, 455, 456
Processing indicator 261
Processing key 194
Procurement quantity 35, 39
Procurement type 42, 85, 95, 304
  Both procurement types (X) 85
  Consignment 86
  Direct procurement 86
  Direct production/collective order 86

534

Index

Procurement type (Cont.)
External procurement (F) 85
In-house production (E) 85, 88
Phantom assembly 86
Production in alternative plant 86
Stock transfer 86
Subcontracting 86
Withdrawal from alternative plant 86
Product 380
Product classification 382, 386, 388, 409
Product group 199
Product group planning 271
Production date 47, 106
Production in alternative plant 86, 139
Production order 268, 285, 303, 319, 413
Production Planning and Detailed Scheduling
 (PP/DS) 22, 25, 96, 192, 211, 221, 223,
 517, 521
Production storage location,
 Customizing 162
Production version 50, 96, 97, 107, 324,
 443, 511
Change 108
Changing 495
Consistency check 110
Creating 108
Locking 108
Production/process order 264
Program
PPH_MRP_START 216, 462
PPH_SETUP_MRPRECORDS 128
RLD05000 310
RM60FORC 371
RM60ROLL 373
RM60RR20 373
RM60RR30 373
RM60RR40 374
RMCBDISP 434
RMMDBOM1 158
RMMDEKS1 434
RMMDKP01 262
RMMPS000 .... 209, 463
RMMRP000 .... 209, 462
RMMRP010 .... 421, 463
SAPLM61K 173
Project 264

Project stock requirements grouping
Customizing 168
Purchase order 268
Purchase requisition 268, 323, 413, 420, 495
Changing 499
Releasing 496
Purchase requisition (object BANF) 134–136
Purchasing contract 118
Purchasing document 472
Inconsistency 472
Purchasing group 150
Purchasing processing time 49, 150

Q

Qualified spike demand 402
Quota agreement
Changing 121
Quota arrangement 43, 50, 96, 121, 125
Creating 121

R

Range of coverage data 257
Range of coverage profile 341, 344
Creating 341
Rate-based scheduling 147
Raw material 56, 104, 347, 380, 414, 441
Readiness Check 505
Receipt element 264
Red base 383
Red buffer zone 383
Red safety 383
Reference ID 446
Regenerative planning 36, 194
Release period 89
Reorder point 33, 34, 70, 173, 267, 402
Reorder point calculation 383
Reorder point procedure 45
Repetitive manufacturing 303, 471
Repetitive manufacturing dependent
 requirements 471
Replenish to maximum stock level
 procedure 40
Replenishment element 416
Replenishment execution 385

535

Index

Replenishment Execution app 404
Replenishment Execution by On-Hand
   Status app 385
Replenishment lead time 239
Replenishment planning 385
Replenishment Planning app 404
Replenishment Planning by Planning
   Priority app 385
Replenishment proposal 35, 39, 43, 76, 85
   Changing 290
Replenishment proposal type 41
Report
   ATP_VBBE_CONSISTENCY 468
   CS_BOM_PRODVER_MIGRATION ... 111, 112
   CS_BOM_PRODVER_
     MIGRATION02 .... 111, 512
   MRP_AREA_STORAGE_LOC_
     MIGRATION 509
   PMRP_CREATE_ENVIRONMENT_MAT ... 442
   PPBICO40 314
   PPBICOR8 314
   PPH_CONVERT_MRPRECORDS 508
   PPH_CONVERT_MRPRECORDS_SIMU ... 508
   PPH_MRP_SET_CACHE 275
   PPH_MRP_START 483
   PPH_SETUP_MRPRECORDS 328, 460
   PPH_SETUP_MRPRECORDS_SIMU ... 418
   PPIO_ENTRY 319
   PPMRP_CHANGE_REQUEST_DELETE ... 293
   RM06C020 469
   RM06HL04 473
   RMCVPLRQ 317
   RMMD07NEW 256
   RMMDDIBE 94, 185
   RMMDERRO 262, 263, 464
   RMMDFD00 436
   RMMDKP01 464
   RMMDMONI 479, 480, 497
   RMMDPERF 480
   RMMDVM10 508
   RMPLAF00 436
   RMPLSC00 436
   SDRQCR21 .... 468, 515
   YMRPAREO 184
   ZCHECKRESB1 471
   ZDELFLGINRES 472

Report (Cont.)
   ZINCON_REPROC 472
   ZPSFCO99 472
   ZRMBF06 472
Reporting
   Customizing 136
Reprocessing record 471
Requirement class 354, 374
Requirement date 176
Requirement type 352, 354, 374, 375
Requirements plan 368
Rescheduling
   Customizing 151, 161
   Exception message 202
   Exceptions 228
Rescheduling check 151, 230, 232
Rescheduling horizon 231
   Long 232
   Short 233
Rescheduling message 280
Reservation 134–136
   Inconsistency 472
Restricted use stock 153
Rolling interval 397
Rough-cut scheduling 147
Rounding profile 41, 84, 125
Rounding value 41, 84
Routing 47, 105, 306, 429, 443
Routing selection ID 147

S

Safety stock 34, 90, 341, 383
   Customizing 165
   Dynamic 341, 343
Safety time 91, 239
Sales and operations planning (S&OP) ... 20, 199, 347, 371
Sales forecast 347
Sales order 264, 347, 350
   Customizing 354
   Inconsistency 467
Sales order BOM 146
   Creating 98
SAP Advanced Planning and Optimization
   (SAP APO) 20, 221, 246, 252

Index

SAP Customizing Implementation Guide
   (SAP IMG) 131
SAP ERP 20, 36
SAP Fiori 26, 441
   Applications for MRP 260, 272, 275, 518
   Extensibility 501
   Recommendation 506
   Roles 26
SAP Fiori launchpad 26, 216, 275, 279,
   284, 442
SAP Fiori Library 501
SAP HANA 25, 190, 473
SAP Integrated Business Planning
   (SAP IBP) 20, 222, 347, 372
SAP S/4HANA migration 500
Schedule Buffer Proposal Calculation
   app 385, 396
Schedule Copying Total Forecast Runs
   app 371
Schedule Lead Time Classification of
   Products app 384
Schedule Lead Time of Products (DD) app ... 392
Schedule line 42, 329, 369, 469
Schedule MRP Runs app 216, 219, 222, 462
Schedule PIR Reorganizing Runs app 374
Schedule pMRP Simulation Creation
   app 442, 444
Schedule Product Classification (DD) app 386
Schedule Product Classification app 384
Scheduling 43, 46
   External procurement 48
   In-house production 46
Scheduling agreement 118, 268, 420
   Creating 118
   Standard type LP 118
Scheduling horizon 148
Scheduling margin key 46, 89
Scheduling type 149
Scope of planning 206, 214
Selection group 226
   Customizing 229
Selection rule 245, 255
   Custom 245
Semifinished product 56, 104, 222, 323, 380
Shortage 273, 303
Shortage calculation 273

Shortage definition 273, 283
   Custom 273
Short-term simulation 415
Simplification 507
   Creation indicator 191
   External procurement 512
   Planning file 507
   Production version 511
   Storage location 248
   Storage location planning 509
   Subcontracting 248, 511
   Total requirements 513
Simplification item 506
Simplified sourcing 115, 118, 121, 511
Simulation
   Changing 446
   Creating 446
   Logging 446
   Processing 448
Simulation creation 444
Simulation ID 446
Simulation scenario 414
Simulative dependent requirements 134
Simulative MRP 413
Simulative planned order 413, 422
   Firming 423, 435
   Scheduling 423
Single-item planning 202, 339, 424
Single-item/multilevel planning 199, 201,
   209, 419, 421
Single-item/single-level planning 197, 199,
   209, 419, 421
Situation handling 235, 293, 300, 521
   Setup 294
Situation template 298
Situation type 296
   Creating 298
   Enabling 300
Sizing 506
Source list 96, 115
Source of supply 115, 324, 441, 453, 512
   Changing 453, 495
   Determination 96, 117
   Determining 499
Special procurement
   Customizing 139

537

Special procurement type 42, 86, 132, 304
   Custom 139
Special stock segment 204
Spike horizon 402
Spike horizon constant 402
Spike horizon DLT multiplier 402
Spike threshold 403
Splitting quota 123
SQLScript 498
Start in past 156
   Customizing 156, 167
Static assembly 367
Static lot-sizing procedure 40, 77
   Fixed order quantity (FX) 77
   Lot-for-lot order quantity (EX) 77
Stock buffer 380
Stock in transfer 153
Stock separation 325, 511
   Partial 325
Stock transfer 43, 139
Stock transfer requirement 499
Stock type 38
Stock/Requirements List 426
   Collective access 254
   Data selection 235
   Exceptions 226
   Filters 242
   Grouping 246
   Individual access 236
   Navigation profile 251
   Order report 267
   Selection rules 242
Storage cost 83
Storage cost code 83
Storage location 162, 182, 305, 509
   Customizing 184
Strategy group 348, 353
   Creating 375
   Defining 357
Subcontracting 50, 86, 97, 323–325, 468, 506
   Logic 495, 499
Subcontracting requirement 327
   Inconsistency 468, 470
Subcontracting requisition BOM 324
Subcontractor 323
Supersession chain 246

Supply element 273
Supply profile 273
Support functions 473
Syntax error 475

T

Table
   DBVL 127
   DBVM 127, 507, 509, 516
   DVER 172
   EKBE 473
   EKES 473
   EKET 473
   MATDOC 172
   MDKP 191, 515
   MDMA 184
   MDTB 156, 191, 515
   MDTC 156, 191
   MDVL 127
   MDVM 127, 507, 509, 516
   MVER 172
   PLAF 422, 471
   PPH_DBVM 127, 418, 507, 516
   PPHDBVMSET 477
   PPHMRPSET 486, 490
   RESB 422, 468, 471, 480, 491
   RQIT 513
   VBBE 468, 513
   VBBS 513
Third-party subcontracting 328, 329
Time fence 161, 404
   Customizing 161
Time horizon 243
Today scheduling 44, 156
Tolerance value 233
Top-down pegging 268
Top-down planning 347
Total planning run 206, 207, 209
Total requirements 513
Transaction
   /UI2/FLP 275
   C223 108
   CA97N 88, 107
   CM38 429
   CO06 136

Transaction (Cont.)
- CO40 ... 312
- CO41 ... 313
- COGI ... 471
- COHV ... 311, 319
- COHVPI ... 319
- COMAC ... 319
- COOIS ... 318
- COOISPI ... 318
- COR7 ... 312
- COR8 ... 314
- CS01 ... 98, 99
- CS02 ... 98
- CS03 ... 98
- CS61 ... 98
- CS71 ... 98
- KSOP ... 435
- M03 ... 209
- MCB ... 433
- MCB& ... 433, 434
- MCEA ... 431
- MCEB ... 431
- MCEC ... 431
- MD_FORCE_MRP_CLASSIC ... 211
- MD_MRP_FORCE_CLASSIC ... 192, 263, 276, 464, 465, 482, 488, 498
- MD_MRP_PERFLOG ... 214, 484, 490
- MD01 ... 167, 207, 208, 419, 498
- md01 ... 209
- MD01N ... 191, 192, 213, 214, 219, 474, 483, 486, 501
- MD02 ... 167, 199, 209, 215, 419, 496, 513
- MD03 ... 167, 197, 496
- MD04 ... 92, 235, 236, 251, 254, 278, 426, 473
- MD05 ... 261
- MD07 ... 254, 256, 257
- MD08 ... 262, 464
- MD09 ... 268
- MD11 ... 304, 308
- MD12 ... 308
- MD14 ... 315
- MD15 ... 142, 315
- MD16 ... 317
- MD20 ... 127
- MD21 ... 126, 466
- MD25 ... 330

Transaction (Cont.)
- MD26 ... 330
- MD27 ... 330
- MD40 ... 167, 209
- MD41 ... 209
- MD42 ... 209
- MD43 ... 202, 424, 466
- MD44 ... 270
- MD45 ... 270
- MD46 ... 270
- MD47 ... 271
- MD48 ... 271, 429
- MD4C ... 264, 267
- MD50 ... 204
- MD51 ... 205
- MD61 ... 349, 368
- MD62 ... 370, 457
- MD67 ... 373
- MD70 ... 371, 457
- MD73 ... 372
- MD74 ... 373
- MD75 ... 373
- MD76 ... 374
- MDBS ... 209
- MDBT ... 208
- MDSP ... 333
- MDUM ... 317
- MDVP ... 308, 317
- ME01 ... 115
- ME11 ... 113
- ME31 ... 118, 329
- ME32 ... 329
- MEQ1 ... 121
- MF47 ... 471
- MFBF ... 472
- MM01 ... 56, 336
- MM02 ... 513
- MP30 ... 62, 75
- MP38 ... 75
- MS01 ... 419, 421
- MS02 ... 419, 421
- MS03 ... 421
- MS04 ... 426
- MS05 ... 429
- MS06 ... 429
- MS07 ... 427

Transaction (Cont.)
MS11 ... 422
MS12 ... 422
MS13 ... 422
MS31 ... 414
MS32 ... 436
MS44 ... 429
MS47 ... 429
MS50 ... 421
MS51 ... 421
MS70 ... 430, 434
MS71 ... 433
MSBT ... 421
OM0E ... 206
OM0I ... 245
OM0J ... 243
OM0K ... 252
OM0L ... 229
OM0N ... 255, 265
OM0O ... 259
OMD3 ... 229
OMD9 ... 87
OMDC ... 89
OMDQ ... 30, 171
OMDU ... 132
OMDW ... 232
OMI1 ... 91
OMI2 ... 134
OMI4 ... 82, 83, 123, 174
OMIA ... 341
OMIL ... 258
OMIO ... 173, 240
OMIQ ... 185
OMIX ... 208, 498
OMIY ... 127
OMIZ ... 180
OMIZA ... 184
OMIZB ... 184
OMJJ ... 377
OMP1 ... 374
OMP4 ... 369
OMPH ... 164, 373
OMPN ... 337
OMPO ... 374
OMS4 ... 422
OPP1 ... 132

Transaction (Cont.)
OPPJ ... 179
OPPQ ... 132, 134, 335, 492
OPPS ... 375
OPU3 ... 107
OS20 ... 418
OS24 ... 100
OS28 ... 100
OS31 ... 144, 418
OSP2 ... 513
OVZ2 ... 513
OVZG ... 375
OVZH ... 375
OVZI ... 354, 375
OWD1 ... 84
PICO1 ... 337
PPH_MDAB ... 128
PPH_MDRE ... 460
SE18 ... 494, 500, 502
SE38 ... 515
SM36 ... 209
SM37 ... 209, 462
SM51 ... 186
SM56 ... 136
SM59 ... 186
ST22 ... 463, 475
Transactional data ... 55

U

Unfirmed planning elements ... 231
Upstream ... 391
Usage value (ABC classification) ... 381, 386, 388, 409
User exit ... 208, 497, 498
User interface improvement ... 25, 260
User role SAP_BR_MATL_PLNR_EXT_PROC ... 275
User role SAP_BR_PRODN_PLNR ... 275

V

Validity period ... 122
Variability (XYZ classification) ... 381, 386, 389, 409

Variability factor 34
Variant configuration 51

W

Warning message 136
WBS BOM 146
   Creating 98
WBS element 264

Weekly lot size procedure (WM) 40, 81, 330
Withdrawal from alternative plant 86, 139
Work center 307, 429, 443, 446
Work center capacity 429, 441

Y

Yellow buffer zone 383, 401

- Configure embedded PP-DS in SAP S/4HANA for advanced manufacturing
- Run production planning and detailed scheduling step by step
- Master planning, service, and scheduling heuristics

Mahesh Babu MG

PP-DS with SAP S/4HANA

Are you ready for embedded PP-DS? Advance your production planning and detailed scheduling with this comprehensive guide! Discover how the PP-DS integration model has been simplified with SAP S/4HANA. Then follow step-by-step instructions for configuring and running PP-DS in your system, from determining your requirements to monitoring your results. With details on advanced features, troubleshooting, and migration, this is your all-in-one PP-DS resource.

476 pages, pub. 02/2020
E-Book: $79.99 | **Print:** $89.95 | **Bundle:** $99.99

www.sap-press.com/4951

- Configure purchasing, sourcing, invoicing, evaluation, and more
- Run your sourcing and procurement processes in SAP S/4HANA
- Analyze your procurement operations

Justin Ashlock

Sourcing and Procurement with SAP S/4HANA

Your comprehensive guide to SAP S/4HANA sourcing and procurement is here! Get step-by-step instructions to configure sourcing, invoicing, supplier management and evaluation, and centralized procurement. Learn how to integrate SAP S/4HANA with SAP Ariba, SAP Fieldglass, and more. Then, expertly run your system after go-live with predictive analysis and machine learning. See the future of sourcing and procurement!

716 pages, 2nd edition, pub. 02/2020
E-Book: $79.99 | **Print:** $89.95 | **Bundle:** $99.99

www.sap-press.com/5003

Interested in reading more?

Please visit our website for all new book
and e-book releases from SAP PRESS.

www.sap-press.com